CHINA STUDIES

JOINT-STOCK REFORM OF CHINA'S MAJOR COMMERCIAL BANKS

Chief Editor
Jiang Jianqing

Deputy Chief Editor
Zhan Xiangyang

Translated by
Ernst & Young Hua Ming LLP

First Edition 2023

ISBN 978-7-119-13680-6
© Foreign Languages Press Co. Ltd, Beijing, China, 2023
Published by Foreign Languages Press Co. Ltd
24 Baiwanzhuang Road, Beijing 100037, China
http://www.flp.com.cn
Email: flp@CIPG.org.cn
Distributed by China International Book Trading Corporation
35 Chegongzhuang Xilu, Beijing 100044, China
P.O. Box 399, Beijing, China

Printed in the People's Republic of China

Editorial Board

Advisors (in the alphabetic order)

Chang Zhenming	Chen Siqing	Dai Xianglong
Fan Yifei	Gu Shu	Guo Shuqing
He Di	Hu Xiaolian	Jiang Chaoliang
Li Lihui	Liu Liange	Liu Mingkang
Liu Shiyu	Lou Jiwei	Niu Ximing
Pan Gongsheng	Peng Chun	Qian Wenhui
Qin Xiao	Ren Deqi	Shang Fulin
Tian Guoli	Wang Hongzhang	Wang Jianxi
Wang Zuji	Wu Xiaoling	Xiang Huaicheng
Xiao Gang	Xie Ping	Yang Kaisheng
Yi Huiman	Zhang Jianguo	Zhang Yanling
Zhao Huan	Zhou Mubing	Zhou Xiaochuan
Zhu Min		

Chief Editor   Jiang Jianqing
Deputy Chief Editor Zhan Xiangyang

Writing Team

Head Zhan Xiangyang

Members
Wang Qi	Wu Zhenhua	Jia Tiezhen
Jiang Shoutao	Zhang Yun	Xu Wenbing
Jiang Lichang	Zhang Chao	Zheng Yanwen
Chen Yang	Li Luxia	Liu Kang
Ha Jing		

Preface

The year 2018 marks the 40th anniversary of China's reform and opening up, an initiative that has catapulted China, the world's most populous country and once home to the greatest number of people in poverty, to spectacular successes. Such an achievement has never been seen anywhere else in the world. In these four decades, China's financial industry, the beating heart of the nation's modern economy, has likewise undergone transformative changes as breathtaking in their outcomes as the meteoric rise of the Chinese economy.

Rewinding the clock to the beginning of the 21st century, who could have predicted that China's banking industry, once labeled "technically insolvent," would push through joint-stock reform and other transformations and leapfrog to the forefront of global banking? Even in the broad sweep of global economic history, the joint-stock reform of China's state-owned banks from 2003 to 2010 was a singular innovation, one that is worthy of a place in the annals of finance for its hugely successful, market-oriented outcomes. Documenting and recapping this history is, therefore, of significance not only to China's banking industry, but also to the country's wider reforms and even to the development of the global banking industry. As a 40-year veteran in the financial industry, I consider myself very fortunate to have witnessed and taken part in this reform – a do-or-die effort that simply could not be allowed to fail – and even more so to have been graced with the support of the leadership, among them the Governor of the People's Bank of China Zhou Xiaochuan, so that a team gathered from each of the Big Five commercial banks could jointly compile this book to document this monumental era.

This book, comprising ten chapters – "Introduction," "Epilogue" and eight others – is a historical recount of the joint-stock reform. The first three chapters treat the 30 years of reforms of state-owned banks as a cohesive effort heralding the joint-stock reform itself. Specifically, Chapter 1 addresses the general background of these early reforms and, above all, China's economic and banking reform from the late 1970s to the mid-1990s. Chapter 2 retraces the rise and evolution of non-performing assets in China's banking industry and in state-owned banks especially, and identifies their direct as well as root causes. Chapter 3 focuses on the two conferences pivotal to China's banking reform, namely the first National Financial Work Conference held in 1997 and the second such gathering in 2002, in particular the decisions made at these meetings.

The core of this book is Chapters 4 through 6, which give a full account of the joint-stock reform of China's Big Five banks – the Industrial and Commercial Bank of China (ICBC), Agricultural Bank of China (ABC), Bank of China (BOC), China Construction Bank (CCB), and Bank of Communications (BoCom). Chapter 4 covers the discussion, formulation, and introduction of the reform plan following the decision at the second National Financial Work Conference, to launch the reform as a pilot program, giving both a detailed account and a behind-the-scene look at the development of the top-level designs. Chapters 5 and 6 recall the full implementation of the reform, from its pilot stage at BOC and CCB, to its intensification and expansion at BoCom and ICBC, and lastly to its conclusion at ABC. While noting the four-step process common to the joint-stock reform of these banks – financial restructuring, creation of a joint-stock company, introduction of strategic investors, and public listing – attention was also given to the differences.

Chapter 7 summarizes the effort and progress made by the Big Five in corporate governance, risk management, and internal controls following the joint-stock reform. Chapter 8 explicates the eight chief effects of the reform and contains a quantitative cost-benefit analysis which shows, with real data, that the post-reform benefits have outweighed the costs borne by the state, and that the reform has breathed new life into the banks. Lastly, in "Epilogue" we sum up the lessons from the reform and voice some general issues and expectations that may help shape further and more extensive changes for China's major commercial banks.

This book is compiled based on the following principles:

First, continuity of banking reform. Reforms over the years in China's banking industry, and in state-owned banks in particular, have all been for achieving Deng Xiaoping's vision of "having banks perform all the functions of banks." In four decades, state-owned banks have been successively transformed into national specialized banks, state-owned commercial banks (SOCBs), and finally state-controlled joint-stock commercial banks, driven, respectively in each step, by the corporate reform, market-oriented reform, and joint-stock reform. This is a logical and inherently coherent process. While the joint-stock reform from 2003 to 2010 ultimately put state-owned banks into the trajectory of market-oriented and modern operations, it is the creation of an independent banking system starting from 1978, the transformation of national specialized banks into SOCBs in 1994, and the initial injection of state funds into state-owned banks and the carve-out of their non-performing assets in 1998 that laid the foundation for the joint-stock reform. Consequently, to illustrate why the banks carried out the joint-stock reform and why they did it that way, it is not enough to simply focus on the period from 2003 to 2010; the changes in the banking industry in the 30 years before that, which laid the groundwork for the reform, and the general background of China's reform and opening up must also be explained. As such, the first three chapters give a broad overview of the developments in the 30 years before the reform.

Second, historical accuracy. This book retells the entire joint-stock reform based on facts. We have relied on the following sources of information: public documents of the CPC Central Committee and the State Council as well as the regulatory documents released by China's central bank and the former China Banking Regulatory Commission; the plans and chronicles of the joint-stock reform of the Big Five; and the recollections of the reform plans' designers, leaders, and executors. This has allowed us to document and recreate the whole history and key phases of the reform – including the conception, discussion, design, development, and implementation of the reform plans and the introduction of the pilot programs and the expansion and successful conclusion of the reform – as well as the little-known twists and turns along the way. The history and facts as they appear in this work have been rigorously vetted by each of the five banks for accuracy.

Third, theory-centric approach. The joint-stock reform was the first attempt of its kind and, like "crossing the river by feeling the stones," had to be done without historical guidance, making it a subject of considerable public attention throughout the process. We do not shy away from the questions, theoretical or practical, that have been raised by the public, choosing rather to address them with facts and figures. Here are some examples: What is the real cause of the banks' non-performing assets? Why did the government bail out these banks? Why did their financial restructuring involve capital injection in a foreign currency? Why were foreign strategic investors brought into the reform? Did state-owned banks sell their shares for pennies on the dollar during restructuring and IPO? Was the joint-stock reform successful? How should we assess the reform? Answering these questions is essential to the faithful recreation of the history, and even more so to an objective assessment of the program and the furtherance of banking reforms in China.

Fourth, focus on the lessons learned. This unprecedented reform contains many lessons which are enormously valuable to both China and the world. In this book, particularly in "Epilogue," we have summed up these lessons, hoping they would play a bigger role in China's reforms and banking development as well as in other parts of the world. We also recognize that reform is a perpetual and continuous endeavor, and this is no exception in relation to China's banking industry and major commercial banks; under the leadership of the CPC Central Committee with Xi Jinping at the core, they will reach greater heights.

This book, having gone through several rounds of revision, is the culmination of over two years of effort from a team of 50 writers from the Big Five, based on the interviews with some 30 leaders and participants of the joint-stock reform and the input of 37 advisors and 50 experts and scholars. We hope this book will preserve the true history of the joint-stock reform of China's state-owned banks, and shed some light for a new generation of reformers.

We dedicate this book to the 40th anniversary of China's reform and opening-up initiative, the witnesses and participants of the 40 years of reform of state-owned banks, and to the 70th anniversary of the founding of the People's Republic of China and to the people who have dedicated themselves to China's financial success in those 70 years.

Jiang Jianqing
November 15, 2018
Shanghai

Contents

CHAPTER I STARTING POINT
– CARVING OUT AN INDEPENDENT FINANCIAL SYSTEM FROM THE STATE TREASURY

Section I Launch of Reform and Opening Up	2
I. Reflecting on the Path of Economic Development	2
II. Sounding the Clarion Call for Reform and Opening Up	6
III. Laying the Theoretical Foundation for Socialist Economic Structural Reform	8
IV. Setting the Goals for Building a Socialist Market Economy at the 14th CPC National Congress	10
V. Economic Reform Called for Banking Reform	12
Section II Banks Emerged as Main Channels of Investment and Financing	17
I. Diminishing Fiscal Inputs	19
II. Issuing Government Bonds and Tapping Foreign Capital	22
III. Bank Financing Inevitably Overtaking Fiscal Appropriations	23
Section III Institutional Reform as Starting Point of Financial Reform	31
I. Reopening and Establishment of Specialized Banks	32
II. Birth of Joint-Stock Banks	38
Section IV Bank Reform Invigorated the Economy	40

CHAPTER II IMPETUS FOR REFORM
– FINANCIAL SECTOR REMEDIATION AND SURFACING OF NON-PERFORMING ASSETS

Section I Macro-Finance and Governance	47
Section II The Non-Performing Loan Quandary	55
I. Crisis in Bank Asset Quality	55
II. Direct Causes of NPAs	69
III. Root Causes of NPAs	101
Section III Early Explorations at Reform	108
I. Bringing Corporate Approaches to Specialized Bank Operation	109
II. Separating Policy-Based Lending from Commercial Activities	111
III. Promulgating Banking Laws	114
IV. Transforming the Operating and Management Philosophy of State-Owned Banks	115

CHAPTER III RESPONDING TO CRISIS
– THE ASIAN FINANCIAL CRISIS USHERED IN A NEW ROUND OF FINANCIAL REFORM

Section I The Asian Financial Crisis	120
I. Financial Turmoil in Southeast Asia Under the Speculative Attacks of International Capital	120
II. Lessons Learned	123
Section II The First National Financial Work Conference	131
I. Drafting the Blueprint of Financial Reform	136
II. Significance of the First National Financial Work Conference	140

III. Joint-Stock Reform of State-Owned Banks: The Conference's Neglected Topic	144
Section III The Five Pillars of Deepening Reform	**147**
I. Centralizing the Financial Regulatory System	147
II. Establishing the Industry-Segregated Operation and Management Framework	151
III. The First Round of Capital Injection	153
IV. Assessing the Loan Situation and Implementing the Five-Category Classification Scheme	159
V. Establishing Financial Asset Management Companies and the First Round of NPL Divestiture	166

CHAPTER IV BREAKTHROUGHS IN JOINT-STOCK REFORM – FINALIZATION OF THE PATH AND PROPOSAL OF THE JOINT-STOCK REFORM

Section I Theoretical Studies and Breakthroughs	**184**
I. Discussions and Controversies of Choosing a Path for Joint-Stock Reform	184
II. Theoretical Breakthrough at the National Level	193
Section II Finalization of the Path for the Joint-Stock Reform of State-Owned Banks	**201**
I. Favorable Timing and Conditions	201
II. Reform Urgent Amidst Changing Landscape	217
III. Final Decision: Holding of the Second National Financial Work Conference	222
Section III Regulatory Reform Creating Conditions for the Joint-Stock Reform	**232**
I. New Arrangements for Financial Regulatory Reform	233
II. Establishment of the CBRC	234

Section IV Formulation and Implementation of Joint-Stock Reform Plans of State-Owned Banks	237
I. No Agreement on the RMB 970 Billion NPL Divestiture Plan	238
II. Experimental and Exploratory Efforts	249
Section V Release of the Plan for the Joint-Stock Reform	280
I. A Report to the State Council	280
II. Follow-Up Discussions and Refinement	307

CHAPTER V   LAUNCH OF PILOT REFORM – JOINT-STOCK REFORMS AND IPOS OF CCB, BOC, AND BOCOM

Section I Establishment of Central Huijin and Capital Injection	315
I. Establishment of Central Huijin	315
II. Capital Injection with Foreign Reserves	321
III. Discussions and Debates	323
Section II Joint-Stock Reform and Listing of CCB	329
I. Preparations	331
II. Financial Restructuring and Establishment of the Joint-Stock Company	341
III. Involvement of Foreign Strategic Investors	362
IV. Public Listing	370
Section III Joint-Stock Reform and Listing of BOC	374
I. Becoming One of the First Pilot Banks for Joint-Stock Reform	376
II. Financial Restructuring and Establishment of the Joint-Stock Company	387
III. Introduction of Strategic Investors	394

IV. A Challenging Journey to Listing	403
V. IPO	409
VI. Significance of BOC's Joint-Stock Reform and Listing	413
Section IV Advancing the Joint-Stock Reform of BoCom	**415**
I. Unique Features of BoCom's Reform	416
II. Financial Restructuring	429
III. Engagement of Foreign Strategic Investors	443
IV. Listing in Shanghai and Hong Kong	453
Section V Accusation of "Gross Underpricing" of State-Owned Banks	**468**

CHAPTER VI EXPANSION AND CONCLUSION
– JOINT-STOCK REFORMS AND IPOS OF ICBC AND ABC

Section I Joint-Stock Reform and IPO of ICBC	**476**
I. Sounding a Strong Prelude to the Joint-Stock Reform	481
II. Innovative Joint-Stock Reform Plan Based on the "Special Joint Fund" Account	505
III. Financial Restructuring, Group-Wide Restructuring, and Introduction of Strategic Investors	514
IV. ICBC's "IPO of the Century"	531
Section II Joint-Stock Reform and IPO of ABC	**541**
I. The Uniqueness of ABC's Joint-Stock Reform	542
II. Four Revisions of the Joint-Stock Reform Plan	557
III. Financial Restructuring and Creation of the Joint-Stock Company	563
IV. Innovative Introduction of Strategic Investors	571
V. ABC's IPO	573

CHAPTER VII STRENGTHENING THE FOUNDATION – DEVELOPMENT OF CORPORATE GOVERNANCE AND INTERNAL RISK CONTROLS IN MAJOR COMMERCIAL BANKS

Section I Development of Corporate Governance Systems	587
I. Building an Effective and Accountable Governance Structure	589
II. Developing a Sound Corporate Governance System and Mechanism	611
Section II Development of ERM System	625
I. Developing Robust RM Culture	626
II. Creating Sound RM Frameworks	628
III. Building Rigorous Delegation and Limit Management Systems	632
IV. Building Empirical Risk Identification and Measurement Systems	637
V. Creating Effective Risk Monitoring Systems	646
Section III Development of Internal Control System	647
I. Defining Organizational Structure of and Responsibilities for Compliance Management	649
II. Building Compliance Systems and Mechanisms	651
III. Identifying Responsibilities for and Handling of Risk Events and Violations	652
IV. Boosting Compliance Culture and Awareness	655
V. Establishing ICC Methods to Improve Risk Control Capability	656
VI. Facilitating Efficient Internal Control Management	658

CHAPTER VIII POST-REFORM REJUVENATION
– AN ANALYSIS OF THE EFFECTIVENESS OF THE JOINT-STOCK REFORM

Section I Post-Reform Rebirths of Major Banks	663
I. Transformation of Operating Model	663
II. Pillars for the Real Economy	687
Section II The Financial Cost and Benefit of the Joint-Stock Reform	698
I. Evaluation Framework	699
II. Cost-Benefit Analysis	701
Epilogue	713
Afterword	728

CHAPTER I
STARTING POINT
– Carving Out an Independent Financial System from the State Treasury

China's financial reform began as part of the broader economic reform following the Third Plenary Session of the 11th CPC Central Committee in 1978. Driven by Deng Xiaoping's call to "have banks perform all the functions of banks," China's financial system, including its banking sector where state-owned banks have been predominant, has since 1979 embarked on the path of reform which has led to profound transformations and progress. The reform of state-owned banks was carried out as a part of, and in tandem with, the wider ecnomic and financial reforms. Although originally launched as an explorative attempt, this early-stage banking reform would later serve as an essential step toward the joint-stock reform.

Section I
Launch of Reform and Opening Up

In the early days after its founding, the People's Republic of China was a war-ravaged country with a ruined economy, plagued by scarcity of materials and financial resources, severe inflation, and all the other qualities of a shortage economy. To recover its economic footing, China opted for a Soviet-style, highly centralized planning system. By allocating productive and economic resources through planning and administrative means, China developed an independent economic system and a relatively complete range of industries, buoying the country to a swift economic recovery. This is not to say that everything was following a strictly upward trajectory in the 30 years leading up to reform and opening up; the decade-long Cultural Revolution, for example, left the economy in tatters. In its aftermath, the 11th CPC Central Committee recognized, at its Third Plenary Session, that China's socio-economic development was hampered by the economic system and started to reflect on what changes were needed to build a brighter future.

I. Reflecting on the Path of Economic Development

(I) A Daunting Task: Catching Up with the Modern World Economy

After the Second World War, the technological revolution brought on by the advent of electronics and information technology catalyzed the cross-border diffusion of the factors of production and kicked off a new wave of economic globalization. Even as their economies became globally integrated, countries were locked into cutthroat competition for the prize of economic development. Some developed market economies seized the opportunities and prospered. Between 1954 and 1974, Japan, the U.K., West Germany, France, and the U.S. saw their fixed asset investment grow 49, 17, 16, 11, and 4 times, respectively. Capitalist countries grew at an average annual rate of 6% in industrial output, while emerging economies such as the Four Asian Tigers successfully joined the ranks of the industrialized countries.

In comparison, China, having just emerged from the Cultural Revolution, found itself falling further behind in economic development and standard of living. In 1980, the Western countries recorded a per capita GNP of USD 10,000, while China's was only USD 300 according to the official exchange rate, or a mere one-tenth that of developed countries at the offshore rate. In the two decades between 1957 and 1976, the average annual pay in China remained flat, while cash-based pay even dropped from RMB 624 to RMB 575[1]. Poverty was even more striking in rural areas. According to the former Bureau of People's Communes of the Ministry of Agriculture, on average each farmer received only RMB 74.67 from his collective in 1978. On an annual basis, 200 million farmers had an average income of less than RMB 50; measured by the day, 112 million people earned RMB 0.11 per day; 190 million earned RMB 0.13 per day; and 270 million earned RMB 0.14 per day.

"Poverty is not socialism."[2] During a visit to China's three northeastern provinces in September 1978, Deng Xiaoping remarked, "Foreigners are discussing how long we can hold on. We should be alerted by what

---

1   Zeng Peiyan: *Five Decades of China's Economy (1949-1999)*, China Planning Press, 1999, pp. 897-898.
2   At a meeting with international guests on June 30, 1984, Deng Xiaoping said, "Socialism means eliminating poverty. Pauperism is not socialism, still less communism." At a meeting with the Prime Minister of the Czechoslovak Socialist Republic, Lubomír Štrougal, on April 26, 1987, Deng further noted, "to build socialism it is necessary to develop the productive forces. Poverty is not socialism. To uphold socialism, a socialism that is to be superior to capitalism, it is imperative first and foremost to eliminate poverty."

they say. We should ask ourselves how much we have done for the people." "We are too poor, too backward. And frankly speaking, we have failed our people." "Socialism must demonstrate its superiority. Things should not continue as they are." These questions challenged China to revisit two essential issues: What is socialism? And how to achieve it?

Surviving the chaos of the Cultural Revolution, China was eager to reboot its economy through reform. The government sent officials all over the world on study tours. In 1978 alone, 20 senior officials including Vice Premiers of the State Council and Vice Chairmen of the NPC Standing Committee paid visits to over 50 countries[1]. At the inception of reform and opening up, China did not have a clear roadmap of reform. Later at the Central Working Conference on December 16, 1980, Vice Premier Chen Yun delivered an important speech titled "The Economic Situation and the Lessons We Have Learned," elaborating on the principles and methods, distilled from past experiences, that should be adopted in reform and opening up. He noted, "We must carry out reform, but we must proceed cautiously. This is because our reform is complicated and we must not act impetuously. It is true that reform depends on theoretical research and on economic statistics and prediction. More importantly, we should start with reform in selected areas and then always evaluate our experience. In other words, we should 'cross the river cautiously.' In the beginning it is necessary to advance slowly."[2] At the closing ceremony on December 25, Deng Xiaoping commented that Chen's speech has "correctly summed up our experience in handling a series of problems in economic work over the

---

1 Quoted from Wu Jinglian: *Thoughts on China's Reform*, Commercial Press, 2017.
2 *Selected Works of Chen Yun*, Vol. III, Foreign Languages Press, 1999, p. 278.

past 31 years and the lessons we have drawn from it. His statement will serve as our guide in this field for a long time."[1]

(II) Exploring a Suitable Roadmap of Reform After the Disintegration of the Soviet Union

After the 1960s, the Soviet Union and eastern European countries experienced declining growth momentum and widening gaps with capitalist countries, prompting reflections on the planned economy and possible reforms. Unfortunately, they failed to find a socialism-based solution that would both deliver higher productivity and modernization and suit their own circumstances. This failure led to the collapse of their communist parties and the dissolution of their countries. Evidently, the economic, political, and national crises of the Soviet Union and Eastern Europe in the 1980s and 1990s were a failure of the Soviet model, not of the underlying socialist system and principles. The Soviet model rejected the role of the market, disregarded the law of value, was slow to react to market demand, suppressed individual initiative, and limited economic vitality; it sought economic progress at the expense of future growth potential, which would inevitably cause supply shortage and throttle productivity and innovation. History, if not forgotten, can serve as a guide for the future. China's four-decade reform and opening up is a process of continually examining the two-part question "what is socialism and how can it be built?" and a process of integrating the foundational principles of Marxism with the realities of China's circumstances.

---

1 *Selected Works of Deng Xiaoping*, Vol. II, Foreign Languages Press, 1995, p. 350.

(III) A Peaceful International Environment Conducive to China's Reform

The collapse of the Soviet Union and the revolutions in Eastern Europe in the late 1980s and early 1990s transformed political and economic landscapes across the world. The world became multipolar instead of being dominated by the U.S. and the Soviet Union. Military alliances turned away from tense confrontation to political, economic, and trade cooperation. The cross-border monopolies held by a few conglomerates became eclipsed by regional economic integration and market globalization. Despite sporadic regional conflicts, the international environment was generally peaceful. Having observed the changed world economic and political landscapes, Deng Xiaoping possessed the acute awareness to reach the timely conclusion that the theme of the era had changed from war and revolution to peace and development. In his view, it was possible for China to secure long-lasting peace, focus on economic development, and marshal resources towards socialist modernization. To escape poverty and embark on a fast track of building a modern socialist power, China needed to align itself with global economic and social development. The changed external environment of world economic and political landscapes created the possibility for the transition of China's development path.

II. Sounding the Clarion Call for Reform and Opening Up

After the Cultural Revolution, *Theoretical Trends*, an internal journal of the Party School of the Central Committee of the CPC, published an article on May 10, 1978, titled "Practice Is the Only Criterion for Testing Truth," which was reprinted by *Guangming Daily* on the following day. It was part of China's effort to quickly correct past mistakes and break free from the shackles of "Two Whatevers."[1] The article pointed out that the sole arbiter of truth is practice, that the integration of theory and practice is a fundamental principle of Marxism, and that any theory has to be continuously proven by practice. This article triggered a nationwide debate on the subject. The discussions promoted the idea of "seeking truth from facts" in dialectical materialism, liberated minds from the shackles of doctrinarism, and ushered in a "thought revolution."

This groundswell of liberated thinking prompted a re-examination of the nearly 30 years of socialist programs since the founding of the People's Republic of China, and gradually led to a consensus on reform and opening up. At the Third Plenary Session of the 11th CPC Central Committee in December 1978, the Party resolutely shifted its priorities toward building a modern socialist country. The Party disavowed obeisance to either existing dogmas or foreign development models, calling instead for seeking guidance from Marxism and testing ideas through practice to be the guiding lights for subsequent economic programs. The Party also removed certain conceptual blinders by accepting the objective existence of the material interests principle (recognizing the interaction of the respective material interests of the state, collective enterprises, and the individual) and the law of value, affirming the necessity of developing goods production and the decisive role of productivity in economic development, and proposing to manage the economy with economic mechanisms and approaches to build a socialist society superior to those based on capitalism. The Third Plenary Session of the 12th CPC Central Committee held in 1984 noted that "it should be clearly understood that

---

1   The February 7, 1997 issues of the *People's Daily*, *PLA Daily*, and *The Red Flag* published the editorial "Understanding Official Documents and Key Policies," which wrote, "We support whatever decision Chairman Mao makes and follow whatever instruction he gives."

a socialist economy must consciously follow and apply the law of value and is a plan-centric, public-ownership-based commodity economy," indicating that China's reform would incorporate more market-oriented elements.

III. Laying the Theoretical Foundation for Socialist Economic Structural Reform

Socialist economy had long been viewed as synonymous with planned economy – a specific form of Soviet-style planned economy marked by a high degree of centralization and mandatory plans. However, with the expansion of social production, China's planned economy began to show its limitations[1].

The first was the inconsistency between production and demand. This was because the unified planning center could not accurately capture the complex profile of public demand for various products: on the one hand, what was produced according to plan was often not needed and became surplus; on the other hand, the country also showed signs of a shortage economy in which vital goods were not produced in sufficient quantities. In a system where the state oversees every aspect of the economy – the allocation of funds, purchase and sale of products, and distribution of the means of production – market feedback was not available to remedy disconnects among production, supply, and sales.

Secondly, inconsistency between price and value. Due to the persistent and significant gap between the planning-derived prices and the actual values of products, business indicators were oftentimes a poor mea-

---

1 This part has referenced the works of the famous economist Liu Guoguang. See Liu Guoguang: *Collection of Liu Guoguang's Works on Economic Reform*, China Development Press, 2008.

sure of the operating results and partly to blame for the low operational efficiency. For China as a whole, irrationally priced products contributed to a general lack of coordination in production growth and an imbalanced industrial structure.

Thirdly, inconsistency between material benefits and operating results. Companies adopted a financial system under which revenue and expenditures were balanced out at a higher level by the government rather than internally (*shouzhi liangtiaoxian*) and neither the material interests of the companies nor those of their employees were tied to operating results. These dragged heavily on production efficiency, product quality improvements, and employee motivation.

Lastly, egalitarianism in resource distribution. As the quantity and quality of work became decoupled from the ultimate rewards or punishments, it was impossible to coax better performance from businesses and individuals.

Discussions on these limitations convinced the leadership that it would be for the best if central planning was supplemented by a market-driven system. This line of thinking can be traced back to the Third Plenary Session of the 12th CPC Central Committee in October 1984, during which the goal of reform was set to "[build] a plan-centric, public-ownership-based commodity economy," even though the basic framework and model for achieving this was still in debate. Further progress came at the International Symposium on Macroeconomic Management (the Yangtze River Cruise Conference) held by the State Commission for Restructuring the Economic System, the Chinese Academy of Social Sciences, and the World Bank in September 1985, as experts agreed that controlled market-based adjustments would be the optimal solution. The goal of socialist market reform was then made more specific at a CPC plenary session in the same month, where the Party determined, in its guidelines for the seventh Five-Year Plan (1986-1990), to "further develop a socialist plan-centric commodity economy (*shangpin jingji*) and gradually improve the market system"; "strengthen indirect state control over economic activities … [and] determine the scope, degree, and steps by which direct state control over microeconomic activities should be reduced"; and "invigorate enterprises, especially large and medium-sized enterprises that are owned by the whole people, and turn them into relatively independent socialist producers and operators that are responsible for their own management, profit, and losses."

The relation between the planned and market aspects of the economy was elucidated by Deng Xiaoping during his Southern Tour in 1992, in that socialism and capitalism are not fundamentally distinguished by the relative proportion of planning in the economy. A planned economy does not equate to socialism because capitalist countries also make plans, in much the same way as a market economy does not equate to capitalism because socialist countries also operate markets. His insight that both types of economies are means of economic development uprooted the long-standing dogma that the two are different and incompatible social regimes, thereby helping build a theoretical foundation from which reform of the planned economy could forge ahead.

IV. Setting the Goals for Building a Socialist Market Economy at the 14th CPC National Congress

The precarious international and domestic situation after 1989 did not deter the CPC Central Committee from pursuing further reform and opening up. In order to provide a clear direction for economic structural reform at the upcoming 14th CPC National Congress and the guiding principles of reform and opening up to be issued at the Third Plenary Session of the 14th CPC Central Committee, the CPC Central Committee with General Secretary Jiang Zemin at the core and the State Council organized a series of theoretical discussions and assessments[1].

Leading economists of the day held 11 symposiums on 3 topics – the development of Western capitalist countries after WWII and why capitalism had managed to remain viable, the evolution of and lessons from the Soviet Union and the Eastern European countries, and how to build a socialist economy with Chinese characteristics. They also weighed the various options and objectives of the reform of China's economic structure, and coined the term "socialist market economy." They proposed that the market should play a fundamental role in resource allocation and discussed the basic qualities that a socialist market economy should possess. Following consultations with Deng Xiaoping and other CPC members, the term "socialist market economy" gained widespread acceptance among the senior Party leadership.

At the 14th CPC National Congress held in October 1992, it was proclaimed that "the goal of economic structural reform is to establish a socialist market economy." The "Decision on Issues Concerning the Establishment of a Socialist Market Economy," adopted at the Third Plenary Session of the 14th CPC Central Committee in November 1993, contains 50 specific directives and a comprehensive framework for building the new economy.

The report at the 14th CPC National Congress unequivocally stated

---

1   Quoted from Chen Jun and Hong Nan: *Jiang Zemin and the Proposal of the Socialist Market Economy*, Central Party Literature Press, 2012.

that China would establish a socialist market economy, which, under the state's macroeconomic regulation, would empower the market to play a fundamental role in allocating resources, so as to let economic activities be shaped by the law of value and the forces of supply and demand. This would bring at least two benefits. First, the efficacy of price levers and the competition mechanism would funnel resources to where they are most efficiently utilized and at once motivate enterprises and force them to compete for survival. Second, production and consumption could achieve equilibrium faster because the market responds more quickly to economic signals. But the report also warned that market forces alone have certain deficiencies and negative externalities, which would require stronger and improved macroeconomic regulation to counteract.

To sum up, the 12th CPC National Congress advocated for a principally planned economy supplemented by the market economy; the Third Plenary Session of the 12th CPC Central Committee proposed the idea of a commodity economy based on central planning and public ownership; the 13th CPC National Congress clarified that a socialist planning-based commodity economy is one which organically combines planning and commodity factors; and, finally, the 14th CPC National Congress prescribed that China's economic structural reform was to establish a socialist market economy. Through iterations of proposal-validation-adjustment cycles, the goal of China's economic structural reform was finally established.

V. Economic Reform Called for Banking Reform

Before reform and opening up, China's banking industry, just like the national economy, operated under a highly centralized and plan-based model. While the roots of China's modern-day financial industry can be traced back to the First Civil War (1924-1927), it wasn't until the War of Liberation period (1945-1949) that the industry took shape in earnest. On December 1, 1948, the People's Bank of China (PBOC) was established in Shijiazhuang, with the head office of Huabei Bank serving as its head office. The first series of Renminbi also went into circulation, marking the birth of the PRC's financial system.

After the founding of the People's Republic of China in 1949, the government curbed speculation and inflation to maintain economic, financial, and monetary stability. It took over, consolidated, and transformed banks run by bureaucratic capital, as well as thousands of other Chinese and foreign banks, to carry out the socialist transformation of the private financial industry. Financial institutions of all types were reorganized according to the Soviet model, quickly creating a unitary system with the PBOC as the sole bank in the country.

In the first Five-Year Plan period (1953-1957), the Chinese government made PBOC a "credit, cash, and settlement center" in line with the highly centralized planning system and the principle that all credit should be managed by the national bank. In this capacity, the PBOC was responsible for managing funds and exercising monetary oversight as a central bank, as well as taking deposits and issuing loans as a commercial bank. It functioned as both a state financial administrator and a banking service monopolist, reflecting the then highly centralized banking system.

The year 1953 saw the creation of a centralized and integrated credit planning and management system for lending and deposit-taking activities, which incorporated the bank credit plan into the national economic plan to provide overall financial supervision and services for economic development. This system facilitated coordination, policy implementation, and holistic control, and achieved great efficiency during the first Five-Year Plan period and the period of economic adjustment in the early 1960s.

In the three decades before reform and opening up in 1978, the few commercial banks operating in the country – such as the Bank of China, the Agricultural Bank of China, and China Construction Bank – went through multiple corporate mergers and divisions. China's banking industry likewise went through the recovery of the national economy, the Great Leap Forward, economic adjustment in the 1960s, and the turmoil of the Cultural Revolution. But the monolithic financial system remained unaffected, bona fide commercial banks continued to be absent, and the role of finance and banks was negligible.

In July 1969, the PBOC shared offices with – and was essentially merged into – the Ministry of Finance while externally retaining its name and functions. Its local branches were also merged into the local fiscal departments, setting an extreme example of the imbalance between banking and fiscal functions in favor of the latter. Under the planned economy, the forces of value and markets were suppressed by the financial system. Banks neither performed economic accounting nor conducted performance evaluation. They were reduced to a cashier for the planned economy and the fiscal authority, a tool for implementing and supporting the state's plan for the allocation and management of funds, and an administrative agency for issuing money. Their local branches, lacking both vitality and motivation, were internally managed like an administrative agency. There were to be no credit transactions between banks or between enterprises. Serious "financial repression" existed between banks and enterprises and even in the whole country. The limited range of financial services and products on offer was abjectly inadequate for productivity growth.

After the start of the economic structural reform in 1977, the many flaws of planned finance came to light, and it became apparent that the existing financial systems and models were hampering economic and social development and changes were urgently needed. At the time, however, the ideological fetters of the planned economy still held strong within the population: the familiar notions and approaches learned and applied in the past were often heavily tinted by the planned economy, and there was a widespread fear of taking a misstep down the capitalist road.

On December 31, 1977, the State Council decided to make the PBOC head office a ministerial agency independent from the Ministry of Finance. The two would operate from separate offices starting from January 1, 1978. This economic reform entailed the reform of the traditional financial system to boost both the efficiency of funds utilization and the effectiveness of enterprises that had gained greater operational autonomy. Deng Xiaoping was deeply aware of the defects of the financial system, a result of decades under the planned economy. When he visited Tianjin on August 9, 1978, the local CPC committee reported a funds shortage. He replied, "It is ill-advised for the state to provide funds. In the future, bank loans may offer a way out. State investment is a lazy approach. When a company takes out a loan, it must pay interest and therefore will plan more carefully."[1] In this statement, Deng Xiaoping clearly indicated that enterprises should source their funds from banks at a cost instead of from the state free of charge. Such a change would definitively reinforce the role of finance in the economy and transform the banking system.

---

1   See Wu Shihong and Gao Yi: *Deng Xiaoping and Historical Milestones of China*, People's Publishing House, 2000.

At a meeting with the first secretaries of Party committees at the provincial level on October 4, 1979, Deng Xiaoping said: "We must truly operate our banks on a commercial basis. Why have so many unmarketable products been stockpiling in every province and city? One reason for this is that under our present financial system we allocate funds rather than grant loans by banks. This system must be reformed. Any company that wants to purchase materials should obtain loans from banks, repaying them with interest."[1] His view implied that banks had to become fund-managing institutions that issue loans for interest.

At the same meeting on October 8, Deng reiterated: "We may consider changing the fiscal-based financing system to a bank-centric one in which banks would accelerate economic and technological development. Banks are meant to earn interest, but our banks are just bookkeepers and not performing the functions that real banks would. For instance, it is natural for a company to borrow from banks at a particular interest rate, and be held legally liable for default. We need to talk in terms of economic laws. Banks are meant to charge interest – why else would they exist?"[2] Here, Deng made it clear that banks should be for-profit entities that, in essence, exchange "goods" with enterprises: Enterprises purchase the right to use funds for a certain period at the price of interest, and repay the principal plus interest to the bank upon maturity. Deng's speech was enlightening and poignant as to the crux of reform. He required officials at all levels to understand the role and value of banks and to put them at the service of economic and technological development, resource allocation,

---

1 *Selected Works of Deng Xiaoping*, Vol. II, Foreign Languages Press, 1995, p. 207.
2 See Wu Shihong and Gao Yi: *Deng Xiaoping and Historical Milestones of China*, People's Publishing House, 2000.

and macroeconomic regulation.

As the former Vice President of the Agricultural Bank of China Liu Hongru recalled, "At that time, Deng Xiaoping's speech was not published in an official document. We found it by chance in a central committee bulletin at the Confidential Materials Office. Many of us saw the significance of the speech and were thrilled that it went straight to the heart of the issue. After the official directive was issued, we, the reform front-liners finally knew which direction to head."[1] This speech jumpstarted China's financial reform and ushered in a new era of finance in the country. Despite heated debates on each of the subsequent reforms, the general direction never changed.

Section II
Banks Emerged as Main Channels of Investment and Financing

Prior to reform and opening up, China's economy had been devastated by the Cultural Revolution. At the national planning conference in December 1977, Li Xiannian estimated that the losses to national income during the decade-long turmoil amounted to RMB 500 billion[2]. This figure is equal to 80% of China's total capital investment in the three decades following the founding of the PRC and exceeded the total value of fixed assets created in the same period. After the 11th CPC Central Committee

---

1   See Liu Shiping: *Review of China's Three-Decade Banking Reform and Opening Up (1978-2008)*, Economic Science Press, 2009.
2   See Xi Xuan: *A Brief History of the Cultural Revolution*, History of Chinese Communist Party Publishing House, 1996.

named, at its Third Plenary Session, economic development as the Party's top priority, the first challenge facing Chinese leaders in rebuilding the economy was sourcing funds, as dependence on fiscal appropriations had become unsustainable and the impetus for change unstoppable.

Instead of the radical approach adopted by the Soviet Union and Eastern European countries, China embraced gradual reform. Without resorting to "shock therapy," China's policymakers strived to grow the economy and raise living standards in a measured way at relatively low public cost and minimal social repercussions. This gradual reform is akin to "crossing the river by feeling for the stones." That is to say, China would solve problems as they arose during the course of its ongoing self-improvement. After the Third Plenary Session of the 11th CPC Central Committee, new challenges arose as the reform unfolded. Decentralization efforts to invigorate the economy shifted national income away from the treasury and toward enterprises and the private sector, even as the accompanying industrial restructuring raised new demands for state investment and transfer payments. All of this created severe fiscal strains on the state. The strategic goal of balancing transition with development posed a dilemma for the state: either to loosen fiscal constraints and invigorate enterprises or to tighten them up to shed its heavy fiscal burdens.

To address the dilemma, China had in the early stage of economic transition decided to shift toward a new financial system where economic development and business operation are financed with bank loans rather than fiscal appropriations. This bank-driven financial system was intended to convert idle savings into investments. Thanks to this bold institutional reform, China managed to secure resources for its economic transition despite having insufficient fiscal capacity. State-owned banks emerged as the main source of capital for economic reform and business development. This new financial system, dominated by indirect financing through banks, vigorously drove forward the nation's economy and was a logical choice considering the historical constraints.

I. Diminishing Fiscal Inputs

In the first three decades after its founding, the People's Republic of China – emulating the Soviet Union – was a planned economy in which the state made production plans and the treasury allocated investment funds. In this manner, the state fiscal system performed the core function of resource allocation. It funded almost all infrastructure projects. Before 1978, over 77% of such projects were financed through state appropriations. Particularly, in the first Five-Year Plan period (1953-1957), 90% of the RMB 58.8 billion of capital investment was funded by the government (79% by the central government). Investment directly managed by the central government made up 86.5% of the total investment during this period.[1]

Back then, banks were prohibited not only from financing infrastructure projects, but also from supplementing the government-appropriated, fixed-quota working capital (*ding'e liudong zijin*) of state-owned enterprises (SOEs) that was necessary for production. Under this system of "big national treasury, small banks," government finance commanded far more power to mobilize financial resources than the banks. In most years, the total fiscal revenue was over five times the amount of urban and rural savings deposits or more than ten times the amount of urban term deposits. Limited

---

1 Wu Taichang, Wu Li, et al.: *Analysis of China's State Capital History*, China Social Sciences Press, 2012.

by however much of the private capital that happened to be sitting idle at the moment, banks could only issue small loans to SOEs to help them meet the seasonal and *ad hoc* financial needs beyond their fixed-quota working capital, playing a wholly subordinate role in resource allocation.

China's economic reform is essentially a transition from the planned economy to a market-based one, or, from the angle of how resources are allocated, a process of decentralization. After the Third Plenary Session of the 11th CPC Central Committee, the "decentralization and profit-sharing" campaign (*fangquan rangli*) encouraged local governments and enterprises to reform and invigorated the national economy that had long been smothered by the old economic system. At the inception of reform, the only power and profit that the central government could (and did) relinquish was fiscal management authority and the national treasury's share of national income. With the introduction of various decentralization and profit-sharing policies – tax cuts, economic incentives, and distribution adjustments – the once highly centralized national-income distribution system started to loosen its grip. For instance, SOEs were now permitted to retain more of their profit (instead of surrendering it to the government) to set up employee benefit funds and finance future development. As a result, the profit retention rate of SOEs increased from 2% in 1978 to 7.6% in 1979 and 36.96% in 1989.[1] While this invigorated the enterprises, the state treasury was receiving less and less of their profits. Fiscal revenue as a share of GDP also plummeted from 31.1% in 1978 to 25.5% in 1980,

---

1 Yang Zhiyong and Yang Zhigang: *Three Decades of China's Fiscal Reform*, Truth & Wisdom Press and Shanghai People's Press, 2008.

22.2% in 1985, and 15.7% in 1990.[1]

"Decentralization and profit-sharing" also opened the spigots of fiscal expenditure, such as price subsidies for agricultural products and byproducts and additional funds dedicated to boosting the salary level at administrative and public institutions. Subsidies to plug the losses of SOEs also increased. Indeed, fiscal expenditure surged from RMB 112.209 billion in 1978 to RMB 308.36 billion in 1990, up 170% in 12 years.[2] Fiscal deficits were recorded for almost every year of the 1980s and 1990s and increased from RMB 6.89 billion in 1980 to RMB 14.69 billion in 1990. Considering the treasury's shrinking share in national income distribution and the yawning gap between fiscal revenue and spending (Fig. 1.1), economic stimulus through leveraging the state balance sheet had already reached its natural limit.

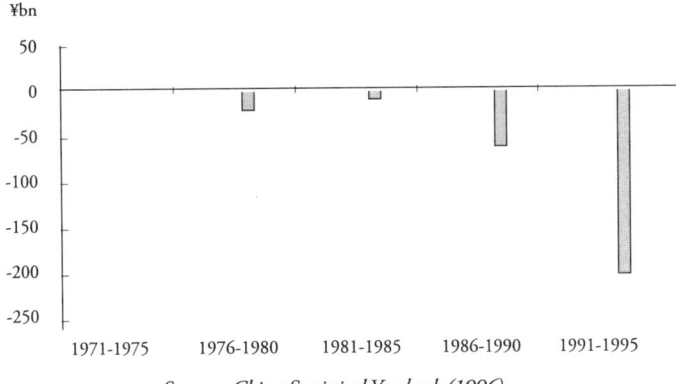

Source: *China Statistical Yearbook (1996)*.

Fig. 1.1: Gap Between Fiscal Revenue and Expenditure (1971-1995)

---

1   Quoted from Gao Peiyong: "From 'Decentralization and Profit-Sharing' to 'Public Finance': Three Decades of China's Fiscal and Tax Reform," *Theory Research*, 2008 (20).
2   National Bureau of Statistics: *China Statistical Yearbook (2007)*, China Statistics Press.

II. Issuing Government Bonds and Tapping Foreign Capital

In 1979, the Chinese government restarted bond issuance after a 20-year hiatus to raise capital for economic development. The government bonds issued in 1981 were followed by key infrastructure project bonds (*zhongdian jianshe zhaiquan*), fiscal bonds (*caizheng zhaiquan*, i.e., bonds issued by the Ministry of Finance to raise funds for infrastructure projects and the state treasury), national infrastructure project bonds, special government bonds, and inflation-indexed bonds. In 1993, the central government's revenue from bond issuance reached RMB 73.922 billion, hitting a debt dependence[1] of 59.63% – among the highest in the world[2]. That is to say, more than half of the expenditure of central government in the year was financed by debts or loans.

China's reforms always went hand in hand with opening up. However, intake of foreign capital was moderate in the early years (1978-1988). From 1979 to 1982, for example, foreign direct investment (FDI) totaled only USD 6.01 billion, of which only USD 1.166 billion was utilized. While it is hard to identify an industry-level pattern in the destination of foreign capital, they primarily flowed into manufacturing and tertiary sectors. From 1983 to 1988, FDI reached USD 22.155 billion on aggregate, including USD 12.095 billion in the industrial sector and USD 9.579 billion in the tertiary sector.[3]

---

1 Central government debt dependence = proceeds from debt issuance / (expenditure + debt repayment).
2 Quoted from Gao Peiyong: "From 'Decentralization and Profit-Sharing' to 'Public Finance': Three Decades of China's Fiscal and Tax Reform," *Theory Research*, 2008 (20).
3 National Bureau of Statistics: *China Statistical Yearbook (1990)*, China Statistics Press.

III. Bank Financing Inevitably Overtaking Fiscal Appropriations

Following reform and opening up, China resumed the bonus system for enterprises and administrative and public institutions, offered price subsidies for non-staple food, and launched pilot programs to link employee salary levels to an enterprise's business performance. These programs substantially increased the salaries of urban employees, which rose from RMB 615 in 1978 to RMB 1,148 in 1985, an 86.7% increase in gross terms or 34.5% net of inflation[1].

Shrinking claims to business profits throttled fiscal revenues. Financial resources previously sequestered in the state coffers flowed to enterprises and individual citizens, handing a larger slice of GDP to the households. The surge in income left people with more money to spend. In 1978, the government, enterprises, and household sectors captured 33.9%, 11.1%, and 55.0% of the national income respectively. In 1990, these ratios changed to 21.5%, 9.1%, and 69.4%. In other words, these 12 years mark a 14.4 percentage point gain by the households, concurrent with 12.4 percentage point and 2 percentage point retreats by the government and enterprise sectors, respectively[2].

Bereft of developed financial markets or a comprehensive social security system, enterprises and households mostly directed their savings to the banks, driving exponential growth in bank deposits (Table 1.1). Urban and rural savings increased from RMB 20.1 billion in 1978 to RMB 703.4 billion in 1990; and their share among the total deposits at national banks and rural credit cooperatives rose from 18% to 51%. Unsurprisingly,

---

1 National Bureau of Statistics: *China Statistical Yearbook (1998)*, China Statistics Press.
2 Quoted from Shi Faqi: *Five Issues of Income Distribution: How to Strike a Balance Between Fairness and Efficiency*, Shanghai Securities News, September 15, 2005.

banks took on the mandate of financing economic development as the supply of fiscal funds tapered off. It turned out that the sole, and therefore inevitable, solution for economic development was channeling savings into investment and creating an effective bank financing mechanism.

Table 1.1: Increase of Urban and Rural Personal Savings (1978-1989)

Year	Balance of Savings (¥bn)	Annual Growth (¥bn)	Annual Growth of Savings as Share of National Income (%)
1978	21.05	2.9	0.96
1979	28.10	7.05	2.10
1980	39.95	11.85	3.21
1981	52.37	12.42	3.15
1982	67.54	15.17	3.56
1983	89.25	21.71	4.59
1984	121.47	32.22	5.70
1985	162.26	40.79	5.80
1986	223.76	61.50	7.80
1987	307.33	83.57	8.97
1988	380.15	72.82	6.31
1989	514.69	134.54	10.35

Source: *Almanac of China's Finance and Banking (1990)*.

As can be seen from Table 1.1, household savings as share of national income increased from less than 1% at the beginning of the reform and opening-up initiative to over 10% in the late 1980s, implying that banks had become the most important reservoir of capital.

As the urgent financing needs arose in the economy and banks became the major pools of unoccupied capital, the state treasury could not keep up. As aggregate investment and financing grew substantially, the banks gradually supplanted this role of the treasury (Fig. 1.2).

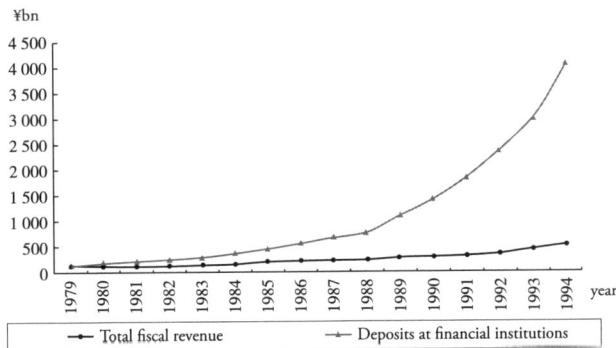

Source: Zhan Xiangyang, Fan Zhigang, and Jiang Ye: "Revisiting Working Capital Loans in Economic Transition," *Finance Forum*, 2006 (9).

Fig. 1.2: Treasury vs. Banks in Funds Mobilization, 1979-1994

Under the planned economy, state finance allocated a working capital quota to each enterprise, and banks were charged with funding and managing any amounts required in excess. Banks themselves could only mobilize a small amount of idle capital entrusted by the public, and the state plan gave them discretion over only a small portion of fiscal appropriations and deposits. They could only extend small working capital loans to meet the seasonal and *ad hoc* needs of enterprises. Meanwhile, the government was the country's sole investing entity, with business production and construction primarily funded by fiscal appropriations (Table 1.2).

Table 1.2: Treasury vs. Financial System in Funds Mobilization and Allocation (1952-1997) (¥bn)

Year	Total Fiscal Revenue	Domestic Infrastructure Expenditure	Innovation Funds and Science and Technology Promotion Funds	Additional Working Capital Appropriations	Urban and Rural Savings Deposits	Urban Term Deposits
1952	17.39	4.67	—	1.86	0.86	0.48
1953	21.32	7.03	—	1.38	1.23	0.68
1954	25.35	8.43	0.18	2.63	1.59	0.98

1955	25.55	8.85	0.31	3.08	1.99	1.33
1956	28.63	13.96	0.25	1.08	2.67	1.56
1957	31.00	12.37	0.23	2.08	3.52	1.96
1958	38.76	22.94	0.08	2.57	5.52	2.39
1959	48.71	30.23	0.22	5.43	6.83	3.16
1960	57.23	35.45	0.26	6.75	6.63	3.73
1961	35.61	11.02	0.27	2.94	5.54	2.97
1962	31.36	5.57	1.47	4.78	4.11	2.56
1963	34.23	8.02	1.83	3.67	4.57	2.94
1964	39.95	12.38	2.09	2.34	5.55	3.70
1965	47.33	15.85	2.52	2.76	6.52	4.34
1966	55.87	19.10	2.75	4.03	7.23	4.69
1967	41.94	16.13	1.03	2.91	7.39	4.89
1968	36.13	11.79	0.57	1.20	7.83	5.03
1969	52.68	20.62	1.07	2.66	7.59	4.94
1970	66.29	29.84	1.48	3.12	7.95	5.38
1971	74.47	30.96	2.64	3.53	9.03	6.14
1972	76.66	30.91	2.55	4.30	10.52	6.96
1973	80.97	31.72	2.55	5.38	12.12	7.77
1974	78.31	31.28	2.72	4.48	13.65	8.67
1975	81.56	32.70	3.15	4.18	14.96	9.45
1976	77.66	-31.13	3.43	4.54	15.91	10.06
1977	87.45	30.09	3.95	6.57	18.16	11.17
1978	113.23	45.19	6.32	6.66	21.06	12.89
1979	114.64	44.37	7.18	5.21	28.10	16.64
1980	115.99	34.64	8.05	3.67	39.95	30.49
1981	117.58	25.76	6.53	2.28	52.37	39.64
1982	121.23	26.91	6.90	2.36	67.54	51.93
1983	136.70	34.50	7.87	1.29	89.25	68.23
1984	164.29	45.41	11.18	1.00	121.47	90.09
1985	200.48	55.46	10.34	1.43	162.26	122.52
1986	212.20	59.61	12.99	0.99	223.85	172.97
1987	219.94	52.16	12.50	1.21	308.14	236.13
1988	235.72	49.48	15.10	0.96	382.22	284.85
1989	266.49	48.17	14.63	1.21	519.64	421.54

1990	293.71	54.74	15.39	1.09	711.98	591.12
1991	314.95	55.96	18.08	1.31	924.16	769.17
1992	348.34	55.59	22.36	1.06	1,175.94	942.52
1993	434.90	59.19	42.14	1.85	1,520.35	1,197.10
1994	521.81	63.97	41.51	1.73	2,151.88	1,683.87
1995	624.22	78.92	49.45	3.48	2,966.23	2,377.82
1996	740.80	90.74	52.30	4.29	3,852.08	3,087.34
1997	865.11	101.95	64.32	5.22	4,627.98	3,622.67

Notes: 1. Price subsidies were subtracted from fiscal revenue until 1985 when they were separately listed as fiscal expenditure. Figures before 1985 were adjusted accordingly for consistency.

2. Domestic infrastructure expenditure, innovation funds and science and technology promotion funds, as well as additional working capital appropriations are all fiscal expenditure.

3. Data taken from the National Bureau of Statistics: *China Statistical Yearbook (1986)*, *China Statistical Yearbook (1998)*, and Hu Shudong: *The Central-Local Relationship in Economic Development – A Study on the Transformation of China's Fiscal System*, Shanghai People's Press, 2002.

After issuing the first technological upgrade loan in 1979, banks began to make official lending plans, with specified funding amounts, for such loans and became increasingly involved in state fixed asset investment and infrastructure investment. At the same time, the state launched the program to substitute fiscal appropriations with bank loans in the area of fixed asset investment (*bogaidai*, "Appropriation-to-Loan Program"), in order to add teeth to the budget constraints placed on enterprises, enhance the sense of responsibility among the construction enterprises, and increase return of investment. As an important part in transforming how fixed asset investment was to be managed, the program was piloted by the textiles, tourism, and light industries in Beijing, Shanghai, and Guangdong. It was rolled out for all sectors nationwide from January 1985.

In contrast to fiscal funds, bank credit is given to enterprises that are essentially required to repay the principal and accrued interest, comprising a unique type of compensated funding activity that operates according to its own internal logic. The Appropriation-to-Loan Program was intended to, through this activity, prod SOEs to evolve into commercial and market-based entities that pursue investment return and efficiency. After the program was introduced, infrastructure loans supported the planned capital projects and guaranteed the funding of key projects carried out after 1985. Such loans have played a pivotal role in continuously promoting China's investment and economic boom over the past four decades since reform and opening up.

The shift to banking lending reform was carried out nearly simultaneously with the working capital system reform. In 1982, the fiscal appropriations for SOEs to use as working capital fell by 64.5% from 1978. Conversely, from 1979 to 1982, the working capital of industrial and commercial enterprises increased more than RMB 70 billion, a growth financed 82% by bank loans and only 18% by fiscal appropriations[1].

In June 1983, the State Council issued the "Notice on Approving and Forwarding the Report of the People's Bank of China on Taking over the Management of SOE Working Capital," authorizing banks to be solely responsible for managing businesses' working capital. The Notice

---

[1] Quoted from Chen Xudong: "Analysis on the Conflicts Between China's Fiscal Funds and Bank Loans," *Journal of Henan College of Financial Management Cadres*, 2005 (4).

clarified that SOEs would no longer be receiving working capital appropriations from the treasury, but could retain previously received funds as their proprietary capital, which would be subject to management by the banks. Banks subsequently became responsible for developing the working capital management system, approving quotas and plans and evaluating capital utilization efficiency. Their role as the "steward" of working capital was further consolidated as their balance of savings deposits grew quickly. In fact, the share of bank loans in total SOE working capital increased to 98.6% in 1994 and ultimately reached 100%[1]. Outstanding working capital loans skyrocketed from RMB 403.47 billion at the end of 1984 to RMB 1,807.743 billion at the end of 1994, representing a compound annual growth rate (CAGR) of 16.18% over the decade[2].

In becoming the "financier" of the economy, banks emerged as a key driver of China's rapid growth since reform and opening up. Between 1978 and 1997, credit issued by national specialized banks steadily increased from RMB 185 billion to RMB 5,931.8 billion, a CAGR of 20.0% or a cumulative 32-fold increase; loans to industrial producers soared from RMB 35.2 billion to RMB 1,543.4 billion, a 22.0% CAGR or 43 times cumulatively (Fig. 1.3). It's not hard to see that the banking sector had become a fundamental impetus to economic development and opening up in the two decades after 1978 by successfully converting savings into investment in the real economy, particularly for industrial enterprises.

---

1   Quoted from Zhan Xiangyang, Fan Zhigang, and Jiang Ye: "Revisiting Working Capital Loans in Economic Transition," *Finance Forum*, 2006 (9).
2   Quoted from Jiang Jianqing and Wei Guoxiong: *Origin and Management of "Evergreen Loans,"* China Financial Publishing House, 2009.

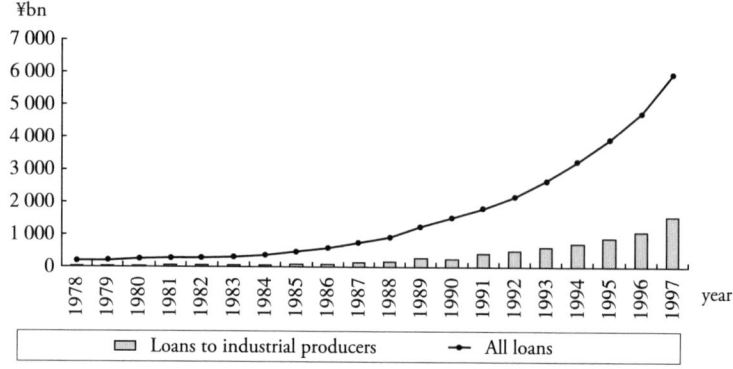

Source: *Almanac of China's Finance and Banking*, figures compiled by the author.

Fig. 1.3: Outstanding Credit Assets of State-Owned Banks (1978-1997)

Fixed asset loans from China's banking system for boosting production capacity increased from RMB 8.3 billion to 1,472.5 billion between 1978 and 1997, or 51.9% CAGR resulting in a 1,858-fold increase over 20 years (Fig. 1.4). Banks had become the engine that would power the country's reinvestment and productivity-improvement cycle.

The above two reforms, all centering on enterprises' working capital, transformed the way financial resources were marshaled to support economic development and business operation. In this transition, fiscal appropriations gave way to a new financial system dominated by bank lending. This vital institutional change made banks (and by extension, savings) an additional, and ultimately, primary source of investment capital in addition to fiscal funds. It maintained a continuous and sufficient supply of private capital for China's reform and transition, thus preventing the country from falling into the poverty trap and fueling four decades of economic boom.

The two reforms, however, also had adverse effects. After the cessation of fiscal appropriations, enterprises faced persistent fund shortages whenever they were unable to timely tap new sources of capital. They became highly indebted and dependent on bank loans, which occupied bank balance sheets for long periods and became a sort of disguised capital cushion for the enterprises. Whenever these loans ultimately turned sour, they would lead to massive build-up of non-performing loans.

Section III
Institutional Reform as Starting Point of Financial Reform

Theoretically, there are two approaches to financial reform: the institutional approach and the functional approach. The former is concerned with raising the operating efficiency of existing financial institutions through the chain of structure-function-performance. By establishing, adjusting, opening, and reforming financial institutions, this approach improves their functional capacity and hence their service levels, ultimately enhancing efficiency and promoting economic development. Over the years, China's financial reform has followed the doctrine of institutional reform. It started with banking institutions when the banking sector was made the main source of capital for economic reform and development. This doctrine underscores all subsequent developments, including the creation of specialized banks and policy banks, the joint-stock reform of state-owned banks, the establishment of joint-stock commercial banks and urban and rural commercial banks, the reorganization of credit cooperatives, as well as the development of private banks stretching into the present day. The institutional approach has guided China's financial reform over the years and spurred rapid financial development.

I. Reopening and Establishment of Specialized Banks

Within a few years following the Third Plenary Session of the 11th CPC Central Committee, the Bank of China (BOC), the Agricultural Bank of China (ABC), and the People's Construction Bank of China were each separated from the PBOC and the fiscal functions. Established in Shanghai in 1912, BOC is one of the oldest banks in China and served as the central bank until 1928, when it became a government-chartered international exchange bank until 1942. It is the first Chinese financial institution to expand internationally with branches opened in London, Singapore, New York, among other global financial centers. When the People's Republic of China was founded in 1949, BOC was taken over by the new government, and its General Administration Office was relocated from Shanghai to Beijing in December of that year. Later, it was merged into the PBOC as the overseas business department but still retained its business name and operated as the foreign exchange bank of China. In 1979, BOC was the first department of the PBOC that was spun off to become a specialized bank. In June 1979, the CPC Central Committee appointed Qiao Peixin as BOC Chairman and Bu Ming as BOC President who was also named the Administrator of the State Administration of Foreign Exchange (SAFE).

In February 1979, ABC – a bank that had witnessed three establishments and three dissolutions in its history – was approved to be reopened, becoming the first bank specialized in rural finance after the reform and opening-up initiative. Fang Gao was appointed as its first President. ABC was the successor of the Bank of Agricultural Cooperation which was set up in 1951 as the first specialized bank after the founding of the PRC. In 1996, rural credit cooperatives ceased to be affiliated to ABC.

China Construction Bank (CCB) was set up on October 1, 1954 to support China's first Five-Year Plan and full-scale economic development spearheaded by 156 key projects. Affiliated to the Ministry of Finance, CCB was responsible for managing a substantial amount of construction funds. It performed fiscal functions from 1954 to 1978 before assuming banking functions, which unveiled a new chapter in its history. Vice Minister of Finance Wu Boshan served concurrently as its first President. In 1996, the bank shortened its name to the current form from the original People's Construction Bank of China.

In early 1982, the PBOC established a reform steering group to develop a conceptual design of China's central bank as mandated by the State Council. In September 1983, the State Council officially designated the PBOC as China's central bank and decided to establish another bank to take over the PBOC's savings deposit and commercial credit business. On January 1, 1984, the PBOC started to independently perform its central bank functions and the Industrial and Commercial Bank of China (ICBC) was formed to take over its industrial and commercial credit, urban savings deposit, and settlement business, as well as its urban and rural branches across the country. Zhu Tianshun, PBOC Vice Governor in charge of credit business, was to concurrently serve as the ICBC Chairman; and Chen Li, PBOC Vice Governor in charge of deposit and accounting businesses, became the first ICBC President.

Bank of Communications (BoCom) was established in 1908 with headquarters in Shanghai. It is one of the oldest state-owned commercial banks (SOCBs) in China and one of the note-issuing banks during the Republic of China era. In 1951, BoCom's head office was relocated from Chongqing back to Shanghai. In 1958, except for the Hong Kong branch, all domestic businesses of BoCom were merged into PBOC local offices or BoCom's newly created successor – the People's Construction Bank of China. To promote economic reform and development, on July 24, 1986, the State Council approved the re-establishment of BoCom as a pilot financial reform program. On April 1, 1987, the re-established BoCom opened officially, becoming China's first state-owned joint-stock commercial bank with nationwide operations. Former President of PBOC Shanghai Branch Li Xiangrui served as its Chairman and President.

The separation of ICBC from the PBOC is a milestone marking the creation of China's central bank system. Since then, the PBOC started to independently perform central bank functions as the country jettisoned the monobank system in the planned economy in favor of a two-tier system. This change reshaped the financial landscape, with the PBOC taking a leadership role supported by the national specialized banks, and joined by a wide array of other banking and non-banking institutions such as insurance companies, trusts, and securities brokers.

National specialized banks sprung up between the 1980s and the mid-1990s. The number of domestic banking institutions reached 199,618 in 1993, an increase of 80,280 or 59.7% over 1985[1]. Banks also made progress in internal reforms. For instance, national specialized banks, mimicking the SOE reform, began assigning performance targets to their

---

[1] Quoted from *History of the Industrial and Commercial Bank of China (1984-1993)*, China Financial Publishing House, 2008, pp. 28-29.

savings-oriented outlets in the 1980s. Their aim was to improve efficiency and performance and drive business and product innovations to meet the economy's diversified demands.

Unlike the situation in corporate reform, in the early years of financial reform, only a few financial institutions were created outside the existing system. The four specialized banks were all spin-offs of the PBOC or the Ministry of Finance. At the beginning, banks were a part or extension of the government and more like administrative bodies than commercial banks. Their responsibility was to "serve as the cashier for the state and make loans and payments according to mandatory state plans."[1] In fact, specialized banks were positioned as "independent accounting entities"[2] directly under the State Council when they were first created.

It wasn't until March 1986 at the Fourth Session of the Sixth National People's Congress (NPC), with the approval of the "Seventh Five-Year Plan of the People's Republic of China for Economic and Social Development," that a roadmap was given to turn specialized banks into true corporations. The NPC recognized that for the banks to function as an economic multiplier, they must operate as enterprises driven by economic interest in providing credit services. "Only in this manner will banks have the autonomy in making loans"[3] and will "specialized banks no longer help themselves from the communal trough while retaining a monopoly in

---

1   Quoted from the speech of then PBOC Governor Chen Muhua delivered at the National Banking Work Conference on April 27, 1985, *China Finance*, 1985 (6).
2   See the "Interim Regulations on Bank Administration" released by the State Council in January 1986.
3   Quoted from Chen Muhua: "Speeding up Financial System Reform" (November 10, 1986), *Zhejiang Finance*, 1987 (1).

their market."[1] Enterprises needed to pay for access to capital and be subject to robust budget constraints. They should not mistake bank loans for government appropriations and should not chase after borrowing opportunities unless they can put forward a solid repayment plan. Such disregard for economic performance is a blatant flaw of the planned economy which must be fixed to increase economic and production efficiency.

In this period, although banks were transformed from administrative bodies into economic entities, national specialized banks still shouldered the responsibility to support SOEs and maintain social stability. Externally, it was not yet possible for banks to operate as enterprises. Internally, banks continued to cling to plans in managing their internal affairs and did not face pressures to take sole responsibility for their own profits and losses. Despite various efforts at self-transformation, they still had a long way to go before becoming truly independent managers of capital.

After the creation of specialized banks, China's credit management system evolved from the PBOC exercising unified control over income and expenditure (*tongshou tongzhi*) to specialized banks exercising unified control over deposits and loans (*tongcun tongdai*), to control loan-deposit difference (*cha'e kongzhi*) and the assignment of performance target based on loan-deposit difference (*cha'e baogan*). Starting from 1985, China started to implement the loan-deposit linkage (*shidai shicun*) system[2].

---

1   Quoted from the "Overall Plan of the State Commission for Restructuring the Economic System on Deepening Economic Structural Reform in 1988" (February 23, 1988).
2   In October 1984, the PBOC, ICBC, ABC, and BOC held the Seminar on the Reform of National Credit Management System, which laid out the principles of "central planning, differentiation of funds, linkage of loan volume to total deposits, and mutual financing." These principles were implemented in 1985.

The circulation of funds between specialized banks and the central bank had since been driven by commercial lending rather than appropriation[1], and this principle was cascaded down to become operative between local branches of the specialized banks and between these local branches and their higher-tiered branches and head offices. The reformed credit management system granted specialized banks the authority to run their own credit operations and made them accountable for their credit portfolios.

Under the planned economy, bank loans only served as a tool for funds allocation under the national economic plan and enterprises' production plans. They were granted according to state plans and policies. Since most enterprises were state-run and free from the risk of bankruptcy, banks were oblivious to credit risk. As China transitioned towards a market economy, SOEs had to follow market rules and some went bankrupt, exposing banks to credit risk. Since the late 1980s and early 1990s, increasing risk awareness prompted specialized banks to put their loan management procedures in order by focusing on the "three independent credit reviews,"[2] and put into place complete loan risk accountability and bad loan write-off systems.

China's banking reform, however, was yet to set the goal of "Four Independents." Loan risk management focused on controlling and evaluating the ratio of non-performing loans (NPLs) and was a reactive and retrospective exercise. The banking sector was still in its infancy with

---

1 Specialized banks maintained a funds segregation system (*fenzao chifan*) for cash management both between themselves and with the PBOC. They were prohibited from overdrafting their accounts at the PBOC. Should a shortfall arise, a bank could borrow from another bank or from the PBOC.
2 The "three reviews" refers to pre-lending, in-lending, and post-lending reviews. "Independent" means that reviewers should act independently and supervise each other.

regard to developing quantitative risk research and management, loan risk accountability systems, and internal controls.

II. Birth of Joint-Stock Banks

From 1987 to 1988, in support of the financial reform, the first wave of joint-stock banks opened business as market-based financial institutions. They broke the oligopoly of the specialized banks and transformed the financial landscape.

When BoCom was established in April 1987, a nationwide joint-stock commercial bank – CITIC Industrial Bank (now CITIC Bank) – was also unveiled in Beijing. While it was a state-run, comprehensive bank affiliated to CITIC Group, it was an independent business in terms of operations and accounting. In April 1987, the Administrative Committee of the Shekou Industrial Zone established the China Merchants Bank following government approval in August 1986. In January 1987, the preparation team for Shenzhen City Credit Bank (now Shenzhen Development Bank) was organized and, for the first time in China's banking history, issued ordinary shares to the public for subscription, forming an equity structure in which state and corporations were the major shareholders but the public formed the bulk of the shareholder base. In April 1988, Shenzhen Securities Corporation was founded, and Shenzhen Development Bank became the first bank to have its shares listed for trading through securities firms. Subsequently, many other joint-stock banks were also launched, such as Yantai and Bengbu housing savings banks, Guangdong Development Bank, and Fujian Industrial Bank.

During his inspection tour to Shanghai in 1991, Deng Xiaoping remarked, "Finance is very important, because it is the core of the modern economy. Handling financial affairs well is the key to success in this sphere."[1] After the pronouncement in 1992 that China would build a socialist market economy and embrace financial reform and opening up, the banking sector ushered in a new round of expansion. In 1992, China Everbright Bank, Huaxia Bank, Shanghai Pudong Development Bank, and Minsheng Bank were green lit for launch.

Other institutions such as urban and rural credit cooperatives and trusts developed even more rapidly than national specialized banks and joint-stock banks. In 1982, the CPC Central Committee's instruction of "making credit cooperatives into real financial collectives" was implemented with back-to-fundamentals reforms to restore the "three features" deemed essential for rural credit cooperatives.[2] In 1984, the reform was carried out at 48,365 rural credit cooperatives, accounting for 82% of the total number. Established in 1979, Henan Luohe City Credit Cooperative was the first urban credit cooperative to emerge since reform and opening up began. By the end of 1988, there were 3,265 urban cooperatives in China with 49,700 employees. Over years of rapid growth, urban credit cooperatives began to push their limits in organization, operations, and management. In a campaign to restore order to the financial sector launched in 1995, China further reformed urban credit cooperatives by reorganizing some into Shanghai, Beijing, and Shenzhen city cooperative banks. Later, more cities lent their namesake to such newly established banks.

---

1 *Selected Works of Deng Xiaoping*, Vol. III, Foreign Languages Press, 1994, p. 353.
2 "Three features" refers to public participation, democratic management, and flexible business operation.

Section IV
Bank Reform Invigorated the Economy

By separating the financial system from the fiscal system, the bank reform enabled banks to recover and reinforce their financing and other functions, empowering them to better promote economic development and technological upgrades. Banks ensured a continuous supply of capital for China's reform and transition, thus fueling four decades of economic boom.

For the period between 1978 and 1994, national specialized banks grew both their assets and deposits over 100 times, which allowed them to fully mobilize financial resources to support economic growth. As intermediaries in this indirect financing system, they financed a significant proportion of fixed asset investment and production activities. They also began to assume the responsibility of supporting the real economy and social progress and drove rapid economic development. To meet diversified financing needs, they broadened their loan portfolios from working capital loans to fixed asset loans. The scope of eligible loan recipients also expanded from producers to distributers and then to larger sectors such as science and technology, education, culture, and healthcare.

In supporting economic growth, banks extended loans for fixed asset investment and introduced new loan products such as short- and medium-term equipment loans, technological upgrade loans, and infrastructure loans. In particular, technological upgrade loans, initially issued to the consumer goods industry, were extended to other sectors like automobile, chemical, electromechanical, and transportation. The purpose of this loan product was changed from supporting production expansion to encouraging enterprises to adopt new technologies, processes, equipment, and materials, so that they could improve technical capacity, energy and environmental performance, and product quality, as well as introduce new products. In a shortage economy, bank credit played an irreplaceable role in promoting active markets; supplying much-needed consumer goods, textiles and exports; creating jobs; withdrawing currency from circulation; and maintaining market stability. In addition to SOEs, banks also extended loans to collective enterprises and in turn to individuals.

By the end of 1991, more than 700,000 township and village enterprises (TVEs) borrowed from ABC and credit cooperatives, accounting for 60% of the total number of TVEs. Between 1992 and 1996, loans from ABC to TVEs amounted to RMB 567.74 billion cumulatively, up 1.58 times over the previous five years[1]. ABC issued agricultural loans to 170 million farming households, up from 5.6 million commune brigades[2]. By the end of 1993, the balance of collective industrial loans issued by ICBC reached RMB 69.217 billion, up 3.2 times over the end of 1984[3].

A more diversified offering of savings products attracted more capital for the banks to mobilize. Official statistics show that the total amount of savings deposited at national specialized banks increased from RMB 113.5 billion in 1978 to RMB 6,000.3 billion in 1997, up 52 times in 20 years, or 23.2% CAGR (Fig. 1.5).

---

1   Wu Chengji: *History of the Agricultural Bank of China*, Economic Science Press, 2000, pp. 340-342.
2   Ibid, pp. 135-138.
3   Quoted from *History of the Industrial and Commercial Bank of China (1984-1993)*, China Financial Publishing House, 2008, pp. 175-177.

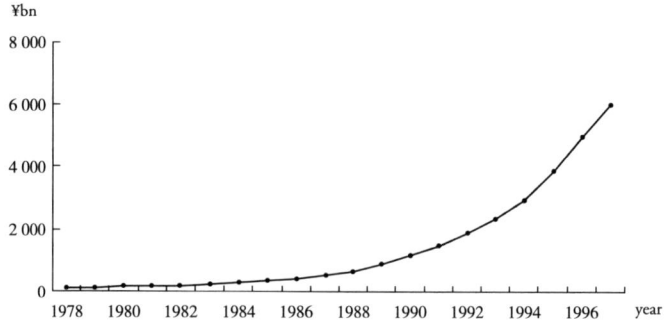

Source: *Almanac of China's Finance and Banking*; figures compiled by the author.

Fig. 1.5: Deposits at State-Owned Banks (1978-1997)

Since 1978, China's steadily rising savings rate has been a key driver of economic growth – acclaimed internationally as the "China miracle." Savings became a significant source of funds for issuing loans (Table 1.3). By 1997, savings made up more than half of the total funds of national specialized banks, up 38 percentage points over 1980 and 47 percentage points over 1960.

Table 1.3: Savings as a Share of Funds at National Specialized Banks (%)

Year	Savings as a share of total deposits	Savings as a share of total funds
1960	14.41	6.90
1970	11.28	7.60
1975	15.34	10.07
1980	24.04	15.22
1985	35.34	23.65
1986	37.93	25.04
1987	41.34	27.29
1988	44.83	28.98
1989	49.38	32.82
1990	51.89	35.89

1991	53.57	38.63
1992	58.57	43.59
1993	58.66	46.81
1994	60.61	48.98
1995	62.04	48.42
1996	63.82	51.81
1997	64.33	53.96

Source: 1. Consolidated figures from the PBOC, China Development Bank, Export-Import Bank of China, Agricultural Development Bank of China, ICBC, ABC, BOC, CCB, BoCom, CITIC Industrial Bank, and rural credit cooperatives.

2. *Almanac of China's Finance and Banking (1996-1998)*; figures compiled and calculated by the author.

The growing contribution of savings as a source of bank funds brought about at least two benefits. First, savings reflected the supply and demand of monetary capital and created a pool of funds that could be channeled to investment – this savings-to-investment model dampened household consumption but proved vital to China's capital formation and rapid economic growth after the reform and opening up. Second, the growth of savings increased the self-sufficiency of national specialized banks and weaned them from loans issued by the PBOC. By matching supply with demand, banks increased their profitability, soundness, and liquidity.

As Table 1.4 shows, between 1978 and 1990, China's GDP increased 4.22 times from RMB 362.4 billion to RMB 1.89 trillion; fiscal revenue grew by 1.59 times from RMB 113.2 billion to RMB 293.7 billion; and foreign reserves expanded by 65.43 times from USD 167 million to USD 11.093 billion. In financing the economy, banks themselves also grew rapidly. Over the same period, bank deposits increased 11 times from RMB 115.5 billion to RMB 1.39 trillion. Equally significant growth also took place in credit supply. During the same period, the total amount of bank loans increased 8.26 times from RMB 189 billion to RMB 1.75 trillion. It is fair to say that the great achievements of the reform and opening-up initiative would not have been possible without the expanding financial industry that provided credit to the economy.

The bank-dominated financial system converted savings into capital on a massive scale. The resulting rapid improvements to the financial sector, financing services, and resource allocation capabilities were critical to and well-aligned with China's successful economic transition. However, finance is also a double-edged sword. In fulfilling its mission to support the economy, the sector also took on significant risks. Excessive, prolonged financing support to SOEs weakened constraints on SOCBs and engendered significant asset risks. Over the past four decades of reform and opening up, China's financial industry had faced many serious risks but fortunately managed to overcome them through bold reforms.

Table 1.4: China's Macroeconomic Indicators (1978-1990)

Indicator	1978	1990	Growth
GDP	¥362.4 billion	¥1.89 trillion	522%
Fiscal revenue	¥113.2 billion	¥293.7 billion	259%
Foreign reserves	$167 million	$11.093 billion	6,643%
Bank deposits	¥115.5 billion	¥1.39 trillion	1,203%
Loans	¥189 billion	¥1.75 trillion	926%

Source: National Bureau of Statistics website (http://www.stats.gov.cn/).

Put simply, state-owned banks have played three important roles in China's economic development: (i) they supplied the credit capital essential to economic growth; (ii) they offered innovative products and services that met the needs of a broad group of businesses and individuals; and (iii) they supported the SOE reform and macroeconomic regulation by establishing a market-based system for funds allocation. While the first two roles were fulfilled before the joint-stock reform, the third came into play after it.

CHAPTER II
IMPETUS FOR REFORM

– Financial Sector Remediation and Surfacing of Non-Performing Assets

The 1990s was a defining period for China's economic reform. The decade is marked by radical political, economic, and social changes, both at home and abroad, that forcefully propelled China forward from a plan-centric commodity economy *(shangpin jingji)* to a socialist market economy *(shehuizhuyi shichang jingji)*. During those extraordinary times, China's financial system was also charged with a historic mission. As a major developing country aspiring to quickly catch up and surpass others, China had its hands full juggling the domestic savings rate, investment-to-GDP ratio, and the interactions between the two. The mounting cost of risk that accompanied China's drastic reforms and economic transitioning was posing major challenges to the traditional systems for financial operation, financial management, and risk control. For this reason, financial reform was a must, or else China's financial system wouldn't merely lag behind the fast-growing economy, but actually directly slow down economic progress due to accumulated risks. The big questions were what, when, and how to reform. These were questions as much about strategies and theories as about tactics and practices. For China to find the right direction and approach for financial reform and development, all industry sectors needed to be on a path of continuous improvement, not only leveraging past successes and failures, but also boldly embracing trial-and-error approaches. In retrospect, the discussion and debate of this decade-long reform period laid the groundwork for a national consensus to emerge on how to push forward with financial reforms.

Section I
Macro-Finance and Governance

It took time for China to understand and develop banking in a socialist context. In the early years of reform, the hope was for banks to fuel economic growth by helping expand the money supply and the scale of lending. This goal was indeed achieved by allowing banks to set up new business entities, to operate more freely and retain surplus profits, to expand their scope of business, and to change how funds were managed. As a result, during the ten-odd years (1978-1990) before the reform, loans grew at 20.38% annually on average and the economy at 14.6%. Excessive lending did supercharge the economy, but it also put too much money in circulation which led to inflation – a fundamentally monetary phenomenon that was, in the case of China, compounded by structural imbalances. Outstanding loan balances climbed alongside the fiscal deficits that had resulted from relative decline in government revenue, together leading to economic overheating and bouts of inflation from the late 1980s to the early 1990s. The wide range of social issues caused by the soaring inflation rate drew the attention of China's decision-makers, who, for the first time since the separation of the financial industry from the state fiscal apparatus, began to contemplate another round of financial reform, in particular how the financial system should be restructured to achieve better operation and management.

China has in fact experienced three periods of major inflation since reform and opening up.

The first occurred at the beginning of reform and opening up, during the country's economic recovery and adjustment between 1978 and 1981. A surge in economic growth, investment, and fiscal expenditure caused a major deficit, while unchecked import growth led to a trade deficit that quickly depleted China's foreign reserves. Consumer prices rose significantly in 1979 and 1980 – the inflation rate in 1980 reached 6%. Although measures including reduction of capital investments, monetary tightening, and price controls were effective at curbing inflation, GDP growth was also affected, plunging from 11.7% in 1978 to 5.2% in 1981.

The second inflation period, taking place in the 1980s, was triggered by two rounds of economic overheating from a dramatic increase in infrastructure investment and outstanding loans. Indications of the first round of overheating came in the second half of 1984. In that and the following year, total investment in fixed assets increased by 28.2% and 38.8%, and total retail sales rose by 18.5% and 27.5%, respectively. In 1985, the retail price index (for goods) saw a 6-percentage-point hike year-on-year, to 8.8%. The nation responded by limiting fixed-asset investment, strengthening price supervision and management, and taking inventory of the amount of credit outstanding. However, the actual implementation of these countermeasures was not robust.

The second round of overheating started from the second quarter of 1986, when GDP growth picked up momentum and both investment and consumption went up. This coincided with the price reforms (*jiage chuangguan*) of 1988 and 1989, during which the retail price index (for goods) surged by 18.5% and 17.8%, up 11.2 and 10.5 percentage points from 1986. RMB 213.4 billion of cash was in circulation by 1988 – RMB 68 billion of which was issued in that year alone – an astonishing 46.8% increase from 1987. This emergency prompted the 13th CPC Central Committee to convene its Fifth Plenary Session to restore economic order by clamping down on government expenditure, credit expansion, fixed-asset investment, and controlling the increase in both aggregate wages and the monetary base. These measures brought inflation under control, but due to their heavy-handedness and tightly spaced implementation schedule, the GDP growth rate also plummeted.

The third inflation occurred between 1992 and 1995. The Chinese economy welcomed a new period of rapid growth in 1992. But because issues deeply embedded in the economic structure had not been fully resolved, overheating flared back up, marked by a rampant rise in the money supply, loans, and fixed-asset investment; income inequality and fiscal deficits suffered as well. By the end of 1995, cash in circulation (M0) shot up to RMB 788.5 billion, M1 reached RMB 2,398.7 billion, and M2 hit RMB 6,074.9 billion, an increase of RMB 524.1 billion, RMB 1,645.8 billion, and RMB 4,421.7 billion from 1990, corresponding to 24.4%, 26%, and 29.7% CAGR. In October 1994, the retail price index (for goods) rose 25.2% year-on-year (24.6% from September 1993 to September 1994). The central government tried to curtail credit expansion through its state-owned banks; but local governments, taking advantage of new freedoms afforded by devolution of authority (*fenquan guanli*) and revenue-sharing policies (*fenzao chifan*), were eager to interfere with the financial system to their own benefit. This led to a proliferation of short-term lending exchanges in various locations, while sizeable, unsanctioned off-balance-sheet lending and financing business lines were being set up by trust companies, credit cooperatives and funds, becoming in effect the earliest shadow banks in the People's Republic of China.

In the absence of strong supervision, many banks partnered with these institutions and engaged in non-compliant lending activities, exacerbating monetary and credit expansion and inflation. The situation was succinctly summarized by contemporaries as "four overheated markets" (overheating of real estate, development zones, fundraising, and stocks), "four highs" (high rates of growth in investment, industry, currency and loan issuance, and consumer prices), "four shortages" (shortages of transport capacity, energy supplies, key raw materials, and funds), and "one poor regulation" (poor regulation of economic activities, the financial sector in particular).

The last of these issues was marked during this time by poor regulation of fundraising, short-term lending, and establishment of financial institutions (colloquially the "three unruly areas"). With regard to fundraising, the shadow banks mentioned earlier would, through various disguised approaches, offer high interest rates to attract deposits, simultaneously putting a massive amount of funds into circulation outside the banking system and starving local bank branches of the cash needed for customer withdrawals, which in turn forced the central bank to make more loans. With regard to short-term lending, there was a prevalence of these exchanges, large and small, and altogether loosely regulated, which would provide funding to financial institutions of any kind and at any level, enabling them to make new loans beyond the prescribed limits. Lastly, with regard to the establishment of financial institutions, because there was no restriction on mixing business lines under the same roof, financial institutions expanded into every market – real estate, trusts, securities brokerage, and more. Worse still, even banks created a large number of financial and non-financial entities. Financial institutions leveraged their substantial capital to feed the unfettered growth of their subsidiaries, all without stringent management frameworks or firewalls.

The central government was alarmed by the unruly financial sector and structural issues in the economy, noting that "[China was faced with a] precarious macroeconomic situation and growing challenges. We must deepen reform and implement macroeconomic controls in a timely manner, or the issues will cause severe imbalance between supply and demand, worsening inflation, and even economic shocks and social instability."[1]

On the whole, the two rounds of inflation at the beginning of reform and opening up and in the 1980s were mainly attributed to the combined effect of excessive infrastructure investment and unconstrained money creation. Controlling the money supply, therefore, was the "antidote" to economic overheating and inflation. The inflation in the 1990s, by contrast, was exacerbated by poor regulation of the financial sector. Taming it required

---

1 "Opinions of the CPC Central Committee and State Council on the Current Economic Situation and on Strengthening Macroeconomic Controls," June 1993.

China to additionally and firstly restore order to the financial sector.

To this end, the national authorities issued the "Opinions of the CPC Central Committee and State Council on the Current Economic Situation and on Strengthening Macroeconomic Controls" (the "Opinions") in June 1993. Out of the 16 measures it proposed, 8 were for reforming the financial system, including: (1) strictly controlling the issuance of money, and "maintaining control of the monetary base" in particular; (2) rectifying unauthorized short-term lending by requiring the PBOC to stop making loans to non-banking financial institutions, imposing stricter requirements on short-term lending by banks, and other measures; (3) increasing aggregate bank deposits through higher interest rates while cracking down on unreasonably high rates; (4) putting an end to unruly fundraising activities by cleaning up illegitimate fundraising using newly defined identification criteria; (5) strictly controlling the amount of outstanding loans, enhancing the central bank's macroeconomic controls, and more effectively managing the destination of loans; (6) requiring the head offices of specialized banks to develop cash redistribution plans to ensure their local branches could always meet customers' withdrawal requests; (7) expediting financial reform by boosting the central bank's capacities in macroeconomic control, stripping provincial PBOC branches of the power to allocate loan quotas, controlling the amount of central bank loans, closing down unlawful financial institutions, and decoupling the central bank and specialized banks from the non-banking financial institutions and other economic entities they had established; and (8) integrating the financial reform with the reform of the investment framework, and establishing policy banks to separate policy lending from commercial finance.

At its third plenary session in November 1993, the 14th CPC Central Committee adopted the "Decision on Issues Concerning the Establishment of a Socialist Market Economy" (the "Socialist Market Economy Decisions"). This was followed up by the State Council on December 1993 with the release of the "Decision of the State Council on Reform of the Financial System," which was meant to supplement the 16 measures it had earlier proposed. In this latter document, the State Council set down four priorities for the financial reform.

First, to establish a sound framework for macroeconomic regulation and control ("macro-control") overseen by the central bank. This entailed (1) repurposing the PBOC by turning it into a *bona fide* central bank and relieving its branches of all levels from their operational duties; (2) reforming monetary policies, by decreeing that the PBOC shall direct monetary policy toward promoting monetary stability and economic growth, and giving it more tools, beyond that of central bank loans which it had, to help it achieve this objective; and (3) enhancing the PBOC's authority in financial supervision and controlling the establishment of financial institutions.

Second, to set up policy banks to take over the policy-driven businesses of state-owned banks, thereby cutting off the direct ties between government-directed lending and the monetary base.

Third, to transform national specialized banks into state-owned commercial banks (SOCBs), upon which SOCBs would be expected to achieve "independent operations, self-assumption of risk, self-assumption of profits and losses, and self-discipline," and would be allowed to cross into other business lines and compete with each other. Additionally, SOCBs would be assigned greater responsibilities in managing funds, redistributing them among their branches, and managing liquidity; and be prohibited from investing in non-financial enterprises and running distinct lines of business under a single corporate entity.

Fourth, to create a unified, open, orderly, and strictly regulated financial market. This task involved the following aspects: (1) better regulating the money market by strengthening access controls and preventing capital from being diverted into securities or real estate markets; (2) regulating short-term lending and clearing by financial institutions, including setting a limit on the term of such loans; (3) tasking the PBOC to set ceiling and floor interest rates on deposits and loans and developing a market-based interest rate system that is anchored to the PBOC rates; and (4) requiring the PBOC to strengthen the monitoring of financing activities among financial institutions.

The financial remediation and reform campaign in 1993 marked the beginning of financial reform in China. Its immense and lasting influence would shape the financial reforms in the years that followed and even the financial framework of the present day.

To fully implement the Socialist Market Economy Decisions, starting from 1994, the central government carried out wide-ranging complementary reforms which covered the fiscal, taxation, financial, foreign exchange, foreign trade, planning, investment, and wholesale and retail systems, the pricing mechanisms, and SOEs. In the financial sphere, the banking sector was segregated from the securities, insurance, trust, and real estate sectors, with each subsequently under separate regulation and supervision, as directed by the "Decision of the State Council on Reform of the Financial System." The decoupling of banks from the economic entities they had established and also from trust companies was correspondingly put on an accelerated timetable. At the same time, the government created the three policy banks in the first half of 1994, achieving the tentative separation of policy lending and commercial finance. Moreover, several foundational laws governing the financial industry – *Law on the People's Bank of China*, *Law on Commercial Banks*, *Negotiable Instruments Law*, and *Insurance Law* – were enacted, helping develop the various markets and expedite China's market-oriented development.

The combined effect of these programs stabilized the economy. By 1996, the high inflation had been tamed and prices returned to a relatively low level, indicating a successful "soft landing." Following this round of reform, China has been maintaining a low rate of inflation for 20 years and counting, building a solid foundation for further economic and financial reform and development.

Section II
The Non-Performing Loan Quandary

In the late 1980s, as China's economy took off and currency creation surged, bank loans expanded exponentially. While businesses and banks started to reinvent themselves as market-based enterprises, non-performing loans (NPLs) began to accumulate and became a major obstacle to China's economic and financial growth.

I. Crisis in Bank Asset Quality
(I) Historical Burdens

In addition to bouts of overheating and generally high inflation at the macro-finance level, starting from the early 1990s, problems at the micro-finance level also surfaced. Specifically, the first campaign to remediate the financial industry in 1993 had revealed to the government and regulators a major threat in the banking industry – the continuous creation and build-up of NPLs, a problem made all the more apparent by regulatory reforms, commercial reform of banks, and greater public scrutiny and research into the quality of bank assets. By the mid-1990s, NPLs had pushed state-owned banks to the edge of a precipice. In June 1995, at the Conference on the Operation and Management of Banking Industry convened by the PBOC, Governor Dai Xianglong ordered ICBC, ABC, BOC, and CCB to lower their average NPL ratio from 20.4% to below 17% in two to three years[1]. But by the end of 1995, the aggregate NPLs of the four banks would climb to RMB 850 billion, further raising the NPL ratio to 21.4%[2].

Both regulators and banks then attempted to halt the upsurge of NPLs. In 1995, the PBOC strengthened its monitoring and supervision of banks' asset quality. The banks, for their part, tried to enhance credit discipline while reducing their overhang of NPLs, including cascading profit and NPL targets from the head office to each lower level of branches and sub-branches through enhanced performance assessments. Nonetheless, both internal and external circumstances conspired to prevent these efforts from reaching the desired outcome.

To better understand the nature and cause of this issue, the PBOC organized a series of surveys. In May 1997, the PBOC head office looked into financial institutions in six prefecture-level cities in two southern provinces. The survey showed that: (1) NPLs had become "a deeply en-

---

1 Figures from Dai Xianglong's report "Comprehensively Strengthening the Operation and Management of China's Banking Industry."
2 Derived from data in the August 1999, PBOC report on the causes of NPLs of the four wholly state-owned commercial banks.

twined social issue"; as such, the measures taken by the PBOC and banks at various levels to reverse the deterioration of assets were doomed to be ineffective, as demonstrated by the rising NPL ratio of the banks surveyed; (2) insolvent enterprises repaid less than 10% of their loans on average at the time of their bankruptcy;[1] even if the loans were secured by guarantee or collateral, banks were at best only able to recover a miniscule portion of their claim; and (3) bank branches at all levels, to various extents, were able to sail through various assessments and inspections by extending the term of loans, adjusting the amount of principal, allowing enterprises to pay off existing loans with new ones, adjusting accounts under which the loans were recorded, and keeping loans off their balance sheets, among other evasive tactics. Fraudulent, withheld, or erroneous reporting on NPLs was prevalent, revealing an issue that was much grimmer than appeared in the books. To a certain extent, the NPL situation at the surveyed banks in the six cities was indicative of the asset quality and risk control shortfalls of the whole banking industry.

The Asian financial crisis in the mid-1997 was another major blow to the loan quality of China's state-owned banks. As of the end of 1998, NPLs on the books of ICBC, ABC, BOC, and CCB totaled RMB 1.97 trillion, more than double the figure in 1995; the NPL ratio soared to 31.3%, a 10 percentage point increase from 1995[2].

It should be mentioned that the NPL balance and ratio noted above were calculated based on a four-category classification scheme that categorized the non-performing loans as either overdue, doubtful, or unrecoverable,

---

1 *Almanac of China's Finance and Banking (1998)*.
2 Derived from data in the appendix to the "Plan for the Comprehensive Reform of Wholly State-Owned Commercial Banks" released by the PBOC in 2002.

in accordance with the criteria set forth in the "Financial System for Financial and Insurance Enterprises" issued by the Ministry of Finance (MOF) in 1993 (though these criteria had been in effect since the late 1980s). Pursuant to the "General Rules on Loans (Provisional)" of 1995[1]:

- "Overdue" meant any loan (excluding doubtful or unrecoverable category) that remained unpaid upon the date of maturity as specified in the loan contract or subsequently extended;
- "Doubtful" meant any loan (excluding unrecoverable category) that, per MOF regulations, was overdue beyond a prescribed period after the date of maturity (either the original date or as subsequently extended), or was overdue for less than that prescribed period (including not overdue), but the business operation or the project for which the loan was taken had already been terminated;
- "Unrecoverable" meant any loan that had been recognized as a loss per MOF regulations.

As evident from the above, the classification depended chiefly on the length of overdue period rather than on borrowers' repayment capacity. While it certainly helped banks manage the quality of their loans, this simplified classification scheme often grossly underestimated the amount of NPLs due to the following reasons: (1) some loans would be misleadingly considered "performing" because they were not overdue, even though future recovery was in jeopardy; (2) banks could easily circumvent the time-

---

1 The 1995 edition was for trial implementation. The official edition was published one year later in 1996.

based threshold for overdue loans by granting an extension or rolling over the loan, sweeping the doubtful loans under the rug. Due to its lackluster design and rigor, this classification scheme could not give an objective and accurate picture of the actual quality of bank loans.

> **Related Topic: Problems of the Four-Category Classification Scheme**[1]
>
> ABC and other specialized banks began to explore ways of classifying the quality of loans in the late 1980s. Around the same time, the MOF, in the interest of financial management, developed the preliminary classification rules, based on which the PBOC issued the "Interim Measures for the Administration and Evaluation of Commercial Bank's Asset-Liability Ratios" in 1994 and the "General Rules on Loans (Provisional)" in 1995. All of these documents classified and measured the quality of loans based on the length of the overdue period, and determined the unrecoverable loans due for write-off according to the criteria laid down by the MOF in 1988. This would be later known as the four-category classification scheme (*yiyu liangdai*).
>
> Notwithstanding the provision in the "General Rules on Loans (Provisional)" that stated that a non-delinquent loan taken out for a project shall be treated as doubtful if the project is terminated and repayment becomes impossible, fundamentally, the general framework for classifying the quality of loans was based on the overdue period. Attention was not being paid to the risks of the enterprises and risks were not being assessed in terms of repayment capacity. While the MOF had specified the criteria for unrecoverable loans, because there was no social safety net and, as a result,

---

1   From Dai Xianglong's speech "Better Loan Classification and Asset Quality for a Stronger Foundation for the Modern Banking System," delivered at a mobilization meeting in 1998 for the "loan review and classification (*qingfen*)" pilot program.

enterprises that would have otherwise gone bankrupt were not allowed to do so, banks did not classify the credit extended to these enterprises as unrecoverable loans. Consequently, a significant amount of incurred losses was not recognized as such, leading to mischaracterization of asset quality. While this classification scheme was easy to use and conducive overall to credit management, it was still a product of the then underdeveloped corporate, financial, and accounting frameworks. Given the circumstances to which it was to be now applied, it could no longer objectively reflect the quality of loans or timely identify, contain, and resolve financial risks, and was in fact increasingly incompatible with the new financial system.

In addition to on-balance-sheet NPLs, state-owned banks also suffered off-balance-sheet non-credit losses of hundreds of billions of yuan. These losses were incurred from, among other sources: (1) losses on companies established by the banks before the remediation of the financial industry that were unlawfully left unrecorded and losses upon the disposal of such companies; (2) devaluation or destruction of assets pledged as collateral for loans; (3) losses from on-balance-sheet interest receivables; and (4) unrecoverable receivables. These losses were in essence an alternate form of credit risk, and together with NPLs, were an onerous stain on the books of state-owned banks.

The size of NPLs and losses easily dwarfed the capital and the corresponding allowances made by the state-owned banks. This dire problem was very much obscured before 1997. Even at the end of 1997, because the accounting methods under the then International Accounting Standards (IAS, later included and superseded by the International Financial Reporting Standards (IFRS)) had not been adopted in China, each of the

Big Five was able to report a small book profit (Fig. 2.1). But this was realized because at 1997 year-end they had recorded only RMB 39.65 billion in NPL allowance, a pittance compared to the balance of NPLs as measured under the four-category classification scheme.

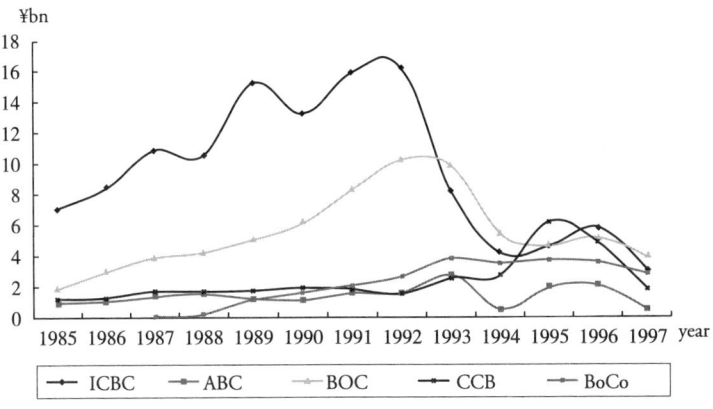

Fig. 2.1: Big Five's Book Profit (1985-1997)

At this time, IAS mandated that the ultimate losses on NPLs should be written off against the bank's capital in the event of allowance shortfalls. But as of the end of 1997, the Big Five only had a total equity of RMB 297.3 billion and no supplementary capital. This means that even a mere 20% uncollectible ratio on the near RMB 2 trillion of NPLs would exceed the banks' total allowance and capital – subsequent evaluations and disclosures by the banks showed that 80% of their NPLs arising before or during 1997 were unrecoverable. Once their enormous uncovered asset losses were taken into account, the Big Five were in fact in severe financial stress or even "technically insolvent."

Moreover, the Big Five's NPLs were reckoned according to a lax standard. If the quality of their assets were retrospectively evaluated using strict accounting standards, losses on their NPLs (and therefore the amount of additional allowance required) would reach trillions of yuan. This figure would far exceed what the Chinese economy and state-owned banks could bear at the time.

(II) Enormous NPLs as a Hidden "Minefield"

The build-up of NPLs in state-owned banks devoured the fruits of their operations and put them at the brink of financial unsustainability; more importantly, it would engender financial dysfunction and disarray. The resulting financial instability would in turn stall China's economic reform and progress.

NPLs brought four major risks. Firstly, they trapped state-owned banks in a vicious circle that diminished their ability to support the economy. NPLs and profitability were interdependent. Resolving the NPLs required higher earnings, but higher earnings could only be achieved after reduction of NPLs. Without external assistance, the banks would spiral toward ever-worsening financial condition and take an eternity to work off the enormous amount of NPLs and non-credit losses with their then meager profit level; and without resolving the NPLs, their profitability, and therefore capacity to build up supplementary capital and provide financing, would be impaired indefinitely. Because state-owned banks would continue to be the primary source of financing in the foreseeable years, their declining lending capacity would be out of sync with the country's rising credit demand. Consequently, the NPL situation of state-owned banks would ultimately weaken their support for the real economy.

Secondly, the NPLs would further erode financial discipline. The NPL issue involved highly complex causes, many excessively delinquent loans, and an entangled web of bank managers, loan officers, and borrowers (who may have acquired such a status after the initial loan had changed hands multiple times), making financial accountability an impossible task. Some banks had a 90% NPL ratio, and neither could hold the relevant personnel responsible nor tried to timely recover the loans. This issue made local bank branches complacent about their reckless lending practices, and gave unscrupulous enterprises the perfect excuse for non-payment. In fact, this erosion of financial discipline was itself partly responsible for the deterioration of loan quality.

This trend coincided with the critical period for the SOE reform. For the purpose of supporting that program and maintaining economic stability, insolvent SOEs with no chance of recovery were allowed to stay alive, as some sort of "zombie business," through continuous injection of capital from banks. This life support could no more be removed than the substantial stock of NPLs could be quickly resolved. As such, the banks had to mitigate their risks and financial pressure by allowing SOEs to take out new loans to pay off existing ones and by extending or collecting only the interest on unqualified loans. The lax restraints on corporate financing led to significant misuse or squandering of capital. The various compromises made were self-defeating acts of desperation, which rather than curbing the NPLs, caused them to snowball, dealing a significant blow to the credit environment as well as to the banks' credit culture and culture of accurate bookkeeping and rigorous financial and compliance management[1].

---

1   The culture of accurate bookkeeping and rigorous financial and compliance management ("*santie*") was first proposed by the PBOC and gradually became the mantra for China's banking industry and the broader financial industry on compliance operation and strict internal management.

Thirdly, the NPLs both distorted the execution and reduced the efficiency of capital allocation. Banks act as funding intermediaries between the demand side, i.e., enterprises and individuals in need of capital, and the supply side, i.e., enterprises, organizations, and individuals willing to make bank deposits. They help balance capital surpluses and shortfalls and promote productive activities. During this process, the occurrence of a small amount of NPLs can be viewed as a cost component of banks' operational risk and need not negatively impact the overall allocation of capital. Too much NPLs, however, means that a large portion of bank deposits are not being directed to where they can generate economic benefits. This inefficiency, if allowed to persist, will create an unhealthy gap between the amount taken in by the banks and the amount they lend out. Once the gap exceeds the banks' capital, the resulting losses will have to be borne by the banks' creditors – the depositors. Accordingly, a serious NPL situation means the shrinking wealth of depositors, which, if not timely addressed, will undermine the public's confidence in the financial system and lead to less deposits or even a bank run. The end result will be financial turbulence and panic that disrupt the circulation of private capital and various productive activities.

Fourthly, the NPLs had made macro-control more difficult. Banks are a credit intermediary and their lending activities impact the effectiveness of money supply and macro-control policies. If the banking system is bogged down with NPLs, which do not result in additional credit formation, and there is little transparency into the actual quality of loans, authorities will face significant difficulty in determining the deposit multiplier, developing appropriate credit policies, and exercising effective macro-control. From 1991 to 1997, bank credit ballooned from RMB 2.1

trillion to RMB 7.5 trillion, equating to an annual average growth rate of 23.3%, and M2 spiked from RMB 1.9 trillion to RMB 9.1 trillion at an average rate of 29.4%. Despite this, capital was in short supply, which was partly due to the sharp decline of performing loans which could be used to power the economy. The build-up of NPLs led to a shortage of effective credit in the market, forcing the monetary authority to greatly increase the money supply to sustain economic growth. This expansionary policy inevitably resulted in inflation.

Related Topic: Negative Coverage by Foreign Media: An Excerpt from *The Economist*[1]

"The concern now is that China's economy is entering a dangerous period of sluggish growth… the economy may well be growing at only 3-4% a year. For this vast, chaotic land such a slowdown amounts, in effect, to a recession… Though China is at a very different stage of development, its current predicament brings to mind Japan's experience in the 1990s… Both countries have banking systems that are riddled with bad debts. China's banks are burdened with dud loans both to state enterprises… The condition of the big four state banks mirrors the appalling state of the enterprises, to whom over four-fifths of their lending is directed… The real picture is undoubtedly much bleaker, for China has a lax system of accounting for bad loans, and unpaid interest on non-performing loans is usually booked as profit… No one knows how far China might be from a full-blown domestic banking crisis. But a further slowdown in the country's economic growth will surely bring one closer."

---

1   "Red Alert," *The Economist*, October 24, 1998.

Related Topic: The Real Size of NPLs[1]

In the 1990s, there was a significant discrepancy between the NPL data published by Chinese banks and the NPL ratio estimated by foreign institutions. There are primarily three reasons for this:

The first was the different classification and statistical standards for NPLs. Traditionally, China classified bank loans into four quality categories: performing, overdue, doubtful, and unrecoverable. NPLs were loans of the latter three categories, which refer to, respectively, loans that are past the due date of the loan agreements, that have been overdue for more than one year, and that are wholly unrecoverable. In 1998, China switched to the internationally accepted five-category classification scheme (i.e., pass, special-mention, substandard, doubtful, and loss; loans in the substandard, doubtful, and loss categories are NPLs).

This difference of classification gave rise to the wildly divergent NPL estimates. To take ICBC as an example, in 1999, ICBC began to officially measure its NPLs with both classification schemes. According to comparable data before the first disposal of NPLs (1999-2000), in 1999, ICBC's outstanding NPLs totaled RMB 776.6 billion, or a 33.11% NPL ratio, according to the four-category classification scheme; and were RMB 1,116.33 billion and 47.59% according to the five-category system. This gave a difference of 14.48 percentage points or RMB 339.7 billion. A similar pattern could presumably be found in the other state-owned banks as well. According to the 2005 estimate by Tang Shuangning – who

---

1   From Jiang Jianqing and Wei Guoxiong: "ICBC Manages Its 'Evergreen' Loans," *Financial News*, April 10, 2009.

had held leadership positions at the PBOC and China Securities Regulatory Commission (CSRC), and was later the chairman of China Everbright Bank – the combined NPL ratio of the Big Four in 1999 was 40% under the four-category system and 50% under the five-category system; if non-performing non-credit assets were accounted for, the non-performing asset (NPA) ratio would have shot up to 60%. When calculated according to outstanding NPLs, at the end of 1999, the Big Four had RMB 7.37 trillion of credit assets and RMB 3.32 trillion of NPLs, or 45% NPL ratio, under the five-category classification system. With the addition of about RMB 500 billion of non-performing non-credit assets, the total amount of NPAs was RMB 3.82 trillion.

The second factor was the difference in accounting standards. As discussed above, the foregoing NPL figures did not include non-performing non-credit assets. Historically, China's state-owned banks adopted progressively sophisticated standards for preparing financial reports: starting with the "Financial System for Financial and Insurance Enterprises (1993 edition)", then the "Accounting System for Financial Enterprises (2001 edition)", and lastly the International Financial Reporting Standards (IFRS). But before universally embracing the IFRS and its predecessor International Accounting Standards (IAS), these banks measured outstanding NPLs, allowances, and owners' equity differently. They each had, to varying degrees, concealed losses on credit and non-credit assets in supplementary capital, allowances, on-balance-sheet interest receivable, repossessed collateral, and other receivables; in addition to such other items as unrecorded losses, advances for benefits payable, and shortfalls in interest payable. Thus, despite their nominal book profit, they were in fact deep in the red and insolvent.

Adding to their financial woes, state-owned banks had to help rescue the state from its own fiscal difficulties. From 1984 to 2001, the banks turned over RMB 487.7 billion in profits and taxes to the state. A small portion of this was for income tax, due to the banks' minimal book profit; while the bulk of this amount – several times the income tax in the 1990s – was due to the 8% business tax, a tax category rarely assessed on banks internationally. Under this fiscal policy, banks had to surrender more "profit" than what they earned, with devastating effect on risk provisioning, profitability, and potential losses. It also crippled banks' ability to improve the asset quality on their own.

The third factor, a source of future NPLs, was that borrowers were allowed to take out new loans to repay existing ones *ad infinitum*, giving rise to the term "evergreen loans." For the most part, China's SOEs had neither any normal means for recapitalization nor a framework to handle operating and financial losses, and therefore had to subsist on bank loans. Consequently, rather than for productive uses, a sizeable portion of bank loans were being sunk into "zombie enterprises" with no hope of recovery or even just making the interest payments. To make the NPL situation worse, some local bank branches made loans with the sole intent of collecting interest. Given the lax budgeting practices of both SOEs and banks, whenever loans could not be repaid upon maturity, the banks had to turn them into evergreen loans or otherwise extend the term, effectively making them part of the baseline working capital for the SOEs.

During China's economic restructuring, evergreen loans were the go-to option for replenishing the working capital of SOEs. Over time, they became a long-term "capitalized" credit and inextricably bound the fate of banks to that of the SOEs. Repayment was never on the table as the loans had to be revolved indefinitely. Diversion and misappropriation were commonplace. Some of the loans were turned into investments or land or equipment; some became receivables, overstocked inventories, bad debts, or unpaid taxes, profits, and charges, i.e., *de facto* NPAs. Many of the evergreen loans should have been recognized as NPLs; but because banks were already overwhelmed by the overhang that had already developed and apprehensive about compounding the issue, they resorted to roll-over by drawing up a new loan agreement whenever the maturity date was reached. For example, at the end of 2000, ICBC had RMB 1,090 billion loans that were issued to replace old ones, and half of these were not considered NPLs.

II. Direct Causes of NPAs

NPAs had grown from a headache at state-owned banks into a stumbling block to China's economic development. What were the exact causes for this development? The answer to this question had been a focus of domestic research since the mid-1990s, as it must be well understood to mitigate the financial risks to which China was exposed. The consensus from these studies is that there were four major contributing factors: financial hardships of SOEs during China's transition to a market economy, the use of credit as a quasi-fiscal tool, the relaxation of internal and external restraints, and unsuitable choice of accounting system.

(I) Financial Hardships of SOEs During Economic Transitioning

China's transition from a planned economy to a market economy, and the resulting profound social and economic changes, was a stupendously costly affair. This comprehensive transformation took place in the 1990s and revitalized the economy and market competition. Concurrent with this program was a new stage of opening up, attracting an inflow of foreign capital which trickled from coastal to inland regions.

As a result, the SOEs were suddenly pitted against foreign capital in the form of wholly foreign-owned enterprises and joint ventures; and in each market segment, against home-grown private, individually owned, and township and village businesses which flourished in both urban and rural areas. Increased competition and expanded market space led to product and technological innovation as businesses of various types fought for market share on quality, service, and price; "survival of the fittest" was now the new guiding principle that shaped market activities and ecosystems. Unfortunately, SOEs were weighed down in this race by their generally blurry ownership structure and principal-agent relations, as well as by the many debilitating non-business-related social responsibilities. Many were too slow to adapt to market changes and adjust their internal mechanisms, becoming, along with their products, casualties of the now intensified market competition.

Following the introduction, in the 1980s, of the Appropriation-to-Loan Program and of bank-assisted management of SOEs' working capital, national policies did not provide any replacement arrangements through which SOEs could obtain supplementary capital, placing many in a difficult position to meet their capital needs. Moreover, due to the slow development of the capital market, state-owned banks became the main source of financing for SOEs, resulting in an unhealthily high proportion of indirect financing and the overuse of monetary and banking measures. In a financial system dominated by indirect financing, SOEs had been the main recipients of banks' credit support. In fact, 80% of all household deposits were held by banks and 90% of their total loans were to SOEs.

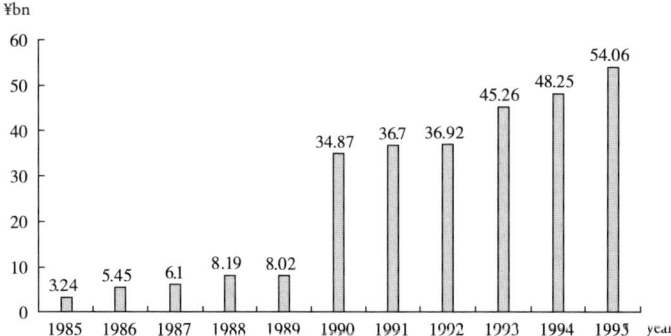

Source: *China Statistical Yearbook (1996)* from the National Bureau of Statistics.

Fig. 2.2: Losses of SOEs (1985-1995)

By the mid-1990s, the situation had become bleak for SOEs: the percentage of loss-making enterprises went up from 16% in 1989 to over 44% in 1995; and between 1989 and 1995, the total losses of SOEs amounted to RMB 287.06 billion (Fig. 2.2). For industrial SOEs, the potential losses were even greater than that suggested by the books due to their fudged accounting of costs. According to an illustrative survey taken by one bank, 30% of industrial SOEs were publicly operating at a loss, and another 30% were doing so secretly, giving a total percentage of 60% or more (see Related Topic: "A Bank's Special Survey Report on the Potential Losses of State-Run Industrial Enterprises").

SOEs suffered greater hardships after 1995 as the SOE reform intensified. A survey of 1,830 SOEs across ten provinces (municipalities) by the PBOC at the end of 1998 found that, losses and inventories to be written off, accumulated losses, and unrecoverable receivables of the surveyed subjects totaled RMB 400 billion, or 21% of their RMB 1,870 billion of book assets. Assuming this is a representative figure, SOEs would have racked up

RMB 3 trillion in losses based on SOEs and state-controlled enterprises' total assets of RMB 14.9 trillion in 1998. Almost all of the SOEs closed down during the wave of reform were customers of state-owned banks. "The vast majority of their unrecorded losses [incurred during China's system transformation, restructuring, and industrial upgrading] were linked to bank credit, causing banks' NPLs to skyrocket."[1] Consequently, state-owned banks assumed a significant portion of the cost of the SOE reform.

Related Topic: A Bank's Special Survey Report on the Potential Losses of State-Run Industrial Enterprises[2]

According to a survey conducted by 40 branches of a certain state-owned bank, as of the end of June 1990, 6,625 of the 10,580 (63%) state-run industrial enterprises analyzed were operating at a potential deficit or loss, 1.96 times the number of those reporting book losses; total unrecognized, forward-looking expected deficits and losses arising from inaccurate accounting, missing or damaged properties, bad loans, and false profits, etc. amounted to RMB 10.83 billion, equaling 1.72 times the aggregate book losses of the surveyed enterprises. By the end of June, the book and potential losses of these 10,580 enterprises had reached RMB 17.12 billion, or 61% of the working capital they held (coming from either state appropriation or the enterprises themselves) and 56% of their realized profit and taxes in that year.

Given that the surveyed enterprises were from major industrial centers and had mostly satisfactory management practices, it is reasonable to assume that operating losses were a more salient issue in the smaller cities,

---

1   From the 1999 PBOC report on the causes of NPLs of the four wholly state-owned commercial banks.
2   From the internal survey report of a state-owned bank.

where competent management was rarer. Regarding these potential losses, the survey identified six main contributing factors.

First, inaccurate accounting of the prices of production inputs. The price of principal production inputs was 82% higher at the end of June 1990 than at the end of 1985. In view of the higher cost of raw materials due to the price hike, a proportionate amount of profits should have been set aside as a reserve to shore up working capital, as required by regulations, but instead was either handed over to the state as profit and taxes, or distributed as dividends. Additionally, the enormous price differential on the high-priced materials purchased as inputs for the following production cycle would tank profitability if recognized in the current period, and so were kept off the books indefinitely.

Second, significant shrinkage of raw materials and product inventories. Due to poor management, inventory wastage and loss were an acute issue at some enterprises, but such inventory inconsistencies were not truthfully reflected in the book value noted in the accounts. Because of the loosely enforced warehouse and periodic inventory-taking protocols, shortage in materials and finished goods alone contributed to an RMB 520 million loss.

Third, a general disregard for the necessary allowances, depreciations, and amortizations. To pad their bottom line in the short term, enterprises misreported their production management expenses, made little or no provision or allowance for depreciation and for the major repairs fund, and even adopted the periodic inventory system to artificially suppress the expenses to be amortized and window-dress current period profitability. Surveys showed that with these tactics, 6,625 enterprises wrestled another RMB 2.68 billion of "profit" by not recognizing the aforementioned incurred expenses and allowances.

Fourth, unrecorded inventory obsolescence. The blind pursuit of manufacturing output by local governments and enterprises had generated a mass of obsolete products and works-in-progress that needed to be scrapped, but these were not written off against capitalized costs as required. Works-in-progress and finished goods made obsolete by their shoddy manufacturing, performance, or quality failures accounted for an RMB 2.05 billion loss.

Fifth, substantial inherent losses due production costs exceeding the selling prices. Some enterprises continued to produce legacy products in small batches, pushing up the cost of production, but had to sell them at increasingly lower prices. The survey estimated that due to these negative margins, total loss from the sale of finished goods would amount to RMB 2.89 billion.

Sixth, receivables turned sour. Lackluster sales forced enterprises to accept extended payment terms such as sales on credit, commission, or consignment basis, putting them at risk of fraud and unrecoverable receivables. In fact, the aggregate unrecoverable receivables of the surveyed enterprises amounted to RMB 890 million.

Indicative of the complex issues underlying China's economic transformation, the abovementioned potential deficit and losses were partly attributable to SOEs' lack of self-discipline during their pursuit of the committed performance targets. The target commitment system was profit-driven, such that it required an enterprise to turn over a mandatory RMB amount to the state, with any excess in the bottom line retained by the enterprise and any shortfall to be made up, and it also linked the enterprise's total available payroll to its performance. This system stimulated manufacturing output but also short-sighted business pursuits. Another contributor of the deficit and losses was the absence of effective public supervision and rigorous performance evaluation. Having limited regard for legal and disciplinary restraints, enterprises took liberties in adjusting costs and expenses to bring them closer to the desired profit target.

(II) Use of Credit as Quasi-Fiscal Tool

In the three decades before reform and opening up, China's financial system was virtually an appendage to its fiscal system, serving as a mere "cashier" for the planned economy, and accordingly inheriting all the traits characteristic of government agencies. With the launch of reform and opening up, national leadership was determined to resolve the heavy dependence of capital investments on government appropriation. Measures were introduced to put banks in a position to mediate between deposits and investment, so that bank credit would gradually replace fiscal appropriation as the engine to power economic growth.

It should be said that at the beginning of reform and opening up, neither capital accumulation nor the government coffers were sufficient to fund the country's economic development, so it was a matter of practical necessity to let bank credit fill the role formerly played by government appropriations. While this institutional change proved to be effective at averting capital shortfall and any resulting wider consequences, the fundamental differences between bank credit and fiscal funds – that the former is concerned with recoverability of the principal, liquidity, and profitability to the banks – were handily ignored. The overemphasis on credit's ability to boost the economy made credit a quasi-fiscal tool, sowing the seeds for a build-up of financial risks.

In the 1980s, China introduced the Appropriation-to-Loan Program to replace interest-free government appropriations to SOEs with interest-bearing bank loans. It was hoped that the program would lead to better accounting practices and funds utilization, as well as shore up the insufficient equity reserves of the SOEs. However, because SOEs had not completed their transition to market-based operations, and both they and banks paid little regard to budget constraints, they ended up treating bank loans in the same way as they would government appropriations. As a result, the interest-bearing bank loans failed to cure SOEs' addiction to government funds.

The frequent recurrence of investment fevers since 1984 makes it clear that bank loans failed to correct the problems of government appropriation: an insatiable drive to make investments, even as returns were low[1]. Under the new program, SOEs were mandated to repay the loans first with their own funds; but an overwhelming majority chose instead to repay from their pre-tax earnings, as new projects had yet to turn a profit and expansion and technological upgrade projects were not bound by any prescribed ratio of own funds to be earmarked for repayment. Based on the amount of profits retained by SOEs in 1984 (rather than turned over to the state), the overall retention ratio of SOEs nationwide was about 30%; excluding those with the autonomy to negotiate their product sales prices, most had a retention ratio of 20% and would pay down their loans with pre-tax earnings. This means that for every RMB 100 paid back to the government, 70 to 80 actually came out of the government's own pocket, or even as high as 90 in some cases.

---

1   In the first half of 1985, capital investment made by SOEs increased by 43.5% year-on-year, funded partly by a 158.2% increase in loans. SOEs also scrambled for bank loans for projects that would bring little benefits to themselves and the public. Incurred and potential losses represented 10% of the outstanding bank loans. These figures are taken from the speech of Tian Chunsheng, Director of Investment Research Institute at CCB head office, delivered at the 1985 Annual Meeting of Zhejiang Financial Association, titled "Breaking away from the Egalitarian Loans to SOEs to Unleash the Power of Capital."

Moreover, for SOEs the repayment of project loans was only a short-term burden; once the principal and interest were paid off, they stood to continuously profit from the projects. Seeing this opportunity for arbitrage, SOEs were tempted to make unsound "impulse investments," leading to duplicate projects, low returns, or even failed investments. Indeed, many projects had to be terminated as soon as the construction phase was completed, resulting in the total loss of indirect government investments and bad debts for the banks. This moral hazard also plagued other forms of loans, including those for infrastructure construction and retrofit projects issued by CCB with funds from business and household deposits, as well as the short- and medium-term loans for equipment and technological upgrades issued by ICBC and other financial institutions.

SOEs also took advantage of the generous "egalitarian nature" of bank loans to replenish their working capital. In the 1980s, government policies had instituted bank-assisted management of SOEs' working capital, requiring SOEs to set aside their own working capital out of their own funds and at a minimum level of 30% of their original quota-based working capital. In practice, SOEs were neither willing nor able to build up this new liquidity pool and continued to fully rely on bank loans to maintain their working capital. According to a survey conducted by ICBC on its clients, working capital loans to industrial SOEs had increased by 380% between 1985 and 1992, averaging 25% per annum, far outpacing the 71.4% growth (8% per annum) in self-owned working capital of the SOEs over the same period. Records show that self-owned funds accounted for 28% of SOEs' total working capital in the early 1980s; but by the end of 1992, this figure had dropped to a mere 9.7%, while the percentage of bank loans climbed to 45.3%. By the late 1990s, SOEs' working capital was almost entirely funded by bank loans, which they tapped for everything from purchasing raw materials to paying salaries and taxes. Recalling those loans would have triggered instant collapse of these businesses. Since SOEs could help themselves to this smorgasbord of bank loans with little restrictions, the supposedly short-term (generally one year or less) supplements to working capital became, in effect, perpetual loans. Accordingly, there was no buffer to absorb any shocks and loan losses immediately resulted when borrowing SOEs suffered from poor sales, operating losses, or even insolvency and bankruptcy.

Following government policy, in the early 1990s state-owned banks sought to break this cycle and began to offer preferential credit, interest rate, and settlement policies to medium and large SOEs.[1] While these policies were moderately successful, they did not address the deep-seated structural and systematic issues within the SOEs. Although the SOEs enjoyed this financial reprieve, their inventories piled up and profitability remained weak. Many even became dependent on the bailout loans from banks, wastefully tying up a large portion of available bank credit.

After 1993, as the domestic economy slowed from breakneck growth

---

1   The principal measures were: (1) Credit expansion. For example, the State Council allowed state-owned banks to increase loans from RMB 30 billion to RMB 60 billion in the first half of 1990 and from RMB 170 billion to RMB 270 billion during the entire year. Medium and large SOEs were among the beneficiaries of this increase. ICBC reported that it lent an additional RMB 37.7 billion to 7,000 medium and large industrial SOEs during the year, RMB 6.4 billion more than the year before. From April 1990, ICBC issued more than RMB 20 billion of low-interest loans for the purchase of reserve commodities (*tiaojiexing chubeishangpin daikuan*) from medium and large SOEs; and (2) Provision of additional emergency loans to medium and large SOEs and "Two Guarantees" (i.e., guarantee of funding and of supply of state-allocated raw materials) enterprises. These loans were channeled into the SOEs, either directly or indirectly through agencies that handled goods supply and commerce, on a basis that placed more emphasis on the number of enterprises assisted than on the exact amount of loans they each needed.

for a period of remediation and adjustment, China began to strategically restructure and transform SOEs by shifting support to large businesses only and shutting down, suspending, merging, or repurposing businesses that performed poorly. Amid these changes, a sizable proportion of SOEs, being ill-prepared to operate in a market-driven economy, suffered from operating difficulties, evidenced by sharp declines in profitability, mounting losses, late payment of salaries, and many other problems. These problems made it almost impossible for the banks to recover the principal and interest, ruining their balance sheets. Although the loss-making SOEs had no hope of paying off existing loans, they still expected banks to keep them afloat with new loans. Some pleaded to the government in the hope that banks would be ordered to provide the "stability and solidarity loans" – including what were known as "dumpling loans (*jiaozi daikuan*)" and "heating coal loans (*kaohuomei daikuan*)" – to help cover employees' payroll, settling-in allowances, and essential living expenses. As such, some of the government's responsibilities were shouldered by state-owned banks whose stock of NPLs was, to a large extent, the cost of the SOE reform. The government also faced a dilemma. It wanted to address the immediate difficulties which would require banks to share part of its responsibilities; it also hoped that the reform would resolve once and for all the lax financial discipline of SOEs and state-owned banks.

Various ideas were tried to achieve the dual objective of supporting the SOE reform and protecting the banks' interests. In 1996, China introduced the "main bank program (*zhubanhang zhidu*)." Under this program, a medium or large SOE would pair up with a commercial bank, whereby the bank would undertake to provide credit, settlement and payment, and other financial services according to a specified quota and interest rate, and the SOE would undertake to replenish its working capital, pay off its loans from the bank, and refrain from diverting or falling into arrears on existing or future loans. A total of 300 SOEs enrolled in the program that year, and another 212 did so the following year. While this program did help advance the SOE reform, it failed to fundamentally break SOEs' reliance on bank handouts, as SOEs didn't hold up to their end of the bargain simply because they were in a strong position to avoid doing so. In fact, banks would assume an increasing share of the cost of SOE reform as the initiative expanded.

In 1997, China launched a three-year campaign to turn around struggling SOEs. To ensure success, the PBOC issued the "Notice on Further Assisting Struggling Enterprises in Paying Late Salaries" (Yin Chuan [1997] No. 76), drafted in view of the main bank program and relevant state policies. The Notice provided that any SOE that had been late on salary payments beyond a certain period was to open a salary reserve account, to which sales proceeds and recouped project payments would be transferred, until its balance could cover three months of salary. This reserve was to be used toward payment of salaries to current employees and of essential living expenses to laid-off employees. For SOEs that were in severe and perhaps long-standing financial distress, and for whom the salary reserve account and local bailout funds were ineffective at reversing fortunes, they would continue to be supported by the trio of aid from the local competent authorities, interest subsidies from local tax revenues, and salary loans from banks, ensuring coverage of the essential living expenses.

As evident from the account of events above, in the 1980s and the 1990s, state-owned banks' support to the economy, and to the SOEs especially, had gone beyond what is normal from a purely business perspective.

A large portion of bank loans were in fact policy lending, becoming an alternative form of government subsidies aimed to keep SOEs afloat at all costs. This practice, however, led to the mushrooming of NPAs in the state-owned banks. Although in the early 1990s China began to remove government functions from businesses, because of fiscal difficulties and the importance of banks in the private capital ecosystem, banks remained the "lifeline" for SOEs.

A 1999 survey by the PBOC named the use of credit in place of fiscal expenditures as the main culprit for the buildup of NPLs in state-owned banks. Specifically, the stock of NPLs came from three sources: (1) policy lending proposed by the central and local governments for social stability, poverty alleviation, employment, development and bailout programs. For example, 54.8% of ICBC's NPLs as of 1997 was due to such policy lending; (2) loans – which later became unrecoverable – to SOEs to replenish their capital and baseline working capital; and (3) loans used to pay taxes. Local governments would order banks to loan to SOEs that, due to operating difficulties, fell behind on tax payments. Those SOEs would later acknowledge the loans but refuse to repay them.[1]

In fact, this use of bank credit as a quasi-fiscal tool actually made it more difficult to transform SOEs into fully market-based entities. This is because as long as banks were committed to providing capital as a matter of fiscal policy, SOEs would never voluntarily shed their dependence on policy-based bank loans and switch to more market-based options.

---

1   From the 1999 PBOC report on the causes of NPLs of the four wholly state-owned commercial banks.

Related Topic: A Bank's Investigation and Analysis Report on Policy Lending[1]

In June 2003, one state-owned bank conducted a survey on its policy lending, as directed by the PBOC. The survey showed that, as of the end of 2002, policy lending, including principal and interest, totaled RMB 312.887 billion. This figure comprised RMB 226.812 billion of outstanding loans, RMB 9.347 billion of overdue on-balance-sheet interest, and RMB 76.729 billion of overdue off-balance-sheet interest. Loans made before 1995, between 1996 and 1999, and after 2000 amounted to RMB 116.243 billion, RMB 101.731 billion, and RMB 8.838 billion, respectively, representing 51%, 45%, and 4% of the total. This shows that an overwhelming proportion of its policy lending was made before 1999.

The bank's statistical standard classified policy lending as special-purpose loans issued at the direction of the State Council, the MOF, the State Development Planning Commission (SDPC), the PBOC, other ministries and commissions, as well as the Party and state leadership. Instrumental in helping SOEs cast off their financial burdens and turn a profit, policy lending is a broad term for 50 types of loans, including, among others, those for purchasing fertilizers, cotton, grain, rubber, steel, non-ferrous metals, and other goods and materials for the national stockpile; those for resolving triangular debts; and those for consolidating accounts by trust companies. These loans can be classified by origin into seven categories:

(1) loans approved by the State Council, totaling (principal and interest) RMB 110.111 billion (35% of the total);

(2) loans approved by the SDPC, totaling RMB 35.523 billion (11%);

---

[1] From internal documents of a state-owned bank.

(3) loans approved by the MOF, totaling RMB 1.068 billion (0.3%);

(4) loans approved by the PBOC, totaling RMB 128.822 billion (41.2%);

(5) loans transferred from policy banks, totaling RMB 25.769 billion (8.2%);

(6) loans transferred from the PBOC, totaling RMB 7.473 billion (2.4%);

(7) loans directed by the Party and state leadership, totaling RMB 4.223 billion (1.4%).

Those loans were issued in specific historical contexts, and mainly for the following purposes: maintaining the stability and growth of commercial and industrial SOEs; assisting key medium-sized and large SOEs, maintaining the national stockpile of key goods and materials; financing special agricultural programs and public welfare programs; and maintaining social and economic order and stability. As such, the loans had all the hallmarks of fiscal expenditure. In addition, to support the restoration of the economic order, this particular bank underwrote loans transferred in from other institutions, loans which had marginal chance of recovery. Estimate puts those loans at 34% of the bank's total NPLs in 2002, and overdue interest on those loans at 23% of the bank's total overdue interest.

(III) Loose Financial Restraints on SOEs and Banks

1. Loose restraints on SOEs' activities due to underdeveloped credit framework

The ambiguous nature of bank credit, as described above, meant that the statutory obligations of repayment were rarely enforced, giving SOEs a free pass to evade bank debts at will. From the latter half of the 1980s to the early 1990s, the occurrence of so-called "triangular debts" (i.e., three or more entities forming a chain of indebtedness where each is behind in its payment to another) among SOEs caused a breakdown of the system of trade credit. A substantial amount of bank loans was pumped into the system, only to create new delinquent loans as quickly as existing ones were cleared. The result was that SOEs actually owed more to the banks than before, pushing up the banks' debt ratio to sky-high levels.

To reverse this trend, the central government launched three extensive campaigns – in 1988-1989, 1990-1991, and 1992 – to clear triangular debts. The first of these was partly prompted by figures reported from the banks, which indicated that overdue payments among SOEs were as high as RMB 110 billion at the end of March 1989. Consequently, starting from the second quarter the PBOC helped SOEs cut down their debts by providing the necessary funds, with due regard given to the conditions of each geographical region. In all, nearly 4 billion yuan of funding was committed into the program in this phase, helping clear more than RMB 80 billion of debts. This, however, did not effectively address the issue of new arrears, and was therefore followed by a second campaign in 1990, clearing another RMB 160 billion in debts but leaving the issue of inter-enterprise payables in arrears standing. Accordingly, in 1992 the State Council initiated the third campaign, with state-owned banks issuing RMB 21.3 billion of loans specifically targeting new debts. While the three campaigns somewhat reversed the damage on business operations and the societal credit system caused by the widespread delinquency among SOEs, they did not address at a fundamental level the issues that jeopardized the system. Moreover, clearing debts with new loans failed to put a stop to new arrears, and burdened state-owned banks with additional non-performing assets and even losses.

The years after the mid-1990s were also a period when China had inadequate legal means to protect banks as creditors and to deal with corporate bankruptcies, and when intervention and protectionism by local governments were commonplace. During the campaign to shut down, suspend, merge, or repurpose struggling SOEs, some of them exploited legal loopholes to intentionally evade repayment, further exacerbating the NPL problem. ICBC's report shows that, of the 133,500 SOEs that had taken out loans from the bank as of the end of 1998, 19,900 had evaded payment obligations, accounting for 15% of ICBC's SOE clients under reform; the amount of principal and interest concerned totaled RMB 139 billion, or 41% of the total principal owed to ICBC by SOE clients under reform and 14.5% of its then outstanding NPLs. According to ABC's investigation in the same year, 45.5% of its SOE clients under reform took opportunity of the SOE reform to evade repayment of RMB 61 billion of loans, or 50% of ABC's total loans to its SOE clients under reform. For BOC, the evasion rate was 65% by the number of SOE clients and 60% by the amount of total outstanding loans; for CCB from 1995 to 1998, it was 37% by the amount of total outstanding loans. The PBOC found that, at the close of 2000, the Big Four maintained 62,700 accounts for SOEs under reform, 32,100 or 51.3% of which were identified by a financial claim management authority as having evaded a total of RMB 185.1 billion in principal and interest payments, or 32.0% of the RMB 579.2 billion of principal and interest owed by SOEs under reform.[1]

Local protectionism for insolvent SOEs presented another hurdle for the lawful recovery of loans. For example, in 1998, the Big Four won 99% of the court cases on delinquent loans, but only 45.4% of those were

---

1 Data from *Report on Evasion of Financial Debts by Enterprises* and the *Almanac of China's Finance and Banking (2002)*.

enforced and only 25.5% of the loans were recoverable. In cases involving bankrupt SOEs, the recovery rate was less than 10%.[1]

Case Study: Debt Evasion by Hainan XX Sugar Refinery[2]

XX sugar refinery, an SOE in Hainan Province and a major borrower of ICBC Hainan Branch, had suffered a string of operating losses due to mismanagement, forcing ICBC Hainan to cut off loans to the factory in July 1994. By the end of June 1997, the refinery was overdue on all its loans totaling RMB 12.78 million. With an additional RMB 8.85 million in overdue interest and RMB 750,000 in lease and late fee, the refinery owed ICBC Hainan RMB 22.38 million in total.

To bail out the refinery, the local government decided to place it under the management of a third party. Not wanting to see the refinery fail, ICBC Hainan was supportive of the decision to the extent that the loan payments were not jeopardized, and even sent the responsible manager to attend relevant meetings. ICBC Hainan also repeatedly approached the new management team for details of the handover, but such attempts at proactive intervention was in vain. Later, at a meeting attended by top local officials and all members of the new management team, a draft management contract created by the local State-owned Assets Supervision and Administration Bureau was put forward for discussion. It was the first time that ICBC Hainan had seen it, and the branch immediately raised the following objections and concerns: (1) The contract proposed to exempt the new

---

1   From the 1999 PBOC report on the causes of NPLs of the four wholly state-owned commercial banks.
2   Ma Jing: *A Study of Typical Cases of Evasion of Financial Debts*, China Financial Publishing House, 2003.

operator from paying interest during 1997-1998. But ICBC Hainan was sole claimant on interest during this period and, as such, the interest could not be reduced or exempted by anyone other than a state-designated authority. (2) The contract stipulated that the new operator would not be responsible for the existing debts of the refinery, leaving unanswered the question of whose responsibility it would be. (3) The contract did not specify who would be responsible for any interest accrued after the change of the refinery's legal representative. ICBC Hainan asked for this detail to be added in, but this resulted in an impasse and the issue was left unresolved.

Sometime later, ICBC Hainan chanced upon news that the management contract had been formally signed without its knowledge. It immediately notified the local government and at the subsequent meeting, reiterated that its claims must be respected. It proposed two recommendations but both were ignored. Undeterred, ICBC Hainan submitted to the local government a "Report on Requiring Repayment by XX Sugar Refinery," containing the following five demands: (1) for the debts owed by the refinery to be borne by the new operator (Haikou South XX Chemical Company); (2) for the original operator to open a basic settlement account at ICBC Hainan to facilitate oversight and prevent debt evasion through diversion of funds; (3) for the new operator to formulate a detailed installment payment plan to ensure, at a minimum, that full payment would be made on interest accrued during the management period; (4) for the handover of assets to the new operator to be suspended until the party to be responsible for the debts was determined; and (5) for vehicles leased by ICBC Hainan to the refinery (under contracts) not to be disposed of without the branch's permission.

In the end, at an executive meeting the government declared that the terms of the contract were final, and on this basis rejected the recommendations and demands of ICBC Hainan.

Related Topic: How Some SOEs Evaded Bank Loans[1]

Many SOEs took advantage of their joint-stock reform to avoid paying back loans. For example, when a Shenzhen-based SOE was restructured into a company limited by shares through capital increase, it concealed the 600-million-yuan loan it had taken out from CCB, and later refused to acknowledge the loan and even moved assets to ensure it was beyond attempts of recovery. In another instance, Jilin Municipal Pipeline Gas Company in Jilin Province invested RMB 124.88 million in a joint venture, Xinjimei, co-established with Hong Kong GeoMaxima Energy Company and China Xinxing Oil Company, and transferred another RMB 40.98 million of assets to its subordinate installation company, design institute, and trade company which were only just re-registered with the commerce authority. Following these two transactions, RMB 70.99 million in principal and interest owed to ICBC became unrecoverable.

Declaring bankruptcy was another method. SOEs faked bankruptcy to erase debts. XX County in Beijing even made this approach the preferred way of "solving" the legacy and difficult issues of SOEs and collective enterprises. In the county, 131 of the 148 SOEs under reform, a staggering 88.51%, evaded debts owed to ICBC, ABC, BOC, and CCB. Those SOEs escaped their financial troubles at the expense of state-owned banks.

Corporate split-ups were yet another alternative. Ordinarily in a split-up the companies involved would assume the debts of the original company

---

[1] From "SOEs Under Reform Are 'Principal Culprits' in Evading Repayment of Bank Loans," *China Securities Journal*, July 10, 2001.

according to the relative ratio of their capital and assets or according to the split-up agreement. But in practice, the original company would cede its good assets to the new companies and retain the debts. As such, the indebted company was stripped of its assets and the new companies that held the assets were freed from any obligation to repay any debt. One example where this scheme was used was a corporate group from Yancheng, Jiangsu Province, which set up three new companies to escape debts during its reform.

Other schemes included not repaying banks with the proceeds obtained from auctioning off or selling assets, or evading debts through custody, contracting, leasing, or other arrangements.

2. Loose internal management at banks

Many of the risks and problems that emerged in China's financial institutions in the 1990s could be attributed to issues with internal management. The bankruptcy of the China Agribusiness Development Trust and Investment Corporation and the Guangdong International Trust & Investment Company reveal the potentially disastrous consequences of loose organizational structure and internal management. State-owned banks likewise suffered from weak management practices, especially in the following two respects:

Firstly, the ownership structure of state-owned banks meant that their operators had different and even diverging operating objectives. This difficulty in separating government function from corporate management was in fact one of the institutional causes for the mushrooming policy loans. Due to their ownership structure, wholly state-owned banks were treated as responsible for funding SOEs on behalf of the state, making it easy for

SOEs to blur the line between banks and fiscal functions and, thus, to never appreciate the cost of borrowed capital.

Since the state was the owner of banks, it was solely responsible for their operational risks. However, because in practice there was no actor or entity to exercise that ownership, no single person could realistically be held responsible for those risks. For the longest time, state-owned banks were operating without a consolidated legal personality and unified management structure, and rather adopted a multi-level management model that was marked by strong horizontal government influence and weak vertical internal management. Strong horizontal government influence here refers to the heavy intervention of local governments into the affairs of local branches of state-owned banks. Before 1998, both build-up of the Party apparatus and appointment of officials at a local branch were jointly managed by both the CPC committee of the bank's head office and the regional CPC committee of where the branch was located. As a result, local governments held a strong sway over the appointment and evaluation of the heads of bank branches. This setup allowed some local governments to frequently encroach on the decision-making of state-owned banks and impose their own policy on them. Whenever there was a conflict between the operating objectives imposed by a higher-level branch and the administrative objectives imposed by the local government, the head of a local branch, for political and career considerations, would more often than not prioritize the administrative ones, which were frequently at odds with commercial principles.

Weak vertical internal management refers to the weak control exerted by higher-level branches over lower-level ones. Ineffective transmission of operating philosophy, inadequate feedback, and lax management frameworks gave little leverage for higher-level branches to manage their subordinates. Strict management would make them stagnant, and loose management, reckless. Since the 1980s, when the corporatization of banks gathered momentum, state-owned banks, attempting to encourage their branches to compete in the market, delegated operating powers to their lower-level branches in order to break away from the highly centralized, rigid, and conservative planned economic system. Notwithstanding the good original intention of this reform, conditions on the ground did not allow for accountability for performance to accompany the delegation of powers, and thus branches approved loans beyond their powers, expanded their business, and engaged in business operations in violation of rules. The 1990s saw frequent financial chaos, giving rise to the situation of the "three new unruly areas" (illegal fund-raising, illegal provision of financial services, and illegal establishment of financial institutions). By 1998, ICBC, ABC, BOC and CCB, together with more than 7,600 economic entities established by them, made investments and issued loans totaling more than RMB 160 billion, resulting in heavy losses to them[1].

Since the remediation of the financial industry in 1993, the creation of a framework for managing state-owned banks as consolidated legal persons had been a top priority of the government. The *Law on Commercial Banks* of 1995 explicitly requires every commercial bank and its branches to be consolidated into and incorporated as a single legal person. However, the process of regaining previously delegated powers and remediating financial misconduct was a lengthy one. This process, occurring alongside

---

1   From the 1999 PBOC report on the causes of NPLs of the four wholly state-owned commercial banks.

significant external events such as the Asian financial crisis and the expedited reform of SOEs, accelerated the deterioration of asset quality and financial conditions of state-owned banks. Consequently, state-owned banks were unable to make allowance for doubtful loans and dispose of their NPLs. Moreover, applicable fiscal rules allowed for only a limited amount of loans to SOEs to be written off on account of bankruptcy. Thus, NPLs continued to build up on state-owned banks' balance sheets year after year.

Secondly, state-owned banks did not have robust risk management and internal control mechanisms in place. At the time, the state required the banks to primarily support economic development, in particular the development of SOEs, while leaving empty any specific requirement for the banks' own risks and profitability. The banks, therefore, prioritized the funding of SOEs over their own risk management and internal control, which was the internal reason for their increasing NPLs. A specific analysis of this reason is provided below:

First, state-owned banks had a flawed credit management system: (1) The credit management system of state-owned banks failed to keep up with the pace of economic reform and to adapt to changes in business arrangements. In particular, their pre-lending review and evaluation were not performed based on rigorous standards because most of their clients were SOEs. This conspicuous shortcoming alone created many NPLs. (2) Lending officers had a weak sense of responsibility because they would not be liable for the loans they had issued. As a result, the pre-lending review was mostly perfunctory and made for a porous first line of defense against risks. (3) Broadly neglecting methods to secure loan repayment, state-owned banks issued massive unsecured loans to SOEs. Even for the loans that were secured by collateral, the banks often failed to execute effective post-lending management and ensure possession of collateral. (4) When issuing loans, some banks would skip certain necessary procedures, fail to fully enforce the conditions for loan, or allow the loan applicants to retroactively complete certain procedures after the loan had been disbursed. Moreover, state-owned banks frequently provided financing to SOEs through off-balance-sheet channels or even rule-breaking off-the-book arrangements.

During the peak of the "loan-frenzy" years in the 1990s, SOEs were champing at the bit to obtain financing. After the remediation of the financial industry in 1993, the PBOC strengthened its management of lending amounts, but some state-owned banks, wishing to maintain their relationship with SOEs, continued to issue loans frequently through off-balance-sheet channels, through trusts and securities firms to circumvent regulation, or even through unrecorded lending, creating risks neither recognized in their balance sheets nor in their accounts. According to a PBOC's survey, in the two years between 1995 and 1996, the branches of ICBC, ABC, BOC, and CCB issued RMB 180 billion more loans than permitted by the quota and RMB 43 billion of off-the-book loans. The non-performing ratio of such loans was much higher than that of the banks' overall loan portfolios[1].

Second, state-owned banks failed to establish robust internal control. Weak managerial practices, unsound decision-making processes, unchecked authorities, poor accountability, and even illegal or non-compliant operations were also major causes of NPLs. These shortcomings were

---

1 From the 1999 PBOC report on the causes of NPLs of the four wholly state-owned commercial banks.

evidenced by the banks' underdeveloped business management rules. The rules that did exist prescribed few sanctions against rule-breaking activities and the responsible individuals. For example, according to CCB's 1998 survey on its guarantee business, some of its branches approved guarantees beyond their powers. Although the head office had established specific rules on the powers and procedures of its branches to approve guarantees, they were simply ignored by some branches, indicating a lax management of the delegated and undelegated powers.

State-owned banks had other problems, including ineffective guarantee management rules and poorly designed approval forms; the lack of an effective accounting and monitoring system for letters of guarantee, performance bonds, premium income, etc.; failure to make the required allowance for bad debts and to cover losses of advances to borrowers; disorderly accounts, incomplete archival materials, and late compilation of operational data[1]. During its joint-stock reform, BOC analyzed management factors contributing to its NPLs based on 208 archetypal cases of late or non-repayment. According to this analysis, the bank's NPLs were 52.5% due to its credit culture, operational mechanisms, and management practices, and 47.5% due to operation and execution. However, operational shortcomings were found in 55.7% of all cases, higher than credit mismanagement (44.1%). The specific impact of each factor was as follows: 12.5% for pre-lending investigation and review, 6.8% loan issuance, 28.2% post-loan management, 22.1% credit culture development, 20.7% credit operations, and 9.7% credit management practices.[2]

---

1 The "Survey on CCB's Guarantee Business," the *Almanac of China's Finance and Banking* (1998).
2 Xiao Gang: *Changing Bank of China*, China CITIC Press, 2011.

After three years of remediation across the industry, state-owned banks' NPLs arising from rule-breaking and off-the-book transactions and loans to their own economic entities were kept under control. But those created by information asymmetry, decentralized decision-making, backward credit management, credit structure adjustment, and delayed repayment recovery became a salient issue. Credit-related decision-making was left to the local branches who, for regional and short-term interests, often recklessly offered loans in regions that did not have the necessary credit environment. Furthermore, state-owned banks were slow to build the risk prevention capacity needed during economic transition, especially in the areas of operational mechanisms, internal controls, use of financial technologies, and personnel quality.

Thus, it's clear that there were multiple causes for the eruption of problems – in particular the continuous deterioration of state-owned banks' asset quality – in the financial industry in the 1990s, including external and systematic factors and weaknesses in the banks' own governance and management. Which cause, then, was the most significant one? Finding an answer to this question was essential because that answer would lead to the heart of the problem and help the country overcome the obstacles to financial development.

From the late 1990s, the PBOC conducted multiple surveys on the causes and composition of state-owned commercial banks' NPLs that arose along with China's reform and opening up. According to the surveys, among all the NPLs of state-owned commercial banks, about 30% resulted from intervention from the central and local governments; 30% from credit support to SOEs; 10% from China's underdeveloped legal environment, low awareness for legal compliance, and, in some regions, weak law enforcement; 10% from industrial restructuring resulting from the shutdown, suspension, merging, and repurposing of SOEs; and only 20% from mismanagement of credit by the banks[1]. Investigations conducted by the state-owned banks themselves also brought them to similar conclusions. For example, according to a BOC analysis of the causes of its corporate clients' historical NPLs, external factors accounted for 43.3% of the NPLs; borrowers, 27.4%; and BOC's own lax internal management, 29.3%[2]. This analysis basically corroborated the PBOC's judgment at the time.

(IV) Unsuitable Accounting System Increased the Buildup of NPLs

The formation and accumulation of NPLs are inevitable in banking operations. But as long as the NPLs are timely disposed of, banks can maintain a healthy balance sheet. However, before the 21st century, China's financial accounting regime could not help banks to timely deal with their NPLs for two reasons. First, the criteria for recognizing NPLs were not rigorous, as the base NPL level was chronically underestimated due to the maturity-based four-category classification scheme[3]. And second, there was no robust policy on creating allowances for bad debts. Such creation sets aside a portion of a financial institution's profit in anticipation of a future write-off on uncollectible loans, helping it fine-tune and stabilize its operations across long time periods. But the provisioning ratio for Chinese financial institutions was kept low until China began to converge with In-

---

1 Zhou Xiaochuan: "Issues Concerning the Reform of State-Owned Commercial Banks," *Financial News*, May 31, 2004. The original text was from Zhou's speech at the Shanghai IIF Spring Annual Meeting Luncheon on April 16, 2004.
2 Xiao Gang: *Reform of the One-Hundred-Year Old Bank of China*, China CITIC Press, 2011.
3 See previous sections.

ternational Financial Reporting Standards (IFRS) in 2001.

For example, although the state had raised the allowance ratio required of financial institutions on several occasions after 1992, that ratio was still a mere 1% of their loan book as late as 1998. According to reported data, the book balance of ICBC, ABC, BOC, CCB, and BoCom's allowances for bad debts totaled RMB 39.65 billion in 1997, or 0.71% of their total loans, and RMB 52.31 billion in 1998, or 0.80% of their total loans. Comparing this figure with their NPL ratio of between 30% and 40% during the same period revealed that there was an enormous gap to fill. Moreover, in and before 1998, the state strictly controlled the write-offs of NPLs by state-owned banks, requiring that such write-offs should be recognized by the State Council unless the borrower was bankrupt, deceased, or had otherwise became evidently insolvent. This imposed a lengthy process on the write-off even if the banks were able to do so.

Related Topic: Interview with Dai Xianglong, Then PBOC Governor, on the Causes of NPLs[1]

Dai believes the NPLs had the following eight causes:

First, credit was used for fiscal expenditure. To maintain social stability, state-owned banks issued massive policy-based loans to support poverty alleviation, employment, and economic development. In some cases, they also needed to help SOEs pay taxes and bail out distressed SOEs. According to ICBC's analysis, by August 1997, RMB 308.6 billion or 54.8% of its RMB 562.7 billion NPLs were attributable to policy-based loans. The banks also

---

1   From the interviews with Dai Xianglong on April 14, 2017, January 17, 2018, and August 13, 2018.

gave substantial advances to SOEs to supplement their baseline working capital. For example, for building a seamless steel pipe plant in Tianjin, the estimated investment was RMB 3.49 billion, but the actual investment reached RMB 13.46 billion which, excluding the value of the land allocated by the government for the plant, came entirely in the form of bank loans and receivables.

Second, substantial losses were not recognized. In 1998, SOEs and state-controlled enterprises nationwide (excluding those in the financial industry) comprised aggregate assets of around RMB 15 trillion, but as much as RMB 3 trillion of losses were not formally recognized. Therefore, it was necessary for those enterprises to take out a large amount of loans to mask the losses.

Third, the nationwide rush from 1992 to 1993 to develop real estate and development zones also left a mountain of NPLs in its wake. Marginal NPL increases due to real estate development in Guangdong Province, Hainan Province, and Beihai City of Guangxi Zhuang Autonomous Region alone totaled RMB 150 billion.

Fourth, losses on redundant construction projects. According to a survey of 202 national key projects during the seventh Five-Year Plan period, the combined investment amount of these projects was RMB 348.2 billion, of which RMB 109.1 billion were from loans (excluding those categorized by the investors as "self-raised funds"), and about one-quarter of these projects were unable to make repayments. In August 1997, the state ordered ten types of small local plants to be closed down, which also created a significant amount of NPLs for the state-owned banks.

Fifth, some local governments and SOEs evaded their bank debts under the guise of SOE reform. According to ICBC, by the end of 1998,

19,939 of the 133,459 SOEs that had taken out a loan from it had actively or passively evaded their debts, representing 15% of the SOEs under reform; the principal and interest involved totaled RMB 139 billion, or 41% of the principal owed by SOEs under reform. According to ABC's statistics, 45.46% of the SOEs under reform evaded loans and 50% of ABC's loans were actively or passively evaded. BOC's data showed that 65% of the SOEs under reform evaded loans. And for CCB, it was 37%. In total, SOEs evaded RMB 266.2 billion of loans from the Big Four on the pretext of reform.

Sixth, banks' claims were not effectively enforceable as a result of local protectionism and SOEs' insolvency. In 1998, the legal and compliance departments of the Big Four filed 148,819 lawsuits to recover RMB 184.1 billion of loans. Although the banks won 99% of the concluded cases involving a total amount of RMB 87.5 billion, they could only recover RMB 22 billion of their principal, or 25% of the claims sought. Worse still, to secure these "empty victories" they had to pay RMB 1.5 billion in legal fees.

Seventh, state-owned banks were more interested in issuing loans than managing them, and they also issued loans in violation of rules. In 1997, the PBOC spot-checked loan issuance by the Big Four and found that in 41% of the loans, the borrower did not meet lending criteria. The Big Four issued RMB 224.6 billion of loans beyond the prescribed quota or off-the-book, and also invested RMB 165.6 billion to establish economic entities, both of which led to heavy losses.

Eighth, the PBOC was lax in its supervision of state-owned commercial banks. It did not timely impose effective sanctions for rule-breaking lending activities, and some of its branches even established their own economic entities, undermining their authority as a regulator.

Related Topic: Evolution of the Policy on Allowances for Bad Debts[1]

In 1988, to ensure the integrity of the national credit funds and press specialized banks to enhance loan management, the MOF issued regulations to require specialized banks to create allowance for bad debts at 1‰, 1.5‰, and 2‰ of the year-start outstanding loan balance, according to the nature of the borrowing enterprises, their industries, and the purpose and type of the loans. Because these provisioning ratios and the stringent conditions for NPL write-offs were not aligned with the needs of the specialized banks to dispose of their NPLs, the MOF issued more regulations from 1992 to 1994 to increase their provisioning ratio and their powers to write off NPLs. In 1998, the MOF issued the "Notice on Modifying the Number of Years for Calculating Interest Receivable by Financial Institutions and Methods for Provisioning for Bad Debts" (Cai Shang Zi [1998] No. 302), which raised the baseline allowance ratio to 1% of the financial institutions' year-end outstanding loan balance, and such a higher ratio within the year was needed to provide full coverage of the actual bad loan ratio. Despite the MOF's efforts to relax the provisioning policy (e.g., from year-start balance to year-end balance), the provisioning was still based off the four-category classification scheme, and there was a gap between the provisioning criteria and the real asset risk level of financial institutions at that time, especially state-owned banks.

To become a WTO member, China began to bring its accounting standards into alignment with international accounting standards at the turn of the century, thereby pushing forward the reform of its financial accounting system. In May 2001, the MOF issued the "Administrative Measures for the Provisioning and Write-Off of Bad Debts by Financial Enterprises." The Admin-

---

1 From relevant materials of the Ministry of Finance and the PBOC.

istrative Measures expanded the basis of provisioning to include all claims and equity assets subject to risk and loss, required bad debt allowances to be created at different ratios according to the risk level of assets, and combined the allowances for doubtful loans with those for bad loans.

Pursuant to relevant MOF policies, the PBOC issued the "Guidance on Loan Loss Allowance" in 2002, changing the allowance for bad debts to the loan loss allowance. The Guidance requires commercial banks to make a general allowance (*yiban zhunbei*) at a certain percentage of their loan portfolio (no less than 1%) and specific allowances (*zhuanxiang zhunbei*) at 2%, 25%, 50%, and 100%, respectively, of special-mention, substandard, doubtful, and loss loans as classified according to the five-category classification scheme and according to the year-end loan balance.

III. Root Causes of NPAs

Further analysis showed that administrative interventions and lax management not only hindered the development of state-owned banks, but also ran other SOEs into operating difficulties in the 1990s, making them two universal issues. Therefore, if we extend our focus from state-owned banks to the economy as a whole, SOEs included, we will touch on the systematic issues – the deeper-seated causes – in addition to the direct ones already mentioned. These issues were also the reason that the costs of the SOE reform were ultimately passed onto state-owned banks, and that the banks' rights as creditors were for the longest time not effectively protected.

(I) Entanglement of Policy and Commercial Functions

State-owned banks were born when China was transitioning from a planned economy to a market economy, and thus were tasked with supporting economic and social development. For a rather long period after their establishment, state-owned banks were not widely recognized as commercial banking institutions in their own right, but rather as money lenders supplementing and substituting for functions of the fiscal system. In fact, the banks did not separate business with a commercial orientation from policy-based initiatives, with the latter even accounting for a relatively high proportion of their operations. As stated earlier, during China's transition into a market economy, many policy tasks, and those supporting the restructuring of SOEs in particular, often produced no profits and even incurred losses, dealing a significant blow to the performance of the state-owned banks. Moreover, because the policy-based activities were not clearly separated from commercial business, the losses incurred by the former could not be accounted for separately from a bank's overall performance. It was thus impossible to either assess the influence of policy business on state-owned banks, or to accurately evaluate the soundness of their commercial business. As a result, lower requirements were placed on the banks in terms of profitability and risk control than otherwise would have been.

After the overhaul of the financial sector in 1993, the state leadership became aware of the issues from the commingling of the political and commercial aspects of state-owned banks and began to separate them and to transform the banks into truly commercial entities. However, the reform was in the early stage and did not produce much result, and SOEs faced various difficulties during the critical stage of the economic transition. Because of this lack of necessary external conditions, the state-owned banks could not be realistically changed from mere government-directed money lenders into genuine financial actors, and still had to undertake the burdensome policy-based tasks. In this critical phase of economic reform, when China had yet to separate its functions of public administration from those of managing state-owned assets, and state-owned banks had yet to establish themselves as autonomous financial operators, the state, governments at various levels, and state-owned banks were all unable to harmonize policy initiatives with the commercial nature of the banks. In conclusion, the entanglement of policy function and commercial function within state-owned banks during this special period contributed significantly to what would become their longstanding woes, and was the fundamental reason that they had to bear the costs of the economic reform.

(II) Unclear Ownership Rights Structure

Unclear ownership right relations actually comprised two underlying challenges. One was that the national government lacked a definite entity through which to exercise its ownership interests in state-owned banks, even though it was legally their sole shareholder; and the other was the lack of segregation between the government's roles in discharging the functions of public administration and in managing state-owned assets. In fact, since 1992, when considering how to develop the public sector and how to carry out the SOE reform, the central government had become conscious of the ownership rights issue as well as its impact on the restructuring of SOEs. In November 1993 at the Third Plenary Session of the 14th CPC Central Committee, the Party decided to establish a modern enterprise system with "clear ownership rights, well-defined functions and responsibilities, separation of government from business activities, and rational management frameworks" that met the needs of the market economy, and set clarifying ownership rights as the priority of the SOE reform. But before the mid-1990s, given the special nature and status of state-owned banks, discussions about the causes of their issues rarely touched upon the question of ownership rights, and instead focused mainly on the banks' internal management. Nevertheless, many of the problems that plagued state-owned banks could be traced to the ambiguity in their ownership.

First, it blurred the boundary between banks and the state. Until the 1990s, the state had exclusive ownership of the state-owned banks and, as such, could rightfully possess, use, derive income from, and dispose of their assets. But the state is only an abstract entity and did not delegate any organization to exercise those rights on its behalf. As a result, governments at various levels, as administrators of the land and having wielded administrative powers and built an extensive administrative network, became *de facto* controllers of the state-owned banks – intervening in the banks' operations within their jurisdiction not only on an "as-needed basis," but essentially as an obligation.

Second, it necessarily shifted the costs of the SOE reform to the banks. State-owned banks had to accomplish both operational and administrative goals due to the aforementioned issue of vague boundaries. The government, as the *de facto* agent for the state-owned assets, and exercising no distinction between its function of public administration and its function of management of state-owned capital, inevitably assigned its administrative objectives to state-owned banks. The finance system and the state-owned banks – two apparatuses commanding major resources – were merely the "left pocket" and "right pocket" out of which the government took money to allocate public resources. When the finance system was short of funds for the SOE reform, state-owned banks had to step up to shoulder the costs. Moreover, because the banks could issue monetary loans, it was technically easier to leverage them to support the

SOE reform and maintain stability.

Third, the status of blurry ownership made it difficult for banks to enforce their rights as a creditor. State-owned banks had difficulty in recovering their loans, for they had neither independent right to claim ownership of loans, nor any ownership representatives with whom they shared the same interests over loans. Both local governments and SOEs believed that the money they owed to the banks were money owed to the state and, as such, needed not be repaid. The statutes before the mid-1990s gave specific protections to banks as creditors, but were not effectively enforced. If an enterprise defaulted on its loans, the local government, despite having the power to investigate the circumstances and determine the liabilities and consequences, considered adjudicating any sanctions as nothing more than a game of taking money out of one pocket and putting it into the other.

Fourth, difficulty in establishing a governance system coordinating incentives and restraints. Due to unclear ownership rights, state-owned banks suffered from incessant management problems until the 1990s. Clearly defined ownership rights were needed as the foundation upon which the state-owned banks could build their incentive and restraint mechanisms, and which also defined an ownership-centered responsibility system for all stakeholders within those establishments. In the absence of such clarity, governments at various levels were in a position to displace the state to exercise such rights and determine the incentive and restraint systems for those banks. The incentives and restraints were thus necessarily linked to the functions of the government, imparting a strong administrative tint to the management goals and division of functions and responsibilities at state-owned banks. In the course of their transformation into market-based and commercial entities, state-owned banks implemented a performance evaluation, compensation management, and promotion system similar to those of administrative organs, which made their executives and employees aloof to market principles. Furthermore, the restraint mechanisms, unconnected to market principles, provided a free pass to the institutions and leaders with poor performance, which fueled complacency and slackness in their work, or incited unconstrained expansion and non-compliant activities.

Though it was not the only cause of the longstanding issues of state-owned banks, the unclear ownership rights structure was undoubtedly a key one, for that structure very much defines the corporate organization and management. As in the case of SOEs, the ownership rights of state-owned banks were established back in the planned economy era. When China began its transition from a planned economy to a market economy, the then relatively simple business structures did not make ownership rights a prominent issue, and economic development was not directly or seriously impacted. However, as SOEs and state-owned banks accelerated their market-based transformation, defects in the ownership rights structure became more manifest and led to productivity and other challenges. The 1997 Asian financial crisis was a wake-up call to the stakeholders that risks were looming in China's financial industry and the state-owned banks had to be reformed. More and more attention was then directed to the ownership rights situation. Later, the banks would also begin their reform by first tackling the ownership rights, which ultimately put them on the path to the joint-stock reform.

Related Topic: Directions of the Structural Reform of Specialized Banks[1]

The specialized banks were all state-owned banks whose assets were wholly owned by the state. In China, state-ownership is also called "ownership by the whole people," meaning that every citizen has a share in the state-owned assets. But the "whole people" are only nominal owners, because no individual citizen can exercise his ownership rights over, or be held responsible for the loss or profit on, his share of the assets, and thus has no rights over any portion of the assets at all. The assets owned by the whole people are instead held by the state on their behalf. Being an abstract construct, the state cannot exercise any civil right or assume any civil obligation like a real asset owner. Therefore, the assets owned by the whole people are actually owned by the government, the administrator of the state. However, even the government itself cannot exercise the ownership rights, either – it cannot be held accountable for the profits and losses. This dilemma gave rise to serious theoretical and practical issues in state-owned specialized banks:

(1) Specialized banks from the head office to the local branches were integrated with, reliant upon, and even considered subordinate to, the governments at the corresponding levels, making them easy targets for government control and intervention. Given their nature as state-owned enterprises, they must undertake the policy tasks assigned by government... Due to this lack of autonomy, specialized banks to a certain extent actually fulfilled government functions, and could not transform into real commercial banks.

(2) Unlike commercial banks, specialized banks could not be purely profit-driven, but rather had to undertake the policy objectives assigned

---

1   Dong Fureng: "Banking System Reform in China and Some Issues about the Joint-Stock Reform of Banks," *Economic Research Journal*, 1994 (1).

by the government without considerations to their bottom line. Accordingly, they could not assume full responsibility for their performance... It can be seen that a large proportion of the business of specialized banks was not profit-driven. Commingling of for-profit and non-profit goals resulted in disorderly management and prevented them from becoming bona fide banks. Some specialized banks even used the losses from policy-driven initiatives to mask those that had separately arisen from underperformance and mismanagement.

Section III
Early Explorations at Reform

The central authorities had always attached great importance to the reform and development of state-owned banks. As the country advanced the reform of the socialist economic system with Chinese characteristics, its state-owned banks explored their own path towards commercialized and market-based development. However, given the unique features of China's state-owned banks, there was no domestic or foreign precedent for their reform. Within a broader context, the state leadership placed high priority on reforming the economic system, with particular focus on SOEs, and state-owned banks yielded to the SOEs as part of their essential supporting role. Consequently, before the mid-1990s, the SOE reform was the only model available to state-owned banks placed in the position to "cross the river by feeling the stones" in their own endeavor. Similar to other SOEs, state-owned banks focused on corporatization, the separation of policy initiatives and commercial activities, and changes in other essential areas. Judging from the outcomes, at various stages these efforts had promoted the wellbeing of the banks and resolved some prominent issues. As the economic reform pushed forward, state-owned banks went through rapid changes and had to meet new requirements. Their initial efforts proved to be inadequate to address the fundamental problems confronting them. To fully transform state-owned banks into market-oriented, modern banks, other approaches were needed.

I. Bringing Corporate Approaches to Specialized Bank Operation

From the 1980s to the 1990s, a key objective of the SOE reform was to reinvent SOEs as true corporations. The main approach to achieving this was to allow enterprises to operate more freely and retain surplus profit and to enhance their competitiveness. This approach also set the tone for the reform of state-owned banks.

The first round of the SOE reform, right after the reform and opening up, was about giving enterprises greater autonomy. With it, the state aimed to address issues such as low level of operating vigor and efficiency caused by the lack of autonomy and incentives under the legacy economic system. Starting as a pilot program in Sichuan Province in 1978, enhanced enterprise autonomy remained a key part of the SOE reform until 1984. As a subset of SOEs, state-owned banks also implemented the same principles, policies, rules, and measures during that period to promote greater autonomy. The four major national specialized banks – ICBC, ABC, BOC, and CCB – all made proactive and productive efforts. However, without certain prerequisite conditions in place, such as the single-legal entity corporate structure and capable IT management systems, and without well-developed internal management frameworks and restraints, potential risks skyrocketed.

Furthermore, the reform for greater autonomy was targeting the internal operation and management system of state-owned banks, and no policy regarding their relationship with the state or the ownership rights was introduced. Without the separation of policy-driven and commercial operations, the various branches of state-owned banks paradoxically suffered from more, rather than less, administrative interventions, owing to the greater autonomy they each now had. Enhanced autonomy and profit retention, while both counting as major reform actions, were nonetheless insufficient to resolve the underlying problems of state-owned banks.

The commitment target system (*chengbao zerenzhi* or *chengbaozhi*) was another approach adopted in the SOE reform. From 1981 when the State Council first approved the Shougang Group to pilot the system to the end of 1988, 90.8% of industrial SOEs had implemented the system[1]. In the 1980s, at the promotion of the PBOC, some branches of specialized banks integrated the commitment target system into their retail banking business to attract deposits and encourage savings. Starting from 1988 when the commitment target system was implemented within ABC across all its branches, national specialized banks had each switched to a comprehensive commitment target system that centered on the cascaded assignment and commitment of profit targets. The adoption of the commitment target system was an exploratory initiative by the banks aimed at advancing their corporate reform, including re-establishing the relationship between the state and state-owned banks and separating ownership rights from the operational decision-making powers. Moreover, once higher standards of

---

1   Xiao Donglian: "The Road of SOE Restructuring: From Decentralization of Power and Transfer of Profits to Institutional Innovation," *Journal of Chinese Communist Party History Studies*, 2014 (3).

accountability over internal operations had been put in place, branches and sub-branches began to weigh cost-benefit tradeoffs and find solutions that balanced the duties, authorities, and interests of stakeholders. This helped shed old habits learned from "feeding at the communal trough" of the traditional distribution system, allowed their system-wide reforms to take deeper root, and improved their management system.

However, the commitment target system, like the reform to grant greater autonomy to the enterprises, left some issues unresolved. Namely, the relationship between state-owned banks and the state remained unaltered, the commingling of policy-based finance and commercial banking meant that fiscal functions could not be carved out from banking operations, and banks were still called upon to extend loans to whomever the traditional economic system demanded. This meant that state-owned banks were still very much bound to finance the SOEs and to fulfill the obligations of the country's finance system when it was unable to. Furthermore, the commitment target system did not change the monolithic asset structure tying together the state-owned banks and the state. Because the banks did not autonomously hold independent ownership rights that would facilitate the alignment of their interests to the nation as a whole, the process of dividing up profits under the commitment target system easily devolved into interest-seeking machinations. These circumstances overshadowed any hopes that tweaking the profit distribution scheme would invigorate the state-owned banks to reach their full potential.

II. Separating Policy-Based Lending from Commercial Activities

The emergence of the NPA troubles in the early 1990s spelled the end of the greater autonomy reform and of the commitment target system.

When analyzing and reflecting on the issue of NPAs, policymakers began to realize that the roots of the problem could not all be traced to the internal workings of the state-owned banks, but might also be related to the external environment and frameworks in which state-owned banks operated. Though the leadership had become aware of the issue of ownership rights and had organized relevant studies, because of the special position and nature of state-owned banks – which created a highly entangled ownership rights structure – it would be overly risky and difficult to tackle the issue before achieving a breakthrough in the reform of the real economy. Against this background, the government decided to push forward the commercial transformation of state-owned banks by addressing another root issue constraining them – the commingling of policy and commercial functions.

The "Decision of the State Council on Reform of the Financial System," released at the end of 1993, called for establishing three policy banks – the China Development Bank (CDB), the Export-Import Bank of China (China Eximbank)[1], and the Agricultural Development Bank of China (ADBC) – to carve out the policy-based initiatives then lodged with the national specialized banks. The three policy banks were each established in the first half of 1994. In particular, CDB took over from CCB part of the loans and interest subsidies to national key infrastructure projects; ADBC picked up some agriculture-oriented policy lending unloaded from ABC and ICBC; and China Eximbank accepted transfer of BOC's subsidized loans and credit guarantee business for export of ready-for-sale mechanical and electrical products.

---

1 Originally the "Import-Export Credit Bank" in the "Decision of the State Council on Reform of the Financial System."

The decoupling of policy-oriented finance was a milestone event in the reform of state-owned banks and particularly significant to subsequent reforms. Firstly, it enabled the commercial transformation of national specialized banks. Although the initial batch of policy-oriented initiatives offloaded from the state-owned banks was small – for example, as of the end of 1994, the policy loans issued by CDB, ADBC, and China Eximbank were only RMB 81.8 billion, RMB 350 billion, and RMB 2 billion, respectively – the policy banks, by their very existence and design, were able to alleviate the state-owned banks of onerous policy-related tasks, and effectively created a barrier from local government interference at the branch level. Following the creation of the policy banks, governments at different levels seeking funds for their policy-based projects could now turn to policy banks instead of the SOCBs, enabling the latter to avoid administrative meddling, improve their relations with government entities, and boost asset quality.

Secondly, the decoupling drove the commercial transformation of state-owned banks by helping improve their performance assessment systems and create a profit-driven system of operation.

Thirdly, it severed the direct link between policy loans and the monetary base, strengthening the PBOC's control of the monetary base[1] and inflation, and helping create a stable loan market for the reform of state-owned banks.

Fourthly, it set a precedent for cooperation between policy banks and SOCBs and facilitated the commercial transformation of state-owned banks. For instance, under the leadership of President Chen Yuan, CDB

---

1   From the "Decision of the State Council on Reform of the Financial System" issued on December 25, 1993.

began to pay commissions to SOCBs for issuing policy loans to national key infrastructure projects on its behalf. This new model of cooperation not only ensured adequate funding for such projects, but also helped advance the commercial transformation of state-owned banks.

Despite its impact and significance, the decoupling still did not resolve the fundamental problems facing state-owned banks for two reasons. (1) It was incomplete, because SOCBs still retained massive policy loans which were concealed within broader commercial operations. (2) The government had not separated its function of public administration from the function of managing state-owned assets, meaning that it would still impose various demands on the state-owned banks, and that these banks were still charged with allocating funds according to needs of the public administration. As a result, from the establishment of the policy banks in 1994 to the close of that decade, state-owned banks continued to engage in policy lending. For example, in 1998-1999, ICBC issued special-purpose loans (*fengbi daikuan*) to help enterprises improve their operations and loans to address the liquidity difficulties of the coal industry. The NPLs thus incurred accounted for 30.3% of the bank's total new NPLs in the first half of 2000[1]. In retrospect, the conversion of state-owned banks into true commercial banks would require multiple rounds of reform and the implementation of a comprehensive set of supporting measures.

III. Promulgating Banking Laws

In addition to the measures mentioned above, China advanced the reform of state-owned banks by legislative means.

---

1   From ICBC's internal report on new NPLs in the first half of 2000.

To establish the status of the PBOC and clarify its responsibilities, ensure the formulation and implementation of monetary policies, develop a sound macro-control system for the central bank, and maintain financial stability, at its third session on March 18, 1995, the Eighth National People's Congress adopted the *Law on the People's Bank of China* which came into effect on the same date. Two months later on May 10, 1995, the *Law on Commercial Banks* was promulgated by the Standing Committee of China's National People's Congress to better protect the legal rights and interests of commercial banks, depositors, and other bank customers; regulate the activities of commercial banks; enhance the quality of loan assets; strengthen supervision and administration; ensure operational soundness of commercial banks; maintain financial order; and promote the development of the socialist market economy. The latter came into effect as of July 1, 1995.

Based on the two laws, several administrative regulations and ministry-level rules were then issued to enhance supervision over the banking industry. Covering such matters as market access, qualification of industry employees, operation, corporate governance, and finance and accounting, they formed a basic legal framework governing the supervision of China's banking industry.

IV. Transforming the Operating and Management Philosophy of State-Owned Banks

State-owned banks are a creation of the planned economy, and their executives and employees had become accustomed to the way of administrative organs. Therefore, to turn state-owned banks into true corporations that operate by market rules, it was essential to ensure their executives and employees recognize and reach consensus on the significance and goals of the reform. Following the issuance of the "Decision of the State Council on Reform of the Financial System" and the *Law on Commercial Banks*, to expedite the transformation of national specialized banks into SOCBs, in June 1995, the PBOC organized the Conference on the Operation and Management of Banking Industry, during which all banks were urged to revise their operating philosophy to be more commercial-oriented.

At the meeting, Vice Premier Zhu Rongji pushed for a shift in priorities towards enhancing the operation and management of banks and using funds more effectively, with the aim of turning specialized banks into commercial banks that would be operated and managed like their global peers. In addition to the eight requirements for commercial banks, the top concern for changing mindset and advancing reform was also established – the reduction of NPL ratio. This meeting was a milestone event for the PBOC. It helped state-owned banks orient their operating philosophy and identify their position at the crucial stage of their transformation into commercial entities, as well as make the shift in mindset needed for later reforms[1].

Recalling the explorative reform measures of state-owned banks in the 1980s and the 1990s, we see two problems remained unresolved by the stakeholders:

Firstly, how to completely decouple the operations of banks from those of the government. Attempts to simultaneously pursue both had exposed the state-owned banks to severe administrative interventions, operational distortions, and asset quality deterioration. Enabling the banks

---

1 From the interviews with Dai Xianglong on April 14, 2017, January 17, 2018, and August 13, 2018.

to fully embrace commercial operations by offloading the policy functions and avoiding unreasonable administrative interventions became both the focus and the challenge of the reforms.

In the early attempts at reform, the government, as the representative and investor of state-owned assets, was in fact the administrator of state-owned banks and had significant control over their human resources, financial affairs, and assets. In this sense, the reform – whether by means of enhanced autonomy or the commitment target system – was in nature only an adjustment to the degree of autonomy granted to banks, rather than a surrender of the government's power to directly intervene. The government, as public administrators, is primarily responsible for social stability and unity, economic development, and employment, and therefore often took advantage of their direct control to hold state-owned banks accountable for public administration objectives, resulting in divergent operating goals and distorted business operations at the banks. Separating policy business from state-owned banks, a substantive reform in the bank-government relationship, was an important initiative that laid the foundation for subsequent reforms. Due to the complexity of that relationship, however, the reform could only help better define the business and functions of banks, but was powerless at dislodging the administrative and fiscal duties assumed by the banks.

Secondly, how to create an effective incentive and restraint mechanism and corporate governance structure for state-owned banks. The common goal for greater autonomy and profit retention, the commitment target system, and the separation of policy-based lending and commercial business was to make state-owned banks into market players structured as corporate entities operating through "independent operations, self-assumption of profits and losses, self-assumption of risk, and self-discipline." However, due to the lack of clear ownership rights structure and independent ownership rights, state-owned banks were unable to harmonize their own commercial interest with the duties of supporting the economy and protecting and growing the value of state-owned assets. Without a well-defined bank-government relationship, state-owned banks would often chase policy goals at the expense of their own commercial interests and risk management. Therefore, to stimulate state-owned banks and enhance their self-autonomy, China had to address the root cause of ownership rights, and seek breakthroughs in the ownership rights structure and corporate governance structure.

CHAPTER III
RESPONDING TO CRISIS

– The Asian Financial Crisis Ushered in a New Round of Financial Reform

The eruption of the Asian financial crisis in 1997 dealt a heavy blow to Asian economies, and created great concern among China's policymakers. In its aftermath, questions of how to prevent and manage financial risks were recognized as not only vital to the stability of China's financial system, and also to its broader economic development. Reform was no longer a yes-no proposition and the focus of debate soon shifted to *how* the state-owned banks should be reformed.

Nevertheless, it was a question difficult to answer. As demonstrated by the explorations from the 1980s to the mid-1990s, given the nature, economic role, and complex history of state-owned banks, their reform would necessarily involve many stakeholders and disrupt the underlying economic and financial architecture and system. For this reason, patchwork improvements would never yield long-term effects, and without breakthroughs in the top-level design and vigorous implementation, transformation of state-owned banks would have been simply impossible.

Section I
The Asian Financial Crisis

History is a story of cause-and-effect and chance. While cause-and-effect shapes the general direction of events, chance creates the twists and turns. Despite the strong impetus for financial reform at the turn of the century, the importance and necessity of finance were still not adequately appreciated, and opinions over the significance, direction, magnitude, and timing of China's financial reform diverged. Such differences of opinion created frictions to reform, and despite the significant changes to domestic and international contexts and the growing consensus among policymakers, China's financial reform was still waiting for a "trigger event" that would set it in motion. But the drumbeat of history would be sounded sooner or later. As the calendar flipped over from 1996 to 1997, a series of events erupted in Southeast Asia and forever changed the course of China's financial reform.

I. Financial Turmoil in Southeast Asia Under the Speculative Attacks of International Capital

The period from the 1970s to the 1990s saw the rising of the Four Asian Tigers – Singapore, China's Hong Kong, South Korea, and China's

Taiwan – and the Tiger Club Economies of Thailand, Indonesia, Malaysia, and the Philippines. These fast-growing economies, together with Japan, already an economic powerhouse, became the new drivers of world economic growth. For almost two decades from the 1980s to the 1990s, the Four Asian Tigers and the Tiger Club Economies maintained a blistering average annual rate of above 8%. Their economic successes were applauded as the "East Asian miracle."[1] In 1997, however, while people were still expecting the dividends from Asia's economic boom to continue, Southeast Asian countries faced premeditated financial attacks on an unprecedented scale.

In January 1997, international speculators led by George Soros sold the Thai baht in a bear raid, taking massive short positions on Thailand's blue-chip stocks and index futures. As a result, the baht fell sharply against the U.S. dollar, and the Thai government was left with no option except to dig into its foreign reserves to shore up the value of its currency. By July 2, the Thai government had exhausted its foreign reserves and was forced to adopt the managed-float exchange rate. In November, Thailand's prime minister resigned; in December, 56 Thai financial companies went bankrupt.

Almost at the same time, the other members of the Four Asian Tigers and the Tiger Club Economies also suffered similar attacks. The Philippines, Malaysia, and South Korea were forced to abandon their fixed exchange rates, and the value of both their currencies and stock markets plunged. South Korea applied for assistance from the IMF. Although this financial tsunami swept across Southeast Asia without directly hitting

---

1   The term came from the World Bank's 1993 publication *The East Asian Miracle*.

Japan, the sudden collapse of the financial markets in Southeast Asia made matters worse for Japan's already beleaguered financial industry. From October to November, Japan's Kyoto Kyoei Bank, Yamaichi Securities, Sanyo Securities, Hokkaido Takushoku Bank, and Tokuyo City Bank successively declared bankruptcy.

From the exuberant mood at the beginning of the year to the widespread upheaval at the year-end, 1997 was the "Waterloo" moment in Southeast Asia's economic and financial history. However, the nightmare did not end there. In 1998, international speculators launched additional salvos. On February 11, the Indonesian government abandoned its fixed exchange rate against the U.S. dollar. Later, Suharto's Administration was forced to permit banks to declare bankruptcy and foreign capital to hold controlling shares in banks, thus partially ceding its economic sovereignty. By June, international speculators had turned their sights to their next target: Hong Kong.

At this critical juncture, the Chinese government pledged to maintain the value of the renminbi, thus stabilizing market expectations, and extended full support to the Hong Kong government to help the newly established Special Administrative Region overcome the crisis. The Hong Kong government also promptly reversed its "positive non-interventionist" stance and fought back against the international speculators. On August 28 – a critical date for it was when many stock-index futures would be delivered – the Hong Kong government launched the final campaign against international speculators over the Hang Seng Index (HSI) and ultimately thwarted their conspiracy, scoring a decisive victory that forced the speculators to withdraw from the Hong Kong market in September.

II. Lessons Learned

(I) Devastating Effects of a Crisis

The Asian financial crisis ultimately ended with the defeat of the speculators, but it left a bitter aftertaste for the Southeast Asian countries and beyond in their aspirations for economic and financial progress. First, investors suffered tremendous losses. Collapses of foreign exchange, stock, and futures markets wiped off trillions of dollars in global investors' wealth and inflicted huge losses on millions of families and companies. In Hong Kong alone, HSI plummeted from the peak of 16,820 points before the crisis to 6,544 points at the lowest in August 1998, with market cap nose-diving from over HKD 4.7 trillion to HKD 1.89 trillion at the lowest point, down nearly HKD 3 trillion.

Second, banks were saddled with a surge in non-performing loans. As international capital fled the capital markets in Southeast Asia, banks faced a deteriorated credit environment marked by collapsing housing markets and widespread wealth destruction. For instance, when the crisis had run its course by the end of 1998, Hong Kong's housing price index almost halved compared with its peak in the first half of 1997. Homeowners saw the value of their housing properties plunge below zero when considered net of outstanding mortgages. Therefore, many of them stopped repaying their mortgage loans, and naturally, the NPL ratio of Hong Kong's local banks spiked.

Third, the mass bankruptcies of financial institutions wrought havoc on the societal credit system. The financial crisis struck a deadly blow to the financial institutions of Southeast Asian countries. During the crisis, Thailand suffered a wave of bank runs with 56 banks forced into closure. After the eruption of the crisis, around 40% of financial enterprises in South Korea declared bankruptcy. Only 19 of its 33 national banks survived, and less than 12% of its investment companies managed to stay afloat. The serial bankruptcies of financial institutions led to the collapse of the societal credit system, paralyzed the financial system, and worsened the post-crisis economic recessions in Southeast Asia.

Fourth, the crisis reshaped Southeast Asia's economic landscape. Most countries and regions struck by the crisis were forced to abandon their fixed exchange rate. In order to qualify for the IMF's bailout, some countries, in deference to the Western rules of economic liberalization, had no choice but to cede the control of domestic financial institutions and enterprises to foreign capital, further sacrificing their economic and financial autonomy.

Fifth, the crisis disrupted the political stability of Southeast Asian countries. Mass protests broke out in many countries, including Thailand, South Korea, Indonesia, and Malaysia, as public confidence in their governments faltered. Cabinet members of Thailand, Indonesia and Japan resigned. The political turmoil threatened their national security.

(II) Root Cause Analysis and Lessons Learned

In the aftermath of the Asian financial crisis, the global community conducted an in-depth autopsy of the root causes of the crisis and came to a series of consensus views. In particular, it was generally agreed that the crisis mainly stemmed from imbalances in the international monetary system and the inherent problems in the model of the Southeast Asian countries for economic and financial development.

A major external factor that contributed to the Asian financial crisis was the unipolar international monetary system which became dominated by the U.S. dollar after the collapse of the Bretton Woods system. Leveraging the dollar's position as a world currency, the U.S. adopted an easy monetary policy to gobble up global resources and commodities, creating excessive global liquidity. The excess international capital, in search of investment opportunities, thus flooded international financial markets and fueled speculation.

In 1997, for instance, aggregate daily transaction volume in global foreign exchange markets fell in the range of USD 1.5 trillion to USD 2 trillion, over 95% of which were speculative transactions[1]. In such an environment, financial risks would inevitably become manifest once dollar liquidity receded. Furthermore, over the years, Southeast Asian countries had been maintaining huge surpluses on their trade accounts with the U.S. and receiving substantial capital inflows even as they failed to patch up loopholes in their financial systems; all these made them targets for international speculative capital.

From an economic perspective, the export-oriented economic development model adopted by Southeast Asian countries was deeply flawed. As the costs of labor and resources rose and production capabilities in the region became homogenized, their export profit margins kept being squeezed, and economic bubbles occurred well before the crisis. In the 1990s, many economies in the region experienced a trade slump. For instance, Thailand's exports of goods and services shrank by 5.5% in 1996.

The financial system was host to even more problems that could be blamed for the eruption of the crisis.

First, to promote economic development, Southeast Asian countries opted to open their capital accounts and adopt fixed exchange rates. According to Paul Krugman's "impossible trinity" theory, whenever there is

---

1   Source: *Almanac of China's Finance and Banking (1998)*.

free flow of capital, countries must make compromises in their monetary policy if they wish to maintain stability of their exchange rates. That is to say, whenever the exchange rate fluctuates, central banks must intervene in the foreign exchange markets to bring exchange rates back to "parity."

At the time, foreign reserves comprised the primary resource for central banks to regulate exchange rates. Before 1997, however, of the said jurisdictions, only Japan, South Korea, and Hong Kong enjoyed foreign reserves above USD 100 billion; the Philippines, Thailand, and Indonesia's foreign reserves were USD 2 billion, USD 37 billion and USD 16 billion respectively, and the ratios between their short-term foreign debts and their foreign reserves were calculated at 1.03, 1.26, and 2.26 times, respectively. It was their paltry resources for regulating foreign exchange markets and maintaining the fixed exchange rates that made themselves easy targets for international speculators.

Second, the unchecked relaxation and removal of restrictions on capital account transactions offered a wide-open playing field for USD 7 trillion in international capital to engage in speculation. From 1993 to 1996, USD 50 billion to USD 100 billion of capital, mostly private capital, flooded into Southeast Asian countries. Massive capital inflows overwhelmed the weak financial regulatory systems of some Southeast Asian countries, which failed to effectively distinguish different types of capital and regulate them accordingly. The hot money did not enter into the real economy as the countries wished and instead fueled asset bubbles in the housing and capital markets.

Before 1997, the stock markets of all these economies climbed to record highs. On the last trading day of 1996, HSI reached 13,451.5 points, up 33.5% over the closing price on the last trading day of the year before.

Real estate prices were at an all-time high, with Tokyo, Hong Kong, and Seoul joining the ranks of the most expensive housing markets in the world.

Third, the banking systems were fragile. Intrinsic problems in the banking systems of Southeast Asian countries not only allowed the Asian financial crisis to spread, but also increased its geographical reach and severity. Before the crisis struck, almost all Southeast Asian economies were experiencing a credit binge. Domestic credit as a share of GDP reached between 115% to 200% for Japan, South Korea, Thailand, and Malaysia. However, the scale of credit expansion was not matched by adequate risk resilience of the banking system as the financial markets were underdeveloped and lacking regulatory oversight and bank governance, and the governments and conglomerates of Southeast Asian countries were inextricably entangled with the banks.

By the end of 1996, the NPAs of banks in South Korea and Thailand represented 34% to 40% of their GDP. However, the problem of NPAs received little attention in some Southeast Asian countries that prioritized economic growth. To take the Philippines as an example, despite annual loan growth of above 10% in the three years leading up to the crisis, the provision coverage ratio fell from 3.5% to 1.5%. Among Southeast Asian countries, Malaysia had the highest provision coverage ratio, which was only 2%[1].

As the whole financial system rested on their weak shoulders, the fragile banks caused the crisis to spread faster and with more devastating effects. Although the crisis originated from the foreign exchange markets and

---

1   Here, the provision coverage ratio refers to the ratio of allowance for loan losses to the balance of loans.

tore through the capital markets, its destructive power came squarely from the banking sector. Closures of banks accelerated credit contraction and the collapse of confidence. Southeast Asian economies struck by the attacks suffered the most after banks and large financial institutions had gone bust, and indeed crushing the banking system was precisely what international speculators aimed to achieve. It was also through the banking system that Soros and his followers, in first attacking Thailand, breached Thailand's financial defensive line. In March 1997, the Thai government was forced to disclose the non-performing housing loans of its banking sector – this revelation shattered public confidence in Thailand's financial system.

Fourth, financial distortions stemming from administrative intervention also contributed to the crisis. For more sophisticated market economies such as Japan and South Korea, lack of financial professionals and operational experience – or other factors at the micro level – were obviously not the most important causes, and the root cause can only be traced down to the macro level of financial systems. Reflections by politicians and experts from countries involved in the crisis may offer an answer to this question.

As then South Korean President Kim Dae-Jung said at the Asia-Europe Meeting (ASEM) in 1998, "The financial crisis of South Korea was the culmination of all-round problems of the economy. Government intervention in bank lending disrupted the financial order and diminished corporate competitiveness." Chung Duck-Koo, South Korean vice minister for finance, expressed similar views in his book *The Korean Economy Beyond the Crisis*. He believed that although South Korea considered itself a market economy, the government still gave implicit guarantees to businesses and intervened in bank operations from behind the scenes, which led to a contagion of moral hazard. South Korean vice minister for industry and technology Ahn Hyun-Ho summed up the situation by noting that the outdated financial system was unable to effectively guide investment, and cronyism among big firms, the government and banks allowed for the losses of firms to be transferred onto bank balance sheets. A flawed financial system – particularly the distortions from administrative interventions – pushed South Korea to the edge of an abyss.

Therefore, among the four reform initiatives launched by the South Korean government after the crisis, financial reform came first. Kim Dae-Jung remarked that "only when banks restore their functions will firms thrive; only with healthy firms will the nation gain its strength."[1] Evidently, improper government intervention in financial institutions was a deep-seated factor behind the eruption of the Asian financial crisis. Proceeding from such analysis, we may infer the chain of events in the crisis as follows: government intervenes – banking operations become distorted – banking systems become fragile – problem banks collapse – surviving banks pull back on lending and cut lines of credit – credit and liquidity freeze up – crisis intensifies.

All in all, the Asian financial crisis shattered the narrative of the "economic miracle" that had been a source of pride for Southeast Asian countries and changed the trajectory of economic development for Southeast Asia and other emerging economies. Unlike any previous global or regional economic crisis, the Asian financial crisis made for a costly lesson about how financial loopholes could be exploited to magnify economic fragility and threaten economic security.

---

1   Information and statements in this paragraph are referenced from Ren Zeping's "Review: South Korea's Belated Reform Triggered the Financial Crisis of 1997," which was published on hexun.com on March 2, 2016.

Compared with the Southeast Asian economies struck by the crisis, China was spared the brunt of direct repercussions mainly due to its adherence to a prudent financial policy. Unlike some Southeast Asian countries, China did not prematurely open its capital account and instead pursued a prudent foreign exchange policy. In responding to the crisis, China promptly adopted a basket of countermeasures, including increasing the money supply, ramping up fixed asset investment, and lowering interest rates to spur growth. China also promised not to devalue its currency, enhanced foreign exchange market regulation to stabilize expectations, actively worked with the IMF in offering financial assistance to the crisis-hit Southeast Asian economies, and implemented financial risk mitigations.

Despite these countermeasures, China still paid a heavy price for the Asian financial crisis. While the Chinese government contributed to stabilizing the financial situation by not devaluing its currency, the trade environment deteriorated as neighboring economies all took the opposite path. From 1998 to 2000, China's annual growth of foreign trade export slowed to 10.8%, down 16.5 percentage points compared with the average growth rate during 1990-1997, and China's GDP growth dropped from an average of 20.4% during 1990-1997 to 6.3% at the lowest. The crisis created financial hardships for some Chinese exporters and took its toll on the asset quality of financial institutions, giving rise to financial risks. The crisis made the Chinese government and people intensely aware of the material risks to a country's economic, political, and social development that may arise from financial flaws. A deep appreciation grew for the importance of financial security to economic and national security. As in the words of then Premier Li Peng, "This crisis has heightened our understanding of the vital importance of finance and the devastating consequences that we may suffer once a crisis erupts."[1]

China will not cease its economic development nor change the course of its opening-up endeavors. Sooner or later, China's economy, like a giant vessel navigating the sea, will head for deep oceans and must be fully braced for tides and torrents and be able to draw upon its own strength to overcome challenges. For China, with its sails fully open, there was not much time left to prepare. The Asian financial crisis that stormed abruptly at the turn of the century sounded the alarm for China, sweeping away the last remnant of hesitation about financial reform. The trigger event for hastening China's financial reform had appeared.

Section II
The First National Financial Work Conference

At the turn of the new century, China's financial industry found itself at a crossroads, where the choice of direction outweighed all other decisions. As Dai Xianglong, former Governor of the PBOC recalled, on August 5, 1996, the PBOC delivered a report on the issue of financial risks to the Central Leading Group for Financial and Economic Affairs. The report identified three risks that had accumulated in China's financial system over the years. First, the NPAs of the four SOCBs had grown to over

---

1   Quoted from a speech of then Premier Li Peng delivered at the first National Financial Work Conference. See the PBOC and the CPC Central Committee's Party Literature Research Office: *Selected Financial Policy Documents (1978-2005)*, China Financial Publishing House, 2005, p. 276.

RMB 840 billion, or close to 1/4 of their total assets[1]. Some banks were *de facto* insolvent. Second, the rural financial system was facing daunting challenges with 44.7% of rural cooperatives nationwide reporting losses and some rural cooperative funds already in bankruptcy. Third, life insurance companies could possibly have difficulties in making full payments as they came due. While no major payment crisis was expected in the short run, a systemic payment crisis on a broad scale would be a matter of time if financial risks persisted[2].

The report drew the full attention of the central government. On February 19, 1997, the Central Leading Group for Financial and Economic Affairs held another meeting to hear a report by the PBOC and the MOF on financial risk mitigations. At the meeting, the central government decided to hold a national conference on financial issues to raise awareness among senior Party and government officials and the executives of large financial institutions on the prevention and mitigation of financial risks, explore countermeasures, and ensure national financial security. The first National Financial Work Conference was thus put on the agenda.

Notably, two incidents occurred during the preparation for the first National Financial Work Conference that profoundly influenced the agenda and priorities of the Conference. The first was the Asian financial crisis, which drew scrutiny – both in China and internationally – to the quality of bank assets and the vulnerability of banking systems in Asia. Naturally, because China was a new engine of the Asian economy, its banking sector

---

1   The amount of NPLs and the NPL ratio here are both calculated by the four-category classification scheme based on loan portfolios of the Big Four at the end of June 1996.
2   Dai Xianglong: "Review of the 1997 National Financial Work Conference," *China Finance*, 2009 (19-20).

also came into the spotlight. From then on, China's banking sector NPLs would only grow in importance in the eyes of the media and analysts around the world. Chinese and foreign newspapers were awash with questions like whether China would reshuffle its banking sector in the manner of countries like Thailand and South Korea, whether a financial crisis would erupt in China, and whether the problem of NPAs would force China to abort its economic reforms. The tragic lessons experienced by Southeast Asian economies highlighted the urgency of preventing financial risks and safeguarding financial security. The CPC Central Committee and the State Council closely followed the developments of the crisis; held numerous meetings to discuss its trends, ramifications, causes, and countermeasures; and intensively re-analyzed the path of China's financial reform. Those efforts formed the basis for the decisions made at the first National Financial Work Conference.

The other incident was a financial scandal in Enping, Guangdong Province in 1996, which incurred a loss of some RMB 10 billion to local financial institutions. More importantly, it arose from local government interventions in financial institutions. The scandal prompted the central leadership to reassess the importance of enhancing Party oversight over financial affairs, a topic that was soon put on the agenda of the first National Financial Work Conference.

Related Topic: Enping Financial Scandal and the CPC Central Committee's Decision to Enhance the Party's Leadership over the Financial System[1]

The financial scandal in Enping, Guangdong Province in 1996 was one

---

1 Compiled based on an interview with Dai Xianglong and relevant historical materials.

of the reasons behind the CPC Central Committee's decision to enhance the Party's leadership over the financial system. After Deng Xiaoping completed his inspection tour in southern China, Enping's local government – eager to seize the opportunities presented by the reforms to develop the local economy – offered an exorbitant investment incentive by promising a cash reward of RMB 15 for each RMB 100 worth of investment. The incentive drove local enterprises to take out high-interest loans from the banks to build nothing but cement plants. To meet this massive demand for loans, local banks in turn offered high deposit rates. In just a few years, cement plants sprang up like mushrooms after the rain in nearly all townships and villages within Enping, and all of them suffered dismal performance due to overcapacity. In the subsequent campaign to restore financial order, many plants went bankrupt, leaving a mountain of loans unpaid. From January 1990 to August 1996, financial institutions in Enping used high interest rates to bring in RMB 13.6 billion of deposits and illegally issued RMB 10 billion in loans. By the end of 1996, the balance of overdue loans exceeded RMB 4.6 billion, including bad loans in excess of RMB 800 million and overdue interest of over RMB 1.2 billion.

The loan defaults impaired the solvency of the banks. In June 1995, angry depositors attacked the banks and staged sit-ins, and once more in August 1996. When the first payment crisis occurred in Enping, the central government dispatched personnel to investigate the incident and warned the Guangdong provincial government and Party committee of the risks. Nevertheless, the manager of the CCB Enping Branch, who was responsible for the disaster, was not only spared punishment, but even landed a nice promotion to vice mayor of Enping until the next payment crisis struck.

The two payment crises caused the Enping Rural Credit Cooperative and the county branches of CCB and ABC to suffer an estimated loss of RMB 10 billion. The ensuing bank run led to the bankruptcy of the cooperative and the business suspension of the county branches. The headquarters of the two banks were forced to allocate funds to the county branches to guarantee payments to depositors. The Enping incident made the central decision-makers aware of the excessive influence over finance held by local governments and the risks that may arise once the central government loses control over the financial sector. Consequently, the central government took steps to strengthen its central leadership over the Party organizations of the financial system nationwide.

Under the guidance of Zhu Rongji, then member of the Standing Committee of the Central Political Bureau ("Politburo Standing Committee") and Vice Premier, the State Development Planning Commission led an effort with the participation of the MOF and the PBOC to draft the "Circular on Deepening Financial Reform, Restoring Financial Order, and Preventing and Resolving Financial Risks." The Circular proposed the roadmap for the next stage of financial reform and laid the groundwork for the convening of the first National Financial Work Conference.

On November 17-19, 1997, the first National Financial Work Conference was held in Beijing. General Secretary of the CPC Central Committee and President of China Jiang Zemin, Premier Li Peng, and Vice Premier Zhu Rongji attended the conference and delivered speeches. The conference enjoyed the extensive engagement of principal government officials of various provinces, autonomous regions and municipalities; leaders of relevant departments of the State Council; heads and deputy heads of the PBOC, policy banks, and SOCBs; the principal leaders of the China

Securities Regulatory Commission, the People's Insurance Company (Group) of China (PICC), and other large financial institutions; presidents of the provincial branches of the PBOC; as well as the general managers of some branches and subsidiaries of large national financial institutions. Backed with a strong strategic mandate from the central decision-makers for the financial sector, this conference set a new high-water mark in terms of the scope, number, and seniority of participants.

I. Drafting the Blueprint of Financial Reform

The first National Financial Work Conference was the first of its kind held by the CPC Central Committee specifically on the planning of the financial reform. The Conference adopted 15 major decisions that shaped China's financial reform and development in the long run. Among them, decisions on the banking reform were the top priorities.

First, the Conference identified the guiding principle that "banks should perform all the functions of banks" as a priority of the reform and proposed the actions that would make it a reality. It was stressed that financial reform must "address both the symptoms and root cause." Here, the "root cause" was referring to the fundamental reasons behind the disorderly financial sector, i.e., "problems within the financial systems and mechanisms," particularly those within the banking system. To create the top-level architecture needed for the banking reform, the Conference called for restructuring the PBOC's supervisory setup by reorganizing its provincial branches into regional branches that cover a larger geographical area, so as to enhance the overall management of the financial affairs within each region. In addition, the supervisory focus of the county (city) branches of the PBOC was redirected to rural credit cooperatives. To accelerate state-owned banks' transformation into commercial entities, aside from improvements to policy-related financial frameworks, the Conference also set the direction of reforming how state-owned banks were to be administered. The priorities included:

- consolidating provincial branches of state-owned banks with branches established in provincial capitals;
- disbanding and consolidating prefecture- and county-level institutions to reduce layers of management hierarchy in the state-owned banks and boost managerial efficiency;
- reforming management over credit lines extended by state-owned commercial banks, and implementing management over the assets-to-liabilities ratio and of risk, to increase operational equilibrium and robustness;
- reforming personnel management, worker relations, and income distribution, and creating a board of supervisors to enhance internal incentives and supervision;
- enhancing centralized management by implementing central accounting and funds allocation and hierarchical financial management for branches, and by strengthening the oversight of the authorities delegated to branches; and
- expediting IT development to increase managerial efficiency.

Second, to enhance the Party's central leadership over the financial system, the Conference established the CPC Central Financial Work Commission and the Central Financial Discipline Inspection Commission. Meanwhile, the Party organizations of large state-owned financial institutions were to be reorganized into CPC committees to enable the CPC Central Committee's vertical leadership over Party building and personnel-related programs at lower levels, which would facilitate the consolidation of state-owned banks and other financial institutions into single corporate entities.

Lastly, the Conference called for a reform to improve the risk management of banks. Given the poor management and inadequate oversight of financial institutions, stronger financial regulation and supervision was needed to prevent financial risks. The importance of separating banking from securities, insurance, and other types of financial services ("industry-segregated operation") and implementing sector-based regulation was reiterated, as banks were urged to decouple from their trust, securities and insurance arms and other economic entities.

The Conference determined that external supervision should be integrated with internal oversight. As regulatory authorities would be called upon to enhance their auditing, inspection, and regulatory functions, so too the banks would be expected to develop independent internal auditing and supervision functions under the top-down leadership of their head offices, so as to improve their internal control and tighten self-discipline.

The Conference also called for reform of financial management. It required financial institutions to adopt unified and stringent financial accounting, data reporting, and information disclosure frameworks, and required banks to defend their reputation for "accurate book-keeping and rigorous financial management and systems." The Conference specified requirements on the capital funds of banks and the quality of their credit assets. It required state-owned banks to maintain their capital adequacy ratio above 8% and reduce the ratio of non-performing credit assets by 2 to 3 percentage points on an annual average basis.

Moreover, banks were also required to improve their loan structure and segregate credit review from loan issuance. The Conference reaffirmed the need for credit discipline, emphasizing that no organization or individual should be in a position to force banks or other financial institutions to issue loans, or provide guarantees or other financial services. The government should not turn to bank loans to cover fiscal shortfalls, and banks should not be hindered in any form from exercising their claims.

The Conference planned for a new round of campaigns to crack down on "illegal fund-raising, illegal provision of financial services, and illegal establishment of financial institutions (the 'three new unruly areas'),"[1] requiring the closure of all illegal financial institutions, the prohibition of all illegal financial activities, and greater supervision over entry requirements for the industry.

The Conference also ordered the following actions: comprehensively rectifying illegal financial organizations or those in disguised forms, including rural cooperative funds, mutual assistance groups (*huzhuhui*), and rural mutual savings funds (*chujinhui*); prohibiting and combatting illegal fund-raising, urging fiscal authorities at all levels to separate from their subsidiary trusts and securities companies; eliminating and imposing sanctions for the off-the-book activities and other illegal operations of financial institutions; and enhancing financial law enforcement and punishing financial crimes and violations. Although these measures themselves were not directly related to the banking reform, they helped establish a

---

1 The "three new unruly areas" paralleled the old "three unruly areas" in the early 1990s, viz., illegal fund-raising, illegal short-term lending, and illegal establishment of financial institutions.

favorable market environment for it.

II. Significance of the First National Financial Work Conference

For the first time, the Conference brought the issues of financial risks and risk prevention onto the central government's agenda, shifting the government's focus of attention to financial risks and financial security. Before the Conference, finance was widely regarded as a lever to spur economic development, while its risks were not fully appreciated. For the first time, a systematic framework for reforming the state-owned banks and the remedies for addressing their deep-seated ills were laid out. As such, the Conference marks a milestone in the history of the reform of state-owned banks.

First, the Conference identified potential risks in China's financial system – an essential step for risk mitigation. At the Conference, the CPC Central Committee analyzed domestic financial risks and their root causes, and made it clear that it was necessary and urgent to accelerate the financial reform. In his speech, Zhu Rongji identified five risks to which China's financial industry was exposed. (1) The financial system was no longer suitable for the changed situations of reform and development. (2) The development of real estate and industrial zones was overheated and created massive non-performing credit assets. (3) SOEs' excessive reliance on loans from state-owned banks obstructed the progress and reform of both. (4) Economic structural issues had created difficulties for SOEs. (5) The misappropriation of credit funds had become a serious problem.

"For the risks that have accumulated in the financial sector over the years," Zhu concluded, "if nothing is done to prevent and resolve them, they may someday cause financial turbulence that disrupts the economy as a whole [and] even lead to an upheaval and shake the foundation of our country."[1] This remark was the first strongly worded warning made at a major Party conference about the dangers lurking in the country's financial operations and industry and indicated that the central decision-makers had taken to heart the potential consequences of financial risks. The statement made maintaining financial stability and security a national strategic concern and identified financial reforms and risk mitigation as priorities in economic reform.

Second, the Conference established reshaping the banking-government relationship as the core issue of financial reform. While previous central economic work conferences had also analyzed this relationship, none of them explained the nature and crux of this issue with such clarity and insight as did the first National Financial Work Conference. On November 19, 1997, Jiang Zemin said in his concluding remarks at the first National Financial Work Conference that "Yet ours have not been banks in the true sense of the word; they have only issued currency and held reserves."[2] He stressed that "The main task in financial restructuring is to have banks perform all the functions of genuine banks. Since the onset of reform and opening up, Comrade Deng Xiaoping has clearly pointed out, on a number of occasions, the need for banks to function as such."[3] Thus, "The core issue in having China's banks perform all the functions of genuine banks is the need to correctly understand and handle the relationships

---

1 Quoted from Zhu Rongji's speech "Deepen Financial Reform and Prevent Financial Risks to Break New Ground in Financial Programs" at the first National Financial Work Conference on November 18, 1997.
2 *Selected Works of Jiang Zemin*, Vol. II, Foreign Languages Press, 2012, p. 73. See also *Selected Works of Deng Xiaoping*, Vol. III, Foreign Languages Press, 1994, p. 193.
3 Ibid.

between governments, enterprises and banks."[1]

In his analysis of the deep-seated problems in the financial sector, Zhu Rongji noted that "the government is not separated from banks and enterprises. Too much intervention by the government in the workings of banks and other financial institutions prevented the PBOC from lawfully performing its duties and responsibilities and the state-owned commercial banks from operating independently. These problems can be resolved only with thorough reform." His remarks attributed the state-owned banks' institutional problems to the blurred boundaries and improper relationship between banks and the government. It marked a significant breakthrough in theory and policy and implied that the central government had started to refocus the reform from the internal management of the state-owned banks to the relationship between banks and the government and between ownership and routine operational decision-making. For the first time, the reform started to address the top-level design issues such as the financial operation at the macro level.

Third, the Conference created an organizational framework for centralized administration of the financial sector. The first National Financial Work Conference made an important decision to centralize financial regulation. Local governments and CPC committees – which were in charge of the personnel management and Party committees of banks – often interfered with the business operations of banks by ordering them to issue loans to specific borrowers. This created a funds shortage at banks at various levels, forcing the PBOC to issue more money. This became a key reason behind the excessive currency creation, credit binge, and high inflation in the 1990s. Thus,

---

1   *Selected Works of Jiang Zemin*, Vol. II, Foreign Languages Press, 2012, p. 74.

freeing banks from the administrative meddling of local CPC committees and governments became a priority in reforming the financial system.

In this respect, the Conference made two groundbreaking changes. The first was to adopt top-down administration of the agencies, personnel, and decision-making of the banks. In his speech at the Conference, Zhu Rongji explained the objectives of this initiative: "In establishing the Central Financial Work Commission, the Central Financial Discipline Inspection Commission, and the CPC committees at all financial institutions, our goal is to enhance the Party's central leadership over financial affairs, capitalize on the Party's strength in promoting theories and political programs, and ensure that the CPC Central Committee's guidelines, principles, policies and national financial laws and regulations are implemented in the financial sector."[1]

In line with the principles laid out at the Conference, the Party leadership groups of state-owned banks at various levels were reorganized into CPC committees, which have the authority to approve and establish Party organizations at lower-level branches which would report to the CPC committees directly. In this manner, the banks regained control over the Party networks at the lower levels which were frequently taken advantage of by local governments and Party organizations for their own purposes.

The second groundbreaking change was that the reform harmonized the relationship between the central and local governments. Aside from the centralized administration of state-owned banks, the Conference put forward a new approach to enhance the development of local banks and urban-rural cooperative banks. Development of regional financial institutions

---

1 Excerpt from Zhu Rongji's speech at the first National Financial Work Conference.

boosted the local economy and reduced potential barriers to the continued institutional reform of state-owned banks.

Fourth, the Conference reinforced the core restraints and requirements under standardized financial management. The first National Financial Work Conference issued clearer, stricter, and more specific requirements on the industry-segregated operation, credit management, capital adequacy, financial and accounting practices, and IT development at commercial banks, most of which are still in effect to this day. The Conference stressed that regulators must play an effective role of supervision and guidance, clarified responsibilities of various entities and systems of accountability, and ensured the implementation of administrative reform measures.

III. Joint-Stock Reform of State-Owned Banks: The Conference's Neglected Topic

At the macroscopic level, the first National Financial Work Conference addressed the independence of the central bank and the state-owned banks. It severed unwanted administrative ties among the central bank, state-owned banks, and local governments, and resolved a host of issues, including the weakened control of the central government over financial affairs, pressures created by local governments for currency creation by the central bank, and excessive lending by state-owned banks that led to economic overheating and high inflation.

At the microscopic level, the Conference explored such problems as the shortage of capital for state-owned banks and the accumulation of non-performing assets and risks. However, the Conference did not take any position on the joint-stock reform of state-owned banks – a topic already on the minds of central policymakers – due to various considerations.

First, policymakers believed that changes should be introduced through a step-by-step approach to not jeopardize the consensus on launching the financial reform that only just took shape. The first National Financial Work Conference made a series of major changes such as the redesign of the PBOC's division of regulatory boundaries and creation of the Central Financial Work Commission, the Central Financial Discipline Inspection Commission, as well as CPC committees at all financial institutions including state-owned banks. These reforms aimed to restructure the government-banking relationship and redefine the boundaries of central-versus-local authority for financial administration. The magnitude of proposed reforms exceeded public expectations and created concerns. Skeptics raised questions such as "Will the reform lead to chaos?" "Is it feasible to accomplish in one step what otherwise takes a decade?" "Is the Western model suitable for China?" "Will a banking system crossing administrative zones impede economic development in central and western regions of China?"[1]

These concerns revealed that the public did not yet share a unified vision on how the financial reform should proceed. In making decisions, the central government must consider the reaction of all stakeholders. It was necessary to build consensus before reform could be carried out prudently. Moreover, the joint-stock reform of SOEs was still at an experimental stage, making it too early to proceed onto the state-owned banks. Hence, reforms proposed at the Conference instead aimed to remove external barriers to the development of state-owned banks, chiefly by first straightening out the relationship among CPC committees, local governments, and

---

1 Excerpt from Zhu Rongji's speech at the first National Financial Work Conference.

banks, and between the central and local governments. Furthermore, the financial reform needed to be a smooth and gradual process. The chaotic state of the financial sector pointed to defects in the governance of financial institutions, which needed to be addressed first before deeper-level reforms were introduced.

The second reason has to do with priorities. Any major reform decision must conform to the contexts and the priorities of its times. Being aware of the many issues in the financial sector, the central leadership indeed had the impulse to accelerate the financial reform immediately. However, at the critical juncture of 1997, when the Asian financial crisis threatened to decimate the economy and the SOE reform had just entered a crucial stage, the central leadership had no choice but to balance financial reform with the SOE reform and the prevention of financial risks with the maintenance of economic stability. "With success of the SOE reform still elusive, can we truly proceed to financial reform?" This question was raised but not satisfactorily answered before the first National Financial Work Conference. At the Conference, Zhu Rongji explained the relationship between the SOE reform and financial reform and affirmed the latter's importance to the former.[1] However, given the greater urgency and economic consequences of the issues with SOEs, the central government had to prioritize the bailout of SOEs and the real economy, so as to ensure a steady level of financial support was available throughout the process.

The third reason was the cost of reform. A more drastic joint-stock reform would be tremendously expensive. Without a turnaround in the

---

[1] For details, please refer to Zhu Rongji's speech at the first National Financial Work Conference.

economy and improvements to the weak fiscal conditions and loose budgetary constraints on enterprises, it would be by no means easy to dispose of the massive NPAs of state-owned banks without leaving legacy problems – in which case subsequent reforms, even if carried out, might not have achieved any meaningful breakthrough.

Section III
The Five Pillars of Deepening Reform

After the first National Financial Work Conference, a new round of financial reform was set in motion according to the plan of the CPC Central Committee. The reform consisted of five pillars: centralizing the financial regulatory system; implementing industry-segregated operation for the banking sector; injecting capital into state-owned banks; reforming the risk management system of banks and creating financial asset management companies; and stripping NPAs off state-owned banks.

I. Centralizing the Financial Regulatory System

Establishing an appropriately centralized financial regulatory system was named at the first National Financial Work Conference as a key principle of financial reform. Adhering to the guidelines of the "Circular on Deepening Financial Reform, Restoring Financial Order, and Preventing and Resolving Financial Risks," the Chinese government started to push forward with financial reform in 1998 at three levels, namely Party organizations in the financial industry, regulatory framework, and internal management of financial institutions.

First, build-up of Party organizations in the financial system. June

1998 saw the creation of the Central Financial Work Commission and the Central Financial Discipline Inspection Commission. Serving as the direct delegate of the CPC Central Committee to financial circles, the Central Financial Work Commission oversaw CPC committees at financial institutions and was responsible for supervising the implementation of Party policies and principles, assisting the CPC Central Committee in managing "centrally managed officials" (*zhongguan ganbu*)[1], and coordinating with the CPC committees of financial institutions and local governments, i.e., involving heavily in the day-to-day activities of the subordinate Party organizations. By contrast, the Central Financial Discipline Inspection Commission took a more supervisory role, and was charged with overseeing the implementation of the Party's guidelines, principles and policies, and identifying and prosecuting violations of laws, regulations, and discipline, as directly delegated by the Central Commission for Discipline Inspection (CCDI). This organizational change prevented local governments from intervening in the Party and personnel affairs of banking institutions in their respective jurisdictions. It also enabled financial institutions to exercise top-down leadership over their Party organizations and officials.

Second, institutional reforms for the central bank. Following the State Council's arrangement, the PBOC carried out institutional reforms for its head office and branches from May 1998. At the head office level, seeking to "unify management and enhance supervision" as directed by the first National Financial Work Conference, departments and bureaus were consolidated and new ones were created to enhance the central bank's

---

[1] This refers to officials whose appointment and dismissal is directly managed by the CPC Central Committee.

functions. The PBOC's securities and insurance regulatory functions, together with its Asian Development Bank business, were split off to the China Securities Regulatory Commission (CSRC), the China Insurance Regulatory Commission, and the MOF, respectively.

The branch-level reform focused on streamlining organizational setup and adjusting functions. Within one month from November 18 to December 18, 1998, the PBOC closed 32 provincial branches and created 9 regional branches in Tianjin, Shenyang, Shanghai, Nanjing, Jinan, Wuhan, Guangzhou, Chengdu, and Xi'an. In provinces and autonomous regions where no regional branches were established, the PBOC set up financial regulatory offices under the regional branches. The PBOC also created central sub-branches in the capitals of provinces and autonomous regions.

With these changes, the PBOC created a four-level organizational structure encompassing the head office, regional branches, central sub-branches, and sub-branches. While monetary policy and lending remained powers of the head office, the regional branches are responsible for implementing financial regulatory policies within their jurisdictions that span across provinces, autonomous regions, and municipalities, and maintained a high degree of autonomy. The central sub-branches are business offices that provide local financial services under the management of regional branches.

Third, reform of the administration of state-owned banks. This reform aimed to consolidate the branches and head office of each state-owned bank into a single corporation. Following relevant regulations[1], all

---

1   The "Interim Regulations on the Board of Supervisors for Solely State-Owned Commercial Banks" released and took effect on November 12, 1997.

state-owned banks started to create their own board of supervisors in 1998. Each board of supervisors answers to the PBOC, and consists of representatives from the PBOC, the MOF, the State Economic and Trade Commission, the National Audit Office, and the State Assets Supervision and Administration Bureau, among other regulatory and ministerial agencies. The board of supervisors is responsible for supervising banks' management of state-owned assets to ensure their value is maintained and increased.

In addition, under the PBOC's leadership, the state-owned banks started to reform their subordinate organizations, focusing on consolidating provincial branches and provincial-capital branches and closing or merging inefficient and loss-making branches[1]. In 1998, the four state-owned banks merged over 100 subsidiaries with overlapped regional coverage and shuttered over 9,000 underperforming outlets[2].

The reform also extended to credit management. As of January 1, 1998, the PBOC removed the cap on incremental loan growth from state-owned banks and replaced the quarterly "directive" plans with annual guidance plans, putting an end to the quantitative control over loan issuance that had been in place for nearly 20 years. The PBOC also required state-owned banks to balance the obtainment and application of funds under the coordination of their head offices, implement a management regime centering on the assets-to-liabilities ratio at the head office level, and maintain an appropriate loan-to-deposit ratio.

Lastly, the reform enhanced the state-owned banks' discretion to ex-

---

1   After the institutional reform, the provincial-capital branches of state-owned banks were renamed into provincial branch business departments and managed as second-level branches.
2   Source: *Almanac of China's Finance and Banking (1999)*.

tend credit, so that credit decision-making authority was no longer subject to the administrative rank of the institution making that decision.

The reforms at this stage did result in the devolution of power to state-owned banks, which partially addressed the needs of the market. But it was a conditional increase of the banks' operational autonomy after they were each re-organized into a single corporation, reflecting the key objective set by the first National Financial Work Conference that was to restore financial order and prevent financial risks. The reform strengthened the vertical management by the head offices of the state-owned banks and reduced the horizontal interference from local governments in the business operation of bank branches.

II. Establishing the Industry-Segregated Operation and Management Framework

In line with the first National Financial Work Conference's decisions on implementing the industry-segregated operation and management in the banking sector, the central government adjusted the securities and insurance regulatory frameworks in 1998 to bring them in sync with the banking reform, and the PBOC's securities regulatory function was off-loaded to the CSRC. On November 18, 1998, the State Council approved the creation of the China Insurance Regulatory Commission (CIRC) to regulate the national insurance market, institutions, and services, functions originally assigned to the PBOC. The establishment of the CIRC marks the full segregation of operation and regulation of the banking, securities, and insurance sectors.

Meanwhile, the State Council released a circular in 1998 requiring central Party and government agencies to cut loose their affiliated economic entities and enterprises, so as to straighten out the bank-enterprise relationship and prevent risks. The PBOC and the Central Financial Work Commission supervised the split-off. By the end of 1998, all financial institutions, including state-owned banks, had cut ties with their previously affiliated economic entities through handovers, reorganizations, revocations, and closures. This task paved the way for implementing industry-segregated operation for financial institutions and preventing financial risks.

Furthermore, in the 1990s, many trust companies went bankrupt, including the China Agribusiness Development Trust and Investment Corporation, Guangdong International Trust & Investment Company (GITIC), and China New Technology Investment Corporation. Their bankruptcies highlighted risks in the trust industry. After the bankruptcy of GITIC was wrapped up in 1998 under the leadership of Wang Qishan, then Vice Governor of Guangdong Province, the State Council General Office issued a circular in February 1999[1] to initiate the fifth round of remediation of the trust industry[2], focusing on ensuring trust businesses would be segregated from banking and securities services. In 1999, 8 trust companies were disbanded, merged or reorganized, and over 100 securities business divisions were closed down or made compliant.

The strict segregation of banking, securities, and insurance sectors was particularly significant given the financial environment at that time. In the 1990s, it was widely believed that "given the public's limited aware-

---

1 "Circular of the State Council General Office on Forwarding the PBOC's Plan for Rectifying Problems in Trust and Investment Companies" (Guo Ban Fa [1999] No. 12).
2 The previous four rounds of remediation campaigns were carried out for the trust industry in 1982, 1985, 1988, and 1993.

ness in this regard and the inadequate regulation of financial entities at the time, mixed business would only lead to chaos."[1] By implementing segregated operation, the financial institutions clarified the boundary of their businesses and responsibilities, which allowed them to focus on their primary businesses for enhanced efficiency and risk management. Segregated operation created more stable and orderly market and institutional environments for the subsequent reform and development of the state-owned banks. As PBOC's former Vice Governor Wu Xiaoling recalled, "It took China ten years – from the outbreak of the Asian financial crisis in 1997 to 2007 – to clean up its financial market and create a reasonably sophisticated financial system."[2] Segregated operation helped create an overall financial framework in line with China's financial maturity and reform priorities at the time.

III. The First Round of Capital Injection

Apart from financial system restructuring, implementation of the reform plan for the state-owned banks laid out at the National Financial Work Conference was another priority task. The eruption of the Asian financial crisis invited many international predictions about the collapse of China's banking sector. Some argued that Chinese state-owned banks were "technically bankrupt." In this context, China's central decision-makers decided to first address the capital shortage and asset quality problems of the state-owned banks. Of the two, capital injection was a more urgent task given the importance of capital funds to banking operations and the need

---

1 From the interview with Lou Jiwei on March 18, 2017. The original statement was Zhu Rongji's assessment of industry-segregated operation.
2 From the interview with Wu Xiaoling on February 8, 2017.

to protect the banks' reputation as they were planning to seek financing from global financial markets.

Because the banks in question were wholly state-owned, capital replenishment had to be done in the form of injection by the state. Based on the criteria for and balance of NPAs, the capital adequacy ratio of the Big Four was less than 3% in 1997. To meet the 8% capital adequacy ratio set by the Basel Accord, a capital injection of roughly RMB 270 billion would be necessary. But China's total fiscal revenue that year was just about RMB 1.1 trillion; revenue for the central government was even smaller and even less than the expenditure. Therefore, the central government did not have sufficient fiscal resources to pump RMB 270 billion into the state-owned banks. In fact, similar dilemmas also haunted the subsequent joint-stock reform of the state-owned banks.

The central decision-makers, the PBOC and the state-owned banks had no choice but to face the challenge. They could not afford to wait for a solution and so the only option was to find an innovative way to recapitalize the banks without incurring actual fiscal spending. The PBOC organized an expert study and held multiple rounds of consultation with the MOF to finally settle on a solution. The MOF would issue special government bonds to the Big Four through private placement. In this manner, the additional capital would not come directly from the treasury, but from the payment made by the Big Four for the government bonds. The difficulty was that the banks should not be asked to pay for the special government bonds with any marginal increase in funds that could be otherwise used for their business operation, as doing so would reduce their ability to support the economy and take a toll on their financial performance.

Facing the impossibility of utilizing additional funds, the PBOC thought about leveraging the funds already on hand. After careful review and comparison of monetary policy instruments, the PBOC picked the reserve ratio as tool of choice. At the time, the statutory reserve ratio was set at 13%, and the PBOC estimated that if the reserve ratio were lowered by five percentage points to 8%, the Big Four would free exactly RMB 270 billion in statutory reserve funds which could be used to purchase the special government bonds. Without affecting the supply of business capital for the banks, this solution created a way for capital injection to work. Furthermore, in the context of the Asian financial crisis, a substantial reduction of deposit reserve ratio could bring forth a robust effect of monetary easing. Additional liquidity from China's banking sector served the secondary purposes of stimulating economic growth and coping with the crisis.

However, neither the fiscal authorities nor the central bank had any experience with this novel approach of pumping capital into the state-owned banks through a combination of issuing special government bonds and lowering the reserve ratio. The MOF had never issued any special treasury funds before, and the central bank also had no experience in supplying liquidity for capital injection by lowering the reserve ratio – a practice that leverages the balance sheets of both the central bank and commercial banks. This decision was too important and unprecedented for the PBOC and the MOF to make on their own. They needed the green light from the central government.

Consequently, PBOC Governor Dai Xianglong prepared a report to Vice Premier Zhu Rongji, who heard the report on a weekend in January 1998. Zhu recognized the feasibility of this proposal and asked Dai to explain to the National People's Congress (NPC) the importance of capital injection and how it works, so as to get the NPC's approval.

At Zhu's instruction, Dai presented the proposal to the NPC Financial and Economic Affairs Committee, which gave its approval. In February 1998, Director of the NPC Financial and Economic Affairs Committee Liu Suinian convened a meeting to hear the PBOC's report on the operational and managerial difficulties of SOCBs and the proposal to replenish their capital through bond issue. Members of the Committee unanimously endorsed the proposal. At Liu's recommendation, Dai exchanged views with Tian Jiyun, Vice Chairman of the NPC Standing Committee in charge of the Economic and Financial Affairs Committee. Recognizing the necessity and feasibility of the proposal, Tian suggested that since the proposal received unanimous support, it should be approved as soon as possible without waiting for the next NPC session. He noted that the proposal could be officially submitted by the State Council to the NPC Standing Committee directly without deliberation at the annual NPC session[1].

Effective communication facilitated debt issuance and capital injection. On February 15, 1998, Premier Li Peng submitted to the NPC Standing Committee the "Proposal of the State Council to Request the Deliberation of the Issuance of Special Government Bonds by the Ministry of Finance to Supplement the Capital of Wholly State-Owned Commercial Banks." On February 28, the capital injection plan was approved by the NPC Standing Committee. In May, the PBOC reduced the statutory reserve ratio by five percentage points and reformed the deposit reserve system by merging the statutory reserve account and provisions custody

---

1 From the interviews with Dai Xianglong on April 14, 2017, January 17, 2018, and August 13, 2018.

account and authorizing payment and settlement operations for the reserve deposits, thus laying the policy and market groundwork necessary to proceed with the capital injection. By June, the Big Four were ready with the funds to purchase the special government bonds. In August, the MOF issued the RMB 270 billion of special government bonds to the Big Four, which were used to recapitalize the banks. This marked the completion of the first capital injection in the history of China's state-owned banks.

Seen within the broad sweep of the history of state-owned bank reforms, the capital injection in 1998 counts as only a small test run, and the RMB 270 billion of capital was in fact insufficient to make up for the bank capital eroded by NPAs. As it was, the injection eased the shortage of capital for state-owned banks only temporarily and exerted only a limited effect on the overall reform of state-owned banks. Nevertheless, being an essential innovation in the reform of state-owned banks, it marks the first attempt to supplement the capital of state-owned banks without directly using fiscal funds, and the first time that it was done by leveraging the central bank's balance sheet. By creating a precedent and serving as a case study for innovations in the subsequent banking reforms, this event holds both theoretical and practical significance.

Related Topic: Xiang Huaicheng on the First Capital Injection of China's State-Owned Banks[1]

"The first problem encountered in the banking reform was a shortage of capital funds, which required a capital injection. As I [Xiang Huaicheng] recalled, back then (before the capital injection in 1997), the ratio of banks'

---

1 Quoted from the interview with Xiang Huaicheng on March 18, 2017.

own funds was less than 3% at a time when international standards required an 8% minimum, a shortfall which translates to a needed capital injection of RMB 270 billion. In 1998, our national fiscal revenue was about RMB 1 trillion, by which I mean the total fiscal revenue rather than the central government's fiscal revenue. The MOF was unable to afford such a huge outlay to replenish bank capital and bring their capital adequacy ratios to 8%. Actually, the central government was running a deficit and could not provide that much cash. In this situation, we came up with a solution: to lower the reserve ratio for banks from 13% to 8%, which means that banks could release RMB 270 billion from reserve funds. Then, the MOF issued special government bonds to the banks, and the money thus released was used to purchase those bonds, and then applied by the MOF to supplement the banks' capital funds."

Related Topic: Evolution of the Deposit Reserve System[1]

Deposit reserves are funds set aside by financial institutions to meet their customers' needs to withdraw deposits and settle transactions. The cash held by financial institutions as reserves at the central bank as a share of their total deposits is the required reserve ratio (RRR), or reserve ratio for short. The level of the reserve ratio determines the proportion of funds that are available for lending by a financial institution and is used as a major monetary operation instrument by the central bank.

The U.S. is the first country to introduce legislation requiring commercial banks to place their deposit reserves with the central bank. This practice

---

1   Based on information on the website of the People's Bank of China and other relevant materials.

was later adopted in other countries. China started to implement the deposit reserve system in 1984 when the PBOC set deposit ratios according to the type of deposits. In 1985, the statutory reserve ratio was reset to a uniform 10%. The March 1998 initiatives mark one of the most important reforms in the development of China's deposit reserve system. This reform included the following elements: (1) the statutory reserve account and provisions custody account of financial institutions at the PBOC were merged into one; (2) the statutory reserve ratio was lowered from 13% to 8%; (3) the PBOC ensured that the required reserve ratios of financial institutions would be applied on a single-corporate entity basis; (4) the deposit reserves of financial institutions would be checked on a 10-day cycle; (5) the PBOC would impose penalties whenever a financial institution fell short of the reserve requirement; (6) the interest rate paid to financial institutions for their required reserves was lowered; and (7) the general scope of applicable deposits for financial institutions was adjusted to include the deposits of government institutions and extrabudgetary fiscal deposits as part of fiscal deposits held on the half of the PBOC, and deposit reserves were accordingly required to be set aside at the specified ratio. This reform laid the groundwork for China's deposit reserve system, enhanced the function of deposit reserves as a monetary policy instrument and the regulation thereof, and supported the ongoing financial reform.

IV. Assessing the Loan Situation and Implementing the Five-Category Classification Scheme

While the capital injection somewhat eased the capital shortage of the state-owned banks at the technical level, a more demanding and crucial task was to improve their asset quality.

To dispose of NPAs, the first step is to create an empirical and logical system for classifying loans by quality. In fact, the four specialized banks had already started to explore a differentiated management system from the late 1980s. ABC was the first among them to classify loans into the four categories – performing, overdue, doubtful, and bad. The PBOC itself used this four-category classification scheme in accounting for NPLs until 1998. As mentioned in the previous chapter, this classification scheme was based on the loan payment overdue period rather than the borrowers' underlying ability to pay. Thus, it could not reflect the real quality of the loans. After thorough analysis following the first National Financial Work Conference, the PBOC decided to adopt a five-category classification scheme referencing the general loan quality classification criteria of the international banking industry.

The five categories are pass, special-mention, substandard, doubtful, and loss, the last three of which are considered non-performing. In contrast to the old system, the five-category classification determines the risk level of loans according to the solvency of enterprises and the probability of loan loss for the banks. In simple words, "pass" refers to loans for which borrowers are repaying interest and principal to the loan contract schedule. "Special-mention" refers to loans for which borrowers are able to repay interest and principal but adverse factors that may affect loan repayment also exist. "Substandard" refers to loans for which borrowers are unable to repay interest and principal from regular income. "Doubtful" refers to loans for which borrowers are unable to make full repayment of interest and principal and certain losses may be incurred even if all recourse to collateral or guarantees is executed. "Loss" refers to loans that cannot be recovered even after all possible means have been exhausted. By these criteria, although the five-category classification still looks at the overdue timing of the loan repayment, the standard is much more complex and stringent than days-in-arrears alone. For instance, under the five-category classification system, loans for which the borrowers have become insolvent cannot appear in the "pass" category through repayment with newly borrowed loans or through loan extension, and potential losses from NPLs will be revealed.

Introduction of the five-category loan classification system was a critical reform which not only improved the credit management of banks and but also enhanced the regulation by the central bank. At a time in which credit lending accounted for 80% of financing to the real economy, reforming the credit classification system was conducive to improving capital efficiency through better credit management. The reform of loan classification also facilitated the reform of the corporate system and of the economic system as a whole[1].

Related Topic: Significance of the Five-Category Classification System[2]

The risk-based loan quality classification is superior to the four-category scheme in the following significant ways:

(1) Reflecting a real picture of loan quality. By the four-category method, an overdue loan may not suggest significant risks if the repayment schedule was unreasonable in the first place; conversely, a loan not overdue is not necessarily free of repayment risk. By the new standard, a borrower's repayment probability must be analyzed based on its business activities, giving

---

1 Quoted from Dai Xianglong's speech at the National Mobilization Conference for Pilot Program for Bank Loan Assessment in 1998, *Collections on Banking and Monetary Policy of Dai Xianglong (Vol. 1)*, China Financial Publishing House, 2008, pp. 339-354.
2 Ibid.

a more accurate assessment of the intrinsic risks and quality of the loan.

(2) Enabling proactive management of loan risks by the banks. Under the new classification system, a bank must perform due diligence on a borrower's business operation in order to classify a loan. This due diligence process enables banks to identify problems early on and adopt proactive credit risk mitigations to protect their claims.

(3) Enabling effective regulation by the central bank. Following the five-category loan quality classification, the central bank will know the net value of the assets of commercial banks after deducting losses. In this manner, the central bank will have reliable accounting information to support decisions to recapitalize the banks, approve well-run banks to merge with troubled banks, or approve financially distressed or insolvent banks to declare bankruptcy.

(4) Safeguarding national economic security. Without real actions to implement a clear and reliable loan classification system, it would be difficult for China's banking sector to join the world arena in an equal and confident manner and raise capital from the international market without paying an exorbitant premium.

(5) Promoting resource allocation and corporate reform.

(6) Clarifying the operational and management responsibilities of banks, and paving the way for reform of the personnel, compensation, and other systems of banks.

The first step in implementing the loan classification system was to verify the amount of NPAs against the new classification criteria. In April 1998, the PBOC released the "Circular on Assessing Credit Assets and Improving Loan Classification"[1] and the "Circular on the Release of the 'Guidelines on Risk-Based Loan Classification'."[2] In May, the PBOC convened a mobilization meeting in Guangzhou to officially launch the program to assess the credit assets and improve loan classification in banks across the nation. In addition to investigating the credit asset quality of banks, the program also aimed to find out the reasons behind the rise of NPAs and enhance the management of bank credit assets and the central bank's supervision of the loan quality of commercial banks.

Placed under the coordination and supervision of the PBOC Guangdong Branch, the program was launched in Guangdong in May 1998 on a pilot basis, starting with the local branches of ICBC, ABC, BOC, CCB, and BoCom. Following the completion of the pilot phase in July 1998, the program was rolled out nationwide involving all policy banks, state-owned banks, and commercial banks.

Priorities of the program included:

(1) Assessing the value of assets, particularly credit assets. The financial institutions were required to verify the compliance with lending requirements and in particular verify and analyze the cause of loans in the "loss" category based on the solvency of each borrower. These results would facilitate reclassification into the five categories.

(2) Recovering loans lawfully. Parallel to taking inventory of credit assets, the banks should exercise their claim to NPLs and safeguard their legal rights as creditors.

---

1 Yin Fa [1998] No. 150.
2 Yin Fa [1998] No. 151.

(3) Creating systems and rules. Commercial banks were given a deadline of 1998 year-end to separately account for old and new loans and to demarcate responsibilities. Furthermore, they should hold the bank presidents and managers accountable for improvement of loan quality, i.e., the head of every bank or bank branch should be responsible for not only the quality of new loans during his term of office but also for disposal of legacy NPLs as well. The PBOC was charged with developing the systems for asset quality reporting, supervision, inspection, analysis, and information disclosure to enhance supervision over asset quality.

(4) Finally and most importantly, the banks were told to implement the five-category loan classification based on material risks and to improve the loan loss provisioning system to make general and specific allowances for bad loans.

At the initial phase of the program, the PBOC did not specify a deadline for implementing the five-category classification. The reasons were twofold. First, after the "Guidelines on Risk-Based Loan Classification (Provisional)" was released in 1998, a track record was needed to gain experience and make improvements. Moreover, a transition period was required to ensure stability in the management of loans as the five-category classification was set to replace the four-category classification. Through the loan assessment program, the PBOC and commercial banks developed a clearer picture about the amount and status of NPLs and gained experience in their management and disposal. They also improved loan classification principles, criteria, and practices.

After the pilot program had run for half a year, the PBOC decided that the five-category classification should be rolled out completely and submitted the "Request for Implementing the Five-Category Loan Classification Scheme on a Full-Scale in 1999," which was approved by the State Council. In July 1999, the PBOC released the "Circular on Full-Scale Rollout of the Five-Category Loan Classification,"[1] which contained program-specific guiding principles and timetables. The Circular required that by the end of 1999, ICBC, ABC, BOC, and CCB, together with the three policy banks, should complete loan classification using the new standard, and the other commercial banks should do so before the end of 2000. The release of this Circular marked the formation of China's risk-based credit asset quality management system for the banking sector at the turn of the new century.

The assessment program achieved its objectives. Thanks to the program, the government was able to unveil the real balance of NPAs held by the state-owned banks, which brought the severity of the issue to light. By the five-category loan classification criteria, for instance, the balance of ICBC's NPLs stood at RMB 1.12 trillion at the end of June 1999, which was RMB 340 billion higher, or 1.44 times, the amount recognized under the previous four-category standard, pushing the NPL ratio up 14 percentage points[2].

Second, the assessment revealed asset quality problems previously concealed in various forms. For instance, ICBC found out that as of 2000 year-end, from among the RMB 1.09 trillion of new loans borrowed for repayment of old ones, businesses borrowing RMB 123.47 billion were experiencing abnormal business conditions, such as production that was

---

1 Yin Fa [1999] No. 263.
2 From ICBC's internal report.

suspended, semi-suspended, or closed altogether. Among those new loans borrowed to repay old ones, NPLs accounted for RMB 215.6 billion, marking an NPL ratio of 21.4%. This category of rolled-over loans also tended to deteriorate rapidly. In the three years from 1997 to 1999, RMB 158 billion of such loans turned into bad loans, becoming a significant source of new NPLs[1]. Third, the assessment initiative allowed the state-owned banks to develop a detailed understanding[2] of the reasons behind the rise in NPLs, enabling targeted reform initiatives.

V. Establishing Financial Asset Management Companies and the First Round of NPL Divestiture

The assessment program and adoption of the five-category classification scheme laid the groundwork for the disposal of NPAs. However, it was expected that the state-owned banks would require a long time to dispose of their massive NPAs if working alone. This was not an option. As the central decision-makers vividly described at the National Financial Work Conference, the NPAs would impede the financial intermediation process and economic reforms as a whole just like sludge could block up a river. Given the urgency of the task, it was necessary to call for assistance outside the banking industry. Work on exploring new avenues for the disposal of NPAs was essentially started in parallel with the nationwide NPL assessment.

In fact, as early as from the mid-1990s, Chinese experts and scholars had been exploring new ways for disposing of the NPAs of the state-owned

---

1   Jiang Jianqing and Wei Guoxiong: *Origin and Resolution of Evergreen Loans*, China Financial Publishing House, 2009.
2   See the analysis of the causes of NPLs in Section I of Chapter II.

banks, such as debt restructuring, debt-for-equity swaps, and capital injections. By 1998, when the issue had become a priority, these ideas finally found an opportunity to be tested in practice.

(I) Creation of the Four AMCs

As early as in the mid-1990s, Zhu Rongji, in charge of financial affairs, had been mulling over the creation of specialized agencies for the disposal of NPAs. Likewise, the state-owned banks were beginning to address the same question at a pragmatic level. In 1998, the CPC Central Committee appointed Zhou Xiaochuan, Vice Governor of PBOC and Administrator of SAFE, as the President of CCB. After taking his new post, Zhou immediately set out to form a research team to work out how the NPA issue might be resolved through restructuring. To this end, Zhou and his team compiled case studies of bank restructuring in the U.S., Nordic countries, countries in Central Eastern Europe transitioning from Soviet to Western economic models, Latin America, Japan, Southeast Asia, and France. CCB even invited senior executives of banks with successful restructuring track records from the U.S., Poland, Hungary, and other countries for knowledge sharing and exchange.

Ultimately, CCB decided to create a specialized company modeled after the Resolution Trust Corporation (RTC). After shedding its NPAs, CCB would become a financially healthy "good bank." According to the plan submitted by CCB to the PBOC, an AMC was to be created to purchase, manage and dispose of the NPAs divested from the bank, inherit and exercise its claims on NPLs, and, to the maximum extent, preserve the value of those assets and minimize risks.

Related Topic: RTC and the Good-Bank/Bad-Bank Model[1]

RTC was a specialized agency created by the Federal Deposit Insurance Corporation in 1989 to address the closure or operational difficulties of some 1,300 savings and loan (S&L) institutions. To complete its mission, RTC adopted the "good bank" and "bad bank" approach, i.e., the NPAs of a parent bank are to be transferred to a separately created subsidiary at fair market value together with the associated reserves. After shedding its legacy NPAs, the parent company becomes a "good bank" with superior asset quality and adequate capital, while the subsidiary becomes a "bad bank" for holding the bad assets. The operation of the "bad bank" is limited to the purchase of specific assets from designated banks. It cannot engage in general banking business and must recover and realize those assets in cash within its period of existence. Prior to dissolution in 1994, RTC's five years of operation involved taking over and disposing of over USD 400 billion in assets at 747 S&L institutions. It played a critical role in solving problems arising from the closure of those S&L institutions.

The PBOC accepted the proposal and held multiple rounds of consultation with the MOF and other ministerial agencies over the creation of such an asset management company, followed up with a report to the central government. In October 1998, the 22nd Premier Office Meeting of the State Council decided to organize a specialized agency for the disposal of NPAs. On April 2, 1999, the PBOC, the MOF, and CSRC jointly issued the "Opinions on Establishing China Cinda Asset Management Cor-

---

1   Zhou Xiaochuan: *Reconstruction and Rebirth: International Experiences on Resolving the Non-Performing Assets of Banks*, China Financial Publishing House, 1999.

poration," which was distributed by the State Council General Office for implementation. On April 20, China Cinda Asset Management Corporation was unveiled in Beijing as the first company in China engaged in the purchase and disposal of commercial banks' NPAs. On July 8, the three ministerial agencies jointly released the "Opinions on the Establishment of China Huarong Asset Management Corp., China Great Wall Asset Management Corp., and China Oriental Asset Management Corp." On October 15, 18 and 19, the three corporations were established for disposing of the NPAs of BOC, ABC, and ICBC respectively. These dates mark the debut of financial AMCs acting as an important participant in the banking reform by disposing of and restructuring the NPAs of the state-owned banks. To enhance coordination between the banks and the AMCs, the presidents and Party secretaries of the four banks served concurrently as the Party secretaries of the corresponding AMCs.

Yang Kaisheng, President of Huarong, wrote that creating AMCs for disposing of non-performing bank assets is a generally accepted international practice. Other than the U.S. which created the RTC in 1989, Germany, Sweden, Finland, and countries in Eastern Europe, Latin America, and Africa had also adopted similar measures. Within Asia, South Korea's KAMCO and Malaysia's Danaharta had been successful AMCs.

While making adjustments for domestic circumstances, China's AMCs patterned themselves on international forerunners with respect to the following operational approaches: taking the form of independent legal entities and non-banking financial institutions, enjoying preferential tax and fee treatment, and carrying a mandate for professional management and disposal of NPLs using a wide variety of tools.

China's AMCs also distinguished themselves from overseas counterparts in the following aspects:

First, the organizational structure for the management and disposal. In other countries, usually only one AMC was set up to purchase, manage, and dispose of NPLs of all problem banks. But given the large size of NPAs of the Big Four, China did not opt for this monopolistic architecture. Instead, AMCs were separately created for each of the four banks, allowing for both cooperation and division of work.

Second, corporate governance and operational goals. Foreign AMCs are generally joint-stock companies with mixed funding from the government, original creditor banks, and other stakeholders; and their boards of directors have decision-making authority on major issues such as the purchase, management, and disposal of assets. Their operational goals are also simple: to minimize the cost of disposal while maximizing recovery rates. China's AMCs, by contrast, are wholly state-owned, subject to many policy requirements in their business operation, and have diversified operational goals.

Third, operational approaches. Most foreign AMCs purchase assets in iterative cycles, i.e., they initially use funds raised from bond issue or borrowed from the central bank to purchase the first batch of NPAs and then use cash collected from disposal of those assets to purchase the next batch. China sought to solve the NPL issue as soon as possible and therefore had its AMCs buy out the mountain of NPAs from the state-owned banks in one go. This required them to pool together more funds initially and to bear a higher interest cost going forward. Even more significant was that while foreign AMCs usually purchased NPLs at an evaluated price or simulated market price, China's AMCs purchased them at their book values.

Fourth, the quality of purchased assets. Foreign AMCs generally fall into two categories. They either purchase all the assets off a troubled financial institution, including both performing and non-performing assets, or they would sift through the target loan portfolios and purchase only those NPLs showing potential for recovery and restructuring. Usually, they would not purchase valueless bad loans. In contrast, the quality of assets purchased by China's AMCs was rather poor and much more challenging to manage and dispose of.

Fifth, legal environment and the AMCs' authority. Most countries enacted special legislation to establish the special legal status of AMCs. In China, the State Council adopted the *Regulations on Financial Asset Management Companies* to regulate the AMCs. Because this document is only an administrative regulation, subordinate in legal force to laws enacted by the NPC, it had to work with and within the constraints of existing laws and was not able to wholly reconcile the business operations of the AMCs with the legal provisions.

(II) The First Round of NPL Divestiture

Creation of the four AMCs set the stage for the state-owned banks to shed their NPAs, but challenges remained. Considering the magnitude of tasks before them, the AMCs were only equipped with scant fiscal resources – a problem reminiscent of the first round of capital injection. Unlike the RTC, the AMCs were instructed by the central government to purchase the NPAs at book value rather than market value to avoid realizing hefty losses on the accounts of state-owned banks that might otherwise derail the banking reform. Since allowances for potential loss on loans were utterly insufficient, the book value of the NPAs remained roughly equal to their outstanding balance, i.e., payment was almost 1:1 to the size of the gross claim value, far higher than the actual value net of incurred losses. At the time of their founding, the four AMCs had a total paid-in capital of only RMB 40 billion. On the other side of the balance sheet, the PBOC's preliminary budget forecasts called for about gross RMB 1.4 trillion in loans to be offloaded from the Big Four, a figure only slightly diminished by deducting the allowances for loss of loans. Policymakers puzzled over how to finance the purchase of this mountain of NPLs at book value. An alternative to outright payment from the state coffers was needed.

Fortunately, these factors had been considered from the outset, and the PBOC improved the plan for creating the AMCs through subsequent consultation with the MOF. Ultimately, it was agreed that the AMCs would take financing from two sources. First, the four AMCs would each issue financial bonds to their corresponding state-owned banks through private placement, RMB 820 billion in aggregate. Second, the PBOC would transfer to the AMCs the loans of some RMB 570 billion it had granted to the four state-owned banks. The financial bonds would pay for NPLs primarily granted for policy reasons, and thus would be guaranteed by the MOF. In other words, if an AMC could not repay a state-owned bank at a bond's maturity, the MOF would do so as the guarantor. Hence, the state treasury-guaranteed bonds with a high credit rating were swapped for the same amount of NPLs of the Big Four, i.e., replacing "bad assets" with "good assets."

With the institutions, plan, and funds in place, the first round of NPL divestiture was kicked off. As the goal was to reduce the NPL burden of state-owned banks arising from policy and historical reasons, the central government, in distinguishing the existing and new NPAs, limited the scope of NPLs to be transferred to the AMCs: doubtful loans issued before the end of 1995 and overdue for more than one year as at 1998 year-end; bad loans as of September 1999 month-end; and loans issued by the state-owned banks after 1995 and approved by the State Council for debt-for-equity swaps. Since Cinda was established before the other three AMCs, CCB was able to lead the pack by transferring RMB 200 billion of NPAs in 1999 while the other three banks spent most of the remaining months in the year on NPA assessments and appraisal.

In 2000, the first round of divestiture came to a completion. In this round, the Big Four transferred loans worth RMB 1,393.2 billion to the AMCs. Specifically, Huarong purchased RMB 407.7 billion of NPLs from ICBC, Great Wall RMB 345.8 billion from ABC, Oriental RMB 264.1 billion from BOC, and Cinda RMB 375.6 billion from CCB. After the transfers, the NPL ratio of the Big Four dropped by 10 percentage points as measured by the four-category classification standard[1]. Out of the nearly RMB 1.4 trillion of divested loans, more than RMB 400 billion were swapped for equities in over 400 companies. From 1999 to the end of 2001, the debt-for-equity swap program resulted in a removal of RMB 216.8 billion in bad loans, providing strong support for SOE reforms, reorganizations, mergers, and bankruptcies. In the end, AMCs recovered over RMB 200 billion with an average recovery rate of 15%[2]. The meager recovery rate points to the poor quality of the loans granted by the state-owned banks; however, compared with traditional methods, the centralized disposal of NPLs through specialized agencies like AMCs was still a more efficient approach.

---

1 Source: *Almanac of China's Finance and Banking (2001)*.
2 Quoted from interviews with Dai Xianglong on April 14, 2017, January 17, 2018, and August 13, 2018.

Related Topic: The First Round of NPAs Divestitures and Recovery Rate[1]

During the first round of divestitures, ICBC, ABC, BOC, and CCB were transitioning from specialized banks to commercial banks. However, the bulk of their asset portfolios had been formed during the transition from the monolithic banking system to specialized banks. As a result, the NPL conditions of the banks varied, and so did the recovery rates in the first round of divestiture. When it was a specialized bank, CCB focused on infrastructure loans. With loans backed by project assets and revenues, CCB reported the highest NPL recovery rate. ICBC, which lent to industrial and commercial enterprises backed by factory premises and land, had the second highest recovery rate. BOC and ABC, given their borrowers and nature of loans, were characterized by relatively low recovery rates. Considering such differences, the MOF set different target recovery rates for the four AMCs: 17% for Cinda, 16% for Huarong, 9% for Oriental, and 7% for Great Wall. In the first round of divestiture, the overall recovery rate reached around 15% and beat expectations.

Related Topic: Comparative Advantage of AMCs in Disposing of NPLs[2]

Without the involvement of AMCs, banks and enterprises would fall into the chicken-or-egg conundrum. As a third party, the AMCs were able to bypass this pitfall, leaving behind a healthy bank-enterprise relationship. In a relaxed policy environment, the AMCs were allowed to hold equities, invest in firms, and experiment with all sorts of ideas. They also helped reduce public grumbles about "losses on state assets."

---

1   Based on documents of the AMCs.
2   Quoted from the interview with Tian Guoli on May 5, 2017.

The first divestiture program has great significance. From 1995 to 2000, annual NPL growth of the Big Four averaged 3.2%. Following this trend, by 2002, their combined NPL ratio as measured by the four-category system would have reached 44.8%, and under the five-category system, a staggering 50%[1], if not for the divestiture program. There is no doubt that the first round of divestiture was a great relief to the state-owned banks, enabling them to make progress in resolving NPLs and reducing the burden of subsequent reforms.

However, it should be noted that in the two years following the first divestiture program, it came to light that there had been a rebound in the NPLs of some state-owned banks. In late June 1999, ICBC disclosed that the balance of its NPLs before the divestiture was over RMB 770 billion, whereas in 2000 and 2001, i.e., after the divestiture, it disclosed an even higher balance in excess of RMB 800 billion. Public concerns over rising NPLs attracted the attention of the central leadership. Overnight, the public began casting doubt over the prospect of banking reform, and criticisms over the effectiveness of their internal management grew harsher.

Why did the first round of divestiture apparently backfire and result in a rebound in NPLs? The reasons can be summarized as follows[2]:

First, the definition of NPLs had been revised. The amount of NPLs for disposal was determined based on the four-category standard, and the 10% drop in the NPL ratio after the divestiture was also calculated by the same standard, which led to an underestimation of NPLs. In 2000 after the divestiture, however, the state-owned banks turned to the five-category

---

1 Source: Appendices of the PBOC's "Plan for the Comprehensive Reform of Wholly State-Owned Commercial Banks."
2 Ibid.

classification in estimating and disclosing NPLs. The first divestiture indeed led to a decrease in the relative proportion of NPLs under the five-category standard, together with a smaller gap in the absolute size of NPLs between the two standards. According to an article by Yang Kaisheng, former president of ICBC, since the older data collection standards were less stringent, some assets previously not recognized as NPLs were later recognized as such under the new classification system, causing a numerical discrepancy (for some banks, the difference could be as much as 15 percentage points). Thus, people were left with the false impression that "bank NPLs keep piling up." According to the PBOC, a marginal RMB 395.9 billion can be attributed to the discrepancy between the two classification standards.

Second, not all NPAs were offloaded to the AMCs. Expecting that banks would assume some liabilities and thus reduce fiscal pressures, policymakers set a limit on the amount of NPAs to be stripped off[1]. Moreover, debt-for-equity swaps were carried out for some borrowers as a method to dispose of their loans. Those loans accounted for a non-trivial percentage of the limited quota for NPL divestiture, even though some portion of them were actually generating interest income and thus not considered NPLs by the banks. Consequently, the NPL "principal" stripped off from the Big Four was far less than the headline reported amount. Moreover, the divested assets of RMB 1.4 trillion included a substantial amount of NPLs of policy banks held by the state-owned banks on the former's behalf. For instance, the NPLs taken from CCB included RMB 100 billion loans belonging to the China Development Bank, over RMB 110 billion in capitalized interest, and over RMB 133 billion performing loans sub-

---

1   Quoted from Yang Kaisheng: *Financial Notes*, People's Publishing House, 2016.

jected to equity swaps. These divested assets included not only NPLs but also other non-performing assets. The actual amount of NPLs offloaded from the state-owned banks was only RMB 1.05 trillion.

Third, subsequent examinations into the substantive nature of the loans found many hidden NPLs. Apart from the additional NPLs arising from switch of classification schemes, as mentioned before, the Big Four also had over RMB 1 trillion in loans borrowed for repayment of old loans which came to light only in follow-up audits into the nature of the loans. Under regulatory pressures, some bank branches also took the initiative to come clean with their hidden NPLs. According to the PBOC, NPLs revealed in this manner was close to RMB 300 billion.

Fourth, since the root cause of NPLs was not addressed, and the SOE reform was yet to produce results, some RMB 400 billion in legacy loans granted before 1998 continued to rapidly deteriorate, contributing to the growth of the NPL pool. Moreover, the new loans granted after 1998 also generated NPLs exceeding RMB 160 billion. Also, among the loans transferred by policy banks to the state-owned banks, over RMB 100 billion deteriorated after 1999. In fact, if the state-owned banks had followed a stricter standard for identifying which loans had been borrowed for repayment of old loans, even more loans would have been considered NPLs.

Given the above factors, the actual amount of NPLs discovered at the time of divestiture was far more than what was presented in the accounts. The real figure for NPLs was much higher than the PBOC's tally of RMB 1.97 trillion set collectively for the Big Four before divestiture. Despite the efforts, therefore, the NPL divestiture was far from sufficient. After the first round of divestiture, the NPLs of the Big Four still totaled RMB 2.16 trillion by the end of 2001 – even higher than the amount recognized before the stripping-off took place.

(III) Debt-For-Equity Swap and Initial Exploration of Joint-Stock Reform

AMCs were originally created with a mandate to purchase NPAs taken off the balance sheets of the state-owned banks; their strategic intention as new platforms, however, went beyond the disposal of NPAs. They also served as a critical testbed for the banking reform, in particular, to use debt restructuring to resolve SOE debts and the NPAs of the state-owned banks. As a major form of debt restructuring, "debt-for-equity swaps" were written into the governing documents of the four AMCs as a priority task following their establishment.

The debt-for-equity swap program was especially important at the time because it was aimed to facilitate the SOE reform. Eager to turn around struggling SOEs within three years, the central government not only accelerated the internal changes by SOEs themselves, but also looked for external help to reduce their debt overhang. Through debt-for-equity swaps, SOEs were relieved of immediate pressures to repay principal and interest and gained the necessary room for the reform.

By the end of 2000, the State Economic and Trade Commission had recommended 601 medium and large SOEs to the four AMCs as candidates for swaps. The State Economic and Trade Commission, the MOF, and the PBOC jointly reviewed and oversaw contract execution for 580 of them, involving more than RMB 400 billion of loans. According to a survey in the first half of 2000 by the National Bureau of Statistics on enterprises that had executed the framework agreements on debt-for-equity swaps, the program was expected to reduce the enterprises' total monthly interest payment by RMB 3.723 billion on average and bring their debt ratio to below 45.6%. After the swap, 87% of enterprises became profitable, while the rest saw substantial reductions in their losses[1]. According to a subsequent PBOC survey, from the cessation of interest payment in April 2000 to September 2002, the participating SOEs saw a reduction in their financial expenditure by about RMB 50 billion with the average debt ratio down from 73% to less than 50%[2].

Case Study: Debt-for-Equity Swap for Tianjin Pipe Company[3]

As the industry headed for restructuring in the 1990s, Tianjin Pipe Company (TPCO), a well-known SOE, ran into financial difficulties after reckless expansion and a loan-fueled investment binge, which led to huge repayment pressures. In November 1999, the company was approved for a debt-for-equity swap, erasing RMB 14.53 billion of debt which lowered its annual debt servicing burden by RMB 706 million. After asset auditing and verification, the annual depreciation was also reduced by RMB 287 million due to the now lowered capitalized interest that was previously added to the cost of assets. Altogether, the company saved RMB 993 million in annual expenditure through the program, allowing it to regain its footing for a more secure financial future. After the debt-for-equity swap, the company followed up with technology upgrades, operational transformation, and improvement of corporate governance, becoming profitable in 2000.

---

1 Source: *Almanac of China's Finance and Banking (2001)*.
2 Source: Appendices of the PBOC's "Plan for the Comprehensive Reform of Wholly State-Owned Commercial Banks."
3 Data are taken from Hong Chen: "Steel Pipe Juggernaut Breaking Waves: Chronicle of Tianjin Steel Pipe Co.'s Endeavor to Become a World-Class Enterprise," *Management and Administration*, 2002 (2).

In other aspects, the debt-for-equity swap program marked an important attempt to revitalize SOEs and tighten their internal constraints at the levels of shareholding and corporate governance. In 1999, Zhou Xiaochuan wrote an article titled "Thoughts on Debt-for-Equity Swaps."[1] The article blamed SOEs' under-capitalization – caused by over-expansion when the industry and economy were not yet ready for fully market-based operations – for the debt burden of SOEs and the NPLs of the state-owned banks. "Under-capitalization syndrome," the article contends, led to various SOE problems such as the poor corporate governance structures, insider control, lax budgetary constraints, and excessive risk appetite. This shortfall of capital cannot be addressed by the usual financial means; but debt-for-equity swaps offer a way out by enabling an enterprise to improve corporate governance, rebuild its balance sheet, and remedy low-quality financial assets.

Zhou also noted in the article that "debt-for-equity swaps and the subsequent sale of equities by AMCs may pave the way toward the joint-stock reform and ownership diversification." To some extent, the views expressed in this article reflected new thinking of the top leadership on the path of the SOE reform, i.e., begin with diversification of the shareholder base and focus on reforming the corporate governance system. Without a doubt, these ideas hold significance not only to the reform of SOEs, but also to that of state-owned banks, and can be viewed as the unofficial starting point for the joint-stock reform of the state-owned banks.

---

1 Published in *Comparison of Economic and Social Systems*, 1999 (6).

Related Topic: China's Conditions and Debt-for-Equity Swaps[1]

China's current conditions are characterized by a shortage of capital for some enterprises, which usually stem from the excessive expansion of enterprises, industries, or the economy as a whole when they are not ready for fully market-based operations. Due to underdeveloped capital markets and the lack of private investors or even the awareness of the concept of capital, enterprises naturally turned to banks for financing. The enterprises were oblivious to the risks of overreliance on bank loans, while the banks lacked awareness of their lending risks. The problem was compounded by the plethora of administrative interventions in all types of economic affairs at the time. After SOEs expanded rapidly using the bank loans, the previously hidden capital shortfall existing before the reform came under the spotlight.

Under-capitalization can lead to many complications, including weak corporate governance structures. Small or nonexistent share capital is a sure sign that corporate governance is sloppy or even absent. Other significant complications include blatant insider control, as well as lax budgetary constraints and excessive risk appetite. Under-capitalization cannot be addressed simply by the usual financial means, but instead requires integrated measures and a well-designed reorganization plan. Most importantly, corporate governance needed to be improved as a matter of priority – something the debt-for-equity swap program was targeted to achieve.

The debt-for-equity swaps created conditions and opportunities for establishing and improving corporate governance structure. They allow firms to overcome their difficulties through restructuring and remedy the NPAs.

---

1   Excerpts from Zhou Xiaochuan's "Thoughts on Debt-for-Equity Swaps," *Comparison of Economic and Social Systems*, 1999 (6). Some sections have been edited out for relevance.

China in its current practice has created AMCs to carry out debt-for-equity swaps. From the perspective of ownership interests in assets, the AMCs and the banks remain independent from each other, but they also cooperate with each other and share common interests. Debt-for-equity swaps are an instrument for the banks to recover NPAs. Under the current framework of industry-segregated operation and regulation, however, the banks may only transfer NPAs to the AMCs to be swapped for equities.

Debt-for-equity swaps and the subsequent sale of equities by AMCs may pave the way toward the joint-stock reform and ownership diversification. Through the debt-for-equity swaps, wholly state-owned enterprises will be changed into joint-stock companies, thus improving their corporate governance structure. Subsequent to being held for a certain period, the equities can be transferred to new domestic investors, foreign investors, and corporate entities, thus diversifying the ownership. The AMCs are also able to recover non-performing assets during this process.

Despite the achievements, debt-for-equity swaps in this stage also had limitations: they were intended to help SOEs overcome their debt dilemma, and the methods of implementation were tentative; the State Economic and Trade Commission determined the list of in-scope enterprises for debt-for-equity swaps without consulting the state-owned banks; and some debt-for-equity swaps were not carried out using market-based pricing or in accordance with the law. As a result, some debt-for-equity swap programs were exploited by enterprises to shirk their bank liabilities and reduce their financial expenses, and resulting losses were passed onto the state-owned banks as part of the economic reform cost. Without fundamentally improving their corporate governance and development model, some enterprises ran into trouble again soon after debt-for-equity swaps.

CHAPTER IV
BREAKTHROUGHS IN JOINT-STOCK REFORM

– Finalization of the Path and Proposal of the Joint-Stock Reform

After long discussions and debates at the conceptual level, all sectors of society – encouraged by the success of the joint-stock reform of SOEs, especially the 15th CPC National Congress' affirmation that the joint-stock form was a viable arrangement for public ownership – came to the consensus that a similar reform for state-owned banks was both essential and necessary and that such reform was a way for the banks to transform their business model. After the second National Financial Work Conference, the reform of state-owned banks unfolded according to the CPC Central Committee's plans, laying the groundwork to turn the vision of joint-stock reform into reality. However, the new round of banking reform was destined to be challenging given the unprecedented nature of the practices, mind-boggling cost of financial restructuring, and sharp criticisms lodged by stakeholders of all types. The joint-stock reform of state-owned banks posed an enormous risk because of their outsized role and influence in the economy, and in some ways, was a "back against the wall" effort that simply could not afford to fail – as Premier Wen Jiabao put it, it was a "do-or-die" mission. To succeed in this effort, policymakers needed to come up with proper top-level planning, an appropriate implementation approach, and solutions to key challenges. Before state-owned banks set sail for the voyage of joint-stock reform, charting a well-designed course would be crucial to their success.

Section I
Theoretical Studies and Breakthroughs

I. Discussions and Controversies of Choosing a Path for Joint-Stock Reform

In the early 1980s, there were some SOEs attempting to operate as joint-stock companies. In 1984, Beijing Tianqiao Department Store became China's first commercial joint-stock company. By the mid-1980s, thousands of small SOEs, collective enterprises, and township and village enterprises had experimented with the joint-stock system. In 1986, Shenzhen became a pioneer by piloting joint-stock reform for large SOEs. After the creation of the Shanghai Stock Exchange and the Shenzhen Stock Exchange in 1990 and 1991, some SOEs began to issue and list their shares on the two stock exchanges.

China's theoretical discussions on reforming SOEs into joint-stock companies can be traced back to the 1980s. The idea was formally proposed by the State Commission for Restructuring the Economic System after the Third Plenary Session of the 12th CPC Central Committee, taking place in 1984. In 1987, the Commission organized top Chinese economists into eight working groups to discuss the plan for the SOE reform, culminating into seven proposals favoring the joint-stock reform[1]. However, the reform was dismissed by most for being "ahead of its time," and so remained only a subject of theoretical research and a few scattered pilot programs. Particularly after 1989, the joint-stock system was even labeled "potential variant of privatization,"[2] which framed it in direct opposition to a public or socialist economy. Against this backdrop, it seemed a fairy tale that the joint-stock reform would take root at state-owned banks which are vital to the national security and economy of China.

Fortunately, Deng Xiaoping's speeches during his inspection tour of southern China reopened the door for the joint-stock reform of SOEs. The "Decision on Issues Concerning the Establishment of a Socialist Market Economy" adopted at the Third Plenary Session of the 14th CPC Central Committee characterized corporatization as a "beneficial attempt" for the SOE reform. Nevertheless, policymakers were still very cautious about pursuing the joint-stock reform of state-owned banks. For instance, the "Decision of the State Council on Reform of the Financial System" released at the end of 1993 made no mention of whether state-owned banks could launch

---

1 Yang Qixian: "The Third Breakthrough in Reform Theory – Notion of 'Ownership Rights'," *Property Rights Guide*, 2003 (11).
2 Xiao Donglian: "The Road of SOE Restructuring: From Decentralization of Power and Transfer of Profits to Institutional Innovation," *Journal of Chinese Communist Party History Studies*, 2014 (3).

a corporatization reform of their own. Therefore, progress in the joint-stock reform of state-owned banks hinged upon further theoretical breakthroughs.

(I) Joint-Stock System: Key to Resolving the Problems of State-Owned Banks

The key theoretical questions to be answered when discussing the joint-stock reform of state-owned banks were whether they could operate as joint-stock banks and whether the joint-stock system could address their major operational and developmental challenges. If it was difficult to demonstrate even on paper what defined the joint-stock system and how joint-stock banks would be beneficial, then the reform would forever remain a theoretical exercise. Although the implementation of a bank joint-stock reform had been postponed time and again, the theoretical research had not and in fact had even thrived since the 1980s as the SOE reform was pushed forward. In the mid-1990s, publicity about the ownership reform of SOEs had educated the public on the vital role of the joint-stock system in the ownership reform and on whether the system could help address the problems of state-owned banks. These developments helped build the following areas of consensus:

First, the joint-stock system would help wean state-owned banks off reliance on fiscal appropriations for their capital. Historically, fiscal appropriations were the only source of capital for state-owned banks. This would mean that no matter what sort of dividing line was drawn between the interests of state finance and state-owned banks, state finance would ultimately cover the operating losses of the banks because by nature their risks would be borne by their owner, the state. In this sense, state finance was an unlimited liability shareholder of state-owned banks. The joint-stock system could allow the banks to diversify their equity structure by bringing in other, select investors, and to attract investment from the general public by converting net assets into readily transferable shares. The joint-stock reform could demonstrably make state-owned banks less dependent on fiscal appropriations for their capital. Since gaining operational autonomy would also mean cutting away the safety net offered by the state, the banks would need to solely assume their operational risks and appropriately send signals of stability to the public to win the public's confidence in their solvency.

Second, the joint-stock system would create conditions for the separation of ownership and management, helping free state-owned banks from government interventions. The oligarchy of state-owned banks stifled market competition that could otherwise stimulate them to operate more efficiently. Compared with other reform options, the biggest advantage of the joint-stock system was that it enabled the separation of the ownership of state-owned banks from their management.

Ownership, as it relates to SOEs such as the state-owned banks, is the right of the asset owner – the state – to possess, use, benefit from, and dispose of state-owned assets. Management, by contrast, is the right of state-owned banks to lawfully possess, use, and dispose of corporate properties. Under the joint-stock system, the owners (i.e., shareholders) of a state-owned bank would, while retaining ultimate control and residual claim over the bank' properties, grant other rights to the bank's management team to run the bank according to market-based principles. Compared with the quick alternative of devolution and economic incentives, the joint-stock system could enable the state to delegate more authorities to state-owned banks. And compared with the commitment target system, the joint-stock system could allow the state to reasonably participate in the business operation of state-owned banks as a shareholder. Under the joint-stock system, the diverse shareholders of state-owned banks, including both state and non-state shareholders, would provide mutual checks and balances which would enable the banks to operate independently from policy mandates and from direct interventions by the government.

Third, the joint-stock system would help improve corporate governance. Under the joint-stock system, the management team of a state-owned bank would be responsible to its shareholders who, having a direct interest in the bank, would be ready to replace the management team if the bank underperforms. This would put management under greater oversight and accountability in this principal-agent relationship, thereby pressuring the bank to maximize efficiency and profitability and not only maintain independent operations and be responsible for its own profits and losses, but also assume its own risks and exercise self-discipline as a modern corporation.

(II) Controversies of the Joint-Stock Reform of State-Owned Banks

Early debates on the joint-stock reform of state-owned banks, like those on the joint-stock reform of SOES, focused on the theoretical question of whether it would privatize the banks. However, with the revelation of enormous NPLs and operating difficulties of the banks, the focus soon shifted to a more practical aspect – the cost of the reform.

1. Privatization

The initial and most prevalent concern about the joint-stock reform of state-owned banks was whether it would change the nature of state ownership. In fact, the very same concern came to the fore when the joint-stock system was contemplated for the SOE reform. In 1992, when CSRC Chairman Liu Hongru, and Chen Jinhua, Director of the State Commission for Restructuring the Economic System, delivered a report on the joint-stock system and stock market to the NPC Financial and Economic Affairs Committee, they were intensely questioned by certain members of the NPC Standing Committee, who commented that no country in the world that had embraced the joint-stock system had not also gone down the path of privatization, and that selling stakes in well-performing SOEs would be a loss of state-owned assets[1].

These concerns were by no means unjustified at the time. Wholesale privatization was believed to be a key contributor to the collapse of the Soviet Union at the end of 1991, serving as an all-too-recent cautionary tale for the Chinese leadership. More importantly, given that a theoretical reconciliation of public ownership and non-public ownership under the socialist economic system was yet to be achieved, if the joint-stock system was characterized as a form of privatization, no further practical discussion could be held, for that characterization alone would have invited accusations of substituting private ownership for public ownership.

Even the understanding of the SOEs' joint-stock reform had been very limited, to say nothing of the joint-stock reform of state-owned banks that made up more than 70% of the financial sector's assets and liabilities and formed the economic lifeline of the country. There were two prevailing views at the time. One was that converting state-owned banks into joint-stock companies would be an open invitation for the private sector and even foreign capital to intervene in China's financial affairs, thus threatening its financial security. The second view was that the reform would

---

1   From Xiao Donglian: "The Road of SOE Restructuring: From Decentralization of Power and Transfer of Profits to Institutional Innovation," *Journal of Chinese Communist Party History Studies*, 2014 (3).

essentially be a sale, and thus loss, of state-owned assets. Most of those holding the first view were underinformed about the joint-stock system, wrongly equating owning shares with having a controlling interest and thus taking an alarmist view of the reform. Those holding the second view had only a partial understanding of the basic economic system in a socialist country, and a static and limited knowledge of the potential effect of the reform and the methods of realizing the value of state-owned assets.

2. Capital-raising

The Asian financial crisis in 1997 gave an important lesson to China's banking sector on the importance of capital adequacy. The central leadership now realized that undercapitalization of state-owned banks could give rise to risks and even a financial crisis. And the people were concerned with one question: Given China's scant fiscal resources, if the state-owned banks were to go bankrupt, who would bear the resulting losses? In the situation where neither the state treasury nor the profit margin of state-owned banks could be relied upon for addressing the banks' capital shortfall, the only remaining option was to obtain external funds. As such, while some scholars agreed that it was necessary to transform state-owned banks into joint-stock companies, they believed the reform could only help supply that additional capital but not necessarily address the banks' structural issues. For this reason, they maintained that the joint-stock reform of state-owned banks should be carried out on a limited scale, that the banks' stocks should only be offered to other SOEs or collective enterprises, and that the restructuring should be a purely financial arrangement not affecting the operation and decision-making power of the banks.

3. Control

The lingering conundrum hanging over the SOE reform was how to address the absence of an executor of state ownership rights. Even during the joint-stock reform of SOEs, opinions differed over who should act on behalf of the state to carry out the duties and functions of a capital contributor[1]. This issue was all the more poignant during the feasibility study on a joint-stock reform of state-owned banks, because the sheer size and highly specialized nature of state-owned banks made it even harder to find that executor. Without it, an effective internal governance structure and mechanism would also be out of the question even if the joint-stock system was implemented. And absent of robust internal governance, the reduced government control over the banks would make them more susceptible to collusion by their decision makers (i.e., insider control) and, therefore, pose greater risks to the economy. This possible loss of control was a common concern about the joint-stock reform of state-owned banks.

4. Cost constraints

The cost constraint argument first emerged in the wake of the series of public exposures of NPLs at state-owned banks and continued to hold sway until the completion of the joint-stock reform. Its main point was that state-owned banks must maintain a robust performance and operation before even attempting to attract investors and go public. This precondition was at odds with the banks' massive NPLs which had already threatened their viability as a going concern. State-owned banks needed to effectively dispose of their outstanding NPLs for the joint-stock reform. Obviously, their meager financial resources were a far cry from what was needed for this self-rescue – external resources had to be tapped.

---

1   The State-Owned Assets Supervision and Administration Commission (SASAC) was established later, in 2003. Before that, state ownership was represented and managed by different agencies.

At the time, the state fiscal authorities were looked upon as the "angel" most likely to bail out the banks. However, the central government was running a fiscal deficit throughout the 1990s, which had increased from RMB 23.7 billion in 1991 to RMB 58.2 billion in 1997[1]. Fiscal revenue accounted for 15.8% of China's GDP in 1991, but dropped to 11.6% in 1997. At the end of 1997, China's fiscal revenue amounted to a mere RMB 1.11 trillion, not enough to cover the banks' losses from NPLs even if the revenue was used for nothing else. It was evident that the state treasury was unable to afford the cost of reform of state-owned banks, especially the cost of disposal of their NPLs. But if the state treasury could not bear the cost, who could (and should)? And how? These questions were used by some as the main arguments against the joint-stock reform of state-owned banks.

Although opposing voices still existed, more and more people from academia and industry started to endorse the joint-stock reform of state-owned banks. Particularly after the Asian financial crisis, overhauling state-owned banks became the mainstream viewpoint. For instance, the noted economist Zeng Kanglin pointed out that restructuring commercial banks into joint-stock companies may help open a channel for public supervision over capital, income and risks and separate ownership of bank assets from their usage rights, so that a principal-agency arrangement could be introduced into the banks' operation and management[2]. Li Yining proposed that public investment funds could invest more do-

---

1 In 1998, the deficit widened to RMB 92.2 billion.
2 From Zeng Kanglin: "On the Development of Commercial Banks Based on the Modern Enterprise System," *Journal of Financial Research*, 1999 (9).

mestically to promote the joint-stock reform of the Big Four[1]. And in his paper[2], Wang Kejing said that the joint-stock reform of commercial banks was necessary as they shared the characteristics of ordinary enterprises, and that "the banks should adapt their ownership structure to the needs of commercial operations, have in place an operation framework based on the joint-stock system, and promote the integration of industrial capital and bank capital."

II. Theoretical Breakthrough at the National Level

The more debate there is, the clearer truth becomes. Controversies and debates on the joint-stock reform of state-owned banks sparked broader and more profound reflections on this topic. As theories on the socialist economic system and SOE reform continued to mature through various reform initiatives, those on the reform of state-owned banks did as well. The Asian financial crisis swept away any remaining doubt about whether state-owned banks should be reformed. The only remaining question, then, was *how*.

(I) The Nature of the Joint-Stock System Determined at the 15th CPC National Congress

The 15th CPC National Congress was held in September 1997 when China's economic system reform, particularly the SOE reform, was entering a critical stage, and when the financial crisis was sweeping across

---

1 From *Information for Deciders*, 1999 (48).
2 Wang Kejing, Lü Zhou, et al.: "Embracing the Joint-Stock System: Realistic Choice for the Reform of China's State-Owned Commercial Banks," *Finance & Trade Economics*, 1998 (4). Wang Kejing was President of the Central University of Finance and Economics.

Southeast Asia. It was convened earlier than usual, but at just the right time called for by the circumstances. This Congress further expanded the fundamental theories guiding China's economic system reform and set the direction for economic development. The following three decisions made at this Congress decided the path of the reform of SOEs, including state-owned banks.

1. Relationship between public ownership and non-public ownership

As China advanced the reform of the economic system, the public sector declined as a percentage share of the economy, and integrated and competed with the private sector in a varied, multi-layered, and complex manner, prompting theorists to question whether it could retain its once dominant position. The public also had concerns that some initiatives, including the joint-stock reform, could lead to privatization.

To address the public's doubt over the relationship between public and non-public ownership under the new circumstances, the 15th CPC National Congress gave a timely and clear answer, stating that: "We must have a thorough understanding of the significance of the public sector of the economy. The public sector includes not only the state and collective sectors, but also state- and collectively-owned portions of mixed-ownership enterprises. The dominant position of public ownership manifests itself chiefly as follows: Public assets dominate among the total assets of society, and the state sector controls the lifeblood of the national economy and plays a leading role in economic development. This is in terms of the national level, as differences may exist in some localities and industries. The dominance of public assets should be evident in quantitative terms, but more so in qualitative terms. The state sector should play a leading role mainly through its ability to exercise control.

We need to strategically adjust the structure of the state sector. The state sector must dominate major industries and key areas affecting the lifeblood of the national economy. But in other areas, efforts should focus on reorganizing assets and adjusting the structure in order to give greater emphasis to priorities and improve the quality of state assets as a whole. As long as public ownership remains the dominant form of ownership, the state will control the lifeblood of the national economy and the state sector will have more control and will be more competitive. Even if the state sector were to account for a smaller portion of the overall economy, this will not affect the socialist nature of China."[1]

This statement elevated the public's understanding of the dominance of public ownership from a "tactical level," i.e., the simple measurement of the proportions of publicly owned assets and capital and other quantitative metrics, to a "strategic level," i.e., attention to the *de facto* control of public ownership. It also changed how public ownership was determined and treated: from the formulaic criteria and uniform treatment to substantive criteria and differentiated treatment, thus providing the theoretical underpinning that enabled the marriage, integration, and mutual support and development of public and non-public sectors, removing the biggest obstacle to implementing the joint-stock system.

2. Essence of the joint-stock system

The Report to the 15th CPC National Congress stated: "Public ownership can and should diversify. All governance methods and organizational forms that reflect the laws of socialized production may be boldly employed. We must strive to find ways to achieve public ownership that

---

[1] *Selected Works of Jiang Zemin*, Vol. II, Foreign Languages Press, 2012, p.18.

can greatly promote growth of the productive forces. The joint-stock system is a way of organizing capital in modern enterprises. It helps separate ownership from management and increases the operating efficiencies of enterprises and capital. It can be used under both capitalism and socialism. We cannot generally say that the joint-stock system is either public or private, for the key to this lies in who holds the controlling interest. If the state or a collective holds a controlling interest, it is clearly a form of public ownership, which is favorable to expanding the area controlled by public capital and enhancing the dominant role of public ownership. Currently, a large number of diverse forms of joint stock partnerships have appeared in both urban and rural areas. They are new things arising from the course of reform. We need to support and guide these partnerships and constantly learn from their experiences in order to improve them. We need to particularly advocate and encourage the collective sector based on the pooling of the labor and capital of workers."[1]

In contrast with what was stated about the joint-stock system at the 14th CPC National Congress, the report at the 15th Congress acknowledged the role and significance of the joint-stock system in the reform of SOEs, clarified its nature, and made it clear that, as a form of capital organization, the joint-stock system was not directly associated with either capitalism or socialism. Theoretically, this statement refuted those doctrines that confused the joint-stock system with privatization and completely rejected joint-stock reform.

3. Relationship between corporatization reform and SOE reform

The Report further stated: "The goal of SOE reform is to establish a

---

1 *Selected Works of Jiang Zemin*, Vol. II, Foreign Languages Press, 2012, p. 20.

modern corporate structure. We will incorporate large and medium-sized SOEs in accordance with the requirements of clearly established ownership, well-defined powers and responsibilities, separate government administration and enterprise management as well as scientific management to make them corporate entities and competitors adapted to the market. We will more clearly define the powers and responsibilities of the state and enterprises. The state will enjoy owner's equity in an enterprise based on the amount it invests in it and will bear limited liability for the enterprise's debt obligations. Enterprises will operate independently in accordance with the law and be responsible for profits and losses. The government cannot directly intervene in the operations of an enterprise; enterprises must accept restraints imposed by their owners and should not jeopardize their owner's equity. We will adopt various means for funding enterprises, including direct financing. We will cultivate and develop diverse investment sources in order to promote the separation of government administration and enterprise management and the transformation of the way in which enterprises operate."[1]

Pursuant to the *Company Law* enacted in 1993, the two types of companies in China are limited liability companies and companies limited by shares, both of which are organized as joint-stock enterprises. In view of this, the 15th CPC National Congress in fact identified the joint-stock system as a key component of the SOE reform. Unlike previous policy initiatives which piloted the joint-stock reform mainly among small and medium-sized SOEs, the 15th CPC National Congress expanded the scope to include medium and large ones as well, thus

---

1   *Selected Works of Jiang Zemin*, Vol. II, Foreign Languages Press, 2012, pp. 20-21.

providing a policy basis for the joint-stock reform of large SOEs, including state-owned banks.

The major theoretical breakthroughs by the 15th CPC National Congress removed substantial barriers to the joint-stock reform of state-owned banks and reform subsequently accelerated. The focus of research and discussions on the reform soon shifted from theoretical questions of feasibility to practical questions of objectives and methods.

(II) Key Tasks in the Joint-Stock Reform of State-Owned Banks

The first issue to be addressed was to determine the primary tasks in the joint-stock reform of state-owned banks. Based on previous experiences of reform, theoretical and practical reformers all turned their eyes to the following four long-standing strategic, institutional, and fundamental issues which were centered on the adjustment of ownership structure.

First, how to address the lack of an agent to execute the rights and duties of state ownership. The theorist community had repeatedly demonstrated the necessity to reform the ownership structure of state-owned banks and to separate asset ownership and management. Now that the policymakers decided to pilot the joint-stock reform, it became imperative to answer the key questions raised by those concerned with loss of control. Under the joint-stock system, the state would become a shareholder of state-owned banks, but who should act as this shareholder and by what means exercise voting rights at their shareholders' meetings and board of directors' meetings on behalf of the state? If an administrative agency was designated to be the representative of the state, how to ensure it could appropriately exercise the shareholder's rights? And more importantly, how to ensure its professionalism? The PBOC would be the most suitable candidate by professional competence, but this would conflict with the independent role of the central bank. Consequently, although it had been settled in theory that the state could and should be a shareholder, in practice there was no one to *act* as one.

Second, how to set reform objectives and plans. One view held by some – including those believing the reform should be primarily for raising capital – was that the reform of state-owned banks was for a single, tactical purpose. However, the broader context was that the state ultimately intended the SOE reform (which included state-owned banks) to create a modern enterprise system, achieve effective separation of ownership and management, and invigorate the SOEs by incorporating a market orientation. According to the policy direction of the state, the joint-stock reform of state-owned banks needed to be a comprehensive package of reforms focusing on ownership right-related changes, and required a holistic design covering the overhaul of frameworks, mechanisms, business, and management.

Third, how to modernize the corporate governance framework. By separating ownership from management and creating new power structures and responsible bodies such as shareholders' meeting and board of directors, the joint-stock reform would materially transform the original power, decision-making, and organizational structures and managerial procedures of state-owned banks. How to dismantle the traditional operation and management systems of state-owned banks so that a new balance of interests could be established was undoubtedly a significant challenge before the state-owned banks. Furthermore, how to improve administrative and corporate frameworks, define the scope of responsibilities, and prevent renewed administrative interventions was another hard nut to be cracked by the state's decision makers, regulators, and state-owned banks.

Fourth, how to resolve the NPL burden. The joint-stock reform of state-owned banks would subject their assets to rigid quality standards. To meet the financial conditions required of modern companies, state-owned banks first needed to address their NPA issue. For this, two options were put forward. The first was an internal but slower solution, i.e., the banks would rely on their own financial resources to dispose of their NPAs, which would take at least ten years, while controlling marginal NPA increases. However, given that financial problems had already throttled economic progress, such a slow and measured response was evidently unviable. The other option involved asset divestiture, i.e., bad assets would be offloaded from the state-owned banking system to leave a "clean" balance sheet for the state-owned banks. If this solution was chosen, the key issue then would be who should bear the actual losses resulting from the bad assets. At a time when the state had little spare fiscal resources, concerns like those raised by the "cost constraint" faction were not without justification.

When the joint-stock system became a viable option instead of a mere theoretical possibility, the state's decision makers and financial authorities needed to consider these four questions as a whole. For the state-owned banks, the most pressing matter was to work down their existing NPAs and rein in the growth of new NPAs so that their total NPAs would not increase.

Section II
Finalization of the Path for the Joint-Stock Reform of State-Owned Banks

I. Favorable Timing and Conditions

(I) China's Stable Economic Growth

The wellbeing of the financial sector and the success of the reform of state-owned banks are dependent upon economic fundamentals. After withstanding the shocks of the Asian financial crisis, China's economy showed clear signs of stabilization and recovery starting from 2000. GDP growth in 2000 increased by 0.9 percentage points from the interim low of 7.1% in 1999. In 2001, this figure stood at 7.3%. Total investment in fixed assets showed an even stronger recovery: it grew by only 5.1% in 1999, but by 10.3% in 2000 and 13% in 2001. After declining for two consecutive years, the consumer price index (CPI) rebounded in 2000 and 2001, sweeping away concerns that China's economy would slide into a deflationary quagmire. And after bottoming out in 1999, the exports rapidly increased by an annual average of 13% until 2001. In addition, expansion of fiscal deficit slowed down in 2001 as revenue grew faster than expenditure, an encore to the same feat achieved in 1997.

Table 4.1: Changes in Major Macroeconomic Indicators of China (1998-2001)

Indicator	1998	1999	2000	2001
GDP (¥bn)	7,834.52	8,206.75	8,944.22	9,593.33
GDP index (previous year = 100)	107.8	107.1	108.0	107.3
Investment in fixed assets (¥bn)	2,840.62	2,985.47	3,291.77	3,721.35
CPI (previous year = 100)	99.2	98.6	100.4	100.7

Export (¥bn)	1,523.16	1,615.98	2,063.52	2,202.91
Fiscal revenue (¥bn)	987.60	1,144.41	1,339.52	1,638.60
Fiscal balance (¥bn)	-92.22	-174.36	-249.13	-251.65

Source: *China Statistical Yearbooks.*

China's stabilizing economic performance suggested that it had successfully shaken off the impact of the Asian financial crisis. China's economic reforms after the 15th CPC National Congress also had improved the economic fundamentals and created new impetus for growth. All these trends implied potential opportunities for a new round of economic development, creating a favorable economic environment for the reform of state-owned banks.

(II) Substantive Progress in the Joint-Stock Reform of SOEs

1. Finalization of the path for the joint-stock reform of SOEs

SOE reform was the linchpin of the reform policies adopted at the 15th CPC National Congress. Initiated in 1997, the three-year effort to lift SOEs out of financial difficulties was an overriding political and economic task. The path for the reform of state-owned banks, themselves SOEs, was necessarily dependent upon and subordinate to the design of SOE reform. From September 19 to 22, 1999, at the Fourth Plenary Session of the 15th CPC Central Committee held in Beijing, a key resolution in the history of SOEs – the "Decision of the CPC Central Committee on Major Issues Concerning the Reform and Development of SOEs" ("Decision") – was adopted. As a follow-up to the reform policies proposed at the 15th CPC National Congress and the goal of building a socialist market economy, the Decision was aimed at charting a course for the SOE reform based on the history, characteristics, and experiences from previous SOE reforms since China's reform and opening up. The Decision expanded on existing theories and policies on the reform and development of SOEs in general, and contained two resolutions which would provide more clear and explicit guidance for the reform of state-owned banks.

First, the Decision explicitly recognized the suitability and necessity of the joint-stock system in the strategic re-adjustment of the state-owned sector. According to the Decision, while the state-owned sector should contribute to the economy through wholly state-owned enterprises, it should also do so through joint-stock state-controlled and state-invested enterprises. The joint-stock system could turn state-owned capital into "seed funds" that could mobilize a much larger amount of private capital and that could both enhance the effectiveness of state-owned capital and the control, influence, and leadership role of the state-owned sector. Medium-sized and large SOEs, particularly the dominant ones, should be transformed into joint-stock companies if possible, so as to promote the mixed ownership economy. Potential options for this included public listing, creation of Sino-foreign joint ventures, and cross-shareholding, among others.

Second, the Decision affirmed that the modern enterprise system would be built mainly through ownership and governance reforms. The Decision crystallized the criteria for modern enterprises set forth at the 15th CPC National Congress – clear ownership rights, well-defined functions and responsibilities, separation of government from business activities, and rational management frameworks – into the following four tasks that outlined the basic framework and rules for the operation and management of joint-stock SOEs:

(i) Promoting the separation of enterprise from government. For enterprises that were funded or partially owned by the state, the government should perform its shareholder's functions through a representative and exercise its rights, such as to receive a return on assets, make major decisions, and select managers, according to the amount of its capital contribution. Party organs and government agencies at all levels should be completely separated – in human, financial, and material resources – from the economic entities established by them and enterprises directly managed by them. This requirement was intended to reshape the government-SOE relationship into an equity-based one and limit the government's management power over enterprises to its proportion of equity-holding in them.

(ii) Separating the state's function of public administration from its function as a contributor of state-owned capital and finding effective means to manage state-owned assets. Steps needed to be taken to create the frameworks for managing, supervising, and operating state-owned assets, as well as a rigorous accountability program. The State-owned Assets Supervision and Administration Commission (SASAC) was created to exclusively exercise ownership rights over state-owned assets on behalf of the state. State-owned assets were to be managed by the central and local governments according to a hierarchical setup, and to be operated by large enterprises, conglomerates, and holding companies. This measure assigned to each level of government a specific scope of responsibility over state-owned assets and established a specific mechanism for separating ownership from management.

(iii) Reforming medium-sized and large SOEs into soundly designed corporations by defining the responsibilities of the shareholders' meeting, board of directors, board of supervisors, and management, thereby creating a coordinated system of governance bodies with well-defined responsibilities and effective checks and balances. This measure clarified the decision-making procedures, restraints, and other fundamental management frameworks of joint-stock SOEs.

(iv) Transforming SOEs into market-oriented businesses in such areas as personnel management, compensation, and reward allocation, with a focus on establishing a sound internal incentive system for SOEs.

With the issuance of the Decision, the priority of SOE reform had officially shifted to implementing the joint-stock reform. State-owned banks, being major SOEs in a competitive industry, fully match the Decision's criteria for implementation of the joint-stock reform and now had a clear path laid ahead of them. In January 2000, when being asked "Will SOCBs undergo the joint-stock reform?" in an interview with the *Financial News*, PBOC Governor Dai Xianglong said, "Wholly state-owned commercial banks operate in the competitive market of commercial lending. According to the decisions made at the Fourth Plenary Session of the 15th CPC Central Committee, there are no policy barriers to reforming wholly state-owned commercial banks into state-controlled joint-stock commercial banks."[1] At the 21st Century Forum held in June 2000, Dai gave an even more direct answer, stating that "We will try to reform qualified wholly state-owned commercial banks into state-controlled joint-stock commercial banks."

Remarks by the PBOC Governor on various occasions reflected the positive attitude of the central leadership toward the joint-stock reform of state-owned banks. The earliest explicit official statement to that effect appeared in the *Tenth Five-Year Plan for National Economic and Social Development* published in March 2001 ("10th Five-Year Plan"). The 10th Five-Year Plan called for "the comprehensive reform of wholly state-owned

---

[1] From a news report in the *Financial News* dated January 21, 2000.

commercial banks and the transformation of qualified ones into state-controlled joint-stock commercial banks," thus elevating the status of the reform to be part of the greater economic system reform for the medium term.

2. Progress of the three-year effort to turn around struggling SOEs

The costs of SOE reform passed on to state-owned banks were a primary source of their NPLs. However, this situation started to improve with the three-year effort to turn around struggling SOEs. Although SOEs still faced operational difficulties at the turn of the century, their prospect became brighter. By the end of 1999, the textile industry which had been a key target of the three-year effort had phased out 9.06 million obsolete cotton spindles, essentially achieving the original objectives for reducing capacity and headcount and increasing efficiency, and reversed its six-year loss-making performance one year ahead of schedule. Nonferrous metal and building materials industries also became profitable; the petrochemical industry had mostly kept its total capacity under control[1].

In 2000, state-owned and state-controlled industrial enterprises saw a 20.5% year-on-year increase in sales revenue, up 12.8 percentage points over 1999. They also recorded a total profit of RMB 239.2 billion, up 140% from 1999 and 290% from 1997. Among the 14 closely monitored sectors, 12 turned loss into profit or reported growth in profits, and the losses of coal and defense industry fell by 26.7% year-on-year. As a whole, state-owned and state-controlled enterprises in 31 provinces, municipalities, and autonomous regions all turned loss into profit, and most

---

1　Jiang Jianqing and Wei Guoxiong: *Origin and Resolution of Evergreen Loans*, China Financial Publishing House, 2009.

loss-making medium-sized and large SOEs became profitable. Among the 6,599 SOEs that reported losses in 1997, 4,799 or 72.7% were turned around through bankruptcy, restructuring, performance improvements, or other means.[1]

In 2001, the SOE reform cemented its progress. State-owned and state-controlled enterprises with an operating revenue of RMB 20 million and above reported a total industrial output of RMB 4.24 trillion, up 4.57% over 2000, despite a decrease in their number from 53,500 to 46,800. This meant the per-enterprise output rose from RMB 75.82 million to RMB 90.68 million, up by nearly 20%, illustrating the early benefits of the restructuring and reform of the SOEs.

Many factors helped make the SOE reform the success it was, and the joint-stock reform was undoubtedly one of the most decisive. The three-year effort to turn around struggling SOEs coincided with their three-year transition into modern companies through the joint-stock reform. The vast majority of the 2,770 SOEs nationwide piloting the modern enterprise system completed the corporatization reform. And among the 514 SOEs approved by the State Council for the pilot, 430 did so. Over those three years, 307 SOEs became listed domestically, raising RMB 272.3 billion. After bringing themselves in line with international standards on corporate structure and governance, 22 large SOEs, including PetroChina, China Unicom and Sinopec, went public overseas,

---

[1] *Almanac of China's Finance and Banking (2001)* and Wu Xiaoling: "SOE Reform at Crucial Stage (1992-2002): The Modern Enterprise System and the Three-Year Effort to Lift SOEs out of Financial Difficulties," *Three Decades of Economic Development in the Eyes of 50 Chinese Economists*, 2012.

raising USD 26.7 billion[1]. After creating an appropriate parent-subsidiary structure, many large SOEs had made ownership the foundation of their management and operational frameworks, enabling further structural improvements. The joint-stock reform was instrumental in helping SOEs change their operational mechanisms and overcome financial difficulties. According to a report of Xinhua News Agency in 2000[2], after Jilin Province – home to a significant number of medium-sized and large SOEs – included 130 such SOEs into its plan for a modern enterprise makeover, the 82 of them that had undergone the transformation recorded a 30-percentage point higher growth in total assets than the remaining 48 that had not; the former group also reported a 76% year-on-year increase in investment returns, versus a 46% decline by those in the latter group.

The success of the SOE reform created favorable conditions for the reform of state-owned banks: (i) improving performance and efficiency of SOEs enabled state-owned banks to enhance asset quality and promote business development; (ii) the three-year turnaround program had mostly achieved its objectives, enabling the central decision makers to focus on the reform of state-owned banks; and (iii) the experiences and success of the joint-stock and corporatization reforms of SOEs provided valuable precedents for the state-owned banks and boosted their conviction at implementing their own joint-stock reform.

---

1 Wu Xiaoling: "SOE Reform at Crucial Stage (1992-2002): The Modern Enterprise System and the Three-Year Effort to Lift SOEs out of Financial Difficulties," *Three Decades of Economic Development in the Eyes of 50 Chinese Economists*, 2012.
2 Xinhua News Agency: "Arduous Journey, Brilliant Achievements: Reporting at the Time When the Objectives of the SOE Reform and Three-Year Effort to Lift SOEs out of Financial Difficulties will Basically Be Achieved," December 12, 2000.

Related Topic: Sinopec Went Public in Hong Kong, New York, and London[1]

China Petroleum and Chemical Corporation (Sinopec) was listed on the New York Stock Exchange on October 18, 2000 and on the Hong Kong Stock Exchange and the London Stock Exchange on October 19, making it the only super-large SOE listed simultaneously in Hong Kong, New York, and London. It was also the only SOE listed overseas that year after PetroChina and China Unicom. It is said that the enthusiasm of investors during the IPO led to Sinopec exercising an over-allotment option and raising USD 3.73 billion in total.

After the IPO, Sinopec's parent company China Petrochemical Corporation (Sinopec Group) was left holding 56.06% of Sinopec's shares, domestic AMCs and China Development Bank 22.73%, and overseas shareholders 21.2%.

Before the IPO, Sinopec was incorporated (in accordance with the *Company Law*) by, and a wholly owned subsidiary of, Sinopec Group, which ranked 58th on the 2000 edition of the Global 500 list. Its creation was made possible after Sinopec Group restructured its business, assets, debts and claims, organizational structure, and personnel to separate main business from auxiliary business, performing assets from non-performing assets, and corporate functions from societal functions.

To promote the strategic restructuring of SOEs, China has in recent years introduced a series of policies favorable to the reform of the petroleum and petrochemical industries. Among them are those aimed to bring the price of domestic petroleum products closer to international levels, removing barriers to market-based operations. Many companies and investors at

---

1 From an article with the same title published in *China Petrochemical News*, October 20, 2000.

home and abroad were optimistic about Sinopec's IPO. ExxonMobil, Royal Dutch Shell, BP, ABB, and Hong Kong-based companies including CK Asset Holdings Ltd. and Henderson Investment Ltd., had each entered into an agreement with Sinopec for the purchase of its IPO shares, thus becoming its strategic investors or financial investors. Some large foreign companies also entered into strategic alliances with Sinopec, bringing Sinopec one step closer to forming joint ventures that may leverage foreign capital, resources, technologies, and managerial expertise to compete with foreign giants.

Sinopec's Board Chairman Li Yizhong said, "Sinopec now unveils a new chapter in its history. Sinopec will be committed to operational compliance in accordance with the operational practices for internationally listed companies and the regulatory requirements in international capital markets. To create high growth and return for our investors, Sinopec will shape itself into an internationally competitive public company with robust principal business, high-quality assets, innovative technologies, sound management practices, and rigorous financial control."

(III) Improved Operational Foundations of State-Owned Banks

Notwithstanding the lingering NPAs and unsatisfactory financial performance of state-owned banks, a comprehensive analysis of the various aspects of their reform after the first National Financial Work Conference showed that they were making strides toward becoming modern commercial banks.

First, state-owned banks became more motivated and capable of managing risks. With the industry-wide re-classification of credit assets and the trial implementation of the five-category classification scheme, the banks obtained an in-depth understanding of the state and causes of their asset quality woes. Under the guidance of the banking regulator and the risk management models of modern commercial banks, they quickly established the protocols for credit approval, loan loss provisioning, NPA recovery and disposal, and credit accountability. For this progress, they committed tremendous resources and made many innovations. In particular, they shored up their allowances and came up with many effective solutions to resolve the legacy NPLs, truthfully reflect credit risks, and prevent the continuing deterioration of credit assets. These efforts paved the way for improving credit asset quality and promoting a prudent and rigorous credit culture. For example, after classifying legacy NPLs as "old" and "new" according to years outstanding, they set targets for resolving each of the two types of loans to enhance accountability in NPL management.

In addition, state-owned banks also internally cascaded their targets for NPL management. In 2000, for instance, ICBC created an asset quality management framework to reverse asset deterioration. Under this framework, ICBC required the control of the total amount of NPAs ("total amount lock-down," *quan'e suoding*); the evaluation of both the proportion and absolute reduction of NPLs ("two-metric evaluation," *shuangxiang kaohe*); loan quality monitoring under both the four-category and the five-category classification ("dual-standard control," *liangtiaoxian kongzhi*); and award and penalty at year-end (*nianzhong duixian jiangcheng*). NPL reduction targets were incorporated into the evaluation and incentive system for heads of branches, and risk control responsibilities were also cascaded down to its branches. Furthermore, state-owned banks worked with the PBOC to more effectively identify potential high-risk loans. For instance, the banks redefined the criteria for identifying loans repaid with new ones, thus allowing problematic loans to be recognized as NPLs through graduated steps. Such criteria not only better reflect the risky nature of this type of loans, but also offered breathing room to banks and smoothed out potential shocks to the financial system from a sudden surge in NPLs.

More rigorous risk management had notably improved the quality of loans issued after 1999. For instance, in 1999, 2000, and 2001, ICBC kept the NPL ratio of its newly issued loans to 1.1%, 0.47%, and 0.22% respectively[1]. Data showed that state-owned banks started to make remarkable progress in preventing the formation of NPLs at the stage of loan issuance. Despite their overhang of legacy NPLs that could not be resolved in the short run, state-owned banks had plugged the loopholes that jeopardized the quality of newly issued loans. After completely resolving the legacy NPAs, they would be expected to reverse their poor asset quality and business performance by establishing a revamped credit risk control and credit culture.

Case Study: How ICBC Strengthened Its Credit Risk Management[2]

ICBC has achieved the historical milestone of lowering both the proportion and absolute amount of its NPLs by: (1) creating a Risk Management Committee to further improve its organizational system for bank-wide risk management; (2) putting in place a system for the management and monitoring of asset quality, under which each branch manages the branches at one immediate lower level and oversees those at two immediate lower levels, to evaluate bank-wide NPAs and extend the coverage of its risk control

---

1 Data taken from *ICBC Annual Report (2001)*.
2 Excerpt from *ICBC Annual Report (2001)*.

from credit assets to all assets; (3) establishing a risk management reporting system to regularly analyze and report the quality of its bank-wide credit assets; (4) relying on sophisticated IT tools to improve the functionality of its integrated credit management system for achieving real-time monitoring of credit operations and quality; (5) establishing a mechanism for early warning and transformation of risks to give an early warning, followed by transaction suspension and remediation, of its home loans, personal consumption loans, bank acceptance bills, and bank card issuances; (6) improving and enhancing its authorization and credit management, defining the scope of credit issuance, and controlling its maximum credit lines, customer credit lines, and itemized credit lines; (7) reforming its credit decision-making process and setting up a credit policy committee at its head office, which further established a credit approval center, composed of credit experts, that would implement the chief reviewer accountability mechanism to improve review efficiency and decision-making; (8) fully implementing a new credit rating method for corporate customers to apply the same rating procedures and criteria on a bank-wide basis and assessing the credit ratings of 211,605 key customers; and (9) creating a risk provision system for personal consumption loans according to international standards to increase the bank's operational robustness and the fidelity of its financials.

Second, state-owned banks ramped up their profitability. With an improving external economic environment, state-owned banks improved both their loan quality and business performance after divesting and writing off part of their NPLs. In addition, the development of new markets and businesses, low cost of capital, and other favorable external factors allowed them to further improve their profitability. In 1998 and 1999, the

Big Four posted two years of combined book losses totaling RMB 9 billion. By 2000, the Big Four achieved a book profit of RMB 15.35 billion, or an operating profit[1] of RMB 77.3 billion calculated exclusive of legacy costs such as loan write-offs and uncollected interest receivables. In 2001, the Big Four made a book profit of RMB 23 billion, or (exclusive of legacy cost) an operating profit of RMB 84.7 billion, up around 10% year-on-year. The improved profitability of state-owned banks brought in more financial resources that could be used to speed up the disposal of NPAs and the replenishment of capital.

Related Topic: Reasons for the Falling Losses, Rising Profits, and Lower Book Profits of State-Owned Banks[2]

In 2000, the Big Four reduced losses and raised profits mainly for the following reasons: (1) the NPL write-offs lowered their allowances for bad and doubtful debts, reducing their operational burden; (2) falling interest rates led to a significant reduction in interest rates paid on deposits; (3) they generally downsized their staff for greater efficiency; (4) they recovered more interest receivable; and (5) they enhanced financial management and discipline.

To enable commercial banks to be more capable in defusing financial risks, China had, since 1997, implemented a range of prudent financial and accounting practices, including changing the provisioning rule for bad debts, shortening the grace period to account for interest receivable but not received, adjusting the business tax rate, and reducing interest margins for

---

1 "Operating profit" is an accounting term for profit used by state-owned banks after 2000 and before the joint-stock reform to reflect their real profitability. It means book profit plus all costs and expenses incurred in dealing with their legacy financial burdens.
2 Excerpt from *Almanac of China's Finance and Banking (2001)*.

the benefit of enterprises. Nonetheless, these practices also increased the costs of the Big Four and dented their book profits accordingly.

Third, state-owned banks enhanced their internal control. In May 1997, the PBOC for the first time incorporated internal control into the program for the enhanced management and risk prevention of financial institutions; operational compliance and self-discipline have since been rising steadily at domestic commercial banks. Since 2000, in response to the PBOC's new requirements, state-owned banks have established an independent internal audit system by creating cross-regional audit offices operating independent of the banks' branches and reporting to their immediate higher supervising departments, an upgrade in internal supervision as well as inspection and sanctions. By 2001, the Big Four had 18,700 internal auditors in total and had achieved an audit coverage of 71%. Internal control frameworks were bolstered as well with the introduction of specific rules and regulations, such as methods for evaluating their internal controls and auditing branch managers' performance, and of loan management handbooks. These efforts helped create a rule-based and proper internal management frame at the banks.

Fourth, state-owned banks overhauled their internal organization. Following the policy requirements to streamline organizational structures and improve efficiency, state-owned banks started their streamlining efforts in 1998. From 1998 to 2001, they closed and consolidated 45,000 inefficient and redundant organizations (primarily banking outlets), reducing the number of business establishments from the peak of 150,000 to fewer than 100,000. Such efforts boosted their efficiency and slashed their operating costs.

In sum, despite their heavy legacy burden, state-owned banks managed to resolve some of the problems created by the original system. They established a preliminary, risk-oriented internal management structure, learned, tested and incorporated the basic operation and management frameworks of modern commercial banks, and gained managerial experience. These efforts laid a solid groundwork for their subsequent reforms.

(IV) Essential Personnel Arrangements for the Reform

In February 2000, the central government made additional personnel changes within the financial system, including the Big Four. Zhou Xiaochuan, then CCB President, was appointed CSRC Chairman responsible for promoting the capital market reforms; Jiang Jianqing was promoted from ICBC Vice President to ICBC President. Shang Fulin was reassigned from PBOC Deputy Governor to ABC President, Liu Mingkang from Chairman of Everbright Group to BOC President, and Wang Xuebing from BOC Chairman and President to CCB President. This round of significant reshuffling of top banking executives was completed within just one month, setting the stage for further reform of state-owned banks and indicating the central government's strong resolve in this initiative.

(V) Recovery of Chinese and Global Stock Markets

Following stabilization after the Asian financial crisis and the deepening of global economic and trade development, global and China's stock markets started to recover in the second half of 1999. China's A-share indices began to rebound in mid-1999 and, by the end of 2000, had risen significantly from early 1999. After being hammered by the Asian financial crisis, Hong Kong's stock market too recovered, sending the Hang Seng

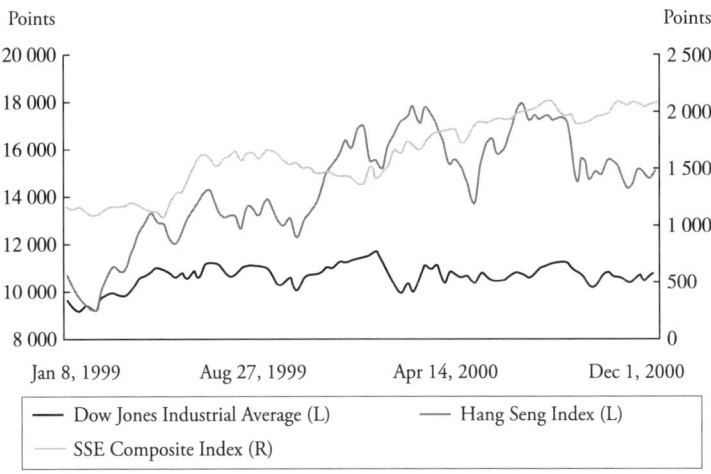

Fig. 4.1: Change in Three Stock Indices from 1999 to 2000

Index upward. These capital market trends created an ideal window for the reform of state-owned banks.

II. Reform Urgent Amidst Changing Landscape

Domestic and international economic and financial landscapes in the new millennium witnessed rapid and profound changes which, while creating favorable conditions for the reform of state-owned banks, also made it more urgent. Affecting the reform were the potential changes in the financial competitive environment brought about by China's WTO accession and shifts in international perception resulting from renewed attention paid to China.

(I) Accelerated SOCB Reform Prerequisite for WTO Accession

On September 17, 2001, the WTO Working Party on the Accession of China adopted the legal documents for China's accession to the WTO. On December 11, China officially joined the WTO. A milestone in

China's opening-up initiative, the accession was a strategic necessity to building socialism with Chinese characteristics and promoting China's economic and financial development. In the financial domain, WTO membership "helps attract international capital into China, import the management practices and new products of modern banks, further open up China's financial industry to the world, and promote financial reform and development."[1]

However, the accession also posed unprecedented short- and medium-term challenges to China's financial industry, especially to its banking sector. Under the WTO agreement, China undertook to: (1) relax market entry requirements and expand the scope of permitted business for foreign banks within five years, including allowing them to provide foreign exchange services to Chinese enterprises and residents; (2) expand the scope of permitted renminbi business of foreign banks and, within five years, completely remove relevant restrictions in all geographical regions; (3) relax cross-regional restrictions to allow any foreign banks approved to engage in renminbi business in one city to provide such services in other cities where renminbi business was permitted for foreign banks; and (4) remove restrictions on the permitted customers of renminbi business within five years to allow foreign banks to serve all Chinese customers. These and other commitments under the agreement meant that Chinese and foreign banks would follow the same set of rules after the end of the transition period and that the domestic banking sector would be competing with overseas banks in all respects – customers, banking professionals, and services.

---

1   From Dai Xianglong's speech at the sixth World Chinese Entrepreneurs Conference.

For China's banking sector at the turn of the century, there were significant challenges. In March 2001, the international rating agency Moody's upgraded BOC's financial strength rating from E+ to D–, a welcome improvement if not for the fact that it was still far below the top A+ rating on Moody's scale. Even so, BOC's rating was the highest among the Big Four. According to the ratings published by Moody's in November of that year, BoCom and CITIC Industrial Bank (later renamed as China CITIC Bank) were the highest-rated Chinese banks with a D rating. Although the ratings did not fully capture the operational and financial strengths of state-owned banks at the time, they did help illustrate the gap between Chinese and foreign banks under international banking standards.

It was impossible for the Chinese government, financial regulators, and state-owned banks to turn a blind eye to such a gap. WTO membership requires China's banking sector to address its credit quality issues and financial losses and engage in fair competition in accordance with international rules to remain viable in the markets, and this had to be done in just five years. This meant that state-owned banks needed to not only advance their own reform, but also produce tangible results before the rigid deadline, which was further shortened by the time needed to see the effects of any newly introduced policies. These pressures spurred the banks on to speed up their reforms.

(II) Nudge from International Public Sentiment and the IMF

Another external impetus was from international public sentiment. After the outbreak of the Asian financial crisis, China's economy and banking sector came under the scrutiny of observers across the world, many of whom viewed state-owned banks with pessimism. To compound the issue, due to enhanced regulatory oversight and management practices brought on by China's financial reforms, state-owned banks became more transparent, and their previously hidden heap of NPAs more visible to outsiders. Even with all the foreshadowing, the 25% NPL ratio of state-owned banks, published by the PBOC in 2000 and calculated by the four-category classification method, still came as a shock to everyone, especially considering that this figure was after the divestiture of RMB 1.4 trillion NPLs which lowered the NPL ratio by ten percentage points. The size of state-owned banks' remaining NPAs would become a subject of much speculation, research, discussion and debate by domestic and foreign observers inside and outside the banking sector.

Starting in 2001, some international investment banks started to publish research reports on the potential financial crisis of China. This topic was eyecatching and quickly became a focus of public attention. Alongside impersonal and impartial analyses and comments, hyperbole also abounded. A whiff of panic about a looming crisis of China's banking sector permeated the international community. It was believed that China's state-owned banks would be unable to continue operation and were on the brink of failure, or could even trigger a financial crisis.

Related Topic: News Reports from Certain Media Between 2000 and 2002 on the Possibility of NPLs Triggering a Financial Crisis in China[1]

In a June 2001 article of the *Financial Times*, Nicholas R. Lardy, a senior fellow at the Brookings Institution, said that China's NPLs was about 40% to 75% of its GDP in 2000, and that China had to accelerate the restructuring of

---

1 From international media reports.

its loss-making state-owned manufacturers and build a commercial credit environment, or it would find itself in a full-blown fiscal and banking crisis.

Christopher Lingle, in an article in the *Far Eastern Economic Review* published in October 2001, commented that China's problems were far graver than Japan's and that if 50% of China's outstanding loans were NPLs, half of the savings in China's banks would be in peril.

In an article in the *Far Eastern Economic Review* published in July 2002, Gordon G. Chang argued that the NPL ratio of China's banking sector was close to 50% or even higher, and that a large amount of newly issued loans were NPLs. He estimated that China's NPL recovery ratio stood at a mere 20%, making China highly susceptible to a banking crisis.

When looking at the asset quality of China's state-owned banks, international analysts overlooked key facts, such as that China had its unique national conditions, a strong government trusted by the people, sufficient cash flows of deposits, and a banking sector continuously undergoing reform over the years. Although China was fully confident and positioned to end its banking woes, these analysts put undue emphasis on the "insolvency" of the banking sector at the level of the balance sheet and financial statements, fueling the illusion that China's state-owned banks had become "technically insolvent." This mischaracterization, created from one-sided views, had a certain adverse impact on the reform of state-owned banks during this special historical period.

Speculations and misunderstandings regarding China's banking risks went beyond the public imagination. In 2001, during its consultation in China over China's accession to WTO, the IMF claimed that upon assessment, its professional staff put China's NPLs at 45% to 70% of its GDP.

The PBOC immediately pointed out the inaccuracies and protested the inappropriateness of their assessment method, and reported the matter to the central government. This incident made clear that a quick disposal of NPLs and improvement of financial performance would be needed to dispel the doubt over the banks and to create the right conditions for their development and reform.

Consequently, it was the combination of various factors at a critical juncture that both made necessary and created opportunities for accelerating the joint-stock reform of state-owned banks. Having sensed this opportunity amid the complex and evolving environment, China's central decision makers set in motion a grand vision for the joint-stock reform of state-owned banks in 2001.

III. Final Decision: Holding of the Second National Financial Work Conference

The reform of state-owned banks was an immense process involving arduous, urgent, and challenging tasks. The tone and direction of the reform had been set, but to implement the reform, it was necessary to set down guidelines, build consensus, and mobilize and organize personnel. In this context, the central government decided to convene another National Financial Work Conference.

(I) Unusual Preparations

During Premier Zhu Rongji's inspection tour of Zhejiang Province in December 2000, departmental heads in his entourage proposed – and Zhu agreed – to hold another National Financial Work Conference to address major questions in financial reform and development. Preparations for the second National Financial Work Conference went underway at Xiaobailou[1] in Tianjin soon after the Chinese New Year in 2001. Among the many topics being proposed for the Conference agenda, the most widely discussed one was the reform of the financial regulatory system, i.e., readjustment of the PBOC's regulatory functions. The rationale was that, in the central government's judgment, more rigorous regulation was needed to better control financial risks and promote operational compliance of financial institutions, both prerequisites for advancing the financial reform.

At a meeting on March 2, 2001, Vice Premier Wen Jiabao told relevant ministries and commissions, including the PBOC, the State Council's decision to convene a National Financial Work Conference before the end of 2001. At the meeting, he noted that the two key items on the agenda were to discuss the challenges facing China's financial industry after China's accession to the WTO and to draft a clear guidance document for the next phase of China's financial reform and development, as was done at the first National Financial Work Conference. After the meeting, the State Council set up nine research groups. The PBOC was responsible for five topics, including the reforms of financial regulatory system, SOCBs, and rural credit cooperatives. In just a few months, the PBOC put forward proposals for the reform of the financial regulatory system and SOCBs.

On this basis, Zhu Rongji, Wen Jiabao, Deputy Secretary-General of the Central Leading Group for Financial and Economic Affairs Hua Jianmin, and other central leadership members held meetings to discuss those proposals. These discussions reshaped the agenda of the upcoming

---

1 Xiaobailou ("Small White Building") refers to a landmark commercial area in Heping District of Tianjin that is named after a white building in the area.

National Financial Work Conference, elevating the reform of state-owned banks to the top. This change was made because the central leadership, having developed a better understanding of the circumstances and challenges of the reform through discussions with the ministries, now believed the reform to be the most pressing issue. In November 2001, Zhu convened a meeting (where President Jiang Zemin gave the opening address) to discuss the agenda of the forthcoming Conference, and the focus was all on the reform of state-owned banks. Such a change in priority reflected the central decision makers' accurate assessment of circumstances, courage to rise to the challenge, and pragmatic disposition.

On January 24, 2002, Zhu held another meeting on the reform and management of commercial banks, during which the objectives of the joint-stock reform were set. At the meeting, the presidents of the Big Four reported the banks' assets, liabilities, and NPLs and pitched their suggestions on the subsequent reforms. Zhu stressed that the upcoming Conference was meant to overhaul the commercial banks, and noted that to address the banks' problems and promote their sustainability, they needed to embrace additional reforms and the five-category classification scheme, to increase transparency into their operation and management, including disclosure of losses, and to raise their capital adequacy ratio. This was the final pre-Conference meeting and the final round of revision to the Conference documents. Zhu's remarks illustrated the central government's resolve to promote the joint-stock reform of state-owned banks.

(II) Historic Decisions

After systematic, in-depth research and preparations, the second National Financial Work Conference was held in Beijing on February 5-7,

2002. Participants included Jiang Zemin and Zhu Rongji, who each gave a speech, as well as the principal leaders at the provincial level and in charge of government departments and central financial institutions. The Conference set forth the ten priorities of China's financial reform during the 10th Five-Year Plan period[1], three of which on the banking reform showed major innovations in theory and practice.

1. Decision to comprehensively reform wholly state-owned commercial banks

The Conference identified the comprehensive reform of wholly state-owned commercial banks as the top priority of the financial reform. Based on the experience of SOEs in building a modern enterprise system, and with a view to turning the banks into modern enterprises with clear ownership rights, well-defined functions and responsibilities, separation of government from business activities, and rational management frameworks, the Conference required the banks to be reformed into internationally competitive modern financial institutions with sophisticated governance structures and operational mechanisms, clear business goals, and robust financial conditions.

Recognizing the joint-stock system as a key component of the banking reform, the Conference noted, "The joint-stock reform of wholly state-owned commercial banks will be an important test of the diverse forms of public ownership. Eligible wholly state-owned commercial banks may be

---

[1] The ten priorities were enhancing financial regulation, promoting the comprehensive reform of SOCBs, furthering the reform of rural credit cooperatives, increasing AMCs' efficiency of NPL disposal, regulating the securities market, accelerating the reform and development of the insurance sector, improving financial macro-regulation, developing the social credit system, raising the competence of financial professionals as a whole, and reinforcing the Party's leadership.

reorganized into state-controlled joint-stock commercial banks to improve corporate governance, and if conditions permit, may go public." These words swept away all doubts, controversies, hesitations, and uncertainties over the joint-stock reform of state-owned banks, heralding its immediate start.

In addition to the external institutional reform, the Conference, echoing the guidelines determined at the previous Conference, also required the banks to improve internally. Compared with previous policy measures, the new ones highlighted the operational principles for modern commercial banks by requiring state-owned banks to:

(i) set clear business goals and increase profits while ensuring the security of assets;

(ii) enhance credit management and reduce NPA ratios: reduce the banks' NPA ratios by an average of two to three percentage points per year during the 10th Five-Year Plan period; recover NPLs and dispose of them in various ways; strictly control the quality of newly issued loans; and improve the protocols for writing off bad debts, including performing independent but rule-based write-offs and safeguarding the right of collection against debtors;

(iii) enhance financial management and profitability: put in place an integrated evaluation system focusing on profit targets and asset quality, define the responsibilities of branch managers, and ensure the value of state-owned assets were maintained and increased; enforce strict cost management and reduce operating expenses; improve the taxation policies; and place the banks under stricter capital rationing so as to meet the required capital adequacy ratio;

(iv) optimize organizational structures and develop sound rules and regulations and business procedures; streamline management hierarchies and enhance autonomous management as a single incorporated entity; exercise strict governance and reinforce internal restraint and supervision; and improve the position responsibility system to implement strict accountability and effective incentives; and

(v) promote the use of information technology to support management and service improvements.

2. Reform of the operations of AMCs

Considering the challenges faced by the AMCs when they took over and disposed of the NPAs from state-owned banks, the Conference also decided to reform their operations to be more market-oriented by requiring them to:

(i) hasten the disposal of NPAs and of equities acquired from debt-for-equity swaps, while preventing the loss of state-owned assets;

(ii) introduce a bidding mechanism and explore alternative methods of disposal such as restructuring, winding-up procedures, and auctions. The state would also lower the qualification requirements for the asset disposal market to allow foreign and private capital to purchase debts, equities, and physical assets held by the AMCs; and

(iii) strengthen their internal management and performance evaluation and increase the transparency and public supervision of the NPA disposal process. Regulators would comprehensively evaluate the AMCs to see whether they had increased the recovery and realization rates and reduced the operating cost.

While these reforms were aimed at the AMCs, they also contributed to the subsequent reform of state-owned banks, particularly for the effective resolution of legacy NPAs, for two reasons.

One, they helped strengthen the business ties between state-owned banks and the AMCs. The first round of NPL divestiture involved swapping performing assets for non-performing ones at book value. Though necessary, this approach could not be replicated because exchanging assets of unequal values contravenes market principles, and the difference would ultimately have to be absorbed by the state. It was proven, within the few years after the creation of the AMCs, that NPA disposal through AMCs had its advantages, not least in easing the burden of state-owned banks as they attempted to reform. Therefore, AMCs were very much a necessary part of the solution to the banks' NPA problem. But their relationship with the banks had to be clarified for them to remain viable and effective. This means future transactions between the two sides had to respect market principles. Thus, the Conference called for the adoption of a bidding mechanism and a market-based approach for NPL disposal.

Two, they increased the efficiency of disposal, and therefore helped reduce the cost of banking reform. The performance of AMCs had shown that, without the proper restraints and incentives, efficiency would often cede to other priorities, leading directly to lower recovery rates and higher disposal costs. To promote the reform of state-owned banks, therefore, it was necessary to figure efficiency more prominently in AMCs' performance evaluations, enhance accountability of personnel at all levels, and create proper incentives.

3. Development of the social credit system

Asset quality woes of state-owned banks hinted at deficiencies within China's social credit system. Aiming to promote the reform of the economic system – and especially to fix the rampant evasion of bank debts during the three-year effort to turn around struggling SOEs and the loss of credibility of local governments – the Conference, for the first time in China's history, proposed measures for the overhaul of the social credit system. Specifically, the Conference stressed that (i) rule of law and economic and financial legal frameworks had to be bolstered, so as to ensure debt-evading entities and individuals and government employees who had condoned or supported such actions would be prosecuted for criminal liabilities; (ii) a national credit database for enterprises and individuals should be established; and (iii) more efforts should be put into public outreach, education, and public opinion monitoring, and to expose enterprises who had evaded their obligations to financial enterprises and regions where such evasion was rampant.

The Conference's stern statements on the breach of financial obligations and effective measures for the implementation of sanctions clearly showed the state's resolve to rectify debt evasion and protect the lawful rights and interests of financial institutions. In particular, by clarifying the consequences for government agencies and their personnel at all levels for breach of credibility, the Conference had created strong deterrent, which helped rein in the activities of local governments, dispel local protectionism, and curb debt evasion. The protection of financial debts and of credit environment also helped improve the sustainability of state-owned banks.

(III) Major Breakthroughs

Launching the joint-stock reform of state-owned banks was unquestionably one of the most important decisions made at the second National Financial Work Conference. In the history of banking reforms, this decision is significant for affirming the joint-stock reform as the immediate concern; and more importantly, it signified that China now possessed better conceived and more definitive solutions for fundamental issues relating to the economic and financial systems, the social responsibility and self-development of financial institutions, and the relationship between government and financial institutions. In addition, the Conference addressed, in unequivocal terms, two key questions regarding the roadmap for state-owned banks.

First, the objectives of the reform. As Jiang Zemin said at the Conference: "By our laws, commercial banks are corporate legal entities, but whether SOCBs are also enterprises has been a long-standing theoretical and practical issue. Many see SOCBs as part of the administrative or fiscal system and, as a result, believe that loans from SOCBs need not be repaid. This is the root cause behind government interference, debt evasion by SOEs, and the sky-high NPA ratios. Since commercial banks are enterprises, they must establish a profit-centered performance evaluation system to reduce their NPA ratios and protect and increase the value of state-owned assets. Our banks cannot be unprofitable because most of their funds are deposits of the general public rather than fiscal appropriations."

This statement revealed two goals at two different levels. The first, at the banks level through institutional reforms, was to restore and protect the status of state-owned banks as enterprise legal persons and empower them to operate independently and outside government influence. Of the four specific goals proposed at the Conference – clear ownership rights, well-defined functions and responsibilities, separation of government administration from business activities, and rational management frameworks – three pertained to the relationship between state-owned banks and the government, making clear the priority assigned by the state was to reform the operation and management of state-owned banks.

The second, at the national level, was to re-align the interest of the state, the public, and state-owned banks so that the pursuit of profitability by the banks would also economically benefit the state and the public. In his speech at the Conference, Zhu said, "The profit pursuit of SOCBs does not conflict with their mandate to support the economy. Rapid and sustained economic growth is needed to ensure the robust and efficient operations of the banks, and safe and stable banking operations are needed for economic development."

The decisions of the Conference on the reform of state-owned banks were not intended solely to resolve prominent and surface issues in banking operations, but also to dig deeper into the underlying mechanisms and dynamics to uncover the root cause of their legacy problems, so as to help them form well-defined, sound, and sustainable operating frameworks and goals that would gradually transform them into modern commercial banks. The two objectives meant that while the joint-stock reform was still focused on settling the ownership of state-owned assets, it would have a broader and deeper impact on China's financial and economic system as a whole.

Second, the policy that the disposal of NPAs should be conducted concurrently with the reform of state-owned banks. Legacy NPLs had been a major obstacle to the reform of state-owned banks. As mentioned earlier, one solution was to require the banks to resolve legacy burdens themselves before reforms were launched in other areas. But Jiang opposed this view at the Conference, stating that "[State-owned banks] must reduce their NPAs while supporting economic development. These two priorities complement each other. Proposals pitting one against the other are untenable. … The increasing NPAs of state-owned banks will inevitably endanger their wellbeing or even survival as well as undermine financial stability and economic security. If they are unable to maintain normal operations, how can they support our enterprises and the economy?"

This showed that the central government was acutely aware of the immense danger posed by the banks' NPLs to the economy, and that it had decided to tackle this issue and other necessary reforms at the same time, rather than the more conservative approach of putting one in front of the other. Obviously, this simultaneous approach meant a more rigid schedule and more demanding tasks, tasks that state-owned banks could not accomplish without the public's support. The central leadership chose to race against time because of the shrinking transition period following China's accession to the WTO. It was a bumpy road that China had to traverse, and would profoundly shape the progress and achievements of the joint-stock reform of state-owned banks.

Section III
Regulatory Reform Creating Conditions for the Joint-Stock Reform

The closing of the second National Financial Work Conference signaled the immediate start of the joint-stock reform of state-owned banks – a complex project requiring thorough and careful preparations. For a period after the Conference, the main task for the reform was to develop a detailed plan. During this period, other financial reforms were launched whenever conditions permit, creating the progresses necessary for the reform of state-owned banks. Among these reforms, the establishment of the China Banking Regulatory Commission (CBRC) had the most immediate and profound impact.

I. New Arrangements for Financial Regulatory Reform

While the key agenda of the Conference was changed from the reform of the financial regulatory system to the reform of state-owned banks, this did not mean that the former had lost its prominence. On the contrary, at the Conference the central leadership continued to view regulatory reform as a top priority and made arrangements which gave birth to China's new financial regulatory structure and a regulatory environment that would make the joint-stock reform possible.

The Conference set forth five tasks for the financial regulatory reform: (i) improving regulatory legislation. In accordance with its WTO commitments, China would revise the fundamental financial laws, such as the *Law on the People's Bank of China* and the *Law on Commercial Banks*, and administrative regulations, and regulate financial institutions and markets by sector; (ii) adopting a stringent regulatory framework and improving accounting, information disclosure, and credit rating systems in line with international practices; for each type of financial institutions, developing dedicated regulatory indicators, risk monitoring and evaluation systems, and early warning indicators of financial system risks; and establishing a multi-level and comprehensive monitoring system; (iii) improving the regulatory approach and enhancing the oversight of risks from financial enterprises and of their internal control and risk management systems; (iv) adopting sophisticated monitoring and inspection techniques, improving the sanction and market exit mechanisms for financial enterprises, and granting necessary law enforcement powers to financial regulators; and (v) improving the regulatory system and collaboration between regulators, in particular those between different sectors.

The Conference coincided with the election of central government officials; and an agreement on the specifics of the reform of the banking regulatory system was yet to be reached. For these reasons, the final Conference documents made no mention of the reform. However, the intention to create a new regulatory framework was evident from the Conference's mandates for the financial regulatory reform. Specifically, the directives for revising the *Law on the People's Bank of China* and the *Law on Commercial Banks,* regulating financial enterprises and markets by sector, and enhancing collaboration between regulators all pointed to a new financial regulatory framework. The directives regarding the financial regulatory system, approaches, and techniques signaled a shift in regulatory philosophy and model – from review and approval of matters to the oversight of financial enterprises and markets – highlighting the aim for professional, law- and rule-based regulation. As a result, the Conference had offered general guidance over how to define regulatory boundaries and how to transform state-owned banks into modern commercial banks while ensuring regulatory effectiveness.

II. Establishment of the CBRC

The second National Financial Work Conference's decision on the reform of the financial regulatory system was in fact built upon the programs of the first conference in 1997. The key tasks then were to reform the PBOC system by establishing branches with regional jurisdiction, assigning regulatory responsibilities to each branch by its level, and transferring certain regulatory responsibilities regarding non-banking institutions to other agencies. These measures had greatly enhanced the PBOC's autonomy in determining monetary policies, reduced interference by local governments, and promoted banking reform and progress. With the rapidly changing landscape of financial reform, however, the PBOC's management system was exposed to three new challenges.

First, in the context of China's region-based (i.e., provincial) administration of economic affairs, the replacement of provincial branches with cross-regional ones had weakened the branches' linkage with the provincial governments, leading to communication and coordination issues when the new branches tried to perform their local regulatory functions.

Second, after the Asian financial crisis, the central government gave increasingly higher priority to financial risk prevention and financial macro-regulation. As the monetary policy agency, the PBOC was required to operate with greater autonomy and professionalism and to shoulder a greater mandate – maintaining financial stability. If it was concurrently performing micro-regulatory functions, it might be worse-positioned to control systemic risks due to the diffusion of resources.

Third, international financial regulation practices and collective experiences indicate that a central bank should be the lender of last resort. The central bank has the authority, responsibility, and obligation to offer bailouts when required by a financial crisis and to prevent or contain such a crisis. As such, retaining micro-regulatory responsibilities might give rise to conflicts of interests and ethical risks, especially in a bailout. Therefore, to allow the PBOC to better play its role as the lender of last resort and to prevent ineffective bailouts, the PBOC had to remain independent, without being burdened by responsibilities of micro-regulation.

Due to these considerations, the regulatory system reform became a major topic during the preparations for the second National Financial Work Conference in 2001. Because it had become clear after the first National Financial Work Conference that the different financial sectors were to be separately operated and regulated, and that the central decision makerss had resolved to further improve the banking regulatory system, the idea of creating a dedicated banking regulator was already widely accepted. However, a major disagreement was whether the regulator should be independent of the PBOC like the CSRC and the CIRC, or affiliated to the PBOC like the SAFE.

Discussions on the form of the new banking regulator continued up to the 16th CPC National Congress in November 2002. The Congress stressed the strategic goal of strengthening macroeconomic regulation and ordered greater reform of the administrative system. According to the Congress, the top priority in any functional adjustment of the financial authorities was to ensure the effectiveness of macro-regulation, and institutional streamlining should be combined with the creation of any new, necessary organizations to effectively implement the state's economic development strategies. These directives helped clarify the specific approach for the reform of the financial regulatory system. To enable the PBOC to better exercise its functions of macro financial regulation, it was necessary to establish an independent regulator responsible for micro-regulation of the banking sector.

On March 10, 2003, the First Session of the 10th National People's Congress adopted the "Decision on the Organizational Structure Reform of the State Council." The Decision contained a package of measures for the reform of administrative agencies, including the decision to establish the China Banking Regulatory Commission (CBRC) as a banking watchdog. On April 26, the Standing Committee of the National People's Congress approved the proposal to allow the CBRC to provisionally exercise the PBOC's financial regulatory powers. The official opening of the CBRC on April 28 marked the formation of China's sector-based regulatory system composed of the CSRC, CIRC, and CBRC.

As a public institution directly affiliated to the State Council, the CBRC took over the PBOC's former functions of regulating commercial banks, AMCs, trust investment companies, and other depository financial institutions. Meanwhile, the PBOC took on more monetary functions, with a focus on enhancing the macro-regulation of the financial industry, preventing and resolving financial systemic risks, and coordinating the regulatory efforts in the banking, securities, and insurance sectors.

Section IV
Formulation and Implementation of Joint-Stock Reform Plans of State-Owned Banks

As the top priority of China's financial reform during the 10th Five-Year Plan period, the development of a plan for the comprehensive reform of state-owned banks started immediately after the second National Financial Work Conference. The focus during this stage was to identify and address key obstacles to the joint-stock reform and the long-term development of state-owned banks, in order to arrive at a sound reform plan that maximized the benefits and minimized the cost. However, due to the complexity and breadth of the program, the formulation of this plan was bound to be faced with unforeseeable risks and challenges that required wisdom, courage, innovation, and experimentation to overcome.

I. No Agreement on the RMB 970 Billion NPL Divestiture Plan

In March 2002, Vice Premier and Secretary of the Central Financial Work Commission Wen Jiabao chaired a follow-up meeting for the second National Financial Work Conference, proposing that the State Council should set up 12 teams to implement the 12 reform measures put forward at the Conference. After the meeting, on April 2, the Work Group on the Comprehensive Reform of Wholly State-Owned Commercial Banks ("Comprehensive Reform Group") – led by the PBOC and composed of the Central Financial Work Commission, the MOF, the Ministry of Personnel, the Ministry of Labor and Social Security, the State Taxation Administration, the Office of the State Council for Restructuring the Economic System, the State Council Research Office as well as ICBC, ABC, BOC, and CCB – was officially created and held its first meeting chaired by PBOC Governor Dai Xianglong to discuss the work plan and schedule. The creation of the Comprehensive Reform Group marked the official start of the preparations for the comprehensive reform of state-owned banks with a focus on the joint-stock reform. In this way, relevant research for the reform took shape.

(I) Identification of Reform Tasks

The first step was to identify the key questions to be addressed during these studies in relation to the reform objectives and the realities of state-owned banks' operations. In the two weeks of preparation leading up to its official creation, the Comprehensive Reform Group developed a work plan which identified seven primary tasks for the reform.

First, how to push forward the joint-stock reform of state-owned banks. This was the core question and a prerequisite for other tasks. For this question, the Comprehensive Reform Group further identified the following four priorities: (i) the objectives and conditions for the reform, i.e., setting the basic orientation of the reform and, on the basis of such orientation, evaluating the potential difficulties and challenges to be faced by state-owned banks during implementation; (ii) the selection of a reform approach and specific steps, i.e., the path of the reform should be clearly defined because different paths varied in cost, feasibility, and expected results. The path needed to be thoroughly discussed in advance, as a wrong choice would be costly to correct; (iii) the relative proportion of state-owned shares and other shares at different stages. Given that the joint-stock reform would inevitably bring in non-state-owned equity capital and impact the decision-making of state-owned banks, the reform plan should evaluate the impact of the post-reform equity structure of state-owned banks on state interests, the preservation and growth of the value of state-owned assets, and the banks' own operation and development; and (iv) the procedures, criteria, and timetable for listing, i.e., early preparations should be made and based on a thorough evaluation of the necessity and basic requirements for the listing of state-owned banks after the joint-stock reform.

Second, how to improve the corporate governance structure of state-owned banks. Per the outcomes of the second National Financial Conference, the most important objective for the banking reform was to establish the modern enterprise system, and improving their governance structure was the top priority. Hence, the second major topic of study for the

Comprehensive Reform Group was to determine how to optimize the internal governance of state-owned banks. In its work plan, the Comprehensive Reform Group identified the following six topics for discussion: (i) the selection of a corporate governance model for state-owned banks, i.e., on the basis of the joint-stock reform, comparing Chinese and international banking practices to find out which governance model was better suited to the reform objectives and domestic circumstances; (ii) major roadblocks to modernizing the corporate governance structure of state-owned banks, i.e., developing forward-looking strategies to reconcile new governance structures with the existing policies, regulations, as well as the operation and management practices of state-owned banks; (iii) the internal components of the new governance structure and the interactions and division of responsibilities between them; (iv) the creation and composition of boards of directors. If state-owned banks were to be reorganized into joint-stock companies, the board of directors would become the governing body of a bank and materially impact other aspects of the bank. The nomination, election, and management of directors and the rules of procedures for board meetings needed to be studied to ensure the banks' decision-making mechanism was optimized without diminishing the state's absolute control over the banks; (v) the reform and composition of boards of supervisors. The first National Financial Work Conference had ordered the governance reform of state-owned banks by requiring every bank to establish a board of supervisors to oversee the activities of the management team and the implementation of state policies. The joint-stock reform would need to consider the division of responsibilities between the newly created shareholders' meeting and board of directors and the existing board of supervisors, and redefine the responsibilities of the latter accordingly; and (vi) the creation and status of management teams, i.e., evaluate how to properly constrain and incentivize professional managers while banks' ownership was separated from their management, in order to prevent principal-agent conflict in operating objectives and increase the operational efficiency of the banks.

Third, how to resolve the legacy burden of state-owned banks. This was the most challenging and critical issue to be considered in planning the banking reform and, therefore, to be tackled by the Comprehensive Reform Group. To reduce banks' NPL ratio by two to three percentage points per year as required by the second National Financial Work Conference, the Comprehensive Reform Group believed the solution depended on an accurate and thorough evaluation of the banks' credit assets and losses on the myriad types of non-credit assets.

Fourth, how to create a dynamic capital replenishment system. To effectively remedy capital deficiencies, raise the capital adequacy ratio, and strengthen capital rationing at state-owned banks, the Comprehensive Reform Group devoted much effort to studying how to establish a dynamic capital replenishment system for them. These efforts included: (i) measuring the potential impact of changes in the amount of risky assets on the bank capital by verifying the year-by-year amount of fiscal appropriations received by the banks and the year-by-year total and structure of capital of each bank; and (ii) investigating the feasibility of various dynamic mechanisms that would improve the banks' capital adequacy, such as risky assets control, earnings accumulation, issuance of subordinated bonds, and share issue.

Fifth, how to improve the internal management of state-owned banks. To encourage banks to modernize their management practices and enhance vitality and self-restraint, the Comprehensive Reform Group believed it was necessary to improve the banks' internal management frameworks. This task covered all aspects of operation and management, including systems for internal audit, credit management, financial accounting, risk management, provisioning for and write-offs of bad debts, classification and evaluation of credit asset quality, and business innovation and development. Some were follow-ups to the initiatives proposed after the first National Financial Work Conference, and some were new proposals on objectives of the banks after the joint-stock reform.

Sixth, how to reform the personnel system of state-owned banks. Considering the potential impact of the banking reform on the banks' original personnel system, the Comprehensive Reform Group analyzed the establishment of a competitive election and appointment system, the improvement of incentives and constraints, and the introduction of market-based compensation programs in the context of the new governance framework.

Seventh, what external environment was needed to support the reform of state-owned banks. Given that reform would be a systematic project and redefine the relations between stakeholders, both of which could not take place in a vacuum, the Comprehensive Reform Group studied the external conditions necessary to the reform, including the relationship between the self-development of commercial banks and the development of the economy as a whole, the launch of fee-based services at commercial banks, the complementary overhaul of the taxation system, and capacity building to compete with foreign banks.

The meticulous efforts made by the Comprehensive Reform Group in identifying the tasks of the reform attested the more comprehensive and systematic planning and consideration of the central decision makers over the reform of state-owned banks. Despite their breadth, these tasks all revolved around the five critical issues that would define the success of the reform. (i) How much the reform would cost. The work plan contained new thoughts on the bearer of the cost of the joint-stock reform and the composition of such cost. (ii) How to dispose of NPAs. The plan made a much more detailed analysis for the disposal of NPAs and proposed that the solution might consider differentiated responses based on asset type and bank branch level. (iii) Where to obtain the required resources. The plan highlighted not only the need for self-accumulation of resources at the banks, but also the more important need to tap the capital markets and other external sources, which outlined an efficiency-oriented general approach. (iv) How to ensure the effectiveness of the reform. The tasks proposed in the work plan reflected the purpose of the reform, that is, while short-term issues would also be addressed, the reform was more concerned with transforming state-owned banks into market-oriented entities and making them internally motivated to compete in the market. (v) How to maintain economic, financial, market, and social stability, protect the state's core interests, and strike a balance among reform, development, and stability.

(II) The First Draft Plan Caused Controversies

1. Proposition of the RMB 970 billion NPL divestiture plan

On April 4, 2002, the PBOC submitted the work plan of the Comprehensive Reform Group and reported the planned tasks and arrangements for the reform of state-owned banks. Per the plan, the Comprehensive Reform Group sent a questionnaire to state-owned banks in April regarding the critical and difficult questions such as the selection of corporate governance models. The Group also analyzed the theories and laws related to the banking reform, and compared domestic and foreign banking systems. Symposiums and other meetings were then held to discuss the resolution of banks' legacy burdens, the replenishment of bank capital, governance structure, joint-stock reform, internal institutional reform, and personnel system reform.

After extensive gathering of feedback from all stakeholders, on August 1, 2002, a draft of the "Plan for the Comprehensive Reform of Wholly State-Owned Commercial Banks" was completed under the leadership of the PBOC. The draft plan then underwent multiple rounds of revisions from August to September based on comments from government ministries, commissions, and state-owned banks. On October 31, the Comprehensive Reform Group finalized the submission copy to be presented to the State Council. This version became the first preliminary plan for the joint-stock reform of state-owned banks.

The reform plan, consisting of 5 parts and 24 measures, provided an overarching framework for the joint-stock reform. The first part argued for the necessity of comprehensively reforming the Big Four. The reform plan recognized the Big Four's historical contributions and irreplaceable role in China's financial system. After the first National Financial Work Conference, the Big Four enhanced their operation, development, and risk management competencies through reforms, but the heavy NPL and financial burdens were left unresolved, necessitating a more comprehensive reform. In the first part of its plan, the Comprehensive Reform Group primarily analyzed the Big Four's NPA situation. According to its calculations, as of the end of 2001, the Big Four's total losses had reached RMB 1.4 trillion, including RMB 970 billion loss on credit assets and RMB 430 billion loss on on-the-book non-credit assets. In other words, after the first round of NPA divestiture totaling RMB 1.4 trillion, the Big Four had another RMB 1.4 trillion of loss assets at least. This was especially jarring considering that the Big Four had only RMB 700 billion in capital. If the loans and non-credit assets that had been recognized as losses were written off against capital, they would be nearly RMB 250 billion below solvency; and if estimated losses from doubtful loans (calculated at a 40% loss ratio) were also accounted for, they would be RMB 700 billion below solvency.

The second part of the reform plan laid out the objectives and tasks of the comprehensive reform. Echoing the decisions at the second National Financial Work Conference, the reform plan called for improving the asset-liability indicators of the Big Four, such that they would be transformed into modern, globally competitive commercial banks by the end of 2006. The specific objectives included: (i) disposing of the Big Four's RMB 1.4 trillion of asset losses; (ii) turning each of the Big Four into a joint-stock company through a step-by-step, tailored approach, while ensuring the controlling stake of the state and diversification of ownership, so that their capital adequacy ratio could be brought up to 8%. Subject to the condition that the state would maintain a minimum 50% controlling interest, the Big Four could attract investments from eligible domestic commercial and industrial enterprises; (iii) allowing the state to make capital contribution either by establishing four financial holding companies (with the help of private capital) to control each of the Big Four, or by creating one financial holding company to centrally manage the Big Four; (iv) allowing overseas investors to invest in the Big Four in principle, subject to any decision made at the end of the 10th Five-Year Plan period based on the progress of the joint-stock reform; and (v) creating conditions for the Big Four to be listed on domestic stock exchanges and then overseas ones after standardizing their joint-stock reform and improving their operations and management.

The third part of the reform plan discussed how to strengthen the internal management of the Big Four. The plan proposed the establishment of a profit-driven operation and performance evaluation system by state-owned banks and named several key financial performance indicators, including that the Big Four: (i) should ensure that, starting from 2002, their NPL ratio would decline by two to three percentage points per year and, by 2006, would be reined in below 6%; (ii) by 2006, would derive more than 20% of their income from fees and commissions from financial services; (iii) by 2006, would strive to control the annual average growth in administrative expenses to within 5%; and (iv) by 2006, would, through efforts to increase income and reduce expenditures, dispose of RMB 430 billion non-credit asset losses through accumulated earnings.

The fourth part of the reform plan recommended the conditional divestiture of the RMB 970 billion of loss loans – calculated in the first part and named as the single biggest challenge to the joint-stock reform – to create conditions for the comprehensive reform of the Big Four. This recommendation followed an assessment of the pros and cons of all available options. Such divestiture would be made in the same way as was done by the four AMCs in 1999. The reform plan also estimated the profits of the Big Four after the proposed divestiture: an expected total income of RMB 1 trillion by 2010 which could cover the reform cost.

The fifth part of the reform plan stressed the need to strengthen regulatory oversight and the social credit environment. When the reform plan was drafted, the PBOC's banking regulatory functions were yet to be offloaded to the CBRC. Thus, the PBOC proposed measures for greater regulatory oversight of the Big Four. As required by the second National Financial Work Conference, to protect banks' creditor's rights and create a good business environment, the reform plan also presented measures for the development of the social credit environment in support of the banking reform.

All estimations and designs of the reform plan aimed to achieve the most expeditious launch of the banking reform, as required by the CPC Central Committee and the State Council, without sacrificing the necessary prudence. The plan provided an important basis for the decision makers and interested parties to conduct further studies on the reform.

2. Controversies over the reform plan

Discussions on the first reform plan grounded to a halt. In fact, throughout the drafting process, the PBOC had maintained close communications with government agencies, who had raised no objections over the direction and steps of the joint-stock reform, or the design of the banks' governance structure and operation and management frameworks. But they disagreed on how to deal with the NPAs. There were three views on this issue: (i) The Big Four should absorb the losses with their future earnings and take steps to rebuild their balance sheets so as to raise their capital adequacy ratio to 8%; (ii) The MOF should issue another series of special government bonds to recapitalize the Big Four to absorb the write-off; and (iii) The Big Four's RMB 970 billion of loss loans should be once again offloaded to the four AMCs, as was done in 1999-2000.

The PBOC considered the first option unfit for the reform environment and objective because it was overly time-consuming. When the first reform plan was prepared, according to the PBOC's calculation under the assumption that the Big Four would record an annual NPL growth of 5% and an annual profit growth of 10%[1], it would take 10 years for ICBC, 28 years for ABC, 8 years for BOC, and 7 years for CCB to dispose of their NPLs wholly by themselves.

The second option entailed the issuance of a massive amount of special government bonds which needed to be backed by good quality assets and would require a bona fide corporate governance improvement at state-owned banks. Given uncertainties in the banks' asset quality and the prospects of their reform, such bond issue could invite many challenges and doubts. In view of these factors, the PBOC considered the third option as more feasible and suggested that the central government should publicly undertake to cover the final losses of the Big Four, but would have them make up their actual losses with future earnings and taxes after resolving their legacy burden[2]. Hence, the PBOC proposed the further divestiture of RMB 970 billion in NPLs to the AMCs.

The third option, however, was much harder to push forward than it seemed at first. Soon after the draft reform plan was finalized, the top officials of the PBOC and the MOF came together in mid-August 2002 to discuss the plan, without reaching a consensus. According to the MOF,

---

1   Although the Big Four turned out to be in a much better financial shape than the assumptions on which the calculations were based, those assumptions were a prudent and reasonable choice considering their NPL overhang.
2   Similar to a "jointly managed account," i.e., profits and taxes of the Big Four would be deposited into a special account to cover the final losses of the AMCs.

the proposal to offload nearly RMB 1 trillion of NPLs, within less than three years after it issued RMB 270 billion special government bonds to recapitalize the state-owned banks in 1997 and the previous divestiture of RMB 1.4 trillion of NPLs in 1999, would be met with tremendous resistance, questioning, and public pressure, which would muddy the external environment for the joint-stock reform of state-owned banks. The MOF also contended that other solutions were available to resolve the NPAs. As a result, discussions on the draft plan stopped.

II. Experimental and Exploratory Efforts

If the banking reform was to be successful, empirical research would be just as important as theoretical research. Experimentation not only helps verify whether a policy will work, but also helps uncover problems and gather data and experience, thereby providing an important basis for improving the policy. In fact, from as early as in 2000, the state began to conduct experimental and exploratory initiatives in domestic and overseas markets, all while mulling over the joint-stock reform. Among these initiatives, the successful restructuring and listing of the Bank of China Group, Hong Kong-Macao Region (BOCHKMR) as the Bank of China (Hong Kong) Limited[1] (BOCHK) offered valuable experience and had steeled the resolve of the central decision makers to roll out the joint-stock reform of state-owned banks.

---

1   BOCHK is the short name of Bank of China (Hong Kong) Limited reorganized from BOCHKMR. It was formerly known as BOCHKMR, Bank of China Group (Hong Kong), or Bank of China Group.

(I) Causes of BOCHKMR's Restructuring and Listing

BOCHKMR was a banking conglomerate composed of 13 banks[1] and several financial companies. Most of these banks boasted illustrious histories and played an important role in China's modern banking history. Of the 13 banks, except for BOC Hong Kong Branch and Macao Branch, 7 banks (including Sin Hua Bank) were registered in Beijing without business operations in the Chinese mainland but operated through their Hong Kong branches; 4 other banks (including Nanyang Commercial Bank) were registered and operated in Hong Kong. BOC managed these affiliates through its General Audit Office in Hong Kong and BOC HK and Macao Regional Office.

Related Topic: BOC HK and Macao Regional Office

With the State Council's approval, BOC managed its banking operations in Hong Kong and Macao as a banking group through its regional office. In the early days, the general regional office was the General Audit Office. In December 1982, with the PBOC's approval, the BOC's General Audit Office in Hong Kong was changed into BOC HK and Macao Regional Office ("BOCHKMRO") to enhance BOC's management over its affiliates in Hong Kong and Macao. The BOCHKMRO was responsible for directing, managing, supervising, and coordinating BOC's affiliated banks, offices, and agencies in Hong Kong and Macao to strengthen the banking conglomerate, enhance their competitiveness, and promote their business development. On behalf

---

1 Including Bank of China HK Branch, Bank of China Macao Branch, Sin Hua Bank HK Branch, China & South Sea Bank HK Branch, Kincheng Bank HK Branch, China State Bank HK Branch, National Commercial Bank HK Branch, Yien Yieh Commercial Bank HK Branch, Kwangtung Provincial Bank HK Branch, Nanyang Commercial Bank, Po Sang Bank, Hua Chiao Commercial Bank, and Chiyu Banking Corporation.

of BOCHKMR, the BOCHKMRO actively participated in economic, financial and banking exchanges in Hong Kong and Macao and maintained ties with local financial regulators. Thanks to a decade of efforts by BOCHKMRO, BOCHKMR had quickly grown into the second largest financial corporation in Hong Kong. The BOCHKMRO-centered management structure had paved the way for the restructuring and smooth transition of BOCHKMR into BOCHK. During the return of Hong Kong and Macao to China, the BOCHKMRO contributed to their financial stability and smooth transition.

BOCHKMR's organizational structure came into shape under special historical circumstances. For a long period after the founding of the People's Republic of China, BOCHKMR had played an important role in counteracting the West's economic blockade against China, maintaining China's financial linkage with the rest of the world, and supporting economic development in the Chinese mainland. However, strategically, with economic and social progress, BOCHKMR's "1+N" business strategy could not meet its needs for sustainable development, primarily because of the following three issues:

First, unclear ownership relationships. BOCHKMR was not a legal entity in and of itself, but a nominal consortium of multiple independent incorporated banking institutions. Due to historical reasons, the ownership of these banks and their relation to BOC were highly complicated and opaque. After the founding of the People's Republic of China, BOCHKMR's member banks were gradually transformed into state-owned banks funded and controlled by the Chinese government. But instead of direct state ownership, historical circumstances and the needs for overseas operation at the time required the equity of these member banks (except for BOC

Hong Kong Branch and Macao Branch) to be held by ten funds nominally established by individuals and placed under the management of BOC on their behalf.

Such discrepancy in nominal and true ownership structure created problems. (i) The state's ownership of these banks was not effectively protected by law which, over time, would expose these state assets to potential risk of loss. (ii) The compliance of the local operations of these banks were called into question. Hong Kong's financial regulator required the seven banks registered in the Chinese mainland to submit their financial statements and corporate management reports each year. They were also required to complete many procedures in the mainland, such as annual business inspections and registration of changes in board members. However, without compliant operations of their board of directors and well-established governance mechanisms, the seven banks found it hard to prepare compliant financial reports to fully meet the regulatory requirements. (iii) Unclear equity structure caused markets and the public to question the legitimacy of BOC's control over the member banks or even BOCHKMR itself. In addition, with the return of Hong Kong and Macao, BOC Macao Branch became a note-issuing bank in Macao, and thus it made more sense to bring the branch under the direct management of BOC head office.

Second, unsatisfactory corporate governance of member banks and ineffectiveness of BOCHKMR's internal management and resource allocation. Although the member banks were independent legal entities in form, they did not wholly meet the local regulatory requirements for corporations due to their unsatisfactory governance structure and limited role of their boards of directors. The bureaucratic style of management by

BOC head office through BOCHKMRO was cumbersome and impaired the control over member banks due to multiple management layers. While operating under the same group, the member banks were significantly different in management efficiency due to their different management competencies and culture. Moreover, given that they operated in the same market, it was difficult for them not to overlap in terms of customers, services, outlet locations, and management positions. The resulting horizontal competition affected the efficient allocation of BOCHKMR's internal resources and made it hard to achieve economies of scale.

Third, lack of competitiveness and resilience of these member banks. While BOCHKMR as a whole was regarded as a key banking player in Hong Kong's financial market on a par with HSBC and Standard Chartered, individually, its member banks other than BOC Hong Kong Branch and Macao Branch were not sufficiently capitalized, and raised most of the funds for their development through accumulated earnings rather than from capital markets. Restricted by these factors, they had a limited balance sheet, catered more to small and medium-sized businesses and general public clients, could only command a tiny share of the high-net-worth corporate and private client market, and had low business development potential. Consequently, their actual competitiveness and resilience against risks in local and international financial markets paled in comparison with major rivals like HSBC, Standard Chartered, and Hang Seng Bank. This, in turn, took a toll on BOCHKMR's overall strength, particularly during market volatilities or a financial crisis.

The flaws in BOCHKMR's management model had impeded the bank's growth. To create synergy among the member banks, boost business in Hong Kong and Macao, and provide stronger support for Hong Kong's financial stability and development, BOC sought to reform BOCHKMR. The reform aimed to reorganize the member banks in Hong Kong into a large bank controlled by BOC and then pick the right timing for public listing.

(II) Restructuring Designed to Enhance Corporate Governance

In the late 1980s, BOC head office started to mull over BOCHKMR's restructuring. However, with the return of Hong Kong approaching, all efforts had to be directed toward ensuring a smooth transition. BOC therefore put the reorganization of BOCHKMR on hold until 1998. This timing was due in part to the factors mentioned above, but also to four major changes in the external environment.

First, Hong Kong's return offered political assurance for the restructuring and merger of financial institutions between the mainland and Hong Kong. After the return, the Hong Kong Government expected BOCHKMR to play a more prominent role in safeguarding local financial stability and economic prosperity, and therefore encouraged it to quicken the restructuring process.

Second, financial innovations and accelerating financial globalization changed the operating and regulatory environment in which banks operated, intensified market competition, and made reform more urgent than ever. After the 1990s, driven by technological advancement and innovations, the international banking sector became more globalized, IT-powered, and expansive, increasing both market competition and regulatory pressure. These changes pushed banks to expand their business scope and sharpen their competitive edge through horizontal or even cross-industry acquisition.

Third, the Asian financial crisis was a major test for Hong Kong's economy and financial industry and forced the banking sector to change its business models, respond to market volatility, and adapt to new regulatory rules. During the crisis, the flaws of BOCHKMR's management model were made all the more apparent, as evidenced by the soaring NPA ratios and credit risks of several member banks and even operating difficulties. The financial crisis compelled BOCHKMR to accelerate its reform and revive its business through restructuring.

Fourth, as the joint-stock reform of state-owned banks was about to start in the mainland, BOC was encouraged to leverage Hong Kong's developed financial market and BOCHK's restructuring and listing to accrue valuable experience for the joint-stock reform. Against the backdrop of China entering a new stage of building the socialist market economy and having applied for WTO accession, the domestic financial industry was fast becoming more market-based and accessible. And to build the modern enterprise system, it was imperative to reform state-owned banks in alignment with the building of the socialist market economy and in response to the challenges of WTO accession. With its roots in Hong Kong, BOCHKMR could spearhead those efforts by leveraging Hong Kong's internationally aligned practices in regulatory oversight, legislation, and markets.

As conditions became ripe, the time had come for the restructuring of BOCHKMR. In 1998, BOC proposed the restructuring and listing of BOCHKMR to the central government, which treated the matter as a top priority. Zhu Rongji approved the idea and encouraged BOCHK to conduct institutional reforms to contribute to Hong Kong's future prosperity, competitiveness and market stability. Accordingly, BOC created a steering committee for restructuring and listing led by executives of BOC head office and BOCHKMRO. Shortly afterward, BOC head office and BOCHKMRO each created a restructuring office as a working body of the steering committee to be responsible for making preparations for the restructuring.

In July 1999, BOC officially submitted to the PBOC an application and a plan for the restructuring of BOCHKMR. In December that year, based on feedback from the PBOC and relevant agencies, BOC revised the restructuring plan, proposing to fold all its overseas operations into BOCHK for listing. Zhu endorsed the revised plan in principle, but, believing this important matter warranted careful consideration, required BOC to conduct more policy studies and discussions to ensure that the plan was consistent with the direction and policies of China's financial reform and SOE reform, and to account for legal, regulatory, and other factors, enhance the policy feasibility study, and extensively solicit feedback. Vice Premier Wen Jiabao, in charge of financial affairs, also approved the restructuring and listing, and believed that it would be an important exploration for the joint-stock reform of state-owned banks. He required BOC to create a thorough and prudent plan that incorporated feedback from all stakeholders, and to analyze and judge market trends to anticipate the problems that may arise during the joint-stock reform and listing of BOCHKMR.

BOC's research and explorations in 1998 and 1999 for the restructuring was of great significance and marked the beginning of the joint-stock reform of state-owned banks in practice. However, given that state-owned financial enterprises, as players in a special industry, had no precedent of listing overseas, many theoretical and practical issues in areas such as policy approval, legal arrangements, regulatory coordination, and technical details needed to be addressed. More importantly, opinions differed over how BOC's overseas operations were to be packaged for listing. Some argued that assigning high-quality assets to an overseas entity for listing and low-quality ones to the BOC head office would arouse concerns from overseas regulators and rating agencies and lower the overall rating of BOC. As news circulated that BOCHKMR was thinking about restructuring and listing, rumors that BOC would put all its best assets into its overseas listed company aroused public pushback to the reform. Impacted by internal and external factors, BOCHKMR's reform made no headway in the near term, but BOC's efforts to explore and research such reform continued.

After being appointed as BOC's President in February 2000, Liu Mingkang prioritized BOCHKMR's restructuring and listing. Through a series of meetings, the Party committee at BOC greenlighted the full restructuring of BOC's overseas operations and BOC's subsequent listing at the appropriate time. The committee decided that the objective was to establish effective corporate governance and efficient operation and management system to increase BOC's competitiveness and capital strength.

In that year, milestone progress was also achieved to lift SOEs out of financial difficulties, giving the central government the breathing room to ponder and promote the joint-stock reform of state-owned banks. The central government intended to carry out a pilot reform in some institutions to test the waters for the full-fledged reform of state-owned banks. In a presentation to Zhu Rongji, Liu Mingkang suggested that BOCHKMR could be that trailblazer. He identified the following advantages of doing so: (i) the substantial size of BOCHKMR would make its restructuring and listing beneficial to cementing the market influence of Chinese-funded banks in Hong Kong; (ii) because BOCHKMR shared many of the same institutional problems as the other state-owned banks, the restructuring would provide experience for the subsequent large-scale restructuring of the state-owned banks; and (iii) the restructuring would offer a peep into capital operation rules in international markets. Well acquainted with the history of BOCHKMR and supportive of its series of reforms, Zhu accepted Liu Mingkang's proposal for its broad implications. At this point, BOCHKMR's restructuring, elevated to the status of a critical pilot program for the joint-stock reform of state-owned banks, was re-initiated.

Because BOC's plan to restructure and package its overseas operations for IPO and listing through BOCHKMR had sparked controversies, BOC decided to confine the restructuring to BOCHKMR itself and focus on aligning such restructuring with the reform of state-owned banks. Under the new mandate and policy orientation, the first and foremost task was to redefine the objectives of BOCHKMR's restructuring.

Considering BOCHKMR's major problems and challenges, BOC set the following objectives for BOCHKMR: (i) clarifying its equity and ownership structure through institutional restructuring to ensure the effective protection, supervision, and operation of state-owned assets; (ii) creating a well-structured and manageable operation framework backed by a large pool of assets and capital to increase its market competitiveness, influence, and efficiency; (iii) establishing centralized and unified risk control, business development, marketing, and technology application systems; (iv) streamlining its organizations and staff and fine-tuning the locations of its branches to conserve and efficiently utilize its resource and reduce operating cost; (v) establishing an organizational framework and ownership structure in line with international regulatory requirements and enhance its disclosure capability and operational transparency; (vi) raising capital for its development and increasing its capital adequacy ratio; and (vii) offering managerial, technical, and other support to promote BOC's overall business development.

Based on these objectives, BOC set out to develop a detailed restructuring plan. To this end, BOC had to address two key questions. The first was how to restructure the 12 banks in Hong Kong under BOCHKMR[1], for which BOC came up with two solutions. The first solution was to combine them into a large BOC HK Branch, which would facilitate the state and BOC head office to exercise centralized control and management, unify and harmonize the once fragmented operational and management rules, facilitate future strategic adjustments, and resolve capital adequacy and NPA issues. The second solution was to reorganize the 12 banks into BOC Hong Kong incorporated in Hong Kong. This would help the latter to fully leverage its autonomy as an overseas bank and the overseas environment, to truly reinvent itself and quickly establish the governance structure of a modern bank.

BOC initially leaned toward the first solution, i.e., creating a large Hong Kong branch. However, as the plan for the joint-stock reform of state-owned banks began to take shape, BOC, considering the relative merits of the two solutions, switched to the second solution to pioneer the reform and provide guidance to the restructuring and IPO to domestic banks.

---

1   Excluding BOC Macao Branch.

BOC proposed to implement the second solution by (i) merging the head offices of the seven banks registered in the mainland into BOC head office and their Hong Kong branches into BOC HK Branch ("seven-into-one"); and (ii) restructuring and merging the four banks registered in Hong Kong into one bank ("four-into-one"), after which Nanyang Commercial Bank (NCB) would retain its own licenses and be directly controlled by BOC.

After discussions, however, BOC believed that this approach could neither completely resolve the fragmentation of BOC's Hong Kong affiliates nor fully exploit their economies of scale and overall competitiveness. Therefore, BOC proposed to implement a "10+3" approach. Under this approach, operations of 10 of the 12 banks under BOCHKMR (the two exceptions were NCB and Chiyu Bank) would be consolidated into Po Sang Bank which would then be rebranded as Bank of China (Hong Kong) Limited (BOCHK). All assets and liabilities of the 10 banks and BOC Credit Card (International) Limited ("BOC Credit Card") would be transferred to BOCHK; and NCB, Chiyu Bank and BOC Credit Card, as BOCHK's affiliates, would continue to operate as relatively independent subsidiaries. NCB and Chiyu Bank were excluded from the merger per the wishes of their founders or shareholders, and because the two banks represented the entrepreneurial spirit of overseas Chinese and were valuable to be retained as national brands.

The "10+3" approach was more thorough. Though this approach would not fully merge BOC's Hong Kong affiliates into BOCHK due to political and cultural considerations, it would allow most of them operate under a single brand and a uniform management framework, which would help increase BOCHK's influence and efficiency in Hong Kong and create conditions for governance improvement. Ultimately, BOCHKMR's restructuring followed the "10+3" approach.

The second question was whether BOCHKMRO should be retained. Initially, BOC intended to merge its Hong Kong affiliates into one bank under the management of BOCHKMRO. But this proposal was rejected by Zhu Rongji who believed that this structure had too many management layers and was more like a government than a bank. Zhu's opinion revealed the central government's intention to remove administrative influences from commercial banks. Therefore, BOC modified its approach and decided to transfer BOCHKMRO's functions to the restructured bank more gradually and to ultimately replace BOCHKMRO with a holding company to manage BOC's Hong Kong affiliates through equity and corporate governance system.

The success of a well-designed plan depends on its implementation, but the finalization of the restructuring plan did not necessarily mean easy implementation. BOCHKMR's restructuring – which could be given the labels of "precedent-setting," "overseas challenges," "institutional problems," "prominent governance issues," and "excessively high NPL ratio" – was bound to encounter a string of challenges.

The first was how to efficiently transfer its customer relations and lawfully complete the restructuring. According to the restructuring plan, there would be an extensive merger of BOC's Hong Kong affiliates, which would involve the lawful transfer of the customer assets and liabilities of all member banks. The conventional approach would require the signing of new agreements with all customers; but considering the large customer base of BOCHKMR, it was obviously untenable. The success of restructuring hinged on the legality of its processes, and BOC was eager to find an optimal and lawful solution. Based on Hong Kong's judicial practices, a private bill[1] would be the best solution for achieving the smooth, safe and efficient transfer of all assets, liabilities, and debts between the merged banks and their customers and for protecting the interests of all interested parties. Thus, following this line of thought, BOC proposed to transfer all assets and liabilities under Hong Kong's jurisdiction to the new bank through a private bill, thereby legally completing the "wholesale" transfer of their customer relations.

Pursuant to Hong Kong's judicial procedures, BOC's promotion of a private bill needed to be approved by the Hong Kong Monetary Authority, the Department of Justice, the Legislative Council (LegCo), and the Chief Executive. When BOC promoted a private bill for the restructuring of BOCHKMR, LegCo was about to enter its summer recess. According to Hong Kong's legal system and the restructuring schedule, if the bill could not be passed before September 2001, all accounting statements of the new bank would need to be prepared anew, it would then be impossible for the restructuring to be completed on schedule. Time, then, was of the essence.

Having been operating in Hong Kong for many years, BOCHKMR was a major part of the local economy and financial market and had broad societal influences. After its unveiling, the restructuring plan drew different reactions in Hong Kong. While most people supported the plan, some worried that if the restructuring failed, the failure might destabilize Hong Kong's financial market. They also feared that BOC would use the restructuring to expand its influence and suppress market competition. LegCo

---

1 "Private bill" refers to any legislative bill applicable to a specific entity.

also exercised prudence when reviewing the private bill, though it was more concerned with whether the interests of the customers and employees could be protected during the restructuring.

To complete the restructuring on schedule, BOC head office, BOCHKMRO, and the restructuring team held extensive and in-depth dialogues with the officials and legislators in the four agencies as well as with other stakeholders, painstakingly explained to them the restructuring plan, and provided detailed responses to questions about the capital adequacy ratio of the new entity, safeguards for customers' assets and interests, potential impact of the restructuring on the market, and the protection of employees' rights and interests. Thanks to these efforts, their doubts as well as those of the market were dispelled. LegCo then set up an *ad hoc* committee to review the private bill for the restructuring. Tung Chee-hwa, the Chief Executive of Hong Kong, also supported the restructuring. Fortunately, on July 12, 2001, just one day before LegCo's summer recess, "Bank of China (Hong Kong) Limited (Merger) Ordinance" was approved by LegCo and signed into law, clearing the legal barrier to BOCHKMR's restructuring.

After the restructuring, the trade names of BOCHKMR's several subsidiaries, including the seven banks registered in the mainland, ceased to exist. Their former assets, liabilities, and customer relations were all handed over to the new entity. While the adoption of the private bill legalized all contractual rights and obligations of BOC under the laws of Hong Kong, its contractual rights and obligations under the mainland's jurisdiction had to be handled in accordance with the laws of the mainland. For this purpose, the Supreme People's Court held a special meeting to deliberate on BOC's request and legal documents and ultimately decided to notify, through a public announcement, all BOC's domestic and overseas debtors and creditors of changes in their rights and liabilities. This was the first announcement for corporate restructuring issued – in both Chinese and English no less – by the Supreme People's Court since the reform and opening up of China. Support from the Supreme People's Court demonstrated the level of priority placed by the state on BOCHKMR's restructuring and the central government's resolve to promote the reform of state-owned banks.

The second challenge of restructuring was how to eliminate BOCHKMR's legacy burden. BOCHKMR's massive NPAs were the biggest obstacle to restructuring, which could not be addressed in such a short amount of time with BOCHKMR's financial resources alone. For this reason, BOC redoubled loan recovery efforts and, at the same time, quickly disposed of BOCHKMR's NPAs by: (i) divesting BOCHKMR's non-banking assets after an asset assessment, recovering its direct investments, real estate investments, and any financing provided to its own financial companies, and closing down all financial trust companies it directly or indirectly owned; and (ii) divesting its NPLs. BOCHKMR's NPLs were internally absorbed by BOC, i.e., a portion of the NPLs was sold as a bundle to the AMC under BOC head office. In addition, BOCHKMR established a department for special assets management which was responsible for recovering and disposing of its remaining NPAs.

The third challenge was how to strengthen management. During restructuring, apart from organizational adjustment, BOCHKMR improved its governance by: (i) streamlining organizations to increase management efficiency. It compacted its 5-layer management structure before the restructuring into 3 layers and consolidated the 295 departments under the original 13 entities into 16, which enabled more optimal setup of management positions and personnel, a reasonable "reach" of each management layer, and higher management efficiency; (ii) redesigning the business process. It created three front-office business units for retail banking, corporate banking, and financial market, and the complementary mid-office management units and back-office support units, with each evaluated for cost efficiency and performance. It unified back-office services by consolidating the 55 processing centers into 5; (iii) adjusting the location and functions of outlets. It optimized the distribution of the original 13 institutions' branches by shutting down or merging some 40 outlets and adjusted outlets' services and functions; and (iv) integrating IT systems. It ensured that the disjointed computer systems of the former member banks would be retrofitted with uniform interfaces and software used by BOCHKMR's computing center and prepared a new IT development plan.

The fourth challenge was how to reform its human resources framework. As BOCHKMR's restructuring involved 14,000 employees, maintaining staff stability, retaining key personnel, ensuring business continuity, and avoiding mass incidents were major challenges and key to the success of the restructuring. Therefore, as part of the restructuring program, BOCHKMR strived to build a new personnel system by: (i) putting in place a merit-based appointment system and a performance-based employment policy to break the so-called "iron rice bowl" of guaranteed employment, and providing market-oriented incentives to attract key professionals; (ii) improving the professional knowledge of its management personnel at all levels and the overall competency of its employees; (iii) building a corporate culture to promote a positive attitude and excellence to enhance employee loyalty and cohesion; (iv) streamlining its staff to reduce operating cost and raise efficiency; (v) selecting and appointing senior executives in a fair, just, and reasonable manner, ensuring the suitability of the selected individuals and the optimization of the overall management structure, and putting in place a comprehensive accountability system. After the restructuring, BOCHK entered into an agreement with each of its senior and mid-level officials to define their authorities and responsibilities; and (vi) imposing higher requirements in performance evaluations and on ethics and skills in connection with the selection and employment of ordinary employees and ensuring the transparency of the selection process. Moreover, BOCHKMR developed a resettlement plan for employees who were let go. By protecting the legitimate interests of these employees through financial compensation and other means, BOCHKMR won their understanding and support for the restructuring.

BOCHKMR's restructuring kicked off in 1999. On October 1, 2001, BOC (Hong Kong) Limited was established. On that day, BOCHKMRO was officially shut down and turned all its functions over to BOCHK, which marked the completion of BOCHKMR's restructuring and the inauguration of BOCHK.

(III) Bumpy Road to IPO and Listing

After overcoming many challenges, BOCHKMR achieved the intended restructuring targets, but the mission was only half accomplished. According to BOCHK's tight reform schedule, BOC had no time to rest. As soon as BOCHK was unveiled, the restructuring and IPO team started to prepare for the IPO and listing of BOCHK in Hong Kong. However, just when the team was expecting that their hard work would pay off and make for the smooth listing of BOCHK, a series of events casted a shadow over the IPO and listing.

About ten days after the completion of BOCHK's restructuring, USD 483 million were found missing from BOC Guangdong Branch's account after an IT system upgrade. Initially, the problem was thought to be a system error. However, investigation revealed unsettling misconduct behind the missing funds at Kaiping Sub-branch, BOC Guangdong Branch. Three branch heads in a row had stolen from the funds in nine years and fled with their families overseas before the theft came to light. The Kaiping incident occurred at the outset of BOCHK's IPO and listing preparation and caused a sensation due to the enormous amount of funds involved. More importantly, the case revealed material loopholes in BOC's internal control and put a significant dent on BOCHK's IPO and listing program.

As investigators struggled to unravel clues about the Kaiping case, BOC was hit by another scandal. On January 11, 2002, Wang Xuebing, former President of BOC and then of CCB, was reported to be under investigation. On January 15, he was removed as President of CCB. Wang Xuebing's fall was attributed to his illegal activities while he was at BOC. The downfall of BOC's former top executive was undoubtedly another major blow to BOCHK's IPO and listing process.

Before recovering from those incidents, people were struck by a third blow. On January 18, 2002, the U.S. Office of the Comptroller of the Currency (OCC) and the PBOC issued a joint notice to impose a heavy fine on BOC New York Branch for misconduct. Though Zhou Qiang, a customer with BOC New York Branch, was the mastermind, Wang Xuebing was in charge of BOC New York Branch when the misconduct occurred and was "directly or indirectly responsible" for it. This was one of the causes leading to the investigation on Wang Xuebing.

These three incidents occurred one after another over a short time span, presenting a severe challenge to BOCHK's IPO aspirations. Investor confidence would make or sink an IPO; and those incidents might raise serious doubts among investors about BOCHK's internal management and discourage them from buying its shares. This would significantly affect such efforts as IPO share pricing, marketing to institutional investors, and share offering.

Those incidents, occurring at the beginning of BOCHK's preparation for IPO, would normally have caused BOCHK to suspend its IPO program out of prudence and to restart the process once the situations are defused. However, BOCHK's IPO and listing concerned not only a subsidiary under BOC, but also the effort to blaze a trail for the joint-stock reform of state-owned banks, which could not wait. Therefore, BOCHK needed to overcome the challenges and ensure the success of its IPO and listing.

Those incidents were taken seriously by the central leadership who required relevant agencies to assist BOC in resolving them and asked BOCHK to overcome the difficulties and complete its IPO and listing as planned. Following the central leadership's direction, then BOC President Liu Mingkang adopted a two-front strategy:

The first front was to deal with the aftermath of those incidents and reduce their impact on BOCHK. To this end, BOC took the following actions: (i) fully cooperating with Chinese and overseas regulators and police authorities during investigations to minimize resulting losses; (ii) making proactive remediation. Considering the adverse impact of the incidents, Liu set down a rule – BOC should disclose as much information about the incidents as possible and actively resolve them, as well as take concrete measures to ramp up its risk management and internal controls. According to the rule, BOCHK invited prominent individuals in Hong Kong and the U.S. to join its board directors and structured its board of directors as a modern bank to make its corporate governance more transparent. Furthermore, it invited risk management experts from the top 10 banks in the world to Hong Kong to share their risk management experience, so as to help improve its internal risk management frameworks; and (iii) winning over the confidence of authoritative industry experts. As advised by a consultancy agency, BOC engaged a group of authoritative experts in the relevant sectors to survey BOC's branches in Shanghai, New York, Hong Kong, and other cities. Through field visits, these experts obtained a full understanding of BOC's operations and management, and issued a fair statement afterward. Ultimately, they reached conclusions favorable to BOC. Their opinions, though unable to sway public attitude immediately, had legal effect and provided support for BOCHK's IPO and listing.

BOC's efforts paid off. First, the bank made heartening progress on the Kaiping incident. Through 11 civil lawsuits, BOC recovered RMB 840 million of frozen funds. In April 2002, the U.S. court issued a default judgment in absentia against the three defendants that they should compensate BOC for all its losses. This judgment paved the way for BOC to win in the subsequent proceedings and recover the assets in question.

Second, BOC New York Branch also won its case. During BOCHK's global roadshows, the United States District Court for the Southern District of New York made a decision in July 2002 to support all of BOC's claims against Zhou Qiang et al. and ordered the latter to pay punitive damages of USD 100 million for "[acting] with a malicious and fraudulent design to injure the plaintiff [i.e., BOC]." Meanwhile, the OCC concluded its hearing of the case between Wang Xuebing and BOC New York Branch and lowered the fine on the branch from USD 60 million to USD 20 million, of which USD 10 million should be paid to the PBOC. Losses from the case were thus substantially reduced.

BOC's responses to the incidents were applauded by domestic and international media. "The victory in New York has removed the cloud over BOCHK's IPO and listing," said a CNN report. Repercussions from the BOC New York Branch case were minimized to such an extent that no investor asked about it during BOCHK's final roadshow.

The second front was to expedite BOCHK's IPO and listing, which was part of a grand strategy that could not be delayed. With the adverse effects of the incidents in mind, BOC began to make full preparation for the IPO and listing. Looking back on the IPO and listing of BOCHK, BOC's efforts on this second front were confronted with many tough challenges.

First, how to ensure BOCHK's capital adequacy and NPA ratios would meet Hong Kong's regulatory requirements. BOCHK's capital strength and asset quality were two correlated metrics that investors cared about the most during IPO and listing. To ensure that its capital adequacy ratio would reach the regulatory threshold, BOCHK greatly supplemented its capital through re-evaluating its property assets, accumulating profits and surplus reserves held by its branches, recovering dividends already distributed to the head office, and receiving special dividend payouts from Nanyang Commercial Bank and Chiyu Bank.

At the same time, BOCHK aggressively disposed of its NPAs to reduce its risky assets and improve capital utilization. It was estimated that to bring BOCHK's NPL ratio down to the regulatory requirement and the average level of its local peers, BOCHKMR had to dispose of over RMB

10 billion NPAs, excluding the NPLs that were likely to be recovered and NPLs for which allowances for write-off had already been made. If those NPAs were all to be written off by BOCHKMR, it would significantly impact BOCHK's prospect of meeting the required capital adequacy ratio. In other words, BOCHK had an acute capital shortfall.

To ensure both the capital adequacy and NPA ratios of BOCHK would meet regulatory requirements, BOC head office decided to sell those NPAs to Zhong Gang (Cayman) Company Limited, an AMC under BOC Cayman Branch. Soon afterward, new state policies and BOC's market operations permitted BOC head office to write off those NPAs against a portion of its future profits. This practice of smoothing out the disposal process by tapping into future earnings was an innovation which would resolve the legacy NPAs and ensure that BOCHK's capital adequacy and NPL ratios meet the regulatory requirements and investor expectations. Retrospectively, this practice had offered important inspiration for the subsequent restructuring and listing of state-owned banks, i.e., one of the challenges in the joint-stock reform of state-owned banks was that their capital adequacy ratio needed to reach the required threshold, but considering their operational conditions, they had to be supported by state policies to do so.

Second, how to determine BOCHK's place of listing. As the listing rules and procedures vary from place to place, the place of listing had to be decided from the outset. To broaden the scope of potential investors and promote BOCHK's corporate image, BOC initially planned for a concurrent listing of BOCHK in Hong Kong and the U.S., but later decided for a Hong Kong listing only, for two reasons. The first one was that the BOC New York Branch case increased the uncertainties of a U.S.

listing. The second one was that the Enron scandal in 2001 had ruined the reputation of their audit firm Arthur Andersen LLP, and pushed it to the verge of bankruptcy. As it happened, Arthur Andersen was also BOCHK's external auditor and IPO auditor. The scandal made it impossible for BOCHK to complete, within the pre-determined schedule, the preparation of its financial statements according to U.S. accounting standards and of its IPO in New York. After multiple consultations with its financial advisers and other intermediaries, BOC decided to abandon a public listing of BOCHK shares in the U.S., going instead for a Rule 144A offering[1].

Third, which strategic investors should be approached. During the preparation for the IPO and listing of BOCHK, BOC decided to bring in strategic investors for the following three purposes: (i) it was necessary to enlist renowned financial institutions as an endorsement of BOCHK's credibility because the public had concerns over whether BOCHK was fit to go public and how it would perform thereafter due to its legacy NPAs and legal battles; (ii) additional capital could be raised from strategic investors; and (iii) BOC hoped to improve BOCHK's internal governance by working with the strategic investors.

BOC set the following principles which would govern the introduction of strategic investors for BOCHK: (i) they should be well-known international financial institutions, preferably commercial banks; (ii) they should be able to bring sophisticated technology and product development and management experience to BOCHK and help improve its governance

---

1   Rule 144A regulates the "private resales of securities to institutions," i.e., an issuer may issue securities to qualified institutional buyers through private placement which will be exempted from SEC's registration and disclosure requirements.

structure; (iii) they should make long-term commitments to BOC and the Chinese market; and (iv) they would not participate in the day-to-day operation and management of BOCHK.

After contacting and exchanging views with many well-known institutions, BOC finally decided to accept Standard Chartered as BOCHK's strategic investor. Standard Chartered is a well-established British bank counting among Hong Kong's top three banks and authorized to issue currency. BOC's decision came as a surprise in Hong Kong, but significantly boosted investor and market confidence.

Fourth, how to valuate BOCHK. For the overseas IPO debut of a state-owned bank, the valuation of BOCHK was of great significance – it concerned how to maintain and increase the value of state-owned assets, and it was likely to serve as a benchmark for the valuation of other Chinese banks when they sought overseas IPO themselves. Thus, BOC exercised great prudence in BOCHK's IPO pricing. At the start of the preparatory stage, Liu Mingkang consulted with Zhou Xiaochuan, then CSRC Chairman, about the pricing issue. Zhou supported BOCHK's IPO and listing and hoped the IPO price would become a benchmark. Liu replied that the price would be set on par with that of Standard Chartered, namely, BOCHK's price-to-book ratio (P/B ratio)[1] would not be lower than Standard Chartered's, so that BOCHK's equity would not be underpriced.

Underwriters including UBS and Goldman Sachs worried that BOCHK shares were overpriced. As David Chin, head of the BOCHK project team at UBS, recalled, during IPO pricing negotiations, members of the underwriting syndicate originally wanted to lower the P/B ratio, but

---

1 Ratio between share price and net assets per share.

Liu Mingkang refused to budge. The IPO price was eventually set at HKD 8.5 per share, close to Standard Chartered's, and at the upper end of the original price band of HKD 6.93 to HKD 9.5.

Fifth, how to persuade investors to subscribe for BOCHK shares during the roadshows. The final roadshows began in July 2002 under extremely difficult market conditions. In 2002, international stock markets were highly volatile with many indices nosediving. By the time of BOCHK's IPO, the Dow Jones, the NASDAQ Composite, S&P 500, the Hang Seng Index, and the FTSE 100 had fallen by 20%, 32.4%, 26.2%, 9.4%, and 21.4% respectively. During the roadshows, the five indices plummeted by 14.5%, 8.9%, 14.3%, 4.4%, and 11.27%. On July 19, the last day of the roadshows, the Dow Jones Industrial Average plunged by 390 points, aggravating the market environment. Faced with the complex market conditions, BOC's teams visited more than 750 institutional investors in the 16 financial centers of 11 countries within 11 days to make a final pitch for the IPO.

In the most important Hong Kong market, BOC carried out one-to-one conversations with institutional investors and received support from local businessmen, including Li Ka-shing, Lee Shau-kee, Henry Fok, Robert Kuok, and Walter Kwok. To ensure the success of its IPO, BOCHK joined forces with Hong Kong's largest banks (including HSBC, Bank of East Asia, and Standard Chartered) in offering its shares to retail investors. Partnership with large banks further increased investors' confidence. The persistent drizzle during the offering period did not dampen investors' enthusiasm at all. For many days in a row, retail investors stood, undeterred by the rain, in a long queue stretching over 100 meters to subscribe for BOCHK shares.

(IV) Success Beyond Expectations

BOC's hard work paid off. By the end of the roadshows on July 19, 2002, share subscription by international investors totaled USD 18.8 billion, giving an overall subscription ratio of 7.5 and an oversubscription ratio of 26.5 in Hong Kong's retail market. BOCHK's IPO became the first successful major public offering in international markets that year, and was also the largest one in Asia since October 2000 and the third largest one in the world in 2002. On July 25, 2002, BOCHK was listed on the Hong Kong Stock Exchange[1] – a milestone success in the experimental stage of the joint-stock reform of state-owned banks.

Vice Premier Wen Jiabao personally congratulated BOCHK on its success. "BOCHK has worked tirelessly for its IPO and listing. It has achieved remarkable results under challenging market conditions and gained experience for the joint-stock reform and listing of SOCBs," wrote Wen Jiabao, "but we should remember that BOCHK's success is only the first step on the road to reform, restructuring, and listing. More difficult challenges lie ahead, particularly those related to internal operation and management. We must remain sober-minded and cannot become conceited or impetuous. We must continue to work hard for a new chapter in the reform and development of Chinese banks."

As pointed out by Wen Jiabao, the listing of BOCHK shares on the Hong Kong Stock Exchange only signaled that BOCHK had passed the "entrance exam." The success of its reform depended on whether its shares would stand the test of time and market by continuing to perform well after the IPO. Subsequent development of BOCHK proved the success

---

1　The company was listed as BOCHK Holdings.

of its reform. (i) Its asset quality steadily improved. At the time of IPO, BOCHK had an NPL ratio (after the divestiture of NPLs) of 8%; despite its promise of additional and rapid improvement, many investors remained unconvinced. BOCHK's data proved the promise was kept, showing that its NPL ratio was declining steadily for three consecutive years after listing, to less than 3% in 2005, and the bank's asset quality outperformed that of its Hong Kong peers. (ii) BOCHK enhanced its profit-earning capacity. In 2002, it reported a return on equity (ROE) of 12%, which was below that of its peers. After listing, the ROE rose steadily and reached 18% in 2005, among the highest in the market. (iii) BOCHK's share price climbed. Following its listing, BOCHK saw its share price dip below the issue price at one time due to various factors, but the price started to rebound during the fall of 2003. Commenting on the performance of BOCHK shares, David Chin, Head of UBS Asia Investment Banking, who was involved in the valuation of BOCHK, subsequently said, "In many cases, investment banks take a short-term view on the valuation of a company. They should take a longer view instead. Like other large Chinese SOEs, BOCHK will have a strong execution capability as long as it removes some inherent barriers."[1]

More importantly, BOCHK's joint-stock reform and listing had transformed the bank's operations, enhanced its governance and risk management, and improved its resilience. In May 2003, BOCHK President Liu Jinbao was dismissed and placed under judicial investigation for economic crime. The case also involved three other BOCHK executives. This incident occurred not long after BOCHK's listing and had a major

---

1   From the interview with David Chin on March 1, 2017.

negative impact on BOCHK's operations. However, BOCHK's board of directors – created during its joint-stock reform and listing – played a pivotal role in stabilizing the situation. With strong support from independent directors, BOCHK brought its management system back into order and avoided business stagnation. Despite its materiality, the Liu Jinbao incident could not shake the foundation of BOCHK's operations, which fully demonstrated the strengths of the new corporate design.

(V) Significance of BOCHK's Restructuring and Listing

Under the leadership of the CPC Central Committee and the State Council and the guidance and support of relevant government agencies, BOCHK (BOCHKMR) successfully completed its restructuring and listing and fundamentally transformed its operational framework. The listing had placed BOCHK under more rigorous regulatory oversight and market discipline, which improved its risk management, internal controls, and awareness of market competition; accelerated the transformation of its corporate structure, management mechanisms, and operating mindset; and raised its competitiveness in Hong Kong and international markets. BOCHK's restructuring and listing marked a milestone in China's banking history and set a precedent for the listing of state-owned banks through large-scale restructuring and overseas capital markets. More importantly, this success contributed greatly to the overall joint-stock reform of state-owned banks.

For one, it proved the feasibility of the joint-stock reform and listing of state-owned banks. Under highly adverse conditions, BOCHK worked hard to win the approval of capital markets and investors. It showed that despite the challenging missions posed by the reform, state-owned banks stood a good chance of achieving success if they duly improved their performance and meet market standards. The successful IPO and listing of BOCHK enhanced the central decision makers' confidence and resolve to help state-owned banks rebuild their operation and development frameworks through joint-stock reform and listing.

Second, the success highlighted the urgency of re-engineering the governance and management systems of state-owned banks. Most of the challenges faced by BOCHK in its restructuring and listing as well as in post-listing operation and development, including the legal battles and NPAs, stemmed from unsound governance system or lax management practices. Thanks to improved governance and risk controls, BOCHK ultimately won the acceptance by investors. The experience of BOCHK provided an important lesson for the joint-stock reform of state-owned banks: reshaping organizational, governance, and risk management systems should and had to be a top priority. In particular, the banks' governance frameworks had to be overhauled. The banks had to benchmark against other modern banks and establish a proper governance framework, comprehensive risk management system, and strict internal controls; reform their management and business procedures; increase management transparency; and standardize accounting practices.

Third, the success proved the necessity of policy support. During its restructuring and listing, BOCHK sought assistance from BOC head office and relevant ministries and commissions in disposing of its NPAs and replenishing its capital. Without such external support, it would be impossible for BOCHK to complete the restructuring and listing and transform its operations within such a short time. The post-IPO performance of

BOCHK showed that those supports would be ultimately beneficial and cost efficient. Therefore, as long as it was possible, preferential policies and resource support for the joint-stock reform of state-owned banks would be both necessary and economical.

In testing the waters for the joint-stock reform of state-owned banks, other state-owned banks had also attempted to tap into foreign capital markets. As early as in 2000, ICBC established ICBC (Asia) Limited ("ICBC (Asia)") by acquiring the Union Bank of Hong Kong. Through ICBC (Asia), ICBC made a backdoor listing in the Hong Kong market and became a pioneer among major state-owned banks in overseas listing. Through a series of successful capital transactions – including the injection of capital into ICBC (Asia) and the follow-on offerings and rights issues of ICBC (Asia) – ICBC transformed ICBC (Asia) from a small bank on the verge of bankruptcy during the Asian financial crisis into a mainstream bank in Hong Kong.

Through their overseas ventures, state-owned banks gained valuable experience for their joint-stock reform and listing, including acquiring a working knowledge of the regulatory and listing rules and practices in overseas markets, of the skills needed to work and compete with international intermediaries, and of the structure and preferences of investors. The joint-stock reform of the two state-owned banks and their successful listing in Hong Kong and other capital transactions won them reputation and influence in overseas capital markets, and enabled investors to obtain a direct and impartial understanding of their operations and development, paving the way for the overseas IPOs of other state-owned banks.

Section V
Release of the Plan
for the Joint-Stock Reform

We will now return to the development of the plan for the comprehensive reform of state-owned banks. As mentioned earlier, discussions on the first draft came to a halt during the consultation stage. Although much of the disagreement was over how to dispose of NPAs, the key point of contention was still who should ultimately cover the losses. Given China's substantial fiscal deficit at the time, a second round of carve-out in the same vein as in 1999 would overstretch state finances. However, as the comprehensive reform was ready to be set in motion, if the question of how the fiscal authority should fund the removal of NPAs continued to drag on, the reform would run into a dead end. For this reason, it was imperative for the leadership to work out a plan that would not excessively rely on the fiscal resources, so as to ensure smooth advancement of the joint-stock reform.

I. A Report to the State Council

November 8, 2002 saw the opening of the 16th CPC National Congress. Drawing lessons from the reform of the economic system since the previous Congress, the 16th Congress formulated an overall strategy for advancing the reform. The top priority was still the reform of SOEs. In particular, the report delivered at the Congress wrote that "except for a tiny number of enterprises that must be funded solely by the state, all the others should adopt the joint-stock ownership structure to develop the mixed ownership economy," affirming the goal of the joint-stock reform and highlighting its necessity. The directives of the Congress bolstered state-owned banks' confidence and sense of urgency in pushing forward a comprehensive reform centered on the joint-stock transformation.

Following the Congress, there was a change of leadership at various government departments. In December 2002, CSRC Chairman Zhou Xiaochuan was appointed Governor of the PBOC, and ABC President Shang Fulin assumed Zhou's mantle to forge ahead with the reform of the capital market. In March 2003, then President of BOC Liu Mingkang was appointed Chairman of the CBRC. These changes were aimed at strengthening regulatory leadership. With them, the personnel for advancing the joint-stock reform of state-owned banks were now in place.

Once again, the PBOC was instructed to develop a financial restructuring plan for state-owned banks. Having gained valuable experiences from various leadership positions, Zhou was back to his familiar position at the central bank. At the same time, the critical task of improving the reform plan or, to be more exact, the financial restructuring plan, fell to him and his team. As Zhou recalled, as soon as he took office as Governor of the PBOC, he perceived the emphasis and urgency that members of the State Council had placed on the reform of state-owned banks. As soon as Zhou took office, Vice Premier Huang Ju asked the PBOC to promptly draw up a feasible plan for the reform of state-owned banks.

Zhou had an in-depth understanding of the circumstances surrounding the reform. In the 1990s, he had suggested state-owned banks to embrace market-based operations through joint-stock reform and financing from the capital market. And thanks to experiences gained from his CCB presidency, during which he led the research efforts on NPA disposal and debt-for-equity swaps, and from his years as Chairman of the CSRC, where he supported BOCHK's restructuring and listing, Zhou had become intimately familiar with the bottlenecks in the banking reform and had been mulling over a way out. He did not see the PBOC's previous plan for the carve-out of RMB 970 billion of NPLs as a nonstarter – in fact, he was mostly in agreement. For the point of contention – the source of funds to dispose of NPAs and to recapitalize banks – Zhou believed an alternative solution was needed. Moreover, to convince the stakeholders, he suggested adjusting the framework for the plan to make it more feasible, complete, and rigorous.

After the target had been clarified, the PBOC set out to draft a new plan without delay. Zhou believed that for the most controversial and critical issue – the disposal of NPAs – the PBOC should work with the MOF. Though fiscal resources were off-limits, the problem could not be resolved without fiscal support. Zhou thus decided to adjust the plan, such that the PBOC would shoulder most of the responsibilities but the MOF would offer additional support. Of course, questions like whether the MOF would consent to this idea and what type of support it could offer, were to be further discussed with the MOF.

Communication with the MOF had to be conducted based on clear and mutually recognized understandings. While the new plan was being drafted, Zhou and his team frequently visited the MOF to negotiate with Minister Jin Renqing and Vice Minister Lou Jiwei. The PBOC agreed to secure funds for the restructuring elsewhere but insisted that the MOF provide other forms of support. After the disagreement over fiscal funding was settled, the discussions became much more productive.

In the end, the MOF agreed to support the reform of state-owned banks in three ways. First, allowing the banks to write off asset losses according to accounting standards and supporting them to accelerate the disposal with their own funds. Second, supporting the banks to find a solution for the mismanaged pension, healthcare, and housing benefits programs, so as to alleviate employee anxieties during the reform. Third, providing the banks with necessary tax breaks for the write-off, disposal, and carve-out of NPAs to reduce their financial costs. Though the MOF did not directly allocate fiscal funds for disposal of the NPAs, these support policies gave the banks the latitude they needed to develop a viable disposal plan, and made it technically feasible for the banks to shed their historical burdens in other innovative ways.

By reaching a consensus with the MOF on major issues, the PBOC eliminated the largest uncertainty and sped up the plan drafting process thereafter. Before the annual meetings of the National People's Congress and Chinese People's Political Consultative Conference (*lianghui*, "two sessions") in 2003, the framework for the new plan took shape. The PBOC delivered a presentation to Wen Jiabao, member of the Standing Committee of the Central Political Bureau. Wen immediately decided to convene a special meeting to discuss the plan after the sessions.

However, the road to success was strewn with setbacks. Shortly after the two sessions, SARS broke out in Beijing, which led to postponement of discussions on the new plan. Nonetheless, both the central leadership and those in charge of the development of the plan, including Zhou, were eager to see the reform through.

(I) New Framework for the Reform of State-Owned Banks

By mid-May 2003, SARS had been put under control in Beijing. Wen Jiabao – now the Premier – decided to discuss the plan for the reform of state-owned banks at once. On the morning of May 19, in the State Council's Meeting Room 3 in Zhongnanhai, Wen chaired a small meeting. The meeting was attended by Huang Ju, Vice Premier in charge of finance; Jin Renqing, Minister of Finance; Yan Haiwang, Secretary of the Party Committee at the newly unveiled CBRC; and Liu Mingkang, Chairman of the CBRC. On behalf of the PBOC, Governor Zhou Xiaochuan, Deputy Governor Wu Xiaoling, and Director of the Financial Stability Bureau Xie Ping each delivered a report at the meeting. In particular, Zhou presented the latest reform plan which was carefully crafted by his team.

Despite its brevity, the plan laid out a complete framework for the reform and carried with it the hope of state-owned banks of a rebirth. The plan covered seven aspects.

1. Approach of reform and cost analysis

The plan began with a macro-level discussion of the reform of state-owned banks and proposed a theoretical framework for the initiative.

First, the plan explained the necessity of the reform. It noted that NPAs were the largest financial risk and that the financial restructuring of NPL-ridden state-owned banks would require tremendous resources and dictate the central bank's agenda and policies in the following five years. Revolving around the functions of the central bank, the plan underscored the significance of addressing the issues facing the state-owned banks. Specifically, if the country's major financial institutions were struggling, transmission of monetary policies would be impossible, which means that the central bank would be unable to fulfill its key mandate – keeping the economy stable and the real economy healthy. Hence, to strengthen macroeconomic control, reform of state-owned banks needed to take priority. By stressing the importance of the reform from a macroeconomic perspective, the PBOC was also sending the message that state-owned banks would not be able to conduct the reform without necessary support from the state.

Second, the plan proposed a set of crucial concepts – national balance sheet, fiscal balance sheet, and banking balance sheet – which were crucial because they implied other, non-fiscal means of addressing the financial woes of state-owned banks. As the plan pointed out, at the macro-level, the reform of state-owned banks could be boiled down to the restructuring of the three balance sheets. "The national balance sheet consists of foreign reserves, state-owned capital, potential pension fund assets, and the like," said Zhou, "if the fiscal balance sheet has no available resources, state-owned banks may draw on the national balance sheet to carry out their reform."

In the section that explained how to use the national balance sheet to address the financial predicament of state-owned banks, the plan was essentially analyzing the cost of reform. Generally, there are two accounting methods to report revenues and expenses: accrual basis and cash basis. Under the accrual basis, revenues and expenses are reported in the period in which they incur; under the cash basis, they are recognized when cash is received or paid out. According to China's accounting standard for enterprises at the time, enterprises adopted the accrual basis, whereas administrative agencies followed the cash basis. This difference led to a timing difference in the accounts, which could be taken advantage of by the cost-sharing plan for the reform.

Specifically, with the cash basis, certain costs of reform incurred in an accounting period might not have to be fully paid out in that period, but could instead be disbursed through several future installments and accounted for as such. In this case, costs and losses would not be immediately reflected on the balance sheet of the accounting entity, thereby lessening its burdens. Meanwhile, for state-owned banks which adopted the accrual basis, the carve-out of NPLs would immediately improve their balance sheets, while the liquidation, disposal, and recovery of NPLs could be carried out according to a more relaxed timetable, affording them a relatively generous amount of time to reduce NPLs at their own initiative and pace. In other words, the heart of this strategy was to give state-owned banks the time to resolve the NPLs themselves. Like the MOF, the PBOC operated on the cash basis, enabling it to address the cost of reform more actively through its balance sheet. By taking advantage of the timing difference in the accounts, the cost of reform could be deferred to a certain extent, such that no additional burden would be imposed on the state finance.

Yet, this strategy was not without flaws. First, tinkering with the balance sheet could very well trigger inflation. Second, the cost of reform could not be deferred indefinitely, and ultimately had to be borne by the banks themselves. Consequently, the effectiveness of this strategy hinged squarely on ensuring the banks could reach the expected performance levels following the reform. The PBOC was aware of this, and in the plan it stressed that timing and pace was everything.

"Timing" referred to the short period of low inflation rate and high interest rate spread. From 2000 to 2002, China had a very low rate of inflation and even a decline in the consumer price index. This meant that any adjustment to the central bank's balance sheet would have a minor impact on the economy. Also in 2002, the benchmark one-year interest spread was a high 3.33%. If this could be sustained, state-owned banks would have a reasonable prospect of achieving higher profit, which would also supply more capital to fuel the reform. "Pace" meant that the reform plan should be unveiled in phases and that the cost of reform should be spread out over time to smooth out the impact on stakeholders.

Thirdly, the plan analyzed the resources available to the reform. The plan identified four types of resources – fiscal resources, state-owned assets, as well as the central bank's balance sheet and foreign reserves – and evaluated the availability of each.

The conditions at the time made it difficult to leverage fiscal resources. Due to the sluggish real economy (the state-owned sector in particular), fiscal revenues had only accounted for a small part of the GDP since the mid-1990s. Even by 2002, that percentage was only 18%, making it impractical for the reform to continue to rely on fiscal revenues. Similarly, because the split-share structure reform (*guquan fenzhi gaige*) was yet to be implemented and China's stock market was bearish, the conditions were not ripe for investing the state-owned shares of public companies or other forms of state-owned assets to push forward the reform.

The third option was the central bank's balance sheet. Because the balance sheet includes a variety of line items, it could be expanded in a number of ways. However, it was not appropriate to repeat the feat of 1999 by once again relying on central bank loans. This was because first, such loans would not give the central bank the equity in the banks. And second, such loans were already extensively used, and their low interest rate and long turnover period were at odds with the movement toward a market-driven financial system.

Lastly, the plan analyzed the foreign reserves held by the central bank, proposing – for the first time ever – to use them to fund the joint-stock reform. Foreign reserves offered three benefits. First, as foreign trade and export grew, China had over USD 280 billion in foreign reserves by the end of 2002, or RMB 2.3 trillion at the prevailing exchange rate. This amount was sufficient to support the reform. Second, because the reserves are the central bank's own assets, there would be much less resistance to the reform compared with scenarios where fiscal resources were involved. Third, using the foreign reserves would not cause inflation as long as they were not converted into the home currency, minimizing the adverse effect.

After giving a thorough comparison, Zhou recommended funding the reform with either an expansion of the central bank's balance sheet or the foreign reserves.

Related Topic: The Theoretical Reasoning Behind Using Central Bank's Balance Sheet to Fund the Reform of State-Owned Banks[1]

Whether the expansion of a central bank's balance sheet will result in more money in circulation depends on the particular circumstances. Such an expansion may be carried out in two ways. One is to increase both assets and liabilities at the same time without causing any abnormal change in cash in circulation (M0, which comprises a liability for the central bank), i.e., minimum increase in money supply. For example, if M0 needs to increase by 10% annually to keep pace with economic growth, and the 10% growth rate is maintained after accounting for the expansion of central bank's balance sheet, then no inflation will be directly created because no excessive money is created. The other option is to buy more assets by printing more money. This additional money supply will be put into circu-

---

1 From Zhou Xiaochuan: "Debates Surrounding Bailout During the Financial Crisis," *Journal of Financial Research*, 2012 (9). Though this paper focuses on the bailout of financial institutions after the sub-prime mortgage crisis, it offers a theoretical analysis of how the central bank may use its balance sheet to bail out banks. The same line of reasoning was applied in the solution to the high cost of the joint-stock reform.

lation and create notable inflation. As illustrated above, these two methods are different in their effect.

There is another question to be answered. Liquidity injected into the market by a central bank are liabilities, and will be converted into other forms of liabilities of the central bank when the central bank switches to a contractionary policy. But whose liabilities are they? In any case, they remain the liabilities of the central bank to – most often – commercial banks and other financial institutions which, as market intermediaries, ultimately have obtained their funds from customers, particularly from the household sector. If so, will the household sector eventually demand the liabilities be honored and withdraw the resulting money? And will the liabilities, once so honored, result in excess liquidity? If the answer is yes, it would mean that while inflation may be avoided at the moment, it would become inevitable on a longer time scale.

Of course, for implementing a bailout that is of immediate concern, it is both necessary and expedient to take certain actions, which at least will prevent the spread and worsening of the crisis, alleviate the pressure created by the expansion of the monetary base, and avert an immediate inflation. This will win time for an economic and financial recovery. Later, the central bank may contract its balance sheet and reduce its liabilities by selling off assets in its possession and thus truly rein in the liquidity previously injected into the market. In this regard, China has past experience to rely on. One example is the reform of SOCBs. By injecting capital with its foreign reserves, China's central bank had successfully advanced the reform.

On the basis of past experience, if the central bank were to expand its balance sheet during the bailout, it should: (i) restructure its liabilities to withdraw the excess liquidity created from the bailout, so as to prevent inflation; and (ii) embrace dynamic and long-term adjustment, so as to help the country overcome the crisis and revitalize its economy, while also eliminating the long-term risk of inflation. Inflation may be unavoidable and may even be alarmingly high in the early years of economic recovery. But it must be brought down in later years, such that in the medium and long term, the money supply is commensurate with the economic growth.

2. Nature and steps of restructuring

The plan offered a basic framework for the restructuring of state-owned banks.

It used CCB to illustrate the essential points to be considered during the restructuring. CCB was used as an example because it had a capital of RMB 120 billion and, under the five-category classification scheme, an NPL ratio of 15%, which meant it was the best among the Big Four in terms of asset quality. Although CCB had posted significant non-credit losses, around one-third of these were off-the-book losses from the government-arranged takeover of the ill-fated China Agribusiness Development Trust and Investment Corporation (CADTIC). On the whole, CCB had relatively light "historical baggage."

In light of the state of CCB, the plan proposed a four-step restructuring scheme. First, to the extent practicable, write off unrecoverable losses against existing capital. Second, strip off doubtful and substandard loans. This could be accomplished by expanding the central bank's balance sheet, specifically by transferring a portion of CCB's NPLs at market price (appraised value) to the PBOC, which would raise the money required by issuing bills. The difference between the book value of remaining NPLs balance and the consideration paid by the PBOC for the doubtful and substandard loans would be losses to be recognized by CCB. Third, leverage the central bank's balance sheet again by injecting foreign reserves into CCB to substantially boost its capital adequacy ratio. Fourth, support CCB in raising funds through the issuance of stocks and subordinated debts to push its capital adequacy ratio above the minimum regulatory requirement of 8%. In fact, because external audits might reveal additional NPLs and the Basel Committee on Banking Supervision might raise the minimum requirement during this period, a comfortable buffer above the minimum was required.

The plan further explained the critical steps of the restructuring. It noted that the central idea behind the four-step scheme was to inject foreign reserves into CCB, which would be the critical link between writing off the bank's losses and allowing it to raise capital through an IPO. Without it, the plan would not work. However, there were two issues about the injection that needed to be resolved. First, although the PBOC had accumulated a sizeable amount of foreign reserves, that amount was far from sufficient for a nation the size of China. To ensure the stability of the economy and trade, whatever amount used in the injection needed to be replenished. Second, because CCB primarily operated in the Chinese mainland, it had to gradually convert all but a certain amount of the foreign currency it held into renminbi.

For these reasons, this scheme also needed to consider the "back conversion" of renminbi following the injection. Moreover, conversion of foreign currencies was likely to lead to a larger monetary base and thus inflation. To address these issues, the plan proposed four countermeasures. First, to meet the requirements that bank capital had to be denominated in renminbi, following the injection, CCB would be permitted to gradually sell its foreign currencies in the interbank market over a certain period. Second, the central bank should buy such foreign currencies to restore its reserves. Third, to deal with both issues, after the injection, the PBOC might require CCB to deposit the injected funds in the central bank at a certain interest rate. In this way, the central bank would have the same amount of available foreign reserves before and after the injection, whereas CCB would be able to earn interest on the foreign-currency capital. Fourth, based on the inflation rate, the central bank might relax the requirement for deposit of foreign currencies and take other measures to offset the effect of currency exchange on inflation.

These measures would later enable CCB to hold the majority of its capital in renminbi, and enable the central bank, after buying back the foreign currencies it had injected, to substantially restore its foreign reserves. Since the central bank's foreign reserves would not be significantly reduced by the injection, the cost of the reform could be deferred and minimized as originally envisioned.

Of course, the reform also needed to be supported by other policies. For instance, China's entry into the WTO was followed by rising calls for exchange rate reform. According to the trade situation at that time, liberalization of exchange rate would inevitably lead to appreciation of renminbi and, in turn, losses upon conversion of foreign reserves, offsetting the effect of the injection to some extent. The PBOC had taken this issue into account in making its plans, but it was kept off the meeting agenda because the issue was more related to the most optimal sequence of reform initiatives at the national level.

In the final discussion on the feasibility of injecting capital with foreign reserves, the plan suggested that given its sizeable foreign exchange business, BOC might need to retain more foreign currency capital if it were to be restructured. Though being little more than a footnote to the above-mentioned measures, this suggestion was of particular significance. While using CCB as an example, the plan also took a quick detour to touch upon BOC, indicating that the central bank had already considered adding BOC into the list of pilot banks.

The plan also covered the methods for capital injection. It proposed to diversify the investing entities, that is, the PBOC would also inject foreign reserves into those healthy state-owned financial institutions that were competent at managing investment and financing activities, and these institutions would in turn invest in state-owned banks. This operation was designed for two purposes. First, by making various state-owned financial institutions the shareholders of state-owned banks, the plan helped improve the equity structure and corporate governance of the banks. Second, since 1999, China's foreign reserves had been growing rapidly. Foreign countries thus watched closely China's utilization of foreign reserves and made great efforts to track down related information. Allowing more institutions to participate in the capital injection would help disperse the associated risks and secure a stable return on investment.

In addition, the plan analyzed the feasibility of replicating this scheme, that is, would it only work for CCB and BOC, or could it be equally effective for other state-owned banks and even financial institutions? In fact, even during the plan's formative stages, the PBOC had already presented its key ideas to Huang Ju, who was very concerned about the general applicability of the plan and asked the PBOC to address this question directly in the plan.

In the plan the PBOC offered an affirmative answer to the question for three reasons. First, the bulk of foreign currencies injected could be bought back through the market, so that the injection would have no significant impact on the total amount of foreign reserves, which could then be used to support the reform of other state-owned banks. Second, the injection, conducted by drawing on the central bank's balance sheet, wouldn't require the use of fiscal resources. Third, low inflation as well as deposit reserve ratio and other potent monetary tools at the central bank's disposal would ensure that the impacts of the injection on money supply and prices would be controllable.

3. Estimated effects and policy support

The first two sections of the plan were all about analyzing the cost of the reform and how it would be met. But because the ultimate goal was to improve the performance of state-owned banks, concrete estimates of the potential returns were also needed. Under the assumption that there would be no significant changes in market environment, the plan calculated that the reform would enable CCB to achieve a pre-tax profit of RMB 30 billion and an after-tax profit of RMB 20-23 billion each year. After distribution of dividends, the remaining profits would turn into additional capital, the annual amount of which would even allow the bank to cover the additional demands for capital arising from asset expansion, thus preventing a sharp decline in the bank's capital adequacy ratio. Even if there was a small capital shortfall, CCB could raise additional funds from the capital market following the reform. This meant that the central bank could divest from CCB by selling its equities in the bank to other state-owned asset management institutions or in the market.

The outcome of the reform was predicated on the assumption that there was no material change in major market conditions. Among them, a vital factor was the interest rate, which was mostly under the PBOC's control. In 2002, expectations for the liberalization of interest rates had already been high, and the PBOC had also identified interest rate liberalization as a core measure to heighten the macroeconomic effect of monetary policies. Yet, interest rate volatility arising from the liberalization would adversely affect the reform of state-owned banks. The PBOC therefore needed to take the potential effects of interest rate into account. Accordingly, the plan required the central bank to maintain a stable interest spread for a certain period to ensure that the reform would produce the desired outcomes.

Stable interest spread would help state-owned banks reverse the steady decline in their capital adequacy ratios, sustain an upward profitability trajectory, and accumulate more capital to self-absorb a larger amount of NPLs. From a macroeconomic perspective, in a period when China had sluggish consumption growth and a high savings rate, the low cost of capital would spur consumption and investment. Moreover, a stable interest spread would help the banking system retain more profits, compensating the state-owned banks for the cost of economic reform and allowing domestic banks to recover from the Asian financial crisis. On the basis of these considerations, the plan suggested that during the reform of state-owned banks, China should relax control on the minimum and maximum interest rates while maintaining a stable interest spread.

4. Carve-out and disposal of NPAs

Although the plan devoted merely one page to analyze the disposal of NPAs, it offered fresh ideas about how this issue could be tackled. Specifically, the plan noted that while it was imperative that state-owned banks dispose of their mounting NPLs, it should not be done in the same manner as in 1999, because disposal at book value was not ideal but it was the "only choice under the difficult circumstances of the time."[1] Repeating the same approach now might create moral hazard – state-owned banks might be tempted to offload assets that they could otherwise recover, incurring unnecessary losses. By contrast, if the banks offloaded their NPLs at market value, and booked the resulting losses against capital (or resolved the NPLs by other methods mentioned earlier), their accounts would be more or less balanced without creating additional burden on the state.

5. Policy support from the central bank and the fiscal authority

The PBOC's restructuring plan was mainly based on the use of its balance sheet. However, to ensure legal compliance, efficiency, and effectiveness, three types of supporting measures also needed to be in place. First, as the monetary authority, the PBOC could not directly hold corporate equities. If foreign reserves were injected into state-owned banks, the State Administration of Foreign Exchange (SAFE) should designate an investment entity to take part in the corporate governance of the banks for a period of time. "For a period of time" means that the investment entity affiliated to the central bank would exit at the appropriate time rather than holding the banks' equity on a long-term basis. Second, for the disposal of NPAs, the PBOC intended to establish a wholesale AMC that would be in charge of handling legal affairs and bundling bank assets. Third, the PBOC planned to counteract potential inflation with more liberal use of asset-backed securities. Meanwhile, the PBOC also planned to reform the deposit reserve system. The system – though seldom used internationally – still had value in China. In particular, flexible instruments including special re-

---

1   Quote from an official who helped design the plan.

serves as well as measures armed with greater incentives and sanctions could raise the efficiency of using the deposit reserves and motivate the banks.

Though the PBOC claimed that the new reform plan would not cause additional fiscal burden, the reform of state-owned banks was closely related to the fiscal authority and could not be completely set apart from it. The plan therefore suggested offering necessary fiscal policy support in two aspects. First, enhancing existing policies. In 1998, the MOF injected funds into state-owned banks for the first time by issuing to them interest-free special government bonds. If the state-owned banks went public following the joint-stock reform, their non-interest-bearing assets might be deemed as NPAs according to international accounting standards. For this reason, the plan proposed to set a definite interest rate on the special government bonds. Moreover, during the first round of disposal of NPLs in 1999, AMCs raised RMB 820 billion from bond issue. The fiscal authority should provide greater guarantee on the repayment of these bonds to avoid potential write-downs under international accounting rules.

Second, improving existing policies. In consideration of the two key factors determining the success of the reform – disposal of NPAs and profitability of banks – the plan noted that the policies governing loan loss provisioning and write-off should be adjusted according to international practices, but if the universal application of this adjustment was for the moment untenable, whichever bank that pursued the reform would be approved on a case-by-case basis to set aside sufficient allowances for potential loan losses and write off NPAs according to their particular conditions. Another suggestion was to lower the business tax rate for financial enterprises.

6. Subsequent arrangements and risk assessment

The plan outlined the arrangements for restructured state-owned banks to go public. First, raising sufficient funds. The plan suggested that the banks should adopt a "dual double-insurance" strategy – offering shares through public offering and private placement in both domestic and overseas markets. Private placement was added due to uncertainty in the banks' public offerings; the overseas market was included in view of market capacity and BOC's successful listing in Hong Kong. Second, ensuring no capital shortfall. To that end, the plan proposed to create a new fund. Third, expediting the listing of state-owned banks. The plan set out a schedule consisting of completing recapitalization and restructuring of banks by 2003, preparing for IPO during 2004-2005, and public listing when timing was favorable. Fourth, initiating external audit as soon as possible. This was emphasized as audit is a time-consuming process that would also be the prerequisite to many other tasks.

In his article "How Should State-Owned Commercial Banks Replenish Their Capital"[1] published in 2000, Zhou Xiaochuan had considered the means by which state-owned banks could be listed: "Banks should raise capital in both domestic and foreign capital markets from the retail and institutional investors as well as from special-purpose investment funds," showing that the listing plan, including the part about the "dual double-insurance" strategy and the investment funds, had been long in the making.

Because reform always carries risks, the plan assessed key risks that

---

1 Zhou Xiaochuan: "How Should State-Owned Commercial Banks Replenish Their Capital," *People's Daily*, May 9, 2000.

might arise from the restructuring and subsequent listing of state-owned banks and identified six risks that required special attention and early responses. First, risk from operation of the pilot program. Given the size of the resources needed, it would be cost-efficient to select one pilot bank before instituting the reform of other banks. At the same time, the plan noted that if the pilot program included one bank only, the listed bank, without peers to compete with, was likely to rely on the resources from the state and be less motivated to advance the reform. Though only CCB was mentioned as an example, the plan suggested selecting two pilot banks, in a bid to let competitive rivalry drive both banks to achieve success, or at least ensure that one of them would.

Second, inflation risk. Because the risk might occur throughout the restructuring and listing of state-owned banks, the plan had proposed corresponding countermeasures.

Third, risk associated with the reform of personnel systems. This type of risk consisted of conflicts arising from the streamlining of institutions and employees as well as potential risks brought by post-restructuring and listing adjustments to personnel under new governance structures.

Fourth, the risk of negative public reaction. Exposure of state-owned banks' NPAs and financial difficulties had planted the seeds of endless debate over the reform. Having foreseen the responses, internal and external, to the joint-stock reform, the plan noted that a hostile public opinion might significantly hinder the reform and urged the banks to work out response strategies in advance.

Fifth, the risk of compromises and inefficiency from combining different ideas. The joint-stock reform of state-owned banks was without precedent. As such, no one could say for certain that any single plan would work and it was likely that many alternatives would be proposed. Accordingly, the authorities should work to prevent the different proposals from coalescing into a potpourri of inherently incompatible ideas that would complicate future decision-making and diminish the efficiency of the reform.

Sixth, risk from external audit. To align with international rules and promote greater transparency, the restructuring and listing of state-owned banks must involve international professional auditors. However, a comprehensive audit of the operation of state-owned banks according to international accounting standards might reveal new problems. Banks should therefore develop a contingency plan to cope with the potential impact of such unexpected risks on their restructuring and listing.

The plan also assessed the prospects for further reform, that is, following the reform of the two pilot banks, whether the reform could be rolled out in other state-owned banks. Upon analysis, the plan concluded that as long as inflation was reined in, the four-step reform would also work for other state-owned banks.

7. International experience and domestic context

The reform of state-owned banks is a complex undertaking and there were no established models to draw experience from. Venturing into the unknown was likely to lead to extensive arguments over the reform plan which could sway decision-making. The new plan proposed many novel ideas that were as brilliant as they were likely to be used as ammunition against the plan itself. Creators of the plan worried about dogmatic interference the most – that stakeholders would rather maintain the status quo than embrace an innovative reform plan which had no precedent and carried plenty of potential risks.

To convince the stakeholders, the plan dealt with the following three questions. First, was it possible to find relevant theories and practices from textbooks to guide the reform of state-owned banks? Zhou Xiaochuan said that he had consulted many textbooks, which explained the conventional use of fiscal and monetary policies – that is, the restructuring of financial institutions was all funded by fiscal authorities – but seldom mentioned the restructuring of ailing banks. The implied conclusion was that the reform of state-owned banks could not be guided by textbooks.

Second, should international precedents, assuming they even existed, be transplanted to China's state-owned banks? Given the varying local conditions, such as the binding power of a legislature (NPC or parliament) over the central bank, ownership of foreign reserves, and different inflation rates, different countries may adopt different measures to address the same issue. As a result, the banks needed to adapt established precedents, if any, to their particular conditions in an innovative way.

Third, what determined the success of a reform? To answer this question, the plan cited the failed financial reform of Japan as an example. Similar to China's state-owned banks, Japanese banks had also been plagued by a serious NPL problem which, despite various efforts, remained tenacious and continued to frustrate any progress in the banking industry. This tenacity was due to the ineffective restructuring of the banking system, which in turn was caused by incessant arguing among the stakeholders which, in the end, only created a series of short-lived reform plans that were on the whole ineffective. The lesson here is that though a sound plan is needed for a successful reform, what matters more is resolve and implementation.

In the end, the plan discussed how to handle major relations in connection with the reform.

First, balancing of interests. The reform, involving major public interests, might elicit different responses from various stakeholders, and thus needed to be implemented in a way that was mindful of everyone's interests. Moreover, because the reform involved attracting private capital and pursuing an overseas listing, international investors needed to be convinced to invest in the banks. As a result, investors' confidence in the application of domestic and international policies should also be boosted.

Second, relations with overseas regulators and investors. To be listed overseas, state-owned banks had to satisfy foreign regulators' requirements and bring in foreign investors, and convince them to accept the reform plan. For instance, stakeholders in Europe and the U.S. originally insisted that China adopt the Soviet and East European models of banking reform, because they believed China was not capable of undertaking such a reform on its own and must rely on foreign funds and foreign banks. If China took this "advice," its banks would in the end be controlled by foreign investors. Furthermore, if the banks were to go public in Hong Kong, they must consider the possible responses from regulators and investors. If any difference of opinion threatened to hinder the reform, the banks would be on the hook to persuade the other party of their point of view.

Third, relations with the academia. The reform created extensive debates and misgivings within the academia. The banks needed to build consensus among the academics given their influence.

Fourth, relations with other entities to be reformed. The reform of state-owned banks was but one of the several major reforms at the time. If the limited national resources, such as foreign reserves, were tapped into during the reform of state-owned banks, would other entities compete for the same resources? Decision makers needed to take every consideration into account to ensure that the reform of state-owned banks would continue as planned.

(II) Initial Approval of the Plan

The plan contained many innovations, some of which were ahead of the time. The new analytical framework was also effective in aiding decision-making. In just 19 presentation slides – rather than a detailed written report – the plan outlined the structure of the reform, presenting the novel ideas to the central leadership through a whole new approach.

The meeting was a resounding success. As attendees recalled, Wen Jiabao and Huang Ju listened to the report intently and seldom interrupted the speakers. But upon hearing that the central bank planned to inject foreign reserves into the banks and to hold shares of the banks through an entity[1], they asked which central bank in other countries or regions ever did that, for they worried that the plan would be less convincing to interested parties if there were no precedents outside the Chinese mainland. After they were informed that the Hong Kong Monetary Authority held equity in commercial banks in 1997 and that Japan's central bank also bought bank equities at the end of 2002, their concern was alleviated.

After listening to the report, Wen approved the plan in principle, and the attending heads of ministries and commissions also supported the plan. More encouragingly, Wen and Huang asked that the four-step plan for the joint-stock reform be incorporated into the official document for the Third Plenary Session of the 16th CPC Central Committee, indicating

---

1 Chapter V provides an overview of Central Huijin Investment Ltd. both during and after the joint-stock reform.

that they not only accepted it, but also thought highly of it. The path ahead for the reform thus became clear.

The new plan won wide approval for five reasons.

First, it proposed a creative restructuring model that did not excessively rely on fiscal resources but rather centered on the use of the national balance sheet. As a matter of fact, the idea of leveraging the national balance sheet, especially the central bank's balance sheet, to solve the problems facing the banks had undergone many years of extensive studies. As early as in 1997, after the first National Financial Work Conference concluded, the PBOC had studied how to facilitate the reform of state-owned banks with minimal or zero use of fiscal resources. Back then, however, the concept of national balance sheet was not familiar to the officials of the central bank, until someone found an English textbook on the functions of the fiscal authority and central bank as well as the relations between the two.

Zhou Xiaochuan, then Deputy Governor of the PBOC, learned a great deal from this book and realized that the reform could be directly advanced through the central bank's balance sheet. However, since there was no precedent of using a central bank's balance sheet to address the problems of commercial banks, it was difficult to put the idea into practice. A widely held opinion at the time was that no matter who profited and who suffered in a bank bailout, the cost would be ultimately borne by the state. Thus, another widely held belief was that fiscal funds were the most natural, direct, and effective means to rescue a struggling bank. However, while no one denies that state finances are ultimately footing the bill of a bailout, it does not mean that it is the only solution.

A participant in the drafting of the plan gave an illustrative example of this misconception: "In the past, when discussing productions and services in political economics, some people argued that because ultimately services were rendered and accepted to produce goods, they should be excluded from the national income lest we double count." The line of thinking that would lead one to understand that both production and service should contribute to the national income also led the drafters of the restructuring plan to not overly rely on fiscal resources – because both the fiscal balance sheet and the central bank's balance sheet were part of the national balance sheet and could play a similar function in supporting the reform of state-owned banks. The plan was successful precisely because it made this theoretical breakthrough. As someone said, "Conflicts over the path of reform in essence stem from a difference of analytical frameworks which leads to different conclusions."

Second, it proposed to inject foreign reserves into state-owned banks. This idea was the largest breakthrough at the technical level and was not just the result of a sudden stroke of genius. Since 1999, China's foreign reserves were increasing rapidly each year and the PBOC was considering the most effective way of using them[1]. The innovation in the plan was "connecting the dots" by tapping into those foreign reserves to recapitalize the banks. In effect, the central bank had put idle resources to use, and thus had minimized the cost of reform.

Third, it suggested the second round of disposal of NPLs be conducted at market value. Until state-owned banks had reduced their NPL ratio to a reasonable level and raised their capital adequacy ratio to international standards, it would be extremely difficult for them to attract strategic

---

1 Quoted from Xie Ping's statements between April and October 2012, provided by the Boyuan Economic Research Foundation.

investors, unless the banks were willing to pay exorbitant financing cost. It would be even harder for them to go public, since no investors, domestic or foreign, would be willing to assume a share of the banks' losses that had been incurred previously.

In his book titled *Financial Notes*, Yang Kaisheng mentioned the following options to improve the banks' balance sheet within a short time:

(i) Asking the banks to absorb NPAs on their own using future earnings. This option was feasible in theory, but it meant that the banks could not conduct restructuring and go public in the near term as planned. Saddled with considerable NPAs, state-owned banks would be unable to cope with the challenges brought by greater opening up and ever intensifying competition. Worse, historical issues intertwined with new challenges would make it hard to clarify the responsibilities of banks' management and to put into place accountability for credit asset quality.

(ii) Copying the model used by certain manufacturing enterprises. Under this model, a manufacturing enterprise would set up a corporate group and a joint-stock company, and assign its NPAs to the former and complete IPO with the latter. Yet, this idea overlooked a key difference between banks and typical manufacturing enterprises. During its restructuring, a manufacturing enterprise would often transfer some of its liabilities to the corporate group that was obviously incapable of making repayments, at the same time as transferring the NPAs. This is hardly possible for banks. Because while a joint-stock bank could transfer NPLs to the corporate group, it could not do so with the public deposits. The only solution would be to transfer such deposits as a claim on the corporate group. In this case, when the bank seeks IPO, it must convince investors that it is able to recover the colossal claim, and this is far from easy.

(iii) Removing NPLs from state-owned banks' balance sheet on a one-off basis. This option would completely relieve state-owned banks of their historical burdens, allowing them to get off to a fresh start and establish a new corporate governance system. However, unlike the first round of disposal of NPLs in 1999, during which NPLs were transferred to AMCs at book value, this round of disposal would be conducted at fair value.

Fourth, the plan laid the foundation for introducing modern corporate governance frameworks. While the plan focused on the financial restructuring scheme, in both the design of the four-step reform approach and the mitigation of the risks associated with the restructuring and listing, the goal of establishing a modern corporate governance system for banks was considered. The plan thus put a great premium on compliance with international rules and governance principles and on the importance of creating a sound governance mechanism for the banks through restructuring.

Fifth, the plan struck a fine balance among reform, development, and stability. The plan assessed the benefits, costs, and risks of the reform. For costs and risks, in addition to those in connection with state-owned banks, the plan offered a prudent analysis of social costs and macro risks arising from the reform and proposed countermeasures. In sum, the three factors helped decision makers gain a more comprehensive and direct understanding of the "risk-return profile" of the reform and enabled them to make correct decisions on major issues involved.

II. Follow-Up Discussions and Refinement

As the plan would shape the course of China's economic and financial development, its creation was naturally a long and prudent process. The presentation delivered on May 19, 2003 was only the first step in getting the new plan approved. Having foreseen the problems that might ensue, Wen Jiabao stressed at the meeting that any financial restructuring of state-owned banks that would use major national resources, either the state treasury or the central bank, should be subject to the approval of the National People's Congress (NPC), and that the PBOC should also consult the Legislative Affairs Office of the State Council (LAOSC) about whether any financial restructuring was legally viable. That is to say, before officially releasing the reform plan, the PBOC must run it by various parties for refinement and general consensus. As a result, the PBOC had to set off a new round of discussions and persuasions.

(I) Smooth Communication

As instructed by Wen, the plan needed to be first endorsed by the NPC and the LAOSC. Given the significance and innovativeness of the plan, leaders of the NPC Standing Committee and the LAOSC were cautious in giving their approval. Hence, the PBOC had to make more thorough explanations. Discussions with the LAOSC, mainly focusing on legal issues, soon yielded a result – the LAOSC endorsed the plan. On the other hand, dialogues with the NPC Standing Committee touched upon a much broader range of topics and continued until the end of July 2003. People most heavily involved in these discussions were Liu Jibin and Zhou Zhengqing, both members of the NPC Standing Committee and Deputy Directors of the NPC Financial and Economic Affairs Committee. According to a PBOC official who participated in these discussions, from late July to early August 2003, the relevant heads of the PBOC met with Liu, Zhou, as well as officials of the LAOSC. After exchanges, Liu wrote a letter expressing his support for the plan. Zhou also drafted a report and submitted it to Premier Wen. In the report, Zhou did not object to the plan, but suggested creating a fund for injecting funds into banks, indicating that the proposal of funds injection was acceptable.

In addition to the NPC and the LAOSC, the PBOC sought comment from the Chinese People's Political Consultative Conference (CPPCC). In August 2003, PBOC officials in charge of the plan asked Liu Zhongli, Director of the Committee for Economic Affairs of the CPPCC, for his opinion of the plan. Having served as Minister of Finance and Director of Office of the State Council for Restructuring the Economic System, Liu was well aware of the significance, progress, and challenges of the banking reform. After listening to the PBOC's explanations, he readily endorsed the plan.

The PBOC then reported feedback from the NPC, CPPCC, and LAOSC to Wen Jiabao and Huang Ju, and received their assent. The next step was to prepare for submitting the plan to the Standing Committee of the Political Bureau for consideration. In the interest of prudence, Huang asked the PBOC to report to leaders of the Standing Committee and the State Council individually. However, there were some twists and turns during this process. As recalled by some insiders, while all members of the Standing Committee approved the plan, some leaders of the State Council objected to part of it, especially the capital injection with foreign reserves.

Tens of billions of U.S. dollars would be a colossal sum at any place and time, especially in China shortly after its economic take-off. The objections showed that even among the top decision makers there were still diverging views about the reform. Though these dissenting opinions did not alter the general course of the reform, they still affected certain elements and implementation, notably the selection of the first group of pilot banks for the reform.

(II) Identifying the First Group of Pilot Banks

At the report presentation meeting on May 19, 2003, the plan named CCB and BOC as the pilot banks. However, given the significance of the matter, the meeting did not decide which bank or banks would be included in the pilot program.

Among the Big Four, CCB was the most certain candidate for the first group of banks to participate in the pilot reform. As analyzed in the plan, CCB had a smaller NPL burden and had submitted to the PBOC the plan for the joint-stock reform in February 2003, ahead of all other banks. As a result, if the central leadership finally decided to select only one bank to experiment with the joint-stock reform, CCB was the most likely choice. This also meant that the eligibility of another possible candidate, BOC, remained uncertain, particularly when the decision makers were yet to agree on the cost of reform.

Finally, the central leadership decided to also identify BOC as a pilot bank. Despite increased costs, two pilot banks would offer double insurance, for the reform could not afford to fail. BOC's relative advantages included: smaller size of assets and financial burden; greater internationalization; experiences from BOCHK's restructuring and listing in 2002. Moreover, the bank's preparations for a joint-stock reform started early. At the end of 2002, its head office set up an office for restructuring and listing as well as ten working groups in charge of restructuring and process integration covering strategic planning, IT, human resources, risk control, and operations.

Coincidentally, the plan for the joint-stock reform of BoCom was also finalized during the same period. As early as in 1999, BoCom had attempted to go public through a joint-stock reform, but its plan did not materialize due to lack of financial strength. Yet, the exploration brought the joint-stock reform and listing of BoCom to the central leadership's attention. Before the election of NPC members in 2003, Wen Jiabao consulted CBRC Chairman Liu Mingkang about whether BOC should be included in the first group of pilot banks. After their meeting, Wen told Liu to seek Huang Ju's inputs. During his tenure as Secretary of the CPC Shanghai Municipal Committee, Huang closely followed BoCom's joint-stock reform program. When Liu came to him for his views, Huang asked about the possibility of including BoCom in the joint-stock reform. After analyzing the bank's situation, Liu believed the idea was feasible.

Later, Liu briefed Premier Wen about Huang's suggestion. Liu explained that since BOCHK had been able to complete restructuring and listing, the nimbler BoCom could do the same. Wen accepted Liu's argument and included BoCom as a candidate for pilot banks. However, because of BoCom's different situation compared with the Big Four and the disagreement over the commitment of resources for the joint-stock reform, BoCom adopted a self-funded reform model, which will be discussed later.

In 2003, ICBC also stepped up preparations for the joint-stock reform and restructuring. As Jiang Jianqing, President of ICBC at the time, recalled, after learning that the central leadership decided to launch a pilot program for the joint-stock reform, he felt anxious. He repeatedly requested Huang to include ICBC in the list of the first group of pilot banks and wrote a report to that effect to the central leadership. However, given ICBC's huge asset holdings and heavier NPL burden, if it were to conduct the reform simultaneously with other banks, the state would have to bear a much higher cost. Furthermore, boasting numerous industrial and commercial customers and urban residential customers, ICBC was closely tied with the economy. In this case, if the reform was advanced by multiple banks at the same time, any problem would lead to a shock to the economy. For these considerations, ICBC was not included among the first group of pilot banks.

Because ABC was an integral part of the agricultural industry and had the largest and most complex NPL problem, it was also excluded from the list. After persistent efforts, about one year after the restructuring of CCB and BOC, ICBC's reform plan was approved. ICBC went public only one year after CCB and five months after BOC and could also be recognized as a member of the first group of restructured banks.

(III) Final Touches on the Plan

Because discussions on the plan went smoothly, no significant change was required. This made the revision process much easier. In August 2003, when communication with various parties came to an end, the PBOC had essentially completed the revision, culminating in the "Report on Accelerating the Joint-Stock Reform of Wholly State-Owned Commercial Banks." The Report was to be submitted to the State Council and the Politburo Standing Committee for deliberation.

On September 17, 2003, Premier Wen Jiabao chaired an executive meeting of the State Council to discuss the Report. Because sufficient discussions had been held, consensus had been reached on most matters, and the central leadership had already taken a stand on few controversial issues, the meeting went well and the Report was approved in principle. Wen additionally instructed the PBOC to further revise the Report according to decisions made at the meeting and then submit it to the Politburo Standing Committee for consideration on the following day.

On September 18, 2003, the meeting of the Politburo Standing Committee adopted the banking reform plan in principle, identified CCB and BOC as the pilot banks, and urged the PBOC to complete its injection of funds into the pilot banks by the end of 2003. The Politburo Standing Committee also established a steering group for the joint-stock reform of wholly state-owned commercial banks, led by Huang Ju, to coordinate the reform.

From October 11 to 14, 2003, the Third Plenary Session of the 16th CPC Central Committee was held in Beijing. On October 14, the Session adopted the "Decision of the CPC Central Committee on Issues Concerning the Improvement of the Socialist Market Economic System." The Decision made official the requirement that the pilot program should "select eligible SOCBs to conduct the joint-stock reform" and affirmed the four-step reform approach covering "expediting the disposal of NPLs, replenishing capital, and creating conditions for public listing."

After one year and a half since the first reform plan was drafted in 2002, the plan for the joint-stock reform of state-owned banks was finalized and released. The plan reflected the central leadership's resolve to make state-owned banks stronger, the public's concern for the development of the banks, the stakeholders' vision and wisdom, and the Chinese people's enterprising spirit. It served as guidance for the joint-stock reform of state-owned banks and helped chart out a new future for the banks.

CHAPTER V
LAUNCH OF PILOT REFORM

– Joint-Stock Reforms and IPOs of CCB, BOC, and BoCom

China ushered in its joint-stock reform of state-owned commercial banks at the end of 2003 when the State Council announced BOC and CCB as the first two pilot banks for the program. Supported by policies including capital injection with foreign reserves by the state, they had ultimately made their historic transition to joint-stock banks after revamping their financial structure, disposing of NPAs, reorganizing themselves as joint-stock companies, introducing foreign strategic investors, and completing road-shows and IPOs at home and abroad. During that time, BoCom also made progress in its own joint-stock reform and listing.

Section I
Establishment of Central Huijin and Capital Injection

Following the momentous decision of the Standing Committee of the Political Bureau of the CPC Central Committee, the Steering Group for the Pilot Joint-Stock Reform of Wholly State-Owned Commercial Banks ("State Council Joint-Stock Reform Steering Group") was soon formed to lead the joint-stock reform of the two pilot banks. It comprised Huang Ju as team leader, Hua Jianmin as deputy leader, and members from the PBOC, CBRC, MOF, and other relevant agencies. Its office, named the Joint-Stock Reform Office, was located at the PBOC Financial Stability Bureau and would act as the control center for the reform. Zhou Xiaochuan served as Director of the Office, closely supported by PBOC Assistant Governor Liu Shiyu and Director of the Financial Stability Bureau Xie Ping. The first task before the team was to complete capital injection into BOC and CCB, thus lifting the curtain on the joint-stock reform of state-owned banks.

I. Establishment of Central Huijin

Capital injection with foreign reserves is both a simple and complicated process. It is simple because funds can be transferred electronically in a matter of seconds. It is complicated because Chinese law prevents the PBOC, as an independent monetary policy maker, from directly holding a stake in state-owned banks. The PBOC hence proposed to specifically set up an entity as the intermediary. But deciding the nature and operational framework of that entity was anything but simple. Not only would the legal and policy framework need to be considered, but more importantly, such an entity had to act as an investor on behalf of the state without intervening in the business affairs of state-owned banks. Therefore, the team needed to first develop the foundational and operating rules of the intermediary prior to capital injection.

To inject capital with foreign reserves, the intermediary should be set up by the foreign exchange administrator – the PBOC, which was the natural and only option. But regarding its functions, operations, and management, two different models were proposed.

One was the SASAC model. The State-Owned Assets Supervision and Administration Commission was established in March 2003 as an investor representing the state to manage and supervise state-owned assets. A special-purpose agency of the State Council, SASAC is allowed by law to invest and hold equity interest in SOEs directly. In actual practice, however, for several reasons it does this only indirectly, by using the central state-owned enterprises (*yangqi*) under its management to supervise and manage the SOEs, especially listed ones. Under such a model, the intermediary would not directly participate in the governance of the restructured state-owned banks, and therefore could not fully exercise its rights as an investor. As a result, one goal of the reform – introducing a modern corporate governance system – might be compromised. Therefore, the SASAC model was rejected.

The alternative was the parent company model. Specifically, the PBOC would establish a company to invest and hold equity interest in state-owned banks and thus exercise direct management. This model was proposed by the PBOC in its report on May 19, 2003. Xie Ping recalled that Zhou Xiaochuan had been studying the model for a long time. As early as in 1995, Zhou had the idea of emulating the Eastern European/German model to manage state-owned assets through an entity. This idea was manifested in his plan for establishing asset management companies which he made during his tenure as CCB President. Zhou proposed that a parent company with closer link to the capital market should be established to hold state-owned assets, so that it could directly hold equity and manage SOEs while minimizing administrative intervention.

The establishment of an intermediary involved both theoretical and practical considerations; however, extensive preliminary study of the parent company model convinced the team of its feasibility. The model was adopted. On October 19, 2003, the Joint-Stock Reform Office finalized the plan for implementing the joint-stock reform of BOC and CCB, according to which the Reserves Management Department of SAFE would set up an investment company to inject capital in the banks and manage the capital under the authorization of the State Council. The Office further named the investment company Central Huijin Investment Ltd. in the proposed establishment and operation plan and formulated the "Articles of Association of Central Huijin Investment Ltd." On November 22, 2003, Wen Jiabao, Huang Ju, and Wu Yi[1] approved the Office's "Request for the Establishment of Central Huijin Investment Limited" and the "Articles of Association of Central Huijin Investment Ltd.," and preparation for the new company soon began.

Central Huijin was established on December 16, 2003, with SAFE as its sole investor. Its articles of association provided that it shall, under the authorization of the State Council, acquire equity interests in major state-owned financial enterprises and exercise rights and fulfill obligations as an investor on behalf of the state to the extent of its contributions, for

---

1 Wu Yi was Vice Premier of China principally responsible for foreign trade and health.

the purpose of preserving and enhancing the value of state-owned assets. The company may not conduct any other commercial activities, nor may it intervene in the operations of the financial enterprises. It has a well-established governance structure, including a board of directors comprising no less than five members, with SAFE Administrator and PBOC Vice Governor Guo Shuqing as the first Chairman; a board of supervisors comprising no less than three members; and a management team with SAFE Deputy Administrator Hu Xiaolian as the first President.

Central Huijin had a low-key birth. According to former President Xie Ping, Huijin was established in only one month after the State Council's approval. Since at the time it was sorely understaffed and had no specific mandates, most of the work was done by two officials from the SAFE Reserves Management Department. Despite its humble beginning – looking like a shell company in the early days – Central Huijin would play an irreplaceable role in the joint-stock reform of state-owned banks and even in China's financial reform at large, for several reasons.

First, by appointing directors to the other banks, it represented the state as an investor of those banks. In this way, the absence of an actor that represents state ownership – a long-standing issue of state-owned banks – was addressed, which laid an institutional foundation for rebuilding the government-bank relationship, clarifying rights and responsibilities, reducing administrative intervention, and promoting the business model transformation of state-owned banks. Second, Central Huijin as the parent company can not only influence the banks' business decisions to safeguard national interests and to preserve and enhance the value of state-owned assets, but also share in the dividends resulting from the banks' reform and development. These changes paved the way for a corporate governance system with balanced constraints and incentives, for more independent bank management, and for the market-based transformation of state-owned banks. Third, Central Huijin is specialized in the equity investment and management of financial enterprises. This sharp focus allows it to build management expertise, which further speeds up the building of the governance systems for state-owned banks, leading to more systematic, well-designed, and modern operation and management frameworks.

Related Topic: Functions and History of Central Huijin[1]

Central Huijin was established in December 2003 as a wholly state-owned investment company upon the approval of the State Council and mandated to promote the joint-stock reform of state-owned banks. In addition to supporting the joint-stock reform of ICBC, ABC, BOC, and CCB with capital injection with foreign reserves, Central Huijin has also invested in several other state-owned financial institutions in accordance with China's financial reform policies. It held stakes in 17 such financial institutions as of the end of 2017.

The "Articles of Association of Central Huijin" provide that Central Huijin shall, under the authorization of the State Council, acquire equity interest in major state-owned financial enterprises and exercise rights and fulfill obligations as an investor on behalf of the state to the extent of its contributions, for the purpose of preserving and enhancing the value of state-owned assets. In practice, Central Huijin supervises the investees as their shareholder to protect state-owned assets and helps them optimize their governance structures and systems through such measures as developing better

---

1   Compiled from information on the official site of Central Huijin.

governance rules and participating in their decision-making by sending shareholder representatives. In addition, relying on its market-based equity holding scheme and competitive capital operation, Central Huijin played an active and important role in preventing and mitigating financial risks and maintaining a stable financial market.

In September 2007, the MOF issued special government bonds to buy out Central Huijin from the PBOC and invested the acquired equity into China Investment Corporation (CIC) as part of the MOF's capital contribution. CIC holds 100% interest in Central Huijin on behalf of the state, but CIC's investment activities are completely separated from Central Huijin's shareholder activities on behalf of the state.

When commenting on the acquisition of Central Huijin by the MOF, then Minister of Finance Lou Jiwei said that Central Huijin was a very good idea and was true to the directive of the Third Plenary Session of the 18th CPC Central Committee to "shift focus from managing personnel, affairs, and assets to managing capital."[1] The story of how Central Huijin became a wholly-owned subsidiary of the CIC began in 2006, when China's foreign reserves broke the 1-trillion-dollar mark. The progressively larger monetary base resulting from the purchase of foreign currency had to be brought back down, but the PBOC had no instruments to do so. The PBOC had already issued central bank bills. But for monetary policy tools, the PBOC would ideally choose a third-party instrument over a self-issued instrument, because the latter approach will offset demand for the self-issued instrument upon maturity, which is not a desirable option. But the PBOC did not have that much government bonds or the more preferable AAA-rated corporate bonds. At

---

1 Quoted from the interview with Lou Jiwei on March 18, 2017.

this point, the PBOC reported its conundrum to the State Council and proposed to gradually raise the reserve ratio by 7 percentage points, from 13% to 20%.

Members of the State Council then asked for Lou's suggestions. His idea was to let the MOF issue special government bonds and use the proceeds to purchase foreign currency, then place that foreign currency under the charge of SAFE, as per the usual practice. The average yield reported by SAFE to the MOF over the years was 3.4%, which was higher than the effective rate to be paid for issued bonds. This would create positive cash flow; and because special government bonds only factor into the amount of government bonds outstanding, not the fiscal deficit, this design would rein in liquidity and make raising the reserve ratio unnecessary. Another benefit was that the PBOC could conduct open market operations using its stock of government bonds as a third-party instrument. This proposal was accepted by the State Council.

Later, when reviewing the MOF's proposal to issue special government bonds for purchasing foreign currency and to establish a foreign currency investment company, the NPC suggested that Central Huijin should transform its management model with the bond issue and currency purchase. That is how the current setup of the CIC and Central Huijin came to be.

II. Capital Injection with Foreign Reserves

The establishment of Central Huijin removed all obstacles that prevented the state from injecting capital into state-owned banks. At a meeting on December 30, 2003, Wen Jiabao approved the "Master Plan for Implementing the Joint-Stock Reform of Bank of China and China Construction Bank." Wen stated that the reform would aim for the public listing of the banks in domestic and overseas markets after they become internationally competitive and modern joint-stock commercial banks with sufficient capital, strict internal controls, safe operations, and competitive services and performances. To achieve this, it would be necessary to optimize their corporate governance structures, transform their business models, enhance their internal management, and sustain their development through financial restructuring, internal reforms, and strict external supervision. The decision to proceed with capital injection with foreign reserves was made at the meeting. On December 31, 2003, the day following the meeting, Central Huijin injected USD 22.5 billion each into BOC and CCB, making the first major step toward the joint-stock reform of state-owned banks. The first and critical part of the "four-step process" was completed.

The interesting thing was that Central Huijin also kept a low profile about the capital injection just as it had done for its establishment. Though the capital was injected on the last day of 2003, SAFE and Huijin didn't make that information public until January 6, 2004 when the State Council announced CCB and BOC as pilot banks for the USD 45 billion injection plan.

In stark contrast to the quiet capital injection process, the news of the results immediately grabbed worldwide attention. *Southern Weekly* reported the news "received over 10,000 comments in two days at Sina.com and instantly led to a general rise of the prices of bank stocks listed on the Shanghai and Shenzhen stock markets." Foreign markets also responded quickly. S&P revised the long-term foreign currency outlook of BOC and CCB from stable to positive on January 7, 2004. And Moody's upgraded their financial ratings to stable on January 8, 2004. Experts both in China and abroad also spoke positively about the injection. "[The injection] sets China's bank reform to sail again," commented Tao Dong, Credit Suisse's Chief Regional Economist for non-Japan Asia. Huang Yiping, Greater China Chief Economist at Citigroup Global Markets also remarked, "This will speed up China's bank reform."[1]

III. Discussions and Debates

As the capital injection with foreign reserves and the pilot reform of BOC and CCB were announced, the joint-stock reform of state-owned banks came to the front, telling the world that China's banking reform was underway, carrying with it the determination of the central government and a brand-new model of reform. The news made a global splash. Whether they were experts or laymen, market players or academics, enthusiasts who really cared about the future of state-owned banks or speculators who agitated for their bankruptcy, people discussed and studied the next steps and placed their wagers on the fate of the reform. Many optimists could be counted among them. But skeptics were also high in number since the reform was revolutionary and carried out in a way that went against conventional approaches, which inevitably led to some voices singing a different tune. Differences were also found among the initiators of the reform plan, nevertheless, with the common goal of strengthening state-owned banks, they could easily reach consensus. However, when the public was involved, a hodgepodge of opinions, rational or irrational, well- or ill-intended, would influence public opinion and affect the reform. This made it imperative for

---

1   Quoted from "Behind the 45-Billion-Dollar Capital Injection with Foreign Reserves," *Southern Weekly*, January 15, 2004.

decision-makers to educate and guide the public early, so as to minimize differences and create a favorable social environment for the reform.

Concerns and controversies mainly centered on four areas.

First, should the state pay the bill for state-owned banks? People who are not familiar with the history of China's state-owned banks tend to believe that their NPAs were caused by mismanagement. In the 1990s, the banks, even including their executives, did not understand how NPAs had come into being until they decided to find out the causes for their now conspicuous financial difficulties. In 1999, the state helped state-owned banks offload their NPAs at a significant cost, arousing widespread controversy. And now, only four years later, it further injected USD 45 billion into the banks. Some thought the state was held hostage by state-owned banks whose massive NPAs caused by mismanagement forced the state to rescue them; some believed this was against the basic law of markets and also optimal allocation of society's resources.

Second, is capital injection with foreign reserves reasonable and feasible? In the eyes of the public, the injection was the first substantial activity in the joint-stock reform and was taken at a tremendous cost. Naturally, it triggered a heated public debate. One focus was the appropriateness of the injection. As *Southern Weekly* pointed out, "What is surprising is not the injection – which has long been anticipated – but the source of injection: foreign reserves instead of the traditional fiscal funds." For the traditionally minded onlookers, fiscal funds were always the first choice, for they believed that the state fiscal system should be ultimately responsible for resolving the problems faced by state-owned enterprises. Another focus was the feasibility of the injection. Since an RMB exchange rate reform was in the cards, many experts were concerned about the stability of the value of the injected capital.

Third, would the joint-stock reform kill or cure state-owned banks? Although the reform had worked successfully for SOEs, whether it also worked for the banks, a special type of SOEs, was disputed. Particularly, should their listing be before or after restructuring? And were the restructuring and listing necessary at all? Some experts had argued that reform measures taken after 1997 had failed to fundamentally improve the operational quality of state-owned banks, which revealed defects in their internal structures. In this case, measures such as capital injection, joint-stock reform, and listing, though effective in promoting their development, could not cure all problems. Therefore, rushing to go public without well-established internal management would be risky. In addition, going public means more transparency, even for adverse information, which would make state-owned banks more vulnerable to external influences.

Fourth, would the joint-stock reform of state-owned banks undermine China's financial security or national interests? Some believed that the reform would significantly change the operations and development of state-owned banks and even the financial sector as a whole. If it succeeded, all would win. But if it failed to meet expectations, not only would the state suffer heavy investment loss, the banks might also run into operating difficulties, resulting in a risky and shaky financial sector.

These questions reflected the skepticisms at the time toward the joint-stock reform of state-owned banks. They arose from a lack of holistic insight into the evolution of China's economic and financial systems, the substitution of state fiscal system with banks in financing, the history of the soft budget constraints placed on SOEs and state-owned banks, the necessity and urgency of the reform, and the reform plan with Chinese characteristics. The opinions of skeptics, however, seemed to be "reasonable" and "logical" on surface and hence were accepted by many, painting the whole program in a somewhat negative light. Foreseeing possible concerns, speculation, misinterpretation, and misunderstanding even before announcing the two pilot banks and the capital injection plan, the CPC Central Committee and the State Council immediately launched a campaign to improve public perceptions for the reform.

One target of the campaign was the financial sector. At the Annual Banking, Securities, and Insurance Work Conference held on February 10, 2004, Premier Wen Jiabao shared his insight on some hot topics regarding the reform of state-owned banks. He noted that the banks, with their back against the wall, simply could not afford to fail to reform. The state could only create conditions for them, such as through a capital injection, but the success of their reform would be determined by structural transformation. Banks should use state capital to introduce corporate governance structures and new business models. This process would be a tough and even painful struggle, and not least a panacea. As to the two pilot banks, Wen stressed that both their executives and employees should abandon their old ways of thinking and assume responsibility for results of the financial reform and the safety of state assets. They should carry out the reform in strict accordance with the pilot plan.

The timing of the conference could scarcely be more perfect. Wen affirmed those objective viewpoints held by the public and converted external pressure into forces driving the joint-stock reform, helping the banks better understand the reform and reinforcing their determination to overcome difficulties.[1]

The other target was the public. In fact, a few months before the injection plan was announced, Zhou Xiaochuan and Liu Mingkang had outlined their ideas on the reform on numerous occasions, paving the way for the introduction of subsequent measures. After the news was released, the PBOC, CBRC, and the state-owned banks responded swiftly to public questioning. Particularly, at the Spring Membership Meeting of the Institute of International Finance (IIF) held in Shanghai in April 2004, Zhou Xiaochuan answered the two most controversial questions in his speech.

The first was about the priority of the reform: whether to first enhance management or introduce corporate governance and joint-stock systems? "The major problem faced by state-owned banks is not improper management, but rather that they are more like government bodies than commercial institutions," Zhou stated. "Their personnel, compensation, employee benefit, social insurance, and internal incentive systems are highly bound to administrative ranks and bureaucratic. Furthermore, their officers only have limited power to make decisions, which frustrated their pursuit of market-oriented operations. Since the banks lack sufficient internal incentives and external pressure, relying on management improvement alone will turn the reform into a marathon. The idea of changing how SOEs operate through corporate governance and restructuring has been recognized by the 16th CPC National Congress, and this idea will

---

[1] Quoted from the speech of Premier Wen Jiabao delivered at the 2004 Annual Banking, Securities, and Insurance Work Conference. See the PBOC and the CPC Central Committee's Party Literature Research Office: *Selected Financial Policy Documents (1978-2005)*, China Financial Publishing House, 2005, pp. 609-610.

also work for state-owned banks which essentially are SOEs."

The second question was whether to promote the listing of state-owned commercial banks. "Going public is just the first half of this comprehensive reform program which aims to establish a market-based system of incentives and constraints in the interests of investors," Zhou replied. "Ultimately, state-owned banks, through reasonable performance motivation, adequate risk management, and capital discipline, will break free from quasi-bureaucracy and a government-centric mindset to become real market players. Hence, as an integral part of the reform, listing aims not to raise funds which the state could provide anyway, but to solve legacy ills, especially constraints from bureaucratic bank departments. Only when listing becomes an urgent mission will these government departments cooperate and even reform themselves in areas of taxation, human resources, employee benefits, social insurance, and business independence. In addition, restructuring and listing require the banks to disclose information, placing them under public supervision. Therefore, capital injection serves not just to improve balance sheets, but also to create a new, efficient financial intermediation system. Listing is the only external force which could push the banks to abandon bureaucratic operations and develop corporate governance structures, thus ensuring the success of the reform."

Finally, to dispel pessimism toward the prospect of the reform, Zhou analyzed the favorable factors including the huge growth potential for China's banking sector given the country's population size and a strong propensity for indirect financing, and great profit potential from the generous spreads. His speech was later published in *Financial News* at the end of May 2004 under the title "Issues Concerning the Reform of State-Owned

Commercial Banks," exerting tremendous influence on both theories and practices.

At the Beijing International Financial Forum held in May 2004, Zhou Xiaochuan and Liu Mingkang delivered speeches on the reform. Reviewing the history of the reform, Zhou analyzed the causes of legacy issues, explained the necessity of the reform, and responded to the question of whether the state should foot the bill of the reform. Liu stressed that the joint-stock reform and enhancing corporate governance and improving business models formed an organic whole and should not be treated or evaluated as independent projects. He also clarified the nature and purpose of the reform.

These early discussions and debates were, albeit their negative influence, essential to the reform. Greater debate brings all stakeholders closer to the truth. It is precisely these types of discussions that would dispel misperception and build consensus.

Section II
Joint-Stock Reform and Listing of CCB

CCB was one of the two pilot state-owned banks for joint-stock reform. It had no precedent to follow and faced serious legacy issues, such as financial losses papered over with reported profits, weak internal control, and severe undercapitalization. Nevertheless, supported by state capital and other financial restructuring policies, CCB successfully restructured itself into a joint-stock company, attracted strategic investors, and finally went public, providing a valuable example for its peers. Its reform and listing is internationally considered as a watershed moment in China's bank reform.

Related Topic: A Brief History of China Construction Bank

China Construction Bank (CCB) was founded on October 1, 1954 as the People's Construction Bank of China and was given its current name on March 26, 1996.

The history of CCB can be divided into three stages:

In the first stage, CCB handled fiscal appropriation. In October 1954, CCB was established by the Administration Council of the Central People's Government to allocate budgetary funds to capital projects, and to manage and supervise the use of such funds as well as other funds raised by ministries and organizations. For decades, CCB had made an outstanding contribution to increasing investment returns and speeding up economic development.

In the second stage, CCB functioned as a national specialized bank. Since the mid-1980s, adapting to economic and financial reforms and economic development, CCB successively offered cash receipt and payment services, deposit services, fixed asset loans, business working capital loans, international finance, housing loans, and a range of agency services. These services expanded the functions of CCB and would facilitate its later transformation into a modern commercial bank.

In the third stage, CCB operated as a state-owned commercial bank. In 1994, responding to the investment and financing system reform, CCB transferred its fiscal functions and lending business for policy-based capital projects to the MOF and China Development Bank, respectively. This was an important step in its way into a modern commercial bank.

In 2003, CCB was selected as one of the two pilot banks for the joint-stock reform.

On September 15, 2004, Central Huijin, China Jianyin Investment Company Limited (JIC), State Grid Corporation of China, Shanghai Baosteel Group Corporation, and China Yangtze Power Corporation Limited held a meeting in Beijing, resolving to jointly set up China Construction Bank Corporation. CCB was thus transformed from a commercial bank that is wholly owned by the state to one that is only controlled by the state. Meanwhile, CCB took a series of complementary measures, including introducing foreign strategic investors, enhancing internal management, advancing internal reform, and adjusting its business model.

CCB adopted its current name – China Construction Bank Corporation – after the transformation and succeeded to the commercial banking business as well as taking on all the assets, debts, and equity of its predecessor.

CCB went public at the Hong Kong Stock Exchange and Shanghai Stock Exchange on October 27, 2005 and September 25, 2007, respectively.

I. Preparations

(I) CCB Became One of the First Pilot Banks for Joint-Stock Reform

On September 18, 2003, the Standing Committee of the Political Bureau of the CPC Central Committee approved in principle the framework and master plan of the reform, and designated BOC and CCB as pilot banks. Among the four state-owned commercial banks, these two had relative smaller size of assets and fewer employees and outlets, as well as relatively lighter legacy burdens, and could therefore be expected to exert less impact on society. Their financial indicators also better met the requirements of the reform. CCB was a natural choice because it uniquely had the best management system and more extensive reform track record.

Most importantly, CCB, having capital of RMB 120 billion and an NPA ratio of 15%, was expected to incur the lowest reform cost among the four banks.

(II) Reform of Personnel System and Employee Incentives and Restraints

At the end of 2002, before presenting its intention to pursue joint-stock reform and listing to the State Council, CCB had already begun overhauling its personnel system and employee incentives and restraints. A modern, rational, and effective human resources framework was built, in which promotion, wage, and employment decisions were made based on competition. This reform paved the way for CCB's later joint-stock reform into a modern financial company.

In reforming its employment system, CCB aimed to control headcount and optimize its personnel structure through a compliant, transparent, and humanistic process. CCB proposed to establish a competition-based selection mechanism; attract the most sought-after candidates while removing redundant employees; enhance leadership, management, as well as staff support; and provide multiple options for those terminated from their posts. Through these measures, CCB improved its systems and internal competition, and ultimately achieved its employee headcount and quality targets.

As a result, from the end of 2002 to the beginning of 2004, among medium- and long-term contract employees, the percentage of those with a junior college degree or higher increased from 61.2% to 63.1%, and of those with a bachelor's degree or higher increased from 20.7% to 22.1%; among short-term contract employees, the percentage of those with a junior college degree or higher increased from 32.9% to 35.4%.

In reforming its human resources management, CCB focused on creating a contract employment system for executives based on its new staff hierarchy. A set of rules on regulating the number of branch executives, selecting executives through open competition, announcing the appointment of new executives, and managing executives' fulfillment of performance targets and responsibilities were drafted. In addition, CCB divided its staff into three major categories: managers, tellers and administrative personnel, and banking professionals who would all in the future be selected through competition.

In 2003, 9 vice presidents at the head office, 579 senior-level management personnel and over 3,800 tellers and administrative personnel obtained jobs through competition, while 1,100 managers failed to make the cut and were demoted or dismissed. Managers at tier-one branches and vice presidents or higher positions at the head office were all employed through contracts instead of the previous appointment system.

At the same time, the remuneration system was also improved, primarily covering total payroll management, wage composition, annual salaries for tier-one branch executives, enterprise annuities, and supplementary medical insurance, with the overall goal of replacing housing allocations with monetary payouts. Under this new system, remuneration included employee benefits, so that the total remuneration of branches at each level was linked to their respective performance, and the remuneration of an individual employee was closely related to his or her responsibilities and contributions. Hence, a CCB-style remuneration system with effective incentives and restraints was created.

(III) Comprehensive Self-Assessment

CCB's top priority in the joint-stock reform was to understand and resolve its financial problems, so as to create a standardized, sound, and reliable financial basis. Only when problems were identified could CCB solve them through "surgical interventions," thus pushing forward its reform in all respects.

When CCB started its financial restructuring in 2003, it faced serious difficulties and challenges, including over RMB 3 trillion in assets that hadn't been audited according to international standards, significant undercapitalization and serious legacy issues, a sprawling branch network with a great number of redundant staff, and weak title claims to certain assets and problematic legal relationships. Its restructuring set a record in the history of China's SOE restructuring in terms of the range and complexity of issues.

Accurate diagnosis is the foundation of effective treatment. As early as the end of 2002, CCB had hired financial consultants to make a "diagnosis" by benchmarking it against the business models of leading international banks and had set financial restructuring goals based on the diagnosis. From the second half of 2003, CCB successively engaged external liaisons and professionals like audit, appraisal, and law firms. They developed a detailed financial restructuring plan for CCB by taking a page from the playbook of successfully restructured SOEs and conducted a year-long comprehensive self-assessment in accordance with the International Financial Reporting Standards (IFRS) and overseas listing requirements.

Throughout the organization, the bank provided full support to the external professionals in their financial audit, appraisal, and legal due diligence. On August 11, 2003, the comprehensive self-assessment was kicked off after a one-month pilot at the head office and five representative

Launch of Pilot Reform | 335

branches in Heilongjiang, Shandong, Qingdao, Guangdong, and Shenzhen which collectively held 38% of CCB's total assets. The pilot helped the external firms make a quick assessment of the financial position of CCB and create a targeted to-do list. It also generated interim estimates to the government as required.

After the pilot, the first field audit and appraisal started from the base date of June 30, 2003, checking 38 tier-one branches in over four months. Enormous human and material resources were invested in this "general physical exam." The accounting firm KPMG, together with the land, property, and asset appraisal firms, designed about 200 audit questionnaires and appraisal checklists and trained over 20,000 CCB employees in various provinces to fill out these forms. Tens of thousands of staff members across the organization filled out the forms after checking and verifying each asset and liability. The firms were responsible for providing on-site training, answering questions, and collecting data. KPMG assigned 300 on-site professionals and divided CCB into six regions, each managed by 2 KPMG partners in charge of credit and non-credit auditing work, respectively. Nearly 2,300 professionals from the land, property, and asset appraisal firms carried out asset checks and appraisals across China. Commerce & Finance Law Offices, a Beijing-based law firm, sent dozens of lawyers to conduct thorough investigations at CCB branches and assist and guide them to set up legal document repositories. After collecting large amounts of data regarding the establishment, licenses, business, contracts, land, properties, intellectual properties, external investment, labor, tax, litigation, supervision, and other aspects of the CCB head office and branches, the Law Offices issued a due diligence report of hundreds of pages, identifying potential legal risks and defects in licenses and property rights.

The comprehensive self-assessment covered all the data, legal documents, and property assets of CCB. Such tremendous efforts across the bank were rewarded with a marked improvement in fundamental management practices. After the plan of pilot joint-stock reform was approved, in the first half of 2004, CCB rolled forward the base date to 2003 year-end according to the schedule of the joint-stock reform for a second round of audit and appraisal.

To meet high standards and align with international principles, CCB adopted the new Financial Enterprise Accounting System (FEAS) for this round of audit and appraisal at the very beginning. In auditing particularly, CCB introduced a stricter accounting system and international best practices to review its asset quality and financial position. Before restructuring, CCB had adopted the "Financial System for Financial and Insurance Enterprises" issued by the MOF in 1993 and other relevant regulations for accounting, without making full provision for asset impairment in accordance with the new FEAS introduced in 2001. As a result, its true financial position was unknown, which posed a major obstacle to the joint-stock reform. In addition, according to the disclosure standards of leading international banks, nearly 30% of the information that should be disclosed couldn't be obtained under the outdated accounting system. Therefore, one of the primary tasks of financial restructuring was shifting to the new FEAS.

This shift was very time-consuming. CCB had to update its computer systems and improve its accounting and financial reporting protocols. First, it introduced more rigorous accounting policies which established standards on the provision for the impairment of eight types of assets, and on this basis made provisions for various estimated liabilities. Second, it adopted a more stringent accrual system to make accurate provision for accrued interest income on loans, bonds, and deposits in the central bank, as well as interest expenses on customer deposits, loans, and interbank transactions, which reflected the true and complete income and expenses of each primary business. Third, it replaced the four-category loan classification with "accrual and non-accrual" classification for the purpose of recognizing interest revenue. In accordance with the new FEAS, any loan with payment of principal or interest overdue by 90 days or more would be accounted and assessed separately as a non-accrual loan. This change allowed for earlier recognition of NPLs. Fourth, CCB included capital expenditures such as renovation fees in fixed asset accounting, and made provision for or deferred these expenses in strict accordance with the requirements of the accrual system.

Moreover, CCB classified and made provision for its credit assets – the most important bank assets – according to international standards rather than the new FEAS. That was because the latter only required in principle that "reasonable provision should be made for the possible losses of a loan after analyzing its risk level and recovery possibility," without offering any specific accounting treatment. CCB and KPMG therefore developed a new method for classifying the credit asset risks in October 2003 based on the best practices of international leading banks, and a new method for provisioning for loan losses in accordance with the requirements of IAS 39. CCB also developed a Content Management Interoperability Services (CMIS) program and trained, in a classroom setting, 1,000 employees across the bank responsible for classifying credit risks, to use the program to retrospectively reclassify and make provision for credit assets originated in the four years after 2000. At the end of 2003, this new loan classification and provisioning method was applied. Through nearly two years of effort, CCB significantly increased its capabilities in asset classification and loss provisioning, which meant the reliability of its asset quality data greatly improved. It was estimated that compared with the previous system, the new FEAS would require CCB to make an additional RMB 184.3 billion of provision as of the end of 2003.

In shifting toward the new FEAS, the far-sighted CCB also considered the adoption of IFRS. Since the basic principles and policies of the new FEAS were generally consistent with those of IFRS excepting some technical differences in accounting policies, CCB made special efforts in aligning its accounting policies and disclosure with international leading examples. This led to a much smaller gap with IFRS in terms of accounting, less adjustments in auditing, and higher quality and efficiency of financial disclosure. For example, in 2003, CCB recorded nearly 100 audit adjustments across all its branch levels, but on June 30, 2005, this number decreased to only a dozen, and the difference between the loan loss provisions estimated by CCB and KPMG narrowed to approximately RMB 100 million. CCB's proactive move not only laid a sound foundation for its financial disclosure in overseas listing, but also improved its business operation and management process through international information standards.

Stephen Kin Wah Yiu, former Chairman of KPMG China and lead partner of KPMG Huazhen, recalled, "It was a big challenge to determine CCB's gross NPAs at that time because before 1998 the figure was calculated based on the four-category classification. The standard five-category classification system was not introduced until May 1998, and reclassification would be a massive project. To complete the task, we organized intensive training across the bank and conducted pilots at some branches. Then we designed intuitive yet informative forms for each level of branch so that information would be aggregated by and reported to higher-level branches successively, so as to create consistent standards and database. Usually, classifying a loan as, for example, special-mention or substandard is not a quantitative task of applying hard-and-fast rules but rather a judgment call which requires extensive market and professional experience. At first, CCB's five-category classification was far below the international standard, but when we conducted its annual audit in 2009, the gap had been greatly narrowed."[1]

(IV) Challenges Facing the Joint-Stock Reform

The comprehensive self-assessment helped CCB fully understand the challenges facing its joint-stock reform and revealed the following main findings:

1. Massive NPAs and severe undercapitalization

Due to historical reasons, CCB carried RMB 271 billion of gross NPLs with an NPL ratio as high as 12.4% at the end of 2003 before its restructuring, which led to an allowance (for potential loan losses) of RMB 211.5 billion. In addition, it also needed to post an RMB 91.3 billion allowance for its non-credit asset losses, including RMB 6.4 billion of retirement benefits. In a pro forma financial statement prepared as of the end of 2003 under the assumption of no restructuring, such burdens would have led to a negative net asset value of RMB -115.5 billion and a negative capital adequacy ratio. This massive funding gap was the first barrier to CCB's

---

1   From the interview with Stephen Kin Wah Yiu on February 15, 2017.

joint-stock reform.

2. Complex policy tasks and legacy issues

Before restructuring, CCB was delegated certain policy tasks and had a number of self-invested entities from legacy operations initiated in an earlier, less regulated era. These problems, which hampered its commercial operations, needed to be solved once for all in accordance with relevant regulations. They fall into three categories:

(i) Policy-directed trusteeship over China Agribusiness Development Trust and Investment Corporation (CADTIC). In 1997, CCB took over the head office and 19 branches of CADTIC. CCB checked and disposed of the assets of CADTIC, and started to repay its debts in the same year. In the process of trusteeship, CCB assumed about RMB 21 billion of CADTIC's losses out of its own pocket.

(ii) Policy-directed entrusted loans. Before October 20, 2000, CCB had been entrusted by government departments at various levels and six major investment companies to grant large amounts of policy loans. As of the end of 2003, the book balance of entrusted loans was approximately RMB 149.4 billion. Their long term and complexity created a web of legal relationships that were often nearly impossible to untangle.

(iii) External investment and various types of self-invested entities. Due to incompliant business activities in earlier years and disposal difficulties, before restructuring, CCB still had a large number of self-invested entities (including hotels and guesthouses), credit cooperatives, and equity investments in domestic non-bank enterprises and RMB corporate bonds. According to the *Law on Commercial Banks*, these operations and assets do not fall within the business scope of commercial banks. Furthermore, most self-invested entities were underfunded, and the entities and credit cooperatives all faced severe insolvency, overdue taxes, and incurred losses, exposing CCB to enormous financial burden and risks. It was estimated that by the end of 2003, losses arising from self-invested entities and external investment activities totaled RMB 3.7 billion.

3. Ambiguous property and land titles

Securing clear titles on fixed assets is a basic requirement of compliant business operations, but turned out to be one of the most severe bottlenecks in the restructuring of state-owned enterprises. The comprehensive self-assessment in September 2003 found that CCB had 16,284 parcels of land (including those of subsidiaries and those held as collateral), of which 10,059 (61.77%) had no land use certificate and 11,991 (73.64%) had defective title. As of November 2003, CCB had 24,578 properties, of which 13,175 (54%) had no certificate of property ownership. Ambiguous property and land titles had been a persistent weak point in CCB's management, indicating considerable potential risks.

II. Financial Restructuring and Establishment of the Joint-Stock Company

(I) Capital Injection and Financial Restructuring

1. Foreign currency injection

In the context of severe undercapitalization before restructuring, how to replenish capital to increase capital adequacy ratio became a central issue of the financial restructuring plan, which aimed to increase CCB's core capital adequacy ratio and capital adequacy ratio to above 6% and 8% respectively. Deciding the specific method of capital injection was at the very heart of the plan.

On February 20, 2003, with the support of its financial consultants,

CCB submitted its first joint-stock reform plan. The plan proposed the establishment of China Construction Bank Group (CCB Group) and China Construction Bank Corporation (CCBC). Given the financial position of CCB, CCB Group would need to raise RMB 157.2 billion from the placement of special-purpose bonds to CCBC. From February to June 2003, the PBOC Financial Stability Bureau, architect of the joint-stock reform plan for state-owned banks, had several discussions with CCB about its proposal. The Bureau worried that the injection would constitute a huge related-party transaction between the two parties, and CCB Group didn't have a stable source of income to repay the bonds. For this reason, the market would very likely doubt the thoroughness of the financial restructuring. In April 2003, CCB put forward an alternative plan, proposing that in addition to CCB's own accumulated retained earnings, the MOF was to issue special government bonds to raise the remaining capital needed. However, since the issuance of a government bond would require the NPC's approval – too complex a procedure to be viable – this plan was also abandoned.

In late July 2003, a State Council meeting made a preliminary decision that the central government would inject USD 15 to 25 billion of foreign reserves into CCB, and CCB should write off its losses against its original capital. The state thought that foreign currency injection could not only provide the enormous funds needed for CCB's joint-stock reform, but also alleviate the alarmingly high growth rate of foreign reserves. On December 26, 2003, the PBOC submitted the "Master Plan for Implementing the Joint-Stock Reform of Bank of China and China Construction Bank" to the State Council Joint-Stock Reform Steering Group, proposing capital injection from Central Huijin into BOC and CCB

(USD 22.5 billion for CCB) at the end of 2003 with foreign reserves and part of the gold reserves. On December 30, 2003, Premier Wen Jiabao chaired a meeting at which the Master Plan was approved. On December 31, Central Huijin injected USD 22.5 billion, or RMB 186.2 billion at the prevailing exchange rate into CCB.

To preserve and increase the value of the injected capital, CCB took strict and professional management measures to ensure the security of funds. It set up a Special Fund Management Leading Group as the decision-making body for the management of injection with foreign reserves, and developed procedures to improve investment decision-making and risk management. The injected foreign reserves were separately used, managed and accounted for, with an independent transaction account, reporting, and cash management at the front office; independent weekly risk management and reporting at the middle office; and independent clearing, bond custody account, and accounting treatment at the back office. In addition, CCB introduced a prudent investment strategy for injected capital, which required that an annual investment plan be proposed at the beginning of every year and implemented after approval by the Special Fund Management Leading Group; that the plan should be reviewed and adjusted on a quarterly basis based on market conditions and operating results; and that at the end of each quarter, the risk control department should conduct an on-site comprehensive inspection on the operation of the injected capital.

Although the injection immediately solved CCB's undercapitalization problem, it also significantly exposed CCB's foreign currency assets to exchange risk due to the prospect of renminbi appreciation. Estimates showed that a 10% appreciation of renminbi against the U.S. dollar would shave 0.4 percentage points off CCB's capital adequacy ratio, which would affect CCB's corporate image and investor confidence. For this reason, CCB repeatedly requested for policy support from the state, and prior to the creation of CCBC in 2004, proposed that it would make an appropriate arrangement (e.g., foreign exchange option and other derivative instruments) with SAFE or Central Huijin to mitigate the capital impairment risk that could be triggered by exchange rate fluctuations, or gradually convert the foreign currency into renminbi. On January 12, 2005, with the support of the unified state policy, CCB and Central Huijin entered into a foreign exchange option contract, which stipulated that CCB had the right to sell the USD 22.5 billion to Central Huijin in 12 equal monthly installments in 2007, in which case Central Huijin should pay in renminbi at the exchange rate on the date of injection (8.2767 yuan against 1 U.S. dollar). In return, CCB should pay 3% of the contract price, or RMB 5.587 billion, to Central Huijin as transaction fee, also in 12 equal monthly installments. In this way, the exchange rate risk incurred by the injection was effectively mitigated.

2. Issuance of subordinated bonds

To improve its capital structure and bring its capital adequacy ratio up to regulatory standards, CCB also issued subordinated bonds. In fact, the proposal of issuing subordinated bonds had already been approved by the State Council as early as July 2003, when the restructuring plan was under discussion. After the release of the "Measures for the Administration of the Issuance of Subordinated Bonds by Commercial Banks" in June 2004, upon the approval of the PBOC and CBRC, CCB issued RMB 40 billion of "2004-2005 CCB Bonds" in three offerings in China's interbank bond market from July to December 2004. This brought CCB's capital adequacy ratio up to 11.29% at the end of 2004.

In the issuance process, CCB adopted innovative product design and market promotion strategies, which were well received in the bond market. These innovations included: (i) the first subordinated bond issued in China to use a mix of fixed and floating rates, thus diversifying the product range available to investors; (ii) the first bond issue in China to embed an over-allotment option, thus granting the issuer greater flexibility and a chance to raise additional capital at an overall higher efficiency; (iii) the first issuance of subordinated bonds in China in the interbank market to adopt the book-building approach, which helped CCB better gauge market interest and achieve success on the bond issue through more market-based pricing; (iv) the first bond issue to use a claw-back mechanism, which allowed flexible adjustment of the relative sizes of fixed-rate and floating-rate bonds based on the results of book-building, thus satisfying the needs of different investors; (v) the use of callable bonds. This not only allowed CCB to increase its capital utilization efficiency by treating 100% of the bonds as supplementary capital if it chose to exercise the redemption right at the end of the fifth year, but also expanded the investor pool with the inclusion of insurers, who were prohibited to buy subordinated bank bonds with a maturity of six years or above; (vi) inclusion of an convertibility provision, which allowed investors to convert, in whole or in part, their fixed-rate bonds into floating-rate bonds at the face value after they held the bonds for two years, giving more choices to investors; and (vii) the timely issuance of a new floating-rate bond benchmarked against the interbank 7-day repo rate, which could help investors mitigate interest rate risk, the issuer to lower comprehensive financing cost, and the banks to disperse the risk caused by holding other banks' subordinated bonds.

3. Write-off and transfer of NPAs

Apart from replenishing core capital through capital injection, to address CCB's enormous NPAs, the Master Plan approved CCB to dispose of its NPAs by writing off or selling them at the end of 2003.

(1) Write-off of NPAs at one stroke. At the end of 2003, CCB had written off RMB 56.9 billion of loan losses and RMB 28.1 billion of non-credit asset losses. The entire process, including accounting treatment, was completed in a mere two months from October 30, 2003 to December 30, 2003. After that, the MOF decided to transfer the RMB 56.9 billion NPLs (plus any delinquent interest) written off by CCB to China Cinda Asset Management Co., Ltd. ("Cinda") for free. Under the coordination of the MOF, CCB and Cinda worked together to verify the loans one by one, followed by signing debt transfer agreements, publishing joint announcement, and handing over documents. Before June 15, 2004, all CCB's tier-one branches had signed debt transfer agreements with Cinda, and by June 30, had handed over all documents to Cinda. A total of 107,637 NPLs involving 84,891 accounts and RMB 56.9 billion in principal, comprising RMB 33.507 billion of bad loans and RMB 23.380 billion of loss loans, were transferred. RMB 45.712 billion of overdue interest on the NPLs – RMB 24.256 billion for the bad loans and RMB 21.456 billion for the loss loans – were also transferred.

(2) Sale of doubtful loans. In line with the Master Plan, CCB sold to Cinda doubtful loans in the principal amount of RMB 128.9 billion, including RMB 119.691 billion of corporate loans and RMB 9.209 billion of personal loans, as well as RMB 45.021 billion of overdue interest, among which RMB 604 million was interest receivable and RMB 44.417 billion was interest under collections. To help CCB dispose of its doubtful

loans, the PBOC issued to CCB special central bank bills equaling 50% of the book value of these loans, and transferred the proceeds to Cinda to purchase the principal of these loans. The difference of RMB 35.8 billion between the purchase price and the net book value of these loans was attributed to CCB's capital reserve.

Under the direction of the MOF and PBOC, CCB sold its doubtful loans through public bidding. The bidding ended in June 2004, and Cinda won the contract. Unlike the NPL divestiture in 1999, this carve-out was carried out through a market-based, commercial approach, featuring clearly defined legal relations among the parties, and thus lessened the side effects. CCB arranged many employees to check and clean up the principal and interest of the loans to ensure that information in the account books was consistent with that in the ledgers, and information in the ledgers was consistent with the principal and interest of loans confirmed by the customers. In particular, it collated documents related to the doubtful loans – primarily including legal documents confirming debts or guarantees and documents concerning loans and guarantees that CCB provided to its self-invested entities – and to the best of its ability discharged these guarantees prior to the sale to avoid potential risk. CCB and Cinda executed a written mutual undertaking, stipulating that Cinda would have no recourse against CCB following the transfer, which ticked the boxes for "true sale" of NPLs and completely solved legacy issues. When disposing of doubtful loans, CCB ensured that by assigning priority level to the loans, and those that were long overdue and had high expected losses and severe defects in claims were disposed of earlier, and allocated a disposal quota to each branch based on the value of their loans, in line with the national policies and financial policies.

4. Attribution of fixed assets

Due to historical reasons, use rights or titles to CCB's lands and buildings were highly ambiguous. To make sure that assets to be transferred to the joint-stock company would have good titles and to eliminate related legal risks, with the policy support from the state, CCB branches invested enormous human and material resources into solving their long-standing problems on land and building management, which ingrained in them a greater awareness of ownership rights that would be passed down to the joint-stock company and management practices going forward. At a meeting on December 30, 2003, the State Council approved CCB to implement delegated management of land use rights. Armed with the approval document, CCB obtained the approval of the Ministry of Land and Resources for the delegated management on February 16, 2004. Meanwhile, CCB initiated a bank-wide effort to sort through the use and ownership rights of its lands, buildings, and other assets.

CCB gained a large number of lands and buildings across the country over a long period of time. Most of them were acquired in China's real estate boom in the 1980s and 1990s, and at the time, the industry was not well regulated and the national policy on real property was in a constant state of flux, which made CCB's use or ownership rights to its lands and buildings a highly complex matter. In the process of attribution, CCB needed to properly address the relationships with local governments, real estate development companies, and joint ventures. The interests of the parties were highly intertwined and made the process difficult and time-consuming. To speed up the process, CCB held a bank-wide video conference, requiring all branches to obtain property certificates for 90% of their land and property assets, and report their daily progress. Under the intensive supervision of the head office, the whole bank took active efforts to overcome difficulties, and finally obtained property certificates for 94.7% of its lands and buildings, the highest rate in the history of the joint-stock reform of state-owned enterprises.

5. Solving legacy issues

(1) CCB innovatively designed an account called "state replenishment receivable" to help it recover from accumulated losses. After injection, CCB used all of its capital and reserves to write off its accumulated losses on and as of December 31, 2003. The large capital shortfall formed after CCB had made full allowance for asset impairment on December 31, 2003 was covered by a diverse set of financial resources listed in Table 5.1.

Table 5.1: CCB Data on Total Loss Covered as of December 31, 2003 (¥bn)

Existing financial resources:			
Net assets as at the end of 2002	94.4	Allowance for loan losses	211.5
Pre-allowance profit in 2003	42.0	Including: Loss write-off	56.9
Special allowance for interest on Cinda bond	23.7	Loss on disposal of doubtful loans	64.4
Beginning existent allowance for asset impairment	27.2		
Loss remedies:		Estimated non-credit asset impairment	91.3
Premium from disposal of doubtful loans	35.8	Including: Retiree benefits payable	6.4
Asset valuation gains	14.2	Write-off of partial loss	28.1
State replenishment receivable	65.5		
	302.8		302.8

Source: Compiled from information provided by CCB.

On December 31, 2003, CCB's existent owner's equity was all written off and Central Huijin injected USD 22.5 billion into CCB to replenish its core capital. At that time, CCB was still saddled with RMB 65.5 billion of accumulated losses, but the State Council had clearly stated that the injection could not be used to offset losses. How to offset the losses became a great challenge facing CCB's management and external professionals. Through more than one month of discussion with foreign auditors over bold ideas, CCB proposed an innovative, effective and compliant solution – "state replenishment receivable," i.e., a commitment of the state to cover the losses with CCB's future taxes and profits. This solution complied with international accounting standards, ensured the fidelity of financial statements, and enabled CCB to make full allowance on December 31, 2003 without increasing the fiscal burden. The State Council Joint-Stock Reform Steering Group approved the idea on August 20, 2004, and stated that CCB could use its profits in the second half of 2004 and the first half of 2005 to recover the losses. As of the end of the first half of 2005, the state replenishment receivable had been entirely settled.

(2) Before the joint-stock reform, CCB provided its retirees with not only basic pension and medical insurance, but also additional pension and medical subsidies. When these benefits came under scrutiny during the restructuring, CCB proposed to the MOF to approve the making of a one-off allowance for retirees' additional pension and medical subsidies, in view of the national conditions and the specific circumstances of the banking sector at the time. The allowance was made following the MOF's approval in April 2005. As for its current employees, CCB introduced an annuity policy to ensure their additional post-retirement subsidies, thus avoiding the financial burden from a lump-sum allowance. This approach would be emulated by banks during their reforms.

6. Fair value of special bonds

A prominent problem encountered by CCB during its restructuring was determining the fair value of special bonds.

CCB's balance sheet recorded three types of special bonds – special government bonds, central bank bills, and Cinda bonds. The special government bonds were issued by the state in 1998 to replenish the capital of state-owned banks. CCB held RMB 49.2 billion of the bonds with a maturity of 30 years at an annual rate of 7.2%. Upon the approval of the NPC Standing Committee, the interest was decreased to 2.25% on December 1, 2004.[1] The central bank bills, of a principal amount of RMB 63.4 billion with a maturity of 5 years and an annual interest rate of 1.89%, were bought by CCB from the central bank in 2004 using the proceeds from the sale of its doubtful loans. The Cinda bonds, totaling RMB 247 billion with a maturity of 10 years and an annual interest rate of 2.25%, was bought from Cinda in 1999 with its divested NPLs.

According to IFRS, the three types of bonds should be initially recognized at fair value which is determined based on the future cash flows discounted at the market interest rate. If the discount rate is higher than the coupon rate, the difference should be amortized over the lifetime of the bond. The auditors indicated that the discounted value of the three types of bonds totaled approximately RMB 40 billion, which would reduce the net assets in CCB's financial reports prepared in accordance with IFRS and undermine its valuation and IPO. To solve this problem, CCB worked closely with the external professionals and competent authorities; its external auditors also discussed with their IFRS experts in London. On June 10, 2005, CCB proposed, and the PBOC approved, to treat the central bank bills and special government bonds as eligible assets for excess

---

1   See the report of the State Council on the payment of interest of the 1998 special government bonds at the 12th Session of the Standing Committee of the 10th National People's Congress on October 22, 2004.

deposit reserves and eligible for future clearing and settlement. Regarding Cinda bonds, CCB looked into various bonds issued in 1999, particularly their terms about interest rate and maturity, and found evidence showing that there were interest rates in the market that were comparable with the interest rate of Cinda bonds, and thus solved the fair value problem of Cinda bonds.

Prior to CCB's restructuring, there was uncertainty about the payment of principal and interest on the Cinda bonds held by CCB. External auditors pointed out that given the proceeds received from previous asset disposal by Cinda and the financial strength of the company, without government support, Cinda would be unable to make full repayment. This would mean that CCB had to make RMB 180-230 billion of impairment allowance for the principal of Cinda bonds, which would greatly weaken CCB's capital strength and ran contrary to the original intent of the state policy. For this reason, the State Council Joint-Stock Reform Steering Group helped the MOF and CCB reach an agreement. On September 15, 2004, the MOF released a document, stating that the interest on Cinda bonds included in CCB's special allowance for losses from NPA disposal over the previous years could be used to plug its capital shortfall; that from January 1, 2005, if Cinda could not repay bond interest in full to CCB, the MOF would provide financial support to Cinda; and that if necessary, the MOF would make up any losses incurred by CCB on bond principal. In essence, the government had guaranteed the repayment of Cinda bonds. In preparing the prospectus, the external professionals specifically interviewed MOF personnel regarding the repayment of Cinda bonds, and thus removed all doubts about the issue.

Related Topic: How CCB Dealt with Its "Financial Bonds" as Recounted by Then CCB President Chang Zhenming[1]

"From 1999 to 2000, the four AMCs acquired the Big Four's NPAs at book value by issuing financial bonds to the banks. I [Chang Zhenming] remember that in 2004, the interest rates of these bonds were slightly lower than those of other government bonds with the same maturity. CCB held RMB 200 billion of financial bonds issued by Cinda. KPMG, which audited CCB for listing, questioned Cinda's capability to repay the bonds, for it had only about RMB 20 billion of net assets but carried RMB 200 billion of liabilities, and raised the question of whether the MOF could provide a guarantee on the bonds. KPMG also noted that even if Cinda could repay the bonds as scheduled, since the interest rate was lower than those of government bonds with the same maturity, a loss should be recognized for the difference.

"How was this problem solved then? I asked Cinda President Tian Guoli to confirm to CCB in a letter that Cinda had government backing and would most certainly repay its bonds. I also made a written commitment to Tian, saying that I would assume all responsibilities if anything goes wrong with the letter. Tian's letter 'secured' the financial bonds, and reassured the accounting firm."

(II) Establishment of the Joint-Stock Company

1. Innovative split-up model

CCB adopted a split-up model to implement the joint-stock reform, i.e., establishing China Construction Bank Corporation (CCBC) and

---

1   Quoted from the interview with Chang Zhenming on April 18, 2017.

China Jianyin Investment Co., Ltd. (JIC) to succeed to its corresponding assets and liabilities.

The choice was made because of the following considerations: the specific situation of CCB; lessons learned on successful restructurings at home and abroad; explorations of an effective approach to the joint-stock reform of state-owned banks; requirements of applicable Chinese and foreign laws and regulations; conclusions of comprehensive analysis and rigorous argumentation by internal and external experts; and the guidance and approvals of competent government authorities. In this model, assets and businesses not suitable for CCBC were carved out and transferred to JIC, including CADTIC-related business under policy-directed trusteeship, policy-directed entrusted loans granted before October 20, 2000, non-compliant external equity and bond investments, CCB's self-invested entities and credit cooperatives, and a small number of fixed and mortgaged assets whose ownership status could not be settled in the short term. After the partition of assets was determined, CCB developed a detailed asset and liability division plan. On November 1, 2004, CCBC and JIC created their respective accounts.

SOEs usually conduct their joint-stock reform by establishing or wholly transforming into a joint-stock company. However, under both models, CCB would find no legal basis to divide part of its assets and liabilities pursuant to its master plan for joint-stock reform. As one of the two pilot banks for the joint-stock reform, CCB desired to chart its own course for the reform according to its specific situation and the State Council's vision of "one bank, one strategy," in a bid to blaze a trail for other banks. Based on the lessons from the SOE reform and through rigorous argumentation, CCB created an innovative split-up model, which would allow it to efficiently and lawfully separate core business from non-core business.

At the time, corporate division as a transaction was only just introduced in China to support the country's rapid economic development. It helps enterprises adjust business sizes, specialize, and carve out assets and businesses without liquidation or the active consent of every creditor. Pursuant to the *Company Law*, in the case of a corporate division, the company properties are to be divided accordingly and the company shall notify its creditors within 10 days after the resolution on division is made and publish at least 3 announcements in newspapers within 30 days. Within 30 days after creditors' receipt of the written notice, or (if they have not received any notice) within 90 days after the first announcement, creditors have the right to demand the company to repay debts or provide the corresponding guarantee. After the division, the new (or surviving) companies succeed to the debts incurred by the original company before the division according to the division agreement.

These clauses provided a legal basis for CCB's split-up model, whereby CCB could conduct a one-off carve-out of assets and liabilities not suitable for CCBC. After the notice and announcement procedures were completed, CCBC and JIC succeeded to the assets and liabilities of CCB, and thus CCB solved the problem of debt transfer which had been a major challenge faced by large state-owned financial enterprises during the joint-stock reform.

Since there was no precedent for the split-up model, CCB had to overcome many legal difficulties. The toughest one was that the law did not specify whether CCBC and JIC should be jointly and severally liable for the debts of CCB. If the answer is yes, then CCB could not hope to achieve clear legal relationships and market-based operations – two of the objectives of restructuring – and CCBC would likely be questioned by investors and domestic and foreign regulators for the contingent liabilities. To remedy this problem and eliminate the potential legal risks, CCB management organized knowledgeable staff and external professionals to create a lawful and compliant split-up procedure. The announcement and notice themselves also underwent more than 100 revisions, to ensure that stakeholders clearly understood how CCB was going to be split up, that CCBC and JIC would not be jointly or severally liable for the debts of CCB, and that any creditor opposed to the arrangement should exercise its rights within the statutory period. Appropriate arrangements were also made for the assets and liabilities to be held by JIC, ensuring that the rights of creditors would not be harmed by the split-up.

Meanwhile, CCB also actively sought support from the judiciary and legislature. It frequently exchanged ideas with the Legislative Affairs Commission (LAC) of the NPC Standing Committee, the Supreme People's Court (SPC), Legislative Affairs Office of the State Council (LAOSC) and many others, hoping they could issue a clear comment regarding the issue of joint and several liability and the notification of creditors, after taking into consideration the realities of the commercial bank reform, the protection of creditors, and the operability of the *Company Law*. To this end, CCB invited officials of the SPC, PBOC and CBRC, as well as experts and scholars to two special meetings held on February 7 and 18, 2004. The SPC argued that the issues in question might involve legislation, and thus should be deliberated by the legislative body to ensure the final decision could be carried out.

CCB President wrote to Vice Premier Huang Ju and Deputy Secretary-

General You Quan on February 23 and 24, 2004, requesting that the SPC and LAC jointly resolve these questions. Noting their significance, the State Councilors including Huang pitched in their opinions. On April 19, Sheng Huaren, Vice Chairman and Secretary-General of the NPC Standing Committee, listened to CCB's report and provided clear guidance. The State Council General Office also offered support. Through heated negotiations, the NPC, the State Council and the SPC ultimately reached a consensus on the legal aspect of these issues, and revised and finalized the split-up announcement. On May 28, 2004, the State Council General Office convened a special meeting attended by officials from the LAC, LAOSC, SPC, and CCB, clarifying that while notifying its principal creditors, CCB should also perform its notification obligations under the *Company Law* through announcement; and that if any creditor should require that CCBC and JIC bear joint and several liability after the split-up, the court may, pursuant to the debt arrangement under the announcement, order that obligation of repayment be performed by either CCBC or JIC. As long as CCBC or JIC repaid the debts, there would be no joint and several liabilities to bear, and the major legal obstacle to CCB's split-up would be fundamentally removed.

On June 8, 2004, the CBRC approved the split-up plan. From June 10, CCB released announcements for three consecutive days in national Chinese and English language newspapers such as *People's Daily*, *Financial News* and *China Daily*, accompanied by CCB spokespersons' clear and detailed answers to questions from the press, such as the backdrop of the announcement, the relationship between CCBC and JIC after the split-up, the assumption of CCB's rights and obligations, and changes in principal business and assets. These answers dispelled concerns and doubts, calmed the public's anxiety, and prevented unnecessary market fluctuations. To make sure that everything went smoothly before the end of the objection period on September 8, CCB established a multi-modal incident response system, developed contingency plans and emergency procedures for all its main business lines and key departments, and made meticulous arrangements in areas of organization, management, funds, and internal rules, so as to ensure the well-functioning of outlets and e-banking equipment, the smooth processing of payments, and the protection of customer interest. Over 1,500 employees attended the Q&A training program organized by the head office, and follow-on trainings were conducted at tier-1 branches. In total, over 10,000 employees received relevant training across the bank, such that every outlet and branch was staffed by service personnel and account managers who were familiar with the split-up policies and requirements. During the split-up period, a 24-hour hotline was set up for answering questions, greatly helping CCB to retain customers and stabilize businesses.

During the split-up, both the number and severity of stakeholder-related incidents were lower than anticipated, and there was no major objection to the split-up. This was a testament of the effectiveness of CCB's incident response system. First, preventive measures specified in the contingency plans – such as the inclusion of special provisions regarding the split-up into the split-up contract, funding support, and communication with customers and relevant authorities – were effectively carried out. Second, customers who did have questions were able to receive satisfactory answers over CCB's 95533 hotline. Most of the questions were covered by the Q&A manual, and the few objections raised did not gain traction. Third, information transmission was timely and accurate. All branches strictly followed the daily reporting regime, so that incidents could be efficiently collected and analyzed and objections could be timely handled.

2. Establishment of China Construction Bank Corporation

Completing business registration and receiving business licenses would mark the official establishment of CCBC and JIC; but because the split-up was still a new concept at the time, this process was far from easy. The biggest difficulty was the asset valuation of JIC, owing to the unclear ownership status of most of the assets it had taken over. If this issue was not addressed, it would also jeopardize the creation of CCBC. To address this issue, CCB conducted intensive legal analysis and case studies, and actively worked with the State Administration for Industry and Commerce (SAIC) (which is in charge of business registration), including personal visits by CCB President. At last, upon the approval of the State Council, SAIC permitted JIC to complete registration through an update to the CCB record on file according to the corporate information of JIC, with net assets verified by the MOF as JIC's registered capital.

On September 15, 2004, China Construction Bank Corporation held its founding assembly, at which Central Huijin, CCBC and JIC signed the tripartite split-up agreement. On September 17, 2004, SAIC issued the business license to CCBC, which marked its official establishment. In accordance with the split-up agreement, CCBC took over more than 99.8% of CCB's assets and liabilities and all its commercial banking businesses. Therefore, CCB's joint-stock reform through the split-up model was a bona fide group-wide restructuring.

Through a step-by-step and accelerated timetable, CCBC was established in less than four months in accordance with the *Company Law*, *Law on Commercial Banks*, *Securities Law*, as well as other applicable laws, regulations, and ministry-level rules.

On September 6, 2004, Central Huijin, JIC, State Grid Corporation of China, Shanghai Baosteel Group Corporation and China Yangtze Power Co., Ltd., as CCBC's co-promoters, signed a Promoter Agreement. On September 14, 2004, the CBRC approved the "Request for Splitting up China Construction Bank into China Construction Bank Corporation and China Jianyin Investment Co., Ltd. for the Joint-Stock Reform." On September 15, China Construction Bank Corporation held its founding assembly and first shareholders' meeting in Beijing, attended by the five promoters. CCBC had a registered capital of RMB 194,230.25 million. The meeting deliberated and approved the "Articles of Association of China Construction Bank Corporation," "Rules of Procedure of Shareholders' Meeting of China Construction Bank Corporation," "Rules of Procedure of Board of Directors of China Construction Bank Corporation," "Rules of Procedure of Board of Supervisors of China Construction Bank Corporation," and other corporate governance documents. The meeting elected the First Board of Directors and the First Board of Supervisors. The First Board of Directors had ten members: Zhang Enzhao, Chang Zhenming, Zhu Zhenmin, Jing Xuecheng, Wang Shumin, Wang Yonggang, Liu Shulan, Zhao Lin, Song Fengming and Yashiro Masamoto. The First Board of Supervisors had four members: Xie Duyang, Liu Jin, Jin Panshi and Chen Yueming.

On the same day, the First Meeting of the First Board of Directors elected Zhang Enzhao as the Chairman and Chang Zhenming as the Vice Chairman and appointed Chang Zhenming as the President; Liu Shulan, Zhao Lin, Luo Zhefu and Zheng Zhijie as Vice Presidents on the nomination of Chang Zhenming; Xin Shusen as the Chief Controller; and Chen Zuofu and Fan Yifei as Assistant Presidents. The meeting also authorized the Chairman to sign the "China Construction Bank Split-up Agreement." The First Meeting of the First Board of Supervisors elected Xie Duyang as the Chairman. JIC was also established on the same day. The CBRC appointed Zheng Zhijie as the Deputy Secretary of JIC's internal CPC committee. On September 21, 2004, China Construction Bank Corporation officially announced its establishment, which was a major milestone for CCB's joint-stock reform.

On November 29, 2004, CCBC held its Second Meeting of the First Board of Directors and the First Extraordinary Shareholders' Meeting in Beijing. The board meeting deliberated and approved 23 proposals and resolutions, including revising its articles of association, "Work Rules of the President," and "Work Rules of the Board Secretary." On December 27, 2004, CCBC held its Third Meeting of the First Board of Directors and the Second Extraordinary Shareholders' Meeting in Beijing. The board meeting approved, among others, the "Proposal of China Construction Bank Corporation for Adopting the Articles of Association (H-share) and Authorizing the Board of Directors to Make Amendments," "Outline for the Development Strategy of China Construction Bank Corporation," and "Plan for Reforming and Setting Up Internal Organizations of China Construction Bank Corporation."

3. Significance of the establishment of CCBC

While having no precedent to follow and being saddled with severe legacy issues, unsupported paper profits, weak internal risk control and undercapitalization, CCB carried out its joint-stock reform as a "do-or-die" effort.

In such a context, by pushing forward its joint-stock reform, restructuring its finances and reshaping its management framework, CCB finally incorporated China Construction Bank Corporation. Despite the difficulties and challenges, with the support of the state's capital contribution and other financial restructuring measures, CCB's reform was successfully completed. In this process, CCB incorporated modern management concepts such as economic value added (EVA), economic capital (EC) and key performance indicators (KPI) into its brand new performance evaluation system; preliminarily created a credit management framework featuring review-approval role segregation, risk warnings, credit ratings, and operation-supervision role segregation; and reduced the number of its group entities by one third and its staff by over 20% in three years. CCB's practices guided the path for the joint-stock reform and restructuring of other state-owned banks.

The restructuring into a joint-stock company enabled CCB to improve its corporate governance structure; bring its risk management, internal control, and operating frameworks up to par with modern financial enterprises; streamline its internal organizations; increase business performance; and seek public listing. Furthermore, the joint-stock reform changed the way that foreign investors saw China's state-owned banks, and rekindled the hopes of those banks that were dismissed by foreigners as being "technically insolvent."

III. Involvement of Foreign Strategic Investors

At a State Council executive meeting held on March 2, 2004, "attracting strategic investors" was underlined as "one of the main tasks of CCB's joint-stock reform." On March 11 the same year, CBRC issued the "Guidance on the Corporate Governance Reform and Supervision of BOC and CCB," specifically calling for the introduction of strategic investors into the two banks. Under the leadership of the CPC Central Committee and the State Council, and with the guidance and support of other government agencies, CCB treated the engagement of strategic investors as a top priority of the reform.

After its establishment in September 2004, CCBC started to gain clarity into its existing problems: low profitability and risk management capability, inability to fully implement customer-oriented service procedures and operating model, wide gaps in product innovation with commercial banks in developed countries, lack of professionals skilled in modern financial instruments, and an underdeveloped human resources system and staff incentives and restraints. Foreign investors were necessary to help CCB solve these problems. Such engagement was not the end goal of CCB's reform, but rather a means to boost its corporate governance, management practices, and core competencies. Accordingly, at the very beginning of the investor selection process, CCB created a set of selection criteria, aiming to find investors who, as the CBRC mandated, had a long-term investment horizon and were willing to help CCB improve its governance and to engage in business cooperation without creating direct competition (referred to as the requirements of "long-term shareholding, governance optimization, business cooperation, and non-competition" by CBRC).

Although foreign strategic investors were optimistic about China's economy and the long-term prospect of Chinese banking sector, they were still worried about the risks of investing in Chinese banks. Paraphrased, the *Financial Times* noted in an editorial in early June 2005 that "for multinational banks, the attraction of acquiring a stake in Chinese banks was obvious: they could seize the opportunity before China opened the market. However, the risk was at least as great as the attraction. Although bad debts had been cleaned up and NPL ratios had fallen, the quality of recent loans was still questionable, especially as the economy slowed sharply. Some branches had been closed, but the remainders tended to have a stronger relationship with local officials than with their head offices. Large state-owned banks were still over-staffed despite layoffs, and only a few employees were familiar with modern banking operations. Furthermore, court judgments against defaulters could hardly be enforced."[1]

In fact, foreign investors were not optimistic about CCB at that time. Uncertain about the prospect of cooperation, most foreign institutional investors showed less investment interest and put forth eye-catchingly low bids. On March 16, 2005, CCBC held the Fourth Meeting of the First Board of Directors and the 2005 First Extraordinary Shareholders' Meeting in Beijing, at which the resignation of Zhang Enzhao as CCBC Chairman and Director for personal reasons[2] was accepted. On March 17, 2005, the CPC Central Committee appointed Guo Shuqing as the Secretary of the Party Committee at CCBC. On March 25, 2005, CCBC held the Sixth Meeting of the First Board of Directors, and the 2005 Second Extraordinary Shareholders' Meeting in Beijing, at which Guo Shuqing was elected as the Chairman.

Guo took the office at a critical juncture when CCB was bringing in foreign strategic investors and pushing ahead with its IPO. Faced with the complicated and volatile external environment, CCB's new leadership

---

[1] Li Liming: "Who Are Against the Opening Up of the Banking Sector," *The Economic Observer*, December 3, 2005.
[2] On November 3, 2006, Zhang Enzhao was sentenced to 15 years' imprisonment for bribery by the Beijing No. 1 Intermediate People's Court.

team, headed by Guo, immediately threw themselves into inviting foreign strategic investors, and successively engaged with dozens of strategic investors including Citibank. Through careful comparison of the investors' international influence, business complementarity with CCB, financial strength, and other factors, CCB selected Bank of America (BofA) as its candidate investor, and finally formalized the decision through a strategic investment agreement.

In an exclusive interview with a leading financial press on June 22, 2005, Guo Shuqing talked about CCB's engagement of strategic investors. Guo said, "We set up a strategic investment team composed of our top employees, and started intensive preparations from the second half of 2004. We've met over ten potential investors to see if they meet our needs. In this process, we focused on the following criteria: First, the investors should be willing to develop long-term cooperation with CCB; second, they should be major banks meeting CCB's financing requirements; third, they should have advanced know-how and competitive advantages in banking businesses, and are willing to transfer technologies to and share management experience with CCB; and lastly, they should have no conflict of interest with CCB. Since we needed to simultaneously negotiate with several investors, the whole team was exhausted. However, with the support of Central Huijin, government authorities and the external professionals, we have seen encouraging results and substantial progress in the recent months particularly."[1]

As for the challenges that CCB encountered during the investor

---

1 "Why Bank of America? Inside Look into the Negotiations by Guo Shuqing," *Financial News*, June 22, 2005.

attraction process, Stephen Kin Wah Yiu, former Chairman of KPMG China, recalled, "At first, CCB was in talks with a large U.S. bank for quite a long time. The U.S. bank agreed to provide investment banking services to CCB for its listing and to make a strategic investment in CCB. Their negotiation lasted for a long time, but the U.S. bank finally decided to pull out, probably because of the price. The negotiation breakdown produced a crisis for CCB, because under the pressure of a tight IPO schedule, CCB was urgently in need of an endorsement of a foreign bank. At this juncture, BofA emerged."[1] In fact, CCB had been in contact with BofA since 2004, but their official negotiation began in March 2005, when Guo took the office of CCB Chairman at a time of crisis.

After dozens of rounds of tough but efficient negotiation that lasted for three months, BofA finally agreed to all terms proposed by CCB – including shareholding cap, non-competition, dispatch of directors, and strategic support – and to acquire a stake in CCB as a strategic investor. On June 17, 2005, BofA signed a strategic investment agreement and a seven-year strategic cooperation agreement with CCB, wherein BofA undertook to hold no more than 20% of CCB shares and never seek the controlling interest in CCB. On July 1, 2005, CCB reached an understanding on strategic cooperation with Temasek Holdings (Private) Limited ("Temasek"), made official with the signing of a definitive agreement with Temasek's wholly-owned subsidiary Asia Financial Holdings Limited ("Asia Financial") in Beijing.

In August 2005, BofA purchased 17.5 billion CCB shares, as well as a call option for subscribing to additional shares, for USD 2.5 billion. Lat-

---

1 From the interview with Stephen Kin Wah Yiu on February 15, 2017.

er in October, when CCB went public, it purchased another 1.651 billion CCB shares for USD 500 million, making a total investment of USD 3 billion. The average price of CCB shares for BofA was then RMB 1.27 per share, equaling 1.26 times CCB's net asset value per share in 2004, or over 1.7 times if the option strike price were to be discounted at the 5-year loan rate of 5.85%. Other than the preferential share price, CCB did not offer BofA any additional incentives. After BofA's investment in CCB, *Hong Kong Economic Times* said, "There is no shortage of people in the U.S. who think that BofA overpaid for the deal, indicating that U.S. investors are still conservative about developing the Chinese market."[1]

Through long-term efforts, CCB finally selected BofA and Temasek as its strategic partners, achieving the best results at the lowest cost. The involvement of strategic investors optimized CCB's ownership structure, and brought the experience and technologies of leading international banks to CCB. Directors and experts from BofA assisted CCB in corporate governance, risk management, retail banking, treasury services, and IT systems, narrowing its gap with leading banks. Furthermore, pursuant to its non-competition commitment, BofA closed all its retail banking outlets and strictly restricted its corporate banking services in China, so that its cooperation with CCB in the Chinese market would remain mutually beneficial. The call option to purchase additional shares enhanced their common interests and protected the long-term interests of CCB and its shareholders. BofA also promised that it would not hold a higher than 19.9% stake in CCB, nor would it seek to intervene or control CCB's operations. CCB's cooperation with Temasek also optimized its

---

1   *Hong Kong Economic Times*, June 20, 2005.

corporate governance structure and promoted its overseas expansion.

Eager to learn the skills and experience of BofA in key areas, CCB board of directors held a thematic meeting, attended by directors, supervisors and management, to discuss how to extract maximum benefits from the strategic assistance. On September 28, 2005, the CCB-BofA strategic assistance project was launched. CCB President Chang Zhenming presided over the launching ceremony, and Chairman Guo Shuqing delivered a speech. Subsequently, BofA dispatched experts to CCB to help it improve retail banking services, enabling CCB to upgrade its outlets from centers for payment settlement and transactions to centers for marketing and banking services. In the same year, the two banks signed a global treasury service (GTS) strategic cooperation agreement to carry out extensive cooperation in product management, professional training, and management structure consulting.

The CCB Chairman, Vice Chairman, and directors also led numerous delegations to BofA to study its business processes and management practices, thus preparing for the development of a feasible technical cooperation plan. During the performance of the strategic cooperation agreement, the two banks always maintained productive relations, and flexibly adjusted their scope of cooperation in light of the latest strategic needs instead of being locked into the terms of the original agreement. Their scope of cooperation went beyond the 52 services provided in agreement as new needs arose due to market development.

It turned out that selecting BofA as a major foreign keystone investor was a vital step toward CCB's H-share IPO. As an internationally leading bank, BofA made a substantial long-term investment in CCB at a time when foreign investors looked at the Chinese banking sector with suspicion. Its investment not only increased CCB's capital strength, but also enhanced other foreign investors' confidence in CCB. The business assistance of BofA, which was almost equivalent to an implicit endorsement for the listing, also raised investors' expectations on CCB's future growth and competencies. BofA also took part in CCB's roadshows in cities including New York, Chicago, Boston, and London, greatly contributing to its successful listing and high IPO pricing.

CCB introduced BofA as its strategic investor and built a long-term strategic partnership with it in the early 2000s, when the economic interactions between developed and emerging market economies were becoming increasingly extensive amid the globalization movement. Against this backdrop, China and the U.S., as major representatives of emerging and developed markets, showed strong desires for cooperation and mutual development. Riding on the momentum of China's fast-growing economy, CCB became the country's first major state-owned bank to go public through joint-stock reform, boasting strong financial strength, an immense customer base, and an extensive outlet network across China. Nevertheless, CCB was still far from achieving modern and market-based operation and management. As a leading U.S. financial institution, BofA had been cementing its position in the U.S. market for many years. The two banks complemented each other, pioneering the comprehensive cooperation between the Chinese and U.S. banking industries in equity, corporate governance, business, and culture. They provided a classic case of in-depth China-U.S. financial cooperation, and set a strategic milestone in the history of the Chinese banking sector.

IV. Public Listing

(I) Finalization of the H-Share Listing Plan

On September 29, 2005, CCBC held the 13th Meeting of the First Board of Directors in Beijing. The meeting approved five proposals, including the "Proposal on Approving Matters Related to H-Share Prospectus of China Construction Bank Corporation," "Proposal on Amending Articles of Association and Related Corporate Governance Documents of China Construction Bank Corporation," and "Measures for the Information Disclosure of China Construction Bank Corporation." With these groundworks in place, it then began to prepare for the listing.

(II) Pre-Marketing and Roadshow

From October 5 to 19, 2005, two roadshow teams, led by Chairman Guo Shuqing and President Chang Zhenming respectively, gave 128 presentations in 20 cities around the world and met with more than 500 institutional investors. The teams actively pitched the prospect of investing in CCB, and answered investors' questions and concerns. For investors worrying about China's macroeconomic fluctuations and CCB's asset quality and risk management, CCB's management gave frank, accurate and detailed answers, clearing away their doubts. During the roadshows, the confidence, steadiness, pragmatism, and professionalism of the management team deeply impressed the investors. In addition to leading investment banks like Morgan Stanley, China International Capital Corporation Limited (CICC), and Credit Suisse First Boston, CCB also engaged strong international underwriting syndicate and a Hong Kong underwriting syndicate during pre-marketing and roadshows, in a bid to reach the different segments of institutional investors worldwide. CCB also encouraged competition among members of the underwriting syndicates to maximize investment demand.

CCB made considerable preparations that would help it set a higher IPO price and keep on top of the price discovery process. First, it seized the initiative on IPO pricing, increasing the price range twice during marketing and price discovery. Second, it repeatedly revised documents presented at the analyst meeting, allowing analysts to gain a deeper understanding of CCB's investment value. Third, it carefully studied the analyst reports, investor feedback from pre-marketing, and the market's judgment on the value of CCB. On October 4, 2005, the underwriters set a preliminary price range of HKD 1.7-2.1 which CCB argued was way too conservative. Through over three hours of negotiation, the price range was finally raised to HKD 1.8-2.25.

After the roadshow started, CCB closely tracked the book-building process and the developments of the capital market. As of October 10, 2005, the IPO had been four times subscribed at the top end of the price range. The management of CCB responded briskly and persuaded the underwriters to further raise the price range to HKD 1.9-2.4. CCB proposed the second price hike in Edinburgh, Scotland. CCB Vice President Fan Yifei later recalled, "I barely slept that night. President Chang Zhenming and I summed up the results of our roadshows in Asia and agreed upon a new price range. Early next morning, we called Chairman Guo Shuqing, who was attending a meeting in Beijing, and then discussed with the underwriters about the price raise in a conference call… We felt quite confident at that time, because we had plenty of orders from international investors. We decided to double the top end of the P/B ratio range, so that the upper bound of the price went from HKD 2.25 to 2.40."

New York was the last stop and naturally the venue of the pricing meeting. Fan Yifei recalled, "Since the lead underwriter didn't agree with us on the price, I was expecting to see tit-for-tat bargaining. I had even come up with an alternative plan: if I couldn't manage it, the President would take the field; if he couldn't do it, then the Chairman would take over. Fortunately, the underwriters and I finally reached an agreement."[1]

(III) IPO and Listing on HKEX

On October 14, 2005, CCB Chairman Guo Shuqing announced CCB's H-share listing. On October 27, 2005, CCB was listed on Hong Kong Stock Exchange (HKEX). It planned to sell 26.485 billion H-shares through global offering, including 1.324 billion H-shares (5% of the total issue) in Hong Kong, and grant the underwriters an over-allotment option to buy an additional 3,972 million H-shares. The IPO price range was HKD 1.9-2.4 per share, indicating a potentially HKD 63.6 billion IPO, which would be a new record for the Hong Kong market. The proceeds would be used to strengthen CCB's capital and support the sustainable development of a series of banking activities.

On October 27, 2005, CCB was officially listed on HKEX (stock code: 0939). The shares opened at HKD 2.35 on the first day, topping out at HKD 2.375, and closed at HKD 2.35. The daily trading volume reached 3.637 billion shares, with a total turnover of HKD 8.58 billion. With an IPO price of HKD 2.35, CCB raised approximately HKD 62.2 billion globally, making it the largest public offering in the history

---

1 Xie Heng: "Glory and Cost: Listing of China Construction Bank," *Sanlian Life Week*, November 14, 2005. http://www.lifeweek.com.cn/2005/1114/13707.shtml.

of Hong Kong. As of November 9, 2005, CCB had sold 26,485 million shares as part of the original plan, as well as another 3,970 million shares from over-allotment ("greenshoe" option[1]) priced and sold out at HKD 2.35. Up to this point, CCB had issued 30.5 billion shares, or 13.5% of its total post-IPO equity capital, and raised HKD 71.58 billion in funds, 12.55% higher than the planned figure of HKD 63.6 billion.

On June 14, 2007, two years after CCB entered the H-share market, CCB's Shanghai Stock Exchange (A-share) listing plan was approved at a board meeting. On September 25, 2007, CCB was listed on Shanghai Stock Exchange (SSE). A total of 9 billion A-shares were issued, including 2.7 billion shares under placing tranche and 6.3 billon shares under public subscription tranche, at RMB 6.45 per share, raising RMB 58.05 billion in aggregate. On the first day, the shares opened at RMB 8.55 and closed at RMB 8.62. CCB's return to the A-share market further enhanced its capital strength and optimized its governance structure, which not only contributed to its long-term development, but also offered a new channel for mainland investors to reap the fruits of the banking reform.

(IV) Significance of CCB's Listing

The joint-stock reform and listing of CCB have provided a precedent for the Chinese banking sector, and its listing in Hong Kong is also of great significance.

As the first of the four SOCBs to be listed abroad, CCB not only achieved its own growth, but also set an example for the other banks who

---

1   "Greenshoe" is a colloquial term for the over-allotment option. It was named after U.S. company Green Shoe Manufacturing Co., which first used it in 1963.

intended to follow its footsteps. CCB's listing has substantially ramped up the confidence of domestic and overseas investors on the future of China's banking sector and even its financial system reform as a whole.

The successful listing of CCB had helped propel China's financial system reform; improve the corporate governance, operations, and the management capabilities of state-owned commercial banks; and boost the overall competitiveness of major Chinese commercial banks in the international market. The engagement of foreign strategic investors enabled CCB to transform into a public company, and more importantly, changed its operational frameworks by placing it under the oversight of domestic and foreign investors.

Section III
Joint-Stock Reform and Listing of BOC

BOC was the other pilot bank for the joint-stock reform. It spent over two years to complete financial restructuring, joint-stock reform, and introduction of strategic investors, before making IPO on HKEX and SSE on June 1 and July 5, 2006, respectively, thus becoming the first Chinese company to list fully tradable H-shares (*quanliutong*, also referred to as "full circulation," i.e., formerly unlisted H-shares later converted into H-shares that could be openly traded in the stock market) and A-shares, and transforming from a wholly state-owned commercial bank to a joint-stock commercial bank.

Related Topic: Brief History of BOC

In February 1912, by the approval of Sun Yat-sen, BOC was established to replace the Ta-Ching Bank of the Ministry of Revenue (*daqing hubu yinhang*). From 1912 to 1949, BOC played three different roles. During 1912-1928, BOC functioned as the central bank. In 1928, it was transformed into a government-chartered foreign exchange bank. In 1942, it served as a specialized bank for promoting international trade.

After the founding of the People's Republic of China in 1949, BOC was taken over by the new government. Its general administration division was relocated from Shanghai to Beijing in December of the same year, and later operated under the PBOC in 1950. On October 27, 1953, the Administration Council of the Central People's Government approved the "Ordinance of Bank of China," which stated that BOC was a specialized foreign exchange bank chartered by the Council.

On March 13, 1979, upon the approval of the State Council, BOC was spun off from the PBOC and operated directly under the State Council, performing the functions of SAFE. The original general administration division of BOC was changed to its head office, being responsible for the centralized management of foreign exchange business nationwide. In September 1983, the State Council positioned the PBOC as the central bank; subsequently, BOC and SAFE were separated and BOC was still responsible for foreign exchange. Accordingly, BOC had become a specialized bank for foreign exchange and foreign trade under the supervision of the PBOC.

Since the reform and opening-up initiative was launched, BOC has matured rapidly in all aspects, joining the ranks of leading international banks. In the beginning of 1994, as a part of the financial reform, BOC started transforming to a state-owned commercial bank.

In 2003, the state selected BOC as one of the two pilot banks for the joint-stock reform of wholly state-owned commercial banks.

On August 26, 2004, upon approvals of the State Council and CBRC, BOC was wholly restructured into Bank of China Limited with Central Huijin as the sole promoter. Afterward, the restructured BOC introduced strategic investors, strengthened internal management, promoted internal reforms, and modernized operational frameworks, unveiling a new chapter in its illustrious history.

On June 1 and July 5, 2006, BOC listed its shares on HKEX and SSE respectively.

I. Becoming One of the First Pilot Banks for Joint-Stock Reform

(I) Preparing for the Restructuring

1. Creation of BOC Restructuring and Listing Office

Following the restructuring and listing of BOCHK, BOC immediately turned its attention to its own restructuring and listing. To better prepare for the structuring, at the end of 2002, the Party Committee at the BOC head office decided to set up the Restructuring and Listing Office.

The Restructuring and Listing Office was responsible for the overall planning and day-to-day management and coordination of restructuring and listing efforts. It also performed real-time supervision and inspection of the progress and performance of restructuring and listing units, as well as restructuring-related external liaison.

2. Ten restructuring and listing units

BOC created ten restructuring and listing units (Fig. 5.1) to carry forward its restructuring and listing, covering development strategy, NPL and risk management, organizational structure and process integration, financial accounting, IT, human resources management, public relations, legal affairs, overseas restructuring programs, and general affairs. Those units operated under relevant departments of the head office. Duties of the ten units are illustrated below:

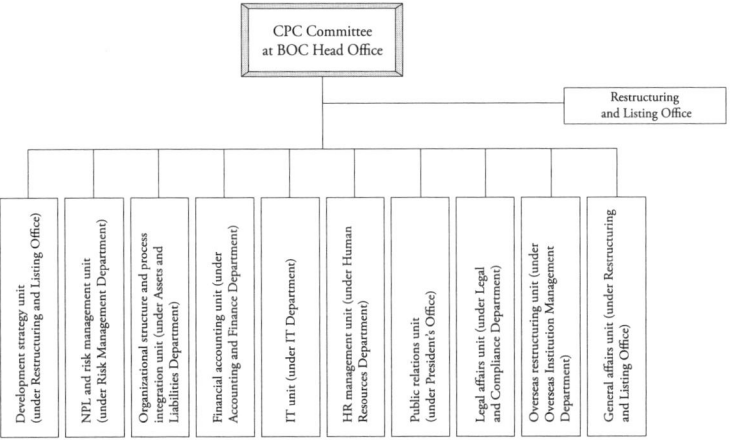

Fig. 5.1: Ten Units for BOC Restructuring and Listing

(1) Development strategy unit

The unit was set up to develop strategies for BOC's joint-stock reform. In 2003, it formulated five-year strategic plans for both domestic and overseas markets. In the second half of 2005, it completely updated BOC's development strategies, and set about working out a rolling three-year business development plan. The unit proposed that BOC should re-position itself as a commercial bank by vigorously developing its retail and corporate banking business and allocating resources to major areas, key accounts, and high value-added services to increase fee-based business revenue.

(2) NPL and risk management unit

The unit mainly assumed the duties of disposing of policy-related NPLs and investigating and auditing non-credit assets; winding down self-invested entities, disposing of sensitive assets and NPAs transferred from BOCHK to BOC Cayman Branch; and steadily pushing forward the establishment of a six-pronged risk management framework (global coverage, comprehensive risk management, full-participation risk management culture, whole-process risk management, new risk management methods, and full-value risk measurement) to improve BOC's long-term mechanism for risk management and internal control.

(3) Organizational structure and process integration unit

The unit integrated processes to promote "multifunctional front office, enhanced middle office, and combined back office" to help BOC achieve more integrated and efficient operations, streamline the management and organization structure, and improve management efficiency. The process integration program mainly covered: (i) clarifying the duties of the front, middle, and back offices to highlight the customer service and marketing functions of the front office; (ii) building a more professional and IT-based middle-office management process; and (iii) promoting back-office integration and resource sharing to lower costs. The unit was also committed to progressively streamlining BOC's internal organization to achieve a flatter management structure, and optimizing outlet distribution and functions to improve revenue.

(4) Financial accounting unit

The unit was mainly responsible for (i) investigating and auditing bank-wide assets and capital, cleaning up NPAs, and attributing ownership to assets based on audit results; (ii) comprehensively updating basic financial accounting systems, and driving innovations in financial management; (iii) facilitating prudent accounting practices and implementing strict information disclosure rules; and (iv) preparing financial statements pursuant to IFRS, and promoting comprehensive, coordinated and sustainable business development to allow BOC to become one of the first domestic banks to meet IFRS requirements.

(5) IT unit

The unit was mainly designed to comprehensively improve BOC's integrated management and service capabilities by developing a new-generation core banking system (CBS) and management information system (MIS), building IT infrastructure, and enhancing overseas IT infrastructures.

(6) Human resources management unit

The unit was mainly responsible for (i) actively reforming the HR system; (ii) eliminating bureaucratic mindset and converting BOC's public institution-influenced human resources system to one more befitting a commercial bank; (iii) replacing seniority-based promotion with merit-based promotion; (iv) replacing permanent employment with market-based employment; (v) replacing fixed compensation with performance-based compensation; (vi) building a rational and optimized performance management system; and (vii) attracting and retaining global professionals and experts.

(7) Public relations unit

The unit mainly assumed the duties of (i) developing and implementing domestic and overseas publicity plans for restructuring and listing; (ii) strengthening leadership and employee training; (iii) enhancing investor relations program; (iv) improving public relations management and emergency response capabilities; and (v) cultivating corporate culture focused on integrity and responsibility.

(8) Legal affairs unit

The unit was mainly tasked with engaging legal advisers to investigate asset ownership, conduct due diligence, and draft reform-related legal documents such as work plans and articles of association.

(9) Overseas restructuring unit

The unit was mainly responsible for (i) collecting basic information of overseas branches to assess and clean up their assets; (ii) developing overseas business strategies and specific plans for the process integration of overseas branches; (iii) driving the creation of an overseas information sharing platform; and (iv) proposing a reform plan for matrix management framework for overseas branches.

(10) General affairs unit

Duties of the unit mainly included (i) researching and improving corporate governance framework and creating a new governance structure with the board of directors as the core; (ii) developing an overall restructuring and listing plan and tracking its implementation; (iii) organizing the selection of strategic investors; and (iv) establishing an information transmission, management and coordination system linking the head office and branches throughout restructuring and listing.

(II) Seeking to Be a Pilot Bank

In a report to the State Council, BOC expatiated over its six comparative advantages to be a pilot bank for the restructuring and listing of state-owned banks: (i) Financial strength. At that time, BOC led other Chinese banks in terms of profitability, capital strength and capital adequacy ratio; (ii) Reputation and brand. Over the years, BOC had built an impressive international reputation and won the admiration of many media outlets. BOC took the lead in disclosing asset quality based on the internationally accepted five-category loan classification, and increased its information transparency each year in line with international standards, which was highly praised by market participants; (iii) Business. As the most international Chinese bank at the time, BOC provided commercial banking, investment banking and insurance services across its global business network; (iv) Human resources. Being the most internationalized among Chinese banks, BOC had more international finance professionals and a higher-quality workforce than any other domestic bank; (v) Experience. Under the leadership of the State Council, BOC successfully restructured and listed BOCHK, the first state-owned financial institution to be listed abroad. In this process, BOC accumulated extensive experience. In addition, BOC's wholly-owned investment bank BOC International also had hands-on experience with the restructuring and listing of SOEs and financial institutions; and (vi) Collaboration. As the world's most well-known Chinese bank, BOC had built long-standing and close ties with many international institutional investors and banks. As a result, BOC was most likely to be accepted by domestic and foreign investors, and better positioned to learn from foreign banks and select strategic investors.

Liu Mingkang, BOC President at the time, later recalled how BOC became a pilot bank. "Soon after the listing of BOCHK in 2002, I submitted a proposal to the central government on the restructuring and listing of BOC – if BOC could do it, so could ICBC and CCB. However, at that time, listing a large SOCB was a major political issue requiring discussion by the Standing Committee of the Political Bureau. The listing of BOC was thus put on hold…

"Later, I was appointed as CBRC Chairman. Before I took office, Premier Wen Jiabao had a talk with me and asked for my plan at CBRC. I told him that we should advance the reform of the banking sector and open it wider to the outside world. We would have two priorities. One was to promote the restructuring, joint-stock reform, and listing of wholly state-owned commercial banks, so that they would be able to recover and become stronger by themselves and in the event of hardship, find market-based solutions rather than asking the Minister of Finance for assistance.

"Premier Wen asked me if BOC could be reformed on a pilot basis. I told him: The success of BOC's reform would be a matter of course, and its failure would also be a failure on our part. If BOC alone were to be reformed, there would be no comparison, competition, and differentiation; so it would be better to add another bank to the pilot program. Wen advised me to seek the opinion of Vice Premier Huang Ju, who was in charge of financial affairs. When I met Huang, I said that without joint-stock reform, banks could never establish incentive and constraint mechanisms. Considering that an average employee of the Big Four had a monthly salary of seven or eight hundred yuan, how could our banks retain top professionals and develop themselves into modern banks? Moreover, employees who had worked harder and shouldered more responsibilities earned as much as those who did not, and thus were not motivated to do more. Most importantly, the reform would free banks from their dependence on MOF. Banking is a risky sector, and banks should bear their own risks and make every effort to replenish their capital by marketing their shares to investors and issuing bonds. Huang agreed with me and suggested, in addition to BOC and CCB, including BoCom into the first group of pilot banks."[1]

On September 17-18, 2003, the State Council and the Standing

---

1 Quoted from the interview with Liu Mingkang on October 31, 2016.

Committee of the Political Bureau each held a meeting, at which BOC and CCB were selected as the pilot banks for the joint-stock reform.

(III) Group-Wide Restructuring into a Joint-Stock Company with a Sole Promoter

Group-wide restructuring is one of the distinguishing features of BOC's joint-stock reform. But historically, during the formulation of the restructuring plan, BOC considered an equity carve-out (ECO) to strip off low-quality assets, creating an entity that was in a stronger position to be listed. This would be an easier option.

But after many rounds of discussions, the Party committee at BOC reached a consensus: BOC should not and had no reason to exclude any assets and personnel from the company to be listed, regardless of the difficulties. The ECO model was proposed primarily because of BOC's serious legacy issues, but BOC was confident that it could withstand and solve these issues.

After the overall listing plan was determined, BOC thoroughly considered whether to include BOCHK in the plan, and decided that although BOCHK was already a public company, it was still an integral part of BOC. If incorporated into the post-reform of BOC, it would build synergy with the rest of BOC and enable BOC to more effectively expand overseas business lines and connect domestic and overseas markets. Admittedly, this integration would make for a more complex listing process, for although BOC was one of the first Chinese banks to adopt internationally accepted accounting standards, it still used a somewhat different set of standards compared with BOCHK.

Following prudent preparations, BOC was restructured as a whole into a joint-stock commercial bank named Bank of China Limited, which succeeded to all assets, liabilities, business, and employees of BOC. This process created no holding company or surviving company, nor was it accompanied by split-off or divestiture. Central Huijin was the sole promoter.

Group-wide restructuring into a joint-stock company with a sole promoter was a wise decision made by BOC in light of historical, practical, and future-impact considerations.

1. Practical considerations

(1) Ensuring the continuity of overseas branches and global business lines

Before the reform, BOC had been operating an extensive network of branches in 27 countries and regions across the world. Maintaining the lawful and continuous operations of these entities was a great concern to BOC – and perhaps even to China's international image. However, according to legal due diligence, in some jurisdictions BOC had to obtain the prior approval of the local regulators before it could change its ownership and organizational structure, and such a process might reduce BOC's overseas business scope or at least put it under greater scrutiny. In addition, BOC had entered into a large number of agreements for "three loans"[1] with foreign governments and economic organizations who could, on the basis that one of the contracting parties had changed due to the reform, demand that BOC assume corresponding legal liabilities, which would adversely affect its overseas business.

---

1 "Three loans" refer to loans to foreign governments, mixed (i.e., with additional contribution from other sources) loans to foreign governments, and buyer's credit to foreign parties. Featuring low interest rates, long terms, and generally favorable terms, "three loans" were mainly issued to promote equipment and technology export and intergovernmental cooperation.

Through group-wide restructuring into a joint-stock company with a sole promoter, BOC avoided the risk of being required by foreign regulators to reapply for business licenses due to change of organization form, and also the risk of breach of contract caused by a change in a contracting party. According to Chinese laws, if a company fully restructures itself into a joint-stock company, subsequent inclusion of additional shareholders will not change the nature or affect the continuity of the company. Therefore, performing relevant approval processes after such restructuring would not affect the legal continuity of BOC's overseas branches and businesses.

(2) Maintaining corporate stability and assuming social responsibility

Group-wide restructuring also avoided the personnel division and reassignment in relation to the 230,000 employees BOC had, and thus prevented the potentially hostile process and safeguarded the business stability of BOC. Furthermore, under the ECO model, the national social security authority would be saddled with a big chunk of resettlement expenses for the retired or laid-off employees, burdening the state and the society. On the date of its listing, BOC decisively took on this social responsibility by creating an allowance for employee benefits for all existing and retired employees.

(3) Improving corporate governance

As a relatively quick path to listing, the ECO model was once favored by many SOEs until the Enron scandal[1]. Since then, this model was used

---

1   The Enron scandal, occurring in 2001 in the U.S., eventually led to the bankruptcy of the Enron Corporation, one of the largest energy, commodity and service providers in the world, and America's seventh largest company ranked by *Fortune*. On December 2, 2001, Enron suddenly filed for bankruptcy in the New York Bankruptcy Court, creating the second largest bankruptcy case in American history.

less and less because it tended to create related-party transactions and information opacity. Both domestic and overseas markets were littered with countless cases where holding companies interfered with the independent operations of joint-stock companies. By contrast, listing as a group can effectively avoid the potential pitfalls of related-party transactions, increase information transparency, and help build a more effective corporate governance structure.

(4) Avoiding legal problems

Pursuant to China's *General Principles of the Civil Law* and the *Contract Law*, BOC's group-wide restructuring into a joint-stock company would not change its legal personality, and thus avoided legal problems such as obtaining the approval of the creditors for transferring claims, liabilities and contracts to the new joint-stock company.

(5) Protecting the national interest and state assets

For the sake of the national interest, BOC adopted group-wide restructuring with Central Huijin as the sole promoter to ensure the preservation and growth of the value of state-owned assets. The *Company Law* provides that "for shares issued in a single offering, the issuing conditions and price for each share shall be the same." If BOC introduced strategic investors or other entities as promoters during its restructuring, these promoters, by law, would enjoy the same share price as that offered to Central Huijin. But if BOC did so after the restructuring, it could issue new shares to strategic investors at a premium per standard investment practices, thereby protecting the national interest and state-owned assets.

2. Future-impact considerations

BOC had operated a business network composed of commercial banking, investment banking and insurance before its joint-stock reform, and a group-wide restructuring would help it maintain the integrity of that network. Moreover, the group-wide restructuring aligned with the industry trend toward customer-centric designs, cross-marketing, and offering a full package of financial services to each individual customer, allowing BOC to maintain its unified brand image and customer network.

3. Historical considerations

Founded nearly a century ago, BOC has witnessed China's recent history from the Qing Dynasty to the Republic of China, and finally to the People's Republic of China. BOC wished to cherish its century-old brand, heritage, culture, and corporate values and to preserve them during the restructuring, and so was fully committed to maintaining its integrity.

On December 30, 2003, the "Master Plan for Implementing the Joint-Stock Reform of Bank of China and China Construction Bank" was officially approved at a meeting chaired by Premier Wen Jiabao, setting the restructuring program into motion.

II. Financial Restructuring and Establishment of the Joint-Stock Company

(I) Financial Restructuring

Financial restructuring, as a prerequisite to the joint-stock reform, is a process where a range of measures – such as capital injection by the state, write-off of loss loans, divestiture of a portion of the NPAs, and issuance of subordinated bonds – were taken to improve the banks' financial health so that they could meet the basic requirements for the reform and listing. Following the principle of "one bank, one strategy," each bank tailored its financial restructuring plan according to its own financial conditions.

1. Capital injection with foreign reserves

At the end of 2003, the State Council decided to inject USD 22.5 billion (including USD 19.6 billion foreign reserves and 7.01 million ounces of gold reserves), or RMB 186.4 billion equivalent, into BOC through Central Huijin. The State Council explicitly required that stricter external supervision and assessment be put in place to ensure that the injected capital would be safe and generate a fair return.

BOC didn't convert the USD 22.5 billion into renminbi, or use it to write off doubtful debts; rather, like foreign reserves, the funds were mainly invested in highly rated and liquid foreign bonds. Through BOC's careful planning and robust management, these funds generated considerable profits, ensuring the maintenance and growth of the value of the state's contributions.

Thanks to the capital injection, BOC greatly improved its financial position and was able to expedite its restructuring and IPO process.

2. Disposal of NPAs

In 1999, before the joint-stock reform, the Big Four had sold RMB 1.4 trillion NPAs to the four AMCs, including RMB 267.4 billion from BOC's domestic branches. This partly helped BOC address its NPAs. However, by the end of 2003, BOC was again troubled by tremendous NPAs. Four factors contributed to this apparent paradox.

First, because the state did not strip off all of BOC's NPAs in 1999, there was still a considerable amount remaining to be resolved by BOC. Compiled figures showed that in 1999, a total of RMB 267.4 billion of NPAs was removed from BOC, representing a decrease of 12.68 percentage points in the percentage of non-performing RMB-denominated credit assets, of 13.81 percentage points in the percentage of non-performing foreign-currency credit assets, and of 13.15 percentage points in the overall NPA ratio. Second, the replacement of the four-category loan classification by the five-category system increased the volume of NPLs. Third, there were loans originated before 2000 that became non-performing in 2000-2003. Fourth, a portion of loans issued after 2000 had also turned into NPAs.

In BOC's financial restructuring, disposal of NPAs was the top priority. However, if BOC were to independently resolve such a huge amount of NPAs on its own, it would take a much longer period, which would incur opportunity cost amid fierce market competition. Given this and based on its specific operational conditions, BOC developed a series of NPA disposal plans.

BOC originally proposed a comprehensive solution based on NPA divestiture, namely the state would help BOC offload RMB 160 billion or RMB 220 billion of NPLs, and BOC would dispose of the remainder. After rounds of discussions with government agencies, BOC finally adopted a financial restructuring plan featuring a mix of divestiture, write-off, and government capital injection.

On December 31, 2003, the MOF issued the "Notice on Financial Treatment of the Restructuring of Bank of China and China Construction Bank," specifying the approach, procedures, and accounting processes for writing off loss loans and non-credit asset losses. In accordance with the Notice, BOC reclassified approximately RMB 220 billion of owner's equity as a special allowance, and pushed forward the financial restructuring in an active, sound, and compliant manner.

In February 2004, BOC specially set up a joint-stock reform asset disposal team and an accountability team to dispose of NPAs. The former was responsible for writing off renminbi and foreign-currency loss loans and selling doubtful loans. From June to September 2004, BOC sold and wrote off its NPLs, policy-directed assets and loss loans totaling RMB 272.02 billion at book value over three rounds, including RMB 148.54 billion of NPLs (RMB 73.430 billion at net book value after deduction of the provision for loan loss impairment), RMB 18.1 billion of policy-directed assets (RMB 18.1 billion at net book value), and RMB 105.38 billion of loss loans (zero at net book value after being fully written off against the state's capital injection). Specifically, for NPLs, the PBOC issued to BOC RMB 73.43 billion of five-year special central bank bills at 50% of the book value of these NPLs, and transferred the proceeds to Cinda to purchase these NPLs. For policy-directed assets, the PBOC issued RMB 18.1 billion of three-year special central bank bills to BOC at 100% of the book value of the assets, and the proceeds raised were used to purchase those assets. Loss loans were fully written off against capital injection by the state, and then "sold" to China Orient Asset Management Co., Ltd. for zero yuan and without recourse.

Identifying NPAs and imposing accountability was an indispensable part of BOC's financial restructuring. The State Council ordered that strict measures be taken to hold relevant bank personnel liable for NPAs, crack down on loan evasion, and prevent moral hazard. For this purpose, the head office's Inspection and Audit Department, with the support of the Risk Management Department and Supervision Department, set up an accountability investigation team for NPA disposal composed of 50 department and branch representatives who consistently maintained high professional and ethical standards. Adopting a historical perspective and an impartial and comprehensive approach, the team analyzed the objective and subjective reasons for the build-up of NPAs, and identified the individuals that should be held accountable. Also, based on thorough studies and intensive discussions, the team issued the "Notice on Issues Regarding Identifying and Pursuing Responsibilities for NPA Disposal during the 2004 Joint-Stock Reform" to all branches. The Notice specified the principles, standards and procedures for identifying and pursuing responsibilities. Furthermore, to strictly prevent moral hazard, BOC created a post-evaluation system to include the outcomes of investigation in its annual performance assessment.

In this regard, then BOC President Li Lihui later said: "BOC did some productive work during the joint-stock reform, including the disposal of NPAs and the divestiture of non-financial assets. Bank personnel who were responsible for NPAs were severely punished, and they were not a small number. Today, this might seem like an overreaction, but at the time, it was absolutely necessary."[1]

3. Issuance of RMB 60 billion of subordinated bonds

Thanks to the divestiture of NPAs and government injection in foreign currency, the capital adequacy ratio of BOC rose significantly. However, it still fell short of regulatory standards. To address this problem, following the approvals of the State Council and government agencies and drawing on international experience, between the second half of 2004 and the first half of 2005, BOC issued four tranches of subordinated bonds with principal amounting to RMB 60 billion to replenish its supplementary capital. This innovative financial product energized the Chinese capital market, and offered investors a new investment product

---

1 From the interview with Li Lihui on February 21, 2017.

and approach to investing, significantly boosting the country's financial reform and innovation.

4. Attribution of assets

During the reform, one of BOC's biggest challenges was the attribution of asset ownerships. Since BOC adopted the group-wide restructuring and listing plan instead of ECO (which was widely used by SOEs during their joint-stock reform), there was no surviving company or entity to take over its unattributed assets and other hard-to-resolve matters, which required a more efficient and thorough attribution of assets. To that end, BOC started a bank-wide initiative for asset appraisal and attribution, which covered all land holdings under its jurisdiction. As of the beginning of 2004, BOC held 12,120 parcels of land in 31 provinces, autonomous regions, and municipalities directly under the central government. However, preliminary survey showed that due to historical complications and different local conditions, only 51.90% of BOC's lands had the corresponding certificates.

To keep up with the group-wide restructuring schedule, BOC needed to complete the land appraisal and attribution as early as possible. To this end, BOC had numerous discussions with the Ministry of Land and Resources and drafted a land asset disposal plan. The Ministry simplified its processing procedure, and also offered strong support in land disposal, land appraisal preliminary review, filing, and land asset disposal approval. In July 2006, BOC had obtained certificates for 90% of its properties, a major improvement from the original 51.90%.

(II) Establishment of Bank of China Limited

On August 23, 2004, Central Huijin held the founding assembly of

Bank of China Limited ("BOC") as its sole promoter. Also, Central Huijin was the sole shareholder of BOC, holding a 100% stake or 186.39 billion shares in BOC on behalf of the state, and exercising rights and fulfilling obligations as a contributor. In accordance with Chinese laws and regulations, BOC drafted a new articles of association, and created a modern governance structure comprising the shareholders' meeting, board of directors, board of supervisors, and management.

The First Board of Directors and the First Board of Supervisors were elected at the founding assembly. The Board of Directors was composed of 11 members: Xiao Gang, Li Lihui, Zhang Jinghua, Yu Erniu, Zhu Yan, Zhang Xinze, Hong Zhihua, Huang Haibo, Hua Qingshan, Li Zaohang and Liang Dingbang. The Board of Supervisors was composed of Liu Ziqiang, Wang Xueqiang, Liu Wanming, and two employee representatives elected by the employee representatives' meeting.

Following the founding assembly, the First Meetings of the First Board of Directors and the First Board of Supervisors were held. At the board meeting, Xiao Gang was elected Chairman of the board and Li Lihui Vice Chairman. At Xiao's nomination, Chen Muhua and Zhuang Shiping were appointed as Honorary Chairman and Honorary Vice Chairman, respectively, and Li Lihui as President. At Li's nomination, Hua Qingshan, Li Zaohang, Zhou Zaiqun, and Zhang Yanling were appointed as Vice Presidents, and Zhu Min, Zhu Xinqiang, and Wang Yongli as Assistant Presidents. At the meeting of board of supervisors, Liu Ziqiang was elected as Chairman.

On August 26, 2004, upon the approval of the State Council, Bank of China Limited was established in Beijing. The century-old company experienced another transformation from a wholly state-owned commercial bank to a state-controlled joint-stock commercial bank. At its inaugural meeting held at the main ceremony venue in Beijing, more than 1,000 people were present, including members of the State Council Joint-Stock Reform Steering Group, leaders of relevant state ministries and commissions, members of BOC board of directors, board of supervisors and senior management, executives and employee representatives of BOC head office, and media representatives from China and abroad.

At the inaugural meeting, the CBRC announced the establishment of Bank of China Limited and issued the financial license, and SAIC issued the business license. PBOC Governor and State Council Joint-Stock Reform Steering Office Director Zhou Xiaochuan, Central Huijin Chairman Guo Shuqing, and BOC Chairman Xiao Gang each delivered a speech. On the same day, Huang Ju, member of the Standing Committee of the Political Bureau and Vice Premier of the State Council, paid a visit to BOC. Huang extended kind greetings to BOC employees and had talks with BOC directors, supervisors, and executives. Huang stressed that BOC should further contribute to the banking reform and strengthen its corporate governance, modernize operational frameworks, and improve business performance, to ensure the success of the pilot joint-stock reform of state-owned banks.

III. Introduction of Strategic Investors

On December 30, 2003, the State Council approved the "Master Plan for Implementing the Joint-Stock Reform of Bank of China and China Construction Bank." The Master Plan required the two banks to "introduce strategic investors from home and abroad to diversify the range of investors," because "only by introducing domestic and overseas investors and restructuring could an effective corporate governance structure and risk management framework be established." Venturing into uncharted territories, BOC quickly dived into engaging foreign strategic investors upon its establishment. From August 2005 to March 2006, BOC successively signed share purchase agreements with investors including Royal Bank of Scotland (RBS), Singapore-based Temasek's wholly-owned subsidiary Asia Financial, UBS, Asian Development Bank (ADB), and National Council for Social Security Fund (NCSSF). The above four foreign strategic investors altogether acquired a 16.85% stake in BOC for USD 5.225 billion, and NCSSF acquired a 3.9% stake for RMB 10 billion.

(I) Necessity of Introducing Strategic Investors

In line with the directives of the State Council and the regulations and requirements of CBRC, BOC intended to achieve five goals through bringing in strategic investors. The first was creating a diversified shareholder structure and optimizing its corporate governance mechanism. The second was enhancing business development and service capabilities to speed up the achievement of strategic business goals through cooperation. The third was improving the competencies of BOC and accelerating the building of a modern operation and management system by learning the managerial expertise and technologies of leading international banks. The fourth was boosting capital strength and capital adequacy ratio. The fifth was gaining the recognition of international investors. The endorsement of international investors would reassure BOC's ordinary investors of the financial soundness of the bank, thus increasing its share subscription and enterprise valuation.

(II) Strategic Investor Selection Criteria

The CBRC mandated that any strategic investors to be engaged by domestic banks should meet the requirements of "long-term shareholding, governance optimization, business cooperation, and non-competition."

In line with these principles, BOC developed its own strategic investor selection criteria. First, the investors should be able to diversify BOC's ownership structure and help it optimize corporate governance. Second, they should be large international commercial banks having no intention to establish independent operations in China and promising all-round cooperation with BOC, so as to enhance BOC's business growth and management capacity. Third, they should appropriately commit to their investments. Fourth, they should have sound corporate governance mechanisms, superior business performance, and strong international reputation.

Speaking about how BOC followed the above criteria when bringing in strategic investors, then BOC Chairman Xiao Gang said, "In the investment agreements, BOC and its strategic investors made commitments to each other and agreed upon binding provisions; our commitments, rights, and obligations were reciprocal. For example, we made three commitments: First, our net asset value per share at the end of 2005, 2006 and 2007 would not be lower than that on December 31, 2004; second, the stock prices offered to our strategic investors would not be higher than the IPO price or other pre-IPO placement prices; and third, should BOC fail to achieve an IPO after the three-year lock-up period, the strategic investors would be allowed to sell their strategic stakes back to BOC at purchase price.

"Likewise, our strategic investors also made commitments. For instance, RBS undertook that first, it would not transfer its shares or increase its shareholding within three years of closing; second, it would pursue a full range of business opportunities with BOC, and would not independently expand its business in China or buy shares of BOC's competitors; third, it would establish an exclusive strategic partnership with BOC; fourth, it would provide technical support and training to BOC in numerous management and business areas; and fifth, it would fulfill all its obligations as an investor (including paying compensation for breach of contract), and unconditionally and irrevocably undertake all its obligations as an investor under the investment agreement."[1]

(III) Introduction of Strategic Investors

1. RBS: the first strategic investor

On August 18, 2005, BOC introduced its first foreign strategic investor RBS, which acquired a 10% stake in BOC for USD 3.1 billion.

The event was reported in two versions the next day. One was RBS alone acquired a 10% stake in BOC for USD 3.1 billion, and the other was RBS, Goldman Sachs and Li Ka Shing Foundation jointly acquired a 10% stake for USD 3.1 billion. This inconsistency came about because that to dilute its investment risk, RBS sold half of its 10% stake to Goldman Sachs and Li Ka Shing Foundation, with each of them paying USD 750 million, and kept the remainder for USD 1.6 billion. The three formed a consortium to jointly hold the 10% stake in BOC, but Goldman Sachs and Li Ka Shing Foundation had no voting rights. The 10% stake was subject to a three-year lock-up period, which indicated a high acceptance of risk by RBS and also its willingness for long-term strategic cooperation.

---

1   From the interview with Xiao Gang on August 25, 2017.

Related Topic: Zhu Min: How BOC Brought in Foreign Strategic Investors[1]

"We [BOC executives] first approached JPMorgan CEO Jamie Dimon and made a deal with him, which, however, was rejected by the board... When we came to RBS, they had never thought of investing in BOC. It was at a meeting in New York or Washington, DC where I [Zhu Min, BOC Assistant President] met Sir Fred Goodwin, CEO of RBS. I asked him directly if he had 15-30 minutes to talk about investing in BOC. He paused for a moment and said that he had never thought of it. I asked if he'd like to give it some thought. He said yes. I knew I had aroused his interest, so I spent half an hour telling him about China's reform and other things. When we met the second time, he came with his advisor Ian. I told him if he was interested in BOC, he may come to China to meet our Chairman. And he did it. He came to Beijing later and met with Chairman Xiao Gang.

"Our negotiation with RBS was a tough one. They had global ambitions. While dealing with us, they were also working on an acquisition in Europe, but they couldn't afford both. Then they asked me if they could halve the investment. I said there was no half deal... There were two things that attracted them most: one was the prospects of the Chinese market, and the other was that BOC operated in both domestic and overseas markets and had a work style close to that of major international banks. At least in their eyes, we had a professional team which talked and behaved in an international manner.

"Goodwin's chief advisor Ian was responsible for the equity investment... We were very candid during discussions with him, because we noticed that BOC and RBS were highly complementary to each other. RBS

---

1 From the interview with Zhu Min on February 23, 2017.

had no major presence in the U.K. except Scotland, so their strategy was to create a 'second home field' in overseas market. In view of this, we tried to entice RBS with the benefits of the Chinese market and our corporate culture. We had rather tough negotiations with RBS, tougher than any negotiation with other strategic investors...

"Our apparent lack of 'credibility' put us in a weaker position. Their offers were all below RMB 1 per share, lower than our net asset [value per share]. And they even doubted the net asset value we provided. Credibility was really everything...

"We asked for RMB 1 per share, but they didn't agree. I told RBS that they could audit the accounts of any of BOC's branches they elected – it was impossible to audit all BOC's assets which were worth hundreds of billions of yuan – and they did what I said. I also told them that BOC had disciplined 60,000 employees for their roles in the build-up of NPLs, and there were 40 tons of NPL write-off documents in our basements. 'Do you want to check them?' I asked with confidence. They said they needed to report to the board to comply with their governance rule and they needed supporting documents to convince the board. Therefore, I gave all relevant documents to them, including the documents describing how we identified and pursued responsibilities for NPAs. After the audit of the selected branch, I went to Scotland again to deliver a presentation to them... At last, they accepted RMB 1 per share – they only offered RMB 0.7 or 0.8 per share at first."

2. Singapore-based Temasek: the second strategic investor

On August 31, 2005, BOC and Singapore's state investor Temasek Holdings (Private) Limited reached a preliminary agreement where Temasek agreed to buy a 10% stake in BOC for USD 3.1 billion through its wholly-owned subsidiary Asia Financial. The 10% stake comprised a 5% stake transferred from Central Huijin, and a 5% stake initially issued by BOC. After further negotiations, BOC allocated 5% of its IPO shares to Temasek. Temasek, as BOC's strategic investor, played a critical role in BOC's joint-stock reform, listing, and development. With its extensive corporate governance experience, Temasek greatly helped improve BOC's corporate governance by dispatching a director to its board. What's more, Temasek's proven track record of investment boosted investors' confidence in BOC's reform and listing. According to the strategic cooperation agreement with BOC, Temasek would help BOC expand business in Asia, and promote BOC's cooperation with its several equity-participating banks in Asia. It also undertook to provide BOC with extensive training and exchange opportunities relying on its industry contacts, recommend managerial and technical professionals needed by BOC, and assist BOC in IT renovation.

3. UBS: the third strategic investor

On September 27, 2005, BOC and UBS entered into an agreement wherein the latter would acquire a 1.61% stake in BOC for USD 500 million. As one of the world's most well-known financial institutions, UBS is at the forefront of global financial management market and provides world-class investment banking and securities services. Pursuant to the agreement, the parties would cooperate in investment banking and securities business, and UBS would share its experience and expertise in risk management and asset and liability management (ALM). David Chin, who was the Asia regional head of UBS, had participated in the listing of BOCHK, BOC and several other companies in Hong Kong. He recalled in an interview the difficulties encountered by BOC when engaging foreign strategic investors.

Related Topic: David Chin: Introduction of Foreign Strategic Investors by BOC[1]

"I [David Chin, UBS] remember that BOCHK went public in July 2002. In 2003, [BOC] was busy with the investigation of Liu Jinbao [former BOC Vice Chairman dismissed and later sentenced for bribery and improper lending], and in the same year, the CBRC and Central Huijin were established, followed by the NPA divestiture from and capital injection into BOC. We maintained close contacts with the BOC head office over the two years, and became good partners during our cooperation. We would share views on some issues, such as the reaction of overseas investors to China's banking reform, and the attitudes we should take toward some events. Around 2004, strategic investment of UBS in BOC was put on the table for discussion, and in 2005, soon after the meeting between UBS and Vice Premier Huang Ju, the project was officially launched.

"In fact, it was a tough process for state-owned banks to seek and negotiate with strategic investors for the joint-stock reform. At that time, BOC and CCB were the first pilot banks. The reform of CCB was by no means easy. Their negotiations with Citibank lasted for a very long time but ended with the withdrawal of Citibank… This indicated that not all foreign investors held a bullish view on Chinese banks – many doubted their prospects.

---

1 From the interview with David Chin on March 1, 2017.

"BOC's effort to seek strategic investors was also not plain sailing. RBS at first agreed to acquire a larger stake in BOC, but as the news spread, it received criticism from many shareholders, and thus had to greatly scale back its shareholding. Since UBS planned to purchase a small stake in BOC and we explicitly proposed our cooperation intention approved by our head office at the very beginning, BOC mainly focused on negotiations with RBS. While BOC reached basic consensus with RBS, they finalized the principal transaction terms. BOC asked UBS if it could accept these terms, and it said yes. In August and September 2005, BOC successively announced its cooperation with several other strategic investors, and by the end of the year, BOC and these investors closed their transactions."

4. ADB: the fourth strategic investor

On October 10, 2005, BOC and ADB reached an agreement under which ADB agreed to acquire a 0.24% stake in BOC for USD 75 million. As a major intergovernmental financial organization in the Asia-Pacific region, ADB is known for promoting social and economic development and cooperation in the region. Due to the restrictions in its charter, ADB only invested USD 75 million in BOC, which was, however, still the largest external investment made by the bank at the time. According to the agreement, ADB would support BOC in anti-money laundering, internal control, and project financing, and cooperate with BOC on specific projects.

5. NCSSF: the fifth strategic investor

On March 8, 2006, BOC concluded an agreement with NCSSF under which the latter would invest RMB 10 billion in BOC, becoming BOC's first Chinese strategic investor.

While the RMB 10 billion of strategic investment was not a particularly large sum for BOC, it was no less significant. First, because funds from NCSSF were equivalent to social security contributions, BOC had to ensure these funds wouldn't suffer any loss. Second, the investment, which was approved by the State Council, came at a critical and sensitive time when the banking reform faced widespread controversy and urgently needed to make progress. This investment showed the state was determined to push forward the reform. Third, the participation of NCSSF also signaled that while opening wider to foreign investors, Chinese banking sector was also welcoming investments from domestic investors. Such a demonstration effect would fundamentally change the ownership structures of state-owned commercial banks.

IV. A Challenging Journey to Listing

The joint-stock reform and listing was a challenging journey for BOC. However, BOC was able to overcome one challenge after another, achieving great success that would spur rapid growth and sustainable profitability.

(I) Business Process Integration and Organizational Restructuring

Taking the opportunity of joint-stock reform, BOC greatly accelerated its business process integration and organizational restructuring to boost its internal efficiency and service offering. In January 2005, BOC issued the "Opinions on Category-Based Business Process Integration and Organizational Restructuring of BOC Domestic Branches." The Opinions contained the general requirements on business process integration and organizational restructuring, the category-based implementation approach, and the focus of integration. It also prescribed that the purpose of process integration was to increase efficiency, lower costs, improve management and internal control, and create a more flexible organizational structure that would better meet customer needs. The program was also aimed to achieve greater business integration and pooling of internal resources and the separation of the front, middle, and back offices with the help of a flatter management structure that was organized based on business and product lines.

The reform consolidated the position of tier-one branches as the centers of regional operations and management, enhanced the oversight and control of the head office, and facilitated the flat management of outlet-level organizations based on business and product lines. Specifically, functions like accounting and audit, post-transaction supervision, risk control, funds settlement, and financial management were centralized in tier-one branches or well-managed tier-two branches; outlets including sub-branches were turned into service and marketing venues to highlight their service and marketing functions; and departments in charge of credit administration, accounting and clearing, and operations were set up to achieve the segregation of front, middle and back offices as well as more effective risk management.

As a result of business process integration and organizational restructuring, BOC optimized its organizational structure; its branches designed business lines according to regional strategies and created functional departments to capitalize on competitive advantages. BOC made an organic integration of business line-based management and region-based management, divided the management of different regions into different levels according to the scale of the respective business and customer structures, and set up specific management units for various business lines, thus improving its efficiency of resource allocation and operations as well as achieving more granular business management.

(II) Human Resources Reform

Within the SOCB reform, the overhaul of the human resources framework was the most far-reaching, complex, and arduous task. The key to becoming a "real bank" is to change mindset and systems; and the success of change lies in people. During BOC's reform, the HR reform was the first yet the most laborious, extensive, time-consuming, and influential step.

Given the stakes involved, and to underscore its determination, BOC started its HR reform at the head office before introducing it to pilot branches, and then the rest of the branches. On November 11, 2003, BOC head office held the BOC Human Resources Consulting Project Launch Meeting, marking the kickoff of its HR reform at the head office. In the following half a year, BOC carried out HR diagnostic review, department responsibility division, and other related measures. By May 2004, BOC head office finalized the standardized internal job positions, determined the preliminary implementation plan for compensation reform, and revamped its employment system and performance management system. Thus, the head office had basically completed its HR reform.

At the branch level, Jiangsu and Sichuan branches were selected as the first pilot sites in view of their geographical locations and state of development. HR reform at the two branches started in September 2004, based on the HR reform plan of the head office but adjusted to the branches' specific situations.

Then, relying on the practices of the head office and pilot branches, in tandem with the business process integration and organizational restructuring, BOC introduced the HR reform across the rest of its domestic branches. Specifically, BOC created three basic platforms comprising position, compensation and performance management systems to support its promotion, recruitment, compensation, and practical training programs. At the branch level, HR reform spread from tier-one branches, to tier-two branches and sub-branches.

Across the bank, BOC reshaped position systems and defined the functions of each position, so that employees could compete through an open and fair process, thus abandoning the so-called "communal pot" system (i.e., performance-independent distribution of benefits) and broadening the career choices for employees. BOC created three career tracks for managerial, professional, and technical personnel; abolished administrative positions at bureau-, section-, and division-levels; and adopted demand-oriented position creation and linked compensation to the duties of the position. In addition, BOC made it a practice to combine public and internal recruitment, which was welcomed by the employees.

Hungry for talent, BOC abolished its internal employee-only promotion policy and opened its door wider to external high-caliber talents, especially senior executives. It employed Lonnie Dounn, former HSBC Hong Kong Chief Credit Officer, as its Chief Credit Officer, the first time since the joint-stock reform that an SOCB offered an executive position to a foreigner. According to then BOC Chairman Xiao Gang, BOC's decision to hire an American executive aroused fierce controversy at the time. Some argued the compensation was too high compared to Chinese executives, and some worried about information security. But BOC stayed firm about its decision. First, to truly break conventions in its HR system, BOC needed a bold breakthrough in talent election, and such a breakthrough at the executive level would greatly promote its market-oriented HR reform. Second, credit management had always been BOC's weak spot – in 2004, BOC divested over RMB 100 billion of NPAs. To become a leading international bank, BOC needed to overcome this weakness. Third, hiring a foreign executive would create opportunities for cross-cultural exchange and management. As the most international Chinese bank, it made sense for BOC to experiment in this area. Fourth, information security could be ensured by laws and regulations, as well as contracts.

With the successful completion of the HR reform, BOC built its new HR management structure and protocols. From its development to the implementation, BOC's HR reform underscored not only BOC's business principles, foresights in market competition, and eagerness to improve employee performance and skillset, but also a human-centric and democratic approach.

While pushing the HR reform, BOC also improved its corporate culture and established its core value of "pursuit of excellence" which includes integrity, performance, responsibility, innovation, and harmony. Furthermore, it conducted a range of educational activities and trainings to integrate the core value into its management process as the common pursuit and code of conduct of employees.

(III) IT Blueprint

In 2004, taking the opportunity of the joint-stock reform, IT unit, one of BOC's ten units for the corporate restructuring and listing, proposed the IT Blueprint project based on a comprehensive and objective evaluation of BOC's existent IT system, development strategies, and business needs; the business philosophy of modern commercial banks; and the practices of global banking leaders. The project included the following aspects:

Application framework: The project treated the building of a well-designed application framework as its priority. It designed BOC's target application framework from the perspectives of delivery channels, customer management, product management, financial accounting and decision support. Moreover, based on the urgency of business needs and the interdependencies among the ten units, the project defined three stages for modernizing the current application framework.

Infrastructure framework: The project assessed existing IT infrastructure development strategies, and put forward numerous plans and guidelines for creating a disaster recovery center.

Management framework: Based on the functional objectives of BOC's IT system, the project created an architecture for the IT system; detailed project management, project prioritization, and annual budgeting procedures; and refined the management framework that would enable smoother interactions between banking businesses and the IT system.

Security framework: The project designed an IT security framework covering security awareness, strategy, organization and facilities.

Taken as a whole, the project provided guidelines and decision-making basis for the building of BOC's IT system. Also, it offered insights into the target application framework, design of transitory stages, construction plans for IT infrastructure and disaster recovery center, management framework featuring smoother interaction between banking businesses and the IT system, and corporate information security system.

V. IPO

(I) Preparations

On December 21, 2004, Vice Premier Huang Ju presided over a State Council Joint-Stock Reform Steering Group meeting to arrange preparatory work for BOC's IPO. Later in 2005, BOC set up an IPO working group, and in September that year, it submitted the "Request for Instructions on the IPO of Bank of China" to the State Council. In February 2006, the State Council approved BOC's overseas listing plan, and agreed that, to the extent that A-share market conditions would allow, BOC should list its A shares as soon as possible. In June 2006, BOC submitted to the State Council the "Request for Instructions on the IPO of Bank of China on the Domestic Market."

On the afternoon of May 23, 2006, BOC's management team in New York and London discussed IPO pricing through video conference. Taking into consideration subscription demand, investor feedback and market changes and upon consultation with Central Huijin, BOC set the H-share IPO price at HKD 2.95 per share, at the upper end of the HKD 2.5-3 price range, and 2.18 times BOC's predicted net asset value per share in 2006. For A shares, through book-building process and considering the interplay between the A-share and H-share markets and prices, BOC set the final A-share IPO price at RMB 3.08 per share.

Related Topic: David Chin: Listing and IPO Pricing of BOC[1]

"Compared with BOCHK, BOC's listing was a breeze. Seven or eight months after preparations started at the end of 2005, BOC went public

---

1 From the interview with David Chin on March 1, 2017.

in 2006, without being troubled by the challenges met by BOCHK. BOC engaged the same investment banks for its listing as those engaged by BOCHK, namely BOC International, UBS and Goldman Sachs. As long-time partners, despite the disputes which were unavoidable, we worked together on the listing, which was completed smoothly. The listing also received positive response from the market that exceeded our expectations. We knew we needed to seize the favorable conditions at the time to complete the IPO as soon as possible.

"Regarding BOC's IPO pricing, given that CCB saw its share price rising after its IPO despite an initial weak P/B ratio lower than 2, BOC set an IPO price slightly lower than CCB's trading price at that time, sweetening the deal for investors. Having witnessed CCB's successful IPO, investors placed a large volume of orders to BOC. Since our issue size was larger than CCB, we invested more time and effort in seeking new investors. Sovereign wealth funds in the Middle East showed strong interest in us, and Saudi Prince Al-waleed finally invested in BOC.

"BOC went public following CCB and BoCom and followed by ICBC. What were the differences between BOC and other banks? How to differentiate BOC from others? What strategies should BOC implement in the future? We spent countless hours to discuss these issues. BOC had a stronger international presence, but was weaker in renminbi business. So our marketing campaign focused on how BOC would increase its market share in that area, as well as how BOC would help individuals and enterprises enter overseas markets. We spent much effort on strategic positioning and investment stories."

(II) Roadshow

BOC conducted its roadshow in Hong Kong from May 11 to 12, 2006, followed by a presentation on May 15 in Singapore. Between May 16 and 18, BOC's red and blue roadshow teams held presentations in the U.S. and Europe respectively. The red team held roadshows in Los Angeles, San Francisco, and New York, and the blue team in Frankfurt, Edinburgh, and London. The markets, media and investors all responded positively.

In speaking of BOC's roadshow, Zhu Min recalled, "Our roadshow was supported by Hong Kong. We also gave presentations in Boston, New York, the U.K., and France, but Hong Kong was our top priority. At that time, the world had little understanding of China's banking sector. Hong Kong helped U.S. and European investors gain a better understanding of BOC."[1]

After the launch of BOC's roadshow on May 11, 2006, global major stock indices slumped across the board. Nevertheless, thanks to the efforts and performance of the roadshow teams, subscription interest kept growing strong. Regarding issues that investors most concerned about, such as exchange rate exposure, asset quality, net interest spread, relationship with BOCHK, cost and tax rates, and corporate loan growth rate, the roadshow teams were very well prepared and provided sincere answers.

(III) The First Company Listed on Both A-Share and H-Share Markets

BOC went public on HKEX and SSE on June 1 and July 5, 2006 respectively. Creating the largest A-share IPO at the time, BOC became

---

1 From the interview with Zhu Min on February 23, 2017.

the first SOCB listed on A-share market, the first A+H share dual-listed bank, and the first company to offer fully tradable A- and H-shares. After the A-share issuance, the state held a 71.95% stake in BOC, retaining its position as controlling shareholder.

BOC was listed in Shanghai just one month after its HKEX debut, making it the shortest interval between the A-share and H-share issuance. Furthermore, as the first bank adopting the "A+H" model (that is, going public in Shanghai and Hong Kong almost simultaneously), BOC avoided potentially adverse changes in markets and the issuer during the interval.

BOC was the first to build a channel connecting A-share and H-share markets, through which funds and shares could circulate between the two markets. In terms of funds, through certain market participants, domestic investors may purchase H-shares and foreign investors may buy A-shares. In terms of shares, A-shares may be sold on HKEX and H-shares may be sold on SSE through dedicated service providers.

Speaking about BOC's listing, then President Li Lihui recalled, "BOC went public almost simultaneously in Hong Kong and Shanghai. As an international bank, BOC had a sizeable overseas business operation, and thus needed to build an international reputation. Therefore, it would have been best for BOC to make listing on the same day in Shanghai and Hong Kong; but this couldn't be achieved due to technical reasons. BOC was listed in Hong Kong on June 1, 2006, and in Shanghai on July 5, which made them almost simultaneous. Simultaneous listing was what we promoted to investors. Of course, we met some technical difficulties, like the circulation of free-floating shares. We did have some regrets about the implementation of the listing plan, but in general, it was good."[1]

Financial News released an in-depth article regarding BOC's successful dual listing, commenting it as a new breakthrough in the joint-stock reform of state-owned banks in that, first, BOC was the first among the Big Four to achieve group-wide restructuring and overseas listing; second, among SOCBs and even in the Chinese banking sector, BOC was the first to adopt the "A+H" listing model, an all-around optimal strategy which would not only strengthen the stock markets in Hong Kong and in the mainland, but also balance the interests of mainland investors and the global investors in Hong Kong.[2]

BOC's successful listing on the two capital markets could be mainly attributed to (i) the promising prospect of China's economy; (ii) the key initiatives taken by the CPC Central Committee and State Council to promote the financial reform, and the active guidance and support from government agencies; (iii) BOC's ability to seize opportunities in international capital markets; and (iv) BOC's brand recognition and a series of reforms that were bearing fruits.

VI. Significance of BOC's Joint-Stock Reform and Listing

During its joint-stock reform and listing, BOC improved its corporate governance through targeted changes to development strategies, decision-making process, accounting standards, talent fostering and training, incentives and restraints, and board composition (Table 5.2), and achieved remarkable progress in each of these areas through reform and listing.

---

1 From the interview with Li Lihui on February 21, 2017.
2 Sun Lingyan, Liu Min, and Zhuo Shangjin: *The Myth of Capital: BOC's Glorious Journey to Going Public*, Unity Publishing House, 2007, pp. 69-71.

Table 5.2: BOC Corporate Governance Pre- and Post-Restructuring

	Before	After
Development strategies	Restrictive internal mechanisms and outdated frameworks and operational systems; bureaucratic governance style; focus on foreign exchange services	Technology-powered corporate banking and retail banking; integrated domestic and global operations and unified credit management; enhanced fee-based services; constant introduction of differentiated products and services
Decision making	Responsibility overlap of the CPC committee, board of directors and management with the positions of Party secretary, chairman, and president being held by the same person; frequent administrative intervention into commercial banking	"3+1" (shareholders' meeting, board of directors and board of supervisors + management) governance structure
Accounting standards	No genuine provision system for loss write-off, resulting in inflated profits	Prudently provisioning for asset impairment in line with the new Financial Enterprise Accounting System; producing financial statements in accordance with international standards
HR training	Cookie-cutter egalitarianism across a three-tier (bureau, section, and division) administrative management system lacking competition and incentive elements	Three career ladders for management personnel, professionals, and skilled personnel; demand-oriented position creation where compensation was tied to the duties of positions
Incentives and restraints	Lax operations where performance assessment focused on gross profits without consideration of loan losses; profit per employee considerations absent	Profitability-, asset quality- and fee-based services as key performance assessment indicators; per-employee profit included; RAROC[1] and SVA[1] added as new indicators; sound balance between business development and risk management, and between short-term and long-term gains
Board composition	Board of directors composed entirely of executive directors	Board of directors composed of non-executive directors (including independent non-executive directors with an international and diverse background) and executive directors, and supported by several specialized committees under it

Source: Compiled based on information provided by BOC.

---

1 RAROC, or risk adjusted return on capital, is the ratio of a financial institution's net operating profit (expected losses deducted) to economic capital. It reflects the risk return profile of a financial institution.
1 SVA refers to shareholder value added.

Section IV
Advancing the Joint-Stock Reform of BoCom

Since the late 1990s, faced with changes in domestic and global business environments, BoCom had made considerable efforts to advance its reform. In June 2004, the state approved BoCom's plan for starting the next stage of its joint-stock reform. After completing financial restructuring, introduction of strategic investors and IPO, BoCom achieved a historic transformation.

Related Topic: Brief History of BoCom

Founded in 1908 in Beijing, BoCom was one of the oldest banks in China. It was headquartered in Beijing in its early years. After the establishment of the Republic of China in 1912, it was mandated by the then central bank to manage, together with BOC, national treasury and the issuance and exchange of currency. In 1928, the Legislative Yuan of the Republic of China passed the "Regulations of the Bank of Communications," turning BoCom into a specialized bank supporting agriculture, mining, industry and commerce. In the same year, as the national political center moved from Beijing to Nanjing, BoCom relocated its head office to No. 14 on the Bund of Shanghai.

After the Chinese People's War of Resistance Against Japanese Aggression broke out in 1931, BoCom moved its head office to Chongqing in 1937. Between 1946 and 1947, BoCom rebuilt its Shanghai head office. In 1951, it moved back to Beijing. In 1958, except for the Hong Kong branch, other BoCom branches were locally merged into the PBOC and the People's Construction Bank of China (later renamed China Construction Bank), a bank spun off from BoCom.

On July 24, 1986, in line with China's economic system reform, the State Council approved the re-establishment of BoCom as a pilot financial reform. On April 1, 1987, the new BoCom opened for business, becoming China's first national joint-stock commercial bank. Its head office was located at Kincheng Bank Building, 200 Jiangxi Middle Road, Shanghai, and later relocated to 188 Yincheng Middle Road, Pudong, Shanghai.

In June 2004, at a stage in which financial reform had gained traction, the State Council approved BoCom's overall plan for advancing its joint-stock reform, aiming to reinvent it into an internationally competitive century-old Chinese brand and a modern financial enterprise with sound governance structure, adequate capital, tight internal control, safe operations, and premier service and performance. As the joint-stock reform progressed, BoCom completed financial restructuring, introduced domestic and foreign strategic investors such as HSBC, NCSSF and Central Huijin, and pushed forward with positive transformations in its operations. On June 23, 2005, BoCom was listed on HKEX, becoming the first mainland commercial bank to be listed overseas. On May 15, 2007, BoCom went public on SSE.

I. Unique Features of BoCom's Reform

Re-established in the 1980s, BoCom positioned itself as a national, socialist joint-stock financial enterprise with majority public ownership. To restructure itself into a setup more suitable for a joint-stock commercial bank, and to clarify the ownership relations between the head office and branches, starting from 1993, BoCom began to consolidate its head office and branches into a single legal person, to replace the original multi-tiered legal person arrangement. This eliminated institutional obstacles for advancing the reform and listing in China and abroad.

(I) Preparations and Unveiling of the Reform Plan

In the mid-to-late 1990s, BoCom was weighed down by China's economic transformation and the Asian financial crisis. To turn around struggling operations, enhance competitiveness, and improve the operational framework, between 1999 and 2004, BoCom embarked on a challenging road toward reform and IPO.

1. 1999-2000: The first attempt at public listing

Since its re-establishment, BoCom had been aggressively exploring a viable growth model as a joint-stock commercial bank. However, from the mid-1990s, it became mired in increasing operating pressures for policy-directed debts caused by the SOE restructuring, a long history of lax management at the branches, a rising NPL ratio, and declining operating efficiency.

In such a context, BoCom's executive team realized that to keep up with trends in the banking sector and address issues at the source, BoCom had to effectuate a fundamental reform rather than an incremental improvement. Therefore, BoCom set about using an IPO and listing to turn around struggling operations, enhance competitiveness, and improve operational frameworks. BoCom made this decision based on three beliefs. First, that listing was an effective method for capital replenishment. For a long time, BoCom replenished capital mainly by private placement, the conversion of retained earnings to capital, and the capitalization of a portion of dividends payable to the MOF. However, with continuous business expansion, these sources could no longer meet its growing capital demands. BoCom's capital adequacy ratio dropped from 11.80% in 1994 to 6.75% at the end of 1998, below the regulatory lower limit and ranking second-to-last among China's ten joint-stock commercial banks. This had become a main obstacle to its integrated business development and robust operations.[1]

Second, that listing could provide an important avenue to standardize its joint-stock system and improve its corporate governance structure. From the very beginning of its establishment, by adopting the standard practice of joint-stock commercial banks, BoCom built a basic framework of modern commercial banks comprising the shareholders' meeting, board of directors, board of supervisors, and management. The four corporate bodies provided mutual checks and balances. However, in its equity structure, BoCom's shareholders encompassed only the state and SOEs, without the participation of any other legal persons or individual investors who could help diversify its corporate governance structure.

Third, that listing would be helpful for it to rise to challenges brought by China's accession to the WTO and improve its capabilities. The five-year grace period provided by the WTO agreement presented an opportunity for BoCom to go public, thus advancing reform and development and solving legacy issues.

And fourth, that listing was a solution for BoCom to compete with emerging joint-stock commercial banks. Between 1987 and 1999, the number of joint-stock commercial banks in China had increased from

---

1 BoCom: "Report on Request for the Authorization of the Executive Committee to Prepare for Listing," October 19, 1999.

one (namely BoCom) to ten. Although BoCom still led the pack in total assets, it had been growing slower than the others by both absolute and relative measures. Around 1999, except for Shenzhen Development Bank and Pudong Development Bank which had gone public, other national joint-stock commercial banks had successively filed applications for listing ahead of BoCom.

On October 17, 1999, the BoCom Executive Committee officially authorized the head office to prepare for IPO and listing. On December 6, 1999, BoCom submitted to the PBOC the "Request for Instructions on the Application of BoCom for IPO and Listing" (Jiao Yin [1999] No. 133). At the same time, it carried out listing preparations both internally and with external parties. However, due to various internal and external factors, the first listing request was denied, mostly on account of BoCom's weak financial position. At that time, listing criteria for financial companies mainly included capital adequacy ratio, asset quality, profitability and internal control. As of the end of 1999, BoCom's capital adequacy ratio had fallen to 5.84%, while NPLs had risen to RMB 58.4 billion, or 22.10% of its loan portfolio, below the prescribed listing criteria. For these reasons, without the government policy support, BoCom was unable to improve its business performance to the level required by the listing criteria in the short term, not to mention hitting a reasonable IPO price and maintaining a stable stock price in the long run. Low capital adequacy ratio and high NPA ratio were the major obstacles that ended BoCom's first IPO and listing attempt.

2. 2001-2003: Introduction of foreign capital

After becoming a WTO member in 2001, China significantly sped up its financial reform and financial internationalization. Although

BoCom was part of this transformative age and already a joint-stock commercial bank, its corporate governance structure was still vastly outdated by the standards of listing rules and international market practices. However, introduction of foreign strategic investors provided a solution – it could not only push BoCom to improve its ownership structure and corporate governance, but also learn from foreign banks' sophisticated organizational structure and operational and management approaches, thus enhancing its institutional, management, technical, and business innovation, and accelerating its convergence with international banking standards.

For this strategic consideration, BoCom decided to bring in foreign investors prior to IPO. On April 12, 2001, BoCom's board of directors authorized the head office to prepare for bringing in foreign investors. On April 27, BoCom submitted a request for instructions on foreign capital injection and a foreign equity participation report to the PBOC. On June 22, the PBOC issued the "Reply of PBOC General Office to Foreign Equity Participation in Bank of Communications" (Yin Ban Han [2001] No. 529), approving BoCom's engagement of strategic foreign investors whose shareholding, however, should account for no more than 15% of BoCom's paid-up capital. On July 10, BoCom set up a Steering Group for Foreign Capital Attraction, headed by President Fang Chengguo and Vice President Qiao Wei as the group's leader and deputy leader respectively, with additional members from relevant departments. Under the group a Foreign Investment Office was also set up.[1] At the beginning of 2002, BoCom announced its plan of taking in foreign capital prior to IPO, and

---

[1] BoCom Foreign Investment Office: "Report on Recent Work Regarding the Involvement of Foreign Investors," July 22, 2001.

engaged Pan-China Assets Appraisal Co., Ltd. for asset appraisal, PricewaterhouseCoopers Zhong Tian LLP (PwC) for IFRS-based audit, Boss & Young Attorneys at Law for legal consulting, and Goldman Sachs Asia LLC for financial consulting.

In the course of dealing with potential foreign individual and institutional investors, BoCom had sounded out the foreign investors, and explored steps to take in investment. On the positive side, China's market potential and business opportunities arising from its WTO accession had appealed to foreign institutional investors. On the negative side, affected by the bankruptcy of American energy giant Enron and loss of credibility by its auditor Arthur Anderson, audit firm PwC as well as potential investors such as Goldman Sachs had become more risk-averse. Furthermore, the approach for net asset appraisal adopted by BoCom was different from that provided in IFRS, which was also seen as a red flag by potential investors.[1] During its preliminary contact with investors in Europe and the U.S., Goldman Sachs found out that their biggest concerns were BoCom's low capital adequacy ratio and high NPA ratio. BoCom also visited mega-conglomerates like GE, Bank of New York, and Bank of America, but due to its tremendous stock of NPAs, negotiation on an equal footing was all but out of the question.

Facing external difficulties, BoCom slowed down its investor attraction program, and shifted focus inward toward boosting its financial strengths. With the assistance of Goldman Sachs and drawing on the best practices of international commercial banks, BoCom carried out preliminary

---

1   Qiao Wei: "Progress on the Foreign Capital Absorption of BoCom," included in 2002 BoCom Tier-One Branch General Manager Regular Meeting Documents, April 13, 2002.

restructuring in governance structure, organizational structure, financial structure, development strategies, and infrastructure. To achieve high credibility and historical continuity in its financial data, BoCom engaged PwC to audit financial statements for periods ending June 30, 2001 and in 2001, 2002, and 2003 in line with IFRS, and retroactively prepared an asset appraisal report and audit report for the period ending in 2000. These efforts were recognized by several potential foreign investors. Also, BoCom took effective measures to improve operational, management, and asset quality across the bank. As of the end of 2002, its capital adequacy ratio went up to 8.83%, and NPL ratio also notably decreased, paving the way for further progress on its joint-stock reform. In 2003, BoCom became a popular investment target, with a number of foreign investors vying for a strategic stake.

3. 2004: Determination of the overall reform plan

During its reach-out of foreign strategic investors, BoCom ascertained its financial conditions through asset appraisal and financial audit. Moreover, it realized that if it clung to conventional approaches, it would take five or six years to make full allowances under regulatory standards, three or four years later than the opening-up date set at the WTO entry and the deadline required by regulatory bodies, which meant a significant slowdown in development. Therefore, BoCom had to come up with new reform ideas and create new opportunities.

In the second half of 2003, China's financial reform entered a new stage. Changes in the economic and financial environments necessitated changes to the reform plans of state-owned banks, one of which was shifting half of the efforts on reducing NPAs to promoting governance structures and operational mechanisms. Against this backdrop, in July 2003, BoCom set out to lay out a plan for advancing the joint-stock reform. This time, aside from financial restructuring which relied on external supports to mitigate risks, other measures such as attracting foreign capital, improving governance structure, reshaping organizational structure, and public listing were also included. During the revision of its plan, BoCom proactively sought the opinions of the PBOC, CBRC, and the MOF, gradually nailing down a comprehensive plan covering financing restructuring, foreign capital attraction and IPO.

As such, BoCom had turned its ideas about joint-stock reform into a comprehensive, feasible and market-oriented plan. Its preliminary report successfully captured the attention of PBOC and CBRC officials. On August 11, 2003, BoCom submitted the "Request for Instructions on Bank of Communications' Overall Plan of Advancing Joint-Stock Reform" (Jiao Yin [2003] No. 40) to the State Council, stating that it would press ahead with the reform by making market-oriented changes to strengthen itself under appropriate government support. The plan outlined three major steps. The first was completing financial restructuring, with particular focus on NPA resolution and capital replenishment, through internal efforts, market-based measures, and governmental support. The second was bringing in foreign strategic investors to promote strategic development, and expedite the integration and upgrade of corporate governance structure, organizational structure, risk management system, IT system, and incentives and restraints. The third was completing listing as a group on the HKEX Main Board or A-share market.

The plan was well received and greatly supported by the departments under the State Council. On February 26, 2004, BoCom submitted the "Request for Instructions on Bank of Communications' Overall Plan of Advancing Joint-Stock Reform" (Jiao Yin [2004] No. 2) to the PBOC. In May 2004, the central government appointed Jiang Chaoliang, former Vice Governor of Hubei Province, as Secretary of the Party Committee at BoCom and Chairman of BoCom; Zhang Jianguo, former BoCom Vice President, as Deputy Secretary of the Party Committee at BoCom and President of BoCom; and Cui Leiping, former ABC Chairman of the Board of Supervisors dispatched by the State Council, as Deputy Secretary of the Party Committee at BoCom and Chairman of the Board of Supervisors. Former BoCom Chairman Yin Jieyan and Vice Chairman and President Fang Chengguo stepped down for age and health reasons.

BoCom thus became the first SOE with a "3+1" (shareholders' meeting, board of directors, board of supervisors, and management) corporate governance structure. Jiang Chaoliang became the first board chairman of a financial institution in China to concurrently serve as the institution's Party secretary and legal representative. (In the past, either the president or the general manager of a state-owned bank (including BoCom) would concurrently serve as Party secretary and legal representative.)

Headed by Chairman Jiang Chaoliang and President Zhang Jianguo, the newly formed BoCom leadership team seized every opportunity to constantly refine and implement BoCom's overall plan for advancing its joint-stock reform, based on thorough analysis and the support of relevant ministries and commissions.

On June 14, 2004, the State Council approved the "Request of the PBOC for Instructions on Bank of Communications' Overall Plan for Advancing Joint-Stock Reform," which had been countersigned by the MOF, CSRC, and CBRC.[1] Upon receiving the approval, BoCom launched its three-step strategy of "financial restructuring – introduction of foreign strategic investors – IPO and listing."

Related Topic: Peng Chun: How BoCom Became a Pilot Bank for the Joint-Stock Reform[2]

"I [Peng Chun, then Assistant President and later Executive Vice President of BoCom] accompanied President Fang Chengguo to report to Dai Xianglong when he was still PBOC Governor. The PBOC first required BoCom to go public, and then proposed the infusion of foreign capital. So BoCom drafted a comprehensive reform plan focusing on the infusion of foreign capital.

"In 2003, the PBOC set out to launch the joint-stock reforms of CCB and BOC, and BoCom was not included as a pilot bank. So, I accompanied President Fang Chengguo and Chairman Yin Jieyan to different governmental bodies several times to submit materials and report on our work. About half a month after we submitted materials to the PBOC, Governor Zhou Xiaochuan asked us to deliver a report in person. PBOC Financial Stability Bureau Director Xie Ping also told us that Zhou was very interested in our plan, because the reform of BOC and CCB would be a difficult process due to their size and the complexity of their financial issues, and any misstep during listing would greatly damage their international reputations. In contrast, BoCom was of a moderate size, and its reform would be much less costly. If BoCom were any larger, a failed reform would have significant

---

1 "Reply of PBOC to Request for Instructions on Bank of Communications' Overall Plan for Advancing Joint-Stock Reform" (Yin Fu [2004] No. 33).
2 From the interview with Peng Chun on March 21, 2017.

repercussions on the industry; and if it were any smaller, the reform would be meaningless. Zhou took an interest in BoCom precisely because it had a moderate size and was already established as a joint-stock commercial bank.

"We formally reported our plan to Zhou at the end of 2003. Then PBOC General Office Director Liu Shiyu, and PBOC Financial Stability Bureau Director Xie Ping and Division Chief Xu Guoping attended the meeting. Zhou instructed Xie Ping to help optimize the reform plan of BoCom. I found that Zhou wanted to lay the groundwork for the reforms of BOC and CCB by leveraging BoCom's experience, so we made a presentation in this regard.

"During the Chinese New Year of 2004, the PBOC sent Xie Ping to BoCom. After the holiday period, Zhou inspected BoCom, and his purposes were clear cut. ... At first only CCB and BOC were on the State Council's list of pilot banks, and BoCom was later added into the list by leaders of the State Council. This was because previously, Zhou had brought us to deliver a report before the leaders of the State Council and convinced them of the merit of our restructuring plan. ...

"BoCom finalized its restructuring plan after an arduous process. The heart of the plan was financial resources which pointed to two key sources: one was the injection of fiscal funds, and the other was NPA write-off. ... BoCom first proposed writing off NPAs against the injected fiscal funds, which was handily rejected by the MOF because that would wipe out the injected funds. Later Vice Premier Huang Ju said that a market-oriented solution would be better, and the parties started to work on it.

"... Finally, we worked out a most market-oriented restructuring plan. At that time, how to obtain the financial resources to dispose of NPAs was a tough problem, mainly because BoCom was not allowed to write off losses with capital injected by the MOF. To solve this problem, Xie Ping, Sun Xiaoxia, Tian Guoli and I met several times, and ultimately Xie Ping figured out a brilliant market-oriented solution which was endorsed by then Cinda President Tian Guoli. The solution was that the PBOC would offer an RMB 3 billion loan to Cinda, and then Central Huijin would purchase 3 billion BoCom shares on behalf of Cinda at RMB 1 per share. The future capital gains on these shares would be used to offset the losses resulting from BoCom's NPA disposal. Specifically, BoCom's RMB 41.4 billion of NPLs were sold to Cinda at a 50% discount for RMB 20.7 billion, but Cinda still needed about another RMB 9 billion for the deal. This gap in funds would be filled by selling these shares, because estimates showed that the share price could reach around RMB 3 per share after the restructuring, indicating a P/B ratio of 3. We all agreed on the solution, and included it into the plan.

"Later on, prior to its restructuring and listing, Cinda had sold these 3 billion shares held on its behalf by Central Huijin to the MOF for cash at about RMB 6 per share. In fact, the resulting premium partly addressed Cinda's legacy issues, facilitating its restructuring and overall listing. Therefore, BoCom's NPL divestiture plan was a classical market-oriented plan which 'killed two birds with one stone' without tapping into the state treasury. I think this is a highlight of BoCom's reform."

(II) Characteristics of BoCom's Reform Plan

Unlike other state-owned banks' reform plans, BoCom's reform plan focused on how to advance its joint-stock reform with some structures already in place, rather than starting it from scratch. At the very beginning of its re-establishment, BoCom, emulating the practices of other joint-stock companies, (i) had built the basic governance framework of a modern commercial bank comprising the shareholders' meeting, board of directors, board of supervisors, and management, which provided mutual checks and balances; (ii) had been working on creating management and operational frameworks suitable for its legal form as a joint-stock company; and (iii) had gradually created a self-reliant business operation featuring self-assumption of profits, losses, and risks, self-discipline in treasury management, and autonomous operations. As of the end of 2003, BoCom had a registered capital of RMB 17 billion, and an owner's equity of RMB 41 billion in which the central government held a 29.08% stake, the local governments 23.98%, and SOEs the remainder. Therefore, building upon previous joint-stock reforms, BoCom's reform plan focused on improving its existing corporate governance and internal systems, and thus was significantly different from the reform plans of other state-owned banks.

BoCom incorporated several innovations into the design and implementation of its reform. The first one was the "self-funded reform" model which was an innovation for the Chinese banking sector. The state closely monitored the reform of BoCom and provided favorable policies, but never funding support. Having to rely on itself and market-based solutions, BoCom developed a creative and highly market-oriented financing solution for its financial restructuring. The second innovation was a comprehensive asset evaluation to ascertain its financial condition. When BoCom was in talks with foreign investors, no fewer than three of the Big Four accounting firms were involved in its audit: KPMG appointed by HSBC, Ernst & Young (EY) by Standard Chartered Bank (SCB), another potential investor, and PwC by BoCom itself. The comprehensive audit helped BoCom gain a clear picture of its financial condition, and produced reliable financial statements acceptable to both domestic and foreign investors. The third innovation was adopting IFRS, a first among domestic banks. BoCom followed international banking industry practices at every stage of processing its accounting data, and thus avoided communication barriers caused by a difference of "accounting languages." Its pioneering practice provided experience for other state-owned commercial banks in adopting IFRS.

The government approval of BoCom's reform followed a bottom-up rather than a top-down route. BoCom was not sitting in the driver's seat of the joint-stock reform like the Big Four; however, being good at seizing opportunities and proactive in taking action, it went out of its way to convince the regulators, and became the first to turn reform ideas into feasible plans. Its plan received attention from the decision-makers, who finally added BoCom to the list of pilot banks. The success of BoCom came from its years of perseverance that finally won over China's top leadership.

II. Financial Restructuring

(I) Framework and Features of the Financial Restructuring Plan

1. Framework

The framework of BoCom's financial restructuring plan, which was adopted at the Eighth Meeting of the Third Board of Directors held in December 2003, was as follows:

(1) Key points

Through self-reliance, market-based solutions, and government support, BoCom resolved its legacy issues about three years ahead of schedule, gaining it valuable time for other self-improvement programs. During the process, the state helped BoCom become financially qualified for listing in

Hong Kong through the following steps: supporting its bulk sale of RMB 41.4 billion of doubtful loans at discount; approving it to write off RMB 35.5 billion of losses on NPAs on a one-off basis; investing in it RMB 30 billion in an appropriate manner; and approving it to issue RMB 18 billion of long-term financial bonds.

(2) Goals

The first goal was to significantly reduce NPLs and make full allowance for bad loans. Given that the state had approved a bulk sale of its doubtful loans at discount, BoCom was to, by using all available financial resources and enhancing recovery efforts, (i) write off, on a one-off basis before tax, loss loans as well as losses from the sale of doubtful loans at their assessed price; (ii) sell doubtful loans to Cinda at 50% of their book value; and (iii) increase the individual allowances and allowance for non-credit asset losses to lower the NPL ratio to below 5% while increasing the provision coverage ratio to above 50%.

The second goal was to greatly increase capital adequacy ratio. Specifically, BoCom was permitted to (i) replenish core capital through investment by foreign strategic investors and appropriately sized government injections, so as to turn around the decline in core capital adequacy ratio and increase it to above 6%; (ii) replenish supplementary capital through issuing subordinated bonds; and (iii) optimize its risk asset portfolio to further boost the capital adequacy ratio to a high level of around 12%.

The third goal was to substantially increase after-tax profit and boost return on capital. To this end, BoCom was to expedite business development and steadily increase profitability, so that it could achieve a 15% annual growth in net profit after the restructuring.

(3) Steps

First, with the support of the state, BoCom divested RMB 20.7 billion of doubtful loans and RMB 14.8 billion of loss loans on a one-off basis at a discount of 50% and 100% respectively, so as to decrease its NPL ratio from 19.65% at the end of 2002 to below 5%, while increasing its provision coverage ratio from 7.69% at the end of 2002 to above 50%.

Given the results of five-category loan classification obtained at the end of 2002, the PBOC provisioning guidance, and audit findings provided by PwC, to achieve the above goals, BoCom was still short of RMB 47.4 billion in NPL write-off and allowance. Its available financial resources totaled RMB 48.3 billion, including valuation gains on fixed assets approved by the state to be recorded, capital reserves from government capital injection, profit in 2003, accumulated capital reserves, accumulated surplus reserves, cash from NPL recovery, and deferred tax.

Second, the state invested RMB 30 billion (including RMB 5 billion of equity investment from the MOF, RMB 3 billion of equity investment from Central Huijin, RMB 10 billion of equity investment from NCSSF, and RMB 12 billion of term subordinated bonds) in BoCom in exchange for another 20 billion shares. In addition, BoCom issued RMB 18 billion of long-term financial bonds to replenish its supplementary capital, boosting capital adequacy ratio to 12% at the end of 2003.

Third, after financial restructuring, all of BoCom's financial indicators met regulatory standards and listing standards of HKEX Main Board, with NPL ratio decreasing to below 5%, provision coverage ratio increasing to above 50%, net assets per share at RMB 1 per share, capital adequacy ratio to 12%, core capital adequacy ratio at above 6%, and after-tax profit reaching RMB 0.17 per share in 2004 after listing.

The steps of BoCom's financial restructuring are illustrated in Figure 5.2.

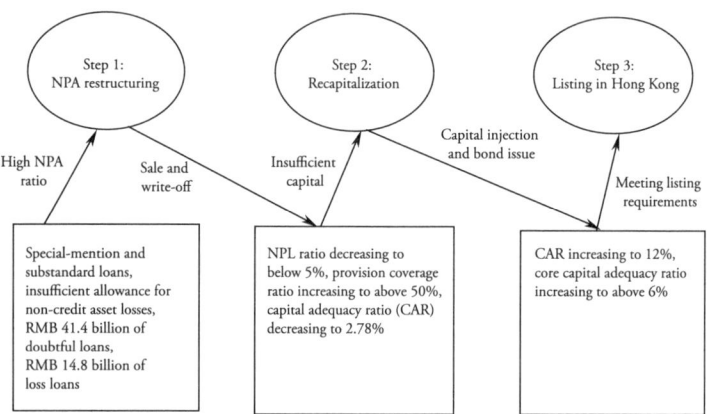

Source: Minutes of the Eighth Meeting of the Third Board of Directors of BoCom.

Fig. 5.2: Steps of BoCom's Financial Restructuring

2. Features of the financial restructuring plan

(1) Protecting the long-term interests of shareholders

First, the financial restructuring plan fully respected the interests of existing shareholders. The state required BoCom to first make all allowances in full using its own resources, including possibly from a reverse stock split at a discounted share price, before it would consider providing policy and resource support to its financial restructuring. If such a reverse stock split was not carried out to make the allowance, then the prevailing capital market practices would require existing shareholders to, before bringing in new shareholders, set aside sufficient undistributed profit as a security deposit against risk of loss on pre-capital-increase assets (including existent and potential NPAs), such that new shareholders could be adequately compensated should that loss materialize following their investment.

Either of the two options above would incur substantial losses to existing shareholders. In view of their contributions, BoCom passionately argued against the discounted reverse stock split, and proposed to fund the security deposit with its profit from 2003 and accumulated surplus and capital reserves, so existing shareholders would not need to make additional contributions either. That is to say, under BoCom's restructuring plan, new and existing shareholders would jointly tackle the pre-capital-increase NPAs and jointly bear the risk of loss on those assets. Therefore, existing shareholders could enjoy the same rights as the new shareholders without putting forward additional investments or assuming liabilities beyond their existing exposure, thus maximizing the protection for their interests.

Second, the plan focused on the long-term interests of shareholders. With the support of the state, BoCom would first swiftly address its legacy issues and then complete financial restructuring. This would substantially drive up the after-tax profit per share, and dividend payout ratio would also grow significantly from the existing 4% or so. And aside from cash dividend, more forms of distribution, like bonus shares, would also be an option. Furthermore, the price of shares held by shareholders would go up after IPO. Thus, the long-term interests of shareholders would be realized by subsequent stock price appreciation and dividend distribution.

Third, the plan would even help maximize shareholders' short-term interests. National laws prohibited Chinese banks from distributing or booking profits before making allowances in full. Without financial restructuring, BoCom's meager profit level meant that it wouldn't be able to set aside adequate allowances until the end of 2006 at the earliest, when it would still be hampered by undercapitalization and need to shore up its reserves. In that case, it was hard to say when existing shareholders could see higher profits. The plan shortened the "zero dividend period" from at least four years to around one and a half years. In other words, if existing shareholders would assent to re-invest the profit that would otherwise be distributed in the subsequent less-than-two-year period into the restructuring, it would not only allow BoCom to strictly comply with financial regulatory policies, but also convey to the State Council of its determination to push on the financial restructuring. In fact, following its IPO in 2004, all of BoCom's financial indicators met regulatory requirements, giving pre-capital-increase shareholders the freedom to choose how profit was to be distributed as well as the same rights as new shareholders. Thus, BoCom was able to make good on its promises to shareholders in less time.

(2) Innovating funding methods for the financial restructuring

First, BoCom creatively addressed the problem of negative net worth by incorporating valuation gains from revisiting its fixed asset and deferred tax accounting policies. The financial restructuring plan estimated that at the end of 2003, BoCom needed to write off and make allowance for asset losses totaling RMB 51.6 billion, comprising a RMB 20.7 billion write-off arising from the bulk sale of RMB 41.4 billion of doubtful loans at 50% book value, RMB 11.8 billon of loss loans to be written off by BoCom head office before tax, and an RMB 19.1 billion allowance for total loss on all non-credit assets and other asset losses.

Current BoCom Chairman Peng Chun, who was then serving as BoCom Assistant President, recalled, "BoCom had RMB 18 billion of share capital and RMB 18.3 billion of net assets. So, how did we offset losses? What policy support did we get? We had basically offset losses with the help of two policies. One was the MOF's policy permitting us to book valuation gains on fixed assets. BoCom was the only bank to benefit from the policy – none of ICBC, ABC, BOC and CCB would. The second was the deferred tax policy. I had a lengthy speech about the two policies. In fact, BoCom had almost depleted its capital to write off NPLs. After restructuring, our provision coverage ratio was a little higher than 40%. Of the RMB 18.3 billion of net assets, over RMB 6 billion was fixed asset valuation gains and RMB 11.9 billion was deferred tax assets. I think the significance of BoCom's reform mostly lies in it paving the way for the reform of state-owned banks. Although the first policy support was not provided to the Big Four, the MOF did set up jointly managed accounts with ICBC and ABC respectively, which played the same role as deferred tax assets."[1]

Second, BoCom raised approximately RMB 50.7 billion for the financial restructuring, including RMB 10 billion of equity investment from NCSSF, RMB 5 billion and RMB 3 billion of equity investment from the MOF and Central Huijin, respectively, RMB 12 billion from term subordinated bonds issued by BoCom, and RMB 20.7 billion paid by Cinda for purchasing BoCom's NPLs.

(II) Preparations for the Financial Restructuring

The first measure was verifying assets. For three consecutive years from the second half of 2001, BoCom had engaged recognized domestic and foreign accounting and appraisal firms such as PwC to conduct

---

1 From the interview with Peng Chun on March 21, 2017.

IFRS-based audits and asset appraisals, thereby ascertaining its financial conditions and verifying its assets and capital.

The second measure was setting up NPA disposal teams and formulating corresponding working rules. Such teams included the NPA Disposal Team under the BoCom Joint-Stock Reform Office, Centralized NPA Disposal Team under the Risk Management Department, and NPA disposal teams at the branch level, which worked together on the preparations for the financial restructuring. For working rules, BoCom established management measures and methods to facilitate the centralized write-off of loss loans and bulk sale of doubtful loans. Specifically, it implemented the "Measures for the Management of Written-Off Assets," and revised the "Methods of BoCom for Identifying and Pursuing Responsibilities for NPAs," providing institutional safeguards for asset preservation and accountability monitoring after the centralized write-off and bulk sale of NPAs.

The third measure was raising funds for NPA restructuring. With government policy support, BoCom absorbed all losses from its NPAs using its own financial resources. For one, through enhanced recovery and write-off efforts, BoCom lowered its NPLs in both absolute and relative amounts, and thus reduced its cash flow pressures arising from financial restructuring. In 2003, BoCom wrote off RMB 9.07 billion of NPLs, accounting for 70.08% of the write-offs over the previous ten years.[1] Furthermore, through the policy support for recognizing fixed asset valuation gains, BoCom was able to show additional financial resources

---

1   "Request for Instructions on Bank of Communications' Overall Plan of Advancing Joint-Stock Reform" (Jiao Yin [2004] No. 2)

for the financial restructuring.

The fourth measure was defining the accounting entities and their responsibilities for the financial restructuring. The accounting entities included the Banking Department and General Affairs Department at the head office, and BoCom branches and sub-branches. The responsibilities of the accounting entities and relevant departments were as follows: (i) Finance Department and Personal Banking Department at the head office oversaw accounting programs, including developing accounting methods, designing accounting procedures, and assisting the accounting entities in resolving accounting issues; (ii) Banking Department and General Affairs Department performed accounting work per the contact sheets provided by the Finance Department; (iii) Various branches and sub-branches performed accounting treatment according to the feedback from the head office.

The fifth measure was signing the NPL Purchase Agreement with Cinda.[1] On April 1, 2004, the PBOC, the MOF, Cinda and BoCom decided upon a purchase framework. On April 2, Cinda's 30 offices across China started due diligence at local branches of BoCom. In the three days from June 3 to 5, BoCom's negotiation team and Cinda engaged in six rounds of substantive negotiations. The two parties had disputes over key issues such as warranty clauses regarding NPL transfer, and the disposal of NPAs of BoCom's self-invested companies and equity-participating companies. To promptly divest NPAs, and completely free themselves of risks and liabilities, BoCom Chairman Jiang Chaoliang and Assistant President Peng Chun insisted that Cinda should include in the agreement

---

1 BoCom and Cinda: "NPL Purchase Agreement," June 7, 2004.

a clause stating that "NPAs sold to Cinda shall not be adjusted, returned or exchanged."[1] Through intense negotiations, BoCom and Cinda finally reached an agreement on the joint disposal of NPAs and signed the NPL Purchase Agreement on June 7. From that date on, BoCom's NPA restructuring plan featuring bulk sale and centralized write-offs entered the implementation stage.

The agreement specified that the assets to be transferred include: doubtful loans with a principal balance of RMB 41.4 billion as of May 31, 2004; loss loans with a principal balance of RMB 14.8 billion written off as a whole before tax in 2004 (subject to the financial restructuring plan approved by the State Council); assets with a principal balance of RMB 9 billion written off in 2003; and the principal and interests of these loans recovered by BoCom from April 1, 2004 to the base date of transfer. By June 20, 2004, Cinda had paid the transfer price to BoCom in a lump sum using an RMB 20.7 billion loan from the PBOC. After the NPA disposal, BoCom created an allowance of the remaining NPLs.

Related Topic: Former Cinda President Tian Guoli: NPA Disposal at BoCom[2]

"When BoCom started its financial restructuring in 2004, the state had attempted to dispose of NPAs through market-based methods – to remove NPAs from the balance sheet by sale at a discount. At that time, BoCom was exposed to RMB 41.4 billion of NPAs in book value, 50% of which, according to foreign appraisal firms hired by relevant government agencies, could be

---

1   Wu Yushan and Wang Haiming: *Twenty Years: Evolution of Bank of Communications and China's Banking Sector*, China Financial Publishing House, 2007, pp. 200-202.
2   From the interview with Tian Guoli on May 5, 2017.

Launch of Pilot Reform | 439

expected to be recovered. BoCom reported the percentage to the State Council, which then approved the financial restructuring plan. As a result, BoCom needed to work hard to recover RMB 20.7 billion of the RMB 41.4 billion of NPAs, or losses would be incurred on state assets.

"When the PBOC asked if any of the four AMCs would be willing to take over these NPAs, none of them assented because the valuation price of credit assets would not necessarily be equal to the market price. It's like you have a set of precious redwood furniture with a certificate of assessment for a high value, but still there is no guarantee that the inherent value would clear the market. Had these NPAs been realizable at a high value, these competing AMCs would have bid for them. However, the 50% recovery rate was too high, even without considering the associated heavy costs. Even when the rate was later reduced to 30%, there was still no reaction. But without solving this problem, BoCom would be unable to continue its restructuring and listing.

"PBOC Governor Zhou Xiaochuan asked Xie Ping to talk to me [Tian Guoli], hoping that Cinda would take over the NPAs. I told Xie that the recovery rate could be 20%-25% at most, but Xie said that changing the recovery rate would lead to changes to the plan, which required more government support, and one more report to the State Council. I knew the process would be lengthy, which meant BoCom might miss the IPO window. Xie asked me to figure out a solution. I told him the solution was to seek innovation in the transaction structure.

"Xie Ping, Sun Xiaoxia, Jiang Chaoliang, Peng Chun and I together came up with a solution: First, Cinda should acquire the RMB 41.4 billion of NPAs in book value for RMB 20.7 billion (i.e., 50% discount) to ensure the listing of BoCom; second, Cinda should be a strategic investor of BoCom; third, the

PBOC should make a loan to Cinda to buy the pre-IPO shares of BoCom; and fourth, Cinda should offset losses arising from NPA recovery against potential future market returns on those shares and assume the corresponding market risks. With this solution, the central bank and BoCom would not be affected should any risk become manifest. I submitted the plan to Zhou, who was satisfied with it. Then, Cinda and BoCom reached an agreement, under which Cinda would buy 3 billion BoCom shares, and acquire RMB 41.4 billion of NPAs for RMB 20.7 billion."

(III) Implementation of the Financial Restructuring Plan

BoCom started to implement the financial restructuring plan immediately upon official approval. Its implementation steps included: First, disposing of its NPAs. Pursuant to the plan schedule, after the approval of the reform plan by the State Council, BoCom only had less than one month to complete the restructuring, which made NPA disposal a tough task. Nevertheless, thanks to sufficient preparations, risk asset management personnel completed the task before the deadline of June 30. Meanwhile, BoCom took actions to hold the responsible employees accountable to the historical NPLs, and launched initiatives to consolidate progress and mitigate risk.

Second, BoCom issued new shares to replenish capital. After the centralized NPL disposal, under the support of the State Council, BoCom launched a recapitalization program to boost its financial strength and capital adequacy ratio. Domestically, BoCom allotted 5 billion shares to the MOF at RMB 1 per share for RMB 5 billion in cash; 3 billion shares to Central Huijin at RMB 1 per share for RMB 3 billion in cash; and 5.56 billion shares to NCSSF at RMB 1.8 per share for RMB 10 billion in cash from NCSSF.

BoCom approached NCSSF at the end of 2003, but the negotiation was slow at first. Approaching the end of May 2004, right before BoCom's leadership change, the two sides finally agreed upon the details of an equity investment – except the all-important price, which remained a hard nut to crack. BoCom insisted that NCSSF should pay RMB 2 per share, the exact price that it had offered to shareholders one year prior. Back then, BoCom's book value of equity per share was RMB 2.3, but the audited value given by PwC was RMB 1 per share, which NCSSF seized to drive down the price. The two parties were thus locked in a stalemate. To solve the thorniest problem, the new BoCom Chairman Jiang Chaoliang decided to talk face-to-face with NCSSF Chairman Xiang Huaicheng. The meeting turned out to be very quick and efficient. The breakthrough occurred when Xiang took a step back, offering RMB 1.8 per share. Jiang thought for a moment and said, "Deal!" The next day, BoCom and NCSSF signed the equity investment agreement. Wu Wei, Deputy General Manager of BoCom's Finance Department, who took part in the negotiation and signing, later said, "The key to Jiang's success was quick decision-making. Back-and-forth bargaining would have irritated Xiang."[1] In fact, NCSSF's investment in BoCom proved to be a lucrative deal, and also piqued the organization's interest in the financial industry, as evidenced by its later investments in BOC and ICBC. By the end of 2006, NCSSF had made nearly RMB 60 billion of investment income from the three banks.

---

1   Wu Yushan and Wang Haiming: *Twenty Years: Evolution of Bank of Communications and China's Banking Sector*, China Financial Publishing House, 2007, pp. 210-211.

Apart from issuing new shares, BoCom placed RMB 630 million shares to some existing shareholders at RMB 1.8 per share in the first half of 2004, raising RMB 1.1 billion.

Third, BoCom issued subordinated bonds to optimize its capital structure. In June and July 2004, BoCom issued RMB 12 billion of subordinated bonds with an annual coupon rate of 4.5% in the interbank bond market, recording the biggest issue size at the lowest interest rate at that time.

(IV) Outcomes of the Financial Restructuring

Financial statements as of June 30, 2004 showed that BoCom's financial restructuring had achieved the desired results in the following areas:

1. Significantly decreased NPL ratio

As of June 30, 2004, BoCom domestic loan portfolio totaled RMB 539.044 billion, including RMB 447.521 billion of pass loans, RMB 72.434 billion of special-mention loans, RMB 13.502 billion of substandard loans, RMB 5.586 billion of doubtful loans, and RMB 1 million of loss loans. NPLs totaled RMB 19.089 billion, with an NPL ratio of 3.54%, 1.46 percentage points lower than the 5% estimate given in the financial restructuring plan. Domestic and foreign loans totaled RMB 577.696 billion, of which there was RMB 13.743 billion of substandard loans, RMB 5.884 billion of doubtful loans, and RMB 173 million of loss loans. NPLs totaled RMB 19.8 billion, with an NPL ratio of 3.43%.

2. Sharply increased provision coverage ratio

As of June 30, 2004, BoCom had made RMB 8.211 billion in general allowance across the bank, including RMB 6.851 billion made by domestic branches (RMB 1.461 billion for bad debts arising from interbank lending and investment, and RMB 5.39 billion for bad debts arising from loans) and RMB 1.36 billion made by foreign branches. According to PBOC standards and BoCom's NPL quality, BoCom increased its domestic specific allowances by RMB 4.428 billion to RMB 5.771 billion, bringing total specific allowances across the bank to RMB 6.198 billion (RMB 427 million of which were made by foreign branches). Allowances for bad debts across the bank totaled RMB 14.409 billion, giving a provision coverage ratio of 72.77%, a weighted average of a 66.12% domestic ratio and a 251.34% foreign ratio.

3. Higher capital adequacy ratio

As of June 30, 2004, BoCom recorded RMB 32.724 billion in accumulated losses across the bank, and RMB 24.962 billion net core capital, with a core capital adequacy ratio (CCAR) of 4.10% and a capital adequacy ratio (CAR) of 7.03%, or 5.89% CCAR and 8.82% CAR as measured under IFRS. As of July 15, 2004, as a result of RMB 1.219 billion additional investments from existing shareholders and the issuance of RMB 12 billion subordinated bonds, BoCom's shares totaled 31.341 billion (31.83% of which were held by the central government, 17.73% by NCSSF, 9.57% by Central Huijin, and 40.87% by other enterprise legal persons), with CCAR and CAR increasing to 4.3% and 7.49% respectively.

III. Engagement of Foreign Strategic Investors

(I) Selection of Foreign Banks as Strategic Investors

BoCom selected strategic investors based on the following criteria: (i) Business size and financial strength. The investors should be among *The Banker*'s Top 50 Banks in 2001, and rated C or above in financial strength by Moody's; (ii) Geographical location. Priority was given to major

European and North American banks for their industry-leading management practices and corporate culture; (iii) Business strengths. The investors should have sophisticated treasury management, risk management, investment banking, and product R&D to provide complementary advantages. BoCom preferred European banks because they are among the first to offer universal banking and have competitive advantages in cross-business sector operation; (iv) Development strategies. Priority was given to strategic investors with branches or representative offices in China, which indicated their long-term strategic commitment to the Chinese market and potential willingness to invest in BoCom; (v) Interbank relationships with BoCom. The investors should have a good interbank relationship with BoCom which would facilitate communication and coordination; and (vi) Credibility. The investors should have respectable reputation and operational style, which would help improve the international reputation of BoCom.

In the second half of 2003, BoCom started formal negotiations with short-listed foreign strategic investors. HSBC and Standard Chartered Bank (SCB) were the main candidates. BoCom was in fact the first bank in China considered for investment by SCB; the formal negotiations between the two banks at the time lasted from September to October of 2002. In the following November and December, led by SCB's CFO, EY conducted loan due diligence at seven or eight BoCom branches. The results showed a severe lack of personal banking customer data, corporate banking customer data, and credit risk assessment data. SCB's financial advisor UBS Securities concluded that investing in BoCom was not an easy thing for SCB, which partly led to the withdrawal of SCB.

The Hongkong and Shanghai Banking Corporation (HSBC) was incorporated in Hong Kong in March 1865 and then in Shanghai one month later. It is the first member of HSBC Group and the flagship of the group in Asia Pacific. It is the largest bank incorporated in Hong Kong, and also one of the three note-issuing banks there. As of December 31, 2004, HSBC registered HKD 2.459 trillion of total assets. It is the wholly-owned subsidiary of HSBC Holdings plc, the holding company for HSBC Group, which, as one of the largest network of banking and financial services in the world, comprises over 9,800 offices in 77 countries and regions and has USD 1.277 trillion in total assets. HSBC's intention to invest in BoCom came from its strategy of long-term development in China. Although it was already holding an 8% stake in Bank of Shanghai, HSBC was still looking for partnership with a Chinese bank commanding a nationwide outlet network. Also, HSBC wanted an inroad to a dominant position in China's credit card market through BoCom's credit card unit, and thus was especially keen to cooperate with BoCom in the personal banking segment. As additional advantage, HSBC had a competitive edge and more robust risk resiliency compared with SCB.

For the reasons behind HSBC's strategic investment in BoCom, HSBC Deputy Chairman and CEO Peter Wong Tung Shun explained, "HSBC had already grown into a large foreign bank in the Chinese mainland. Our efforts in China paid off, turning into successful relationships and trust between HSBC and local customers, employees, communities, regulators, and other related parties. While expanding our own business, we sought cooperation with Chinese banks through equity investment, in a bid to jointly promote the financial reform and economic development of China. Our value proposition was that BoCom was the fifth largest bank in China. It was restructured into a joint-stock company in 1987, and had set up over 2,000 outlets across the mainland. Moreover, BoCom considered HSBC a suitable partner among many foreign banks, and expressed its interest in working with us."[1]

(II) Equity Participation of HSBC in BoCom

1. **Process and pricing basis**

Price was the biggest sticking point in the nearly 30 rounds of tough investment negotiations spread over one year. The negotiations even came to a deadlock where neither side was willing to give in.

When the tension between the two sides was heating up, the new BoCom Chairman Jiang Chaoliang, for his decisiveness, emerged as a key player to break the deadlock. Before Jiang took the helm at BoCom, the negotiations between the two sides tended to be roundabout. When he came to BoCom, he said directly to the head of BoCom's negotiation team, "We need someone to wind up the negotiations… HSBC is now here. This is the last chance. You must conclude the negotiations within one week!" Under the close supervision of decision-makers, the strategic cooperation clauses were finally nailed down following three months of back-and-forth talks.[2] In August 2004, BoCom and HSBC agreed to the size and price of the equity transaction – the net asset value per share of BoCom as of December 31, 2003 would be the benchmark price for HSBC's strategic stake. According to IFRS-based audit results provided by PwC, at the end of 2003, BoCom had RMB 18.081 billion of net assets,

---

1   Quoted from the interview with HSBC Deputy Chairman and CEO Peter Wong Tung Shun (provided by BoCom).
2   Wu Yushan and Wang Haiming: *Twenty Years: Evolution of Bank of Communications and China's Banking Sector*, China Financial Publishing House, 2007, p. 221.

or RMB 1.06 per share. Previous cases where foreign investors bought into Chinese banks had been conducted with a P/B ratio of 1.8 at the high end (consortium led by Hang Seng Bank into Industrial Bank) and 1.54 at the low end (Citibank into Shanghai Pudong Development Bank); BoCom proposed a P/B ratio range of 1.54-1.8. At last, HSBC accepted the ratio of 1.76 which was near the upper limit, and acquired a 19.9% stake (7.775 billion shares) in BoCom at RMB 1.86 per share for RMB 14.461 billion or USD 1.747 billion, becoming the second largest shareholder behind the MOF.

Speaking about the difficulty of courting HSBC, Peng Chun recalled, "BoCom was the first Chinese bank to obtain foreign investment. We launched our foreign capital attraction plan as early as 2001, and specially set up a foreign investment management office. In fact, the first contact between HSBC and BoCom occurred even earlier. At that time, we also met many other potential investors, and a huge quantity of their due diligence documents piled up in several rooms. ICBC, ABC, BOC, and CCB didn't hire foreign institutions to conduct due diligence like us. We didn't have any experience and could only feel our way forward. Before BoCom's joint-stock reform plan was approved, our talks with HSBC had almost broken down. They said that they would accept our offered price, but only net of the bad loan-related costs, but it was unacceptable to us. After the plan was approved on June 14, we told HSBC that the state would deal with BoCom's NPAs through capital injection. I remember that at our last meeting with HSBC at Grand Hotel Beijing, BoCom Chairman Jiang Chaoliang and HSBC Holdings Chairman John Bond talked directly. I was also there. It was supposed to be a 'farewell dinner,' but Jiang and John, with foresight and sagacity, quickly reached a deal, both agreeing that the two companies should think in terms of the next 100 years. On August 18, the parties signed an agreement, under which HSBC would acquire a stake in BoCom for about USD 1.7 billion at RMB 1.86 per share. USD 1.7 billion was a huge sum. It marked the largest single foreign investment in China as well as the largest single investment ever made by HSBC. Such a result really didn't come easy. It demonstrated a great deal of resolve of the State Council leaders who approved a stake very close to the 20% shareholding cap, which made HSBC the second largest shareholder of BoCom."[1]

2. Principal undertakings of HSBC

BoCom and HSBC concluded five agreements – the "Stock Purchase Agreement," "Investor Rights Agreement," "Credit Card Business Cooperation Agreement," "Brand Licensing Agreement," and "Technical Support and Assistance Agreement." HSBC's undertakings regarding its equity participation in BoCom mainly included the following:

(i) HSBC would maintain the MOF's position as the largest shareholder. Even if the 20% foreign shareholding cap was lifted, HSBC would still be required to obtain the approval of the MOF before increasing its stake to a level higher than that of the MOF. (ii) HSBC would maintain BoCom's status as a Chinese-held bank and should keep the status unchanged at all times. (iii) HSBC would not change its shareholding in the next five years. To this end, the "Stock Purchase Agreement" stipulated a three-year suspension period (in which HSBC could not buy shares without approval) and a five-year lock-up period (in which HSBC could not sell shares without approval), and only allowed HSBC to exercise an anti-

---

1 From the interview with Peng Chun on March 21, 2017.

dilution option in the event of the IPO to maintain its shareholding. (iv) Exclusive investment. HSBC would not make any other strategic investment in any company within five years, to the exclusion of previous investments. (v) Jurisdiction. Disputes between the parties should be solved in accordance with the Chinese laws, and disputes over arbitration clauses and the enforcement of arbitral awards should be governed by courts in Shanghai. (vi) License of HSBC's brand. Under the "Brand Licensing Agreement," HSBC granted BoCom a license to use the brands of HSBC and HSBC Group for a three-year period which could be renewed. (vii) Technical assistance and support. HSBC would provide technical support and services in risk management, corporate governance and internal control, financial management, ALM, and human resources management under the "Technical Support and Assistance Agreement." (viii) Credit card business cooperation. The two parties would conduct business cooperation by setting up a credit card unit which would be operated under BoCom and keep separate accounts. Even if future laws would permit HSBC to hold an over 50% stake in a credit card joint venture, HSBC would still be required to negotiate with BoCom in advance.

(III) Results of Bringing in Foreign Investors

The process of bringing in foreign investors forced BoCom to constantly improve corporate governance and internal systems and mechanisms, and to learn advanced management concepts and skills from foreign banks. The participation of HSBC promoted not only the overall reform and long-term development of BoCom, but also the reform and development of the whole financial industry.

For one, HSBC's participation as a foreign strategic investor helped diversify BoCom's equity structure and governance structure. Table 5.3 depicts BoCom's equity structure after the introduction of strategic investors and before H-share listing.

Table 5.3: BoCom Equity Structure Before the H-Share Listing

Shareholder	Shareholding	Percentage (%)
MOF	9,974,982,648	25.53
HSBC	7,774,942,580	19.90
NCSSF	5,555,555,556	14.22
Central Huijin	3,000,000,000	7.68
Capital Airports Holding Company	985,447,500	2.52
Shanghai Tobacco Group	378,328,046	0.97
Hongta Group	345,215,314	0.88
Shandong Electric Power Company	300,000,000	0.77
China Huaneng Group Co., Ltd.	198,041,710	0.51
FAW Group Corporation	177,376,500	0.45
Others (2,585 shareholders)	10,380,173,362	26.57
Total	39,070,063,216	100.00

Source: BoCom H-Share Prospectus.

Furthermore, foreign investors brought in not only capital, but more importantly, sophisticated management concepts, products, and skills, which contributed to a stronger BoCom with optimized frameworks and improved management capabilities. Under the package agreement between BoCom and HSBC, HSBC would directly participate in the operation and management of BoCom, and provide BoCom with technical support and services in risk management, corporate management and internal control, financial management, ALM, and human resources management. This arrangement would help BoCom draw on experience from the world-class commercial bank HSBC, narrow its gap with leading international banks, and build a stronger image both at home and abroad.

Related Topic: Peter Wang Tung Shun: Strategic Cooperation Between HSBC and BoCom[1]

"I [Peter Wang Tung Shun] joined HSBC in April 2005 as an executive director, being responsible for the strategic cooperation between HSBC and BoCom. In August the same year, I became a non-executive director of the board of directors of BoCom. I want to say that I'm very honored to participate in and witness the cooperation between the two banks over the past decade. I remember that to promote multi-level and all-round cooperation, I proposed a strategic communication mechanism and propelled its creation in September 2005. From the top down, the multi-level mechanism comprised semi-annual executive meetings to determine strategic direction, quarterly senior management meetings to develop and advance concrete cooperation plans, and business teams to implement those cooperation plans. Each level worked in close communication, which enhanced mutual trust. Cooperation projects included co-branded credit cards, joint product R&D, IT cooperation, employee exchange, and management personnel training, among others.

"In 2005, HSBC appointed Dicky Peter Yip, its Chief Executive of HSBC China, as Vice President of BoCom responsible for part of personal banking business, such as credit cards and retail loans. During his seven years at BoCom, Dicky dedicated himself to integrating the proven experience of HSBC into the specific local environments and BoCom's business model in

---

1 Quoted from the interview with HSBC Deputy Chairman and CEO Peter Wong Tung Shun (provided by BoCom).

an international development framework. Also, Dicky helped BoCom build the Pacific Credit Card Center, which promoted the development of its credit card business. The two banks' joint achievements in credit cards are a shining example of Sino-foreign cooperation.

"In terms of other business areas, especially key areas, the two banks also took advantage of complementarity. Particularly, we combined our respective advantages in domestic and overseas markets to support Chinese enterprises''going global' programs. I'd like to talk more about the BoCom and HSBC '1+1 global financial service' model, which was a good example of win-win cooperation. In the model, business units of the two banks worked together via a regular communication mechanism to analyze BoCom's market prospects and customer demand, develop projects, and explore new cooperation models and service plans. These efforts have promoted the cooperation between the two. Currently, the two banks are running cooperation programs in 13 key domestic branches, to offer targeted, jointly marketed financial solutions. Meanwhile, the '1+1 service' model has been introduced to major markets in Asia Pacific and Europe, which effectively promoted the implementation of 'going global' projects. On the technical side, the two banks conducted extensive and in-depth cooperation through expert exchange, project training, and work experience sharing. Also, the model was expanded into social service activities, such as the community-based BoCom-HSBC Happy Aging Program, enabling the two banks to jointly assume social responsibility at a higher level of strategic cooperation.

"In general, HSBC and BoCom established trust and strategic partnership over the past decade. Under the principles of 'mutual understanding, mutual benefits, long-term cooperation, and joint development', the two banks have made extensive, notable and widely recognized achievements through joint efforts. I can say proudly that we have set an example of cooperation between Chinese and foreign banks."

While successfully taking in foreign capital, BoCom maintained the dominant positioning of the state in the financial industry, because throughout its investment reach-out and negotiations, maintaining the central government's controlling interest was always the guiding principle. Despite all the challenges and difficulties, BoCom always put the national interest first. As a landmark event in China's financial reform, the successful introduction of foreign investors by BoCom greatly increased the trust of foreign investors on the country's banking reform, demonstrated its determination to speed up the financial reform, and boosted the confidence of foreign investors in its banking sector and financial market.

IV. Listing in Shanghai and Hong Kong

Following the financial restructuring and the participation of strategic investor HSBC, BoCom pushed ahead with its IPO and listing, which was the natural step for it to implement the overall plan for advancing joint-stock reform, embrace the supervision of investors and regulators, and accelerate system and mechanism reforms.

(I) Simultaneous Listing Plan

Creating a well-designed listing plan is essential for successful listing. The success of BoCom's public listing has its roots first in a sophisticated listing plan which can be adjusted to respond to the latest capital market trends. In line with the overall reform plan of BoCom, the "Proposal on the Capital and Share Increase, Financial Restructuring and Introduction of Foreign Strategic Investors of BoCom" adopted at its shareholder's meeting on June 20, 2004, and relevant resolutions, BoCom formulated the "Proposal on the Plan of Simultaneous Listing of BoCom on the H- and A-share Markets and Relevant Authorization Matters," which was deliberated and adopted by the board of directors on August 23, 2004 and approved by CSRC and CBRC at the end of August. On September 23, the final listing plan, revised based on opinions of the regulators, was approved at its shareholders' meeting. The final plan stipulated key matters regarding BoCom's IPO and listing, including listing venues, types of issuance, IPO dates, methods of issuance, IPO sizes, target investors, IPO pricing methods, issuance principles, use of proceeds, and adjustment plans.[1]

1. Listing venues

The proposed listing venues were HKEX and SSE. BoCom selected HKEX for several reasons. First, as Hong Kong is an international financial center, listing there would demonstrate China's resolve to carry through the banking reform, and enhance BoCom's international reputation. Second, Hong Kong is home to a well-established capital market that has easy access to financing. Third, Hong Kong has robust legal and credit environments and a stringent regulatory system. Fourth, Hong Kong as China's special administrative region has unique advantages in information exchange, language, and culture compared with other international capital markets. Fifth, Hong Kong is situated close to the mainland, and thus is more familiar with the mainland's realities, policies, and laws and regula-

---

[1] "Proposal on the Plan of Simultaneous Listing of BoCom on the H- and A-share Markets and Relevant Authorization Matters" adopted at the third meeting of the Fourth Board of Directors on August 23, 2004.

tions. Last, listing in Hong Kong would help BoCom develop its foreign business. BoCom Hong Kong Branch was then the largest Chinese bank branch in Hong Kong. Overall listing on the HKEX Main Board would enable BoCom to obtain the supports from local regulators for its foreign business, thereby achieving its goal of growing into a leading international commercial bank.

SSE, located in Shanghai – China's economic and financial center – is the country's largest capital market with huge market capacity. BoCom mainly operates in the Chinese mainland, therefore, listing on the Shanghai A-share market would increase its credibility, enable mainland investors to share in the results of its reform, and expand its influence on the mainland.

Dual listing in Hong Kong and Shanghai would motivate BoCom to transform its corporate governance and operational mechanisms, build an effective incentive mechanism, and learn from and converge with leading international commercial banks. In Hong Kong, both regulators and investors have high standards on the corporate governance, internal control and information disclosure of listed companies, which meant BoCom needed to enhance its transparency and management as an international public bank. The dual listing would put BoCom under broader supervision of regulators and the general public of the two markets, spurring it to optimize its corporate governance structure and internal management. What's more, by referencing the employee incentive mechanism prevailing in the H-share market, BoCom could develop an effective, long-term incentive plan aligning with international practices to incentivize its management team to maximize shareholder return. Lastly, dual listing would enable BoCom to access two financing channels and build a more efficient capital replenishment system, thus opening up further possibilities for its follow-on financings.

2. IPO size and pricing

Pursuant to HKEX regulations, the publicly offered shares of a listed company must be at least 25% of its total share capital; in the case of a listed company whose total market value worth over HKD 10 billion, a lower percentage between 15% and 25% may be allowed at HKEX's discretion. CSRC also requires a 25% threshold of public float, and lowers the number to 15% for companies with share capital exceeding RMB 400 million. After the financial restructuring and the introduction of foreign investors, BoCom had 39.07 billion shares in total, which meant that taking the 25% threshold as the offer size, it could raise an estimated RMB 20 billion and reach a total market value of over RMB 120 billion. As a result, it might apply the lower thresholds specified by HKEX and CSRC. However, to conduct share offerings on mainland and overseas markets, complete financial restructuring, issue subordinated bonds and expand business, and considering the sustainability of the capital markets, and the earnings dilution associated with the upcoming IPO, BoCom set the preliminary issue size at the thresholds required by HKEX and CSRC or a slightly higher level, namely a size not exceeding 25% of its total shares after IPO.

Since there had been no precedent of simultaneous listing on A- and H-share markets and the two markets adopt different pricing and subscription methods, BoCom priced its IPO shares within price ranges proposed by the lead underwriters based on their valuation. Specifically, it arranged in descending order the subscription prices received from domestic and overseas roadshows and book-building process, and then determined the prices based on subscription data. In particular, the H-share was priced through building an order book and based on the valuations of comparable companies in global capital markets and the prevailing conditions of global capital market, which was an international practice; A-share was priced through a book-building process where institutional investors were invited to submit bids for IPO shares, pursuant to Chinese IPO regulations.

3. Adjustment plans

BoCom's plans to further its joint-stock reform called for going public at an early date. Since BoCom was the first company to conduct simultaneous listing on the H- and A-share markets, to ensure successful IPOs and the implementation of the overall plan of advancing joint-stock reform, it prepared four adjustment plans in consideration of difficulties that might occur during listing: issuing H-shares and A-shares on different dates but based on one approval (Plan I); issuing H-shares and alternative equity certificates (e.g., Chinese depositary receipts) separately (Plan II); issuing H-shares separately (Plan III); and issuing A-shares separately (Plan IV). The adoption of any of the four plans would not affect the remainder of the listing plan.

(II) Preparations for Public Listing

A leading group headed by then Chairman Jiang Chaoliang was created when preparations for public listing started. A well-organized and efficient Unicorn Office (Listing Affairs Office) was set up under the leading group to ensure timely decision-making, handling of IPO matters, and coordination.

Public listing is a series of highly interrelated activities that are subject to rigid requirements and government policies. Over 20 external parties were involved in the public listing of BoCom. To ensure that these activities were conducted as scheduled in an orderly fashion, the Unicorn Office developed a strict work schedule, and created a teamwork system which assigned specific roles to each member and ensured information confidentiality. The office was composed of several special teams which worked closely with various BoCom departments, branches, and sub-branches. The office impressively completed its various tasks as scheduled, including selecting firms to conduct audits and appraisals at domestic and foreign branches, assisting the external firm in their due diligence, prospectus review and editing, preparing legal documents required by regulators of the two markets, replying to regulators' questions, and making preparations for analyst meetings and roadshows. These efforts laid a solid foundation for BoCom to obtain external approvals, pass the listing review of HKEX, and complete a successful listing.

The IPO process witnessed BoCom's constant standardization in its operation according to requirements of the capital markets. To meet the listing criteria of the capital markets, BoCom passed a range of external request and review procedures imposed by each government authority with jurisdiction for its listingrelated matters, including completing business registration, plugging financial deficits, appointing senior management, amending the articles of association, reducing the state's shareholding percentage, transferring tradable shares, clarifying its status as a Chinese-funded bank, submitting listing-related documents, and the final hearing with HKEX.

(III) Listing on the H-Share Market

Considering the subdued market conditions for A-shares in 2005, conditions of the capital markets, and feedback from CSRC, BoCom decided to implement adjustment plan III (issuing H-shares separately) under its simultaneous listing plan. The CBRC and CSRC approved BoCom's application for listing on HKEX on March 22, 2005 and May 12, 2005, respectively. Compared with the "A+H" model, Plan III had the following differences: First, global offering using a mix of a Hong Kong public offering and international placements would be adopted; second, new ordinary shares (excluding additional H-shares offered upon the exercise of the over-allotment option) should not exceed 13.03% of the post-IPO total shares; third, in the case of over-allotment, the size of over-allotted H-shares would not exceed 15% of the post-IPO total shares; fourth, HSBC could exercise an anti-dilution option to maintain its proportional shareholding; fifth, shares held by NCSSF, Central Huijin, and HSBC would be converted into H-shares upon H-share offering; and lastly, the converted H-shares held by Central Huijin could be included in the public float.[1]

1. Rational IPO pricing

For the H-share offering, the valuation of BoCom, the foundation of IPO pricing, was an indispensable step. Specifically, the brokers evaluated and calculated the true intrinsic value of BoCom based on industry analysis, BoCom's financial conditions and development strategies, and other factors. Through quantitative simulation of these factors, the brokers made predictions on BoCom's value, primarily including changes in interest rates, changes in its costs and asset quality, development of its principal business, and changes in its expenses. Based on these forecasts, the brokers

---

1 From BoCom Listing Affairs Office: "Request of Bank of Communications for Instructions on the Plan of Listing on the H-Share Market" (Jiao Yin Han [2005] No. 118), May 9, 2005.

evaluated BoCom's value using an industry-standard method, providing a basis for the final IPO price. Because its successful roadshow had created huge demand, BoCom priced its IPO at HKD 2.5 per share near the top end of the HKD 1.95-2.55 range. The IPO P/E ratio[1] was 14.8, ranking at an intermediate level among mainland Chinese banks. A total of HKD 14.64 billion was raised.

2. Successful roadshow

To protect the interests of existing shareholders and ensure successful public listing, BoCom (i) watched closely the capital market dynamics and actively took diverse marketing measures throughout the listing; (ii) prepared analyst meetings to promote the investment value of BoCom; (iii) allotted shares to institutional investors in accordance with Rule 144A under the U.S. *Securities Act of 1933*; and (iv) sold shares to Japanese investors through a POWL (public offering without listing). During the two-week pre-marketing and roadshow held between June 1 and 18, 2005, the roadshow team, led by then Chairman Jiang Chaoliang and President Zhang Jianguo, directly met 553 investors at 87 presentations in 9 cities around the world. At the presentations, the team showcased China's progress in economic development and banking reform, pitched BoCom's investment stories, and answered questions about China's economic and financial conditions, BoCom's operations and management, and system and mechanism reforms.

The roadshow was a challenging program for BoCom. Internationally, it faced market expectations for RMB appreciation, intensifying China-U.S. trade friction, and rising oil prices; domestically, it encountered

---

1   The ratio of a company's stock price to earnings per share.

growing pressure from expectations for macroeconomic regulation, an increasing number of scandals involving Chinese commercial banks, and the simultaneous listings of large SOEs like Shenhua Group and COSCO Group. In spite of these challenges, BoCom's unique investment value, extensive preparations, inspiring presentations by the management, and rational IPO price range made the roadshow a complete success.

The roadshow ended with a pricing meeting. According to records, on June 17 local time, the roadshow team arrived at the last stop of their global roadshow tour – San Francisco, where the pricing meeting was scheduled to be held. Pricing was a key part of the IPO – the price could not be too high or too low, and had to be accepted by both existing and new shareholders and investment banks. During the global roadshow, global investors showed a strong appetite to subscribe to BoCom shares; by stark contrast, some investors offered low indicative prices during the previous roadshow and the underwriters also offered surprisingly low prices at the pricing meeting. The listing arrived at a key point where BoCom and investment banks disputed fiercely over the IPO price. Since neither side was willing to make concessions, the pricing meeting carried over from June 17 to 1:00 a.m. the next day.

In response to the underwriters' bearish views of the value of BoCom, Jiang Chaoliang stressed, "I have five principles. The first is market-based pricing by reference to the P/E ratios, P/B ratios, and other indicators of our peers. The second is fully protecting the interests of existing shareholders, which means the price cannot be too low. The third is considering the interests of new shareholders which means the price cannot be too high, or the investors will be disappointed if the stock price slumps below the IPO price. The fourth is protecting the national interest and the progress of

China's banking reform, so a rational price must be set to avoid any losses on state assets. The fifth is ensuring the after-market price stability." After reeling off his list, Jiang paused for a second, and concluded, "If the P/B ratio is lower than 1.6, and the P/E ratio is lower than 13, we'll leave for Shanghai tomorrow. And there will be no deal!" At last, BoCom convinced the underwriters, and the price was set at HKD 2.5, or RMB 2.66, near the top end of the price range, corresponding to a P/B ratio of 1.76 and a P/E ratio of 15.2, both higher than the IPO averages of comparable Hong Kong banks at that time.[1]

The above vignette was supported by what Peng Chun recalled, "The whole roadshow was a big challenge for BoCom, especially the question of pricing which put us under tremendous pressure. At many moments, we even fell out with the investment banks. I remember that we had blazing rows in San Francisco and Hong Kong, and Jiang Chaoliang said at last that there was no room for discussion. ... Finally, we pulled through. The issuance was very successful. The subscription ratio was very high."[2]

The H-share issuance included a Hong Kong public offering and international placements. The former targeted public investors in Hong Kong, while the latter was pitched to international institutional investors, private banks, corporate investors, high net-worth investors, and Japanese investors purchasing via a POWL. Public investors in Hong Kong showed great enthusiasm – shares of BoCom were 205 times oversubscribed, corresponding to a subscription amount of HKD 150 billion, the sixth largest IPO subscription on HKEX. Many public investors borrowed funds to

---

1   Wu Yushan and Wang Haiming: *Twenty Years: Evolution of Bank of Communications and China's Banking Sector*, China Financial Publishing House, 2007, pp. 270-272.
2   From the interview with Peng Chun on March 21, 2017.

apply for IPO shares, leading to a sharp increase in short-term loans. The overnight rate rose up to 0.5%, hitting a four-year high. The extremely high oversubscription ratio triggered a claw-back mechanism – the shares allocated to public investors in Hong Kong finally increased from 290 million to 1.17 billion, or from 5% to 20% of the offer size. This meant each public investor could at least acquire 1 lot (1,000 shares). International placing recorded over 1,000 institutional investors at an oversubscription ratio of 20.

3. Listing on the H-share market

On June 23, 2005, BoCom listed H-shares on the Main Board of HKEX. The public offering and international placing registered 6.734 billion shares (including shares offered under over-allotment), accounting for 14.7% of the post-IPO total shares. The offer price was HKD 2.5 (RMB 2.66) per share, corresponding to a P/B ratio of 1.76 and a P/E ratio of 15.2. A total of HKD 16.82 billion (approximately USD 2.163 billion) was raised. The shares closed at HKD 2.825 on the first trading day, an increase of 13% over the initial offering price. Highlights of the H-share issuance included:

First, both the Hong Kong public offering and international placements recorded high oversubscription ratios, ranking second among the IPOs of major Chinese enterprises listed abroad. Of the USD 53.4 billion total demand, USD 19.6 billion (the sixth largest IPO subscription on HKEX) came from the Hong Kong public offering, where shares were 205 times oversubscribed, and USD 33.8 billion was from the international placements, where shares were 20 times oversubscribed.

Second, the offer price was set at a high level after a market-based process. The offer price was finally set at HKD 2.5 per share, near the top end of the 1.95-2.55 range provided to investors. The P/B ratio and P/E ratio were 1.76 and 15.2 respectively, staying above the averages of comparable banks listed in Hong Kong and at a high level among large SOEs listed abroad. In the market environment at the time, the offer price was set to protect the interests of existing shareholders, especially the state as the controlling shareholder; to attract more international investors; and to ensure a stable price level after IPO.

Third, the state had a controlling stake in BoCom where the central government was the largest shareholder. Of the shares issued, 64.74% was held by the state and SOEs. The top four shareholders were the MOF (21.78%), HSBC (19.9%), NCSSF (12.13%) and Central Huijin (6.55%). Public float took up 11.77% of the total shares. After the shares held by NCSSF, Central Huijin, and HSBC were converted into H-shares upon the IPO, H-shares accounted for 50.35% of the total issued shares.

Fourth, shares held by the state increased in value, and shares held by NCSSF and Central Huijin were all converted into H-shares which would become tradable one year later. One year after the issuance, as measured from the offer price, shares held by the MOF and Central Huijin, which injected capital into BoCom during the financial restructuring, increased by 166% in value, and shares held by NCSSF increased by 47.78% in value.

(IV) Listing on the A-Share Market

1. About the issuance

On May 15, 2007, BoCom went public on the SSE A-share market. A total of 3.19 billion shares were issued at RMB 7.9 per share, accounting for 6.51% of the total shares (48.994 billion). With 1.595 billion shares being traded on SSE, BoCom was the tenth Chinese bank listed on the A-share market. The P/B ratio and P/E ratio were approximately 3.42 and 31.6 respectively. After the issuance, the net asset value per share of BoCom increased by RMB 0.38 to RMB 2.31. A total of RMB 25.2 billion was raised, creating the fifth largest IPO in 2007 worldwide, and the fourth largest IPO in the A-share market.

2. Characteristics of the A-share listing

The total subscription funds exceeded RMB 1.45 trillion, a new record in China's capital market, including over RMB 299 billion from placements to institutional investors. In addition, the percentage of bidders that eventually subscribed for shares, interest of investors in the placing tranche, and bids from institutional investors all set records among Chinese banks. A total of RMB 25.2 billon was raised, higher than the expected RMB 18-20 billion. After the IPO, BoCom's capital adequacy ratio exceeded 15%, and core capital adequacy ratio reached 10.5%, increasing by 4.17 and 1.98 percentage points respectively over the beginning of the year.

The circulation of non-tradable shares was also reasonably resolved. BoCom's listing on the A-share market effectively solved the circulation problem of non-tradable shares held by 2,114 legal persons. After the IPO, the 41.9% state-owned shares (including shares held by the MOF, but excluding shares held by NCSSF and Central Huijin which had been converted into H-shares) appreciated in value. The market value of BoCom ranked fifth in the A-share market. The first trading day was busy. The shares opened at RMB 14.2, topping and bottoming out at RMB 14.99 and RMB 13.45 respectively, and closed at RMB 13.54. The daily turnover was RMB 12.828 billion, a record high in the A-share IPO trading. The market value of BoCom reached RMB 663.4 billion when the market closed on May 15, 2007, making the company the world's 17th largest commercial bank by market cap and the 5th largest heavyweight in the A-share market. On May 16, SSE and China Securities Index Co., Ltd. announced that BoCom would be included into the SSE 180 Index, SSE 50 Index, CSI 300 Index, CSI 100 Index, CSI 800 Index, and CSI Well-Off Index on May 29.

(V) Significance and Outcomes of the Listing

BoCom's successful listing in Hong Kong and Shanghai is of far-reaching and great significance for its reform and development and even for that of all state commercial banks, as well as for BoCom to grow into a world-class commercial bank.

BoCom's listing further diversified its ownership structure and improved its corporate governance. To meet the strict requirements under mainland and overseas listing rules and of the stock markets and foreign investors on corporate governance, internal control, and information disclosure, BoCom improved its modern corporate governance structure where the shareholders' meeting, board of directors, board of supervisors and senior management operate independently and are mutually checked and balanced, created a highly professional and international board of directors and a board of supervisors responsible for the general shareholders' meeting, and optimized the specialized committees under the board of directors and board of supervisors in accordance with standards of international listed banks and domestic and foreign regulatory rules. Among Chinese banks and companies listed on the H-share market, BoCom was the first that prepared and disclosed financial statements in accordance with international accounting standards. In addition, though not expressly required by HKEX listing rules, it published financial statements on a quarterly basis, and proactively informed investors of significant information through investor relations management activities, voluntarily accepting the strict supervision of international capital markets and of investors.

The listing further enhanced BoCom's capital strength, and in the short term, solved the undercapitalization problem that had hobbled its development. In the long run, the successful listing had created a new financing channel for BoCom by linking it with the capital markets, and also helped it establish a sustainable capital replenishment mechanism. As of the end of 2007, the owner's equity of BoCom reached RMB 128.379 billion, an increase of 47% over the end of 2006; assets valued RMB 2,103.626 billion, up 22.61% from the end of 2006; capital adequacy ratio and core capital adequacy ratio were 14.44% and 10.27% respectively, up by 3.61 and 1.75 percentage points compared with the end of 2006; after-tax profit was RMB 20.42 billion, an increase of 66.60% over 2006; ROA and ROE reached 1.07% and 17.17% respectively, up 0.27 and 2.75 percentage points from 2006.

The listing remarkably boosted BoCom's corporate image and brand value. As the first major Chinese state commercial bank going public overseas, BoCom attracted the attention of massive international investors. After BoCom's listing on the H-share market, rating agencies like S&P and Fitch successively upgraded its ratings, and some authoritative brand valuation firms selected BoCom as a winner of their awards, including the 2005 Best Commercial Bank in China from *FinanceAsia*, and China's Brands Annual Award (ranked first) from World Brand Lab. The market also responded positively. After BoCom went public, its stock price rose steadily, topping at over twice of the offer price.

BoCom's listing on the H-share market in 2005 was not only a key milestone in promoting the bank's reform, but also a new starting point for it to grow into a world-class commercial bank. Moreover, it improved the international reputation of BoCom, and enhanced the confidence of foreign investors on Chinese banking reform. After BoCom issued A-shares in 2007, its market image and reputation were considerably raised. On the Top 1000 World Banks 2007 list of the U.K. magazine *The Banker*, BoCom moved up to 69th by total assets, and ranked 68th by Tier-1 capital. BoCom was awarded China's Brands Annual Award (ranked first) by World Brand Lab for several years in a row. In 2008, BoCom was named China Buyer's Satisfaction Brand (ranked third) by World Brand Lab, as well as the Most Competitive Brand in the Chinese Market. In 2009, BoCom was selected as one of the 2009 Top 25 Most Respected Listed Chinese Companies in an event (held for the sixth year) jointly organized by the world's leading financial magazines *The Buffett*, *World Economist Weekly*, and authoritative brand valuation institution World Enterprise Competitiveness Lab. The brand value of BoCom had been gradually recognized by the market.

Section V
Accusation of "Gross Underpricing" of State-Owned Banks

CCB and BOC, the two pilot banks for the joint-stock reform, went public in October 2005 and June 2006 respectively, and saw their share prices start to go up steadily after staying poised for a spell. However, six months before their IPO, the market had been abuzz about the "low creditability," "technical insolvency," and "unattractive equity" of state-owned banks, causing the banks to worry about whether their shares would arouse the interest of enough investors. When CCB went public in Hong Kong, its shares were oversubscribed by enthusiastic investors, which made some to realize that the bank sold shares to strategic investors at a price much lower than the IPO price. This soon led to a wide-spread public outcry about the "gross price concession" made by state-owned banks to foreigners. Nevertheless, as the banks had made significant progress after going public, this accusation tapered off.

The pricing of strategic stakes should be analyzed from the perspective of historical conditions and realities. That is to say, the prices at which shares of major Chinese banks were sold to strategic investors had been affected by the prevailing prices in the capital market of that time. It's just like the price of real estate – it would be meaningless to gauge the price of a house traded several years ago based on the current market price. Therefore, whether shares of state-owned banks were underpriced for strategic investors should be judged based on the market environment and the prices of comparable banks at the time.

First, the prices of strategic shares were decided by the prevailing market conditions. Except for ABC, the other four state-owned banks all went public in 2004 or 2005, when the stock markets in Hong Kong and the mainland were in a bear run – the Hang Seng Index (HSI) picked up slowly from around 13,000 to 15,000, and the SSE Composite Index slipped down from around 1,500 to 1,100. The P/B ratios for the shares sold by state-owned banks to strategic investors averaged 1.2 or so, falling within the reasonable valuation range of the global banking sector at the time. Throughout the shareholding period of strategic investors, capital markets in Hong Kong and the Chinese mainland witnessed bullish sentiment – the HSI started to trend upward in 2006 and nearly hit 32,000 in November 2007, which more than doubled from 2005. SSE Composite Index also took off in 2006, and soared to the historical high of 6,124 on October 31, 2007, up nearly fivefold from 2005. Buoyed by the bullish market, the stock prices of large banks went up. For instance, H-shares of CCB rose to above HKD 5 per share, a 1.5-fold increase over the offer price. This market upturn, which arrived unexpectedly, stood in sharp contrast with the downturn when BOC and CCB brought in investors. Therefore, at that time, neither the state-owned banks nor foreign investors could realistically set high prices. In recent years, P/B ratios of the banks have almost fallen below 1, illustrating that market capitalizations of banks are not meant to be held constant, but rather fluctuate over time (Figure 5.3).

Then BOC President Li Lihui later said, "The strategic stakes were priced based on the capital net worth calculated by the accounting firm after the second round of NPA disposal, corresponding to a P/B ratio of around 1.2. Given that international rating agencies considered the state-owned banks to be technically insolvent, it was a reasonable valuation. We cannot compare the price at which strategic investors were brought in with the high share prices state-owned banks achieved following their listing, or else how would you explain that the banks' current stock prices are lower than their net assets? I remember that some scholars criticized the banks for selling state assets like selling scruffy shoes, which was a lopsided opinion I vehemently oppose. In my view, no matter when the foreign strategic investors exited from the banks, they had made contributions to the joint-stock reform of Chinese state-owned banks. We must recognize their merits, which domestic institutional investors cannot provide. Introducing foreign investors was a key component of the reform plans and I think we did a good job in this regard."[1] Historical data have proved that the strategic shares were sold for reasonable prices instead of at grossly undervalued prices.

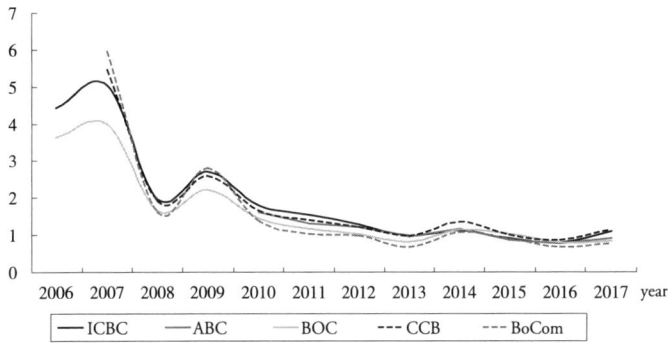

Note: Prepared based on P/B ratios of the Big Five since the joint-stock reform.

Fig. 5.3: Changes in P/B Ratios of Big Five Since the Joint-Stock Reform

Second, the prices were determined through extensive negotiations. When state-owned banks launched efforts to bring in strategic investment and listing after financial restructuring, the net asset value per share of restructured state-owned banks was RMB 1 or a little higher, and the shares were sold at a premium at around 1.2 times the net asset value. After the state-owned banks made their listings, many people, both at home and abroad, still thought that "technically insolvent" state-owned banks went public just after financial restructuring, and thus doubted the thoroughness of the banks' transformation and their sustainable profitability.

During the period of taking in strategic investment, foreign and

---

1 From the interview with Li Lihui on February 21, 2017.

domestic investors faced the same market conditions and made investments on a level playing field. Suffice it to say, price negotiations for strategic shares showed that foreign investors had not been blessed with clairvoyance. RBS initially only offered RMB 0.7-0.8 per share to BOC, and finally agreed to RMB 1.22 per share after rounds of negotiations. What's more, it later sold half of its 10% stake to Goldman Sachs and Li Ka Shing Foundation to dilute its exposure. As for ICBC, when courting strategic investors, it had engaged with several domestic institutional investors, but none of them showed strong interest. ICBC also considered domestic private enterprises but they generally had no financial capacity to invest – Chinese private enterprises in the early 2000s were small in size, with only a few ones having a net profit of over RMB 1 billion, therefore they didn't have enough funds to make large investments. In such a context, ICBC had to turn to foreign strategic investors. Among the over 40 international institutional investors that ICBC invited, only three said they would "think about it." Of the three, Fortis Group finally gave up the plan of investing EUR 1 billion in ICBC, for its shareholders' meeting and board of directors held that the plan was too risky. Another investor Allianz reduced its investment from the original EUR 3 billion to EUR 1 billion. All of these indicated that domestic and foreign investors still had doubts about the effects of the banking reform.

Introducing foreign strategic investors was a pioneering practice in the IPO process of the state-owned banks, because foreign investors would not only underwrite the creditworthiness of the banks and thus boost offer prices, but also be subject to a three-year lock-up period, during which, just like the promoters, they must assume risks of market volatility and stabilize the share prices of the banks.

In short, foreign strategic investors assumed risks in exchange for a share of the future profit of the state-owned banks, and the state-owned banks shored up their credibility as well as reaped other benefits from strategic cooperation. Therefore, the results of the pricing negotiations were objective and fair reflection of the parties' judgments on risks and benefits.

Third, the strategic investors sold shares based on market supply and demand. After the lock-up period expired, early foreign strategic investors successively sold their stakes in the state-owned banks toward various ends under market principles. In fact, they didn't sell shares at the most opportune moments. For instance, UBS sold 3.4 billion H-shares in BOC on December 31, 2008 at HKD 2.12 per share, much lower than the offer price of RMB 2.95 per share. The first wave of selling occurred in 2008 and 2009, when many foreign investors sold part of their strategic shares due to financial troubles amid the global financial crisis. Another wave of sell-off arrived later around 2011, whereas the capital markets in the Chinese mainland and Hong Kong and the share prices of state-owned banks had entered a period of volatility since 2010.

When the early strategic investors were selling shares, other well-known international institutional investors were buying heavily. In August 2011, BofA sold 13.1 billion H-shares in CCB. The buyers included Temasek, Qatar's sovereign wealth fund, and other foreign investors, apart from Central Huijin and NCSSF. Based on the mid-year net asset value per share of CCB in 2011, the P/B ratio was around 1.5, lower than the IPO P/B ratio of 2. Given that major banks were associated with promising performance and stable dividend distribution, it was true that their shares were undervalued, but that was also the overarching reason for both domestic and foreign investors to buy their shares. For another example, when Goldman Sachs was selling its shares in ICBC in 2012, Blackrock Inc. and Temasek were buying shares in ICBC. In short, selling or buying shares in major Chinese banks by foreign investors depended on their judgments on the market value of the banks.

Fourth, when the strategic investors received return on their investments, so did all the other investors. Because shareholders holding the same class of shares enjoy the same rights, the higher post-IPO share prices of the major banks was not "exclusive" to a certain class of shareholders. The post-IPO equity structures of the major banks showed that state-owned shareholders held a bigger stake than foreign investors, therefore, if calculated based on the share price at which strategic investors sold their shares, state-owned shareholders' "capital gains" would be greater (Table 5.4).

Table 5.4: Equity Structures of Banks in the Year of Listing

Bank	Shareholding of foreign strategic investors (%)	Shareholding of the MOF and Central Huijin (%)	Shareholding of state-owned shareholders among the top 10 shareholders (%)
ICBC	7.2	70.6	75.4
BOC	9.78	67.49	70.79
CCB	14.4	61.48	74.26
BoCom	19.9	28.33	45.27

Note: 1. ABC didn't introduce strategic foreign investors and thus is not included in the table.

2. Compiled based on data disclosed by the banks in the year of listing.

CHAPTER VI
EXPANSION AND CONCLUSION

– Joint-Stock Reforms and IPOs of ICBC and ABC

On the basis of successful joint-stock reforms for CCB and BOC and the further reforms of BoCom, China started to carry out joint-stock reforms for other SOCBs. ICBC, thanks to its meticulous preparations and national policy support, successfully launched and completed its joint-stock reform and IPO shortly after the three pilot banks. And ABC, despite many twists and turns, also successfully concluded its reform, marking the completion of the joint-stock reform for all wholly state-owned commercial banks. A new era dawned for China's financial industry.

Section I
Joint-Stock Reform and IPO of ICBC

As the bank with the largest assets – and the largest NPAs – in China's financial industry, and the bank with especially close relationships with both the industrial and commercial enterprises and the public, ICBC faced a string of challenges in its joint-stock reform and IPO. Due to the broad impact, high cost, and difficulties of its restructuring, ICBC was not included in the first group of pilot banks for joint-stock reform and IPO. Undeterred by the difficulties, ICBC accelerated its pace of reform. By improving internal management and risk control, ICBC disposed of its NPAs, improved financial performance, and made progress in its business transition. Through such efforts, ICBC geared up for the joint-stock reform and IPO, which laid a solid foundation for its post-reform development.

As it was well-prepared, ICBC obtained the approval of its joint-stock reform plan in April 2005 and successfully went public in October 2006 – the quickest among the Big Five. Its joint-stock reform yielded remarkable results. On October 28, 2005, ICBC was wholly restructured into a joint-stock limited company. It brought in domestic and overseas strategic investors, and initiated an IPO. On October 27, 2006, ICBC was dual-listed on the A-share and H-share markets in the Chinese mainland and Hong Kong at the same time and same price. Through the joint-stock reform, ICBC transformed from a wholly state-owned commercial bank into a joint-stock commercial bank and indeed also an international public company.

Related Topic: Brief History of ICBC

The Third Plenary Session of the 11th CPC Central Committee in December 1978 unveiled rapid reform of China's financial system. On September 17, 1983, the State Council promulgated the "Decisions on the PBOC's Exercise of Central Bank Functions," which stipulated that "the PBOC shall exclusively exercise the functions of the central bank, and will no longer offer industrial and commercial credit and savings services," and that "the Industrial and Commercial Bank of China shall be established to take over the industrial and commercial credit and savings services from the PBOC."

On December 30, 1983, ICBC's founding ceremony was held in Beijing. On January 1, 1984, the *People's Daily* and Xinhua News Agency announced ICBC's establishment to the world. The *Economic Daily* published a front-page editorial titled "An Important Reform of the Banking System" congratulating on ICBC's establishment, indicating that "ICBC's founding is an important event in China's economic development and marks a major reform of China's banking system." ICBC's founding marks the inauguration of China's system of specialized banks.

From 1984 to 1993, ICBC functioned as a national specialized bank. During this period, ICBC made great strides to run itself as a commercial enterprise. It extensively took in deposits and served as a main source of financing for borrowers. Committed to supporting promising businesses, particularly large and medium-sized SOEs, ICBC made significant progress in its savings, lending, and foreign exchange businesses; developed credit card, international business, and other emerging businesses from scratch; and became China's largest bank. With a well-developed IT system and improved business performance, ICBC completed the tasks of macroeconomic regulation and policy lending assigned by the central government, and vigorously supported China's economic development, reform, and opening up.

From 1994 to 2004, ICBC was a SOCB. After making the transition from a national specialized bank, ICBC accelerated its reforms. Starting in 2000, by enhancing quality, profitability, and management, ICBC transformed its management philosophy and achieved breakthroughs in bank-wide reform and development; and by creating a new operational system based on quality and profitability metrics, ICBC fundamentally improved its bank-wide asset and business performance. Notable progress in capital strength, innovation, cross-border business, IT development, institutional reform, internal control, and risk management paved the way for ICBC's joint-stock reform.

On April 18, 2005, the central government officially approved ICBC's joint-stock reform plan, kicking off ICBC's financial restructuring. On October 28, the Industrial and Commercial Bank of China Limited (ICBC) was inaugurated. All ICBC's businesses, assets, liabilities, outlets, and employees were brought into the scope of joint-stock reform and consolidated into the newly formed joint-stock company.

On January 27, 2006, ICBC and Goldman Sachs signed a strategic agreement on investment and cooperation. Later, ICBC brought in the National Council for Social Security Fund (NCSSF) as a shareholder.

The inclusion of Goldman Sachs and NCSSF would enable ICBC to launch a successful IPO and gain access to international capital markets. On October 27, 2006, ICBC launched a simultaneous dual IPO in Shanghai and Hong Kong, which marked the world's first dual listing on A-share and H-share markets. This IPO thoroughly transformed ICBC and unveiled a new chapter in its history as a modern financial enterprise. ICBC's "IPO of the Century" created or broke 28 records in the capital market. After its IPO, ICBC embraced a golden decade as it experienced its fastest growth since establishment, blazing a unique trail of transition and development.

Related Topic: Birth of ICBC[1]

In its early years, the PBOC assumed dual functions as the central bank and a specialized bank. Even after ABC and BOC had been split off, the PBOC continued to offer industrial and commercial credit and urban savings services. Acting as both the referee and player, the PBOC was not in a position to single-mindedly focus on financial regulation. The profit-seeking specialized banks lacked self-restraint and scrambled to snap up market share, issuing excessive loans that disrupted national economic adjustment and development.

In the second half of 1983, the separation between the PBOC and ICBC and transfer of the relevant institutions, services, and personnel started to be carried out under the guidance of a series of government documents. There were 14 departments, totaling 500 official employee positions, established under ICBC head office. Starting January 1, 1984, the PBOC's branches of provinces, municipalities, and autonomous regions and sub-branches at lower levels put up ICBC's nameplate. The transition followed the principle of "one organization, two names, separate finances, and two sets of accounts." In early 1985, all the provinces and equivalent administrative units, except for Qinghai and Hainan (which were not made provinces until 1988), completed their separation of the PBOC and ICBC. By the end of 1983, the working capital loans transferred from the PBOC to ICBC represented 64.6% of the balance of working capital loans of all Chinese banks. The fixed asset

---

1 Quoted from *History of the Industrial and Commercial Bank of China (2005-2014)*, China Financial Publishing House, 2017.

loans allocated to ICBC made up 86.7% of the balance of fixed asset loans of all Chinese banks. The urban deposits transferred to ICBC accounted for 87.8% of the balance of deposits of all Chinese banks. Specifically, ICBC received, from this transfer, RMB 74.558 billion of deposits from industrial and commercial enterprises, and completed the transfer of relevant cash accounts.

Zhu Tianshun, the PBOC's Vice Governor in charge of credit business, was appointed as ICBC's Board Chairman. Chen Li, the PBOC's Vice Governor in charge of deposit and accounting business, served as ICBC's first President and Secretary of its Party Leadership Group. Zhang Xiao was appointed as ICBC's Vice President and a year later promoted to President and Party Leadership Group Secretary. The PBOC's deputy directors in charge of various businesses were appointed as directors of corresponding departments at ICBC head office. In most cases, the first deputy general managers of the PBOC's branches in charge of the banking business were appointed as general managers of ICBC's branches. Deputy general managers of the PBOC's branches in charge of credit, savings, accounting, and financial affairs were appointed as deputy general managers of ICBC's branches.

At its establishment, ICBC rented a 2,800 m^2 space from the third to the sixth floor of a newly constructed small factory building as its head office. The six-story building was owned by Xicheng District Clothing Company and located at 32 Sanlihe Yuetan South Street, Beijing. Over 200 employees of ICBC head office worked in this poorly equipped and crowded rented office. "Things were hard at the beginning, and it made sense to be frugal. Regretfully, we did not preserve any mementos from this period, and now we only have a blurry black-and-white photo of our first meeting," Chen Li recalled.

I. Sounding a Strong Prelude to the Joint-Stock Reform

"Joint-stock reform is a long journey. It takes long-term commitments to achieve sustainable development. A good bank is not built in one day or on external support only. No matter how much policy support is given by the state, a bank cannot become a good bank without its own effort, and cannot grow into a healthy bank without developing its own 'immune system,'" said Jiang Jianqing, then ICBC President, at a staff meeting, "because we knew our weaknesses at the beginning, we focused on 'cleaning the house' to create better conditions and gear up for the joint-stock reform. What we did in those years is not wasted. Our hard work paved the way for ICBC's joint-stock reform, IPO, and robust development for many years to come."[1]

In 1994, although external conditions were not fully ready, ICBC initiated its transition into a commercial bank following the "Decision of the State Council on Reform of the Financial System." Its head office and branches were consolidated into a single corporation, implemented accountable lending, and put in place asset risk management and asset and liability management (ALM) to focus on quality and efficiency. After officially terminating its role as a national specialized bank, starting from 2000 ICBC accelerated reforms that focused on quality, efficiency, and internal management improvements.

In April 2000, ICBC adopted reform principles of "efficiency, quality, management, development, and innovation." It created a new operational framework based on quality and efficiency metrics. It implemented a

---

1 Jiang Jianqing: "ICBC's Joint-Stock Reform Process and Reflections," *Internal Update Bulletin*, September 29, 2005.

quality evaluation approach of "total-amount lock-down (*quan'e suoding*), two-metric evaluation (*shuangxiang kaohe*), dual-standard control (*liangtiaoxian kongzhi*), and award or penalty at year-end (*nianzhong duixian jiangcheng*)"[1] for the control of NPLs, and an efficiency evaluation approach that focused on "fully segregated profit measurement (*quanfengbi*), results-linked operating expenses and incentives (*shuangguagou*), and separation of operating expenses from financial expenses (*liangfenli*)."[2] These systems fundamentally improved ICBC's asset quality and operational efficiency. Notable progress in capital strength, business innovation, IT-based development, institutional reform, internal control, and risk management paved the way for ICBC's joint-stock reform.

---

1   "Total-amount lock-down" means itemizing and fixing the amounts of NPAs. Each account and transaction should be brought under monitoring and prohibited from being changed without permission. Each entry of new NPAs should be submitted and explained to the asset risk management department and signed by the chief auditor and branch general manager. "Two-metric evaluation" means the evaluation of NPL ratio and absolute amount. "Dual-standard control" means that both NPLs under the four-category loan classification and the three categories of NPLs under the five-category classification should be brought under monitoring. In addition, the quality of both existing loans and new loans should be monitored to assess both the contraction of NPL stock and the control of new NPLs. "Award or penalty at year-end" means that the change in NPLs should be an important element of general manager performance evaluation.

2   "Fully segregated profit measurement" means separately measuring a branch's profits without overstatement. In addition to book profit, the evaluation focused on the true profit level after excluding on-balance-sheet interest and full allowances for interest payables and doubtful and unrecoverable loans in reporting a branch's profits. This requirement aimed to improve ICBC's financial accounting system. "Results-linked operating expenses and incentives" means that the operating expenses of various branches were linked to their operating performance; and that incentives of branch managers were linked with their performance evaluation results. Compensation should be more differentiated to ensure effective incentives. "Separation of operating expenses from financial expenses" means adopting separate accounts for operating expenses and financial expenses at some loss-making banks, which otherwise could use operating funds to finance their financial expenses despite the losses.

(I) Putting Quality and Efficiency First and Consolidating the Foundation of Business Operation

In assuming the role of a national specialized bank, ICBC's mandate was to attract, allocate, and supply funds for China's economic development. Reforms of the national economic system and SOEs in the 1990s laid bare the risk assets that ICBC had built up over the years, adding to the cost of its restructuring. The Asian financial crisis of 1997 dragged China's economy into a downturn. Enterprise bankruptcies led to a spike in doubtful and unrecoverable loans, and ICBC's loan risks came to the spotlight and reached a zenith. By the four-category loan classification, ICBC's overdue, doubtful, and unrecoverable loans surged from RMB 255.77 billion at the end of 1994 to RMB 851.48 billion at the end of 1999, up by RMB 595.71 billion in five years, or 2.3 times. ICBC's NPL ratio also increased from 21.08% in 1994 to 34% in 1999, up 12.92 percentage points.

ICBC's NPL balance and NPL ratio reached their highest levels at the end of 1999. By the newly adopted five-category loan classification, ICBC's NPLs in the latter three quality categories amounted to RMB 1,100 billion, with an NPL ratio of a staggering 47.5%, not to mention various financial losses in excess of RMB 180 billion. Huge NPL and asset losses became a heavy burden for ICBC, adding pressures to its paltry interest income and falling earning power. In fact, ICBC had been reporting net operating losses since 1993. Problems abounded in its risk control, operation, and management. Some branches paid little attention to loan quality and business efficiency, and many of them falsified and frivolously adjusted accounts.

From 1999 to the end of 2000, the first round of NPA divestiture played a pivotal role in reducing ICBC's legacy burden and improving its asset quality and financial position. ICBC cumulatively stripped off RMB 407.7 billion of NPAs and debts (through debt-for-equity swaps) to China Huarong Asset Management Co., Ltd. (Huarong), involving 72,000 industrial and commercial enterprises. Excluding on-balance-sheet interest receivables and performing loans in debt-forequity swaps, ICBC in effect offloaded RMB 294.2 billion of NPLs (by the four-category classification) in principal. By the end of 2000, ICBC's NPL ratio dropped by 6.89 percentage points. It stripped off RMB 42.7 billion on-balance-sheet interest receivables, disposed of a significant part of the legacy burden, and improved its financial position[1].

Shortly after the NPL divestiture, however, the more stringent five-category classification came into effect at the end of 2000. By the new criteria, the last three categories of NPL still stood at RMB 824.59 billion, accounting for 34.43% of total loans[2], a still daunting challenge. Having been excluded from the first group of pilot banks for the joint-stock reform, ICBC had only a few years to write off its NPAs and make up for the capital shortfall by improving internal management and shoring up profits. These challenges were, of course, demoralizing for the workforce. The regulatory environment was changing, too. Ever-tightening capital management rules meant that ICBC could not expand its business free from quality and performance restraints.

Amid these interrelated and mounting pressures, ICBC came to realize that a correct, coherent approach mattered the most. IPO was

---

1 See *Circular on Transmitting General Manager Zhang Geli's Speech at the Working Conference on Asset Risk Management* (Gong Yin Xian Guan [2001] No. 33).
2 Source: Internal information offered by ICBC's Asset Risk Management Department.

not the ultimate goal for the joint-stock reform of state-owned banks. To develop into a modern bank with principles-based management and all-inclusive governance, ICBC needed to address the loopholes in its asset management. Therefore, ICBC gave top priority to quality, efficiency, and competitiveness in its business development, adopted a host of measures to boost financial performance and efficiency, and vowed to refrain from falsifying business performance and to devote all its revenues in the subsequent five years to reduce legacy risks and financial burdens, so as to clear its NPL burden and gear up for restructuring and IPO.

1. Reflecting real profits through the "siloed" performance evaluation system

ICBC came to this conclusion: to muster the financial resources to resolve its NPLs, it must first address operational inefficiencies and the increasingly inflated profits. At that time, China's banking sector had yet to implement international accounting standards. To meet profit targets, many banking institutions – ICBC's branches among them – deliberately made little or no allowance for bad debts and accrued interest payable; and in calculating profits, they overstated accrued interest receivable, effectively manipulating the amount of accounts receivable and payable to inflate profits. This type of profit overstatement, driven by short-term motives, concealed actual losses and led to a build-up of risks in banks. As a result, book profit in the ordinary sense could no longer give a real picture of the operating results of ICBC branches. The misleading elements of book profit must be removed to produce truthful accounting.

To this end, in January 2000 ICBC put in place a performance evaluation system dubbed "fully segregated profit measurement (later known as 'operating profit'), results-linked operating expenses and incentives, and separation of operating expenses from financial expenses."

- "fully segregated profit measurement" means separately measuring a branch's profits without overstatement. In addition to book profit, the evaluation focused on the true profit level after excluding on-balance-sheet interest and full allowances for interest payables and doubtful and unrecoverable loans. False accounts were therefore eliminated to reflect a real picture of bank operation.
- "Results-linked operating expenses and incentives" means that the operating expenses of branches were linked to their operating performance; and that incentives of branch managers were linked with their performance evaluation results. Thus, compensation was more differentiated to ensure effective incentives.
- "Separation of operating expenses from financial expenses" means adopting separate accounts for operating expenses and financial expenses at some loss-making branches, which otherwise could use operating funds to finance their financial expenses despite the losses.

With better incentives and cost control, ICBC enhanced internal management. Requiring branches to report real profits created pressures for them to resolve their legacy burdens.

Referencing the IFRS (then called IAS, the set of standards it subsumed), ICBC adopted a system to reflect real profits without overstatement. It improved the financial accounting system with clearer performance targets and changes. Explicit targets and fair performance evaluation set a clear direction to strive for. Fully segregated profit measurement played a critical role in ICBC's effort to reduce operating losses and inefficiency, and helped prevent additional risks and profit overstatement. In addition to capturing point-in-time profits precisely, it also revealed progress in resolving legacy problems[1]. This transitional system achieved its purpose and was later replaced by IFRS.

As recalled by Jiang Jianqing, "China's banking industry did not fully comply with IFRS until 2002-2003. Before then, there was no reliable method for measuring the profit of banks. At that time, banks which were bold could create a 'book profit' by recording more accruals (i.e., recording less NPL allowances and interest payable, padding the on-balance-sheet interest payable, and 'tinkering' as much as possible with various other receivables and payables).

"To use a metaphor, in order to pad the book profit, some branches would 'dig' deeper into their accounts – and whatever 'asset' or 'income' they could dig up would increase that book profit. Therefore, to reveal a branch's true operating results, we had to reverse those inflated figures. Accordingly, before the implementation of IFRS, I came up with a concept of 'fully segregated profit measurement' – a similar approach to IFRS. It requires banks to make full allowances and eliminate the fictitious income and receivables. By this method, only five to six branches of ICBC showed positive profits. For the seven years before 1999, ICBC ended up making a cumulative loss…"[2]

ICBC examined loss-making branches to find out why losses occurred and how to curb them. It dissolved or merged outlets unable to reverse losses, optimized its regional distribution of outlets, and laid off

---

1 *History of the Industrial and Commercial Bank of China (1994-2004)*, China Financial Publishing House, 2008, p. 116.
2 From the interview with Jiang Jianqing on March 6-7, 2018.

redundant personnel. It elevated the level of financial accounting, rolled out cost management, beefed up real-time and ex-post cost control, and carried out breakeven point analysis for each outlet and business.[1]

2. Turnaround in profitability

The new profit evaluation system played a pivotal role in turning around ICBC's profitability. In 2000, ICBC's domestic institutions made a total operating profit of RMB 9.6 billion, with a book profit of RMB 5.1 billion. In 2001, these figures rose to RMB 34 billion and RMB 5.9 billion, respectively. In 2002, ICBC's operating profit hit RMB 44.3, up by 30.29% YoY, including a book profit of RMB 6.2 billion. In 2003, ICBC's operating profit amounted to RMB 61.6 billion, up 38.92%, and further climbed to RMB 74.6 billion in 2004.

In 2000, only 3 out of ICBC's 36 tier-one branches made both positive operating and book profits. In 2003, 23 branches did so, and 97% of its branches reported positive operating profits. In 2004, ICBC developed the concept of "profit value (*lirun jiazhiliang*)" after revising the definition of operating profit. "Profit value" reflects a risk provision at 1% of current-year new loans, capital cost simulated according to the shortfall of risk provision, and profit structure coefficient estimated by the share of different types of income. Profit value highlights the intrinsic value of operating activities.

In 2005, ICBC reported an operating profit of RMB 89.9 billion, an increase of RMB 16.6 billion over 2004, or 22.68%[2]. By increasing

---

1 *History of the Industrial and Commercial Bank of China (2003-2006)*, China Financial Publishing House, 2014, pp. 192-193.
2 ICBC Finance & Accounting Department: *Report of ICBC's Business Performance and Profit Structure*, 2001-2005, 2006, internal document.

Expansion and Conclusion | 489

operating profit, reducing allowance shortfalls, and boosting its financial strength, ICBC were in a position to calculate operating results based on sufficient provisioning, and laid the foundation for pushing forward with its joint-stock reform and IPO. ICBC officially adopted IFRS in 2006, introduced "pre-allowance profit" and "book profit,"[1] created budgetary metrics based on the book profit rather than operating profit, cancelled the budget for removal of legacy burden, and included core budgetary metrics like pre-allowance profit, book profit, net profit, economic value-added (EVA), and shareholder value-added (SVA). These metrics guided ICBC branches to monitor their cost of risk and capital in proportion to operating revenue.

ICBC's operating revenue materialized into considerable book profits. In 2005, ICBC posted a pre-tax profit of RMB 59.35 billion, with a net profit of RMB 37.7 billion[2]. In 2006, ICBC ramped up profitability with robust growth of after-tax profit, which reached RMB 49.88 billion. All its financial and quality metrics improved and met domestic and international regulatory requirements.[3]

In the five years from 2000 to the first half of 2005 (right before the joint-stock reform), ICBC reported a cumulative operating profit of RMB 267.6 billion. But its "book profit" was a mere RMB 24.7 billion as it used the bulk of operating profits to write off NPLs. "At the 'Most Respected

---

1 "Pre-allowance profit" and "book profit" refer to profit before deduction of asset impairment and profit after deduction of asset impairment. They reflect profit realization before and after full allowance for asset impairment.
2 Editorial committee of ICBC's Yearbook: *Yearbook of the Industrial and Commercial Bank of China (2006)*, China Financial Publishing House, 2006, p. 2.
3 Editorial committee of ICBC's Yearbook: *Yearbook of the Industrial and Commercial Bank of China (2007)*, China Financial Publishing House, 2007, p. 248.

Chinese Enterprise' award ceremony in 2003, I said when answering a reporter's question that ICBC's book profit was only a tip of an iceberg because massive profits lay beneath the surface. After completing NPA disposal, our robust profitability would become manifest. I expected ICBC to contribute RMB 100 billion in book profit each year to our country and investors," said Jiang Jianqing.

"Wang Shi, Chairman of Vanke, a real estate company, was also at the award ceremony. When I said that ICBC's future annual profit was expected to hit RMB 100 billion, he was rather shocked. He also said that he wished his company to achieve RMB 100 billion in annual sales. As it turned out, both of us beat our initial goals. In 2017, ICBC made a net profit – or book profit – of RMB 287.5 billion, while Vanke posted sales revenue of RMB 529.9 billion." Surging operating profit bolstered ICBC's financial strength in disposing of its legacy burden, setting off a campaign to clean up NPAs.

(II) Three Campaigns on Asset Quality

Poor asset quality posed the biggest barrier to ICBC's reform and development. Jiang recalled that "three big mountains" stood in ICBC's way: First, non-performing credit assets totaled RMB 1.14 trillion at the end of 1999, with an NPL ratio of 47.5% by the five-category classification system. Second, non-performing non-credit assets reached RMB 180 billion. Third, loans borrowed to repay old loans or "evergreen loans" stood at about RMB 1 trillion. According to the PBOC's survey, about 70% to 80% of NPLs stemmed from China's economic transition. ICBC reached a similar finding. But serious problems also existed in the guiding philosophy of bank operation and risk and internal management practices. ICBC needed to not only reduce its NPL ratio but develop a strong culture for risk management and internal control as well.[1]

1. Strict control over the quality of new loans

After the first NPA divestiture, ICBC called for launching the three campaigns of "ensuring the quality of new loans, preventing deterioration of existing loans, and disposing of existing NPLs." It decided to, from 2000, adopt separate accounts for loans issued before 1999 – what it called "old loans" – and after 1999[2], and establish accountability with incentives and penalties. ICBC carried out a pilot reform on centralized credit management and developed sound management of credit ledger to monitor the quality of newly issued loans. It put in place a business line suspension and resumption system, and reshaped its risk controls and credit culture. These measures were all highly effective.

As Jiang Jianqing later recalled, in 2000, he asked for the NPL ratio of newly issued loans to be strictly brought under 2% in a conversation with Niu Ximing, then General Manager of ICBC's Credit Management Department, who was later appointed as chairman of BoCom. Niu Ximing believed that 2% was too demanding judging by the circumstances of the past few years. He suggested relaxing the limit to 3% and even 5% instead. Jiang Jianqing did not budge: given the prevailing interest rate spread, he replied, 2% was the bottom line – anything above it would render newly issued loans unprofitable and even loss-making, making it

---

1 Jiang Jianqing: "ICBC's Joint-Stock Reform Process and Reflections," *Internal Update Bulletin*, September 29, 2005.
2 "Old loans" refer to loans issued in 1998 and before; "new loans" refer to loans issued since 1999. For new loans, ICBC put in place risk control and management according to commercial bank operational principles.

impossible to raise profits to resolve NPAs. The message needed to be made clear throughout the bank: the NPL ratio should not exceed the limit, and whoever oversteps the line in whatever manner was to be punished severely.[1] In the five years since 2000, ICBC managed to keep the NPL ratio of its new loans within 1%, which reduced year by year[2], achieving the goal of keeping the NPL ratio in check.

2. Management of "evergreen loans"

During China's economic transition, many SOEs took out "evergreen loans" to keep up with their needs for working capital. Over time, these loans would accumulate and become the "capitalized" credit assets of enterprises that bound the fate of those enterprises with that of state-owned banks. Banks were forced to issue short-term working capital loans to their debtors so that the latter could repay old loans with new ones. In the event that the financial position of these enterprises worsened, or that banks refused to supply them with new loans, the bulk of these loans would deteriorate into NPLs.

Evergreen loans were a means by which banks handled maturing loans, and their emergence – ostensibly a micro finance phenomenon – was in fact tightly intertwined with transitions of China's economic, fiscal, and financial systems. According to the risk management theories of modern commercial banks, evergreen loans go against the nature of bank loans and the basic principles for credit business. The fact that state-owned banks for long were not able to part with them reflected the necessity of a banking reform amid China's economic transformation.

---

1 From the interview with Jiang Jianqing on March 6-7, 2018.
2 *History of the Industrial and Commercial Bank of China (1994-2004)*, China Financial Publishing House, 2008, p. 325.

Over time, many of these rollover loans deteriorated into NPLs, making up the bulk of NPLs for ICBC. The problem needed to be addressed at the source, given its severe impact on the allocation of national economic resources. After an extensive survey, ICBC held a special workshop to address the issue of rollover loans to the tune of over RMB 1 trillion in Shanghai in August 2000. The workshop sought to "redirect credit issuance to high-quality borrowers, tighten credit management to block loopholes, clean up the stock of NPLs, and comprehensively improve credit management,"[1] and unveiled ICBC's campaign to address the issue of rollover loans under this principle.

After over five years of hard work, ICBC successfully resolved the issue of rollover loans, clearing the major obstacle to the final settlement of NPA issues, the successful implementation of the joint-stock reform, and the introduction of strategic investors. By the end of 2005, ICBC had cleaned up RMB 957 billion of rollover loans, and reduced the outstanding balance to RMB 52 billion. Specifically, the rollover loans of high-quality borrowers worth RMB 329.3 billion were being managed in the same manner as new loans issued after 1999, with the NPL ratio strictly kept within 2%. While for potentially at-risk rollover loans worth RMB 376.2 billion borrowed by enterprises with poorer credit ratings but still afloat, ICBC took successive steps to recover them. Lastly, the rollover loans which deteriorated into NPLs were worth RMB 251.5 billion[2].

---

1   ICBC Credit Management Department: *Finding a Solution to Legacy Problems through Development and Innovation: ICBC's Management of Rollover Loans during Joint-Stock Reform*, August 2006, internal document.
2   ICBC Credit Management Department: *Finding a Solution to Legacy Problems through Development and Innovation: ICBC's Management of Rollover Loans during Joint-Stock Reform*, August 2006, internal document.

Following risk management requirements, ICBC took various measures to recover and dispose of such NPLs and minimize loan losses. By March 2006, the balance of ICBC's rollover loans further dropped to RMB 47 billion. At the end of the same year, ICBC completely resolved the issue of rollover loans repaid with newly borrowed working capital loans. Management of rollover loans reflected the transition of China's banking industry and of the allocation of private capital.

3. Disposal and write-off of existent NPLs

While strictly controlling the quality of new loans, ICBC made great efforts to dispose of its existing NPLs through recovery, conversion, and disposal to minimize losses. Specifically, ICBC offered interest exemptions to encourage repayment, allowed borrowers to pay off their debts with assets which formed an "asset pool," wrote off bad loans to increase the recovery ratio, disposed of NPLs in cooperation with the government, and securitized NPLs as the first SOCB to do so.

From 2001 to 2004, ICBC recovered and disposed of more than RMB 361.2 billion of NPLs, including RMB 155.2 billion (43%) recovered in cash; RMB 38.02 billion (11%) repaid with assets; RMB 110.46 billion (31%) written off; and RMB 57.53 billion (15%) disposed in other ways[1]. In 2005, ICBC proactively responded to the initiation of the joint-stock reform and adjusted its NPL disposal strategy. While offloading NPLs to AMC, ICBC enhanced NPL recovery and disposal through innovative ways. For the whole year of 2005, ICBC recovered and disposed of NPLs worth RMB 110.7 billion in parallel to its NPA divestiture pro-

---

1   *History of the Industrial and Commercial Bank of China (1994-2004)*, China Financial Publishing House, 2008, p. 336.

gram[1].

Meanwhile, ICBC proactively disposed of its non-credit NPAs. Prior to 1999, many of ICBC's non-credit assets had already turned into risk assets that incurred actual losses, which put great strains on its operation and became a financial burden that needed to be addressed in gearing up for the joint-stock reform. In early 2000, ICBC launched a host of measures to enhance the monitoring of its at-risk non-credit assets, clean up bank-wide at-risk non-credit assets, and proactively dispose of existent NPAs and control new ones through recovery, conversion, restructuring, and write-off with its own resources. As a result, ICBC's stock of at-risk non-credit assets dropped from RMB 157.9 billion in 1999 to RMB 15.06 billion by the end of 2005. Most of the remaining risk assets were normal items like rights-collateralized assets, on-balance-sheet interest receivables, and as-yet unrecorded receivables.

From 2000 to 2004, ICBC, through its own efforts, managed to reduce the balance of NPAs from RMB 1,017.4 billion to RMB 812.2 billion, down RMB 205.2 billion; the NPL ratio fell from 25.6% to 14.3%, down 11.3 percentage points. According to the five-category classification scheme, ICBC's NPL ratio dropped to 18.99% in 2004, down 28.6 percentage points over the peak of 47.59% at the end of June 1999. Meanwhile, ICBC's NPL ratio for new loans was kept below 1.6% – a stellar figure by international standards[2]. Improving bank-wide asset quality and

---

1   Editorial committee of the ICBC's Yearbook: *Yearbook of the Industrial and Commercial Bank of China (2006)*, China Financial Publishing House, 2006, p. 84.
2   *History of the Industrial and Commercial Bank of China (1994-2004)*, China Financial Publishing House, 2008, p. 9; *History of the Industrial and Commercial Bank of China (Appendices Volume)*, China Financial Publishing House, 2008, p. 264; 2004 Annual Report of ICBC, p. 33.

operating profits set the stage for ICBC's joint-stock reform and historic transformation.

(III) Enhancing Competitiveness and Development through Structural Improvement

Robust and sustainable development of banks hinges upon structural improvement. By optimizing their business structure, banks can increase risk resilience and profitability. In 2000, ICBC vowed to improve its efficiency in allocating business resources and cultivate a group of exemplary branches and premium services. In achieving these goals, ICBC set out to improve its regional outlet locations and credit structure. On the basis of effective risk control, ICBC granted more operational autonomy to major branches and revoked the level-by-level approval system for certain services to make them more responsive to the market.

Credit structure and distribution are vital to banks. They determine the business development, risk profile, profitability, and competitiveness of commercial banks. The credit structure of China's state-owned banks was shaped by their development history as well as by external factors like economic planning, adjustment of economic structure, industrial policy, macroeconomic policy, credit policy, and government intervention. Accordingly, credit structures vary across banks and periods.

ICBC's credit structure had four major problems. First, ICBC did not make proactive credit decisions, adjust its policy on credit issuance, and fine-tune its credit structure for different industries, regions, and products. Second, the credit decisions were scattered across branches without overall coordination at the level of the head office. Third, branches without conditions for developing credit business and lacking risk control capabilities expanded credit size irrespective of the market environment and cost constraints. Lack of coordination for branches led to an overall discordant credit structure. Fourth, ICBC lacked the data and technology to control and intervene in credit issuance and collect post-lending information.

These problems led to a high-risk credit profile with rampant losses. Managing NPAs is like taming a flood: blocking it is futile; it had to be channeled to downstream canals and reservoirs in a controlled manner. Similarly, the head office needed to guide lower-level branches on which industries or companies would make good borrowers, creating a bank-wide credit structure through both top-down and bottom-up approaches.

To address such problems, ICBC drafted a master plan on adjusting its credit structure and issued industry credit guidelines. It stepped up industry credit analysis and credit issuance control, and redirected credit resources to customers and regions with better credit history, state-supported industries, financially robust customers, and high-return credit products. It created a sound credit market entry and exit mechanism, improved credit quality and efficiency, and supported national economic restructuring and industrial upgrade. It carried out forward-looking research and explored emerging credit markets, including consumer credit, note financing, and SME credit markets. It offered working capital loans to Sino-foreign joint ventures, multinational companies, joint-stock companies, and SMEs in a broad range of sectors including electricity, coal, petroleum, petrochemical, and telecom. The head office then adjusted the bank-wide loan structure based on an overall plan.

As recalled by Jiang Jianqing, "To address NPLs and improve asset quality, we should redirect, not block, the issuance of loans. In light of national economic trends, we identified a few credit markets to which credit issuance should be directed. In 1999, ICBC's mortgage loans stood at a mere RMB 20 to 30 billion with a high NPL ratio. Back then, CCB had the biggest share of the mortgage loan market owing to its robust business relating to the housing provident fund. After analyzing the credit structure of leading international banks, we identified mortgage loans as a priority for business growth. At first, we selected eight branches in the coastal region as pilot banks, added another eight banks as backups for step-by-step implementation, and adjusted our approach where necessary. As a result, our mortgage business developed rapidly. By 2005, housing credit and consumer loans amounted to RMB 500 billion with a rapid turnover. Repayment exceeded RMB 100 billion each year, and the NPL ratio was low. The mortgage loan market was the first high-quality market we found.

"Our second target was the note market. We created China's first specialized note institution – the ICBC Notes Operation Department. By 2005, we had fostered a market of RMB 350 billion with NPLs of just a bit over RMB 100 million. The third market we entered was the capital construction market as China was accelerating its infrastructure development. We started by lending to technological upgrade projects and then expanded to capital construction projects in coal, electric power, petroleum, and transportation sectors. By 2005, the balance of our capital construction loans amounted to RMB 700 to 800 billion; and accounting for the loans we had recovered by that point, we had issued over RMB 1 trillion of this type of loans. The NPL ratio for such loans was also very low. These three markets added up to nearly RMB 2 trillion. Business growth diluted the NPL ratio and brought about a significant improvement in asset quality. What we learned from this experience is that finding the right market and customers is the key to credit quality management."[1]

Traditionally, ICBC was specialized in offering working capital loans to industrial and commercial enterprises. It issued working capital loans to SOEs without proper due diligence due to weak budgetary constraints on both the bank and SOEs. Traditional working capital loans for SOEs made up 83% of NPAs carved out from ICBC. To change its credit structure, ICBC needed to lend to well-run industrial and commercial enterprises while restricting credit supply to struggling ones. From 2000 to 2005, ICBC withdrew credit worth over RMB 1 trillion from inferior borrowers, and redirected lending to advanced manufacturing, outperforming listed firms, joint ventures, and SMEs.

As noted by Jiang Jianqing, "Small and micro businesses are not an unfamiliar market for ICBC. We witnessed and gradually learned how small and micro businesses grow. In the economic transition during the 1980s and 1990s, SMEs of state and collective ownership suffered a heavy blow. I remember that when ICBC wrote off loans of loss category in 1999, 100,000 small businesses were involved – wiping out almost all our loans to small businesses. 'Once bitten, twice shy' was what we felt toward small businesses at that time. Having sensed an uptick in the market, ICBC Zhejiang Branch took the initiative to lend to private small businesses starting in 2001 and 2002. In 2002, ICBC Zhejiang Branch, Yuhuan County Sub-branch went all-out to support small and micro businesses with zero NPLs, creating a sensation in China's financial industry.

---

[1] Jiang Jianqing: "ICBC's Joint-Stock Reform Process and Reflections," *Internal Update Bulletin*, September 29, 2005.

ICBC executives at the head office were so surprised about this success story that they dispatched a working group to verify it. Successful experiences boosted ICBC's confidence in small and micro businesses. We expanded the pilot program from Zhejiang Province to the entire eastern region and then nationwide. Finally, small and micro businesses became a new market for credit supply. Today, the balance of ICBC's small business loans has crossed the RMB 2 trillion mark."

Credit market development led to an improvement in ICBC's credit structure. By 2005, personal loans as a share of ICBC's credit business increased from 5% to 16%. Also evolved was the ownership structure of ICBC's corporate customers. Joint-stock enterprises represented 18% of ICBC's loans to corporate customers, up from 13%. Private and foreign-funded enterprises accounted for 21%, up from 10%. The percentage of loans to mixed-ownership enterprises rose from 14% to 23%. The credit ratings of corporate borrowers also improved. The share of loans to at-risk customers at or below A- grade fell from 51% to 14%, and the share of loans to superior customers above A grade jumped from 49% to 86%. In particular, the share of loans to customers at or above AA- grade rose from 37% to 64% while credit rating criteria were raised substantially. By reducing NPLs and addressing the root cause, ICBC reported excellent quality of its new credit assets.

Non-credit assets as a share of total assets increased from 33% five years before to 50%, ending credit assets' dominance in the asset portfolio. Despite passive liabilities (i.e., deposits) still accounting for a dominant share of ICBC's balance sheet, active liabilities – loans, interbank lending, repos, etc. – started to grow. Fee-based business income as a share of net income increased from 5% to 10%. The share of income from bond investments and transactions jumped to 31%, while the share of income earned from interest rate spread dropped to 59%, reducing the bank's reliance on the net interest spread. The share of e-banking business rose from 3% to 26%, and teller-less business expanded, making transactions more expedient and cost-efficient.

(IV) Improving Corporate Governance

ICBC reviewed its internal management and benchmarked against leading global banks to identify gaps. It took a host of measures to improve internal management.

(1) Improving performance review: Referencing international bank management and central bank evaluation models, ICBC established a comprehensive evaluation system. Having integrated factors such as cost, risk, internal control, and capital rationing, this system comprises self-regulatory evaluation, performance review, differentiated management, level-based control, and resource allocation. It puts a premium on risk-adjusted return to capital and economic value-added, and combines the annual performance review with periodic management evaluation.

(2) Enhancing management of branches: ICBC introduced a new hierarchical system to more effectively manage its substantial branch network. Under the new system, each branch would manage the branches at one immediate lower level and oversee those at two immediate lower levels. ICBC devolved authority to branches at all levels based on their management competency and business performance. It adopted a system for the oversight, early warning of risks, remediation, and suspension or

winding-down of its service offerings and branches. It also streamlined, optimized, and consolidated outlets. From 2000 to 2005, the number of ICBC's outlets fell from 31,671 to 18,871.

(3) Implementing sound risk management: ICBC moved risk control to earlier stages of each process to focus on early prevention. It adopted targeted countermeasures for new risk assets, existing risk assets, and NPLs; went beyond management of credit risks to the areas of management of liquidity, market, and operational risks; and put theoretical advances in the entry and exit of credit market into practice. In keeping up with international risk management practices, ICBC set up an office in 2003 for internal ratings-based (IRB) approach to credit risk measurement, and engaged PwC as its advisor on the IRB project.

(4) Establishing the framework of management accounting: ICBC deployed the latest technologies to flatten accounting hierarchies. In 2004, it consolidated accounting for savings-oriented outlets into that of county-level sub-branches, streamlining over 20,000 accounting entities into some 3,000. Later, accounting work was further consolidated to tier-two branches. In this manner, sub-branches and lower-level outlets were no longer independent accounting entities. These measures flattened hierarchies, improved accounting efficiency and quality, and centralized data. By developing a cost accounting system for various branches and outlets, departments, and products, ICBC became the first large commercial bank in China to adopt a comprehensive system for cost accounting.

(5) Reforming internal review system: ICBC made its internal audits and reviews more independent and reliable. It became the first Chinese bank to create an internal audit bureau complemented by ten regional sub-bureaus. It established an internal control and compliance depart-

ment and developed internal regulations and rules. It severely cracked down upon violations and disciplinary breaches, and took firm actions to achieve the goal of "accurate bookkeeping and rigorous financial and compliance management." It employed data and information technologies to transform business processes and risk control systems, adopted technical means to control business operations, and standardized and modernized its management processes. It separated back-office functions, and stepped up oversight and control on front-office business. In 2003, ICBC started to disclose bank-wide financial statements and key data, and included such data as NPLs, related-party transactions, non-credit-risk bearing assets, and quality of new loans. Transparency reassured ICBC's depositors and investors.

(6) Improving corporate governance and decision-making: ICBC established a risk management committee, asset and liability management (ALM) committee, financial approval committee, credit policy committee, and information technology approval committee. These committees are responsible for making most major decisions. Committees for major lending decisions and financial review and approval follow the principle of "one member, one vote," and all members vote anonymously. The ICBC President may veto a committee's approval, but cannot reverse its negative decision. ICBC re-designed its business processes, making them no longer driven entirely by products and departments, improved customer-centered product development and marketing, reformed the compensation system for managers at various levels, and put in place a position-based management system. ICBC ramped up personnel training, and introduced a qualification accreditation system. It revamped logistical management and service systems so that services would be provided by independent

contractors rather than internal departments.

(7) Turning data and information technologies into core competencies: ICBC was faced with a daunting task of managing numerous outlets and business services across various regions. Up-to-date technology is essential to modern bank management. Despite the shortage of funds, ICBC spared no resources when it came to investing in technology. It upgraded from personal computers to small, medium, and large computers, and evolved from standalone computers to regional and bank-wide networks. After more than a decade, ICBC had developed 36 connected computing centers by 1999. Network efficiency, however, was hampered by incompatible computer models, programs, and interfaces. On September 1, 1999, ICBC inaugurated a data aggregation project dubbed the "9991 Project" to address these problems.

In October 2002, ICBC became the first Chinese bank to complete a massive-scale computer information network. By achieving centralized processing and management of bank-wide data, ICBC went from a disjointed organization with respect to IT to a truly unified bank. In 2004, ICBC merged two major data centers into a unified data center, and further extended this IT capability globally. In 2005, ICBC created remote disaster recovery systems in Beijing and Shanghai, achieving the highest international rating for disaster recovery. Data centralization was followed by the deployment of a new-generation integrated business system and a data repository. By creating an electronic credit ledger (i.e., integrated credit management system), corporate customer database, and personal customer database, ICBC upgraded its operation and management processes. Data centralization boosted financial innovation. In 1999, ICBC unveiled China's first telephone banking center that met international standards.

In 2000 and 2003, ICBC launched its corporate and personal online banking systems, respectively. It introduced new applications such as the international settlement system, Bank Securities Express (*yinzhengtong*, i.e., a system that links bank account with securities trading account), and the OTC bond trading system. In its IPO roadshow in 2006, ICBC proudly declared to Chinese and international investors that "ICBC has developed a world-leading IT system over the past few years and become the first Chinese bank to complete data centralization – ahead of its domestic peers by four to five years. Today, all transactions and customer data are brought together at one center with a peak processing capacity of 50 million transactions per day. ICBC also saw its e-banking business surge to 26% of its total business transactions. By the end of 2005, RMB 42 trillion worth of transactions were completed through e-banking, representing 70% of the industry's total. For these achievements, ICBC has been awarded 'Global Best Bank Website,' 'Best Personal Online Bank in China,' and 'Best Corporate Online Bank in China.'"

II. Innovative Joint-Stock Reform Plan Based on the "Special Joint Fund" Account

While improving its internal management, ICBC closely followed CCB and BOC's joint-stock reforms, and quietly prepared for its own. A common challenge facing both pilot reform banks was cost. In ICBC's case, its huge NPAs would make its joint-stock reform even more costly. To develop a viable reform plan, ICBC could not simply copy the approach used by CCB and BOC. Instead, it needed a design that would minimize immediate fiscal spending by the state. On the basis of its pre-reform NPL disposal and drawing upon CCB and BOC's joint-stock reform plans, ICBC developed a unique plan which received the green light from the State Council, thus embarking on a joint-stock reform of its own.

(I) Deliberation on the Joint-Stock Reform Plan

After the 16th CPC National Congress in November 2002, reforming wholly state-owned commercial banks was brought on the agenda, and ICBC set out to formulate its reform plan. After the central government declared CCB and BOC – leaving out ICBC – as the first pilot banks for joint-stock reform, ICBC did not give up and worked tirelessly to reduce its NPAs and improve internal governance to prepare for its own reform. In mid-2004, ICBC completed its reform plan and submitted it to the State Council Joint-Stock Reform Steering Group as an informal document. This plan put forward a financial restructuring approach that leveraged both national policy support and ICBC's own efforts: ICBC would use its existing financial resources to write off loss loans, while the state was to inject additional capital into ICBC. ICBC would cover the losses on doubtful loans with future operating income and reform income and then introduce strategic investors to complete the joint-stock transformation.

(II) Considerations behind the Special Joint Fund

In its financial restructuring plan, ICBC proposed an account named the "Special Joint Fund" ("jointly managed account"). Jiang Jianqing, then ICBC President, who was appointed as ICBC Chairman after the joint-stock reform, recounted the creation of the Special Joint Fund: "Since 2003, I had presented reports to Vice Premier Huang Ju, who was in charge of financial affairs, on many occasions to express ICBC's determination to carry out the joint-stock reform, and explained to him that we were fully prepared – ICBC had improved its profitability and slashed NPAs. In deliberating CCB and BOC's reform plans, some officials expressed reservations about the hefty cost of reforming state-owned banks. With their concern in mind, Huang asked ICBC to come up with a cost-efficient reform proposal.

"According to his requirements, we revised the approach of financial restructuring, and put forward the principle of 'combining national support with ICBC's own efforts.' We proposed to set up a jointly managed account to repay the cost of reform with our future revenues without increasing the immediate burden of the government. This would make it easier for our reform plan to be accepted by various stakeholders. When I presented our revised reform plan, Huang expressed his endorsement and asked me to explain the plan to Finance Minister Jin Renqing and PBOC Governor Zhou Xiaochuan. And we later learned that all the key leaders of the State Council personally walked through our reform plan with each member of the Politburo Standing Committee."[1]

(III) Finalization of the Joint-Stock Reform Plan

At the 61st State Council executive meeting on August 18, 2004, Premier Wen Jiabao proposed that while BOC and CCB were to be converted into joint-stock commercial banks before the end of December, the joint-stock reform plans of ICBC and other banks were also to be considered at the same time. On August 23, the PBOC and the CBRC convened a joint conference on implementing the decisions of the executive meeting, deciding to complete the deliberation of ICBC's reform plan before the

---

1 From the interview with Jiang Jianqing on March 6-7, 2018.

end of the year.

On September 2, 2004, ICBC held the 14th Head Office CPC Committee expanded meeting to study the reform plan and make preparations. The meeting decided that the head office was to set up a leading group for joint-stock reform led by President Jiang Jianqing as director and Vice President Yang Kaisheng as deputy director with other members of the CPC committee serving as members. On November 17, ICBC issued the "Circular on Establishing the Leading Group for Joint-Stock Reform and Daily Working Bodies"[1] ("Circular"). The Circular identified the Leading Group as the leading and decision-making body for ICBC's joint-stock reform. The Leading Group consisted of the Restructuring Office, Joint-Stock Reform Advisory Committee, and 10 specialized working groups responsible for specific affairs.

The 10 working groups included: NPA Disposal Working Group, Asset Appraisal Working Group, Public Communication Working Group, Institutional and Personnel Incentive Reform Working Group, Development Strategy Planning Working Group, IRB Working Group, External Audit Working Group, Legal Affairs Working Group, Overseas Affairs Working Group, and Internal Control and Corporate Governance Working Group. Creation of the Head Office Leading Group and the Restructuring Office signaled the official start of ICBC's joint-stock reform.

From September to December 2004, ICBC proactively communicated with the MOF, PBOC, and CBRC, and revised its reform plan numerous times according to their feedback. Regarding the approach for financial restructuring, ICBC and the MOF agreed to create the Special

---

1 Gong Yin Fa [2004] No. 194.

Joint Fund, which increased the clarity and feasibility of ICBC's reform plan and made it acceptable to various government agencies. On December 21, 2004, the State Council Joint-Stock Reform Steering Group officially submitted the "Master Plan for the Implementation of ICBC's Joint-Stock Reform" (Yin Fa [2004] No. 292) to the State Council.

NPA disposal lay at the heart of ICBC's financial restructuring. Due to its heavier NPA burden, ICBC followed a slightly different method for NPA disposal from BOC and CCB.

Unlike BOC and CCB that fully wrote off their loss loans with the capital injection from the MOF, ICBC divided the RMB 201.6 billion financial resources available to it (including owner's equity and existing risk reserves) into two parts: RMB 124 billion was retained as capital contribution from the MOF, and RMB 77.6 billion was converted into risk reserves. Then, the state injected capital into ICBC with foreign reserves and restructured ICBC's capital.

With respect to the divestiture of NPAs, ICBC classified its NPAs into the "loss" category and the "doubtful" category. Unlike BOC and CCB that fully wrote off their NPAs with capital injections from the MOF, ICBC adopted an innovative accounting system for its financial restructuring by creating a jointly managed account. Specifically, ICBC would sell its loss-category assets worth RMB 246 billion to the MOF who would pay for them in a few installments. The two parties would create a jointly managed account for managing such payment (Fig. 6.1). The sources of funds would include ICBC's dividend distribution to the MOF, income tax payable, and cash proceeds from NPA disposal and recovery.

As for the disposal of doubtful assets, ICBC essentially followed the same approach as BOC and CCB. A slight difference was that the PBOC swapped ICBC's doubtful assets with private placement notes at 100% of their book value, instead of 50% in the case of BOC and CCB.

With its national credibility and fiscal capacity, the Chinese government bought time for the restructuring and joint-stock reform of state-owned banks. ICBC used its future operating income and other incomes from the restructuring to cover the immediate cost of reform. Rather than tapping into existing fiscal resources, the MOF purchased ICBC's loss-category assets in exchange for ICBC's claims on the MOF as recorded by the balance of the jointly managed account. The MOF thus played a dual role as a "shareholder" and "state treasury." The jointly managed account facilitated ICBC's joint-stock reform with minimal cost, and provided a model that can be referenced for the financial restructuring and joint-stock reform of other state-owned banks.

Niu Ximing, Vice President of ICBC, who also once served as chairman of BoCom, made the following remarks on the significance of the innovative jointly managed account: "The jointly managed account was a great innovation in ICBC's NPA disposal plan. Instead of creating a jointly managed account, CCB and BOC wrote off NPAs against all of the capital previously appropriated by the government and received a capital injection from Central Huijin for the joint-stock reform. For ICBC, the MOF no longer agreed to a write-off using equity and asked that the equity be preserved. If we imagine that the idea of setting up a jointly managed account had never been thought up or put into practice, ICBC would have probably been compelled to give up on the reform midway. In addition, if follow-up had been lax in the six months following the joint-stock reform piloted by CCB and BOC, ICBC would have seen its reform postponed to 2011 and even 2012. Therefore, I regard ICBC's idea to create such an account to be an outstanding and significant innovation."[1]

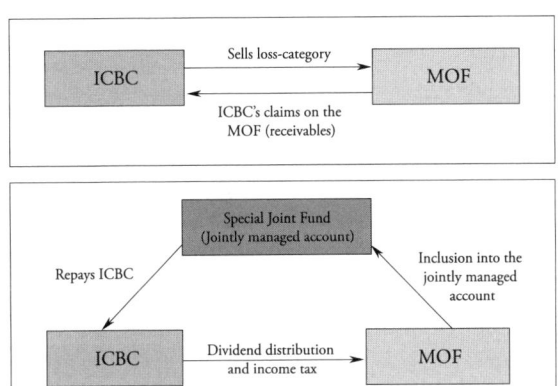

Fig. 6.1: ICBC's Sales of Loss-Category Assets and Debt Repayment Arrangement

(IV) Approval of the Joint-Stock Reform Plan

In 2005, the central government accelerated ICBC's joint-stock reform. Meanwhile, ICBC was making proactive early-stage preparations such as screening external professional firms, creating internal organizations for the joint-stock reform, and developing a document repository. After a few rounds of modifications, ICBC's joint-stock reform plan was officially approved by the central government in April 2005.

On April 18, 2005, the central government officially approved the "Master Plan for the Implementation of ICBC's Joint-Stock Reform." The central government decided to allocate USD 15 billion of foreign reserves for a capital injection into ICBC through Central Huijin. On April 21, the USD 15 billion of foreign-currency funds were credited to the account of Central Huijin.

On the same day, Xinhua News Agency published the government's

---

1   From the interview with Niu Ximing on March 7, 2017.

approval of ICBC's joint-stock reform. "As the commercial bank with the largest asset portfolio in China, ICBC has made tremendous contributions to China's economic development and reform of the economic system. Due to historic reasons, however, ICBC has also developed significant risks. Over recent years, ICBC has made great progress in improving internal control, management, and profitability with its own efforts and the support of national policies, and developed the conditions for implementing the joint-stock reform. To align with the opening up of China's financial sector and economic development and on the basis of the experiences of BOC and CCB, the State Council has decided to implement ICBC's joint-stock reform."[1]

On the same day, ICBC issued a "Notice on the Group-Wide Restructuring of the Industrial and Commercial Bank of China" to overseas regulators and large financial institutions. On April 25, ICBC delivered the "Report on the Arrangements for the Implementation of ICBC's Joint-Stock Reform."

The approved reform plan[2] stipulated that the cost of ICBC's reform was to be covered by its future revenue, thus combining national support with its own resources. The overall goal was to accelerate various reform initiatives, transform business operations, complete the joint-stock reform by 2005, and seek IPO at the right time. Through the reform, ICBC expected that it would turn into a modern commercial bank with sound ownership and corporate governance. Through IPO, ICBC aimed to become a relatively full-fledged modern financial enterprise, develop into an

---

1   Xinhua News Agency, Beijing, April 21 (2005).
2   See the "Master Plan for the Implementation of ICBC's Joint-Stock Reform" (Yin Fa [2004] No. 292).

internationally competitive large commercial bank with adequate capital, stringent internal controls, secure operations, superior services and efficiency, and major operational indicators at or above the average level of international peers.

ICBC identified the following underlying principles for the joint-stock reform:

First, the reform should create a modern financial enterprise. Following the requirements of creating a modern commercial bank, ICBC was to reform its ownership structure, modernize its governance structure, and put in place stringent internal accountability. It should develop sound financial constraints and risk mitigation strategies, and create rules and regulations befitting a modern financial enterprise.

Second, ICBC should match national support with its own resources. With appropriate support of the national policy, ICBC was expected to pay for the cost of reform with its future earnings so as to minimize burden to the government.

Third, ICBC's reform should be carried out through a comprehensive and stable approach. ICBC should carefully plan for its reform and IPO, maintain robust business operations, and contribute to China's economic and financial stability.

Fourth, ICBC should carry out group-wide restructuring following modern and international standards. Benchmarking against the operational and managerial practices of leading international banks, ICBC should reach and maintain above-average levels in governance structure, quality, and efficiency as well as in international financial indicators among top 100 international banks.

III. Financial Restructuring, Group-Wide Restructuring, and Introduction of Strategic Investors

(I) Improvement of Capital Structure

1. State capital injection with foreign reserves and capital structural adjustment

After receiving the USD 15 billion (equivalent to RMB 124 billion) capital injection on April 22, 2005, ICBC immediately developed a plan for the prudent operation and management of foreign-currency funds, so as to ensure the state-injected funds would be secure and generate a reasonable return. On April 25, ICBC held the first meeting of the ALM Committee to review the plan. The meeting identified the "prudent operation and centralized management for the maintenance and appreciation of value of state assets" as the core principle for managing the foreign-currency funds. It called for striking a balance among asset return, risk management, and liquidity, and for selecting a reasonable asset allocation plan to prevent foreign exchange risks and mitigate any adverse impact on ICBC's capital adequacy ratio.

The meeting made arrangements on the following matters: the division of duties for managing the foreign-currency funds, the objectives and risk management of capital market transactions, the selection of foreign-currency-fund portfolios, the planning for the initial stage of capital injection, the accounting of foreign-currency funds, foreign-currency loans, and the settlement (i.e., exchange) of foreign-currency funds into renminbi[1].

ICBC planned to fix the U.S. dollar settlement price through the

---

1 Department of Strategic Management and Investor Relations, ICBC head office: *Chronicle of Events of ICBC's Joint-Stock Reform and IPO*, p. 34, internally distributed in 2007.

purchase of options, so as to avoid exchange losses on the USD 15 billion of capital injection. Following the joint-stock reform principles set by the PBOC, ICBC entered into a three-year hedge agreement with Central Huijin, which granted ICBC the right, but not the obligation, to exchange foreign currency into renminbi over 12 equal quarterly installments. By spreading currency settlement over a period of three years, ICBC aimed to reduce potential shocks to the market and stabilize the inflation rate. ICBC's approach for the operation and management of injected foreign-currency funds was also followed by BOC and CCB during the same period of time.

In accordance with "The Ministry of Finance's Approval of the Adjustment of ICBC's Capital Structure,"[1] the RMB 124 billion capital previously allocated by the MOF were retained as ICBC's equity. As a result, ICBC's core capital reached RMB 248 billion, with the core capital adequacy ratio reaching 6%. On April 30, ICBC successfully completed all financial transactions related to the recapitalization and capital structural adjustment.

2. Issuance of the first series of subordinated bonds

On August 19, 2005, ICBC successfully issued, through an underwriting syndicate, the first series of RMB 35 billion subordinated bonds, including 10-year fixed-rate, 15-year fixed-rate, and 10-year floating-rate bonds. A total of 40 institutions submitted tenders for subscription totaling RMB 85.525 billion, equaling an oversubscription ratio of 2.44. The bond issue was intended to increase ICBC's supplementary capital, improve its capital structure, and raise its capital adequacy ratio. It was the

---

1 Cai Jin [2005] No. 39.

first time that ICBC issued subordinated bonds, which was also the largest single-series subordinated bond issuance ever executed by a commercial bank in China. This bond issue pushed ICBC's capital adequacy ratio above 8%.

(II) Divestiture of NPAs

1. Overall arrangements for the divestiture of NPAs

Following the official approval of the joint-stock reform plan and the one-off capital injection with foreign reserves, ICBC formulated a detailed plan and a set of complementary rules for the divestiture of NPAs in accordance with national policies and regulatory requirements to assign responsibilities at various levels, enhance process control and supervision, and prevent risks from the divestiture.

The divestiture of NPAs was a major undertaking and needed to achieve challenging policy-driven objectives within a demanding timeframe. The degree of success of this task would dictate the success of ICBC's joint-stock reform. On April 19 and 28, 2005, ICBC held two head office meetings to discuss and arrange for the divestiture of bank-wide NPAs. Led by ICBC Vice President Yang Kaisheng, the head office formed a special working group consisting of internal experts to draft two proposals on the planned divestiture of loans of the loss and doubtful categories, respectively. The proposals were submitted to the PBOC and the MOF, which endorsed the suggestions proposed therein by ICBC's Financial Planning Department on the cleanup of bank-wide at-risk non-credit assets.

NPAs were created by both external factors, such as changes in national policy and business environment, and internal factors such as incompliant business operations. ICBC analyzed the causes of at-risk non-credit assets and identified the responsible employees. This analysis helped standardize the procedures for the divestiture and prevent moral hazard, and summarized the lessons from the management of non-credit assets. As part of the divestiture process, 7,623 employees were held accountable for past incompliances. Specifically, 2,930 were given administrative penalties, 2,457 given monetary fines (totaling RMB 4,036,064.63), and 2,236 given other penalties.[1]

A critical step for ICBC in this stage was to enter into a transfer agreement with the AMC to clarify the rights and responsibilities of both parties and stipulate the methods and price for the divestiture. On May 18, the MOF issued the "Circular on the Disposal of Part of ICBC's Non-Performing Assets by China Huarong Asset Management Co., Ltd."

On May 25, in accordance with the principles laid by the MOF document Cai Jin Han [2005] No. 60, ICBC and Huarong jointly issued the "Notice on the Transfer of the Loss-Category Credit Assets and At-Risk Non-Credit Assets between ICBC and Huarong."[2] The Notice stipulated the overall requirements on the asset transfer, timetable for asset handover, document handover procedure, agreement execution and legal document handover time, asset transfer procedures and timeline, contents of the asset transfer agreement, among other matters.

On May 27, ICBC entered into the "Agreement on the Transfer of Loss Loans" and the "Agreement on the Transfer of At-Risk Non-Credit Assets with Huarong." The tier-one (directly affiliated) branches of ICBC also executed relevant transfer agreements with Huarong's local offices on

---

1 Information provided by the ICBC Finance & Accounting Department.
2 Gong Yin Fa [2005] No. 118.

the same day.

As of the end of May, ICBC and Huarong's local offices completed the execution of all agreements and financial account processing. ICBC's RMB 246 billion of loss-category assets, including RMB 176 billion of loss loans and RMB 70 billion of at-risk non-credit assets, were transferred to Huarong at book value without recourse.

On June 3, the MOF released the "Circular on Promulgating the 'Measures for the Administration of the Joint Fund between the Ministry of Finance and ICBC.'"[1] This document stated that the loss-category assets transferred from ICBC to Huarong would entitle ICBC to a corresponding amount of receivables from the MOF, which would pay principal and interest to ICBC in installments through the jointly managed account. By mid-June, ICBC and Huarong had successfully completed legal document handover.

Yang Kaisheng, who previously served as ICBC Vice President and was then Huarong's President, made the following remarks as he recalled the transfer of ICBC's loss-category NPAs: "(During the first round of divestiture in 2000) Huarong's acquisition of ICBC's NPAs was financed by loans from the PBOC and the financial bonds that the company issued to ICBC. In effect, Huarong borrowed funds from ICBC to purchase ICBC's NPLs, and promised to repay ICBC at the book value of the NPLs. What if Huarong fails to make the repayment? According to the *Regulations on Financial Asset Management Companies*, upon maturity of the bonds, the MOF will propose a solution to the State Council. By the time ICBC was ready for IPO, Huarong had yet to fully repay the bonds as it was impos-

---

1   Cai Jin Han [2005] No. 56.

sible to reach a 100% recovery rate on the NPAs. Since Huarong acquired the NPAs at the book value of RMB 400 billion, even if the recovery rate could reach 30%, Huarong would only have recovered about RMB 120 billion, leaving behind a shortfall of RMB 280 billion. The question was what to do with the shortfall? The MOF later issued a statement saying that it would guarantee the payment. But how? The solution was for the MOF and ICBC to set up a jointly managed account and fill the gap with the post-restructuring profits of ICBC."[1]

As Jiang Jianqing, former Board Chairman of ICBC, recalled, the RMB 246 billion obligation of the MOF to ICBC was repaid in just four and a half years after ICBC's joint-stock reform with the income tax and dividends paid into the jointly managed account. Later, Jiang even asked Xie Xuren, then Minister of Finance, whether taxes from ICBC could be used to pay off PBOC's loans to Huarong. Although this loan was legally unrelated to ICBC, it was still incurred by ICBC's reform. The MOF accepted the proposal, and after a few years, that loan was also largely paid off.

2. Transfer of doubtful loans

After proactive consultations and communication, ICBC, with facilitation of the PBOC, successfully held a public bidding for 35 bundles of doubtful loans on June 25, 2005. Comprising professionals and external experts from the PBOC, MOF, and CBRC, a working group opened and evaluated bids on the spot through an open, fair, and merit-based assessment process and announced the winners. On June 27, ICBC executed agreements for the transfer of doubtful credit assets in 35 bundles totaling RMB 459 billion with the four AMCs. According to these agreements, the

---

1 From the interview with Yang Kaisheng on March 15, 2017.

four AMCs would purchase, without recourse, the RMB 459 billion of doubtful loans at book value before allowances for impairment loss.

On June 29, the PBOC entered into the "Agreement on Special Central Bank Bills" with ICBC, under which the PBOC would issue the special central bank bills to subscribe for ICBC's doubtful loans tendered for sale. On June 30, ICBC successfully completed the account processing for the transfer of the doubtful loans, which marked the end of ICBC's financial restructuring program.

(III) Title Confirmation and Valuation of Real Estate

Verification, confirmation of title status, and valuation of land and building properties were usually the most labor-intensive and time-consuming tasks of fundamental importance to the reform of state-owned banks. It was the linchpin of the restructuring and reform process as a whole. To enhance organizational leadership and complete the task with high quality and on schedule, ICBC established steering groups to verify the state and confirm the title status of real estate at various levels. Following the overall arrangements of the joint-stock reform, ICBC's verification, title confirmation and valuation of real estate were carried out in three stages, including asset verification (from September to November 2004), the confirmation of title status of land plots and building properties (from January to July 2005), and valuation (from July to September 2005). These activities were completed in a year and involved over 4,000 ICBC employees.

(IV) Supplemental Allowances for Retired Employees

As employees who retired before the joint-stock reform of the SOCBs were paid less pension compared with those retiring after the reform, the pre-reform retirees needed to be given a certain amount of allowance to make up for the difference. After extensive communication and with the consent of the government, ICBC set aside a supplemental pension fund for more than 120,000 retirees and created a corporate annuity fund for its employees yet to retire at the time of the joint-stock reform.

(V) Establishment of the Joint-Stock Company

1. Intensive preparations for the establishment of the joint-stock company

After ICBC's financial restructuring, work was underway to determine the official name of the joint-stock company, go through government approval procedures, complete business registration, and submit the promoters' agreement for review. On June 24, 2005, ICBC held the ninth President Meeting, which determined the Chinese name of the reformed ICBC to be "中国工商银行股份有限公司" and English name to be "Industrial and Commercial Bank of China Limited," abbreviated as "ICBC."

On August 4, ICBC held a conference on the applications for government approval, and made arrangements on the next step of work regarding the submission of documents for regulatory approval and the division of work among relevant departments.

On August 9, ICBC's relevant departments sent personnel to the State Administration for Industry and Commerce (SAIC) to discuss business registration in connection with incorporating ICBC as a joint-stock company.

On August 22, ICBC submitted the "Report on the Submission of

'Promoters Agreement on the Establishment of Industrial and Commercial Bank of China Limited' for Review"[1] to the MOF and Central Huijin, its two shareholders, for feedback.

On September 20, ICBC submitted the amended "Proposal on the Execution of Promoters Agreement of the Industrial and Commercial Bank of China Limited"[2] to the PBOC and Central Huijin, requesting them to issue a reply on the execution of the promoters agreement.

On October 12, the CBRC issued a letter to the overseas regulatory authorities with jurisdiction over ICBC's overseas institutions, informing them of ICBC's group-wide restructuring into a joint-stock company with the establishment of Industrial and Commercial Bank of China Limited.

On October 24, the "Capital Verification Report for ICBC" and "Audit Report on the Expenses during the Preparation for the Establishment of ICBC" drafted by EY were finalized.

2. Official establishment of ICBC Limited (ICBC)

On October 25, 2005, a string of events were held in Beijing, including the Founding Ceremony and the First Shareholders Meeting, the First Session of the First Board of Directors, as well as the First Session of the First Board of Supervisors of the Industrial and Commercial Bank of China Ltd. Representatives of the MOF and Central Huijin deliberated and voted on various proposals on the establishment of the joint-stock company. The meeting adopted the new (draft) articles of association as well as the (draft) rules of procedure for the shareholders' meeting, the board of directors, and the board of supervisors. It elected the members of

---

1 Gong Yin Bao [2005] No. 94.
2 Gong Yin Bao [2005] No. 121.

the First Board of Directors and First Board of Supervisors, appointed senior executives, and put in place a basic yet standard corporate governance structure. The following 13 members of the First Board of Directors were elected: Jiang Jianqing, Yang Kaisheng, Zhang Furong, Niu Ximing, Fu Zhongjun, Kang Xuejun, Song Zhigang, Wang Wenyan, Zhao Haiying, Zhong Jian'an, Liang Jinsong, John Thornton, and Qian Yingyi. The following four members of the First Board of Supervisors were elected: Wang Weiqiang, Wang Zhixi, Wang DaoCheng, and Miao Gengshu.

At the First Session of ICBC's First Board of Directors, the newly elected board members elected the chairman and vice chairmen of ICBC's First Board of Directors, and deliberated proposals on the appointment of ICBC's president, vice presidents, and board secretary. Jiang Jianqing was appointed as Chairman of ICBC; Yang Kaisheng, Vice Chairman and President; Zhang Furong, Niu Ximing, Zhang Qu, Wang Lili, and Li Xiaopeng, Vice Presidents; and Pan Gongsheng, Board Secretary. The First Session of the First Board of Supervisors deliberated and unanimously approved the "Proposal on the Election of the Chairman of ICBC's Board of Supervisors." The newly elected member of the First Board of Supervisors Wang Weiqiang was elected as Chairman of ICBC's First Board of Supervisors.[1]

On the day following the founding ceremony, Vice Premier Huang Ju paid a visit to ICBC. Huang recognized ICBC's contributions to China's economic and social development as the largest commercial bank in China. "ICBC's financial restructuring, joint-stock reform, and introduction of strategic investors are a means rather than an end. The

---

1   Department of Strategic Management and Investor Relations, ICBC head office: *Chronicle of Events of ICBC's Joint-Stock Reform and IPO*, p. 57, internally distributed in 2007.

establishment of ICBC Limited is only the beginning of a new journey, and many challenges still lie ahead. We must remain sober-minded about the long-term, complex, and arduous nature of reform, aim for new targets and high standards right from the new beginning, and complete various fundamental tasks to ensure the success of reform. We must be guided by the rational outlook on development, further improve corporate governance structure, reform incentives and constraints, and ramp up internal control and risk management," he said.

"We must develop a detailed internal reform plan and accelerate the reform of management and operational mechanisms. We must step up the reform of subsidiaries and branches, and enhance coordination between various levels. We must further improve the credit management system and develop an empirically-grounded enterprise risk management (ERM) system. We must improve independent internal audits, and create standardized and effective internal controls. We must transform our operational and development model, and proactively pursue technological and product innovations in light of international practices, and foster our core competencies and innovation capacity. We must increasingly support the development of leadership and officials' teams at various levels, promote ICBC's growth through its talented workforce, give play to the initiative of various stakeholders, and strive to improve services."[1]

With the approval of the State Council and the CBRC, the Industrial and Commercial Bank of China Limited (ICBC) was officially established on October 28, 2005, with a grand launch ceremony in Beijing presided over by President Yang Kaisheng in the afternoon of the same day. CBRC

---

1 "Huang Ju Visits ICBC," *China Financiers*, 2005 (11).

officials announced the approval for the establishment of ICBC, and conferred the financial license to ICBC. The SAIC conferred the business license to ICBC. PBOC Governor Zhou Xiaochuan and ICBC Chairman Jiang Jianqing unveiled ICBC's nameplate. Zhou Xiaochuan, Vice Minister of Finance Li Yong, and Chairman Jiang Jianqing each delivered a speech. The founding ceremony was attended by around 1,000 people, including members of the State Council Joint-Stock Reform Steering Group, domestic financial institutions and external professional firms, members of ICBC's board of directors, board of supervisors, and senior executives, general managers of various branches and departments, as well as representatives of ICBC's employees and retired leaders and employees.

The establishment of ICBC Limited marks the completion of ICBC's comprehensive reform. The joint-stock reform restructured and consolidated ICBC's bank-wide businesses, assets, liabilities, outlets, and employees into the newly formed joint-stock company. Turning ICBC – the largest commercial bank in China – into a joint-stock company was an important strategic decision of the government, and a milestone event in China's financial and banking reform and in ICBC's own history. For ICBC, the success of the joint-stock reform ushered in a new era of growth.

(VI) Introduction of Strategic Investors

1. Early-stage preparations for introducing strategic investors

A key element of ICBC's joint-stock reform was to introduce overseas strategic investors, which is conducive to diversifying the equity structure and improving corporate governance. But this process involved many complex technicalities and negotiations. In the preparatory stage, ICBC set up a framework for introducing strategic investors, developed repositories of commercial and legal documents and standard working procedures, carried out due diligence, and compiled information memorandums (IM), term sheets, and memorandums of understanding (MOU) on the introduction of strategic investors.

2. Extensive contacts with strategic investors

ICBC's management expressed the utmost sincerity in approaching large international financial institutions. By introducing strategic investors, ICBC aimed to diversify the composition of its future board of directors, adopt advanced managerial concepts, practices, and technologies, and improve corporate governance and risk management. Also, ICBC desired to cooperate with strategic investors in some business areas. From 2003 to 2005, ICBC's leadership and management used every possibility to approach large international financial institutions, engaging the executives of dozens of them over ICBC's joint-stock reform, IPO, and partnership opportunities. These financial institutions include: JPMorgan Chase, Bank of New York, Merrill Lynch, UBS Group, the Dutch bank ABN AMRO, Barclays Bank, KEB Hana Bank, Citigroup, Mizuho Bank, Goldman Sachs Group, Standard Chartered Bank, HSBC, Bank of East Asia, Fortis Bank, Allianz Group, American International Group (AIG), Credit Suisse First Boston (CSFB), and Deutsche Bank.

However, few were willing to place bets on China's state-owned banks. As Jiang Jianqing, then ICBC Chairman, recalled: "From 2004 to 2005, we visited more than 40 large banks, investment banks, fund management firms, and insurance companies around the world, but only 3 expressed an interest to invest in ICBC, including Allianz Group of Germany, Fortis Bank of Belgium, and Goldman Sachs Group from the U.S. No large

Chinese enterprise expressed any interest. Given ICBC's size, the original 20% equity ratio set aside for foreign capital corresponded to a huge investment, and it was hard to find foreign investors able and willing to invest that much. We requested to reduce the target percentage of foreign capital to 10%, which was approved. But even 10% of our equity was no small amount. The chairman of Allianz Group later told me that Allianz planned to invest USD 3 billion in ICBC, but was rejected by German regulators. Allianz ended up joining a consortium led by Goldman Sachs, and invested USD 1 billion.

"Two successive CEOs of Fortis Bank expressed interest to invest in ICBC, but failed to secure approval from their boards of directors. More regretfully, in August 2008, the board of directors and shareholders' meeting of Fortis Bank overwhelmingly approved an investment in the Dutch bank ABN AMRO Bank, a deal which brought Fortis Bank – a bank with a history of 186 years – to the brink of bankruptcy.

"Goldman Sachs was keen on underwriting ICBC's IPO. When I first asked its chairman Hank Paulson on whether he would consider investing in ICBC, he was caught by surprise. After difficult negotiations, Goldman Sachs became the leader of a USD 3.7 billion investment consortium for ICBC, but did not manage to underwrite the IPO. Citigroup and JPMorgan Chase did not send representatives to discuss investment in ICBC until the late stage of investment negotiations. Moreover, both of them intended only to acquire 5% of the shares on offer, and requested that ICBC carve out its credit card business for a 50:50 joint venture. Since the credit card business is the foundation of retail banking and involves customer data, we did not agree to this proposal, so the negotiations failed. As can be seen from these events, Chinese and international investors were indeed jittery about perceived risks in China's commercial banks."[1]

3. Successful engagement of strategic investors

ICBC explained China's economic and banking reforms and development prospects to investors and addressed their concerns. After extensive promotion, ICBC identified a consortium consisting of Goldman Sachs, Allianz Group, and American Express as the potential strategic investors. After more rounds of intense negotiations, ICBC came to an agreement with the consortium over key investment clauses. On August 25, 2005, ICBC submitted the "Report on Matters concerning the Execution of the 'Memorandum of Understanding for Strategic Cooperation between ICBC and Strategic Investors'"[2] to the MOF and Central Huijin on the basic framework for introducing strategic investors, key clauses, and future priorities. Upon securing their approval, ICBC signed the "Memorandum of Understanding for Strategic Cooperation" with the Goldman Sachs Consortium (including Goldman Sachs, Allianz Group, and American Express) on August 30, which marks the official beginning of ICBC's program to introduce overseas strategic investors.

Regarding ICBC's negotiations with strategic investors over the key clauses of the strategic investment agreement, Pan Gongsheng, then Director of ICBC's Restructuring Office and current Vice Governor of the PBOC, wrote as follows in his book *The Transformation: The Road to Rejuvenation of China's Major Commercial Banks*:

"Both Chinese and foreign parties strove to maximize their interests.

---

1   From the interview with Jiang Jianqing on March 6-7, 2018.
2   Gong Yin Bao [2005] No. 101.

Since the foreign parties sought to capture capital gains through an option agreement, ICBC negotiated strenuously over the clauses of the final strategic investment agreement. ICBC's senior management haggled over every penny with their counterparts, and substantially revised MOU clauses to raise the equity purchase price and remove the option to purchase additional shares and the annual compound yield on backup liquidity facilities.

"ICBC achieved such results thanks to the experience of other large Chinese commercial banks that had introduced strategic investors earlier. The final agreement represented the principles of long-term strategic cooperation and mutual benefit. ICBC held firm on critical clauses over investor structure, investment price, maintenance of net asset value, option to purchase additional shares, and compensation for breach of contract."[1]

On January 26, 2006, ICBC held its first extraordinary shareholders' meeting of 2006 in Beijing. Pursuant to the articles of association and rules of procedure, the meeting deliberated and adopted the proposal to introduce the Goldman Sachs consortium as ICBC's strategic investor[2]. In the afternoon of January 27, ICBC and the Goldman Sachs consortium executed a strategic investment and cooperation agreement in Beijing, under which the Goldman Sachs consortium agreed to purchase a USD 3.782 billion stake in ICBC. The strategic investment was to be completed with the purchase of ICBC's newly-issued shares. The Goldman Sachs consortium would appoint a director to sit on ICBC's board of directors, and both parties agreed to carry out strategic cooperation in all areas

---

1   Pan Gongsheng: *The Transformation: The Road to Rejuvenation of China's Major Commercial Banks*, China Financial Publishing House, 2012, p. 135.
2   Department of Strategic Management and Investor Relations, ICBC head office: *Chronicle of Events of ICBC's Joint-Stock Reform and IPO*, p. 112, internally distributed in 2007.

(Fig. 6.2). After investing in ICBC, Goldman Sachs set aside a significant amount of funds for business cooperation with ICBC. ICBC desired to leverage Goldman Sachs' business strengths to develop an integrated financial IT system and ramp up transaction capabilities, and Goldman Sachs agreed to devote financial and human resources to assist. After a few years of collaborative development, the system went live and is still the most sophisticated system of its kind in China today.

Source: ICBC Restructuring Office.

Fig 6.2: "7+1" Strategic Cooperation between ICBC and Goldman Sachs

4. Investment from NCSSF

On June 19, 2006, ICBC entered into a strategic investment and cooperation agreement with NCSSF. Under the agreement, NCSSF would acquire ICBC's newly-issued shares worth RMB 18.028 billion. Thus, ICBC now had six shareholders, further improving its equity structure and shareholder composition (Fig. 6.3). NCSSF's investment not only promoted equity structure diversification and new business development, but also allowed the state to reap the fruits of ICBC's rapid growth through dividends. Such strategic cooperation boosted ICBC's development of emerging business sectors, particularly the business of asset custody.

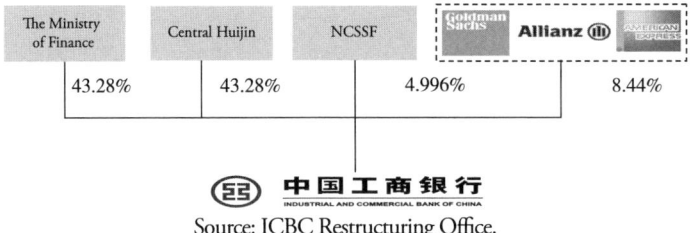

Source: ICBC Restructuring Office.

Fig 6.3: ICBC's Equity Structure and Shareholder Composition (June 29, 2006)

IV. ICBC's "IPO of the Century"

(I) Preparations for the IPO

1. Deliberation of the IPO plan

As the first step in preparing for the IPO, ICBC started to draft an IPO plan, which included such elements as the selection of stock exchanges; the determination of IPO date, the size, proportion, and structure of share offering, the nature of existing shares, and the sale of state-owned shares. These decisions required coordination among the issuer, shareholders, regulators, and external professionals, and consideration of the market environment, regulatory requirements, and economic interests.

Around the time that the joint-stock company was established, ICBC set out to draft its IPO plan, which took the following three stages to complete. Stage 1: Selection of stock exchanges and timing for IPO (June to December 2005). Stage 2: Determination of a preliminary IPO plan to issue H-shares before A-shares (January to May 2006). Stage 3: Deliberation on the relationship between A-shares and H-shares issuances, and the completion of a simultaneous A+H dual offering plan (June to July 2006).

The biggest challenge to ICBC's IPO was the proposed offering of A-shares and H-shares on the same day and at the same price. The simultaneous dual listing was unprecedented for Chinese enterprises. For this reason, Chairman Jiang Jianqing brought a long list of questions to the CSRC for assistance, and was received by Shang Fulin, CSRC Chairman at the time, whose guidance and support paved the way for ICBC's successful offering of A+H shares.

With the support of shareholders and regulators, ICBC made many rounds of revisions before adopting the final IPO plan of "simultaneous roadshows, unified pricing, and simultaneous offering" for A-shares and H-shares based on feedback from various stakeholders. In mid-July 2006, the IPO plan was officially approved by national authorities.

2. Convening the pre-IPO preparatory conference

In March 2006, ICBC initiated pre-IPO preparations. On July 20, ICBC held a kick-off meeting for the A-share offering, and retained China International Capital Corporation Limited (CICC), CITIC Securities, Shenyin & Wanguo Securities, and Guotai Junan Securities as joint sponsors (lead underwriters). ICBC also retained ICBC East Asia and China Galaxy Securities as financial advisors for its A-share offering, and Goldman Sachs as a financial advisor for ICBC's simultaneous offering of H-shares and A-shares in Hong Kong and Shanghai respectively.

After rounds of research and consultation, ICBC disclosed the A-share draft prospectus and H-share data set on September 22, 2006, domestically and internationally. On September 27, ICBC published the "Preliminary Prospectus," "Summary Preliminary Prospectus," "Announcement on Offering Arrangements" and "Preliminary Book Building," as well as "Appendices of Preliminary Prospectus" on the website of Shanghai Stock Exchange (SSE) and four newspapers, namely *China Securities Journal*, *Shanghai Securities News*, *Securities Times*, and *Securities Daily*. On the same day, ICBC updated its H-share information disclosed on the HKEX website.

(II) Domestic and Overseas IPO Roadshows

1. Domestic pre-marketing and preliminary book building

From the end of September to mid-October 2006, ICBC divided its management into three roadshow teams – red, blue, and orange – led by Chairman Jiang Jianqing, President Yang Kaisheng, and Vice President Li Xiaopeng respectively for pre-marketing events in cities including Shanghai, Shenzhen, Guangzhou, and Beijing. During these events, ICBC's management also started to accept preliminary book-building bids. Based on the reports of A-share and H-share lead underwriters on the results of mainland and overseas pre-marketing and preliminary book building, the management determined ICBC's stock price range.

2. Official domestic and overseas roadshows

From October 9 to 18, 2006, teams led by Chairman Jiang Jianqing and President Yang Kaisheng conducted roadshows in 18 major cities in Asia, Europe, and the U.S. over 9 days. The teams met with over 1,000 overseas investors to relate ICBC's investment story.

In Asia: On October 9, ICBC unveiled its IPO global roadshow in Hong Kong. The red and blue teams hosted 12 "one-on-one" meetings and a grand luncheon for 350 investors at the Four Seasons Hotel. On October 11, the red team led by Jiang arrived in Dubai, and the blue team led by Yang arrived in Singapore to pitch ICBC to global institutional investors.

In the U.S. and Europe: On October 13, the red team launched a roadshow in New York – the first stop on its itinerary in the U.S. The blue team arrived in London for roadshows in Europe. At 6:00 p.m. on October 19, ICBC's H-share international book building came to a completion with a total registered demand of USD 323.3 billion and an oversubscription ratio of 39.4 – a record high for an overseas IPO of a Chinese firm.

On October 16, 2006, Vice President Li headed an official A-share offering roadshow in Beijing. On October 17, ICBC released an "Announcement on A-Share Online Roadshow" on *China Securities Journal, Shanghai Securities News, Securities Daily,* and *Securities Times.* From 2:00 to 6:00 p.m. of the same day, the A-share online roadshow took place on China Securities Network. Jiang and Yang, who were still overseas, answered questions from investors over the internet together with the orange team headed by Li who also attended the online roadshow.

Related Topic: ICBC President Yang Kaisheng recalls ICBC's overseas roadshows[1]

"An IPO roadshow is a tough job. Every day, we had seven to eight meetings from morning till evening. Vice President Wang Lili worked with me in the same team. On the busiest day, we had to start the next session in five minutes after lunch arrived, so we had lunch in just five minutes. They said it was unseemly for a banker in pin-stripe to eat from a lunchbox while standing upright, so we had our meal hidden in a tool room down the stair-

---

1 From the interview with Yang Kaisheng on March 15, 2017.

case. We repeated the same message in every meeting and doing the same thing over and over again, which added to the exhaustion. ...

"In London, we held an online press conference with reporters from Hong Kong. Due to time zone difference, the conference took place at one or two o'clock in the morning. To our delight, the roadshow company prepared porridge, pickles, and fried dough stick. ... 'You guys from ICBC are going all-out,' marveled an investment banker, 'we've conducted roadshows for countless firms, and many lasted for just a couple of days. As soon as their shares were over-subscribed, they went playing golf or shopping.' The investment banker asked why we continued delivering presentations after our shares were already over-subscribed so many times, and I told him that this is how ICBC goes about its business."

(III) IPO and Simultaneous A+H Listing

1. Initial Public Offering (IPO)

As the domestic and overseas roadshows unfolded, ICBC's investment value became increasingly recognized by Chinese and foreign investors. On October 16, 2006, ICBC published the "Announcement on ICBC's Initial Offline A-Share Offering" and "Announcement on the Online Subscription in Connection with ICBC's Initial Online A-Share Offering" on *China Securities Journal, Shanghai Securities News, Securities Daily*, and *Securities Times*. On October 17, ICBC released the "Announcement of Initial Public Offering" in connection with the H-share offering to Hong Kong investors.

At 9:00 a.m. on October 16, ICBC initiated the public offering to retail investors in the Chinese mainland and Hong Kong, which was enthusiastically received by institutional and retail investors in both markets.

The A-share online offering was subscribed by 1.55 million investors with a lot winning ratio of about 2.03%, locking up over RMB 650 billion of subscription funds – a record high. Meanwhile, the public offering officially started in Hong Kong and was met with equal enthusiasm on the first day. Investors waiting to collect application forms and prospectus formed a long queue in front of the banks. By noon on October 19, the public offering in Hong Kong concluded with a final subscribers count of 977,000 (977,000 applications were received) and an oversubscription multiple of 78 times, which triggered the claw-back option[1]. The IPO posted the highest number of subscribers (applications) ever in Hong Kong, leading to HKD 425 billion (roughly USD 54.6 billion) of funds being frozen – the highest amount for subscription in a public offering ever in Hong Kong.

With the successful completion of domestic and overseas roadshows, ICBC held a simultaneous teleconference on IPO pricing and share allotment in Beijing, Hong Kong, and Los Angeles on October 20. The meeting summarized the book-building results during A-share and H-share roadshows, deliberated the pricing of A-shares and H-shares, and determined the principles for share allotment. Based on book-building results and demand, ICBC set the price of A-shares and H-shares at RMB 3.12 (HKD 3.07), the upper level of the indicative range. Before exercising the greenshoe option, ICBC had raised a total of USD 19.1 billion from its domestic and overseas offerings – the largest at the time.

---

1   The claw-back option: The issuer asks for bids from corporate investors to set share price, and offers shares to ordinary investors online; based on the subscriptions of ordinary investors, it determines the number of shares allotted to corporate and ordinary investors.

2. "A+H" simultaneous listing

Based on the unified share pricing and public offering, ICBC was listed on SSE and HKEX. The dual listing was intended to increase the circulation of ICBC's shares, fully leverage the financing function of domestic and overseas capital markets, and promote the role of capital markets in corporate governance. On October 23, 2006, ICBC selected its stock codes, which are 601398 for the A-share market and 1398 for the H-share market. The Chinese abbreviation of the listed company is "工商银行," and the English abbreviation is "ICBC."

On October 26, ICBC published the "Announcement on A-Share Initial Public Offering" on *China Securities Journal, Shanghai Securities News, Securities Times, Securities Daily,* and the website of SSE. ICBC's A-shares were scheduled for listing on the SSE on October 27. ICBC planned to issue 13 billion A-shares (provided that the greenshoe option was not exercised), and the total share capital of A-shares and H-shares before the exercise of the greenshoe option stood at RMB 327,821,930,026.00. The announcement also briefly disclosed ICBC's global offering of H-shares.

On October 27, the A-shares and H-shares of ICBC made their debut on SSE and HKEX simultaneously. On the first trading day, ICBC's A-shares closed at RMB 3.28, and H-shares closed at HKD 3.52. At that A-share closing price, ICBC's A-share market capitalization reached RMB 823.2 billion after fully exercising the greenshoe option for its A-shares and H-shares (or RMB 821.9 billion before exercising the option), which was 40.06% higher than the RMB 586.8 billion market capitalization of BOC – the second largest on the A-share market. On the day of listing, ICBC became China's largest A-share company, accounting for 17.35% of SSE's total market capitalization of RMB 4,744.934 billion, indicating its pivotal role for the stability and development of China's capital market. At ICBC's H-share closing price of HKD 3.52 and A-share closing price of RMB 3.28 on October 27, ICBC's A+H share market capitalization totaled USD 141.9 billion after fully exercising the greenshoe option (or USD 139.1 billion before exercising the option), making it the fifth-largest listed bank in the world.

On November 7, ICBC published an announcement on the exercise of H-share greenshoe option on the website of HKEX, *South China Morning Post*, and *Hong Kong Economic Times*. The announcement indicated that ICBC's H-share joint book-runners had fully exercised the greenshoe option on November 6 for a total of 5,308,650,000 H-shares, or 15% of its initial H-share offering. The over-allotted shares were issued at the price of HKD 3.07, which is the same as the issue price of original H-shares. On November 16, ICBC fully exercised the greenshoe option for its 1.95 billion A-shares, with capital raised from the over-allotment fully credited to its account. By then, ICBC's IPO came to a successful completion with a total offering of 14.95 billion A-shares and about 40.7 billion H-shares, raising some USD 22 billion from A-share and H-share markets combined.

3. Significance of ICBC's IPO

The resounding success of IPO brought ICBC to a new and higher starting point. On the morning of October 27, 2006, ICBC Chairman Jiang Jianqing made the following remark at ICBC's listing ceremony at HKEX: "In its full march toward domestic and international capital markets, ICBC has opened a new chapter in its history, becoming a modern financial enterprise and completing the first-ever A-share and H-share simultaneous listing. It has set the record for the initial public offering of a single stock, bringing opportunities and dynamism to the capital markets."

Feted as the "IPO of the century," ICBC's IPO marks a swathe of institutional and technological innovations, setting 28 world records, including:

- world's biggest IPO;
- world's first A+H share simultaneous offering;
- highest valuation multiple for a Chinese state-controlled commercial bank upon share offering;
- biggest demand during book-building for a Chinese financial stock;
- first inclusion of Chinese corporate investors into the allotment category for global institutional investors;
- first Chinese enterprise to stage an IPO roadshow in the Middle East;
- biggest H-share offering;
- first pre-IPO disclosure in the form of a "data set" on the website of HKEX for H-share offering;
- biggest allotment for H-share cornerstone investors;
- highest percentage of H-share order placement at one-on-one international roadshows;
- highest number of H-share subscription applications;
- highest number of electronic H-share subscription applications;
- highest financing quota for new share subscriptions by H-share investors;
- highest number of banks for receiving subscription funds for H-share offering;
- highest amount of funds frozen for subscription of publicly offered

- H-shares;
- highest trading volume on the day of H-share offering with the most transactions;
- highest processing volume at Hong Kong's bank settlement system on the day of H-share offering;
- first case of approval of short-selling on the day of H-share offering with the issuance of futures, options, and warrants;
- biggest A-share offering;
- largest A-share market capitalization;
- first exercise of an over-allotment option in A-share offering;
- first simultaneous disclosure of H-share offering announcement during A-share offering on the website of SSE;
- first to introduce analyst conference call, a standard international practice, in A-share offering;
- broadest coverage of A-share offering roadshows for institutional investors;
- first simultaneous participation by the management team in online A-share roadshows at three places around the world;
- largest amount of funds frozen for the subscription tranche of A-share offering;
- largest amount of funds frozen for the subscription tranche of A-shares under the new book-building system;
- highest trading volume on the day of A-share offering with the most transactions.

Expansion and Conclusion | 541

Section II
Joint-Stock Reform and IPO of ABC

The Agricultural Bank of China (ABC) was the final large state-owned bank to complete joint-stock reform and IPO. Given its status as a specialized bank traditionally focused on agriculture, ABC had followed unique institutional arrangements throughout its reform process. State support, buoyant economy, and the prior success of other state-owned banks created favorable conditions for ABC's joint-stock reform and IPO, enabling it to complete a historical leap.

Related Topic: Brief History of ABC

On July 10, 1951, the Agricultural Cooperation Bank – ABC's predecessor – was established under the leadership of the PBOC to offer financial services for the revitalization and development of the rural economy and society. In July 1952, ABC and its functions were merged into the PBOC. In March 1955, the bank was reincarnated under the name of "Agricultural Bank of China" to provide credit support to agricultural collectivization. In April 1957, ABC was once again merged into the PBOC.

In November 1963, ABC was re-established as an institution directly affiliated to the State Council for the unified management of funds earmarked for agricultural programs. In November 1965, it was merged into the PBOC for the third time. On February 23, 1979, the State Council issued the "Notice on the Resumption of the Agricultural Bank of China," which marks the fourth time that ABC was (re)established.

In December 1993, the State Council made a decision to transform ABC into a SOCB. In April 1994, ABC transferred most of its policy functions to the newly-organized Agricultural Development Bank of China. In August 1996, ABC ceased to be the authority overseeing rural credit cooperatives pursuant to the "Decisions of the State Council on the Reform of Rural Financial System," freeing them from the administrative affiliation to ABC.

In 2004, ABC submitted its joint-stock reform plan for the first time. In January 2007, the third National Financial Work Conference determined that ABC was to "promote the development of *sannong* (i.e., agriculture, farmers, and rural areas), conduct group-wide restructuring, embrace commercial operations, and seek public listing when appropriate," which unveiled a new stage of ABC's joint-stock reform. In October 2008, the State Council executive meeting adopted the "Overall Implementation Plan for the Joint-Stock Reform of Agricultural Bank of China," which brought ABC's joint-stock reform to the stage of implementation.

In November 2008, Central Huijin injected capital into ABC, becoming ABC's largest shareholder together with the MOF. On January 15, 2009, the Agricultural Bank of China Limited was established.

In July 2010, ABC's A-shares and H-shares were listed in Shanghai and Hong Kong on July 15 and 16, respectively, becoming the biggest IPO in the world at that time.

I. The Uniqueness of ABC's Joint-Stock Reform

ABC's joint-stock transformation straddled both China's banking reform and rural financial reform. With its highly complicated history and *sannong* focus, ABC was besieged by a high loss ratio on past policy loans, debilitating operational efficiency, and hefty legacy burden. As a result, ABC's joint-stock reform was full of twists and turns.

(I) Reform of ABC as a State-Owned Bank Specialized in Rural Finance

The difficulty of ABC's joint-stock reform was compounded by its simultaneous involvement in both the reform of China's large state-owned banks and rural financial reform.

First, ABC's joint-stock reform marked the completion of the joint-stock reform of China's major state-owned banks, which, launched in 2003, was advanced through the state's capital injection with foreign reserves. Before it were ABC, listed on HKEX in October 2005, and BOC and ICBC, both listed on SSE and HKEX in 2006.

Second, ABC's joint-stock reform was a key element of China's rural financial reform. ABC's market-based and joint-stock transformation overlapped with progress achieved in the reform of China's rural financial system. Prior to the joint-stock reform, ABC experienced major reforms such as the separation between policy and commercial functions, the spin-off of the Agricultural Development Bank of China, and decoupling from rural credit cooperatives. By the eve of the joint-stock reform, China's countryside had formed a financial system dominated by ABC in which policy banks, regional rural commercial banks and rural credit cooperatives operated in parallel.

In January 2007, the third National Financial Work Conference decided to establish a sound rural financial system, promote innovation among rural financial organizations, lower the licensing requirements of financial institutions that serve the rural market, lower the market entry threshold, and encourage and support the development of financial institutions of various ownership types to meet rural demand. It also decided that the priority of ABC's joint-stock reform was to better support *sannong*, as part of the country's program to promote financial development in rural areas.

(II) Exploring an Effective Path for Serving *Sannong* and Transitioning Toward Commercial Operations

The State Council tasked ABC with the important mission of supporting *sannong*, ABC's traditional business focus. ABC was established after the Third Plenary Session of the 11th CPC Central Committee in 1978 to expedite agricultural development and enhance the fundamental role of agriculture in the economy. In various stages of its history, ABC made great contributions to *sannong* and the rural financial system, including providing accounting guidance for the people's communes and brigades, organizing the operation of rural credit cooperatives, and centrally managing agricultural development funds. It became a primary channel of market-based support to the agricultural industry after its separation from the Agricultural Development Bank of China and rural credit cooperatives. County-level markets and pro-agriculture business comprised a big chunk of ABC's business operations. At the end of 2004, 61.9% of ABC's outlets and 51.5% of its employees were assigned and 34.9% of its loans were issued to the county level or below. Agriculture-related loans of ABC amounted to RMB 975.3 billion, or 38.8% of its loan portfolio. ABC provided credit and other financial services to 70% of leading agricultural enterprises in China.

For many years, rural China has been financially underserved. Extensive and varied demand for rural financial services highlighted the urgency to create a multi-tiered rural financial system. Given the weak rural credit environment and scant commercial financial resources, other Chinese commercial banks exited the rural market during their joint-stock reform and market repositioning; at the same time, financial cooperatives could not keep up with the financial needs of medium and large agriculture-related customers and urban-rural customers because of their limited capital, technology, and service network. Furthermore, the business scope of policy financial institutions was confined to lending related to the supply and management of grain, cotton, and edible oils.

In comparison, ABC boasted a historical advantage in supporting the balanced development of urban and rural areas. With the largest service network connecting these two markets and the broadest customer base, ABC possessed a significant amount of assets and offered a wide range of fee-based services. ABC's strengths included businesses and products with integrated home and foreign currency services, specialized agricultural credit service system, and a modern technology support system. Right from the inception of its reform, ABC had already become the primary channel for offering commercial financial services to the agricultural industry and for bridging the financial gap between rural and urban areas, as well as a major means by which government at all levels could implement *sannong* programs. For this reason, the CPC Central Committee and the State Council set "supporting *sannong*" as the crucial goal of ABC's joint-stock reform and IPO.

ABC strove to balance commercial sustainability with its rural mandate throughout its joint-stock reform. In the process, ABC conducted extensive pilot programs, and after coming up with three possible approaches for supporting *sannong*, chose the one that called for creating *sannong* financial business departments, and then introduced a host of follow-up reforms and innovations.

1. Three approaches for supporting *sannong*

Unlike other large commercial banks, a critical reform priority facing ABC was the design of an organizational structure for supporting both commercial and *sannong* operations. Based on considerations to improve the national financial resource distribution and rural financial system, ABC carefully weighed the three options of organizational reform.

(1) The model of "One Bank, Two Systems"

In 2007, the third National Financial Work Conference prescribed the following principles for ABC's joint-stock reform: "*sannong*-oriented, group-wide restructuring, market-based operations, and [seek] public listing when appropriate." Considering China's urban-rural divide and the different characteristics of urban and rural financial services, ABC proposed to develop a network of county-level sub-branches appropriate for the *sannong* and countywide business parallel to its urban business network, i.e., "One Bank, Two Systems." The vision was to create a single corporation with separate yet coordinated urban and rural businesses under separate accounting.

Specifically, "One Bank" was to be manifested in six aspects: one CPC committee, a single corporation, one brand, one network, one set of financial statements, and one support system. Among them, "one CPC committee" refers to the principle that the bank should be subject to the leadership of the CPC committee of the ABC head office. "Single corporation" means that all operational and management activities of the head office and branches were to be organized with the head office as the singular corporate entity. "One brand" means that ABC should conduct all its business activities under the same corporate image, logo, and brand. "One network" refers to the unified bank-wide service network platform and business system. "One set of financial statements" means that ABC should reflect and disclose all its business activities and financial results in the same set of financial statements. "One support system" refers to that *sannong* and county-level business would share middle- and back-office management system and logistical support system with urban business.

"Two systems" refer to a dual-track system separating the urban business from the *sannong* and county-level business. ABC would introduce special institutional arrangements for the *sannong* and county-level business in terms of organizational structure, performance evaluation, resource allocation, credit management, risk control, human resources, and product innovation, based on the particular characteristics of such business. ABC would also devolve operational authority to lower levels, streamline business processes, shorten the decision-making chain, increase service efficiency, and adopt separate accounting. The next priority was to coordinate urban and rural business development, and complement the advantages and share resources between city banks and county-level banks to enhance support to rural areas.

However, in the long run, this model might cause operational and management authority to gravitate toward the higher levels in the bank-wide organization structure, which would run counter to the goal of devolving operational authority, shortening the decision-making process, and improving service efficiency.

(2) The model of "tier-two subsidiary"

The "secondary subsidiary" model refers to a two-tier corporate structure that aimed to transform some tier-two branches into subsidiaries specializing in *sannong* business. The two tiers of corporations would operate independently under the umbrella of the same joint-stock conglomerate. Theoretically, this model would help ABC better serve *sannong* by devolving operational authority to the outlet-level and shortening the decision-making chain, and would improve accountability as independent subsidiaries would solely assume their own business risks.

Yet this model might weaken urban-rural business coordination and give rise to related-party transactions, which would complicate the IPO process. Subsidiaries in the poorer regions in central and western China might also lack risk resilience and sustainability. Reassigning employees to subsidiary banks may destabilize the workforce.

(3) The model of *sannong* financial business departments

Based on experience of international financial institutions in offering rural financial services, this approach called for creating business departments, under ABC as a single corporation, for managing ABC's *sannong* business. The plan proposed to carry out the reform first in China's central, western, and northeastern regions where *sannong*-related problems were the most prominent (these regions accounted for 91.6% of state-designated poverty-stricken counties (*guojiaji pinkunxian*), 71.4% of provincial-designated poverty-stricken counties, and 59.7% of major grain and cotton-producing counties), before rolling out the program in other parts of China. *Sannong* financial business departments (*sannong* has been variously referred to as "agro-related" and "county area" in official ABC communications) would be responsible for supporting *sannong* and the county-level economy, and for creating a whole set of systems and mechanisms on organization structure, product innovation, resource allocation, performance review, credit management, and risk control especially tailored to this sector.

After much analysis and comparison, ABC chose the third approach, which is a common organizational management model adopted by most leading international companies, including many financial institutions. Creating a dedicated business department would allow ABC to run its *sannong* business more efficiently and sustainably. It would also maximize the effect of national agriculture-related financial policies by demarcating their boundary of application. Compared with the other options, creating separate business departments would create fewer shocks and obstacles as well.

Of course, this approach would present challenges in terms of management cost, horizontal coordination, (lack of) institutional innovation, and technical requirements.

In October 2008, the 32nd executive meeting of the State Council for the year approved the overall plan for ABC's joint-stock reform. According to the State Council's requirements, ABC should reform its county-level business department system to meet the demand for rural financial services, devolve decision-making power to lower levels, and form independent accounting and accountability at the business department level.

2. Conducting the pilot program for supporting *sannong*

(1) Conducting the pilot program on *sannong* financial services

In 2007, ABC formulated the "Overall Implementation Plan of the Agricultural Bank of China for Supporting *Sannong*." To test the feasibility and effect of this plan, ABC launched a pilot program of *sannong* financial services in 116 county-level sub-branches in 17 regions of 8 provinces (municipalities and autonomous regions) in September 2007, including Jilin, Anhui, Fujian, Hunan, Guangxi, Sichuan, Gansu, and Chongqing. In the nine months of the pilot program, ABC extensively reformed the credit system, developed innovative financial products, broadened the scope of guarantee services, increased loan review efficiency, and enhanced risk management. It developed a set of effective practices and case studies, gained the necessary experience, and laid the groundwork for creating *sannong* financial business departments.

(2) Launching *sannong* financial business departments

Based on its mandate to serve both urban and rural markets, ABC decided to create dedicated business departments for managing *sannong* and county-level business. ABC brought its urban and rural businesses, divided at the county level, under separate management to increase specialization and coordination. In March 2008, ABC launched a pilot reform program to test the feasibility of this idea, optimize institutional design, and minimize the risks of the transition. In 2009, ABC released the "Implementation Plan for the Pilot Reform Program of the Sannong Financial Business Department," which laid out the overall reform approach and identified suitable branches for the pilot program. The scope of the pilot program was expanded three times in 2010, 2012, and 2014. In April 2015, ABC rolled out the program across the bank following the PBOC's "Circular on All-Round Implementation of ABC's Sannong Financial Business Department Reform."

3. Exploring an effective model for supporting *sannong*

During its joint-stock reform and after the IPO, ABC has been committed to developing the underserved *sannong* and county-level market segment by continuously improving the operations of its *sannong* financial business departments, and therefore the quality and efficiency of *sannong*-related financial services.

(1) Putting the *sannong* financial business departments to work

First, ABC has adopted a management model of "three-tier supervision, one-tier operation." At the level of the board of directors, ABC created a Sannong Financial Development Committee responsible for strategic decision-making for bank-wide *sannong* programs. At the management level, ABC set up an Administrative Committee for the Sannong Financial Business Department responsible for the decision-making of key matters related to *sannong* services. At the head office level, ABC established the Sannong Financial Business Department, which initially was structured to include three departments and six centers.

The three departments were the specialized departments for *sannong*-related programs, including the Sannong Policy and Planning Department, the Rural Industrial Financial Service Department, and the Farmers' Financial Service Department.

The six centers comprised middle- and back-office management centers, including the Human Resources Management Center, the Accounting and Assessment Center, the Capital and Funding Management Center, the Risk Management Center, the Credit Management Center, and the Product R&D Center.

This architecture has been further developed into a three-department and eight-center architecture.

The Sannong Financial Business Department at the head office is responsible for developing the bank-wide *sannong* services, and conducting business guidance, product innovation, resource allocation, performance review, and risk management.

At the level of provincial and municipal branches, ABC created the *sannong* financial service divisions structured as two departments and six centers. The "two departments" refer to the Rural Industrial Financial Service Department and the Farmers' Financial Service Department. Aligned with the head office, the six centers are primarily responsible for various *sannong* services in the respective jurisdictions of provincial and municipal branches.

All county-level sub-branches hang out an additional nameplate of "(Name of County) County Sannong Business Unit of the Agricultural Bank of China," indicating that they are responsible for the day-to-day management of *sannong* and county-level business for the area.

Second, ABC has adopted an operational mechanism incorporating six types of separation and segregation, including:

(i) Separate capital management: The head office annually determines the operational and economic capital of *sannong* business departments, and breaks down the economic capital quota to be assigned to various *sannong* financial service divisions.

(ii) Separate credit management: ABC has adopted differentiated policy guidelines for *sannong* and county-level credit business. To date, ABC has issued credit policies for over ten agriculture-related sectors and many regional credit policies.

(iii) Separate accounting: ABC has adopted separate accounting and reporting for the *sannong* business departments, and follows independent cost- and profit-sharing rules to ensure that a business department's and the bank's account books are "separate, accurate, and explainable."

(iv) Separate risk provision and write-off: ABC has adopted a differentiated risk provision policy for the *sannong* business, and relaxed write-off conditions for agriculture-related bad loans, such as the amount and recourse period of each loan to be written off.

(v) Separate fund balance and operation: ABC has brought the *sannong*-related funds under separate management, and developed a separate *sannong* credit plan to ensure that the *sannong* business departments increase their loan issuance at a faster pace than bank-wide average.

(vi) Separate evaluation, incentives, and restraints: ABC's head office separately evaluates the performance of the *sannong* business departments of its tier-one branches, and conducts a look-through evaluation of key county-level sub-branches. It also conducts evaluations on the competitiveness of its branches in county-level market, and grants appropriate result-based incentives to help reinforce the branches' *sannong* mandate.

(2) Improving *sannong*-related financial services

After setting supporting *sannong* as the objective of its joint-stock reform, ABC improved its *sannong*-oriented financial services in the following areas:

First, it introduced a "3510" plan for *sannong*-related business with three-year, five-year, and 10-year targets. Specifically, ABC planned to, in the three years from 2008 to 2010, find an effective model for the development of *sannong* business and substantially improve its *sannong*-related financial services. Within about five years, i.e., by 2012, ABC aimed to achieve significant progress in developing the underserved *sannong* and county-level market segment, highlighting its pivotal role in China's rural financial system. In around ten years, i.e., by 2017, ABC aimed to develop *sannong* into a key business segment, consolidate its leadership position in China's rural financial market, and offer superior financial services to *sannong* customers.

Second, ABC focused on priority areas for supporting the *sannong* niche market. Without compromising its commercial sustainability, ABC set a minimum ratio of *sannong*-related loans in relation to its overall loan portfolio, played a leading role in financing agriculture industrialization and rural infrastructure construction, and improved its rural financial services. Meanwhile, ABC vowed to address the difficulties faced by farmers, SMEs, grain and cotton-producing counties, and poor counties in securing loans, and to expand the coverage of services to *sannong*. ABC identified eight priority areas where *sannong*-related credit support should be increased, including agriculture industrialization, rural commodity distribution, agricultural and rural infrastructure construction, small-town development, and unique local resources development. In terms of regional priorities, ABC adopted differentiated policies for major grain and cotton-producing counties, poverty-stricken counties, prosperous counties, and counties in special regions.

Third, ABC developed and introduced innovative financial products and services to meet the diversified financial demand of *sannong* customers. For example, it streamlined quick loans, self-service revolving loans, forestry rights-collateralized loans, specialized cooperative loans, store operating rights-collateralized loans, Golden Agriculture Insurance Policy, and New Simple Personal Insurance. ABC also promoted the Golden Grain credit card, through which the cardholder may access microcredit, fiscal payments, insurance agency, and wealth management services in addition to traditional savings, remittance, and cashing services, offering a "one-stop" solution for farmers to access a full range of financial services.

Fourth, ABC increased the number of business outlets in the countryside, improved financial infrastructure and services, and hired more and more skilled employees to staff the local outlets. Regarding electronic service channels, ABC broadly deployed new service delivery channels that appeal to farmers, such as telephone banking, mobile banking, and online banking. To broaden service coverage, for townships and villages without access to outlets, ABC partnered with rural credit unions and postal savings banks so that transactions might be completed with one of those institutions as agent, or by home visit by a bank employee. ABC also joined hands with local governments, the PBOC, and the banking regulator to promote public awareness about the functions and use of financial products. By creating rural insurance companies and agricultural financial leasing companies, ABC explored new channels for supporting *sannong*.

(III) Challenges Facing ABC's Joint-Stock Reform

Redundant workforce, legacy burden, and inefficiency plagued ABC's joint-stock reform, delaying the reform until after 2008.

First, policy loans accounted for a significant share of ABC's loan losses. ABC's legacy burden was heavier than other banks mainly due to its hefty policy loans, which fall into two categories: first, special loans transferred from the Agricultural Development Bank of China and the PBOC[1]; second, other special-purpose loans issued at the direction of the state. By the end of 2004, ABC's non-performing policy loans accounted for 42% of its total NPLs and 46% of its total losses. In some poorer regions, sub-branches were over-burdened with special loans, which exceeded their holdings of conventional loans. The high NPL ratio and losses from policy loans made it hard for ABC to evaluate the real performance of its

---

1 Pursuant to the "Notice of the Agricultural Bank of China on Enhancing the Management of Special Loans" (Nong Yin Fa [1995] No. 311), after the separation of rural policy financial business from industrial financial business, ABC's special loans shall be commercial loans with a strictly defined scope and purpose. As a special form of commercial loans in ABC's reform toward commercial operations, the special loans primarily include loans to major grain and cotton-producing counties, loans to high-yield, high-quality and efficient agricultural demonstration zones, R&D loans, Spark Program loans, loans to agricultural hydropower, loans to water-efficient irrigation, township water supply loans, trade, industrial and agricultural loans, loans for the development of rural small towns, among others.

sub-branches and to make truthful disclosures without causing adverse effects.

Second, ABC's significant legacy burden, which was reflected in the following aspects: (1) ABC's small-sized, geographically dispersed, and financially distressed customers led to risks in special loans. (2) Systemic risks arose from ABC's conventional loans to township enterprises, supply and marketing cooperatives, rural artisanal workshops and smelters[1], which had built up through various rural reforms and economic transitions. As a result, ABC did not achieve profitability until 2001, and was far less profitable than the other three SOCBs. Thin profit margins made it harder for ABC to dispose of its legacy burden. (3) ABC assumed most of the cost of rural financial transformations, including the separation from credit unions and the creation of the Agricultural Development Bank of China, which added to its financial burden. (4) Before 2000, ABC lacked the operational competence and technical prowess to bring its scattered credit business activities under effective management, giving rise to lending risks.

Third, ABC suffered from inefficiencies. Over the years, ABC created institutions in all administrative regions, and expanded its market from the countryside to cities and from small cities to medium and large cities. To manage its policy loan business, ABC had to develop numerous institutions spread over urban and rural areas and recruit personnel in the less-developed regions in central and western China. Burdened with a massive

---

1   These artisanal workshops and smelters include: artisanal paper mills, leather workshops, dyeing workshops, coking plants, sulfur plants, arsenic smelters, mercury smelters, zinc smelters, oil refineries, gold extraction workshops, pesticide producers, small electroplating workshops, asbestos producers, radioactive producers, and small dyeing workshops. The central government took steps to ban these artisanal workshops and smelters due to concerns over pollution and obsolete technology.

Expansion and Conclusion | 557

organizational system and large headcount, ABC was far less efficient than other banks.

By the end of 2004, ABC's headcount reached 489,425, including 70,683 internally laid-off or re-assigned (*neibu fenliu*) and internally retired (*neitui*) employees. It boasted the largest number of outlets and employees, which were respectively 1.95 times and 1.69 times the average levels of ICBC, BOC, and CCB. ABC's per-customer and per-outlet savings deposit balances were merely 49.7% and 44.5% of the average levels of the three banks. Moreover, ABC's outlet distribution and personnel structure were heavily skewed toward high-farmer-population areas and China's central and western regions, with 31.4% of its outlets located in areas below the county level, and 58.1% in central and western regions. Over 80% of ABC's 8,100 loss-making and unproductive outlets were located in central and western regions. To achieve the average efficiency of other commercial banks, ABC needed to streamline its organization and headcount.

II. Four Revisions of the Joint-Stock Reform Plan

ABC started to develop its joint-stock reform plan in 2002. Based on the joint-stock reforms of other banks and its own circumstances, ABC finalized its comprehensive reform plan to meet national policy requirements and reflect its own characteristics after considering four different approaches.

(I) Creating a Banking Conglomerate and Restructuring of Subsidiaries

In 2002, ABC developed a reform plan to develop itself into a banking conglomerate based on the shareholding system. It vowed to take the initiative of reform to meet the needs arising from China's entry into the

WTO and contribute to the banking reform.

Given its hefty legacy burden, it was challenging for ABC to create a corporate governance structure with diversified equity ownership in a short period. Therefore, the plan suggested that in transforming into a banking conglomerate, ABC should strengthen itself as a wholly state-owned company, establish subsidiaries in which it would hold a controlling interest, carry out joint-stock restructuring of its subsidiaries, and create conditions for an IPO. This corporate governance restructuring and improvement aimed to create a modern banking system with clear shareholding relations, clearly defined rights and responsibilities, and segregated government administration and enterprise management.

The plan was to create the Agricultural Bank of China Group with controlling stakes in ABC and relevant risk asset management company, insurance agency, and securities brokerage. Within the five-year transition period after China's entry into the WTO, ABC expected to complete this reform program in three stages:

Step 1: Establish the Agricultural Bank of China Group with an asset management subsidiary or department to separate ABC's existing good assets from bad assets.

Step 2: Improve the organizational design of the wholly state-owned company, create, when appropriate, an insurance agency and a securities brokerage where part of ABC's workforce would be diverted to, create a governance structure extending throughout the conglomerate and its subsidiaries, and adopt innovative operation and management mechanisms.

Step 3: Carry out the joint-stock reform for some of ABC's subsidiaries, and strive to meet regulatory and listing requirements on profitability and capital adequacy ratio for the separate listing of these companies.

Expansion and Conclusion | 559

(II) Creating a Banking Conglomerate and "Good Bank/Bad Bank" Model

In June 2003, ABC established a restructuring leading group to answer the State Council's call for accelerating the reform of SOCBs. By mobilizing resources and conducting extensive studies, ABC developed a plan for reforming itself into a banking conglomerate and conducting joint-stock reform through the "good bank/bad bank" model.

Based on ABC's circumstances, the plan aimed to, in five years, reform ABC into a modern financial enterprise with sound governance structure, operational mechanisms, and financial position; clear goals; and strong market competitiveness. Specific measures included the restructuring of assets, outlets and personnel, joint-stock reform, and improvement of corporate governance and operation.

The plan laid down three principles: commercial operation-oriented reform, cost minimization, and steady implementation. It also identified three major issues to be tackled: (1) the lack of clear shareholding structure; (2) poor corporate governance; (3) hefty legacy burden. Based on the overall goal and principles, ABC needed to restructure existing assets and relevant personnel and outlets according to the nature and quality of assets, create a financial holding company with an asset management subsidiary, and carry out the joint-stock reform.

(III) Three-Step Approach of "Regional Carve-Out, Reverse Acquisition, and Public Listing"

The difficulty of addressing ABC's woes was compounded by a string of factors, including the hefty size of policy loans, legacy burden, and uneven development between various branches. In 2004, in line with the

State Council's directive for "one bank, one strategy" for the reform of SOCBs, ABC put forward a three-step reform plan of "regional carve-out, group-wide restructuring, and public listing when appropriate."

Step 1: Regional carve-out and creation of a new bank. After disposing of policy loans and burdens, ABC would carve out and restructure its well-performing branches to create a new bank, and establish a holding company with controlling stakes in the new and existing banks. The new bank would receive a state capital injection through the holding company and issue subordinated bonds to raise its core capital adequacy ratio and capital adequacy ratio to over 4% and 8% respectively. External investors would be brought in to transform the institution into a modern joint-stock commercial bank.

Step 2: Reverse acquisition and group-wide restructuring. After the carve-out, the remaining branches would remain within ABC, and continue to reform and dispose of legacy NPAs to create a modern commercial bank. When the net assets of the original ABC are brought up to zero, some outlets would be transformed into rural credit unions, with others to merge into the new bank.

Step 3: Create conditions for an IPO. After the consolidation, the new bank would spend some time to improve its financial condition, optimize its organizational system, transform the operational frameworks, improve its corporate governance, introduce strategic investors, and prepare for a domestic and/or overseas IPO.

The plan identified differentiated measures for the disposal of various NPLs arising from policy-related operations. The basic approach was to compensate for loan losses with fiscal funds, write off loss loans against PBOC loans, swap doubtful and substandard loans for the same amount of central bank bills, and sell off microcredit loans to credit unions, large loans to the AMC, and *sannong* loans of the pass and special-mention categories to the Agricultural Development Bank of China. The goal was to create a business landscape with reasonable division of functions and responsibilities among ABC, the Agricultural Development Bank of China, and rural credit unions within the rural financial system. Transforming some rural outlets into rural credit unions would help reduce competitive pressures for rural credit unions, boost their capital strength, expand service functions, and help the reformed ABC enhance performance and competitiveness.

Yet CBRC Chairman Liu Mingkang opposed ABC's carve-out and IPO, pointing to the value of its existent service network and the unsuccessful experience of splitting a bank into a "good bank" and a "bad bank" in previous SOE reform which left many complications. Such was the background for ABC's final decision to pursue group-wide restructuring and listing.

(IV) "Group-Wide Restructuring" Model

In line with the State Council's requirements on the reform of SOCBs, ABC finalized and submitted its group-wide restructuring plan in 2005 to address its deep-seated problems and enhance performance and competitiveness based on the lessons from other banks' reforms.

The plan identified three basic principles for ABC's joint-stock reform. First, adhere to the principle of group-wide restructuring to prevent systemic financial risks from a business carve-out, maintain economies of scale as a large bank, contribute to economic and financial stability, maintain workforce stability, and avoid waste of resources and related-party transactions. Second, in coordination with the rural financial reform, bring into full play ABC's function to provide commercial financial services to *sannong*. Third, minimize the cost to the state, and strive to cover the cost of reform with future earnings in the shortest possible period.

The plan put forward the approach of financial restructuring, institutional integration, and corporate governance reform. The basic vision of financial restructuring was to first dispose of special loans and strip off ABC's policy functions, then increase its capital adequacy ratio through state capital injection and NPL disposal, and finally seek a public listing. As for the integration of institutional systems and personnel, the plan was to reorganize ABC's organizations in China's underdeveloped regions, consolidate and merge inefficient and loss-making outlets, and streamline redundant personnel in various ways. Moreover, ABC called for overhauling its risk management, business and management process, human resources management, financial accounting system, and IT system, focusing on improving the corporate governance structure to create a modern commercial bank system – a mission of historic significance.

On January 19, 2007, Premier Wen Jiabao fully recognized ABC's substantial contributions to rural social and economic development at the National Financial Work Conference. He called for resolutely advancing ABC's joint-stock reform under the following principles: *sannong*-oriented, group-wide restructuring, market-based operations, and [seek] public listing when appropriate[1]. Subsequently, ABC's joint-stock reform gained momentum. On October 21, 2008, the State Council approved the "Mas-

---

1   Wen Jiabao: "Comprehensively Deepening Financial Reform to Promote Sustained and Sound Financial Industry Development," *Qiushi Journal*, 2007 (5).

ter Plan for the Implementation of ABC's Joint-Stock Reform" – a "full steam ahead" signal to ABC.

III. Financial Restructuring and Creation of the Joint-Stock Company

Following the "one bank, one strategy" requirement of the CPC Central Committee and the State Council and the principles for ABC's joint-stock reform laid out at the National Financial Work Conference in 2007, ABC drafted a timetable for its joint-stock reform. According to the timetable, ABC would complete the review and approval of the reform plan before the end of June 2008, complete the state capital injection and initiate NPA divestiture before the end of July 2008, and complete the registration as a joint-stock company in 2010.

(I) Asset and Capital Verification before the Joint-Stock Reform

In August 2006, ABC started to gear up for financial restructuring. After evaluating its assets and capital, ABC was ready for financial restructuring by January 2008.

1. External audit

ABC retained Deloitte to complete external audits for the three years from 2005 to 2007, and initiated additional external audits with June 30, 2008 as the benchmark date.

2. NPL survey

From March 2007, ABC carried out risk evaluation, classification, and documentation for each doubtful and loss-category loan throughout the bank, and retained external professional firms for verification. Moreover, it assigned responsibility for emergence of the NPLs and held relevant individuals accountable, paving the way for NPL disposal.

3. Verification and disposal of non-operating assets and other categories of assets

After setting the joint-stock reform in motion, ABC proactively carried out asset, land and property appraisals, actuarial analysis, and due diligence. In January 2008, external professionals submitted preliminary appraisal results for relevant assets, land, and properties. Attorneys completed legal due diligence, and drafted the articles of association for the to-be-established joint-stock company, as well as corporate governance documents in collaboration with ABC, including the rules of procedure for the board of directors, the board of supervisors, and shareholders' meeting. Actuaries completed actuarial analysis of expected liabilities for retirees. ABC also stepped up disposal of special assets (i.e., assets that were acquired for special reasons, such as from lawsuit or foreclosure, that are often priced lower than prevailing market rate) and idle fixed assets, and raced to confirm the ownership rights of land and housing properties. By January 2008, ABC had confirmed the integrated ownership rights of over 90% of its land and buildings.

(II) Capital Injection and Financial Restructuring

1. State capital injection for restructuring capital structure

On November 6, 2008, Central Huijin injected foreign-currency assets equivalent to RMB 130 billion into ABC. At this time, ABC developed a plan on operation and management of foreign-currency capital to avoid risks from the injection. It obtained the "Approval of the MOF on the Adjustment of ABC's Capital Structure," and an exemption from complying with statutory procedures for capital injection granted by the

CBRC and SAIC.

2. NPA disposal by swapping for PBOC loan at an equal value and creating a joint management fund

Given its joint-stock reform experience and conditions, ABC chose to dispose of its NPAs by accepting an equal value of the PBOC loan for the NPAs and creating a joint management fund.

(1) ABC's NPA disposal

On November 21, 2008, with the approval from the MOF, ABC shed NPAs worth RMB 815.70 billion at their book value with December 31, 2007 as the benchmark date. The total amount of NPAs included RMB 217.32 billion doubtful loans, RMB 549.45 billion loss-category loans, and RMB 48.93 billion non-credit assets. Part of the NPAs was swapped for the PBOC's interest-free loan of RMB 150.60 billion supplied to ABC on December 31, 2007. The remaining RMB 665.09 billion formed receivables from the MOF with an annual interest of 3.3% on the outstanding balance accruing from January 1, 2008.

The MOF and ABC created a joint management fund to manage the principal and interest components of funding used for the purchase of NPAs. The lifetime of the joint management fund was set at 15 years, and the sources of funds included ABC's share dividend distribution to the MOF, income tax submission to the central government, and funds recovered from the NPAs purchased by the MOF.

After purchasing the NPAs from ABC, the MOF appointed ABC to act as its agent to perform the duties of creditor and asset owner, but reserved for itself the rights to dispose of or collect upon the NPAs starting January 1, 2008. Recovered cash, net of relevant expenses, would flow into the joint management fund. ABC was required to set up a dedicated department in charge of the management and disposal of the assets, to keep the assets entrusted by the MOF under a dedicated account with separate accounting, to report to the MOF on the disposal and recovery of NPAs on a quarterly basis, and to take all possible actions to maximize the recoverable value of the assets.

(2) Considerations behind the unique method for the disposal of NPAs[1]

ABC and ICBC share similarities in terms of the operation and funding source of their respective joint management fund, but differences still exist. Since the receivables of ABC exceeded that of ICBC, the lifespan of ABC's joint management fund was also comparatively longer, at 15 years. In choosing the entity to execute NPL disposal, ABC's restructuring plan also differed from those of other comparable banks in significant ways. After purchasing the NPLs, the MOF appointed ABC to recover the NPLs, instead of assigning the task to an AMC as it did for other banks.

At a practical level, it would have been be difficult to transfer ABC's NPLs to an AMC. First, the four AMCs only had offices in some provincial capitals without presence below the prefectural level, making it a tall order to recover ABC's large, numerous, and geographically dispersed NPLs, which were mostly in small sums. Second, given the uniqueness of such assets, if an AMC were to take over ABC's NPAs, it would have to incur additional costs to sort out and evaluate such loans, conduct surveys, and compile customer files. What is more, the lack of understanding about the NPLs would also cause the AMC to miss the best timing for disposal.

---

1   Pan Gongsheng: *The Transformation: The Road to Rejuvenation of China's Major Commercial Banks*, China Financial Publishing House, 2012, pp. 61-64.

Third, putting ABC in charge of recovering its NPLs would be conducive to holding relevant individuals accountable for creating the NPLs in the first place and thus prevent moral hazard.

Familiar with the origins of its NPLs, ABC had dedicated agencies and personnel responsible for NPL disposal and recovery, and would insist on fewer cumbersome formalities such as public bidding for NPL transfer, making the transaction less costly and creating jobs for surplus personnel. Given these advantages, the MOF appointed ABC to dispose of and recover NPLs after the divestiture.

"As to the differences between ICBC and ABC in their reform programs, I was struck by their different approaches to NPA disposal," recalled Pan Gongsheng, then Vice Governor of ABC and current Vice Governor of the PBOC, "ICBC followed a similar approach as BOC and CCB by transferring doubtful NPAs to a few AMCs for recovery. But instead of following this model, ABC sold its NPAs to the MOF, which then entrusted ABC to dispose of them on its behalf. To that end, ABC set up a special asset management and disposal department to drive forward this task top-down within its system. This was a nice improvement. Unlike other banks, ABC's NPAs were scattered across wider regions, mostly in the countryside."[1]

(III) Creation of the Joint-Stock Company

1. Preparations

First, ABC created favorable conditions for the joint-stock reform by enhancing internal management and boosting profitability. After achieving

---

1   From the interview with Pan Gongsheng on September 30, 2018.

profitability in 2001, ABC realized RMB 259.1 billion in cumulative operating profits by 2007, with an NPL ratio down from 42.8% in 2001 to 23.6% by the end of 2007. The quality of its newly issued loans significantly improved. Furthermore, ABC streamlined its workforce with headcount reduced from 647,000 in 2000 to 448,000 at the end of 2007, down 199,000 on a cumulative basis. By the end of 2007, ABC completed the centralization of nationwide business data and developed the largest financial service network covering China's urban and rural areas.

Second, ABC accelerated its internal reform. To establish the systems appropriate for a modern financial enterprise, ABC drafted the "Plan on Deepening ABC's Internal Reform," which charted a detailed roadmap and implementation plan for the reform of internal corporate systems. Under this plan, ABC would: (i) formulate a mid- and long-term strategic development plan with clear goals and priorities; (ii) put in place structures and mechanisms needed by modern governance; (iii) revamp its resource allocation system. ABC would take steps to improve the management of economic capital, comprehensive risk provisioning, and performance evaluation guided by risk-adjusted return metrics, and would centralize financial work and create a management accounting system; (iv) carry out ERM planning by taking the first steps toward creating an ERM system and making steady progress in the implementation of the IRB approach; (v) strive to improve internal control and prevent risks, focusing on bolstering the control of the head office and program implementation at the branch level; and (vi) ramp up in-house capabilities and corporate culture. ABC would strive to build a more skilled workforce and modern corporate culture. Meanwhile, it would also improve human resources, the application of new accounting standards, its auditing and internal control systems, and its IT system.

Third, ABC applied for the establishment of the joint-stock company. To be specific: (i) ABC applied to the Ministry of Land and Resources for the approval of its overall plan for disposal of land assets. Approval on the overall plan was received right after ABC's joint-stock reform plan was approved. After the completion of the land valuation report, ABC applied to the Ministry for filing of the land valuation results and approval of its land asset-specific disposal plans. (ii) ABC finalized its asset valuation report and applied to the MOF for approval. (iii) After receiving approval on the asset valuation report, ABC applied to the MOF for approval of its plan for management of ABC shares held by the state. (iv) ABC then applied to the CBRC for the establishment of a joint-stock company. (v) Lastly, ABC applied to SAIC for registration as Agricultural Bank of China Limited.

Fourth, ABC made internal preparations for establishing the joint-stock company. Specifically, (i) ABC created a "3+1" corporate governance structure consisting of the board of directors, the board of supervisors, the shareholders' meeting, and senior management. It helped determine the composition and candidates of the joint-stock company's board of directors, board of supervisors, senior management, and special-purpose committees. (ii) ABC entered into a promoters agreement with the promoters. (iii) ABC organized an audit of the expenses for establishing the joint-stock company, for which the auditor issued a special audit report. (iv) After the MOF approved the plan for management of state-owned ABC shares, ABC engaged auditors to complete capital verification.

2. Official creation of Agricultural Bank of China Limited

Various prerequisites for the establishment of the joint-stock company quickly fell into place. On October 28, 2008, the state capital injection came to a completion. On November 24, the Ministry of Land and Resources approved ABC's land valuation report. On November 26, ABC finalized its valuation report. On November 28, ABC completed its NPA divestiture. On December 8, the MOF approved ABC's asset valuation report and the promoters executed the shareholding agreement. On December 11, the MOF approved ABC's plan for management of state-owned ABC shares. On December 22, the CBRC approved the establishment of Agricultural Bank of China Limited. On December 25, ABC completed the registration of the joint-stock company, and obtained the business license. By the end of December 2008, ABC officially unveiled the joint-stock company.

On January 9, 2009, the founding meeting of the Agricultural Bank of China Limited was held in Beijing, attended by representatives of the MOF and Central Huijin as the promoters. The meeting approved the "Articles of Association of the Agricultural Bank of China Limited (Draft)," together with proposals on the composition of the board of directors and the board of supervisors. This finalized the decision to transform the entirety of ABC from a wholly state-owned commercial bank into a state-controlled joint-stock commercial bank, and to rename the bank as "Agricultural Bank of China Limited (ABC)."

After the founding meeting, ABC convened the first session of its First Board of Directors and the first session of its First Board of Supervisors. The First Board of Directors elected Xiang Junbo as Board Chairman and Zhang Yun as Vice Chairman. The First Board of Supervisors elected Che Yingxin as Chairman of the Board of Supervisors. ABC appointed Zhang Yun as President; Yang Kun, Luo Xi, Zhu Hongbo, Guo Haoda, and Pan Gongsheng as Vice Presidents; and Li Zhenjiang as Secretary of the Board of Directors. The board of directors decided to hold a founding ceremony after the completion of the business registration of Agricultural Bank of China Limited.

On January 15, 2009, the SAIC approved ABC's change of registration information (i.e., from Agricultural Bank of China to Agricultural Bank of China Limited, with other associated changes), and issued a new business license to ABC.

On January 16, 2009, the founding ceremony for Agricultural Bank of China Limited was held in Beijing, which unveiled a new era for ABC's reform and development and marked a solid step toward achieving its long-term goal of creating a world-class commercial bank. At the founding ceremony, a CBRC official read the "Approval of the CBRC of the Reform of Agricultural Bank of China into a Joint-Stock Limited Company" and conferred the financial license to ABC. An official from SAIC recounted the conferment of the corporate business license to ABC. An MOF official announced the names of the members of the board of directors and the board of supervisors. The founding ceremony was also addressed by Vice Governor of the PBOC Su Ning, Vice Minister of Finance Li Yong, Board Chairman of Central Huijin Lou Jiwei, and ABC Chairman Xiang Junbo.

IV. Innovative Introduction of Strategic Investors

(I) Selection of A-Share Strategic Investors

Strategic investors refer to legal entities that are permitted by law to strategically invest in an issuer through private placement. Such investment is bound by the strategic investment and placement agreement executed with the issuer. Pursuing long-term strategic interests, strategic investors maintain close business ties with the issuer, and are motivated to participate and capable of participating in corporate governance.

Following the State Council's instructions on the approved joint-stock reform plan, ABC set down the principles for A-share strategic placement: In the screening of strategic investors, priority would be given to reputable, influential, and financially robust large enterprises, large insurance companies, and leading agricultural enterprises. Using these criteria, ABC created a list of candidate strategic investors, including 22 large SOEs, 6 insurance companies and other financial enterprises, and 6 agricultural enterprises. The final list included the following 27 strategic investors:

Aviation Industry Corporation of China (AVIC), CNPC Asset Management Co., Ltd., Dongfeng Motor Corporation, China Three Gorges Corporation, China Huarong Asset Management Co., Ltd., Tsinghua University Education Foundation (TUEF), Jiangsu Huaxi Group Corp., Guangdong Provincial Communication Group Co., Ltd. (GCGC), China Chengtong Holdings Group Ltd., China Shipbuilding Industry Corporation (CSIC), People's Insurance Company of China (PICC), China Aerospace Science & Industry Corporation (CASIC), China Pacific Life Insurance Co., Ltd., China National Nuclear Corporation (CNNC), China National Tobacco Corporation (CNTC), China Life Insurance Co., Ltd., Minmetals Capital Co., Ltd., China Ocean Shipping (Group) Company (COSCO), China National Cereals, Oils and Foodstuffs Corporation (COFCO), China Southern Power Grid (CSG), China Railway Construction Investment Group Co., Ltd. (CRCC), China Co-op Group Co., Ltd., Jiangsu Credit Re-guarantee Group Co., Ltd., China State Construction

Engineering Corporation (CSCEC), State Grid Asset Management Co., Ltd., Anshan Iron and Steel Group Corporation, and Everbright Financial Holding Asset Management Co., Ltd.

(II) Selection of H-Share Cornerstone Investors

In contrast to strategic investors, cornerstone investors refer to first-rate institutional investors, large conglomerates, high-net-worth individuals or enterprises owned by them. By investing in an IPO company, a cornerstone investor affirms the company's fundamentals and development prospects, which will bolster market confidence about the company. A cornerstone investor should undertake to purchase equity with a lock-up period of 3 to 6 months after the IPO and cannot make multiple subscriptions. More importantly, a cornerstone investor needs to disclose relevant information in the issuing company's prospectus.

Based on the principles laid out in the joint-stock reform plan, ABC determined the criteria for H-share placement to cornerstone investors, which encompassed Hong Kong investors, sovereign wealth funds, international financial institutions, Chinese-funded insurance institutions, and large SOEs.

V. ABC's IPO

On March 31, 2010, the State Council approved ABC's IPO plan. The scheduled IPO dates of July 15 and 16, 2010, however, coincided with the most turbulent period of the global financial crisis triggered by sub-prime mortgage loans in the U.S., which inevitably had a major impact on the IPO.

(I) Deliberation of the IPO Plan

1. Global economic and capital market assessments in the context of the economic crisis

ABC began by looking at performance trends in domestic and overseas capital markets. First, ABC investigated volatility in A-share and H-share markets from January to May 2010, as shown in Figure 6.4.

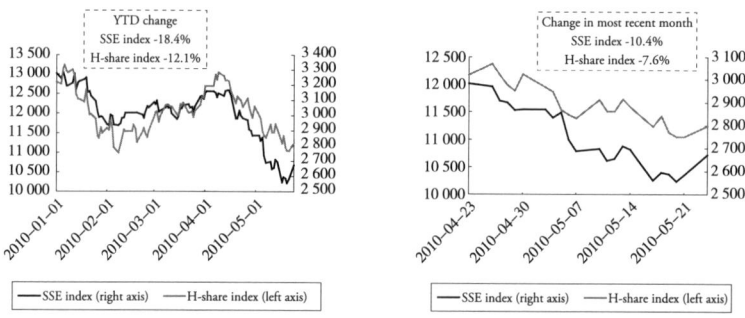

Source: Compiled based on information from ABC.

Fig. 6.4: A-Share and H-Share Market Volatility from January to May 2010

Second, determinants of capital market tendencies. Internationally, the Greek debt crisis was causing market jitters; domestically, uncertainties in macroeconomic regulation were at the forefront, as reflected in the following areas:

(1) Expectations for tightening monetary policies and exchange-rate policies heightened. Market expectations for policy tightening – such as a rate hike – added to the downward pressures. Expectations for renminbi appreciation also gave rise to market uncertainties.

(2) Concerns over the quality of loans from government financing platforms and a credit binge unnerved investors. In 2009, China's banking

sector issued an alarming amount of credit, and particularly, issuance by government financing platforms spiked, raising concerns among domestic and overseas capital markets, especially among foreign investors.

(3) A succession of real estate market regulation policies introduced from mid-April 2010 weighed on the prices of real estate and bank stocks.

(4) As Chinese regulators had yet to release details on follow-up financing of the other major commercial banks, unstable market expectations also suppressed bank stock evaluations.

2. Determination of the IPO plan

After the State Council's special meeting on ABC's reform and development on February 11, 2010, ABC's restructuring leading group drafted the "Request for Instructions on Issues concerning ABC's Joint-Stock Reform" together with relevant government departments, and submitted it to the State Council. The document set a public float between 12% and 18% of ABC's post-IPO total share capital, along with a target date range for ABC's IPO between June and July of the same year.

After the State Council's leaders approved ABC's joint-stock reform plan on March 31, ABC took swift actions to prepare IPO documents for approval and to engage in proactive dialogues with important domestic and overseas investors through various channels, making best efforts to promote ABC's investment value. In this process, the restructuring leading group played a pivotal role. It convened two meetings that settled a number of key matters.

Sufficient early-stage preparations and vigorous government support had expedited ABC's IPO process. On May 4, ABC submitted its IPO materials to the CSRC and HKEX. Based on the IPO timetable and communication with mainland and Hong Kong securities regulators, ABC passed the review of the CSRC's Public Offering Review Committee on June 9 and the HKEX's listing hearing on June 10, and was listed on the two markets on July 15 and 16 respectively.

(1) ABC's public float: The reform plan specified the public float to be in the range of 12% to 18%. In fact, ABC originally considered a 16% target, but in light of market conditions and regulatory requirements, it lowered the ratio to 15%. Considering the performance, capacity, and expected valuations for bank stocks on A-share and H-share markets, ABC decided to offer 7% of its total share capital on the A-share market and 8% on the H-share market.

In terms of the composition of share offering, ABC considered offering around 40% of A-shares and H-shares to strategic investors and cornerstone investors[1] and the rest to ordinary public investors[2] to reduce the impact on capital markets and maintain market stability.

(2) ABC's post-IPO valuation: In gearing up for the IPO, ABC closely followed developments in capital markets. After the global financial crisis in 2008, most leading international banks saw their price-to-book (P/B) ratios dive below 1. The Eurozone sovereign debt crisis increased volatility in international capital markets. A further complicating factor was the aforementioned credit binge and loan issuance from government financing platforms in China, which also aroused concerns among investors about the future asset quality of China's banking sector. On June 9,

---

1   In a strategic placement, the issuer agrees to place a certain number of shares to specific investors at the final issue price, who are required to hold the shares for a lock-up period. Targets for strategic placement of A-shares are called "strategic placement investors"; that for H-shares are called "cornerstone investors."
2   Public investors include A-share offline institutional investors and online retail investors, as well as H-share international institutional investors and Hong Kong's local retail investors.

the average P/B ratio of ICBC, BOC, and CCB was 1.74 (1.80 for ICBC, 1.59 for BOC, and 1.82 for CCB) on the A-share market and 1.85 (2.09 for ICBC, 1.48 for BOC, and 1.97 for CCB) on the H-share market.

(3) The size of ABC's IPO: Based on the assumption of a P/B ratio of roughly 1.6 and a 15% public float before exercising the greenshoe option and a 16.87% public float after exercising it, ABC expected to raise some RMB 145.5 billion from its IPO, including RMB 68.40 billion in A-share offering and RMB 77.10 billion in H-share offering. Excluding the 40% placement for strategic and cornerstone investors, ABC would offer some RMB 41 billion A-shares and RMB 46.30 billion H-shares, or RMB 87.30 billion in total. ABC calibrated the size of its IPO to limit the potential impact on the open market and ensure that its core capital adequacy ratio would be kept above 8.5% and capital adequacy ratio above 11.5% in the subsequent three years.

(4) ABC's strategic placement: Pursuant to the State Council's requirements, ABC approached strategic investors for A-share placement. It succeeded in obtaining letters of intent for share subscription from more than 30 strategic investors with a total share subscription worth RMB 34 billion. These investors mainly included large SOEs, financial institutions, and leading agricultural enterprises with a lock-up period of 12 months for half of them and 18 months for the other half.

Meanwhile, ABC also started to screen H-share cornerstone investors. By region, they included investors from the Middle East, Southeast Asia, Hong Kong, the U.S., Australia, and Europe. By type, they included sovereign wealth funds such as the Qatar Investment Authority (QIA), well-known international institutions as ABC's strategic partners including Rabobank and Standard Chartered Bank, as well as investors and Chinese-funded institutions in Hong Kong, such as Li Ka-shing and China Resources Group. Three types of lock-up period applied, including (1) a 6-month lock-up period for half of the general cornerstone investors and a 12-month lock-up period for the other half; (2) a one-year lock-up period for cornerstone investors having executed a strategic cooperation agreement with ABC; (3) an even longer lock-up period for cornerstone investors with extremely large investments such as the QIA.

(II) Early-Stage Preparations

1. Internal preparations

(1) Selection of external professionals: ABC retained a total of 33 professional firms to work with it on-site. They included:

- Lead underwriters for A-share offering: CICC, CITIC Securities, China Galaxy Securities, and Guotai Junan Securities;
- Financial advisors: China Merchants Securities and Haitong Securities;
- Auditor: Deloitte;
- Issuer's attorney: DeHeng Law Offices;
- Underwriter's attorney: King & Wood Mallesons;
- Financial PR agency: Ever Bloom Investment Consulting Co., Ltd.;
- Underwriters for H-share offering: CICC, Goldman Sachs, Morgan Stanley, JPMorgan Chase, Deutsche Bank, Macquarie, and Agricultural Bank of China International Asset Management Limited;
- Financial advisors: UBS and CITIC Securities International;
- Auditor: Deloitte;
- Issuer's attorneys: Davis Polk and Freshfields law firms;

- Underwriters' attorneys: Herbert Smith, Yang & Associates, and Haiwen & Partners law firms;
- Financial PR agency: Wonderful Sky;
- Roadshow company: Imagination;
- Printing firm: RR Donnelley;
- POWL lead underwriters: Nomura Securities, and Daiwa Securities;
- POWL attorney: Anderson Mori & Tomotsune law firm;
- POWL auditor: Deloitte (Japan);
- POWL printing firm: PRONEXUS.

The underwriting syndicate for ABC's A-share offering consisted of 26 underwriters, including 4 lead underwriters and 22 supporting underwriters; the H-share underwriting syndicate consisted of 34 underwriters, including 7 lead underwriters, 16 co-lead underwriters, and 11 supporting underwriters.

(2) Due diligence: In March 2010, the external parties launched a due diligence program involving 36 departments and 40 branches of ABC[1]. The due diligence focused on six aspects, including bank-wide business, finance, legal compliance, risks, *sannong*, and overall business. They created a due diligence document repository which contained an enormous amount of information, and conducted interviews with the management, departments, branches, and third parties.

(3) Drafting of IPO application documents: Based on the due diligence, ABC worked hard to prepare various application materials. Before

---

1 Including ABC's Changchun Training Institute, Tianjin Training Institute, and Wuhan Training Institute.

May 4, 2010, it prepared a whole set of application documents, including A-share prospectus, H-share prospectus, and documents relating to accountants, attorneys, sponsors, and corporate governance.

(4) Internal review and approval: Since mid-April, ABC held a board of directors meeting and two extraordinary shareholders' meetings to deliberate a host of core proposals, such as investment from the National Council for Social Security Fund (NCSSF) and details of the share offering.

2. External review and approval

(1) Central Huijin: On April 23, Central Huijin provided the seven approval documents to ABC, including the letter of commitment for A-share lock-up period, the letter of commitment for H-share lock-up period, the letter of commitment on state-owned shares transfer, non-compete commitment, photocopy of business license, a letter of declaration, and the PBOC's approval of Central Huijin's functions.

(2) MOF: ABC obtained the MOF's approvals on the domestic and overseas lock-up period commitments and the state-owned equity management plan, approval of an RMB 34.5 billion tax break, approval of state-owned shares transfer, and commitment on the share transfer.

(3) CBRC: ABC obtained the CBRC's approval on information disclosure and other matters, approval of matters related to domestic and overseas public offerings, letter of regulatory opinion, and approval of the qualifications of additional directors.

(4) NCSSF's shareholding and regulatory approval: ABC executed the strategic shareholding agreement with NCSSF, completed the closing of the shareholding transaction, and obtained the CBRC's approval documents in respect of NCSSF's shareholding and the change of regis-

tered capital, as well as the updated business license. ABC also obtained NCSSF's confirmation of state-owned shares transfer.

(5) CSRC: ABC submitted preliminary application and formal application for A-share offering to the public offering department of the CSRC on April 26 and May 4, respectively. The CSRC issued the first round of formal feedback to ABC, which submitted its reply accordingly.

(6) HKEX: ABC submitted preliminary application and formal application for H-share offering to the HKEX on April 26 and May 4, respectively. The HKEX issued the first round of formal feedback to ABC, which submitted its reply accordingly.

(III) The IPO Pitch

1. A-share strategic placement

Pursuant to the joint-stock reform plan, ABC set out the requirements for A-share strategic placement, including the selection criteria for strategic investors, subscription quota, and the lock-up period.

(1) Selection criteria: Priority was given to large SOEs, large insurance companies, and leading agricultural enterprises, particularly well-known, financially robust, and influential enterprises. Following this standard, ABC drafted a list of candidate strategic investors, which included 22 large SOEs, 6 insurance companies and other financial enterprises, and 6 leading agricultural enterprises.

(2) Subscription quota: The subscription quotas were in general set at no less than RMB 2 billion for a large financial institution such as insurance company, in the range from RMB 500 million to RMB 1 billion for a large SOE, and around RMB 500 million for a leading agricultural enterprise or other enterprise. Flexibility was afforded to key strategic investors.

(3) Lock-up period: The lock-up period needed to be as long as possible to maintain stable market price. The lock-up period was set to 12 months for half of the allotted shares and 18 months for the other half. In principle, the lock-up period was to be kept consistent for all strategic investors.

Following the above requirements, ABC sent the letters of invitation and confidentiality undertaking to 34 target investors, who subscribed enthusiastically. Of them, 31 investors subscribed to shares worth a total of RMB 46.60 billion to RMB 54.60 billion, or upwards of RMB 1.5 billion for each investor on average. Some investors placed significant bids. For instance, Huarong placed a bid of RMB 4 billion; China Life Insurance (Group) placed a bid in the range of RMB 3 billion to RMB 8 billion; China National Tobacco Corporation (CNTC) placed a bid in the range of RMB 3 billion to RMB 5 billion.

2. H-Share strategic placement

ABC adopted the following requirements for H-share placement for cornerstone investors: Target investors mainly included Hong Kong's local investors, sovereign wealth funds, well-known international financial institutions, Chinese-funded insurance institutions, and large SOEs. The subscription quota for each cornerstone investor was generally no less than USD 100 million with a lock-up period of one year. Accordingly, ABC sent letters of invitation and confidentiality undertaking to 29 target cornerstone investors.

3. Communication with strategic investors and analysts

According to the listing requirements of SSE and HKEX, ABC's executives held dozens of one-on-one meetings and small group meetings in Hong Kong, Australia, the U.S., Europe, and the Middle East from mid-

April to May, and met with 48 large international investment institutions. In early May, they held dozens of investor meetings in Singapore and Hong Kong, and met with 38 important international investors. They also engaged international institutional investors that had come to China, such as Capital Research.

In addition, recognizing the major influence of the valuation and research reports of analysts on ABC's final valuation and successful IPO, ABC held meetings with analysts from the seven H-share lead underwriters and the four A-share lead underwriters to pitch its investment value and create a positive impression. On May 18, ABC held meetings with analysts from A-share and H-share underwriting syndicates to pitch its investment story and competitive strengths, explain the factors that might influence ABC's investment value, and answer questions. On such basis, analysts from underwriters drafted their research reports from an objective perspective.

(IV) IPO Launch

On July 15, 2010, ABC officially started trading on the A-share market, and on July 16, ABC began trading on the H-share market, thus successfully completing its IPO process. ABC set its A-share issue price range from RMB 2.52 to RMB 2.68 per share, and the final issue price was RMB 2.68 per share, corresponding to a P/B ratio of 1.59 as of 2010 year-end (after the greenshoe option had been fully exercised). ABC set its H-share issue price range to be HKD 2.88 to HKD 3.48 per share, and the final issue price was HKD 3.20 per share, corresponding to a P/B ratio of 1.66 as of 2010 year-end (after the greenshoe option had been fully exercised). ABC's H-share pricing reflected nearly a 4% premium as compared with A-share pricing.

In total, ABC raised the equivalent of USD 22.1 billion from its A+H share offering, succeeding ICBC as the largest IPO in the world and breaking many Chinese and foreign capital market records. For instance, it became the largest A-share IPO (RMB 68.5 billion after the greenshoe option was exercised), the largest H-share cornerstone investment (USD 5.45 billion), the largest H-share single cornerstone investment (the Qatar Investment Agency subscribed to USD 2.8 billion shares), the largest A-share strategic placement (RMB 27.40 billion, accounting for 40% of total proceeds raised from the A-share offering after the greenshoe option was exercised), the largest number of investors for strategic A-share placement (27), as well as the first implementation of the greenshoe option and introduction of strategic placement mechanism for the A-share market after the CSRC's IPO reform in 2009.

Then Vice President of ABC and current Vice Governor of the PBOC Pan Gongsheng made the following remark on ABC's successful IPO under challenging conditions: "ABC raised a total of USD 22.1 billion from its initial public offering, which was the largest in the world at the time. Specifically, it raised USD 10.10 billion from the A-share market and USD 12 billion from the H-share market. ABC's successful IPO amid challenging market conditions presented an instructive case, and can be attributed to the following six factors: first, China's rapid economic growth, restructuring, and upgrade; second, China's banking sector's great growth potential and development prospects; third, the well-crafted IPO plan; fourth, the carefully prepared investment story; fifth, the intensive IPO pre-marketing campaign that reached a broad audience; sixth, well-grounded and reasonable pricing."[1]

Regarding the great significance of ABC's domestic and overseas IPO, Pan Gongsheng wrote in his book *The Transformation: The Road to Rejuvenation of China's Major Commercial Banks*: "ABC's successful IPO marks the successful completion of the reform and public listings of China's large commercial banks after the eight years of hard work following the decision adopted at the second National Financial Work Conference in 2002. This is a milestone achievement in China's financial reform, and is of great significance to bolstering the core competitiveness and opening up of China's financial sector as a whole. It will surely leave an indelible mark in China's financial development history."[2]

---

1 From the interview with Pan Gongsheng on September 30, 2018.
2 Pan Gongsheng: *The Transformation: The Road to Rejuvenation of China's Major Commercial Banks*, China Financial Publishing House, 2012, p. 278.

CHAPTER VII
STRENGTHENING THE FOUNDATION

– Development of Corporate Governance and Internal Risk Controls in Major Commercial Banks

The joint-stock reform not only enabled state-owned banks to complete financial restructuring, offload non-performing assets, and rebuild balance sheets, but, more importantly, also empowered them to reshape the established institutions to create modern corporate governance structures, risk controls, and accountability systems. In conjunction with their financial restructuring, introduction of strategic investors, and public listing, the Big Five focused on developing sound corporate governance, risk management, and internal control systems and bringing themselves up to international standards in the critical areas, such that every management level, process, and person would have clear risk control responsibilities and could be held accountable.

Section I
Development of
Corporate Governance Systems

While financial restructuring, joint-stock reform, and even public listing brought unprecedented institutional changes to China's SOCBs, they each were but only a single part in the sweeping banking reform, not the ultimate goal. Rather, the motivation and ultimate objective of the banking reform is to establish effective corporate governance by creating sound governance structures and mechanisms[1].

Sound structures and effective mechanisms built on the foundation of diversified ownership are at the heart of governance and a deciding factor for governance efficiency. Indeed, ownership diversification, conversion to a joint-stock company, and the subsequent public listing are the path toward building a modern financial institution. Only a diversified ownership structure makes possible the establishment of a governance body with clearly defined authorities and responsibilities as well as effective power of oversight, the creation of a "web of supervision" comprising shareholders, regulators, the public, and other stakeholders, and the synergy of restraints, internal oversight, and market discipline that pressure and motivate a company to enhance its governance.

However, conversion to a diversified ownership structure only contributes to improved governance, but does not necessarily lead to better business operations and performance, or solve all the problems faced by

---

1   Jiang Jianqing: *Banking Footprints – Thought and Reflection on China's Financial Sector Reform*, China Financial Publishing House, 2016.

commercial banks. The facile, dismissive, and ideology-driven correlation often drawn between private ownership and economic efficiency has been proven false by China and many other countries undergoing economic transformation. Capital injection and the joint-stock reform are akin to "giving a man a fish"; to revitalize the banks, it is necessary to "teach them how to fish" by helping them build robust corporate governance structures and mechanisms. Therefore, at the inception of the joint-stock reform, the government unequivocally stated in the "Master Plan for Implementing the Joint-Stock Reform of Bank of China and China Construction Bank" that the principal goal of the reform is to create a modern corporate governance structure and a modern system for financial enterprises.

Related Topic: Excerpt of Liu Mingkang's Speech at the Beijing International Financial Forum in 2004[1]

This round of state capital injection is different from the issuance of RMB 270 billion in special government bonds to replenish the capital of the Big Four in 1998 and the disposal of RMB 1.3 trillion NPAs from 1999 to 2000. The first two rounds of capital injection aimed to mitigate financial risks, and did little to address the banks' institutional problems... The current round of capital injection is only one step in the overall reform of the two banks to improve their asset-liability position and create the conditions for accelerating the joint-stock reform.

In this round of reform, the two banks have focused on deepening internal reforms, creating a sound corporate governance structure, and transforming operational mechanisms. This requires the two pilot commercial

---

1   *Financial News*, May 20, 2004.

banks to give equal importance to reform and management, and speed up NPL disposal...They should race to create a modern corporate governance structure, expedite establishment of internal controls, and enhance external supervision to ensure that state-injected funds remain safe and earn a decent return, and ensure that their investment on the governance mechanism pays off...

The governance problems of SOCBs are closely related to and stem from the development of the modern corporate governance system. Similar issues can also be found in SOEs. At the heart of the problems facing China's SOCBs are defects in their ownership and governance systems... In the current reform of the commercial banks, the core element that we have identified is to create an effective corporate governance system. After the financial restructuring, we will require SOCBs to step up the reform of their corporate governance and overhaul their governance structure, management system, and operational mechanism in a thorough and compliant manner.

I. Building an Effective and Accountable Governance Structure

At the end of 2003, the CPC Central Committee and the State Council chose BOC and CCB as the pilot banks for the joint-stock reform. This decision was officially announced by the State Council in January 2004, marking the start of not only this program which took years in the making, but also the governance reform of the SOCBs. Since then, each SOCB, propelled by the support policies and the pressure that came with the joint-stock reform, would leverage its own adaptation of the reform, the creation of joint-stock companies, and the subsequent domestic and overseas listings to develop its governance structure and workings.

The first state-owned bank to seek better corporate governance practices was in fact BoCom. In 1994, BoCom consolidated its head office, branches, and sub-branches, which had been operating as separate companies in a tiered setup, into a single corporate entity. The bank set up a board of directors and a board of supervisors right at the start, and later added a shareholders' meeting. The board of directors consisted of 19 members, 7 to 9 of whom would serve on the executive committee which performed the powers and duties of the board when not in session. The board of supervisors was composed of shareholder representatives and five employee representatives, and two out of those five would be democratically elected by employees. With these three bodies in place, along with the management, BoCom had established a preliminary "3+1" corporate governance framework that would be typically found in companies at later times. But limited by the prevailing economic environment and the lack of sophisticated regulation and oversight in the area of governance, BoCom's corporate governance model was very much a work-in-progress.

Genuine corporate governance structure was established during the joint-stock reform, and can be given the specific date of August 26, 2004, when BOC completed its reform and was transformed from a wholly state-owned bank into a joint-stock bank. This transformation also signaled the emergence of the first board of directors and board of supervisors among SOCBs, as well as the first true articles of association of a joint-stock company.

By combining their particular circumstances with the internal control-centric German-Japanese governance model and the external control-focused Anglo-American model, BOC and CCB established their standardized shareholders' meeting, board of directors, and board of supervisors in 2004, followed by ICBC in 2005, and thus each created a basic

"3+1" governance structure. Within this structure, the shareholders' meeting is the supreme governing body which has final decision-making power over material matters. The board of directors is the decision-making body which is accountable to the shareholders' meeting. The board of supervisors is the supervisory body which reports to the shareholders' meeting. Management is the executive organ which is accountable to the board of directors.

Later, in 2009 as part of its joint-stock reform, ABC incorporated its agricultural mandates and business objectives into the governance structure, by setting up under its board of directors the Sannong Financial Development Committee, thus creating a modern yet highly distinctive governance structure and operational framework. With it, the Big Five had all established their own "3+1" governance structure. Each component – shareholders' meeting, board of directors, board of supervisors, and management – would play its own part, either as the decision-making body, supervisory body, or executive body, in a coordinated manner to ensure the banks would be well managed (Fig. 7.1).

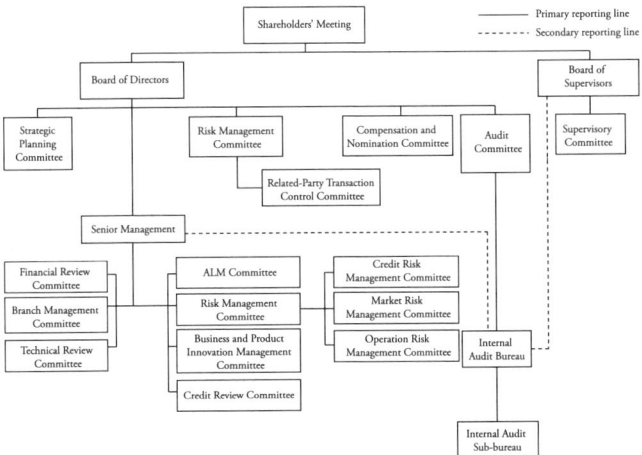

Fig. 7.1: ICBC Corporate Governance Structure after Joint-Stock Reform

(I) Shareholders and Shareholders' Meeting

To create effective and responsible governance structures, China's SOCBs started with the ownership reform. Before the joint-stock reform, the MOF was the capital contributor to the Big Four. After the banks were transformed into joint-stock limited companies and brought in strategic investors, Central Huijin and some overseas strategic partners took stakes in the banks. At the beginning of its restructuring, BoCom's shareholders included local governments and enterprise legal persons, making its equity structure more dispersed than other banks. The Big Five saw their equity structure further diversify after successfully going public. Under the *Company Law*, the shareholders' meeting is the supreme governing body of a company. It has the power to select directors and supervisors and determine their compensation, and make decisions on such important matters as operational strategies, financing, and dividend distribution. Under the new governance structure, major shareholders on behalf of the national interest and other shareholders will take part in the managerial decision-making of major state-owned banks through deliberation and voting at the shareholders' meeting or dispatching directors and supervisors.

(II) Board of Directors

The board of directors is a company's decision-making body answerable to its shareholders' meeting. In an interview with McKinsey[1], then ICBC Board Chairman Jiang Jianqing commented: "I see the board of directors as the company's soul. Effective corporate governance is highly cor-

---

1 Bao Damin, Wang Yi & Ye Mei: "Corporate Governance and Financial Crisis in the Eyes of a Chinese National: An Interview with ICBC Board Chairman," *The McKinsey Quarterly*, 2009 (2).

related with the composition of the board, which influences its operation, decision-making style, and efficiency. The competency of board members determines the authority and performance of the board. A sound board structure should have the qualities of independence, professionalism, ethical conduct, integrity, and dedication." Years later, he added: "Corporate governance makes us reflect upon workplace democracy and listen to different voices in making decisions. Although some suggestions may not be without flaws, this mechanism has produced benefits and created supervision on the use of power."

In reviewing the articles of association of the SOCBs, the CBRC paid special attention to the board structure, requiring the banks to create a professional and diversified board of directors comprising directors representing state-owned shareholders, executive directors concurrently acting as senior officers, directors representing strategic investors, and independent directors, to ensure effective board operation. According to Central Huijin President Xie Ping, he suggested to the former PBOC Governor Zhou Xiaochuan that officials familiar with economic affairs from the MOF, PBOC, SAFE, and other ministries and commissions related to economic affairs should be appointed as independent directors. Under the framework designed by Central Huijin, the board of directors consists of directors representing shareholders, directors concurrently acting as senior officers, and independent directors. In this manner, key matters related to the shareholders' meeting and the board of directors have been settled[1].

The CBRC also emphasized the appointment of foreign directors.

---

1 Quoted from Xie Ping's narrations from April to October 2012, provided by the Boyuan Economic Research Foundation.

After the joint-stock reform, with encouragement from the CBRC and authorizations from the shareholders' meetings, the banks recruited a group of international academic and industry experts to serve as directors or independent directors. For instance, ICBC hired John Thornton, Chairman of the Board of Trustees of the Brookings Institution; BOC recruited Suzanne Labarge, Vice Chairman and Chief Risk Officer of the Royal Bank of Canada; BoCom engaged Peter Nolan, Director of the Centre of Development Studies, University of Cambridge, as independent directors.

Most of the foreign directors were experts with managerial experience in various domains, and some served as senior officers at leading international banks. For instance, Christopher Cole, a shareholder-appointed director from Goldman Sachs to ICBC, boasted some 30 years of experience in investment banking. Laura May Lung Cha, a shareholder-appointed director from HSBC to BoCom, had a 25-year career in the legal field and capital markets. Alberto Togni, an independent director recommended by UBS to BOC, possessed a 40-year track record in bank management. Foreign directors and state-owned shareholder appointed directors breathed new vitality into the corporate governance of the banks, broadened their strategic horizon, and contributed to the performance and decision-making capacity of their boards with their vast experience, expertise, and market insights.

(III) Special Committees under Boards of Directors

Following the CBRC's requirements, the Big Five set up special committees under their board of directors, including a strategic planning committee, a compensation and nomination committee, an audit committee, a risk management committee, and a related-party transaction control committee. Among them, the compensation and nomination committee, the audit committee, and the related-party transaction control committee should, in principle, be chaired by independent directors.

On November 15, 2005, for instance, the second meeting of the first board of directors convened by ICBC Chairman Jiang Jianqing created their audit committee, risk management committee, and related-party transaction control committee chaired by independent director Antony Leung Kam-Chung, as well as compensation committee chaired by independent director Qian Yingyi. These independent directors have provided important consultation and advice to the board of directors, and enhanced checks and balances in its decision-making process.

At a board meeting of ICBC, independent director Leung suggested that the goal stated in ICBC's strategic plan to "develop into a world-class bank" was too vague, and should be decomposed into component-specific concepts and indicators. His proposal was echoed by many directors. After the meeting, ICBC's strategic planning department revised the goal to make it clearer, more specific, and feasible. Establishment of the board special committees ensured a rational and fact-based operation of the board of directors, as well as the exercise of its guiding and supervisory functions.

Throughout 2006, ICBC, BOC, CCB, and BoCom each held close to 10 board meetings and more than 20 special committee meetings. On average, each bank's board of directors deliberated nearly 50 proposals, and their special committees deliberated over 50 proposals. The board of directors could make decisions on major issues, serving as the core of corporate governance. Taking ICBC as an example, from its creation as a joint-stock limited company on October 25, 2005 to the end of 2006, its board of directors and special committees convened 38 meetings and adopted 85 resolutions. Based on its experience of various board meetings, ICBC's board of directors identified problems and improved its work approach, thus ensuring an effective, compliant, and better decision-making process at board meetings.

As then ICBC President Yang Kaisheng recalled, "Some proposals approved by the CPC committee would be denied by the board, but they accounted for a small share. We put them aside. If we considered it necessary to pass a denied proposal, we would persuade the board of directors and suggest that the proposal be deliberated at the subsequent board meeting."[1] By continuously benchmarking internationally advanced corporate governance theories and practices, the board of directors grew out of a mere "rubber stamp" role. Instead, it ensured the participation of all stakeholders in the decision-making process, and vigorously promoted standardized operations, rational and evidence-based decision-making, and risk prevention at the banks.

(IV) Board of Supervisors

Each of the Big Five established a board of supervisors accountable to the shareholders' meeting. As the supervisory body, the board of supervisors is responsible for overseeing the banks' financial activities, risk management, and internal controls, as well as the performance of duties by the board of directors, management, and their members. The board of supervisors consists of professionals, including supervisors appointed by shareholders, external supervisors, and supervisors representing employees. Such a composition ensures considerable independence for the board of

---

[1] From the interview with Yang Kaisheng on March 15, 2017.

supervisors. The major commercial banks each have a board of supervisors that has explored innovative ways of supervision, created and improved supervisory rules and measures for due diligence, established due diligence archives for directors and the senior officers, and followed various approaches in conducting supervision.

By dispatching supervisors to attend shareholders' meetings and board meetings as non-voting participants, the board of supervisors reviewed the performance of duties and due diligence by the members of the board of directors and management, as well as the financial activities and audits of the banks. It scored the members of the board of directors and management by the metrics of mindset and attitude, performance, competency, and contribution.

"Supervisors have the maximum privileges of access to information and documentation," said Wang Chixi, ICBC's supervisor. "We regularly inspect risk management, internal controls, and related-party transactions. Where necessary, we may ask for detailed explanations on suspicious matters. Each year, we ask our external auditors to report four or five times on the bank's financial status and operational metrics such as assets, allowances, asset quality, and risk exposure. We may also challenge the procedure of a specific decision, such as who made a decision for what reason."[1] In addition, retired and former directors, presidents, and other members of the management must receive an audit of the board of supervisors. Any violations of laws and regulations discovered during the audit will be submitted to management and the board of directors for deliberation through

---

1   Cited from the International Institute for Management Development: *ICBC: Oriental Governance Experience Worth Referencing for the West.*

a proposal. If the board of supervisors fails to perform its duty of supervision and inspection, the CBRC will hold a hearing and summon the supervisors to offer an explanation.

Unlike the corporate governance structure prevailing in European and North American banking sectors, China's commercial banks have both a board of directors and a board of supervisors. At the beginning, some expressed doubts over the lack of clarity in the functions and powers of the board of supervisors. Antony Leung Kam-Chung, a former director of ICBC, said: "Initially, I had no idea about why the board of supervisors was set up in parallel to the board of directors for the purposes of managing the banks. Later, I realized the board of supervisors was very useful and clearly not a bad thing. The board of supervisors has the power to monitor the board of directors and its members. Under the Western corporate governance structure, there is no similar institution. Sometimes, though not common, the members of the board of directors at Western companies would be directly appointed by the CEO, and had to defer to the CEO. In China, however, the board of supervisors has legal authority to enforce checks and balances."[1]

Talking about the work procedure, Leung said, "They (supervisors) normally do not participate in discussions of the board of directors. But since they are genuine full-time employees, they may submit motions to help the banks better focus on strategic management. Once again, the exercise of this function relies on the professional qualities of supervisors. As I remember, some supervisors pointed out problems that not even

---

1 Cited from the International Institute for Management Development: *ICBC: Oriental Governance Experience Worth Referencing for the West.*

members of the board of directors had discovered. The reason is that independent directors were part-time directors and shareholder-appointed directors lacked enough experience in the banking sector. Supervisors are more familiar with their banks and boast professional competence and experience. For these reasons, full-time supervisors offer a unique advantage."[1]

"In my opinion, the board of supervisors of major Chinese banks represents a best practice of corporate governance," said Wang Chixi. "With strict implementation, a high degree of authority, and a professional team consisting of full-time and part-time members, the board of supervisors restricts and prevents misconduct and the abuse of power. The board of supervisors is an indispensable force in improving corporate governance."[2] After the Big Five completed the joint-stock reform and IPOs, their boards of supervisors proactively offered opinions and inputs to relevant organs, branches and sub-branches concerning the problems discovered during supervision and inspection. For important matters or matters that required attention, the boards of supervisors timely prompted, consulted, and reported to the boards of directors and management. By deepening the practice of corporate governance and particularly checks and balances, the banks have improved the proactive performance of duties by directors, supervisors, and senior officers, thus contributing to the upgrade of their corporate governance.

---

1 Cited from the International Institute for Management Development: *ICBC: Oriental Governance Experience Worth Referencing for the West.*
2 Ibid.

(V) Senior Officers

After launching the joint-stock reform, the state-owned banks started to plan for market-based recruitment of professionals, calling for veteran international bankers to assist their market-oriented reform and international development. Various banks announced plans to recruit senior officers worldwide. Centrally managed officials were no longer the sole candidates for the management teams of the banks.

BOC took the first bold step in the market-based recruitment of senior officers after the joint-stock reform. In 2004, BOC decided to recruit its chief credit officer globally, and after extensive screening, appointed Lonnie Dounn to take the office. In February 2005, BOC signed a recruitment contract with him.

Under the leadership of BOC's president, Lonnie Dounn was put in charge of the Risk Management Department and Loan Administration Department at the BOC head office. He was responsible for the review and approval of loans, and worked extensively to enhance centralized, professional, and independent risk management. In September 2006, Lonnie Dounn resigned from his position. Despite his short tenure of only over a year, many Chinese colleagues who worked with him spoke highly of his professionalism and significant role in designing BOC's loan business. "When provincial governors came to Xiao Gang asking for loans," recalled Xie Ping, "he referred them to the chief credit officer, Lonnie Dounn, who stood firmly by his principles."[1]

---

1 Quoted from Xie Ping's narrations from April to October 2012, provided by the Boyuan Economic Research Foundation.

(VI) CPC Committee and Discipline Inspection Commission

Under the new governance structure, the CPC committee continued to exist as the political organ of the major commercial banks. By providing opinions on critical business decisions such as the appointment of senior officers, the CPC committee ensures that corporate decisions comply with national policies, guidelines, and regulations. It also supports management decision-making, and maintains its stability. As pilot banks for the joint-stock reform, BOC and CCB created their board of directors, board of supervisors, and shareholders' meeting, forming a basic "3+1" governance framework. As the new governance framework took shape, the two banks faced transient controversies over the necessity of the CPC committee and the discipline inspection department[1].

Despite the controversies, the Big Five retained their CPC committees and discipline inspection departments. Facts have proven that the CPC committee and the discipline inspection commission have played a pivotal role in the corporate governance of the Big Five, which came up with new ways to integrate the CPC committee's leadership with the modern corporate governance system.

First, the CPC committee and the board of directors share common goals in the governance of the banks, which constitute the foundation for balancing their relationship. The CPC committee and the board of directors are two statutory bodies of major commercial banks, and both bodies

---

1 As Wang Hongzhang, then Secretary of the PBOC CPC Discipline Inspection Commission, recalled, CCB and BOC faced controversies during their joint-stock reform. As the two created a standard corporate governance system consisting of the board of directors, the board of supervisors, and the management for their reform and listings, some questioned the necessity of the CPC committee and the discipline inspection commission, the relationship between the CPC committee and the board of directors in corporate governance, among other issues.

share the same goals. The board of directors assumes legal responsibilities for the banks, and performs functions on behalf of shareholders to ensure the sustainable and healthy development of the banks. The CPC committee is a body dispatched by the CPC to the banks in accordance with the *Company Law* and other laws, and shares the goal of ensuring that the banks develop toward the right direction and thrive. In this sense, the two bodies share the same fundamental goals.

The necessity of the CPC committee's leadership was easier to understand for the Chinese officials and employees than for the foreign members involved in the banks' corporate governance structure. As Peng Chun, a BoCom executive, recalled, foreign directors and executives could not make sense of the CPC committee's leadership system at Chinese commercial banks. "Why am I not invited to BoCom's meetings?" asked a vice president of BoCom from HSBC. "These meetings are CPC committee meetings," explained Peng, "only Party members are invited, but you may attend important meetings as an observer." In subsequent meetings, BoCom's CPC committee sometimes invited this vice president to its meetings to help him understand the committee's important role, or briefed him on the meetings afterward. After some time, senior officers from HSBC – including this vice president – came to appreciate BoCom's "Party's leadership over everything" model. "When I mentioned the CPC committee's role in BoCom's corporate governance in a chat with Sir John Bond from HSBC," recalled Peng, "he thought our CPC committee plays a similar role as HSBC's Group Management Board. Our chairman is like the Director of their Group Management Board, which deliberates all important issues before their submission to the shareholders' meeting, the board of directors, or management, a practice which is no different from that of our CPC committee."

Second, the demarcation of responsibilities is the key to coordinating the CPC committee with the board of directors. Despite the same goals, the two bodies have different responsibilities and functions, and cannot replace each other. BOC summarized its governance experience as follows: "For the state-controlled banks, the CPC committee is responsible for matters regarding overall direction, mindset, human resources, coordination, and Party development – these responsibilities are beyond the scope of work for the board of directors. In terms of overall direction, the Committee should ensure that the Party's lines, guidelines, and policies are implemented within the banking system through Party organizations at various levels. In terms of mindset, the Committee should conduct ideological work among Party members and employees, and arouse their enthusiasm, initiative, and creativity. In terms of human resources, the Committee should create a talent pool composed of managers, professionals, and employees at all levels. The board of directors only considers and approves the appointment of personnel above vice president level, leaving the management of department and branch managers to the CPC committees at various levels. In terms of coordination, the Committee should coordinate the interests of the intertwined stakeholders after the creation of the joint-stock company, including the state-owned shareholders, foreign shareholders, and the general public shareholders. In addition, because the banks are supervised by their boards of supervisors, various regulators, as well as internal organizations representing different employee interests, such as the trade union and youth, women and retired officials' organizations, the Committee is also required to coordinate with these stakeholders. In terms of Party development, the Committee should enhance Party organizations and the team of Party members."[1]

Third, the assumption of Party secretary and board chairman positions by the same person is a smart institutional arrangement for coordinating the CPC committee with the board of directors. After the joint-stock reform, the board chairmen of the Big Five have concurrently acted as Party secretaries. Some members of the CPC committee at the head office assume positions at the board of directors, the board of supervisors, and management in accordance with statutory procedures. This institutional arrangement where one person wears two hats facilitates communication and coordination between the board of directors and the CPC committee, and causes both bodies to fulfill their respective responsibilities under the same goals.

Fourth, the deliberation of major issues by the CPC committee before the board of directors is a necessary procedure for adhering to the Party's leadership and coordinating the CPC committee with the board of directors. While improving corporate governance, the Big Five developed a mature operational mechanism, in which the CPC committee supports the board of directors, the board of supervisors, and management in lawfully performing their respective functions. For major decisions and issues, the CPC committee must reach consensus through collective deliberation, listen to feedback from various stakeholders, and submit the matters to the board of directors for deliberation in accordance with prescribed procedures.

"Since its first meeting, ICBC's board of directors has adopted the

---

1   Xiao Gang: *Changing Bank of China*, CITIC Press, 2011.

following principle (which is now called for by President Xi Jinping): in the decision-making procedure, the Party organization should precede the board of directors and management in deliberating major issues. Key business issues must be reviewed by the Party organization before being submitted to the board of directors or management for final decisions. ... This practice not only meets the requirements of modern corporate governance, but reflects Chinese characteristics – upholding the Party's leadership over joint-stock SOEs,"[1] recalled Yang Kaisheng, former President of ICBC. Since 2017, the Big Five have revised their articles of association to establish the "core leadership role of the CPC committee."

Fifth, smooth communication is essential to ensuring consistent understanding between the CPC committee and the board of directors. With different professional backgrounds, knowledge structure, professional experience and personal inclinations, the CPC committee, the board of directors and the board of supervisors may view and handle specific matters in different ways. They are independent from each other, and cannot force each other to agree. The only way to reach a consensus among them is to create a smooth communication mechanism. "Facts have proven that the most effective way to reach an agreement is to communicate repeatedly," said then BOC Chairman Xiao Gang. "We must rely on communication, mechanisms, and checks and balances to align our understanding and bridge our differences."

From their governance experience, the Big Five came to realize that the role of the discipline inspection department should be enhanced rather than diminished after their joint-stock reform and IPOs. Discipline

---

[1] From the interview with Yang Kaisheng on March 15, 2017.

inspection played a significant role in corporate governance, compliance, investigation of violations, and integrity and self-discipline. The discipline inspection system gave play to the CPC committee's pivotal role in political guarantee and leadership. The CPC committee, the discipline inspection department, the board of directors, the board of supervisors and management maintained smooth communication, coordination, and mutual support with each other.

The Big Five defined a reasonable boundary of responsibilities between the CPC committee and the "3+1" governance structure. They effectively maintained the CPC committee's key role in political leadership over corporate governance without excessive intervention in market-based decisions, forming a coordinated, mutually checked and balanced corporate governance system with Chinese characteristics.

(VII) Strategic Investors

Introducing strategic foreign investors was a critical step in reforming the banking sector. Apart from the investment, strategic foreign investors also brought new governance concepts, better governance structure, better business models, advanced technologies, innovative products, and banking expertise to the banks. Associating Chinese banks with reputable international brands also helped their IPOs at the beginning of the joint-stock reform. Central Huijin suggested that a strategic foreign investor may nominate a director if holding a 5% stake, and may nominate two directors and one member of the management if holding a 10% stake.

After CCB inked an investment and strategic assistance agreement with Bank of America (BofA), both sides carried out extensive strategic assistance and cooperation in such areas as corporate governance, risk management, credit card business, personal banking business, global treasury services, and information technology. Among their 26 assistance projects, the transformation of retail outlets, the development of personal loan centers, and the improvement of call centers were the three critical pilot projects in which both sides invested a great deal of human resources.

The transformation of retail outlets, for instance, aimed to shift business lines of CCB outlets from settlement and transactions to marketing and services. By improving sales and service efficiency, CCB's goal was to raise customer satisfaction. Under the guidance of American experts, CCB introduced the "Six Sigma" approach for project implementation and management. Delivering efficient, convenient, and quality services to customers is a basic requirement of business process design and transformation. Before the implementation of three critical projects including the transformation of retail outlets, both sides carried out face-to-face interviews with over 3,200 customers in Beijing, Shanghai and four other cities, interviewed more than 4,500 customers via telephone, and collected 7,400 valid questionnaires. The market survey identified the critical demand of customers for the three projects, offered an important basis for determining project goals, and implemented CCB's customer-centric business approach.

On August 24, 2006, CCB and BofA inked an agreement in Hong Kong for the acquisition of 100% equity of Bank of America (Asia) ("BofA (Asia)"), a wholly-owned Hong Kong subsidiary of Bank of America, and of its affiliates. On December 29, 2006, both sides completed the acquisition, and BofA (Asia) was renamed as China Construction Bank

(Asia) Corporation Limited. "CCB will not copy BofA's experience for project implementation. Based on its unique circumstances and business development strategies, CCB will draw upon BofA's advanced experience to improve its business process and competitiveness," a CCB manager told reporters.

As ICBC's strategic investor, Goldman Sachs agreed to provide technical support, consulting services, and employee training, develop non-lending products, foster a corporate culture with risk awareness, and improve the risk management system and corporate governance structure. Both sides identified seven areas of strategic cooperation and support, including corporate governance, risk management, treasury business, asset management, corporate and investment banking, NPL disposal and training.

Corporate governance: Goldman Sachs presented its corporate governance rules and best practices as instructive materials, and helped ICBC to improve its auditing and reporting systems in line with the latest IFRS, including the design of new procedures and detailed implementation guidance.

Risk management: Goldman Sachs advised ICBC to: create an effective internal reporting system, develop a risk structure for credit, market and operational risks in accordance with the New Basel Capital Accord, and draft rules for the risk management committee.

Treasury business: ICBC and Goldman Sachs jointly developed renminbi-denominated structural investment products linked to foreign exchange derivatives.

NPL disposal: Goldman Sachs designed independent and combined approaches to disposal of NPLs. As part of its strategic support, Goldman Sachs appointed three experts as full-time advisors for ICBC.

Knowledge transfer was more broad-ranging. Goldman Sachs agreed to dispatch at least 50 employees as ICBC's senior advisors responsible for offering training and technical support, and initiate no fewer than 50 training programs for key business areas. ICBC would send at least 50 senior officers to attend leadership development programs at Goldman Sachs, and appoint 50 employees to receive training in key business areas for three to six months at the head office or other locations of Goldman Sachs.

In 2004, BoCom introduced HSBC as its strategic investor, which marked the prelude to their strategic cooperation. Through their cooperation, BoCom expected to learn from the advanced systems and experiences of leading international financial institutions and to make itself, and even the entire Chinese banking sector, more enticing to investors from Hong Kong and international investors. But other considerations were at play, too. "HSBC was familiar with the Asia-Pacific region, and especially China's national conditions and culture," recalled Hu Huaibang, BoCom Chairman at the time. The partnership turned out to be a win-win deal for both sides without causing any cultural conflict, and greatly contributed to BoCom's development.

After partnering with HSBC, BoCom created a set of mechanisms for strategic, business, and structural cooperation to incorporate capital, expertise and systems from HSBC. In August 2004, HSBC bought a USD 1.747 billion stake in BoCom to become its second-largest shareholder after the MOF. This acquisition marked the completion of HSBC's investment in BoCom. Afterward, by incorporating HSBC's expertise, BoCom drew on the first-hand experience and best practices of the leading international financial conglomerate, and by introducing the conglomerate's advanced management systems, achieved comprehensive improvement to its business management.

In terms of risk management, HSBC appointed Cao Guohong as an advisor for BoCom's enterprise risk management (ERM) program. Through mutual visits and exchanges between the leadership and working teams, both sides created a regular communication mechanism at the working level to share risk and compliance management experience and exchange views. After the centralized training and exchange system was put into place, HSBC assisted BoCom in accommodating shareholders' risk preferences, establishing a risk filtering and monitoring list, moving the risk management to the early rather than later stages of each process, adopting advanced systems and tools to measure credit cost and make sufficient and timely provision for losses, and enhancing the risk constraint concept.

HSBC carried out special training for the senior officers of BoCom's domestic and overseas branches to share experience and practices in identifying credit risks, financial statement fraud, trade financing risks and group customer risks, and conducting anti-money laundering (AML) and fraud-countermeasure initiatives. Supported by the strategic cooperation and communication mechanism with HSBC, BoCom optimized various management structures, mechanisms and processes, including risk management.

After implementing the joint-stock reform, the Big Five reported that the clearer responsibilities, greater oversight and stricter restraints enacted under the new corporate governance environment were conducive to fact-based and logical operations and decision-making. After the reform, the Big Five created investor relations management systems consistent with international rules, and effectively boosted the quality and transparency of information disclosure by upgrading the disclosure systems of financial reports and risk factors.

The Big Five also reformed the appointment of senior officers, and implemented market-based global recruitment for key positions such as chief financial officer, chief risk officer, chief credit officer, chief auditor, and board secretary, thus achieving a diversified group of senior officers according to market-based appointment and removal.

II. Developing a Sound Corporate Governance System and Mechanism
(I) Corporate Governance System

Following the joint-stock reform, the Big Five set out to establish their charters and bylaws. They all developed sound corporate governance systems, which covered articles of association, rules of procedure of the shareholders' meeting, governance of the boards of directors and supervisors and management, information disclosure and investor relations (IR) management, risk management and internal controls, and capital and financial management, providing a basis for various governance activities at different levels.

CCB had already started preparing the corporate governance documents when bringing in promoters before the joint-stock reform. Since the listing venue had not yet been determined, CCB drafted governance documents based on the most stringent regulatory standards of the Chinese mainland and Hong Kong, the practices and experience of leading foreign commercial banks and Chinese companies listed abroad, and McKinsey's research results regarding the best practices of corporate governance structures across the world. After the first draft was prepared, CCB sought the opinions of regulators (e.g., the PBOC and Shanghai Stock Exchange), promoter shareholders, and some well-known domestic and overseas professional firms. Then, through intensive deliberation and revisions, CCB worked out a set of corporate governance documents that met both Chinese and foreign regulatory requirements while remaining appropriate for its own circumstances, including the articles of association, rules of procedure of the shareholders' meeting and boards of directors and supervisors, and the implementation rules for board committees. Later, to be eligible for IPO in Hong Kong, CCB amended and updated its articles of association and other corporate governance documents in line with the "Mandatory Provisions for the Articles of Association of the Companies to Be Listed Overseas," "Letter of Opinions on Supplements and Amendments to the Articles of Association of Companies to Be Listed in Hong Kong," and "Listing Rules of the Hong Kong Stock Exchange." Its governance documents featuring "long articles" were thus finalized.

On September 13, 2005, ICBC President Jiang Jianqing presided over the 14th ICBC Head Office President Meeting at which the "ICBC Articles of Association (Draft)" prepared by the ICBC Head Office Joint-Stock Reform Office was discussed and approved. One month later, the first version of "ICBC Articles of Association" was approved by the CBRC, and greatly facilitated the bank's corporate governance.

Afterward, due to the involvement of strategic investors and amendments to the *Company Law*, which imposed requirements on Shanghai-Hong Kong dual listing, ICBC updated its articles of association. After comparisons and analyses, to the extent permitted by the laws, ICBC made major amendments to its articles of association twice before the listing based on the following innovative "four principles." The first was that ICBC should ensure the articles would be compliant, practical, and feasible and govern foundational and constitutional issues. The second was it should consider its specific circumstances and the best practices of its peers. The third was it should analyze in depth the opinions of and, in an impartial and open manner, balance the interests of stakeholders, establish an effective checks and balances system, and be prudent when adjusting and changing any institutional arrangements. The fourth was it should adjust the style, logical sequence and structure of the articles according to preferences and requirements of regulators.

BOC has also been upgrading its corporate governance system according to changes in regulatory requirements and its operating status. In 2015, it reviewed and updated the "Plan of Delegation of Authorities by Shareholders' Meeting to Board of Directors" and the "Plan of Delegation of Authorities by Board of Directors to President," which further regulated the delegation system under the "3+1" governance structure. By the end of 2017, BOC had amended its corporate governance documents 14 times.

BoCom has amended its articles of association five times in accordance with laws and regulations, domestic and foreign regulatory rules, and established a standard corporate governance framework, covering such documents as rules of procedure of the shareholders' meeting and boards of directors and supervisors; working rules of the board of supervisors, special committees under the boards of directors and supervisors, the independent directors, board secretary, and president; measures for the management of information disclosure; internal reporting procedure for material information; and measures for the management of related-party transactions; rules for nomination and election of supervisors; and rules for annual performance evaluation of senior officers (interim).

ABC formulated its articles of association to define core issues like the set-up and division of duties and powers of the "3+1" governance structure, shares and registered capital, financial and accounting systems, internal audit, and profit distribution; and to regulate such issues as information disclosure, employee management, and amendments thereto. The rules of procedure of the shareholders' meeting, board of directors, and board of supervisors further detailed the articles of association. Specifically, these rules provided the composition, duties and powers of the shareholders' meeting and boards of directors and supervisors, as well as their meeting procedures covering convening, proposing, notification, attendance, auditing, voting, recording, and implementation. ABC has also developed working rules for board committees and the president, including the "Working Rules of the ABC Board Sannong Financial Development Committee" which reflect its own characteristics.

With an open attitude, ABC has been upgrading its corporate governance documents in line with laws and regulations, Chinese and foreign regulatory rules, and the latest industry trends, in an effort to optimize its corporate governance framework, enhance management fundamentals, and continuously improve upon its governance capabilities. It has also taken measures to assess the performance of its board, management, and members of them; improve the information disclosure system; standardize investor relations activities; and increase corporate transparency.

These articles of association and working rules, as amended and updated from time to time, have provided critical support and sound institutional guarantees for the business development of the Big Five, thus greatly improving their business growth and corporate governance systems.

(II) "3+1" Governance Structure

At the beginning of their establishment, the board of directors, the board of supervisors, and the management team of the banks had been troubled by inefficient communication. The state-owned banks vigorously developed communication and coordination systems for these three organs in response. According to then CCB President Chang Zhenming, after the joint-stock reform, the banks started to adopt the dual leadership model – the president was responsible for operations and management, and the chairman took charge of board affairs. This model posed a question: Who was the CEO? At CCB's first board meeting, shareholder-appointed directors from Central Huijin, independent directors, and CCB's executive directors had heated discussions. Chang recalled, "An independent director named Yashiro Masamoto[1] asked to have a word with me outside the meeting room, and said he had never participated in such a board meeting where people were arguing about 'who runs the company,' which was 'interesting' to him."[2] Wang Jianxi, then Central Huijin Vice Chairman, has told a similar story. In 2005, after BOC's budget was set, Central Huijin proposed that the cost-income ratio was too high and be cut by two percentage points. The proposal was rejected by BOC President Xiao Gang and also at the board meeting where foreign and independent directors all backed up the management. At last, the proposal was submitted to the shareholders' meeting where both Central Huijin and BOC's management refused to budge. Central Huijin held that as the controlling shareholder, it had the right to veto the proposal[3].

---

1   Former Chairman of Shinsei Bank of Japan.
2   From the interview with Chang Zhenming on April 18, 2017.
3   From the interview with Wang Jianxi on January 19, 2017.

The transformation from old to market-oriented management models, though unavoidably involving small conflicts, especially in the early stage of corporate governance transformation, progressed smoothly with the efforts made by the boards and management to adapt to their new roles. After the transformation, the Big Five highlighted the role of their boards as decision makers and supervisors while also emphasizing communication with the board of supervisors and management, defined the duties and powers of the boards of directors and supervisors (including special committees) and management, and created a sound communication and coordination mechanism among the three organs.

Through improvement in human resources and organizational structure, CCB further defined the powers and duties of the boards of directors and supervisors (including special committees) in corporate governance. With clearly defined functions, sufficient staff, and enhanced professionalism, the special committees greatly assisted the boards in the decision-making of major operation and management issues. Specifically, first, CCB constantly defined and adjusted the functions of special committees. For example, it transferred the nominating power of the Strategy and Nomination Committee to the Compensation and Assessment Committee, so that the former could focus on the development and implementation of strategies. The former was renamed Strategy Committee and later Strategic Development Committee as suggested by the CBRC, and the latter renamed Nomination and Compensation Committee. Second, the bank enlarged the size of the committees. Through two rounds of adjustment, the number of members of the Strategic Development Committee, Audit Committee, Risk Management Committee, and Nomination and Compensation Committee were increased to 12, 7, 7 and 7, respectively. Third, it enhanced the role of independent directors in the board committees by appointing independent directors as the chairmen of the Audit Committee, Nomination and Compensation Committee, and Related-Party Transaction Control Committee. In addition, CCB later established a Supervisory Committee for Duty Performance and Due Diligence and a Supervisory Committee for Financial Affairs and Internal Controls, both under the Board of Supervisors, to create a more professional board of supervisors and a mutually checked and balanced governance system.

ICBC also explored measures to create a communication and coordination mechanism linking its board of directors, board of supervisors and management (Fig. 7.2). On November 25, 2005, ICBC released working rules for its five board committees. The rules stipulated that each special committee should set up a working group composed of heads of relevant departments and offices to facilitate coordination among departments and organize meetings; and that the board office should head the working groups with support from relevant departments. These working groups helped the special committees to discharge their duties, while also enhancing the communication between the board (including special committees) and management. Furthermore, pursuant to the articles of association, the board continued to explore the best ways to engage the management and departments in discussions before meetings, so that it may receive sufficient, necessary, and timely information before formal discussions. The board also prioritized problems reported by the supervisors. The board secretary and board office would timely inform board directors of such problems, who would subsequently work out solutions and seek improvements through careful analysis and intensive communication with the board of supervisors.

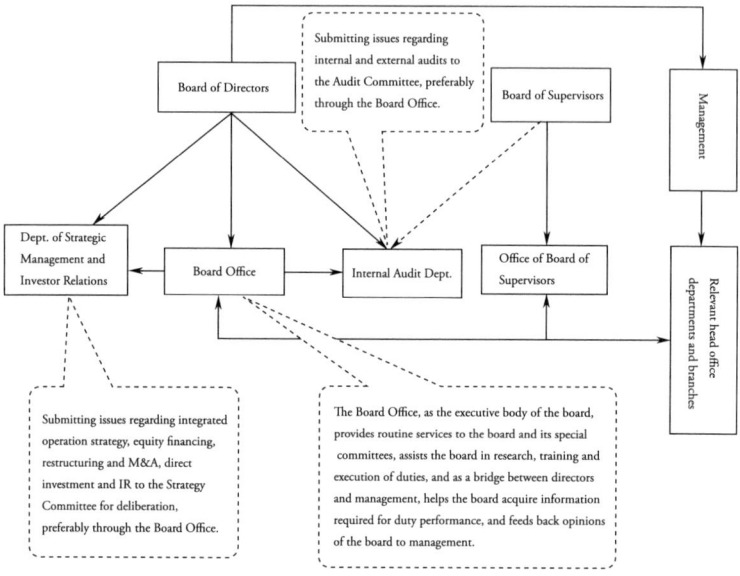

Source: ICBC Board Office.

Fig. 7.2: ICBC Communication Mechanism between the Board and Other Internal Departments

BOC focused on building decision-making and communication mechanisms. Decision-making was enhanced through two ways. For one, (i) directors were entitled to be informed of the operations, financial condition, and material events of the bank, and to supervise the performance of the management team; (ii) independent directors, relying on their expertise in finance, law, risk management, and banking operations management, were entitled to review the reports submitted by management, participate in the discussions of the board and its special committees, and independently give opinions; and (iii) the board was entitled to question management about the implementation of the board's resolutions. For the other, management implemented the board's resolutions and fed results back to the board; and the board of supervisors supervised the implementation of the resolutions. BOC has also set up secretariats to special committees at corresponding head office departments, with department heads as secretaries. This effectively increased the expertise of the secretariats, and thus enabled special committees to better assist the board in decision-making.

BOC also took active measures to promote communication between the board and management. Before a board meeting was held, non-executive directors would listen to reports from management on proposals to be submitted to the board through communication and pre-communication meetings, so as to understand the matters to be deliberated, and at the same time, give their opinions and suggestions.

(III) IR Management

The concept of "investor relations" (IR), originating in the U.S. in the 1960s, refers to strategic management actions whereby companies like GE combine sufficient voluntary information disclosure, finance, and marketing activities to enhance communication with and boost their visibility and reputation among investors, thus maximizing corporate value[1]. Following the joint-stock reform, the Big Five set out to promote IR in line with information disclosure regulatory requirements. ICBC specially set up the Department of Strategic Management and Investor Relations.

---

1   National Investor Relations Institute: NIRI Annual Report 2009.

1. Creating IR management frameworks and systems

ICBC upgraded its information disclosure system after launching the joint-stock reform. At the end of November 2005, ICBC formulated the "ICBC Information Disclosure Rules" which was later approved at the fifth meeting of the first board of directors in March 2006. In May 2007, ICBC prepared the "ICBC Investor Relations Management Rules," which was amended in December 2012 and renamed "ICBC Investor Relations Management Measures (2012 version)." In October 2017, upon the deliberation and approval of the board meeting, the Measures was further amended and renamed "ICBC Investor Relations Management Measures." The latest version specified the purposes, basic principles, target audiences, main communication contents, and information collection procedures of IR management, as well as the IR management responsibilities of relevant head office departments and domestic and foreign branches. Meanwhile, ICBC developed the basic framework for IR management, whereby the board was responsible for developing IR management measures which were implemented under the arrangement of the board secretary and the supervision of the board of supervisors. Furthermore, ICBC created a multi-layer collaborative IR management framework led by the board chairman and management, implemented by the Strategic Investment Department, General Office, Board Office, and Information Department, and supported by over 30 head office departments and domestic and foreign branches.

Like ICBC, the other four banks have also established similar IR management systems and teams headed by board offices. For instance, ABC formulated the "ABC Investment Relations Management Rules" in accordance with the "Working Guidelines for the Relationship Between

Listed Companies and Investors" issued by the CSRC, "Listing Rules" and "Guide on Disclosure of Price-Sensitive Information" released by HKEX, other applicable rules and regulations, and "ABC Articles of Association." The Rules, approved at the 19th meeting of the first ABC board of directors, specified issues regarding IR management, promoting the bank's lawful, compliant, orderly and efficient IR management. The Rules stipulated that the board secretary should be responsible for IR management, including (1) disclosing information; (2) arranging for relevant personnel to develop and implement IR development plans; (3) organizing investor exchange activities; (4) arranging for relevant personnel to collect and analyze information and provide feedback; (5) analyzing the equity structure; (6) conducting investor and capital market research; (7) promoting market value management; and (8) guiding branches and sub-branches in IR management. Tier-one branch offices acted as HR management liaisons, and relevant head office departments and domestic and foreign branches assisted the board office in IR management, primarily including (1) providing information necessary for IR management; (2) participating in drafting publicity materials; (3) attending investor presentations; and (4) participating in IR activities such as roadshows.

2. Enhancing IR management to maximize corporate value

Roadshow promotions, a key communication channel between listed companies and investors, were an important IR management measure taken by the Big Five. Niu Ximing, then ICBC Vice President, recalled that during the bank's overseas roadshow led by Chairman Jiang Jianqing, an American investor asked: "How do Chinese banks delegate the authority to approve loans?" "We delegate the authority according to the types of loan. For small loans, like working capital loans, we authorize the branches to make loans up to RMB 100-200 million, with the grant of other loans being basically under the thumb of the head office. The projects assigned with greater authority are largely infrastructure projects, which are mostly endorsed by the government and will most certainly generate cash revenue in the future. Therefore, the risk of such loans is minimal," said Niu. Even so, this investor still claimed ICBC was taking risk in doing so, insisting that the risks of such loans would be uncontrollable. "We have a credit management system that covers each loan. Even though the approval authority is delegated to branches, the head office, through this system, can keep abreast of how and where each loan is granted and monitor the future changes of each loan. Hence the head office has a way to know the risks of each loan," Chairman Jiang further explained. After this explanation, the investor changed his mind and recognized the reliability of ICBC's risk management. In this sense, the roadshow helped clarify some of the customers' or investors' doubts about the bank. The U.S. roadshow can be called a great success because it updated the understanding of international investors on ICBC and its business management[1].

Stephen Kin Wah Yiu of KPMG once told a story about CCB's roadshow: "During a roadshow presentation, facing the doubts of investors, Guo Shuqing said, 'I know that CCB still has many problems, but that's why we are going public – we want our investors to help us reform the bank.' I observed that many investors there agreed with him and believed the bank had a future, because its management knew very well that going public was just a start, and this would promote its reform."[2]

---

1   From the interview with Niu Ximing on March 7, 2017.
2   Quoted from the interview with Stephen Kin Wah Yiu on February 15, 2017.

Based on experience accumulated since their roadshows, the Big Five have created two-way communication systems through which information was collected from capital markets and fed back to management for decision-making, and business performance was introduced to investors. For instance, following the principle of active, accurate, cooperative and efficient public relationship management, ICBC periodically disclosed business performance and held global and reverse roadshows. Specifically, it (1) timely and adequately disclosed information through business results press conferences and global investor telephone conferences; (2) conducted targeted, multi-level global roadshows according to the distribution of foreign investors to broaden its international investor base; (3) participated in high-profile investment forums held by famous domestic and foreign financial institutions to enhance multi-dimensional communication with investors; (4) held reverse roadshows and open-day theme activities to increase its influence in capital markets and duly manage investors' expectations; and (5) communicated with small and medium-sized investors through diverse channels such as hotlines, dedicated investment-bank email inbox, and SSE's e-interview platform to improve the transparency of information disclosure and duly protect their lawful rights and interests.

BOC created a capital market tracking and analysis framework whereby a dedicated team tracked and studied the number and composition of investors and their changes, as well as the daily transactions of stocks and securities, thus providing data which could inform IR-related decision-making. Other measures included (1) collecting investment bank analysts' opinions, reports, predictions and suggestions, media reports, and other market information; (2) tracking and analyzing macroeconomic data, industry policies, peers' performance, and market trends, and assessing their impacts; and (3) collecting investors' concerns and comments during business results press conferences, roadshows, investment bank forums, and regular visits from other institutions. BOC delivered the above information to its leadership and management through such methods as daily share price reports, IR monthly reports, key market reports, results briefings, roadshow summaries, and periodical IR plans, which each supported the bank's effective absorption of outside information.

ABC promoted voluntary information disclosure in accordance with laws and regulations, as well as its own characteristics. It created a voluntary information disclosure framework featuring separate disclosure of county business, extensive business data, and investors' concerns and corporate culture, to achieve more targeted and effective information disclosure.

On May 19, 2017, BoCom invited over 30 investors and analysts from the U.S., Singapore, Hong Kong and the Chinese mainland to launch a reverse roadshow at Shenzhen Branch together with the Board Office's IR team. At the reverse roadshow, Shenzhen Branch introduced its business performance as well as achievements concerning its further reform and transformation strategy in recent years. The investors and analysts highly praised the branch for its robust profitability, high asset quality, and active efforts in supporting the real economy and private businesses, and expected to see the spread of the branch's experience to the bank's other outlets. After the roadshow, the invited guests visited the branch's banking department and banking service demonstration area to experience smart self-service banking, and were impressed by the bank's use of internet technology, human-centered setup of outlets and channels, and excellent services. Compared with the results presentations and roadshows conducted by the head office, the reverse roadshow, widely appreciated by investors and analysts, unquestionably provided a more direct and intuitive way for them to understand, interact with, and experience the bank and have a more clear picture of the implementation of its further reform and transformation strategy at the branch level.

Having achieved impressive performance in IR management, the Big Five received awards from a host of leading media at home and abroad, such as the League of American Communications Professionals, Annual Report Competition, *IR Magazine*, *Institutional Investor*, *Corporate Governance Asia*, Quamnet, and *Securities Daily*.

Section II
Development of ERM System

Risk management (RM) is one of the bedrock principles of commercial banks. China's SOCBs first incorporated RM into operations in the 1980s to meet financial regulatory requirements and promote their reforms and development. Since then, the banks have been developing, implementing, and modernizing their RM systems. Before 2003, the banks had already created preliminary RM frameworks relying on their own explorations. After its establishment in 2003, the CBRC required the banking sector to implement the New Basel Capital Accord ("Basel II"), which imposed stricter RM requirements on the banks. During their restructuring and joint-stock reform, the Big Five, with one of their core goals being to develop sound RM mechanisms, had all implemented the Basel II to boost their RM capabilities and keep in line with international practice, thereby improving their corporate governance and becoming modern commercial banks.

I. Developing Robust RM Culture

Corporate culture is the soul of a bank. The Big Five, though having their own characteristics, have all developed compliant, rigorous and robust RM cultures.

Clear risk preference (RP) determines risk culture. The Big Five have all developed RP rules to specify RP determination, implementation, monitoring and adjustment policies and procedures. For example, in 2005, BOC stated that at the group level, it preferred moderate risks, and would handle the risk-return relationship in a "rational, robust and prudent" manner. In 2011, the bank formulated the "BOC Risk Preference Statement" and the "BOC Risk Preference Management Rules" and released them across the bank for implementation. When determining the RP indicators provided in the Statement, BOC took into consideration the regulatory standards under the CARPALs model[1] of the CBRC, interests of investors, requirements of the board and management, its RM capability, and consistency in RM among affiliates. In 2014, it amended the Rules and Statement, a revision which expanded previous 10 strategic indicators into 13 strategic indicators and 13 subordinate indicators, covering more types of risk. In 2017, to meet the latest domestic and foreign regulatory requirements and its strategic needs, BOC released the second amendments to the Rules and Statement, which highlighted the transmission and use of RP.

ICBC formulated its "Risk Preference Management Rules (Trial)"

---

1 In early 2010, the CBRC created a regulatory model called "CARPALs" for major banks. This model consists of 13 indicators falling into seven categories of capital adequacy, asset quality, risk concentration, provision coverage, affiliated institutions, liquidity, and swindle prevention and control, supplemented by the limited discretion of banking regulators.

and "Risk Preference Table" in 2010 to promote business development and RM. The documents specified basic issues concerning the bank's business development and RM, such as what types of risk it preferred, how much risk exposures it was willing to take, and what return it expected. In 2017, ICBC upgraded the documents by incorporating monitoring indicators under the CBRC's enhanced regulatory standards to create an RP statement which combined 23 quantitative indicators falling into four categories (capital, incomes, specific risks, and zero tolerance) with corresponding qualitative descriptions.

BoCom had built a set of sound RP indicator systems by the end of 2010. Among them, the market risk management information system (KRM system) is particularly noteworthy – it increased the bank's market risk measurement and monitoring capabilities, providing technical data for the bank-wide quantitative RP profiling and risk limit. With the system, BoCom used Standardized Approach (SA) and Internal Models Approach (IMA) to measure market risk capital requirements and set corresponding market risk limits. While setting the risk limits, BoCom linked RP and value at risk (VaR) with existing product risk limits across the bank, creating a bidirectional (top-down and bottom-up) workflow that runs through the front and middle offices. In this way, the bank was able to use a combination of risk capital-based risk limits and product-based transaction limits, forming an efficient and rigorous market risk limit management system.

The Big Five have been upgrading their risk assessment systems, which had been created pursuant to uniform and specialized assessment standards. In the system, the head office and branches of a bank would analyze and assess the implementation of RM policies and rules and the operation status of the system. With the risk assessment systems, mechanisms, and models, the banks regularly carried out risk assessments to ensure that all types of risk and their management status are identified timely and accurately, so as to facilitate both supervision over different departments and the decision-making.

II. Creating Sound RM Frameworks

RM is built on RM frameworks. Major commercial banks have started to develop and revise ERM frameworks since 2004. For example, ICBC formulated the "Enterprise Risk Management Framework" in 2004 and amended it in 2008 and 2010 to separate the RM of front, middle, and back offices, and specify the framework, contents, and requirements of ERM. In 2011, in view of its new RM demands, ICBC issued the "Enterprise Risk Management Framework (Revision)" to upgrade its RM system. In 2017, the bank formulated the "Enterprise Risk Management Rules" based on the "Guidelines for Comprehensive Risk Management of Banking Financial Institutions" laid down by the CBRC, the new developments of international regulatory reform after the financial crisis, and its RM practice and innovation. The Rules specified the basic elements, principles, policies and procedures of RM; detailed issues including "three lines of defense," RP, risk limits, stress-testing, assessment of risk and capital adequacy, recovery and resolution, and emergency plans; and imposed requirements on the management of primary risks. Furthermore, ICBC has established a set of special RM systems. For example, the credit RM system consisted of rules on three layers – internal rating management rules on the first layer; management measures for corporate customer credit rating, non-retail debt rating, and retail credit asset internal rating on the second layer; and rating implementation rules on the third layer.

Following its centralized disposal of NPLs in 2004, BoCom switched to building its ERM system. In 2005, it issued the "2005-2007 BoCom Comprehensive Risk Management Outline." In 2008, at the fifth meeting of the fifth board of directors, the bank amended the "Regulations on the Work of the Board Strategy Committee," and released the "2008-2010 Comprehensive Risk Management Plan."

BOC developed the "General Rules of BOC for Risk Management" (the "General Rules") in 2005 as its guiding document governing RM, which specified the purposes, basic principles, preference determination, framework, procedure, and team building for its RM. From 2010 to 2017, according to its RM needs and regulatory requirements, BOC amended the General Rules four times to add such items as RM culture building and effective data aggregation, expanding its RM to all important areas.

Major commercial banks have set up risk policy committees under their boards to develop fundamental RM policies and determine core issues like RM strategies, preferences and goals. They have also set up RM committees under the management team, which have credit risk, market risk, and operational risk sub-committees to manage credit, market, operational, liquidity and strategy risks, respectively. The banks also established chief risk officer-led organs and hired domestic and foreign experts to assist the management teams in the supervision and decision-making regarding RM.

As a result of the joint-stock reform, all the major commercial banks have established head office RM departments responsible for ERM. Special RM departments have also been set up to work with the head office RM departments, to separate the RM of front, middle and back offices. At branches, the head offices have built dedicated loan approval teams composed of credit risk directors and professional loan reviewers. Only the head offices and tier-one branches have the right to approve loans, and lower units only act as marketing channels.

ICBC, BOC, CCB, and BoCom had successively explored and built RM organizational structures since early 2003. After the listing of ABC, all the Big Five had in place increasingly sound RM organizational structures, which, being roughly the same, have the following common characteristics:

First, the board of directors, board of supervisors, and management of a bank all assume RM responsibilities. The board of directors, which determines a bank's RM strategy and preference and main RM policies, takes ultimate RM responsibility of the bank and supervises and assesses its RM system and risk level. The risk management committee under the board assists the board in RM. The board of supervisors supervises the duty performance and due diligence of the board and management in RM. The management is responsible for implementing RM decisions made by the board, and organizing RM system development and routine RM activities across the bank, as well as review, assessment, coordination, and supervision regarding RM policies and rules, RM models and tools, risk profile, and RM measures.

Second, each bank has built "three lines of defense" with each line having wide-ranging powers over matters falling within the ambit of its responsibilities. The head office banking department, as the first "line of defense," is responsible for routine RM along its business line. Head office RM, internal control and legal compliance management, credit management, and credit approval departments form the second line to manage corresponding risks. The audit departments, as the third line, operate "vertically" across the organization and are tasked with independently supervising and assessing the effectiveness of the RM system. The banks have also assigned the management of major risks like credit, market and operational risks to specific departments.

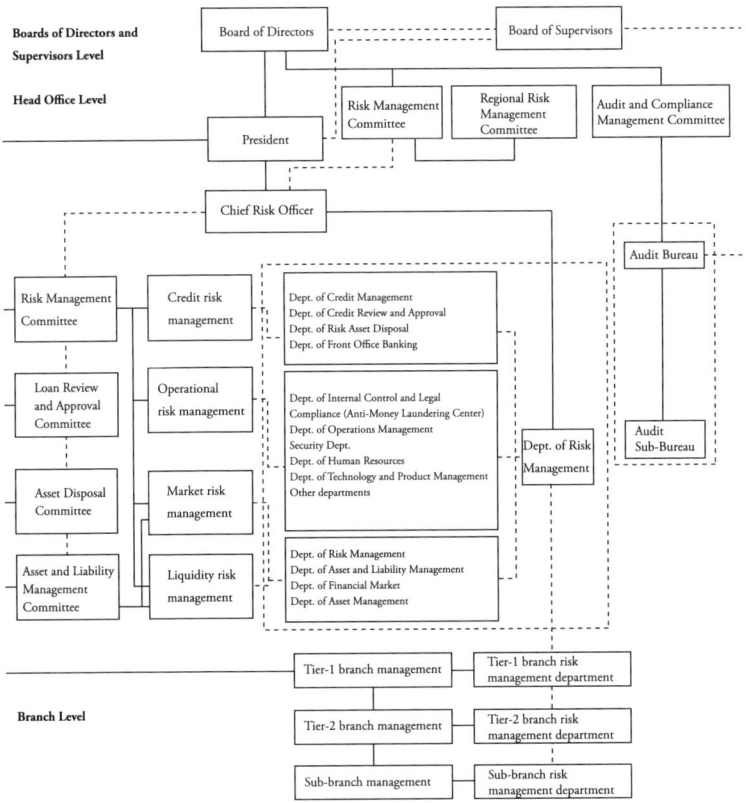

Fig. 7.3 Major Commercial Banks' RM Organizational Structure

Third, each bank has created branch-level RM systems that cover from the highest to the lowest level of the organization. In the RM systems of the Big Five, branch heads have primary responsibilities for RM management, and branch RM officers organize RM activities within their purview. Branches at different levels all have RM committees as deliberation and coordination bodies. ABC, for instance, has set up RM, credit management, and internal control and legal compliance departments at tier-one branches. At tier-two branches, risk and credit management departments are run by the same team, which assumes the responsibility of RM, credit management, and loan review and approval together with the credit review and approval center and personal loan review and approval center under the team. At tier-one sub-branches, RM departments are set up to manage credit and operational risks.

III. Building Rigorous Delegation and Limit Management Systems

It has been proven from reform experience that delegation and limit management provide a direct means to manage risks. Thanks to the "3+1" governance framework, the Big Five have further enhanced their internal delegation framework. Now, the shareholders' meeting grants the necessary authority to the board of directors, which, within the scope of that, grants full authority to management, and finally management grants, through the management hierarchy, such authority to lower organizational levels as appropriate. The banks have also developed annual delegation plans which provide full coverage over the banks and enable dynamic management of delegation.

First, the banks created delegation management frameworks. For example, soon after transforming into a joint-stock company, ICBC defined the duties and powers of the shareholders' meeting, the board of directors, the board of supervisors and the president (the management) in its articles of association. It was also committed to building a sound delegation system, as evidenced by the "Plan of Delegation of Authorities by Shareholders' Meeting to Board of Directors (Trial)" and the "Plan of Delegation of Authorities by Board of Directors to the President (Trial)" released in April 2006. The plans were revised in 2010 based on extensive studies and shareholders' suggestions, to adapt to changes in the market environment and in ICBC's business development and scale. The revised plans enhanced the review and approval powers of the board and president over equity investments, bond investments, fixed asset acquisition and donation to external parties; and further clarified the duties and powers of the shareholders' meeting, the board of directors and management. The two plans have become examples for comparable peers.

Second, the banks created delegation assessment systems to periodically check the implementation of delegation plans. In each bank, the management and the board would analyze assessment results and report their conclusions to the board and shareholders' meeting respectively, which greatly standardized delegation management. For instance, BoCom formulated its "Annual Working Rules for Delegation of Authorities" to assess authorities given by the shareholders' meeting and the board by the end of each year, and submit an assessment report and adjustment suggestions to the board. Such report and suggestions, if adopted at the board meeting, would be summarized into a white paper which is distributed to the management. The president would then issue letters of delegation to other management members, departments of the head office (including departments directly managed by it), provincial branches, and foreign branches and lead the implementation of the white paper. Meanwhile, the president would prepare the management white paper on delegation.

Third, the banks created delegation systems. In ABC's system, for example, the shareholders' meeting delegates authorities to the board; the board to the president; the president to vice presidents, head office department general managers, and tier-one branch general managers; vice presidents to head office department general managers; tier-one branch general managers to tier-two branch general managers; tier-two branch general managers to sub-branch managers; and so on. According to ABC's "Articles of Association," "Rules of Procedure of the Shareholders' Meeting," and "Working Rules of the President," the shareholders' meeting may, where it is necessary, reasonable and lawful, delegate the board to decide relevant issues within the meeting's authority; and the board may, within its power, decide such issues as investment, asset acquisition, asset disposal, asset write-offs, and guarantees, or delegate the president to do so. In terms of business operations, ABC implemented unified corporate management and delegation rules, with branches and employees at various levels all operating within their scope of authority. The president may, under the "Articles of Association" and the board's delegation, grant operational and management authorities to head office managers and branch heads. In addition, under certain circumstances, the president may, on his own initiative or through application, expand the scope or limit of authority that a certain person has for specific operational and management activities.

BOC has continuously improved its three-pronged loan approval rules featuring independent due diligence, rule-driven loan review and rigorous accountability to ensure prudent risk evaluation. Personnel responsible for due diligence, review and approval make judgments based on comprehensive understanding of customers and projects. The loan review committee examines the loan approval process by making clear yes/no decisions. These rigorous control and checks and balances mechanisms helped BOC eliminate non-compliant business operations, ensuring loan quality. In addition, the bank centralizes the loan review and approval powers into the head office and tier-one branches and only allows tier-two branches to originate loans, thus reducing the number of loan approvers from over 300 to 38. Such a flat management procedure ensures loan review quality and efficiency.

In 2009, BOC piloted an industry portfolio and limit management program which, focused on both industries and regions, started with corporate banking of domestic branches. In 2011, it used quantitative models to measure industry limit for the first time. In line with the principle of keeping balance among risks, capital and earnings, BOC created a risk measurement model to allocate capital and calculate the optimal growth rates and credit limits of each industry in the corporate banking industry portfolio, in a bid to maximize the portfolio's RAROC. Recent years saw that the guiding and restraining role of policy instruments like credit issuance policy and portfolio management were growing rapidly.

Fourth, the banks have been constantly adjusting their delegation plans to improve delegation management according to new requirements. For example, BOC, based on valid delegation under rules and measures adopted at or approved by its shareholders' meetings and board of directors meetings after the launch of its joint-stock reform in 2004, and opinions offered by its major shareholders, directors, head office departments, affiliated institutions, and legal counsels after several rounds of communication, supplemented and modified these delegation provisions and formulated the "Plan of Delegation by Shareholders' Meeting to Board of Directors" and the "Plan of Delegation by Board of Directors to the President." The two plans, approved by the bank's board meeting and 2014 annual shareholders' meeting, further defined the powers and duties of the shareholders' meeting, the board of directors and the management, boosting its corporate governance compliance.

Furthermore, after the global financial crisis, the Big Five actively developed and amended risk limit management rules whereby they set reference limit indicators, and specified the methods and procedures to determine, set and implement such limits. For example, ICBC released the "Risk Limit Management Rules" in 2008, and amended the Rules in 2010 and 2012. The Rules defined the division of responsibilities for risk limit management; the composition, setting, review, monitoring, early warning, adjustment of limits; and the handling procedure for limit violation. It also created a limit monitoring framework that defines indicators that account for the types of risk, business lines (products), regions (institutions), industries, customers, and other aspects.

BoCom formulated the "BoCom Market Risk Limit Management Measures" in 2009 to regulate the setting, allocation, implementation, monitoring and reporting procedures of market risk limits. According to the Measures, the Head Office Asset and Liability Management Department would periodically review market risk limit applications for trade services, and based on review results, set the bank-wide market risk limits (including both risk limits and stop-loss limits) for trade services. The risk limits needed to be reviewed by the Market and Liquidity Risk Management Committee before being implemented by the Head Office Financial Banking Center. The Transaction Monitoring Department of the Financial Market Division should monitor daily the implementation of the limits, and prepare and submit risk assessment reports every month. In addition, the bank also made increased efforts on the pricing, evaluation and market risk measurement of various financial products, to assess their market risks, improve limit management and operational strategies, and prevent possible impacts of extreme events on the trade service portfolio. In 2010, the bank had created a sound risk management system for trade services which was suitable for the complexity of its trades. In January the same year, pursuant to requirements under the internal rating standards of the CBRC, it started to implement credit risk limit management for individual borrowers.

IV. Building Empirical Risk Identification and Measurement Systems

Within the RM area, risk measurement has recorded the fastest improvement at major commercial banks in recent years. Chinese commercial banks previously relied on the individual experience of their staff to identify and assess risks, falling far behind their foreign peers in technical strength. By implementing the Basel Accords, the banks enhanced their development of core RM technology, and introduced new RM tools and methods to increase their quantitative measurement and management capabilities. They shifted their risk control focus from single customer to portfolios to control for industry-specific concentration risk, and from qualitative judgment to quantitative analysis to allocate limited RM resources to industries that generate higher returns. They also created centralized data management platforms with IT systems covering the entire business management process. Thanks to the platforms, the banks enhanced centralized risk management by increasing data use efficiency, and achieved systematic RM at the front, middle and back offices by creating sound IT systems covering the whole RM process comprising risk identification and measurement, risk controls, risk monitoring and assessment, and risk reporting.

(I) Internal Ratings-Based (IRB) Approach to Credit Risk

Based on extensive internal data collected over many years, the Big Five created unified data platforms; internal rating models covering corporate customers, institutional customers, individual customers, local governments, and sovereign states; and rating and application systems. Rating results were incorporated into loan application, review and tracking processes to achieve empirically-sound and refined credit management.

BOC established an interdepartmental Basel II research team as early as 2001 to study how to integrate Basel II requirements into its operations. In 2002, BOC set up the Leading Group for Asset Risk Classification and IRB Approach – a preparation for Basel implementation. Later in 2003, based on the Third Quantitative Impact Study (QIS3), BOC formulated the implementation plans for the Basel II and IRB Approach. Then, relying on the experience shared by leading foreign peers, experts' feedback received during overseas investigations, and the assistance of professional consulting firms, BOC launched its global risk management system program to optimize its RM procedure in accordance with the Basel II, IRB Approach and listing requirements. In November 2006, based on adequate preparations, BOC set up the Basel II Implementation Leading Group headed by bank leaders to arrange and coordinate the Basel implementation.

ICBC set up the Basel II Implementation Project Committee in 2003 to lead Basel implementation. The Committee established the IRB Approach Implementation Team, Internal Model Approach Implementation Team, and Capital Measurement Approach to Operational Risk Implementation Team to measure the credit, market and operational risks respectively. While pursuing independent innovation, ICBC also actively drew on sophisticated quantitative risk management models of foreign peers. In 2004, in partnership with PwC, the bank launched the IRB Approach Program (Phase I) to analyze its RM gap with the Basel II requirements and leading international banks, set corporate governance and ERM goals, and create the implementation roadmap covering three transitional implementation plans and 55 projects, creating a general plan for implementing the Basel II and building an ERM system.

CCB has created 458 risk measurement models (292 in use) covering its approximately 140,000 non-retail customers and 80 million retail customers and all trade services in the financial market in recent years. These models helped CCB accurately identify risks, and build a cutting-edge credit management system, up-to-date credit policy system, and efficient credit card and personal loan approval system. In retail banking, for example, CCB created 20 scorecard models to expedite the handling of applications and limit adjustments for private banking, creating a better customer experience. Also, the bank created 89 retail measurement models covering 98% retail loans across the bank. Relying on these models, 44% of loans were reviewed automatically, saving at least RMB 725 million of human resources cost every year; and 98% of telephone credit limit increase applications were handled within three minutes, a rapid response to market needs much shorter than the previous one or two days. In addition, the application of the scorecard brought in notable results in risk prevention and control. Figures showed that scorecard-based automatic loan review greatly decreased the NPL ratio by two-thirds, from 0.54% (manual review) to 0.15%.

(II) Internal Model Approach to Market Risk

To enhance their overall capacity for market risk management, the

Big Five have developed market risk databases, created risk measurement systems focusing on VaR, and independently designed global market risk management systems, and thus achieved ERM covering risk identification, measurement, monitoring, and control.

ICBC, for example, created a set of internal models for market risk, which adopted the VaR model based on historical simulations. Relying on the models, ICBC determined market risk capital charges through calculating the VaR of its theoretical losses in the previous 250 working days, and comprehensively analyzing its VaR under the stress scenarios after 2007. The internal models, namely four types of risk measurement models (valuation, VaR, stress testing and back testing models) were created based on market, transaction and reference data, the first of which included over 300 million data items collected between 1987 and 2012. In 2008, ICBC set out to build its market risk management system relying on its independent exploration on methodology, system and team building. In January 2011, ICBC launched its global market risk management system, becoming the first Chinese bank with an independently-developed market risk management system. This system, covering over 85% of the bank's operations, had such core functions as pricing and valuation, VaR measurement, stress testing, back testing, limit management, risk reporting, and capital calculation. In 2012, the system won the first prize of PBOC Technical Innovation Award.

CCB innovated its stress testing and measurement. Since 2008, it has created 169 stress testing models (30 in use) and a credit risk stress testing system to conduct stress testing for market, liquidity and interest rate risks. With these tools, CCB conducted various stressing tests both top-down and bottom-up. For instance, in 2015 when the country's macroeconomy entered a new normal stage, CCB assessed asset quality through stress tests, and predicted that 2016 would result in RMB 160 billion of NPLs. In response, the management adjusted asset quality management goals, and got prepared for efforts related to credit issuance policy and NPA disposal, seizing the initiative in achieving robust operations.

(III) Advanced Measurement Approach to Operational Risk

The Big Five, based on internal and external loss data, developed advanced measurement approach models and auxiliary systems to systematize operational risk measurement and tool application, thereby increasing their strength in operational risk management.

To develop an appropriate loss data management system, BoCom started to collect loss data across the bank and standardize collection procedures and scope in September 2009. In October 2010, its first collection effort came to an end. In this process, BoCom optimized the scope, method, and channels of its event collection, as well as post-collection management and tracking, thereby accumulating extensive experience in event collection. In April 2010, it started procedure analysis to identify inherent operational risk events in main business procedures and activities and created corresponding control measures, and successively issued the "BoCom Interim Measures for the Management of Loss Events" and the "BoCom Interim Measures for the Management of Operational Risk Events." These Measures stipulated that all events falling into the definition of operational risk should be collected and measured according to statistical standards, and imposed more detailed requirements on the whole-process management of operational risk events.

The first area is risk classification and measurement. In 2010, BoCom incorporated the Basic Indicator Approach (BIA) and Standardized Approach (SA) into periodical calculation of operational risk capital. BIA uses BoCom's gross income as a risk exposure indicator and sets the required level of operational risk capital as a fixed percentage of the gross income. BoCom calculated the operational risk capital arising from the stand-alone financial statements of BoCom Corporation and the consolidated financial statements of BoCom Group using SA, and unified the definitions of products and services to determine SA-based capital calculation methods and procedures. After 2010, in accordance with the CBRC's guidance issued in respect to its application on implementing Basel II, when calculating operational risk capital, BoCom would use SA, while BoCom Group would use a combination of SA and BIA, namely SA for BoCom Corporation and BIA for the subsidiaries. As data accumulation would progress, the Advanced Measurement Approach would be gradually phased in.

The second area is risk control and prevention. In April 2010, BoCom started to promote the Risk Control and Self-Assessment (RCSA), Key Risk Indicators (KRI) and Loss Data Collection (LDC) across the bank, as required by the Basel II compliance and regulatory rules. In the same year, BoCom structurally classified the loss events, risk factors, impact types, event modality, and control measures of operational risk across the bank, to create an operational risk and control dictionary. This tool enabled BoCom to standardize operational risk management and data collection to create a unified operational risk management system. BoCom then released the "Operational Risk Management Policy" and "Measures for the Implementation of Operational Risk Management" to further mitigate and prevent operational risk.

The third area is the development of risk management systems, policies, and tools. In 2010, to meet the Basel II compliance and regulatory requirements, BoCom created an operational risk management system with integrated RCSA, KRI, and LDC functions. Through subsequent upgrades, this system would become the "531 Operational Risk Management System" which better aligned with the bank's risk management needs. Through this system, BoCom implemented risk and control self-assessment for all its operating entities and made such assessment a regular program. It created a three-layer RCSA architecture and assigned dedicated personnel to the head office and branches to regularly monitor changes in KRIs. BoCom's business departments also submitted quarterly KRI analysis to the head office's risk management department, which was then consolidated into, and comprised an essential part of, the quarterly operational risk evaluation report for review by the management.

BOC focused on developing its operational risk management tools and systems to achieve efficient operational risk management across the group.

First, BOC incorporated RCSA, KRI, and LDC into operational risk identification, assessment and monitoring. After its joint-stock reform and listing, BOC developed a set of operational risk management tools like RCSA, KRI and LDC together with its strategic investor RBS, and has been promoting these tools across the bank after piloting them at branches in 2006. At present, BOC mainly relies on RCSA to periodically assess business procedures, voluntarily identifies unacceptable residual risk and detective control, and proposes corrective suggestions. In case of the occurrence of material operational risk events, an immediate assessment is triggered. BOC developed two KRI systems at the head office and branch levels respectively to dynamically monitor KRI changes, in order to detect and prevent operational risk in a timely manner. BOC has also conducted an LDC program across the bank to collect and analyze losses arising from operational risk, and periodically verify loss data to increase their accuracy and integrity.

Second, BOC created an operational risk management system that provides policy framework, management measures, and operational guidelines. In 2008, the bank released the "Operational Risk Management Policy," "Methods for the Classification of Operational Risk," and a series of management measures and procedure guidelines for operational risk management tools. The "Operational Risk Management Policy" approved by the Risk Policy Committee under the board acted as the fundamental document of operational risk management, specifying the basic principles, requirements, purposes, and goals of BOC's operational risk management. "Methods for the Classification of Operational Risk" unified terms of operational risk management across the bank. "Measures for the Management of Operational Risk and Control Assessment," "Measures for the Management of Operational Risk KRIs," "Measures for the Management of Operational Risk Loss Data Collection" and relevant procedure guidelines detailed requirements on the principles, methods, division of responsibilities, and procedures regarding the use of various management tools.

After ten years of preparation (Table 7.1), in October 2013, China was finally assessed as compliant within the Regulatory Consistency Assessment Program (RCAP) by the Basel Committee, becoming the sixth compliant jurisdiction following the U.S., EU, Japan, Singapore, and Switzerland. Specifically, China was graded compliant in 12 of the 14 components, and largely compliant in the remaining two components. The result indicated significant progress made by China in building prudent banking regulatory systems, which increased the confidence of international markets in its banking sector and greatly promoted the internationalization of major Chinese commercial banks.

While building capital management frameworks, state-owned banks also continued preparation for the introduction of Advanced Capital Management Approaches ("Advanced Approaches"). In April 2014, the CBRC approved the use of Advanced Approaches by some commercial banks, including the Big Five. Advanced Approaches, including Pillar 1 Advanced Measurement Approach and Pillar 2 Internal Capital Adequacy Assessment Process (ICAAP), are ways through which commercial banks measure risks and monitor capital using internal models in accordance with Basel II. Compared with SAs, Advanced Approaches feature more rational risk classification and measurement methods, as well as more accurate, stable, and prudent risk quantification results.

Table 7.1 ICBC Progress of Adopting Advanced Approaches to Capital Management

Time	Progress
2003	Launching Phase I of the IRB Approach Program
2005	Starting non-retail projects in Phase II of the IRB Approach Program
2007	Application of non-retail projects outcomes; starting retail projects in Phase II of the IRB Approach Program
2008	Application of retail projects outcomes; launching the Advanced Measurement Approach to Operational Risk Program
2009	Launching the Internal Model Approach to Market Risk Program, Pillar 2 ICAAP Program, and Credit Risk Verification Program
2010	Comprehensive application of risk quantification outcomes such as RAROC rigid control, and of outcomes of Market and Operational Risks Program; launching the Pillar 3 Information Disclosure Program
2011	Application of outcomes of ICAAP and Information Disclosure Programs; launching the Verification Program for Market and Operational Risks

2010-2013	Accepting the CBRC's pre-evaluation, follow-up evaluation, re-evaluation and acceptance evaluation, and rectifying problems discovered during the evaluations
April 2014	CBRC officially approved the adoption of advanced approaches to capital management.

V. Creating Effective Risk Monitoring Systems

In the increasingly complex business environment, end-to-end and forward-looking risk monitoring is the key to prevent financial risk and achieve prudent operations. Major state-owned banks, relying on big data mining techniques and systematic approaches, integrated middle and back office monitoring to timely and effectively identify and control risks.

Credit risk: ICBC set up a credit monitoring center equipped with hundreds of monitoring and analysis personnel. Relying on big data techniques, the center created risk early warning models from the dimensions of customers, products, industries, and so forth, to comprehensively monitor on- and off-balance-sheet financing across the group.

Market risk: The banks adopted pre-transaction control-oriented concepts and methods which covered such elements as traders, counterparties, trading prices, and trading deal limits. They set up independent middle offices to review front-office transactions one by one for real-time control. They also incorporated product control measures into post-transaction control, including three-way (front, middle and back offices) reconciliation, market value verification, cost-benefit analysis, and price monitoring. Through pre-transaction, real-time, and post-transaction control of their financial market business, the banks effectively prevented various risks in banking transactions.

Operational risk: The banks created centralized and efficient operation and risk monitoring systems featuring centralized business operations, remote authorization and optimized supervision. These systems converge fragmented operations in the back office, and employees handling the businesses are physically segregated from those approving them to fundamentally ensure independent authorization. They also created new supervision systems based on big data and quantitative models to prevent and control operational risk. Under the systems, post-transaction supervision was achieved through risk management and quality control, rather than conventional reviews, greatly reducing the rate of violations, number of risk events, and internal risk exposure year by year.

The Big Five share three characteristics in their RM practices. First, they started RM efforts with credit risk management, which, together with the subsequent market, operational and liquidity risk management, gradually formed their fast-growing ERM systems. In parallel with the international and comprehensive development of the banks, country and reputational risks were also incorporated into their RM. Second, they learned new RM concepts and upgraded RM systems amidst or in the wake of significant changes or reforms occurring in external environment, national policies, or themselves. Third, their RM systems have been growing more comprehensive, forward-looking and complex to meet new technical, financial, regulatory, and market disciplinary requirements, highlighting the increasingly vital role of ERM.

Section III
Development of Internal Control System

In 2002, the PBOC issued the "Guidelines for the Internal Controls of Commercial Banks"[1] which set forth the meaning and principles of internal controls. In 2004, the CBRC released the "Interim Measures for Internal Control Evaluation of Commercial Banks," which first integrated the five internal control components of control environment, risk identification and assessment, internal control measures, information exchange and feedback, and monitoring evaluation and correction. The Measures also proposed the full process evaluation of the internal controls of commercial banks. In October 2006, the CBRC issued the "Guidelines for the Compliance Risk Management of Commercial Banks" to promote the effective compliance risk management of banking financial institutions and ensure compliant operations. The CBRC also urged non-bank financial institutions to improve internal control systems through on-site inspections, off-site supervision, and regulatory ratings. In July 2007, the CBRC issued the "Guidelines for the Internal Controls of Commercial Banks."[2] The Guidelines specified the definitions, purposes and requirements of commercial banks' internal controls; incorporated internal control evaluation results into their risk assessment and the market access management over them; and urged the banks to establish dynamic processes and systems for the early prevention, real-time control, and post-event supervision and correction of risks.

Under the guidance of the CBRC, after 2004, the Big Five successively set up separate internal control and compliance (ICC) departments, developed ICC policies, and created overall frameworks for compliance management, providing a general basis for building compliance risk man-

---

1 PBOC Announcement [2002] No. 19.
2 CBRC Decree [2007] No. 6.

agement systems and conducting compliance management. These measures indicated the transformation of the banks' compliance management from decentralized to centralized models, from passive response to active response, from post-event handling to real-time control and comprehensive prevention, and from conventional and single to comprehensive and diverse functions.

The Big Five have been expanding their compliance management functions. Their ICC departments were originally tasked with setting up with internal controls, compliance management, operational risk management, and general auditing. Afterward, they have been placed in charge of AML, insider trading, related-party transaction, the "two lines of defense" for IT, operational risk monitoring, operation outsourcing management, and violation prevention. They also took over such duties as economic accountability audit, supervision-inspection integrated management, integrated management over group rules, ICC monitoring and analysis, foreign compliance management, as required by business development. Since their debut, ICC management systems have been evolving with the development of banks, playing a growing role in the banks' operations.

Under the "Guidelines for Internal Controls of Commercial Banks" of the CBRC, the Big Five have established complete compliance management systems through years of exploration, laying a strong foundation to become leaders among large listed banks.

I. Defining Organizational Structure of and Responsibilities for Compliance Management

To complete their joint-stock reform and listings and build on strengths in corporate governance, operations management, and risk controls, the Big Five have been devoted to creating sound compliance risk management frameworks and clarifying the duties of compliance posts since 2004.

First, they developed the top-level design for the top-down compliance management systems, where everyone involved can be held responsible. Specifically, the board assumes ultimate responsibility for compliance management across the bank; the Audit and Compliance Management Committee under the board is responsible for the day-to-day oversight of compliance management; and the Compliance Management Committee under the management level reviews compliance management plans, systems, measures, and procedures, and coordinates various departments in playing their compliance management roles.

Second, they established compliance management organizational structures. All the Big Five have set up compliance management bodies at the head office, tier-one branch and tier-two branch levels to lead, organize and coordinate compliance management activities. ABC has also assigned risk compliance managers to county-level sub-branches to manage compliance matters.

Third, they reinforced responsibility for compliance management and expanded the scope of ICC. For one, competent business departments at various organizational levels took primary responsibility for the compliance management of their own business lines: They incorporated basic compliance management concepts and basic compliant operation requirements into business procedures and different positions and supervised the implementation of these concepts and requirements, thus increasing each level's compliance management strength of corresponding business line.

Furthermore, the banks duly took a host of new steps, including employee code of conduct education, conduct management and a pilot program for comprehensive AML reform, and thus increased the duties and scope of ICC activities, replacing the old model of post-event examination, remediation and investigation, correction and responsibility identification with pre-event, real-time, and post-event control and conduct management. These steps highlighted the core value of internal control management.

II. Building Compliance Systems and Mechanisms

After creating their ICC management systems, to achieve new internal control targets, the Big Five successively released a series of compliance management guidelines and rules, thereby forming a three-pronged compliance management system comprising system framework, procedure management, and operational guidelines. This system ensured the compliance of bank-wide rules and systems.

ICBC set the overall goal of "accelerating efforts to establish a world-class internal control system" during its joint-stock reform. In early 2010, based on experience accumulated, ICBC laid down the compliance management principles of "compliant conduct, appropriate authorization, full-coverage monitoring, rigorous inspection, and effective control," which, keeping the original goal of compliance management, indicated a shift from overall system building to the development of critical elements, and specified the internal control goals for the subsequent period. In line with these principles, ICBC explored measures to create an ICC system with its own characteristics to achieve higher internal control targets. Then ICBC ICC General Manager Hui Ping recalled, "For bank-wide management, ICBC combined 'three lines of defense' (i.e., preventive risk management, deposit insurance system, and emergency response protocol) with vertical and horizontal supervision. For internal controls, the bank created a full-process ICC management model characterized by pre-process review, real-time verification and post-process inspection. To be specific, it explored and implemented embedded and service-oriented compliance review in pre-operation stage to ensure compliant conduct; focused on risk monitoring and the verification of quasi-risk events during operation to achieve full-coverage monitoring; and enhanced inspections, follow-up examination, investigation, and post-operation remediation to ensure rigorous inspection."

ABC created a uniform process for proposing, drafting, reviewing, approving, releasing, evaluating, revising and repealing its rules; developed annual plans for rule drafting and revision; periodically evaluated and collated its rules; published lists of in-effect rules; strictly followed rule-making procedures and standards; incorporated illustrative diagrams into rules; and created a regulatory framework planning chart for its business lines, thus creating a rule framework featuring four-tier hierarchy of authority and nine business units.

III. Identifying Responsibilities for and Handling of Risk Events and Violations

Following the joint-stock reform, the Big Five created internal control supervision and accountability systems to inspect the integrated planning, process management, and quality evaluation of projects; tighten the identification of accountability for project management and loss; and explore measures to identify accountability for risk events arising from financial asset and other services (e.g., asset management service). In this manner, the banks effectively reined in violations by operating units and employees through inspection. Based on internal control supervision and accountability systems, and rules governing risk events and violations, the Big Five created responsibility identification and accountability systems for risk events and violations, such that every management level, process, and person has clear responsibilities and can be held accountable (Fig. 7.4).

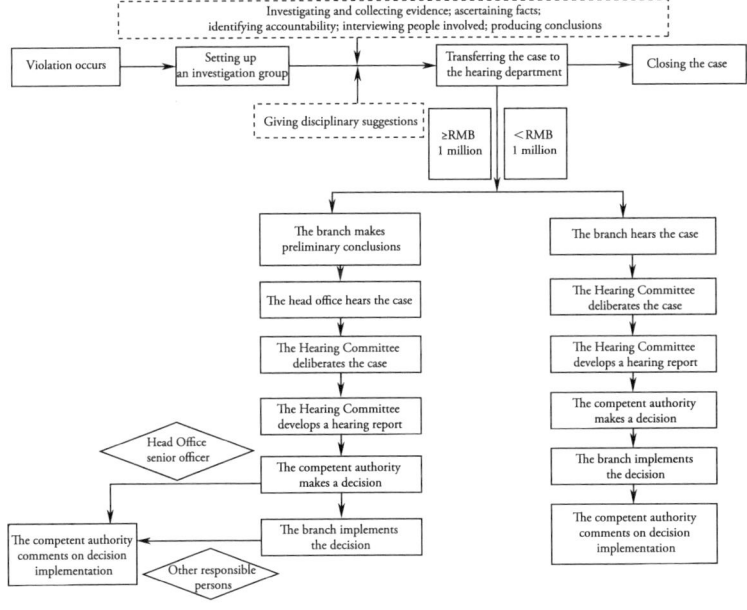

Fig. 7.4: Commercial Bank Procedure for Handling Violations

The Big Five establish violation accountability following the procedure of fact finding, division of accountability, consequence and circumstance assessment, severity assessment, and disciplinary action determination. Specifically, fact finding refers to the process where the investigation body determines facts relevant to detected violations, identifies accountability, and gives disciplinary suggestions. The next step is determining persons to be held responsible for the violation, including the offender(s), directly responsible individual(s), and persons assuming the management, leadership and supervision responsibilities. The third step is assessing consequences and circumstances of the violation, which are grounds for disciplinary actions. The fourth step is assessing the severity level of the violation, which determines whether the people involved would be exempted from or subject to light, medium, heavy and very heavy disciplinary actions. Disciplinary actions mainly include criticism and education, one-on-one disciplinary meeting, disqualification, pay reduction or suspension or dismissal (*richang chuli*), and administrative sanction.

Relying on strict internal control systems, the Big Five have broken away from previous "soft" risk management and accountability constraints. As then ICBC ICC General Manager Hui Ping said, "We established a set of strict accountability systems to restrain behavior and prevent risks. For example, the Three Iron Systems (iron bookkeeping, lending and regulation systems) prompted us to replace 'soft' risk management and accountability constraints with 'hard' constraints. Moreover, based on the principle of 'strict management ensures big benefits,' and 'Rules on Employee Violation Disciplinary Action,' the bank ensured successful identification of risks and violations like NPLs, and held corresponding offenders responsible for violations. The bank will also notify employees of the disciplinary action for a violation, warning them about the consequences of the violation, and urge business units to prevent risks through internal controls, so that employees dare not, cannot, and refuse to violate rules."[1]

IV. Boosting Compliance Culture and Awareness

Since 2010, the Big Five have explored steps to develop compliance culture, an effort to turn compliance concepts and rules into the awareness of compliance among employees. For one, they helped employees develop a correct and in-depth understanding of rules – first, following and respecting rules is essential for protecting their careers, and for promoting steady banking operations; second, rules should not only be understood, but more importantly, be applied in areas like business innovation and market expansion. Furthermore, they created rational, concrete, practical, and effective compliance education systems, which, focusing mainly on new, transferred and promoted employees, help them understand and follow the rules required by new positions, thus promoting steady banking growth.

ICBC started to provide compliance education as early as 2010 to help employees develop compliance awareness. Also, it set "internal controls improve quality and compliance creates value" as the very core of internal controls, and formulated a long-term mechanism for employee code of conduct education. In 2016, it released the "2016-2020 ICBC Plan for Internal Controls and Compliance Culture Development," where the core of internal controls is evolved into "bank-wide compliance and risk controls for robust and efficient growth."

---

[1] Quoted from the writing groups' interview with Hui Ping.

BoCom developed the *Employee Compliance Manual* and standard online training courseware. The *Manual*, created in four-frame comic strips, was emailed across the bank periodically, serialized in internal newspapers, and printed on large bulletin boards to disseminate and promote compliance concepts and requirements, helping employees better understand professional ethics and the code of conduct.

ABC issued a set of documents such as the "2010-2012 Compliance Culture Development Plan" and the "Compliance Culture Development Outline" to create a six-pronged long-term compliance culture development system, which comprised promotion and education, institutional building, intensified implementation, supervision and inspection, correction, and performance-based rewards and punishments. ABC also took other initiatives, such as publicizing compliance culture and violation prevention rules, analyzing typical cases arising from its operations, notably those related to its employees, to help them develop right compliance values.

V. Establishing ICC Methods to Improve Risk Control Capability

The promotion and use of new techniques and E-channels exposed banks to new risks. What's more, off-site supervision – a practice strongly pursued by domestic and foreign regulators – grew alongside the internationalization and integration of banking business, making risk controls a tougher task. In this context, improving methods and capabilities for compliance management became the Big Five's top priority.

Relying on cutting-edge technologies, the Big Five quickly optimized internal control supervision and compliance control measures and methods, to meet the new regulatory requirements. They created ICC management information systems to achieve the timely collection, efficient transmission, convenient sharing and adequate use of ICC information, immensely increasing the efficiency and effectiveness of compliance management.

ICBC has been working on creating an IT-based internal control system to promote IT-based internal controls. After developing a general plan for IT-based ICC in 2010, it created the Internal Control Monitoring and Analysis System and the Supervision and Inspection Management System, forming a basic bank-wide ICC Comprehensive Management Platform. Later, starting with the set-up, accessibility, and running of various systems, ICBC launched the IT-based ICC Program. According to the general plan, it pushed ahead with the building of ICC Comprehensive Management Platform, launched a range of subsystems for internal control monitoring and analysis, supervision and inspection management, and compliance management, released the MOVA System, Historical Data Storage Platform, and EDW Advanced Query System, and connected them to its major professional systems, which greatly increased the efficiency of its ICC management.

ABC launched in 2011 its ICC management information system – a basic, comprehensive, open operational and information platform for ICC management across the bank. Through constant upgrading, the platform has grown into a shared, bank-wide systematic framework which covers the whole ICC management process and supports information integration, data mining, risk monitoring, early warning response, analysis presentation, and other functions. Driven by big data, the framework enormously raised the application degree of IT in ICC management.

BOC's risk management information system debuted domestically and abroad in 2009 and 2012, respectively, achieving full coverage of risk management. Boasting three tools – internal control remediation, internal control inspection and operational risk management – as well as such functions as capital measurement, the system provided technical support for routine management and capital measurement of operational risk, contributing to the centralized and standard information management. In 2013, BOC released the Group Operational Risk Monitoring and Analysis Platform covering all core systems built both domestically and abroad. Designed to provide additional supervision parallel to the process-based supervision beyond individual processes, the platform filters operational data from operational systems of front, middle and back offices based on an early warning model. Also, with the support of manual analysis and judgment, the platform can identify, assess, rectify and control operational risk, thereby increasing business compliance, shortening the period in which material operational risk events could gain in severity, and refining operational procedures and systems.

VI. Facilitating Efficient Internal Control Management

Since the joint-stock reform, the Big Five have taken a number of steps to push forward the efficient management of internal controls.

First, the banks have been following the model of pre-process compliance review, real-time verification and post-process inspection. In terms of procedure, the banks focused on enhancing pre-process and real-time controls through rule-based integrated management, compliance review, internal control monitoring and analysis, and risk verification. In terms of structure, the head offices and tier-one branches carried out compliance review, monitoring and analysis of rules, systems and products, and tier-two branches and lower outlets conducted risk verification, supervision and inspection, thus forming bank-wide compliance systems where head offices and branches operate independently while supporting each other.

Second, the banks combined quantitative data analysis with qualitative event analysis, and incorporated the method into risk identification and assessment. Specifically, they integrated experience and outcomes accumulated via comprehensive application of big data and IT-based banking development with different types of information such as monitoring results, verification results, and risk event information collected in daily operations from different sources, to mine risk clues and detect trends of change relying on specialized systems and tools, thereby increasing their risk identification and assessment capabilities.

Third, the banks established online-plus-offline systems to achieve on-site-plus-off-site supervision. The on-line off-site supervision system enabled internal control supervision and analysis at different structural levels and in different business lines. The off-line on-site supervision system focused on conventional supervision means like violation reporting and customer surveys.

Fourth, the banks reinforced the duty performance capacity and professional ethics of internal control departments. Particularly, they built professional internal control teams in different business lines, thus improving the duty performance capacity in internal controls. They also enhanced employees' awareness of service and efficiency and work ethics, enabling them to perform duties in a proactive, objective and impartial manner.

During the joint-stock reform, SOCBs were required to build a better internal control system to meet modern commercial institutions' business needs, which enabled them to shift from previous critical process-oriented internal controls to the comprehensive development of internal control rules and systems. Through introducing advanced management concepts and techniques from leading foreign peers, innovating management models and procedures, and promoting regulated, standardized, procedure- and IT-based management, the Big Five have created an internal control management system covering every outlet and every operation process, and achieved notable progress in internal controls.

CHAPTER VIII
POST-REFORM REJUVENATION

– An Analysis of the Effectiveness
of the Joint-Stock Reform

It has been more than ten years since China's five major banks set foot on a new path from 2003 with the joint-stock reform. All debates and doubts about the success of this reform will be definitively settled with the passage of time, the fairest and truest judge of all things. While a magnificent undertaking, the joint-stock reform of state-owned banks – the largest as well as the most technical and influential of all financial reforms in the past 40 years, a "battle of the century" that China could not afford to lose – can prove its merits against the original designs only through the test of time.

Looking back at the history of banking reforms and at the uncertainties, complexities, and difficulties along the way, that the state-owned banks would finally embark on the path of joint-stock reform was because the reformers firmly believed that, compared with all other options, only this initiative could maximize the success in catalyzing a market-oriented transformation of the banking system to turn domestic banks into well-capitalized and modern financial institutions featuring sound internal control, robust operations, and excellence in services and performance. It was because they believed that it offered the best chance at empowering banks to become bona fide market players and key distributors of resources, so as to better support China's real economy. And it was because they believed it would increase the competitiveness of the banks. The joint-stock reform was not designed to address any temporary difficulty of the banks, but to help them develop the vitality and incentive mechanisms necessary for a brighter future. Therefore, to evaluate whether the joint-stock reform has been a success, it is not enough to solely look at the performance figures and qualitative improvements at the banks, but more importantly, we must also examine whether they have adopted a development philosophy and model that is different from what they used to pursue.

This chapter discusses the effectiveness of the joint-stock reform at two levels. First, it summarizes the post-reform changes in the development model and operating performance of the Big Five to determine whether the reshaping of the banking system, anchored by the joint-stock reform and public listing of the Big Five, has truly revitalized the banks. And second, through financial simulations, it gauges the net benefit the reform has brought to the state and the general public, in order to validate the financial soundness of the program.

Section I
Post-Reform Rebirths of Major Banks

While the string of programs pursued by the state and state-owned banks before the joint-stock reform led to certain improvements, they never radically freed the banks from the shackles of the old systems. Because of the diverging business objectives and lack of effective incentives and constraints, every state-owned bank faced a string of issues arising from distorted business decisions and actions as well as ineffective institutional frameworks. Eventually, the banks were hounded by high NPL ratios and poor performance, which continued to erode their competitiveness and long-term viability. Beginning with an overhaul of the equity rights, the joint-stock reform aimed to enhance the banks' corporate governance, secure their market status and vitality, foster growth potential, and reshape their business structures and models. During the ten or so years of the joint-stock reform, the major state-owned banks have indeed charted a new development path and lived up to the expectations of the government and the public on the strength of outstanding performance.

I. Transformation of Operating Model
(I) A Leap in Asset Quality

The problem of non-performing assets was most pronounced for the state-owned banking system and also the biggest challenge that had long plagued and stunted the state-owned banks. One of the major tasks of the banking reform was to reduce NPAs and establish a rigorous risk control framework. Thanks to the joint-stock reform, there has been a fundamental improvement in the quality of the assets held by the Big Five, with the

NPL ratio dropping from 18% before the reform to 1.56% in 2017, and the provision coverage ratio soaring from less than 20% to 171.5%. An equally substantial leap was also made in the risk management capacity of the Big Five. For example, in 2008, they had weathered through the international financial crisis, even managing to keep driving down the outstanding balance and relative ratio of NPLs. Since 2013, faced by a changing economic cycle as China transitions from fast growth to the new normal, the Big Five have held their ground by checking the growth of NPL balance and ratio to within 2% compared with 2012 figures. After write-offs and disposal of NPLs over the years, by 2017 the asset quality of the Big Five has stabilized as the NPL ratio has fallen. Adhering to the prudential principles and relevant policies, the Big Five have made adequate allowances for potential loan losses in anticipation of the fluctuations in asset quality and operating results during the change of economic cycle. Before the joint-stock reform, the onerous NPL problem and potentially massive losses pushed state-owned banks to the brink of bankruptcy; but today, the Big Five rival the best of their global peers in terms of asset quality.

Experiencing the operational difficulties arising from the NPAs prior to the joint-stock reform and the hardship of addressing the legacy issues during the reform, the Big Five have developed a profound understanding of the harm of non-performing assets, thus identifying the enhancement of risk management as a core operating principle. Following the joint-stock reform, the Big Five have noticeably increased their investment in risk management. They are the early adopters of enterprise risk management (ERM) frameworks and the Internal Ratings-Based (IRB) Approach, and leaders in developing and using innovative technologies. As a result, within China's banking industry they have become the benchmark for risk management and the guardian for financial stability.

(II) From Administrative Constraints to Institutional Constraints

Though the legacy problems of state-owned banks had many causes, both internal and external, they were all attributable to the lax business constraints on SOEs and state-owned banks. Before the joint-stock reform, state-owned banks had a multitude of business objectives and undertook many policy-related functions. They had also long relied on state appropriations, which gave the government or state finance a strong grip on their activities. This made it impossible to separate government activities from corporate activities, or to put an end to administrative interference. Consequently, the banks could not pursue a purely profit-driven strategy or develop the capacity to bear the risks and consequences of its actions.

The joint-stock reform enabled that separation and a profit-first strategy, and unlocked new sources of capital for the banks. Additionally, investors with differing interests could use their capital and voting rights to shape the activities of banks, creating a system of checks and balances that avoided further administrative meddling and redefined the banks' decision-making process and business practices.

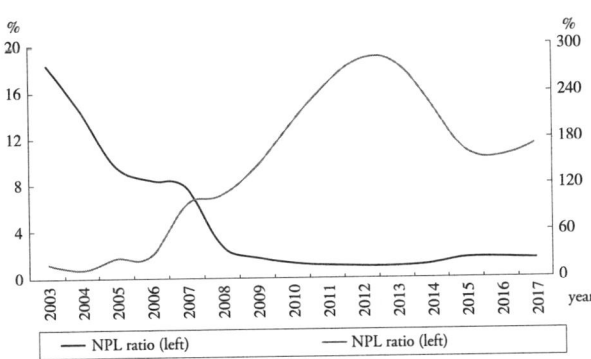

Fig. 8.1: NPL Ratio and Provision Coverage Ratio of Major Banks since the Joint-Stock Reform

Once capital became the measure and "regulator" of banking activities, market rules and internal forces superseded administrative directives and external influences as the guiding light of banks' operations. Confronted with the impersonal but also transparent "ceiling" that was capital, both banks and government authorities had little wiggle room and could not help but play by market rules and strike a balance between expansion and risk control, and between growth and stability. In short, capital was now the most important and scarcest resource for banking operations; and this capital-based business constraint redefined the development path of major Chinese banks.

Since the joint-stock reform, to meet capital requirements and ensure sustainability, the Big Five have integrated capital management into all major aspects of business operations, such as by creating a full suite of capital management systems, developing capital plans on a periodical basis, prospectively and systematically replenishing capital, and actively promoting performance evaluation, resource allocation, and management innovation based on the metrics of economic value added (EVA) and risk-adjusted return on capital (RAROC). Between 2005 and 2017, the net capital of the Big Five increased eightfold from RMB 1 trillion[1] to RMB 8.66 trillion; risk-weighted assets rose by a mere factor of 5.1, and the capital adequacy ratio improved from 11.2% to 14.6%. Capital-based business constraints have set the Big Five on a course of efficient, return-risk balanced, and sustainable business development.

---

[1] This figure does not include the Agricultural Bank of China as it had not begun its joint-stock reform in 2005.

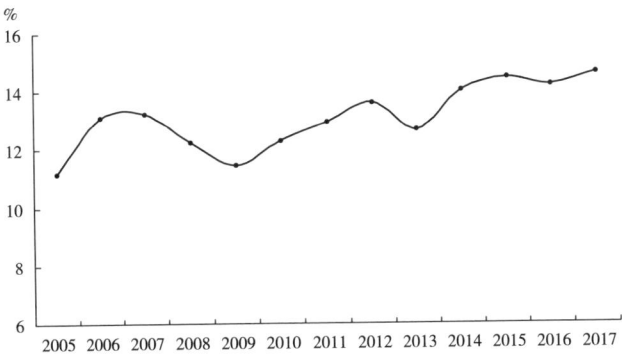

Note: Data before 2008 do not include the Agricultural Bank of China.

Fig. 8.2: Capital Adequacy Ratio of the Big Five since the Joint-Stock Reform

More importantly, the joint-stock reform has fundamentally altered the decision-making and management systems of state-owned banks. Following the reform, the Big Five established a modern governance framework consisting of the shareholders' meeting, the board of directors, the board of supervisors, and the management; and redesigned the corporate decision-making framework. The shareholders' meeting, the board of directors, and the board of supervisors perform their respective duties according to the bank's articles of association. This arrangement has introduced "multilevel oversight" over the conduct of the executive team, reduced the risk of manipulation by insiders and outside influences, created a basic internal operational framework that harmoniously integrates incentives with constraints, and enhanced the soundness and transparency of decision-making. Externally, disclosure requirements and investor relations are two other persistent "regulators" of the activities of listed banks.

Although there is still room for improvement in the banks' governance systems, the joint-stock reform has generally played a critical role in stabilizing the operations of major banks. Because of it, the banks have developed a new model for running modern commercial banks that well balances Party leadership and executive decisions, compliance with national policies and observance of market principles, social responsibilities and commercial interest, and decision-making efficiency and execution efficiency.

(III) From Scale-Oriented to Performance-Oriented Operations

For a long period before the joint-stock reform, state-owned banks had been nominal corporate businesses; in fact, they performed quasi-fiscal functions and were responsible for allocating resources as administrative authorities. This made wholly commercial-based incentives impossible to take root. Due to misdirected business objectives and lack of incentives, state-owned banks were increasingly disconnected from the market, complacent, and inefficient. The government was also challenged by the rising cost of controlling financial assets and maintaining financial security. Extricating itself from these financial ties would be hopeless without a systemic change.

The joint-stock reform and subsequent listing turned the Big Five into public companies, and state-owned shares became free float shares. A more diversified mix of both domestic and foreign investors has dislodged the formerly government-only shareholding structure and re-established the banks as a commercial concern. With these changes, it was both natural and justified for the banks to pursue commercial interest to maximize return to shareholders and other stakeholders. Because the interests of banks' shareholders, management personnel, employees, and customers are now fully aligned with profitability targets, the banks instinctively shifted from a quantitative, scale-oriented strategy to a quality-focused, profit-

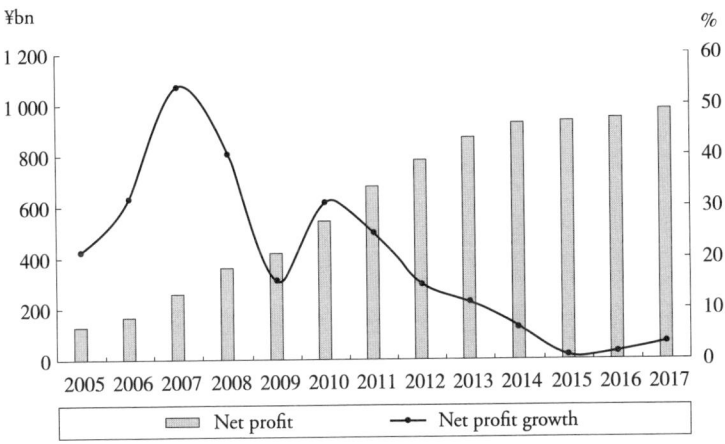

Fig. 8.3: Profitability of the Big Five (2005-2017)

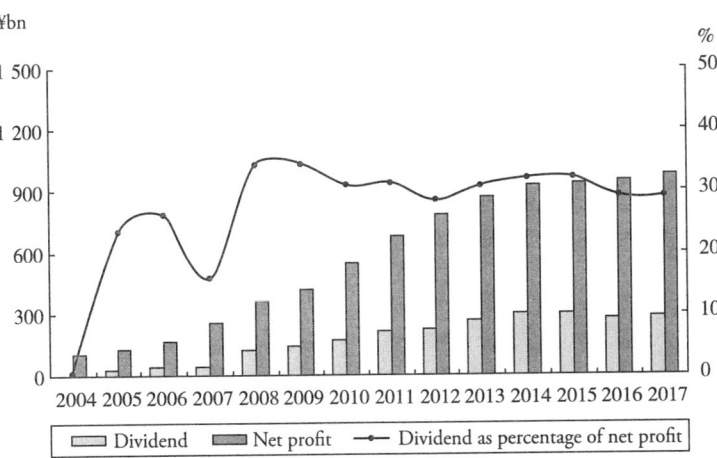

Fig. 8.4: Dividends Distributions of the Big Five (2004-2017)

oriented one. Indeed, the banks enjoyed a renaissance from 2005 to 2017, with annual profit growing 18.7% annually on average and 700% cumulatively, from RMB 122.6 billion to RMB 980.0 billion, creating a golden decade for the domestic industry and "miracle of the East" in the history of global banking. Since 2005, the Big Five have distributed more than RMB 2.4 trillion in dividends, or 29.8% of their net profit in the same period, creating much value for the state and millions of other investors.

(IV) From Single Business Pillar to Diversified Businesses

The joint-stock reform redefined the business objectives and operations of the major banks. The refocus on capital and the bottom line meant that structural optimization was now a higher priority than business expansion. Furthermore, the reform has lifted the legacy financial burdens off the shoulders of the banks, enabling them to more freely reshape their business structures.

The reform has brought three prominent changes to the banks. The first is the optimization of asset structures. Following the reform, the Big Five have been reworking their asset structures according to the macroeconomic environment. In particular, while moderately increasing the share of such assets as investments, they dynamically controlled the pace of credit supply, supported and implemented macroeconomic control policies, and reduced their risk exposures. From 2003 to 2007, China's average annual GDP growth was as high as 18.3%, so China's macroeconomic policy was to "prevent overheating from a rapidly growing economy and inflation from structural price increases." Accordingly, the Big Five voluntarily curbed credit growth, reducing the credit-to-asset ratio from 60.9% in 2003 to 53.3% in 2007 (or 49.5% excluding the loans that were transferred out during the joint-stock reform). After September 2008, the global financial crisis posed increasing threat to the Chinese economy. In response, the Chinese government shifted the macroeconomic policy to "maintaining steady and rapid economic development and controlling price hikes." The five major banks quickly stepped up their credit support for infrastructure, affordable housing, and livelihood projects, bringing their credit-to-asset ratio in 2014 to 54.1%.

Since 2015, in line with the new normal of economic development (i.e., quality over speed), the Big Five have slowed credit expansion to a modest pace and kept the credit-to-asset ratio to around 54%. On the whole, credit assets of the Big Five have fallen appreciably from the 60% level before the joint-stock reform, as have the banks' reliance on such assets. Meanwhile, thanks to the enhanced credit control capabilities, credit turnover and thus efficiency has also improved, allowing the Big Five to provide greater credit support to the real economy, rather than less, as might be predicted from their lower credit-to-asset ratio.

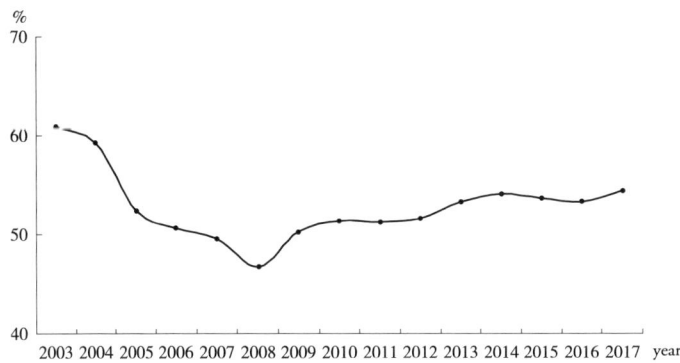

Note: Data do not reflect loans divested during the joint-stock reform.

Fig. 8.5: Loan-to-Asset Ratio of the Big Five (2003-2017)

The second change is the diversification of businesses. After reconnecting with the market with the help of the reform, the banks are now fully aligned with their customers in their interest. Also, the banks can now free up the human and financial resources previously tied to the NPAs, and use them to seize new opportunities and enhance business. Following the reform, the Big Five picked up the pace of business restructuring and innovation to dovetail with the intensifying economic reforms and the increasingly diverse customer needs. With a view to serving customers while conserving capital, increasing profitability, and lowering risks, the banks have ventured into new lines of business including investment banking, asset management, asset custody, financial market services, private banking, special financing, pensions, precious metals, and internet finance. These emerging businesses quickly became a significant part of the banks' operations, forming a sizeable professional services market and substantially diversifying the banks' existing product and service offerings.

Moreover, the joint-stock reform has provided banks with more accessible platforms for capital operations and facilitated the development of their cross-market businesses. Since 2005, the Big Five have either invested in or directly set up fund, leasing, insurance, and trust companies, in an effort to promote pilot integrated operations, improve product design, and test cross-selling and one-stop services. Having the full range of financial licenses opens up new possibilities in improving customer services and business competitiveness.

Table 8.1: Integrated Businesses of the Big Five (as of end of 2017)

Bank	Insurance	Fund	Securities, Investment Banking, Investment	Leasing	Trust	Others
ICBC	ICBC-AXA Life (60%)	ICBC Credit Suisse (80%)	ICBC International (100%)	ICBC Leasing (100%)	—	
			ICBC Financial Service (100%)			
			ICBC Financial Asset Investment (100%)			
ABC	ABC Life (51%)	ABC-CA Fund Management (51.67%)	ABC International (100%)	ABC Financial Leasing (100%)	—	
			ABCI Asset Management (100%)			
BOC	BOC Group Insurance (100%)	BOC Investment Management (83.5%)	BOC International Holdings (100%)	BOC Aviation (70%)	—	
	BOC Life (100%)		BOCI International (China) (37.14%)			
	BOC Insurance (100%)		Bank of China Group Investment (100%)			
	BOC-Samsung Life (51%)		BOC Financial Asset Investment (100%)			
CCB	CCB Life (51%)	CCB Principal Asset Management (65%)	CCB International (100%)	CCB Financial Leasing (100%)	CCB Trust (67%)	CCB Pension Management (85%)
			CCB Financial Asset Investment (100%)			
BoCom	China BOCOM Insurance (100%)	BoCom Schroder Fund Management (65%)	BOCOM International (100%)	BOCOM Financial Leasing (100%)	BOCOM International Trust (85%)	
	BoCommLife Insurance (62.5%)		BOCOM Financial Asset Investment (100%)			

Notes: 1. Information compiled from the 2017 annual reports of the Big Five.

2. Figures in parentheses are the shareholding ratio.

3. This table only lists the top-level, full-service subsidiaries of each bank.

The third change is the potential for the banks to fine-tune their revenue structure. Before the reform, interest spreads were the banks' largest "breadwinner," accounting for as high as 80% of their operating revenue. The reform not only helped banks optimize their asset and business structures, but also created for them additional sources of revenue.

From 2005 to 2017, the average annual growth of fees and commissions at the Big Five was 22.7%[1], 9.8 percentage points higher than that of net interest income, with fees and commissions accounting for 18% of the banks' net profit at the end of the period, up from 7.9%. The Big Five also lowered their reliance on loan interest; as between 2008 and 2017, they had doubled their investment income and optimized the interest structure. These changes in income structure have allowed the banks to reduce the effect of cyclical fluctuations on their revenue, and stabilized their performance and earnings, which have not only helped safeguard the interests of the country and investors, but also boosted market confidence and financial stability.

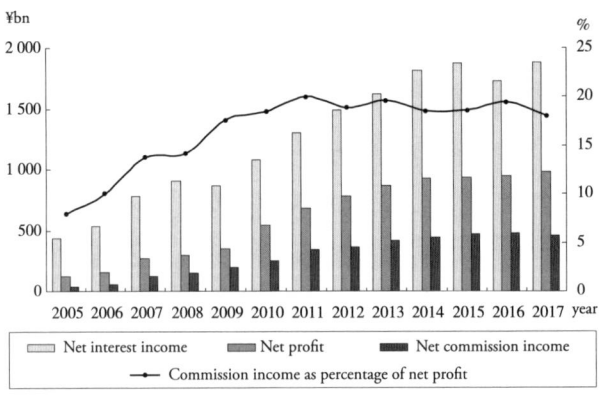

Fig. 8.6: **Profit Structure of the Big Five (2005-2017)**

---

1   Using the 2005 figures as the baseline here and in the following paragraph.

(V) From Local Businesses to Global Operations

Even before the joint-stock reform, the major banks made numerous, albeit modest, attempts to become more international. The reform and listing laid a foundation for them to pursue international presence. Starting with the Hong Kong listing of BOCHK and ICBC Asia, the benefits brought by the joint-stock reform – in terms of greater information availability, brand recognition, management capabilities, and capital strength – have made international expansion easier than before, and boosted the confidence and prospects of the banks to turn their global aspirations into a reality.

Following the reform, the Big Five all accelerated their international plans to keep pace with globalization trends. In particular, as European and American financial institutions scaled down overseas operations in the wake of the global financial crisis, the Chinese commercial banks were faced with a golden opportunity to expand internationally. As of the end of 2017, the Big Five had established more than 1,200 branches and outlets outside the Chinese mainland, creating a global network that covers six continents and all major financial centers. ICBC acquired a 20% stake in Standard Bank, the largest bank in South Africa, and became the latter's controlling shareholder. ABC and institutions from the Republic of the Congo created a joint-venture bank which promises to promote trade and economic cooperation between China and Africa. Under China's "going global" strategy, the Big Five have not only broadened their own business and source of revenue, but also greatly contributed to the national opening-up strategy. As of the end of 2017, the Big Five have set up branches in more than 20 Belt and Road countries, supplying the much-needed financial services for the Initiative.

Table 8.2: Overseas Presence of the Big Five (as of end of 2017)

Bank	Number of Overseas Branches and Outlets	Countries and Regions	Presence in Belt and Road Countries	Others	
ICBC	419	45	129 branches in 20 B&R countries and regions	Indirect coverage of 20 African countries through shareholding in Standard Bank Group	Agent bank agreement with 1,545 foreign banks in 143 countries and regions
ABC	22	17	6 branches in 5 B&R countries and regions	Establishing the Sino-Congolese Bank for Africa in the Republic of the Congo	Agent bank agreement with 1,594 banks in 151 countries and regions
BOC	545	53	Branches in 22 B&R countries and regions	—	Agent bank agreement with nearly 1,600 institutions in 178 countries and regions
CCB	184	29	Branches in 7 B&R countries and regions	—	Agent bank agreement (head office level) with 1,371 banks in 132 countries and regions
BoCom	65	18	Branches in 2 B&R countries – Singapore and Vietnam	—	Agent bank agreement with 1,580 peer institutions in 142 countries and regions

Note: Information compiled from the 2017 annual reports of the Big Five.

Concurrent with the growth of their global banking network, the Big Five are also becoming more proficient at running international businesses. At the end of 2017, each bank's overseas branches accounted for a greater share of the bank's total assets compared with 2006. These gains, notable even contrasted with the banks' rapidly growing domestic business and profit-earning capacity, indicate that their international efforts are beginning to bear fruit.

Table 8.3: Operating Results of Big Five's Overseas Branches Before and After the Joint-Stock Reform

Bank	2006		2017	
	Proportion of total assets (%)	Contribution to total profit (%)	Proportion of total assets (%)	Contribution to total profit (%)
ICBC	2.97	3.67	9.0	7.0
ABC	0.7	0.8	4.42	2.24
BOC	24	43	25.99	29.5
CCB	2.25	0.82	5.4	4.06
BoCom	6.39	10.64	10.41	8.30

Note: Information compiled from the 2017 annual reports of the Big Five.

The joint-stock reform also helped China to create a banking regulatory system that conforms to international best practices, and the major banks to converge with international standards in business philosophy, systems, and tools. The establishment of the China Banking Regulatory Commission, capital management mechanisms, and macro-prudential regulatory framework have elevated the industry to more stringent operational protocols and standards. Of particular note, since 2002 the Chinese accounting standards have gone through multiple major revisions, such that the accounting items, accounting standards and methods, as well as disclosure rules are now substantially converged with the international accounting standards and general practices. These developments have in turn noticeably improved the international recognition and fairness of the financial information of major Chinese banks, made it easier to compare these banks with their international peers in all aspects of business management, and helped them compete internationally.

These banks are now always among the first in the world to comply with and implement international rules on risk and capital management.

Under the leadership of the China Banking Regulatory Commission, the Big Five have duly implemented Basel II and Basel III, and in fact have held themselves to higher standards than the Basel Accords in areas of risk measurement, provisioning, capital management, market discipline and supervision, and arrangements for the transition period. Through listing in both the domestic and international capital markets, the Big Five have proven that they have met the disclosure standards for listed companies and have significantly improved their business transparency.

(VI) From Leaders in Scale to Leaders in Innovation

The history of the reform of state-owned banks is a history of innovation; but the significance and role played by innovation varied as the banks went through different stages of development. Before the joint-stock reform, business and management innovations were mostly designed to support business growth so that the banks could best their peers in corporate size and business scale. Because the reform has fundamentally altered the market environment, galvanized the banks, and reshaped banking operations, innovation now has a higher mandate. Accordingly, the major banks have turned to technical and IT innovations to drive their growth, and in the process, they have turned from leaders in business scale to leaders in innovation.

Notably, innovation has brought benefits to three areas. First, innovation of business channels has made the banks more efficient. The Big Five all went through the ordeal of downsizing during the joint-stock reform, closing down poorly run outlets and establishments to save cost, optimize the use of resources, and raise the overall efficiency of the banks. Following the reform, the Big Five were faced with the even more pressing need of reinventing their business channels: The ever more sophisticated customer needs and the emergence and fast growth of new business lines and new business landscape have posed fresh challenges to the functions and efficiency of existing business channels. In particular, the take-off of mobile technology after 2008 and of internet economy and internet finance after 2011 has dealt a significant blow to the banks' traditional channels and service models. Now under mounting pressure, the Big Five fought back with an innovation-driven revolution of business channels.

For one, the banks have upgraded their IT systems to enable remote, smart, and automated processing of transactions. At the same time, banking outlets have been transformed from offering only limited services to providing a full range of services, and finally to purveyors of smart services.

Secondly, the banks have invested heavily in electronic channels. In response to the growing popularity of smart mobile devices, wireless internet technologies, and online financial services, the Big Five are finding new ways to combine technology with finance. By streamlining websites, transactions, and processes and bringing in robots and other novel service methods, the banks are building more open and intelligent online service channels. By opening text message banking, WeChat banking, mobile banking, and other new service channels, they have made financial services on-the-go both faster and easier. These innovations have resulted in a surge in the proportion of transactions handled outside physical outlets. For instance, in 2017 95.0% of the transactions at ICBC were conducted online, up from 50% before the joint-stock reform. For BOC and BoCom, that figure was 94.2% and 94.5%, respectively. These numbers show that e-banking and mobile banking are now the primary channels for serving bank customers.

Thirdly, the banks have pushed for greater integration of online and offline business. Aiming to provide a consistent service experience, the Big Five are investing in ideas that help bridge the digital divide between online and offline service channels and bring out the best of each. In short, mobile applications, smart banks, QR codes, and other technologies have revolutionized the design and efficiency of banking channels.

Also in terms of benefits, internet-based innovations have reshaped banking operations. One of the biggest challenges before the Big Five following the reform was the rise of internet finance. Emerging in early 2009 and sweeping across the country merely two years later, internet finance has made a spectacular entrance by uprooting the traditional model of banking business. With the dawning of the era of internet finance, the Big Five all sprang into action. ICBC has introduced the "e-ICBC" strategy to pursue a forward-thinking, more intelligent, and more sustainable development strategy. CCB chooses to build a robust financial ecosystem and gradually merge its traditional banking services into a fully integrated e-banking service platform. BOC is committed to building itself into a mobile- and service-oriented internet bank. ABC focuses on expanding its customer base and increasing customer loyalty, supporting the real economy and the agricultural sectors, as well as integrating financial services with real-world scenarios to build synergy. And lastly, BoCom is pursuing a business model that "combines 'financial internet' with 'internet finance.'"

After 2012, the five major banks have all created their own internet finance platforms and steadily improved them based on customer feedback. The Big Five have been committed to giving traditional financial services an "internet makeover" by developing new products and services such as online payment, financing, investment, and trade. The coming of a new wave of standardized, convenient, and inclusive products that complement well with the traditional offerings, has created a vast, promising internet-based financial business landscape that has forever altered the way major banks operate and grow.

Innovations, specifically IT innovations, have also enabled more robust business management. State-owned banks have a long tradition of using technologies to improve how their businesses are managed and operated. In view of the management transformation plan proposed for the joint-stock reform, the Big Five took advantage of the latest-generation information technologies just as they became widespread in the financial industry. These upgraded IT backbones have in turn allowed the banks to improve management systems and efficiency. Specifically targeting their long-standing managerial challenges, for a short period after the joint-stock reform the Big Five were fully focused on building up IT capabilities, in order to strengthen their head office's ability to oversee all businesses, organizations, and risks; make information more transparent; improve the coverage and penetration of management ability; and ensure secure and stable operations.

Adapting to the rise of a new generation of technologies including the internet, big data, and cloud computing, in 2010 the Big Five shifted their near-term objective from IT-equipped banks to fully IT-powered banks. To this end, they have ramped up the development and deployment of the new-breed IT architectures, and begun building enterprise-level databases as well as big data- and cloud computing-based analytical systems. Along with their growing IT capabilities, the banks are bringing technologies to such areas as product design, business marketing, risk control, and lean operations. When combined with the traditional management systems, these IT-enabled applications help the banks make all their management activities smarter and more precise.

In short, the joint-stock reform has created the pre-conditions for business and management innovation, and innovation in turn is the main pathway to a successful reform and more vibrant and sustainable banks. The innovation-driven achievements of the Big Five following the joint-stock reform are a testament to the profound and positive impact of the reform on the banks.

(VII) From Middle-of-the-Pack to Global Leaders

To evaluate the effectiveness of the joint-stock reform, one can conduct a "vertical" comparison of the state of the banks before and after the reform. But a more thorough and objective evaluation is based on a "horizontal" comparison with comparable peers. For many decades the Chinese commercial banks have looked up to the established international banks – Citigroup, JPMorgan Chase, HSBC, and the like – as international benchmarks and role models. In their joint-stock reform plans, the Big Five also used these banks as yardstick for core performance indicators. In retrospect, that the Big Five have been able to recover from being "technically insolvent" before the reform, to being internationally competitive institutions whose post-reform core indicators consistently rival those of the comparable foreign banks, is another convincing proof of the success of the reform.

This progress is most evident in four areas. First, the banks now boost world-leading profit levels. Between 2005 and 2016, the total pre-tax profit of the Big Five soared from USD 23.5 billion to USD 171.7 billion, an increase of 19.8% annually and 630% cumulatively. In the same period, the total profit of the seven comparable international banks rose from USD 122.0 billion to USD 143.8 billion, an increase of merely 1.5% annually and 17.8% cumulatively. Looking at the numbers from another angle: the total profit of the Big Five was 19.2% of that of the seven international banks in 2005, but 120% by the end of 2016.

Table 8.4: Profit Levels of Major International Banks

Bank	Pre-Tax Profit			
	2005		2017	
	Profit ($mn)	Ranking	Profit ($mn)	Ranking
ICBC	7,355	18	52,270	1
CCB	6,860	21	42,476	2
JPMorgan Chase	12,215	6	34,552	3
ABC	976	127	32,608	4
Wells Fargo	11,548	7	32,120	5
BOC	6,668	23	32,002	6
Bank of America	25,155	2	25,153	7
Citigroup	29,433	1	21,398	8
BoCom	1,591	85	12,390	9
BNP Paribas	9,937	10	11,800	10
MUFG Bank	12,786	5	11,631	12
HSBC	20,966	3	7,112	31

Source: *The Banker*'s Top 1000 World Banks. Rankings for 2005 and 2017 are based on data published in 2006 and 2018 respectively for the preceding year.

Second, the Big Five are now among the best capitalized banks in the world. The ten or so years of steady growth following the joint-stock reform have greatly raised the capital strength of the five banks. Indeed, their total tier-1 capital surged from USD 117.5 billion in 2005 to USD 985.3 billion in 2016, a growth of 740%. ICBC, ABC, BOC, and CCB have all joined the list of top ten banks by capitalization; and ICBC has even been holding onto the top spot for many years in a row. For comparison, the total tier-1 capital of the seven international banks rose by only 164% over the same period. In terms of capital ratio[1], the Big Five went from only 4.46% in 2005 to 7.48% in 2016, a gain of 3 percentage points; the seven international banks picked up only 2.1 percentage points, from 5.27% to 7.37%.

Table 8.5: Tier-1 Capital of Major International Banks

Bank	2005		2017	
	T1 Capital ($mn)	Ranking	T1 Capital ($mn)	Ranking
ICBC	31,670	16	281,262	1
CCB	35,647	11	225,838	2
JPMorgan Chase	72,474	4	208,112	3
BOC	31,346	17	199,189	4
Bank of America	74,027	3	190,315	5
ABC	9,864	60	188,624	6
Citigroup	79,407	1	178,387	7
Wells Fargo	29,873	19	171,364	8
HSBC	74,403	2	138,022	9
MUFG Bank	63,898	5	135,944	10
BoCom	8,949	65	90,367	11
BNP Paribas	25,146	24	86,476	14

Source: *The Banker*'s Top 1000 World Banks. Rankings for 2005 and 2017 are based on data published in 2006 and 2018 respectively for the preceding year.

Third, brand competitiveness has improved significantly. For a bank, a brand is built upon its products, services, technologies, and employees, and reflects its market reputation and competitiveness.

---

1 *The Banker* simply calls this indicator the capital adequacy ratio, given by tier-1 capital / total assets. To avoid confusion, this book refers to it as "capital ratio" here and in other parts of this section.

Brand Finance's 2005 brand valuation list did not contain a single Chinese commercial bank. From 2007 to 2017, the brand value of the Big Five rose 530%, compared with 34.2% for the seven international banks. As a result, while the Big Five only represented 19% of the brand value of the international banks in 2007, that figure climbed to 88.8% just ten years later, reflecting the significant headway they have made internationally since the reform. According to *"Brand Finance* Banking 500 2017," ICBC, CCB, BOC, and ABC were among the top ten most valuable brands in the banking industry, overtaking household names such as Citigroup and HSBC Holdings. BoCom gained 44 places on the list, to earn a place in the top 20, thanks to a 340% rise in brand value.

Table 8.6: Brand Value of Major International Banks

Bank	2007		2017	
	Value ($mn)	Ranking	Value ($mn)	Ranking
ICBC	84.27	16	478.32	1
Wells Fargo	131.3	8	416.18	2
CCB	77.86	18	413.77	3
JPMorgan Chase	147.98	6	337.37	4
BOC	67.41	23	312.5	5
Bank of America	254.17	3	302.73	6
ABC	—	—	285.11	7
Citigroup	278.17	2	276.74	8
HSBC	354.56	1	206.88	9
BNP Paribas	146.37	7	136.44	13
MUFG Bank	35.4	52	132.15	14
BoCom	26.64	63	116.32	19

Notes: 1. Data from the brand value reports published by *Brand Finance*.

2. None of the Chinese commercial banks made the list in or before 2007. No information is available on the brand value and ranking of ABC in 2007.

3. JPMorgan is listed separately from Chase on the brand value list. The

figure for 2007 is for Chase. JPMorgan was ranked 13th in 2007 with a brand value of USD 9.064 billion, and 11th in 2017 with a value of USD 15.71 billion.

Fourth, there has been a substantial rise in the banks' market value and international influence. Public listing in particular has made the Big Five more influential in the global capital market. In 2006, aside from ABC which had yet to be listed, ICBC, BOC, and CCB all made the list of top ten banks by market value, with BoCom coming in at the 28th place. For all the ups and downs of the capital market in the years thereafter, the Big Five generally maintained their growth momentum in this metric. By 2017, ICBC, ABC, BOC, and CCB were among the top ten most highly valued listed banks in the world, with BoCom taking the 27th spot. The total market value of ICBC, BOC, CCB, and BoCom rose 28.9% compared with 2006.

Table 8.7: Market Value of Major International Banks

Ranking	2006		2017	
	Bank	Market Value ($bn)	Bank	Market Value ($bn)
1	Citibank	273.7	JPMorgan Chase	371.1
2	ICBC	250.9	ICBC	326.8
3	Bank of America	239.8	Bank of America	307.9
4	HSBC	210.0	Wells Fargo	298.8
5	JPMorgan Chase	167.6	CCB	232.9
6	BOC	165.4	HSBC	207.4
7	CCB	143.0	Citibank	196.7
8	MUFG Bank	132.9	ABC	187.4
9	RBS	123.9	BOC	169.7
10	Wells Fargo	120.0	RBS	119.1
28/27	BoCom	55.6	BoCom	63.5

Source: Data compiled from public information.

The major banks that have undergone the joint-stock reform have become not only the pillars of China's financial market, but also the "stabilizing anchors" of the global financial market. In 2011, the G20 Financial Stability Board identified BOC as one of the latest Global Systemically Important Financial Institutions (G-SIFIs). According to the Basel Committee on Banking Supervision, the recognition of a G-SIFI is based on, among other factors, the size, interconnectedness, and substitutability of the institution in question, and, in particular, its influence on the global market. The recognition of BOC as a G-SIFI means that international regulators are beginning to take note of the global influence of Chinese banks. By 2015, ICBC, ABC, and CCB were also identified G-SIFIs. And by 2017, Chinese banks made up 14% of the 28 global banks on the G-SIFI list.

II. Pillars for the Real Economy

More important than to simply turn around the distressed state-owned banks and reduce potential financial risks, the joint-stock reform was meant to ensure that the banks could support China's economic development long into the future. This is also the primary criterion by which the success of the reform would be judged. In fact, the major banks now continue to be the pillars of the economy, not in any way different from before the reform was launched. Furthermore, with the improved operational frameworks, they are now even more capable than before in providing leverage and in allocating resources, which have been instrumental to the national economic strategy and economic transformation and upgrade.

(I) Improving Financial Services to Power the Economy

The decade following the joint-stock reform coincides with China's golden period of economic development, during which the country's growing and maturing market demanded higher credit supply than the years before. Although the reform had stripped away a considerable amount of NPLs from the banks, causing their credit balance to decline, the banks' ability to provide capital and financial leverage is not at all diminished, but is in fact heightened. From 2006 to 2017, the Big Five's total credit balance more than quadrupled from RMB 12.8 trillion to RMB 53.2 trillion, equaling an annual growth rate of 13.8%. Even accounting for the NPLs that were divested during the reform, the cumulative growth would still be quadrupling, from close to RMB 14 trillion to RMB 55 trillion (Fig. 8.7).

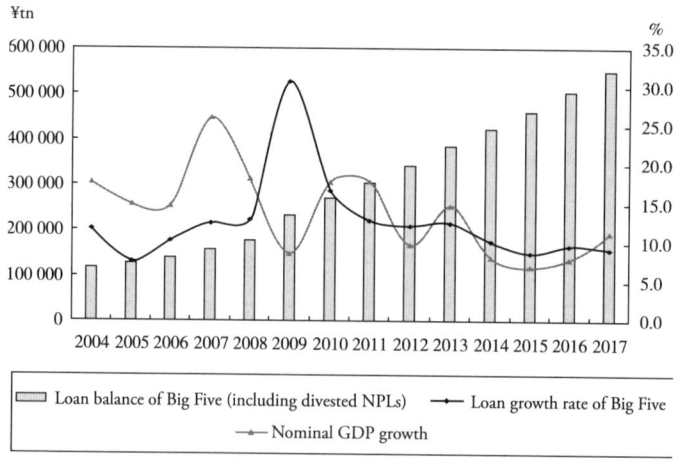

Fig. 8.7: **Credit Supply of the Big Five and Macroeconomic Growth (2004-2017)**

More importantly, the reform has enabled the banks to better manage their credit assets, which helps safeguard economic stability.

1. Remaining the principal channel of social financing following the reform

Although financing channels in China have become increasing diverse in recent years with the development of the multi-layered capital market, bank credit still accounts for nearly 70% of total social financing (aggregate financing to the real economy). Furthermore, 30.5% or nearly one-third of the total is attributable to the Big Five, demonstrating that they are still the main supplier of capital for powering China's economic growth (Fig. 8.8).

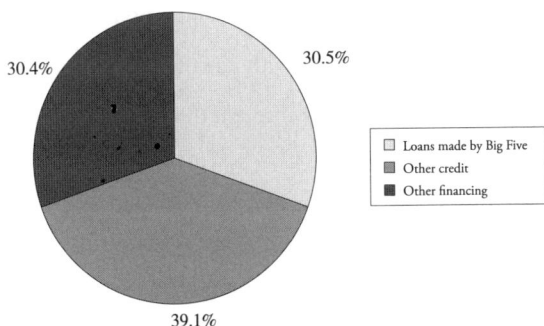

Fig. 8.8: Breakdown of Total Domestic Social Financing in 2017

2. Building resilience against financial crisis

While China's 9.34% GDP annual growth from 2003 to 2017 – and especially the double-digit growth from 2003 to 2013 – may suggest a consistently upward economic trajectory, the reality was not so. The 2007-2008 subprime mortgage crisis that took the world by storm was also taking a heavy toll on China. It started with trade contraction, which battered industries and liquidity and thus quickly led to a precipitous slowdown of the economy as GDP growth dropped to 6.2% in the first quarter of 2008.

To maintain the country's growth momentum in the face of the crisis, the central government rolled out a 4-trillion-yuan stimulus package, which gave rise to complementary investment plans at various local levels, all designed to spur domestic consumption and investment. Major investment projects required credit support; and the Big Five, which contributed over half of the China's total social financing at the time, naturally became the dominant lenders that would help China implement macroeconomic policies and maintain growth rate and investment. In particular, the five banks all increased credit supply to fund infrastructure, post-disaster rebuilding, and other key projects, thereby helping the Chinese economy stabilize from the second quarter of 2009 and rebound before the end of the year, as evidenced by a GDP growth rate of 9.1% that year.

In retrospect, it was precisely through the constructive interaction of various measures and conditions that China was able to weather through the storm in 2008-2009 – a lapse in any part of China's crisis response plan would throw it off course, and an adequate supply of credit from banks was certainly an essential part of that plan. But if the joint-stock reform had not taken place, could the banks have come up with the capital needed to help China ward off a crisis that had ravaged the world? And where then would the Chinese economy be headed? A thought experiment for this hypothetical scenario might offer another perspective that helps one understand the value and necessity of the reform.

In the three-year period from 2009 to 2011, the Big Five extended a net amount of RMB 12.78 trillion of loans, representing an annual growth rate of 21.8% and a great boost to the real economy. Net increase in 2009 alone was over RMB 5.4 trillion, or more than one-third of the five banks' loan balance in 2008.

Assuming a 100% risk weighting and an 8% minimum capital adequacy ratio, an increment of RMB 12.78 trillion of loans would require an additional RMB 1.02 trillion of capital. Assuming the joint-stock reform was displaced by the former plan of the PBOC that required the banks to resolve the legacy NPLs by themselves, and assuming the banks could achieve an optimistic 10% annual profit growth before 2012, then between 2009 and 2011, the Big Five could at most earn RMB 560.0 billion of profit, or a staggering RMB 460.0 billion short of the amount of additional capital needed for the RMB 12.78 trillion of loans.

Without the joint-stock reform, it would be exceedingly difficult for the banks to make up for the capital shortfall. For if they did not go public, the funding gap could only be plugged by issuance of subordinated debt or capital injection by the state. And without the joint-stock reform, the Big Five was nowhere near the financial position needed to issue debts at any time before 2009, while capital injection was also out of the question during the subprime mortgage crisis.

In other words, the joint-stock reform had allowed the Big Five to issue an additional RMB 5.75 trillion (RMB 460 billion/0.08) of loans during the crisis. Based on the historical growth rates for GDP and loans, it can be estimated that before 2011, for every 1 yuan of loan the GDP would increase by 0.7 yuan. Therefore, the additional loans granted during the crisis and as part of the reform would have translated into an additional RMB 4 trillion in GDP or around 5 percentage points in GDP growth. Hence, it is safe to say that without the joint-stock reform which had reshaped the banks' business structure and development model and put the banks in a much stronger position in terms of capital, profitability, and credit management capability, the Big Five would be hard pressed to play a vital economic role as they did during the financial crisis.

3. Boosting credit management capacity

The quintupling of the loan books of the Big Five, from around RMB 10 trillion before the joint-stock reform to RMB 53 trillion after it, has made credit management much more challenging. Assuming a 1:2 new-to-repayment ratio, an annual loan increase of RMB 5 trillion means RMB 15 trillion was actually disbursed each year, if repayments of matured loans are taken into account. This suggests that however large the loan portfolio would be, it would be completely turned over every three to four years, which requires a much more sophisticated credit management system than what state-owned banks could hope to possess before the reform.

History has shown that the system developed during the reform has risen up to the challenge. For more than a decade, the major banks have ensured an adequate credit supply for key development projects and a well-functioning economy, as well as an NPL ratio of within 2% and no outbreak of systemic risks.

(II) Channeling Capital for Economic Transformation and Upgrade

The key to maintaining loan quality during a credit boom lies in choosing the right projects and maintaining a good loan structure. Fine-tuning of the loan structure is also a telltale sign and key component of economic transformation and upgrade. Aligning with the shift in national economic strategies, the major banks not only optimized their loan portfolios, but also played an indispensable role in helping China restructure its real economy by pursuing qualitative development, trimming excess capacity, and addressing economic weaknesses.

First, they supported China's major economic strategies. Since 2003, China has bolstered top-level economic planning and unveiled a series of major regional, sectoral, and industrial policies such as the "Four Regions" strategy, which prescribes tailor-made economic priorities for East, West, Northeast, and Central China, and the "Three Supporting Belts" strategy which consists of the Belt and Road Initiative, the Coordinated Development of Beijing-Tianjin-Hebei Region program, and the Yangtze River Economic Belt program. These strategies, entailing the wide-ranging transport and migration of factors of production as well as cross-regional economic cooperation, requires massive investment and funding support. To promote and secure more private investment for these major national projects, the Big Five each drew up and implemented a highly successful battle plan that covered strategic design, policy guidance, system optimization, and business innovation and made the most out of their role as a financial platform and intermediary.

In terms of strategic design, a central goal of the Big Five's efforts to adjust loan structures and transform corporate business was to promote the coordinated development of economic regions. For instance, ICBC has incorporated the "Four Regions" and "Three Supporting Belts" strategies into its medium- and long-term plan, to better prioritize loans for national strategic programs, build a robust investment banking business, support national cross-regional projects, shape itself into an integrated financial service provider for the "going global" strategy, and help businesses expand overseas. For CCB, it was to leverage its competitive edge in infrastructure projects, project cost consulting, and full range of financial licenses to support major national initiatives.

In terms of policy guidance, the banks have developed targeted policy guidelines to advise local branch activities. BoCom released the "BoCom Guidelines for Aligning with National Key Strategic Policies" and the "Opinions on Implementing the State's Strategy of Accelerating the Building of the Central Plains Economic Zone," among others. It has even integrated the key points of those documents into its sector-specific and regional investment guidelines and market entry strategies. For ABC, the focus in East and Central China is the Yangtze River Golden Waterway and the Multimodal Transportation Corridor of the Yangtze River Economic Belt. Further north, it is the Coordinated Development of Beijing-Tianjin-Hebei Region, in particular projects related to urban infrastructures, rail transit, clean energy, decentralization of Beijing's non-capital functions, and the Winter Olympic Games.

In terms of institutional optimization, the Big Five have been improving the systems for managing the pool of major projects and for cross-regional coordination, believing that those systems would make existing strategies easier to carry out. The aim is to ensure steady progress of key programs and major regional projects. As a result, many economically and socially beneficial projects have been launched to enthusiastic reception from the public.

Second, the banks have promoted industrial restructuring. After the financial crisis, China sped up economic transformation, and a top priority of that transformation was to upgrade industries and manage production capacity. The country's 12th Five-Year Plan laid out the direction and focus of this upgrade and transformation; following the 18th CPC National Congress, the supply-side structural reform was launched to reshape the industrial and economic landscape by "cutting excess capacity, inventories, leverage, and costs, and addressing economic weaknesses." As in the case of other major initiatives, industrial reform requires major financial institutions to provide integrated services, innovative offerings, and more efficient asset allocation and financing models. The recent years have seen the Big Five supplying the financial leverage needed by the national economic policies and industrial restructuring.

For one, the banks have been keen to foster new growth drivers. While ensuring risk manageability and business sustainability, the Big Five have set out the overall loan balance and structure, and continue to optimize their loan portfolios in terms of maturity dates, customers, loan types, and regions, with a view to channeling more capital to strategic emerging industries, advanced manufacturing industries, modern service industries, and other areas promoted by national policies. At the same time, the banks are also offering a wider range of non-credit financing options, such as wealth management products, bonds, leasing, and trusts.

Additionally, the banks are now more attentive to addressing root causes by accelerating the phase-out or transformation of outdated industries and eliminating excess capacity. In particular, the Big Five are discouraging loans and private investment to industries with excess capacity by more effectively enforcing industry-specific loan policies, offering differentiated interest rates, and strengthening capital management. Meanwhile, the banks now provide integrated financial services such as merger and restructuring advisory and debt-for-equity swaps to contain the cost and risks of economic restructuring and to contribute their know-how and plans for industrial transformation.

Related Topic: CCB Brokering Debt-for-Equity Swaps

To help deleverage the real economy and promote debt-for-equity swaps as encouraged by the government, CCB has been committed to experimenting with new business models and practices. Adhering to market and legal principles throughout the process, the bank works with high-quality businesses to find a broad range of investors who are interested in exchanging debts for equities. The proceeds raised are earmarked for paying down high-cost debts. CCB even established a dedicated company for handling these swaps – CCB Financial Asset Investment – at the close of 2016 in Beijing.

In 2016, CCB undertook the market-driven debt-for-equity swaps of a central SOE (Wuhan Iron and Steel Corporation), a local SOE (Yunnan Tin Group), and a private company (Nanjing Nangang Iron and Steel United) – the first in the country for these business types. In addition, it has inked framework agreements with Shandong Energy Group, Shanxi Coking Coal Group, and Chongqing Chemical & Pharmaceutical Holding, among others. By the end of 2016, CCB had signed debt-for-equity swap agreements valued at RMB 222 billion and raised RMB 18.2 billion of investment. Once the funds are in place, the businesses involved are expected to reduce their debt ratio by 5-15 percentage points each and significantly lower their financial costs.

Third, the banks have helped correct the weaknesses in the economy. Since the joint-stock reform, the Big Five have actively answered the government's call for supporting micro and small businesses, the agricultural sector, poverty-stricken areas, and other underdeveloped sectors. To this end, the banks have been adhering to the latest policies, increasing credit and financial support, and generally becoming a role model for helping build a stronger economy.

For example, to promote system and product innovations, the banks have set up inclusive finance divisions, specialized microfinance institutions, and dedicated teams for the agricultural sector. They have also developed specialized products, data collection and accounting practices, and risk management, resource allocation, and project and performance evaluation systems, and increased the use of information technologies in standardized online projects and risk management. Overall, the banks have achieved the goal of "three minimums" (*sange budiyu*)[1] in microfinance for many years in a row. As of 2017, the Big Five maintained a loan balance of RMB 7.42 trillion with domestic micro and small businesses, accounting for 31.8% of all loans issued to them by commercial banks, showing that the Big Five are the primary source of such financing support.

The banks have also increased financial support to address uneven and inadequate economic development as part of the national anti-poverty campaign. Since the joint-stock reform, the Big Five have synergized loans, policy support, and targeted agricultural loan products and improved the related payment and credit systems, which allow them to precisely address the financing needs of poverty-stricken areas and increase the coverage and efficiency of their services.

Related Topic: ICBC Bazhong's "4+1" Targeted Poverty Alleviation Program

Under the "4+1" program that pooled the efforts of ICBC, government anti-poverty departments, villages, and leading enterprises to help poor households, ICBC Bazhong Branch, in Sichuan, introduced a pilot ecological breeding project in 4 villages in Tongjiang and another 19 in Nanjiang. By

---

1 This refers to a goal that the growth rate of loans for micro and small businesses should not be lower than the average growth rate of all loans, and the number of micro and small borrowers as well as their loan approval rate should not be lower than those of the preceding year.

distributing thousands of native Bashan piglets and Nanjiang yellow goats to villagers to develop the local livestock industry, the Bashan Branch blazed a path to a better life for more than 3,500 poverty-stricken people by boosting their per-capita annual income by RMB 740. In addition, the branch has also brought 26 varieties of 20 local specialties such as pork and mushrooms to the ICBC online shopping site to widen sales channels, generating tens of millions of yuan in sales.

Furthermore, the bank also set up service outlets in poverty-ridden towns, townships, and villages to make it easier for local farmers, workers, planters, breeders, and agritourism operators to withdraw cash. With the help of online and mobile banking, the bank also extended online services such as money transfers and phone and utility bill payment to mountain villages. Last but not least, the bank developed RMB 20 million of exclusive financial products for Wanyuan, Sichuan and waived the normally required custody fees and sales commissions to provide quality services to customers in underdeveloped mountainous regions.

Section II
The Financial Cost and Benefit of the Joint-Stock Reform

By reviewing the achievements of the Big Five in reinventing themselves from the perspectives of performance, governance, risk control, management, competitiveness, and contribution to the society, the first section of this chapter has demonstrated the historical significance of the joint-stock reform. However, given that the reform had also incurred colossal costs to both the state and the banks themselves, when evaluating its success, it is further necessary to weigh the benefits against these costs. This section will attempt to give a cost-benefit analysis for the Big Five, to show that the joint-stock system was not only strategically necessary and appropriate, but also economically feasible and intensive.

I. Evaluation Framework

Just like the same object may look different from different perspectives, the outcomes of a cost-benefit analysis will depend on the framework of evaluation. It is therefore necessary to first set down this framework, and then draw conclusions from it.

(I) Perspectives

1. Comparative analysis

The primary motivation, goal, and components of the joint-stock reform were to address the "technical insolvency" of state-owned banks to put them on a financially stable foundation and sustainable path. This was also the primary target which the banks' investors – the state being the most important among them – were concerned with. Accordingly, in evaluating the success of the joint-stock reform, an essential and pragmatic standard is whether the reform has been financially economical, which invites a comparison between the financial cost it incurred and the financial benefit it brings. This question was in fact already a topic of discussion when the reform was first contemplated. And now, more than ten years since the conclusion of the reform, it is possible and necessary to provide an affirmative answer.

2. Baseline

It has been more than a decade since the joint-stock reform was officially launched in 2003. A cost-benefit analysis at present will be different from the one conducted at the start of the reform, in that it no longer needs to rely on assumptions to arrive at only estimated figures. Instead, it should reconstruct the cost and benefit based on the actual cost and benefit that were recorded after 2003.

3. Analytical dimension

Another controversy over the joint-stock reform is whether it has benefited the state, the public, or the banks, i.e., whether the reform was a boon for one party alone or for all stakeholders. This means that the cost-benefit analysis should not dwell solely on the financial statements of the Big Five, but also and particularly on the net "profit" to the state and the public.

(II) Methods

1. Incremental analysis

To simplify the analysis, we lay emphasis on the reform's incremental benefits and incremental costs based on the aforementioned framework for comparative analysis, without taking into account the historical benefits and costs.

2. Correlation analysis

For ease of analysis, this section focuses on the direct benefits and costs of the reform, without considering its indirect and extended impacts.

3. Timeline considerations

Because the five banks launched their respective joint-stock reforms at different times and each reform would take some time to make an impact, the cost-benefit analysis needs to cover a longer timeline than that of any individual bank's reform. To this end, we take 2003, the year when the reform officially began, as the starting point, and extend the analysis all the way to 2017. The reform, then, can be seen as a multi-year, continuous effort, and the cost and benefit can be discounted at a certain rate[1] to 2003 values so as to allow a direct comparison[2].

II. Cost-Benefit Analysis

(I) Benefits

On the basis of the foregoing perspectives and methods, the benefit (or "income") column of the joint-stock reform mainly consists of five components:

1. Profit attributable to domestic shareholders

Net profit is a reflection of the profitability of state-owned banks. Domestic shareholders, by virtue of their stake in the banks, have the right to receive dividends when the net profit is distributed. By definition, the net profit attributable to domestic shareholders is equal to the total net profit of state-owned banks minus the dividends distributed to non-domestic shareholders each year. From the start of the reform[3] to the end of 2017, the Big Five recorded a cumulative net profit of RMB 8.1 trillion[4], of which 8.2%, or RMB 658.0 billion, was distributed to overseas organizations and individuals as dividend. Therefore, the net profit attributable to the state is RMB 7.4 trillion.

---

1 From the end of 2003 to the end of 2017, the average daily yield of the 5-year government bond was 3.246%. In view of the variations in risk premiums, this section uses three discount rates – 3%, 4% and 5% – to convert all benefits and costs to 2003 values. For ease of calculation, the discount rate is held to be a constant.
2 An equivalent way of measurement is to convert the cumulative effects of costs and benefits to end-of-2017 terms using the discount rate.
3 In this section, reform-related data start at 2005 for ICBC, 2008 for ABC, and 2004 for BOC, CCB, and BoCom.
4 For ease of analysis, all figures in this section are, unless otherwise indicated, as before the discount ratio is applied.

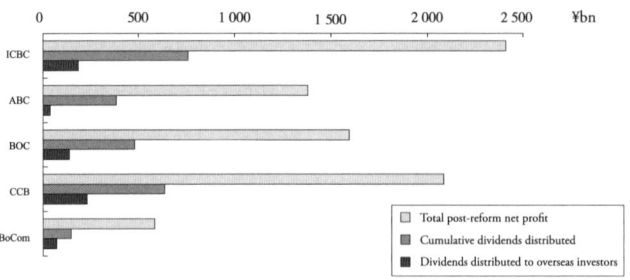

Fig. 8.9: Cumulative Profit and Dividend Distribution since the Joint-Stock Reform

2. Tax revenue

Tax revenue mainly consists of business tax, surcharges, and corporate income tax paid by the Big Five every year. From the start of the reform to the end of 2017, the banks paid a cumulative of RMB 1.05 trillion of business tax and surcharges as well as RMB 2.3 trillion of corporate income tax.

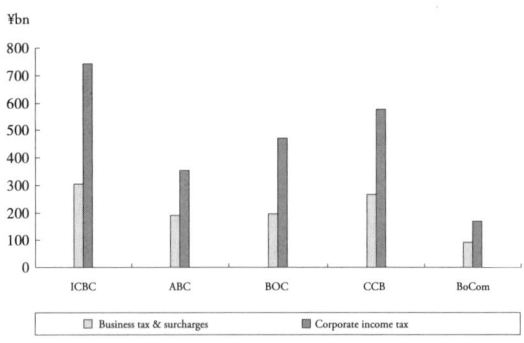

Fig. 8.10: Cumulative Major Taxes Paid by the Big Five since the Joint-Stock Reform

3. Capital appreciation

The potential income brought by the reform to national-level shareholders is the capital appreciation. We take capital appreciation = (P/B ratio – 1) × shareholding ratio of national-level shareholders × owners' equity.

It reflects the appreciation on state-owned assets and the wealth created for domestic investors.

Capital appreciation is linked to the performance of stocks in the stock market. Due to factors such as the global financial crisis and governance reform in the domestic capital market, China's stock market had been in a state of flux since the launch of the joint-stock reform, which made for highly volatile stock prices. To prevent stock price fluctuation in any particular year from throwing off our calculation of stock appreciation, the amount of appreciation each year is calculated using the average P/B ratio of each bank from the start of reform at that bank to 2017. According to this method, the Big Five recorded a total average capital appreciation of RMB 1.33 trillion since their listing.

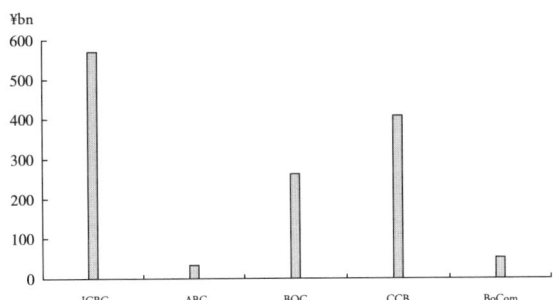

Note: Average capital appreciation = (sum of the bank's P/B ratio each year since listing ÷ years listed − 1) × owners' equity.

Fig. 8.11: Average Capital Appreciation since the Listing of the Big Five

4. Provisioning

Following the joint-stock reform, state-owned banks have set aside a significant amount of allowances in accordance with the regulatory requirements to cover expected losses on non-performing loans. The loan loss allowance is essentially profit set aside as a reserve and it directly reflects the banks' ability to mitigate risks and stabilize asset quality. Additionally, according to capital management regulations, allowances unrelated to specified losses may be recorded as tier-2 capital. However, because accounting standards treat allowances as a pre-tax deduction item and exclude them from the profit attributable to domestic shareholders, the cumulative allowances made by the Big Five since the joint-stock reform should be viewed as income arising from the reform. Since 2003, the Big Five have posted a total allowance (for potential loan losses) of RMB 2.76 trillion.

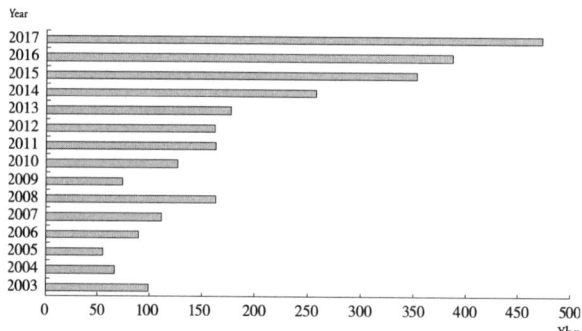

Fig. 8.12: Allowances for Potential Loan Losses Made by the Big Five since the Joint-Stock Reform

5. Brand value appreciation

The joint-stock reform and public listing has a significant and direct impact on the brand value of state-owned banks. For one, by introducing foreign investors and listing in overseas markets, the banks have attracted the attention and interest of more foreign institutions and individuals around the globe. And second, the more transparent disclosures following the reform have made it possible for international third parties to assess the brand value of the banks according to their business performance.

According to the yearly reports on the world's most valuable banks published by *Brand Finance*, no Chinese commercial bank had made the list as of 2006. In 2007, ICBC, CCB, BOC, and BoCom won a spot on the list for the first time, ranking 16th, 18th, 23rd, and 63rd among the world's top 100, respectively. In 2017, ICBC, CCB, BOC, ABC, and BoCom took the 1st, 3rd, 5th, 7th, and 19th place, respectively. If measured by the change between 2006 and 2017, the total brand value of the Big Five has appreciated by USD 160.6 billion, or RMB 1,084.35 billion based on the average USD/RMB exchange rate in 2017. If their brand value in 2007 is taken as the baseline, the gain will be USD 134.98 billion or RMB 889.55 billion. To be prudent, this section measures the appreciation of brand value according to the latter method.

Table 8.8: Change in the Brand Value of the Big Five

Bank	2017		2007		Increase	
	$bn	¥bn	$bn	¥bn	$bn	¥bn
ICBC	47.83	322.95	8.43	64.08	39.41	258.87
ABC	28.51	192.50	—	—	28.51	192.50
BOC	31.25	210.99	6.74	51.26	24.51	159.74
CCB	41.38	279.37	7.79	59.20	33.59	220.16
BoCoM	11.63	78.54	2.66	20.26	8.97	58.28
Total	160.60	1,084.35	25.62	194.80	134.98	889.55

Note: Calculated and compiled from data in the *Brand Finance* Banking 500 reports.

(II) Costs

1. Capital write-offs

To clear the way for the joint-stock reform, BOC and CCB converted all of their capital into allowances for loss on NPAs, writing off doubtful and unrecoverable loans with capital stock. This is equivalent to the state, as the shareholder, supporting the write-off with its original interest at book value, which is therefore one of the input costs of the reform. In the financial restructuring of ICBC, a portion of its original capital contributed by the Ministry of Finance was converted into allowances to offset loss on NPAs, and the remaining portion was converted into capital stock. BoCom and ABC did not convert their original capital into reserves, and thus no write-off cost was incurred. Altogether, the financial restructuring of BOC, CCB, and ICBC involved a capital write-off of approximately RMB 400 billion.

2. Net loss from divestment of NPAs

The Big Five all divested a certain amount of NPAs during the joint-stock reform. While all these divestments would eventually incur losses, due to differences in the banks' restructuring models, how that loss was to be absorbed varied from bank to bank. BOC and CCB converted their original capital into special allowances, part of which was transferred to the asset management companies along with the divested assets to offset the actual losses. Any losses on the NPAs that could not be covered by these allowances are treated as cost borne by the state. For ICBC and ABC which did not fully write off their original capital, and swapped the divested assets with claims of equal value, the difference between their existing allowances and the estimated loss on the divested assets can be treated as cost to the state. Lastly, BoCom did not create any cost to the state because it largely resolved the NPAs internally.

As such, the net loss from disposal of the Big Five's NPAs borne by the public is estimated at RMB 1.3 trillion. When the amount of capital write-off is taken into consideration, the total figure would climb to RMB 1.7 trillion, higher than the RMB 1.4 trillion net asset loss (comprising RMB 970 billion of loss loans and RMB 430 billion of other loss assets) assessed by the PBOC in 2002. Two factors account for this difference. One is that the higher figure also includes the estimated RMB 55 billion of asset loss of BoCom, and the other is that the PBOC estimate was lower than it should have been.

3. Cost of interest on receivables from restructuring

During the reform, some of the divested NPAs were swapped for the PBOC's special bills or the MOF's receivables which would pay interest, thereby allowing the banks to exchange non-interest-bearing bad assets with interest-bearing good assets. The interest paid by the MOF and PBOC each year is in reality a cost item, which has amounted to RMB 240 billion since the launch of the reform.

In particular, the restructuring ABC and ICBC involved the use of a jointly managed account and the swap of NPAs at full book value. Given the large amount of receivables of the two banks, the interest "subsidies" they received from the state were also substantial, roughly accounting for 94% of the interest cost on the receivables from the restructuring (Fig. 8.13).

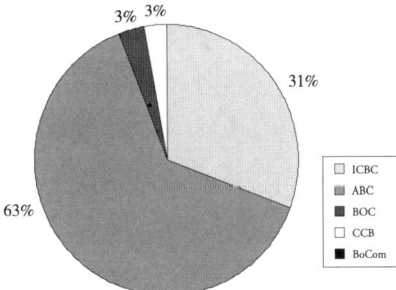

Note: Interest cost on receivables = Cumulative interest payment on receivables for the jointly managed account + cumulative interest payment on bonds (including special central bank bills) swapped for NPAs.

Fig. 8.13: Breakdown of Interest Cost on Receivables from Bank Restructuring

4. Cost of capital injection

The state pumped various amounts of capital into the Big Five, a process that involved three types of cost.

First, the cost of the injected capital, which creates two divergent viewpoints. One viewpoint is that this capital was real cash spent by the state to support the reform and therefore should be treated as a cost. The other view is that capital injection was in essence an investment by the state and hence was not a financial cost. To be on the safe side, this section takes the first and the more conservative of these two viewpoints when analyzing the cost-benefit proposition of the reform.

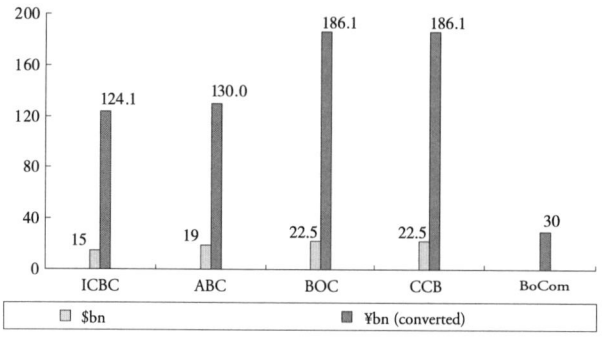

Note: The state injected foreign exchange into ICBC, ABC, BOC, and CCB, and RMB 30 billion directly into BoCom. The foreign currency amounts have been converted into RMB at the then-prevailing exchange rate.

Fig. 8.14: Capital Injections into the Big Five

Second, the opportunity cost of foreign exchange. This arises from the observation that if the foreign reserves had not been injected into the banks, they could have been used in other income-generating activities. To simplify our analysis, we assume the opportunity cost was incurred at the discount rate.

Third, the cost of hedging against foreign exchange risks. The joint-stock reforms and IPOs of BOC, CCB, and ICBC were almost contemporaneous with the exchange rate reform. To mitigate the impact of rate fluctuations on their capital, the three banks each entered into an exchange rate hedge contract with Central Huijin. The difference between the exercise value of the contract and the contract fee is the cost assumed by the state.

Specifically, the contracts with BOC and CCB were for the year 2007; and the one with ICBC was for 2008. The difference between the market exchange rate and the contract exchange rate was to be settled over 12 months in as many installments. To simplify our calculation, we assume a one-time settlement was carried out at the central parity rate at the end of the coverage period of the contract. In this case, the cost borne by the state to minimize the foreign exchange risks for the three banks was around RMB 47 billion.

Undoubtedly, there had been other gains and costs associated with the joint-stock reform, such as asset appreciations and interest on special government bonds. Because these items are not inextricably linked to the joint-stock reform and have already been reflected in the other items (such as profit and capital appreciations), they will not be considered separately.

(III) Evaluation Results

Table 8.9 and Fig. 8.15 show the economic benefits of the joint-stock reform without considering discounts and with a discount rate of 3%, 4%, and 5%.

Table 8.9: Cost-Benefit of the Joint-Stock Reform at Different Discount Rates (¥bn)

Item	No discount	3% discount rate	4% discount rate	5% discount rate
I. Income items				
Profit	8,064.3	6,074.1	5,548.0	5,077.2
Less: Dividends to overseas shareholders	658.8	493.4	449.6	410.4
Tax revenue	3,395.4	2,594.0	2,380.5	2,188.5
Capital gain	967.7	849.5	813.7	779.6
Provisioning	2,286.6	1,785.2	1,651.5	1,531.4
Brand value gain	889.6	588.1	513.7	449.3
II. Cost items				
Net loss of asset divestment borne by the public	1,298.9	1,174.5	1,137.2	1,101.7
Capital write-off	405.5	401.0	399.6	398.3
Income from asset swap	239.2	195.4	183.3	172.1
Capital injection	656.5	631.5	624.0	616.8
Hedging cost of injected assets	46.7	41.1	39.5	37.9
III. Net income	12,297.9	8,953.9	8,074.3	7,288.7
Net of capital gain and brand value income	10,440.6	7,516.4	6,746.9	6,059.9

Note: All amounts are discounted to 2003 values.

The data show that the joint-stock reform has brought considerable net gains to China.

Without considering the time factor: The reform came with a total income of RMB 14.94 trillion and a total cost of RMB 2.64 trillion, equaling a net income of RMB 12.3 trillion for the country, or RMB 10.44 trillion excluding capital and brand value appreciations.

At a 3% discount rate: The income and cost would be RMB 11.40 trillion and RMB 2.44 trillion, respectively, yielding a net income of RMB 8.95 trillion or RMB 7.52 trillion excluding capital and brand value appreciations.

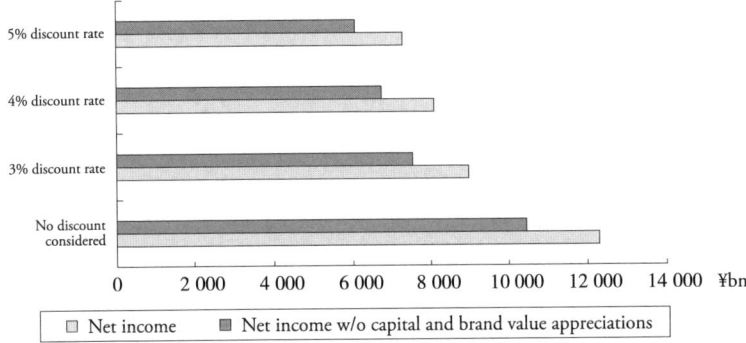

Fig. 8.15: Net Income from the Joint-Stock Reform at Different Discount Rates

At a 4% discount rate: The income and cost would be RMB 10.46 trillion and RMB 2.38 trillion, respectively, yielding a net income of RMB 8.07 trillion or RMB 6.75 trillion excluding capital and brand value appreciations.

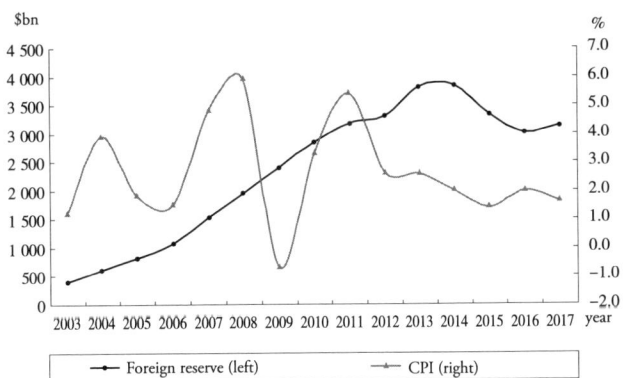

Note: Data taken from the website of National Bureau of Statistics.

Fig. 8.16: Changes in China's Foreign Reserve and CPI after the Joint-Stock Reform

At a 5% discount rate: The income and cost would be RMB 9.62 trillion and RMB 2.32 trillion, respectively, yielding a net income of RMB

7.29 trillion or RMB 6.06 trillion excluding capital and brand value appreciations.

It can be drawn from the analysis that the income brought by the joint-stock reform has completely covered the cost, and even created trillions in net returns for the country. Therefore, the joint-stock reform was economically sound, and has built a foundation from which the Big Five can grow steadily and rapidly under a new paradigm, invigorated them and greatly enhanced their profitability, fundamentally reversed their long-standing financial woes by turning book profit into real profit, and truly turned them into profitable entities and an important source of tax revenue for the state.

In addition, when studying the plan for the joint-stock reform, the architects of the reform also considered the social cost that may arise from the use of foreign exchange – namely inflation and foreign exchange gap – and proposed ideas such as phased settlement and recovery of foreign currency. Outcomes of the reform show that these proposals were also effective. China's foreign reserve has maintained a high rate of growth after the reform. And apart from a temporary uptick in inflation in 2007 and 2008 caused by the massive expansion of money supply and credit in response to the subprime mortgage crisis, the inflation rate within China has been kept at a steady 2% for the rest of the decade.

Epilogue

In the four decades from 1978 to 2018, along with the reform and opening up of the Chinese economy, China's state-owned banks completed their historic transformation from plan- and policy-driven organizations into market-based companies. Having undergone the long journey from the corporate reform, to the market-oriented reform and finally the joint-stock reform, they have achieved Deng Xiaoping's vision of "having banks perform all the functions of banks" that operate under the principles of "independent operations, self-assumption of risk, self-assumption of profits and losses, and self-discipline." An unprecedented undertaking, the joint-stock reform has not only enabled the rebirth of state-owned banks, but also had a profound impact on the reform of China's state-owned economy.

I

The roaring success of the joint-stock reform is due to the following five factors:

The first contributing factor was the brilliant decision-making and vigorous push by the CPC Central Committee and State Council. After China's accession to the WTO in the early 21st century, it was widely agreed that China needed to accelerate the reform of the state-owned banking system. Nevertheless, there were diverging opinions and widespread doubts about two questions: What are root causes of the long-standing issues within the state-owned banks? And is it possible to restructure these banks, which had the state as their sole shareholder, into joint-stock companies?

After the 15th CPC National Congress announced to build SOEs into modern corporations through the joint-stock reform, the Party's central leadership held the second National Financial Work Conference in early 2002, and, while under enormous pressure, made the decision that "wholly state-owned commercial banks are to be turned into joint-stock companies," "eligible wholly state-owned commercial banks may be restructured into state-controlled commercial banks," and "if conditions permit, the banks may go public." This signaled the start of a "do-or-die" effort to resolve the institutional inefficiencies, accumulation of NPAs, and low level of competition within the state-owned banking system in the five-year grace period allowed by the WTO.

These far-sighted and bold decisions silenced all disputes and doubts about the reform. At the executive meeting on December 30, 2003, the State Council announced CCB and BOC as pilot banks for the reform, and injected capital into the two banks the very next day, thus raising the curtain on the joint-stock reform of state-owned banks.

To push forward the reform, the State Council set up the Steering Group for the Pilot Joint-Stock Reform of Wholly State-Owned Commercial Banks, headed by Huang Ju, Vice Premier and member of the Politburo Standing Committee. A series of meetings were then held to plan for and determine the goal and objectives of the reforms at CCB and BOC, and then as the pilot reform progressed, put forward targeted measures and requirements for the joint-stock reform of state-owned banks.

After achieving success in the reform of CCB, BOC, and BoCom, the State Council shifted attention in 2005 to ICBC, which was the largest state-owned bank in China at the time. And later in 2008, ABC, the only remaining major state-owned bank, launched its joint-stock reform in the wake of the global financial crisis. Following their restructuring and IPOs, the Big Five were transformed from wholly state-owned banks into international public companies. And the success of this program owes largely to the astute decision-making of the CPC Central Committee and the strong support of the State Council.

It is important to understand that the four-decade-long reform of state-owned banks has been a continuous and continuing effort. The success of the joint-stock reform was built on the series of changes introduced since 1978, such as the restoration of financial order and the market-oriented reform of state-owned banks in the 1990s, the enactment of the *Law on Commercial Banks*, and particularly the recapitalization and transfer of NPAs of state-owned banks during 1998-2000.

The second factor was timing. Specifically, the reform coincided with China's "golden decade" of economic progress during 2002-2011. The National Bureau of Statistics reported that China's GDP grew at 9.1%, 10.0%, 10.1%, 11.4%, 12.7%, 14.2%, 9.7%, 9.4%, 10.6%, and 9.5% from 2002 to 2011. These give an average growth rate of 10.7%, one percentage point higher than the 9.7% average in the 40 years after 1978, and the fastest growing decade for China. The success of the joint-stock reform came down to China's thriving economy, which supplied the right environment and conditions for the restructuring, listing, and governance reform of the banks. Similarly, the great enthusiasm displayed by investors – especially foreign investors – during the IPOs of the banks was, fundamentally, a vote of confidence in the growth and outlook of China's economy and market. Moreover, in coordination with the efforts to resolve the NPA issue at the banks, the PBOC slowed down the pace of interest rate liberalization, maintaining a 3% interest rate spread over the ten years of the joint-stock reform. This bought time for the banks to divest NPAs, return to profitability, and rebuild their balance sheets, and ultimately helped them maintain a strong business performance and join the ranks of premier international banks after their reforms and IPOs.

The third deciding factor was the bold innovations of the people who designed and carried out the reform. Capital injection with foreign reserves was the key to funding the reform and enabling the banks to restructure financially and to rebuild their balance sheets. Historically, whenever state-owned banks ran into financial difficulties, they had always been bailed out by the central government, whether through recapitalization or divestiture of NPAs. But when the joint-stock reform was being planned during the period from 2001 to 2003, it was realized that, due to budgetary and other reasons, it was no longer possible for state finance to foot the enormous cost of restructuring and balance sheet rebuilding. The rejection of the PBOC's initial proposal which demanded RMB 970 billion from the state's coffers, had sent a clear message that the joint-stock reform must follow a different path, one that would not rely on fiscal resources. Subsequently, the PBOC went back to the drawing board and, under the leadership of Zhou Xiaochuan and with great courage and inventiveness, came up with the second proposal, under which the financial restructuring of the state-owned banks would be supported by China's foreign reserves (i.e., restructuring of the central bank's balance sheet). This proposal capitalized on the fast-growing foreign reserves brought by China's booming economy – and foreign trade in particular – after China joined the WTO, and offered three advantages: It provided adequate funding for the financial restructuring of the banks; it alleviated the pressure on central fiscal resources; and it helped China maintain a steady foreign exchange balance. With the triumph of the reform, China became the first country to successfully rescue major state-owned banks by adjusting the central bank's balance sheet.

Mao Zedong once said, "Cadres are a decisive factor, once the political line is determined."[1] After the central government finalized the plan for the joint-stock reform, how to implement it became the key to success. Transforming state-owned banks into joint-stock companies was an innovation that had never been attempted in the history of China's banking reforms, and had been rarely successful even when carried out abroad. To the leaders of the banks, each step of the reform, from financial restructuring and bringing in strategic investors, to establishing and listing joint-stock companies, was unfamiliar territory the entry of which required great courage and sense of responsibility. To make it even more challenging, the reform was also a "do-or-die" effort that simply could not afford to fail.

Faced with an unprecedented trial, the leaders of the Big Five neither showed hesitation nor backed down in fear, but rather shouldered the responsibilities and pushed forward. Despite the intense pressure and doubts from both within and without, they led the banks to overcome one challenge after another, including offloading the NPAs and pursuing accountability, streamlining the organization and staff, reforming the human resources system, bringing in strategic investors, and completing

---

1 *Selected Works of Mao Tse-tung*, Vol. II, Foreign Languages Press, 1965, p. 202.

share pricing. Eager to learn from international practices and strategic investors, they quickly educated themselves about the international rules and conventions and successfully completed the four major phases of the reform: financial restructuring, introduction of strategic investors, corporate governance overhaul, and public listing. With their efforts, the banks were able to maintain high asset quality and profitability after the reform, performing the miraculous feat of going from "technical insolvency" to becoming part of a leading group of international banks. But behind the miracle, few people know about the hardships and pressure endured by the banks' leadership or the efforts they had made. It is fair to say that the leaders of the Big Five and the employees who took part in the reform were the heroes of the day. Without their commitment, or the support of everyone in the banking industry, the joint-stock reform would not have been a success.

The fourth contributor to success was the focus on rebuilding market-based operations at the banks. While financial restructuring, bringing in strategic investors, and going public were all critical components of the joint-stock reform, they were only the means and ways, not the goal. Succinctly stated, that goal was to introduce mixed ownership to the banks to completely transform them into market-based entities, including replacing government-like management models with modern corporate governance structures, lax risk management practices with internal controls that would enable banks to assume their own business risks, and government- and policy-directed operations with profit-driven objectives.

It was because every change the Big Five made was aimed at this goal that they were able to develop the governance framework, risk management system, and internal controls while completing financial restructuring, bringing in strategic investors, and going public. They paid particular attention to creating robust risk control systems that cover risk identification, risk resolution, and accountability mechanisms, and extend to every organizational level, division, employee, and aspect of operation.

With these improvements in place, the Big Five have been maintaining low NPL ratios of below 2% as well as sustained profitability in the 15 years after the joint-stock reform, even during the 2008 global financial crisis. These performances also put them among the world's top 20 banks, and dispelled all doubts and concerns of domestic and foreign onlookers about whether the Big Five could maintain the asset quality and profitability after the reform.

Lastly, the fifth key to success was China's continuous economic reform and opening up as well as the close coordination between the various reform programs. This is because the banking reform had widespread economic, political, and social implications and in turn relied on the deep-cutting changes to the design and workings of the socioeconomic system. As a key part of China's economic reform, the banking reform could not be separated from or advanced faster or slower than the whole, for the progress of the whole determined the intensity and pace of the banking reform. Over the 40 years of reform and opening up, China's economic system gradually transitioned from a planned economy with market-oriented features, to a plan-centric market economy, and finally to a market economy. The state-owned banks also went through a similar path of evolution: from corporate reform, to market-oriented reform, and finally to the joint-stock reform. In short, the joint-stock reform was feasible because of the environment and conditions created by the economic reform.

If we compare China's economic reform to a game of chess, the banking reform would be an important moving piece. Each step of the joint-stock reform was strongly supported by the National People's Congress and the State Council: The NPC approved the foreign-currency capital injection plan, so that the reform could take advantage of the golden decade of reform and opening up; the Ministry of Finance financially pushed the reform toward success; the Ministry of Land and Resources greatly sped up the re-appraisal and ownership title resolution of tens of trillions of yuan of assets, paving the way for the financial restructuring; and the CSRC worked hard to ensure the successful IPOs on the mainland and overseas markets. In sum, much of the success of the joint-stock reform owed to the continuous reform and opening up of China and to the close coordination of all parties involved.

II

The historical significance and far-reaching influence of the joint-stock reform may be understood from the following aspects:

First, the reform redefined the relationship between the state and state-owned banks. Following the creation of Central Huijin, the capital injection, the attraction of strategic investors, and the joint-stock reform and listing, state-owned banks were now under mixed ownership, which addressed the long-standing issue that the banks only had a nominal shareholder (i.e., the state), but not an actual one with the corresponding powers and responsibilities. Furthermore, the reform reshaped the banks' corporate governance structures and systems, cutting off the direct, administrative connections between the state and the banks. This decoupled ownership from management, which ended improper interventions by various levels of the government and preliminarily stopped the banks' slide into becoming mere agents for the fiscal authorities. These changes in turn enabled the banks to focus on risk management and profit-making, and therefore to run a market-oriented, independent operation with self-assumption of risks.

Second, the reform helped state-owned banks to start afresh without the burden of historical NPAs and financial losses. During China's reform and opening up, while helping jumpstart the economy, the state-owned banks also assumed the cost of the SOE and economic reform by engaging in policy-directed financing. These activities created a staggering amount of NPAs and losses, which remained resilient even after multiple rounds of targeted reforms. In the process of financial restructuring, reasonable write-offs, divestment of NPAs, and capital injection had freed the banks from these historical burdens, unleashing their vitality and innovation capacity. In the ten years following the joint-stock reform, the Big Five maintained an impressive 20% annual growth rate in operating income, further reduced the amount and proportion of NPAs – with the NPA ratio being kept at an internationally leading number of below 2% – and emerged from "technical insolvency" to become the best performing banks in the world.

Third, the reform allowed state-owned banks to establish modern corporate governance, risk management, and accountability systems. The significance of the reform lies not just in financial restructuring, divestment of NPAs, and rebuilding of balance sheets, but, more importantly, in institutional overhaul and substantial convergence with the international standards on governance, risk control, and accountability management, such that every organizational level, process, and person has clear risk control responsibilities and can be held accountable.

Fourth, the reform fostered the development of a large number of professional bankers. Each step of the reform – financial restructuring, NPA divestment, foreign investment, roadshows, and IPOs – brought unprecedented challenges to the leaders and management of state-owned banks. It was these challenges that helped mold many into bankers and internationally minded and technically savvy professionals. By learning and innovating as they put newly acquired knowledge into practice, these people gradually developed the skill to run banking businesses according to market-based principles. This skill allowed them to maintain business performance and asset quality following the joint-stock reform, and to bring the banks up to international standards in the areas of risk management, internal control, capital management, financial management, and performance assessment, thus transforming state-owned banks into modern and market-driven financial institutions.

Fifth, the reform helped stabilize China's economy during the global financial crisis. Even in the most precarious five years after 2008, the Big Five still maintained an average NPA ratio of 1.5% and an average profit growth rate of 23.7%. Their consistently stellar performance during the trying years, like the ballast stones of a ship, helped them as well as the Chinese economy to remain on course throughout the financial crisis with minimum impact. Put another way, if the banks had not undergone the joint-stock reform and achieved timely resolution of their deep-seated issues, they might very well have been sunk by the financial crisis like many other European and American banks, dragging the Chinese economy down with them in the process.

The reform of major state-owned banks could be called the highlight of China's economic transformation in the first ten years of the 21st century. It not only brought China's banking sector back from the brink of "technical insolvency," but also reshaped the banking system. It put China's banking sector on the path of modernization, and greatly contributed to the future reforms and growth of the Chinese economy, especially during the financial crisis. Achieving market-oriented and fully commercial operations marks a major progress for the state-owned banks, who in turn serve as a catalyst for China's further economic reforms and development.

Lastly, the reform showed domestic and international stakeholders how a successful restructuring of financial institutions could be conducted. Following the success of the joint-stock reform, Central Huijin successively brought market-oriented restructuring program to many other state-owned financial institutions, including banks (e.g., China Everbright Bank), three insurance companies (e.g., China Export & Credit Insurance Corporation), and seven securities firms (e.g., Galaxy Securities). How the state-owned banks were able to switch to mixed ownership and market-based operations also gave valuable insights for the ownership reform of other SOEs. More importantly, the restructuring of state-owned banks did not result in the privatization or foreign control of the banks as in the case of their Soviet Union and Eastern European peers. Rather, it upheld the state's control over the banks while turning them into market-based entities. This distinctively Chinese innovation has shown the world another viable path toward bank restructuring and governance modernization.

III

The reform of major state-owned banks is still ongoing, because the joint-stock reform is only the start, not the end. The evolving global economic and financial landscape and China's new normal are bringing many new challenges and presenting a long road ahead of the state-owned banks.

For one, the state-owned banks need to find a new model of corporate governance with Chinese characteristics. During the joint-stock reform, state-owned banks built modern governance frameworks in line with international standards. Under China's unique socialist market economy, however, state-owned banks not only are independent, market-oriented entities, but also are controlled by the state. In such a context, how to harmonize the relations between market-driven activities and state control, how to ensure Party leadership while making the most of the "3+1" governance structure, and how to ensure the Party's control over the management while attracting talents by market practices and through market-based remuneration systems, are all challenges that the banks must address. We cannot wholly copy the corporate governance models of Western companies, but must find new ones that suit the Chinese context. And this will be a major challenge for state-controlled banks in the years to come.

Second, state-owned banks need to continue to support the real economy and strategic emerging industries, as it is one of their historical missions. Economy defines the financial industry; therefore state-owned banks, being operators in that industry, must defer to and serve the real economy. In retrospect, the 2008 global financial crisis, caused by subprime mortgages, was primarily due to an overdeveloped financial industry that was increasingly detached from the real economy. State-owned banks must draw lessons from the crisis, by always putting the needs of the real economy first. Given that China has entered a new normal marked by lower rates of return, it becomes especially important for the banks to support the real economy and strategic emerging industries and to steer private capital into the real economy, so as to promote the sustainable and qualitative development of China.

Third, there is still much room for improvement in risk management. In the second decade after the joint-stock reform, China's economic development has entered a new stage featuring new growth drivers and a focus on quality rather than quantity, as the growth rate dropped from around 10% to within 7%. This shift caused issues like overcapacity and "zombie" businesses to resurface on a broad scale. These issues, together with excess leverage by local governments, an overheated real estate market, and increased stock market volatility, threaten the central role and wellbeing of the real economy. After 40 years of economic boom brought by the reform and opening-up policy, major state-owned banks are facing their first economic downturn, as both their absolute NPL balances and relative ratios have rebounded after ten years of decline. This economic environment is nothing like what the banks faced 30 years ago, and makes mitigating asset risks a much harder task than before. Thus, the risk management framework established during the joint-stock reform is facing a major test. To secure the progress they have made since the reform, the banks must move quickly to resolve various emerging risks and safeguard their asset quality while the economy tries to find and build a new sure footing and switch to new growth drivers.

Fourth, the banks have to become more international, integrated, and IT-powered. Following the joint-stock reform, the Big Five immediately launched initiatives in these three areas which have achieved initial success. But they need to understand that the global financial industry is undergoing profound changes, and not even the financial crisis could dissuade the industry from becoming more international, integrated, and IT-driven. Compared with leading international banks, China's state-owned banks have just taken their first step in these areas. Therefore, how to promote the level of internationalization in the banking industry to support the globalization of the Chinese economy and enterprises, how to promote integrated businesses amid interest rate liberalization and financial disintermediation, and how to promote IT-powered banking in the information age, all the while maintaining compliance with the Basel Accords, the OECD[1] governance principles, and the domestic financial regulations, are the major questions that state-owned banks will need to find an answer to.

Last but not least, effective incentive systems need to be established. An incentive system is not just about compensation, but is an integral part of corporate governance. It helps bind managers and employees to their organization through shared interests, values, and business philosophies. State-owned banks in fact introduced stock incentive plans for executives and employees on a trial basis at the beginning of the joint-stock reform, but for various reasons these programs had to be abandoned. Currently, the executives at major state-owned banks are underpaid, which, if allowed to continue, may lead to an outflow to foreign-funded and private financial institutions not dissimilar to "bad money driving out the good." And this in turn may undermine management competency and employee quality. Therefore, state-owned banks must redesign their executives system and attract professional managers with competitive remuneration packages. In other words, while the banking operations are made to be more market-oriented, the human resources and remuneration systems should be as well – of course, more rigorous assessment and supervision systems should be put in place at the same time. Furthermore, it is necessary to restart the stock incentive plans, to align the interest of executives and employees

---

1   Organisation for Economic Co-operation and Development.

with that of their organization.

In conclusion, the joint-stock reform wrote a heroic tale of the rebirth of China's state-owned banks. Nevertheless, one must remember that this is just a new starting point of China's banking reform which is still ongoing. As China pursues its great rejuvenation and the Two Centenary Goals under the leadership of the CPC Central Committee with Xi Jinping at the core, large state-owned banks must do more; and continuing reform and opening up is the surest means toward sustainable and qualitative development. China's state-owned banks have come a long way, but there is still a long road ahead of them!

Afterword

The *Joint-Stock Reform of China's Major Commercial Banks* is dedicated to the 40th anniversary of China's reform and opening up in the year 2018. We had long thought about writing a book on this part of history, but real work began only in 2016, when Jiang Jianqing retired as the chairman of ICBC and undertook the task.

After sharing our idea with the presidents of the Big Five, we all agreed that the joint-stock reform is a historic event that took place during a very special period of our history – China's transition from planned economy to market economy. This highly successful reform, which launched a heroic tale of the rebirth of China's state-owned banks, is not only unprecedented in Chinese history, but also rarely seen in the banking history anywhere in the world. Therefore, an ode to this part of history is also a dedication to the 40 years of reform and opening up. Recording this history is also an urgent matter, as we still have access to the direct participants and primary materials. Accordingly, we all agreed that the five banks should form a writing team to jointly write this book.

This book received the full support of our advisors. Former Governors of the PBOC, Zhou Xiaochuan and Dai Xianglong; former Ministers of Finance, Xiang Huaicheng and Lou Jiwei; former Chairman of the

CBRC, Liu Mingkang; and other leaders gave guidance and advice during our writing. Additionally, officials from various ministries, the CSRC, CBRC, and PBOC, as well as former and current leaders of the Big Five, totaling nearly 30 people, accepted our requests for interviews. These interviews are the highlight of this book.

Jiang Jianqing serves as the editor of the book and prepared the chapter outlines; Zhan Xiangyang is the associate editor and compiled all drafts. Volume I was completed by a coalition of writers from the Big Five as follows: "Introduction" and "Epilogue" written by Zhan Xiangyang; Chapter 1 drafted by Zhan Xiangyang, Zheng Yanwen, and Li Luxia; Chapters 2 to 4 drafted by Wang Qi, with the assistance of Zhang Yun and Yang Houde for Chapter 4; Chapters 5 and 6 drafted by Jiang Lichang with the assistance of Jia Tiezhen, Zhang Yun, Yang Houde, Jiang Shoutao, and Xu Wenbing; Chapter 7 drafted by Liu Kang with the assistance of Jia Tiezhen, Zhang Yun, Yang Houde, Jiang Shoutao, and Xu Wenbing; Chapter 8 drafted by Wang Qi with the assistance of Jia Tiezhen, Zhang Yun, Yang Houde, Jiang Shoutao, and Xu Wenbing. Wu Zhenhua and Chen Yang edited the book; Jiang Jianqing and Zhang Chao revised all chapters of the book; Zhan Xiangyang compiled all writings for the book.

The writing team received much support from many people and departments at the Big Five banks. The following people took part in writing for the book: Mao Xiaolong, Huang Yanfei, Li Ying, Zhang Liejun, Hu Yanbin, Wu Wen, Zhong Weijie, Lin Jun, Man Mingjun, Lan Yonghai, Tong Li, Huang Xuefei, Liu Di, Liu Chenggang, Li Xiaolong, Wang Ke, Wang Liwei, Liu Miao, Shen Hong, Hao Dongmei, and Zhao Sheng. The following departments provided information and materials:

- PBOC: Head Office;
- ICBC: Head Office, Risk Management Department, Strategy and Investor Relations Department;
- ABC: Office of the Board of Directors, Finance and Accounting Department, Asset and Liability Management Department, Risk Management Department, Internal Control and Compliance Department, International Banking Department, Technology and Product Management Office, Strategic Planning Department;
- BOC: Secretariat to the Board of Directors, Head Office, Financial Management Department, Risk Management Department, Credit Approval Department, Credit Administration Department, Internal Control and Legal & Compliance Department, Human Resources Department, IT Department, Treasurer, Accounting and Information Department;
- CCB: Strategic Planning Department, Board of Directors Office, General Office, Finance and Accounting Department, Human Resources Department, Equity and Investment Management Department, Risk Management Department, Credit Management Department, Internal Control and Compliance Department, Public Relations and Corporate Culture Department;
- BoCom: Head Office, Board of Directors Office, Office of BOCOM Magazine, Budget and Finance Department, Risk Management Department, and Development Research Department.

We would like to express our gratitude to all of them!

In the revision process, many advisors generously contributed their time and advice. The following corporate leaders participated in the review and revision: Shen Rujun, Wu Wei, Huang Yi, and Chen Caihong. Additional contributions came from the following department-level leaders and staff: Liu Ruixia, Hui Ping, Ma Mingjun, Zhang Shouchuan, Zhang Weiming, Zhu Feng, Hua Ruiqi, Lian Ping, Fang Weixing, Lin Zhihong, Zhou Kunping, Po Ying, Wang Chen, Tang Jianwei, E Yongjian, Wang Wei, Wang Qiang, Yu Sha, and Lin Li. We thank all of the above individuals for their support.

This book used *China's Finance – 40 Years of Financial Reform* by former PBOC Chief Economist Cao Yuanzheng, as well as the outlines for the *History of China's Banking Reform* by former ICBC President Yang Kaisheng, as reference materials. They have our gratitude.

We also thank Boyuan Foundation and its Director General He Di, for the financial support, guidance, and help. We also extend our heartfelt thanks to Mr. Kelvin Leung and Mr. Zhang Xu from Ernst & Young, who took charge of the translation work.

This book also received full support from the China Financial Publishing House, particularly the kind attention and guidance from its former President Wei Gejun and Editor-in-Chief Jiang Wanjin. We thank Publishing Editor Li Rong and Art Editor Wu Jinming for making the publication of this book a reality. And finally, our special thanks go to Editor Dai Shuo, for his continued support from the inception of the book to its publication.

This book took two years and three months to reach the final draft, after going through multiple rounds of revisions and ten rounds of rewriting. To solicit feedback, we held 7 symposiums, consulted all 37 of our advisors, and sought comments from over 50 experts from industry and academia. These efforts culminated into the final draft which was completed at the end of November 2018. As requested by Zhou Xiaochuan, we have tried to give equal priority to historical accuracy, theoretical exposition, and readability. We hope this book can inform our readers about the true history of the joint-stock reform, including details from "behind the scenes," answer the related questions and controversies, and retell the history through a flexible structure and highly readable writing. Of course, due to our limited time and expertise, the book may contain errors, omissions, and other flaws; we sincerely welcome corrections from the industry, academics, and our readership.

Writing Team of the *Joint-Stock Reform of China's Major Commercial Banks*
November 2018, Beijing

图书在版编目（CIP）数据

中国大型商业银行股改史：英文 / 姜建清主编. -- 北京：外文出版社，2023.7
（学术中国）
ISBN 978-7-119-13680-6

Ⅰ. ①中… Ⅱ. ①姜… Ⅲ. ①商业银行－股份制－经济体制改革－银行史－中国－现代－英文 Ⅳ. ①F832.97

中国国家版本馆CIP数据核字(2023)第121607号

出版指导：胡开敏
出版统筹：文　芳
责任编辑：熊冰頔　苏佳钰
英文翻译：潘未名　艾　飞
英文审定：梁成杰　张　旭　Michael Hamalainen　王　琴　徐汀汀　李　洋
英文编辑：王　琴　姜防震
装帧设计：一瓢文化 · 邱特聪
印刷监制：章云天

中国大型商业银行股改史

姜建清 主编　　**詹向阳** 副主编

©2023 外文出版社有限责任公司
出 版 人：胡开敏
出版发行：
外文出版社有限责任公司（中国北京西城区百万庄大街24号　100037）
http://www.flp.com.cn
电　　话：008610-68320579（总编室）
　　　　　008610-68996144（编辑部）
　　　　　008610-68995852（发行部）
制　　版：北京维诺传媒文化有限公司
印　　刷：北京中科印刷有限公司
开　　本：700mm×1000mm　1/16
印　　张：47
2023年7月第1版第1次印刷
（英）
ISBN 978-7-119-13680-6
（精）
22800

版权所有　侵权必究　如有印装问题本社负责调换（电话：68329904）